CALIFORNIA GUN LAWS

A Guide to State and Federal Firearm Regulations

COLDAW
PUBLISHING

COLDAW PUBLISHING

©2020 Coldaw Publishing - C.D. Michel
All rights reserved

No part of the original content of this book may be reproduced or
transmitted in any form or by any means now known
or which will become known,
without written permission from the publisher.
Permission is granted for reviewers and others to quote
brief passages for use in newspapers, periodicals,
or broadcasts provided credit is given to: California Gun Laws,
published by Coldaw Publishing. For information contact:

COLDAW PUBLISHING
C. D. Michel
284C E Lake Mead Pkwy, Suite 530
Henderson, NV 89015-5511
calgunlawsbook@coldawpublishing.com
www.CalGunLawsBook.com
www.MichelLawyers.com

Michel & Associates, P.C.
Environmental ~ Land Use ~ Firearms ~ Employment Law
Civil Litigation ~ Criminal Defense

Images Provided Courtesy Of
The National Rifle Association of America, NRA National Firearms Museum,
NRA Firearms Sourcebook, NRA Shooting Illustrated, Defense Distributed,
www.gunfacts.info, CRPA Firing Line, iStock, Bigstock & Bruce Krell, PhD

Cover Design: Jason O. Crye
Project Manager/Editing/Layout: Grace Wu
ISBN: 978-0-9884602-9-4
Library of Congress Control Number: 2020920374

ATTENTION
Contact the publisher for information on quantity discounts!

Printed and bound in the United States of America
at Color House Graphics, Grand Rapids, Michigan

Eighth Edition

DEDICATION

To my father, Carl Robert Michel,
a volunteer NRA Instructor who taught his three sons how to shoot.
And to my mother, Joan Hancock Michel,
who loved us enough to put up with it,
and to occasionally plink a can off the back stoop
with the Crosman 760 herself.

DISCLAIMER

This book is not "the law," and it is not a substitute for "the law." "The law" includes all legal obligations imposed on you as a gun owner and involves a much greater volume of work and opinion than the coverage of firearm statutes and regulations contained in this book. No book can cover everything or replace a competent and experienced lawyer's advice. This book is only a guide, designed to provide general information regarding California gun laws and to provide references to seek additional information. It is not intended to be a legal treatise or a summary of the entire body of law covering firearms.

We expressly disclaim any liability for errors or omissions that may be in this book. There are many legal and technical "gray area" questions about firearms law that have not been decided by the courts and may never be. Although we do our best to identify the gray areas of which we are aware and provide *our* analysis and *likely* or *possible* interpretations as to how courts *may* decide certain issues, by no means should our analysis or interpretations be taken as the law. Despite our efforts in researching, collecting, organizing, writing, and preparing this book, we do not make any claims, promises, or guarantees about the absolute accuracy, completeness, or adequacy of the contents of this book. The opinions of other attorneys, and particularly prosecuting attorneys or judges, may be different from ours.

Many people find laws hard to understand, and gathering all the relevant ones, let alone explaining them, is a lot of work. This book helps you with these chores. Again, while great care has been taken to accomplish this with a high degree of accuracy, *no guarantee of accuracy is expressed or implied, and the explanatory sections of this book are not to be considered legal advice or a restatement of law.*

The exact language of the principal state laws controlling gun use in California is generally not reprinted verbatim in this book. Typically, only edited pieces of laws are included here. The laws and other regulations are expressed in conversational terms for your convenience and are cross-referenced with statutes or published court cases. In using plain English to explain the general meanings of the laws, differences inevitably arise, so *you must always check the actual laws.*

You are fully accountable under the exact words and current official interpretations of all applicable laws, regulations, court precedents, executive orders, and more when you deal with firearms under any circumstances. You are responsible for researching any federal, state, and/or local law(s) that are applicable to your particular inquiry or circumstance, or for hiring an attorney to advise you on your particular question given your particular circumstances. For guidance on how to find a competent attorney, review the "How to Judge a Lawyer" memorandum published on my website, www.CalGunLawsBook.com.

Even though we are attorneys, we are not providing legal advice nor are we rendering other professional services. The use of this book does *not* create an attorney-client relationship. Please do not send us or our law firm any confidential or sensitive information until you speak with an attorney and obtain prior written authorization to send that information to our law office. Guidance on how to communicate with our office so that confidentiality can be preserved is available through our website, www.MichelLawyers.com. Communication of information by, in, to, or through this book and your receipt *or* use of it (1) is *not* provided in the course of and does not create or constitute an attorney-client relationship, (2) is *not* intended as a solicitation, (3) is *not* intended to convey or constitute legal advice, and (4) is *not* a substitute for obtaining legal advice from a qualified attorney. You should not act upon any such information without first seeking qualified professional counsel on your specific matter. The hiring of an attorney is an important decision that should not be based solely upon this book or its promotional materials.

For the most part, local ordinances, rules, regulations, and policies are not covered by this book. This book concerns the general gun laws as they apply to law-abiding private residents in the state of California only. Though this book touches on certain aspects of these topics, it is not intended to and does not describe most situations relating to licensed gun dealers; museums or educational institutions; state or federal military personnel; Native Americans; hunting; foreign nationals; the police or other peace officers; other government employees summoned by a peace officer to help in the performance of official duties; people with special licenses, authorizations or permits; non-residents; bequests or intestate succession; persons under indictment; felons; prisoners; escapees; dangerous or repeat offenders; criminal street gang members; incorrigible juvenile delinquents; or unsupervised juveniles.

While this book discusses possible criminal consequences of improper gun use, it avoids most issues related to deliberate gun crimes, particularly violent ones. This means certain laws are excluded or not explained in the text. Some examples are: 1st degree murder, 2nd degree murder, homicide, manslaughter, gun theft, gun-running, concealment of stolen firearms, enhanced penalties for commission of crimes with firearms (including armed robbery, burglary, theft, kidnapping, drug offenses, assault, and priors), smuggling firearms into public aircraft, threatening flight attendants with firearms, possession of contraband, possession of a firearm in a prison by a prisoner, false application for a firearm, shooting at a building or vehicle, possession of a firearm in association with a criminal street gang, removal of a body after a shooting, drive-by shooting, and retaliation. This is only a partial list.

New laws and regulations may be enacted at any time by federal, state, and local authorities. The authors and publisher make no representation that this book includes all requirements and prohibitions that may exist. Be aware that firearm laws are subject to change anytime. You are strongly urged to consult with a qualified attorney and local authorities to determine the current status and applicability of the law to specific situations you may encounter.

You are accepting this book, and the contents thereof, "as is" without any warranty of any kind, express or implied, including but not limited to the implied warranty of merchantability or fitness for a particular purpose. All liability and/or resulting damages from this book's use are disclaimed. Again, the author and publisher expressly disclaim any liability whatsoever arising out of reliance on information contained in this book. *The Author and the Publisher Shall Not Be Liable for Any Direct, Indirect, Incidental, Special, Exemplary, or Consequential Damages However Caused and on Any Theory of Liability, Whether in Contract, Strict Liability, or Tort, Arising in Any Way out of the Use of this Book.* Damages disclaimed include, but are not limited to, direct, indirect, incidental, compensatory, equitable, exemplary, special, and/or consequential damages, regardless of any cause of action by which the damages may arise.

Again, the information contained in this book is not a substitute for professional advice and does not constitute professional advice, nor is the information contained in this book conveyed or intended to be conveyed as professional advice. Under no circumstances shall you hold the author responsible for any acts you decide to take or not to take. Any decisions you make, and any subsequent consequences, are your own. If you need legal advice or other expert assistance, hire a lawyer familiar with firearms law.

Contents

TABLES xxvii
ABBREVIATIONS xxx
ACKNOWLEDGMENTS xxxii
A SUMMARY OF THE PAST YEAR AND
 WHAT'S NEW IN THE EIGHTH EDITION xxxiv
NEW LAWS FOR 2021 xxxviii

CHAPTER 1: INTRODUCTION 1
I. GUN SAFETY IS YOUR RESPONSIBILITY 1
II. HOW TO USE THIS BOOK... 2
   A. The Materials Posted at www.CalGunLawsBook.com
      and www.crpa.org Complement This Book 3
   B. Symbols Used Throughout This Book 3
III. HOW TO READ LAWS AND DETERMINE WHETHER
    THEY APPLY... 4
   A. Federal Laws, State Laws, and Local Laws 4
   B. Statutory Interpretation Techniques 4
   C. Determining Which Statute Controls When There
      Are Duplicate Laws for the Same Crime 5
   D. How to Read Court Opinions 7
IV. HOW TO JUDGE A LAWYER 7

CHAPTER 2: THE CALIFORNIA REGULATORY ENVIRONMENT 9
I. THE UGLY PROCESS OF GUN LAW POLITICS............ 9
   A. The Legislative Process 9
   B. Local Laws... 11
   C. How the Initiative Process Works 13
   D. The Gun Ban Lobby's "Feel Good" Laws 14
   E. Law Enforcement's Overaggressive Enforcement 15
   F. The Pro-Gun Lobby 15
      1. The National Rifle Association and The California
         Rifle & Pistol Association... 15
   G. Gun Violence Research 16
II. THE RIGHT TO KEEP AND BEAR ARMS AND TO
    SELF-DEFENSE... 19

    A. The United States and California Constitutions 19
    B. Primary Issues Being Addressed in Current Second Amendment Litigation 20
III. THE PREEMPTION DOCTRINE 22
    A. Federal Preemption Doctrine 22
    B. California Preemption Doctrine 23
IV. THE CALIFORNIA LEGAL SCHEME 25
    A. The Dangerous Weapons Control Act (DWCA) 25
    B. Confusion Runs Rampant 25
    C. 2012 Reorganization of the Dangerous Weapons Control Act 27
    D. "Gray Areas" and Test Cases 28
    E. Government Bias in Applying Gun Laws 29

CHAPTER 3: WHAT IS LEGALLY CONSIDERED A "FIREARM" AND "AMMUNITION"? 31

I. "FIREARM" DEFINITIONS 31
    A. Federal Law "Firearm" Definitions 31
        1. The Gun Control Act 32
        2. The National Firearms Act 32
        3. What Is a Frame or Receiver Under Federal Law? 34
        4. Are Precursor (80%) Receivers "Firearms"? 35
        5. Are Non-Functioning Firearms "Firearms"? 35
    B. California Law "Firearm" Definitions 35
        1. History of California's "Firearm" Definition 36
        2. When Is a Frame or Receiver Considered a "Firearm"? 37
        3. What Is a Frame or Receiver Under California Law? 37
        4. Are Non-functioning Firearms "Firearms"? 38
        5. Are Precursor (80%) Receivers "Firearms" Under California Law? 39
II. FIREARM SUBGROUP DEFINITIONS 39
    A. "Handguns" 39
        1. Pistols 40
        2. Revolvers 41
    B. "Rifles," "Shotguns," and "Long Guns" 42
        1. Rifles 42
        2. Shotguns 43

		3. Long Guns..43

      D. Definition of "Weapon" 45
      E. "Antique Firearms" 46
           1. Federal Law Definitions..46
               a. The Gun Control Act 46
               b. The National Firearms Act 48
           2. California Law Definition 49
      F. "Curios or Relics" 49

III. IS THAT THING CONSIDERED A "FIREARM"? 50
      A. Bang Sticks/Shark Killers 51
      B. Coyote Booby Traps 52
      C. Potato Guns a.k.a. "Spud Guns" 52
      D. Flare Guns With Metal Inserts 53
      E. 37mm Flare Launchers 54
      F. Explosive-Powered Nail Guns 55
      G. Items Meeting the "Firearm" Definition, But Expressly Exempted 55

IV. "AMMUNITION"..55
      A. Federal Law "Ammunition" Definition 55
      B. California Law "Ammunition" Definitions................................56
           1. Deactivated Ammunition 57
      C. "Ammunition" Parts 58

CHAPTER 4: WHO CAN OWN AND POSSESS FIREARMS AND AMMUNITION?...............................61

I. WHAT DOES "POSSESSION" MEAN? 62
II. WHAT DOES "OWN" MEAN? 63
III. DETERMINING WHEN FIREARM POSSESSION PROHIBITIONS APPLY DURING FIREARM PURCHASES........63
IV. CALIFORNIA'S ARMED PROHIBITED PERSON SYSTEM (APPS) AND FIREARM DENIALS REPORTED TO LAW ENFORCEMENT 64
V. FIREARM AND AMMUNITION POSSESSION RESTRICTIONS FOR MINORS (UNDER AGE 18) 66
      A. Rifles and Shotguns 66
      B. Handguns 66
      C. Ammunition 67

D. Exemption to Federal Restriction on Handguns and "Handgun Ammunition" 68

VI. CRIMINAL CONVICTIONS RESULTING IN LOSS OF FIREARM POSSESSION RIGHTS 69

    A. Federal Restrictions for Certain State or Federal Convictions 70

    B. California Restrictions for Felony Convictions 71

    C. California Lifetime Restrictions Following Convictions of P.C. Section 273.5 and Certain "Violent Crimes" 71

    D. California Convictions of Offenses Listed in Penal Code Section 23515(a), (b), and (d), or Two or More Convictions Under Penal Code Section 417(a)(2) Resulting in a Lifetime Restriction 72

    E. California Restrictions for Certain Misdemeanor Convictions 74

        1. Misdemeanor Convictions Resulting in a Ten-Year Restriction 74

        2. Misdemeanor Conviction Resulting in a Five-Year Restriction 79

    F. Federal Restrictions for a Misdemeanor Crime of Domestic Violence (MCDV) 80

        1. California Offenses that May Be a Misdemeanor Crime of Domestic Violence 81

            a. Injuring a Spouse, Cohabitant, Fiancé, Etc. 81

            b. Battery Against a Spouse, Cohabitant, Fiancé, Etc. 82

        2. Other California Crimes That May Be Considered a Misdemeanor Crime of Domestic Violence 84

    G. Juvenile Offenses 84

    H. Persons on Probation or Parole 86

    I. Notice Required 88

    J. Unlawful Detainer Actions 89

VII. APPLICATION OF EX POST FACTO PROHIBITIONS ON FIREARM POSSESSION 89

    A. The Effect of a California Conviction in Other States 90

VIII. POSSESSING A FIREARM WHILE BEING A "FUGITIVE FROM JUSTICE" AND THE CALIFORNIA RESTRICTION FOR POSSESSING A FIREARM WHILE HAVING AN OUTSTANDING WARRANT FOR CERTAIN OFFENSES 90

    A. Federal Law for Firearm Prohibitions Based on "Fugitive from Justice" Status 90

	B. California Law for Firearm Prohibitions Based on an Outstanding Warrant for a Felony or for Certain Misdemeanors 91
IX.	DRUG ADDITION FIREARM POSSESSION PROHIBITION 92
	A. Federal Restrictions for Drug Addiction and Use 92
	B. California Restrictions for Drug Addiction 94
X.	MENTAL HEALTH RELATED FIREARM RESTRICTIONS 95
	A. Federal Mental Health Restrictions 96
	1. California Commitments Resulting in Federal Restrictions 97
	B. Dangerous Inpatients 97
	C. Communicating Threats to a Psychotherapist 97
	D. Mental Disorders, Illnesses, or Disordered Sex Offenders 98
	E. Not Guilty by Reason of Insanity 98
	F. Incompetence to Stand Trial 98
	G. Individuals Under Conservatorship 99
	H. Dangerous or Gravely Disabled Persons 99
	I. Those Committed to Intensive Treatment 100
XI.	RESTRAINING ORDERS AND FIREARM POSSESSION RESTRICTIONS 102
	A. Federal Domestic Violence Restraining Orders 102
	B. California Law Restrictions 103
	1. "Gun Violence Restraining Orders" 105
	2. Voluntary Surrender of Firearm Rights for Individuals Facing GVROs 107
XII.	EXCEPTIONS FOR PROHIBITED PERSONS POSSESSING FIREARMS 108
	A. Self-Defense 108
	B. Momentary Possession 110
	C. Justifiable Possession 111
XIII.	OTHER FEDERAL LAW FIREARM POSSESSION RESTRICTIONS 112
	A. Aliens 112
	B. Dishonorable Discharge From the Armed Forces 114
	C. Renouncing United States Citizenship 114
	D. Federal Restrictions Against Indicted Persons Receiving Firearms 114
XIV.	Dealer's Record of Sale (DROS) Delays 115

XV. ACQUIRING YOUR CRIMINAL RECORDS AND
DETERMINING YOUR ELIGIBILITY TO POSSESS
FIREARMS 117
   A. Obtaining Your Criminal History 117
   B. Determining Your Firearm Eligibility 117

CHAPTER 5: OBTAINING FIREARMS AND AMMUNITION 119
I. PURCHASING FIREARMS FROM A LICENSED DEALER 120
   A. Sale Requirements for All Firearms (Both Handguns and Long Guns) 120
      1. Federal Form 4473 Requirements 120
      2. California Dealer's Record of Sale (DROS) Form 121
      3. Proof of Identity, Age, and Address 122
         a. Federal Identification Requirements 123
         b. California Identification Requirements 124
         c. REAL IDs, Non-REAL IDs, and AB 60 125
            i. Eligibility Checks Submitted Via Paper Format .. 127
            ii. Eligibility Checks Submitted Via Electronic Format 128
            iii. DROS Transactions (Firearms and Ammunition Purchases) 128
            iv. Other Eligibility Checks 128
         d. Special Circumstances 129
            i. Members of the Military Stationed in California ... 129
            ii. Non-Citizens (Aliens) 129
            ii. Dual Residency 130
         e. Dealer Record of Sales Fees 131
      4. Background Checks 131
      5. Registration at Time of Purchase 132
         a. Voluntary Registration 132
         b. Confusion Regarding the AFS Requirement for All Firearms After January 1, 2014 133
      6. Waiting Period 133
      7. Required Locking Devices and Warnings 135
      8. Firearm Safety Certificate 137
         a. "Firearm Safety" Certificate Exemptions 137

			b. Firearm Safe-Handling Demonstration 147
		B. Additional Purchase Requirements 149	
			1. Only One Firearm Purchase Every 30 Days 149
			2. Proof of Residency 151
II.	PRIVATE PARTY FIREARM TRANSFERS 155		
III.	DEALER LICENSE REQUIREMENTS AND SELLING YOUR FIREARMS 158		
	A. Federal Law 158		
	B. California Law 159		
		1. Exceptions 160	
IV.	INTERSTATE FIREARM PURCHASES AND TRANSFERS 160		
	A. Transfers From Out-of-State Dealers 160		
	B. Interstate Private Party Transfers 162		
		1. Shipping Firearms 163	
	C. Exemptions to California's Restriction on Out-of-State Transfers 164		
V.	LOANING FIREARMS TO ADULTS 169		
VI.	TRANSFERRING AND LOANING FIREARMS TO YOUNG PEOPLE 176		
	A. Dealer Sales 176		
		1. Federal Law 176	
		2. California Law 177	
	B. Those Under Age 18 177		
		1. Loans and Transfers to Minors 177	
VII.	EXCEPTIONS TO TRANSFERRING FIREARMS THROUGH A FEDERAL FIREARMS LICENSEE IN CALIFORNIA 180		
	A. Federal Law 180		
	B. California Law 180		
		1. Intra-Family Transactions 180	
			a. Change in Law for Long Guns 181
		2. Transfers Between Spouses or Domestic Partners 182	
			a. Firearms and Divorce 182
		3. "Operation of Law" Transfers Other Than Transfers Between Spouses Involving Transmutation of Property 183	
		4. Gun Trusts 185	
			a. NFA Trusts 185
			b. Non-NFA Gun Trusts in California 186

i. California Firearm Transfer Laws in the Context of Gun Trusts 186

ii. Relevant Exceptions to Having to Process Firearm Transfers Through a Licensed Firearms Dealer, As Applied to Non-NFA Gun Trusts 188

Intra-Familial Transfers... 188

Transfers of Firearms Between Spouses 188

Taking Title by Operation of Law 189

Transfers of Long Guns to Minors by Immediate Family Members 189

"Antique Firearms"... 190

iii. Limitation of Non-NFA Gun Trusts: Firearms Cannot be Shared Amongst Trustees, So California Laws on Firearm Loaning Must be Followed If Trustees Want to "Share" Firearms 190

iv. Limitations of Non-NFA Gun Trusts as Applied to "Assault Weapons"/.50 BMG Rifles and "Large-Capacity Magazines" 190

"Assault Weapons" and .50 BMG Rifles.................. 190

"Large-Capacity Magazines" 191

5. Transfers to Those With an Entertainment Firearm Permit (EFP) 191

6. Acquiring Antiques and "Curio or Relic" Firearms 192

   a. Antique Firearms.. 192

   b. "Curio or Relic" Firearms...................................... 192

7. Auction of Non-Handguns 195

8. "Gun Buybacks" 196

9. Other Limited Exceptions 197

VIII. BUILDING YOUR OWN FIREARM 197

  A. Ways to Build Your Own Firearm 198

    1. Creating a Firearm from a Prefabricated Frame or Receiver 198

      a. Requirement that Firearm Precursor Part Sales Be Conducted Through a Licensed Precursor Part Vendor.. 199

      b. Face-to-Face Transaction Requirement................. 200

      c. Exceptions to the Requirement that Firearm Precursor Part Sales Must Be Conducted Through a Licensed Firearm Precursor Part Vendor and Face-to-Face Requirement. 201

d. Recording of Firearm Precursor Part Purchaser or Transferee Information..202

e. Persons Prohibited from Possessing Firearm Precursor Parts. 203

f. Authorization to Purchase Firearm Precursor Parts. 203

g. Restriction Against Bringing Firearm Precursor Parts into California..205

2. Creating a Firearm From an 80% Receiver...................206
3. "Build Parties"...206
4 3D Printing 207

B. Registration Requirements for Manufacturing or Assembling Your Own Firearm 208

1. Submitting Applications for a DOJ-Approved Serial Number 208

2. Engraving the Unique Serial Number and Required Digital Images 210

3. Deadlines to Engrave and Upload Required Digital Images 211

3. Firearms Exempt from AB 857's Serialization Requirements...212

IX. COMING INTO CALIFORNIA WITH FIREARMS......................213
A. Visiting California...213
B. Moving Into California..214

X. FIREARM STORAGE 216
A. Criminal Storage in the First, Second, and Third Degree for Loaded Firearms 216
B. Storage of Firearms..217
C. Exceptions to Criminal Storage in the First, Second, and Third Degree and Storage of Handguns or Any Firearms..217
D. Residing With a Person Who Is Prohibited from Possessing, Receiving, Owning, or Purchasing Firearms..218
E. Storage of Handgun in Unattended Vehicle 219
   1. Storage of Lawfully-Obtained "Unsafe" Handgun in Unattended Vehicle by Certain Law Enforcement Officers...221
F. Local Storage Laws 222
G. Penalties for Community Care Facilities,

Residential Care Facilities, Residential Care Facilities for the Elderly, Family Care Homes, and Day Care Centers ...223
XI. FALSE REPORTS OF LOST OR STOLEN FIREARMS........226
XII. REPORTING LOST OR STOLEN FIREARMS 226
XIII. ACQUIRING AMMUNITION 227
    A. Ammunition Sales & Transfers 228
        1. Requirement that Ammunition Sales Must Be Conducted Through a Licensed Ammunition Vendor ...228
        2. Face-to-Face Transaction Requirement.........................229
        3. Exceptions to the Requirement that Ammunition Sales Must Be Conducted Through a Licensed Ammunition Vendor and Face-to-Face Requirement....230
        4. Recording of Ammunition Purchaser or Transferee Information 231
        5. Required DOJ Electronic Approval 232
            a. Updating AFS Records for Purposes of Obtaining the Required DOJ Electronic Approval.....................233
        6. Exceptions to the Record Keeping and Electronic Approval Requirements...235
    B. Restriction on California Resident's Bringing or Transporting Ammunition Into California 237

CHAPTER 6: CARRYING FIREARMS OPENLY, CONCEALED, AND/OR LOADED............................239
I. WHAT DOES "CARRY" MEAN? 239
II. WHAT DOES "IN A VEHICLE," "ON," OR "UPON THE PERSON" MEAN? 240
III. CONCEALED CARRY LAW..241
    A. Carrying "Concealed" 241
    B. What Does "Concealed" Mean? 243
IV. LOADED CARRY LAW 244
    A. Loaded Firearm Restrictions 247
    B. What Does "Loaded" Mean? 247
        1. General Definition of "Loaded"......................................249
        2. "Loaded" While Committing a Felony or in Sensitive Places 249
        3. Fish and Game's Definition of "Loaded" 249
V. OPEN CARRY OF HANDGUNS RESTRICTION.......................250
VI. RESTRICTION ON CARRYING FIREARMS OTHER THAN HANDGUNS 252

	A.	"Firearm That Is Not a Handgun"..253
	B.	Penalties for Unlawful Carry of Non-Handguns....................253
VII.	PLACES WHERE CARRY RESTRICTIONS APPLY 254	
	A.	What Does "Public Place" Mean? 255
	B.	What Does "Public Street" Mean? 257

CHAPTER 7: FIREARM CARRY RESTRICTION EXEMPTIONS AND TRANSPORTING FIREARMS 263

I. HOW TO USE THIS SECTION 263

II. EXEMPTIONS TO THE GENERAL CARRY RESTRICTIONS IN NON-PUBLIC PLACES: RESIDENCES, PRIVATE PROPERTY, AND PRIVATE PLACES OF BUSINESS 264

    A. Exemptions for Carrying Loaded Firearms and Openly Carrying Unloaded Handguns 264

    B. Exemptions for Carrying a Concealed Handgun 265

    C. Exemptions for Carrying "Firearms That Are Not Handguns"..265

III. EXEMPTIONS TO THE GENERAL CARRY RESTRICTIONS IN PUBLIC PLACES 266

    A. Temporary Residences and Campsites...............................266

    B. Business or Other Privately Owned or Possessed Property Open to the Public 267

    C. Vehicle or Boat as a Residence...268

    D. Vehicle or Boat as a Place of Business 269

    E. Motor Vehicles 269

        1. Locked Container Requirement 270

        2. "Lawful Purpose" Requirement 271

        3. Transporting "Assault Weapons" and .50 BMG Rifles in Motor Vehicles...272

    F. Motorcycles and Bicycles 272

    G. Boats 273

    H. Being in "Grave Danger"...273

        1. Protected by a Restraining Order..................................273

        2. Not Protected by a Restraining Order 274

IV. CARRYING WHILE HUNTING OR FISHING 274

V. ADDITIONAL EXEMPTIONS TO THE GENERAL CARRY RESTRICTIONS 275

    A. Exemptions for Carrying Concealed Handguns 275

        1. Conditional Exemptions for Carrying Concealed Handguns..276

		2.	"Other Exemptions" for Carrying Concealed Handguns 278
	B.	Exemptions for Carrying Loaded Firearms...........................278
	C.	Exemptions to the Restriction on Openly Carrying Handguns in Public 280
	D.	Exemptions to Restriction on Carrying "Firearms That Are Not Handguns" 283
		1.	"Locked Container" or "Encased"..................................283
		2.	Other Exemptions to the Restriction on Carrying "Firearms That Are Not Handguns" 284
VI.	LICENSES TO CARRY A LOADED HANDGUN 288
	A.	Criteria for Issuance 289
		1.	"Good Cause"..290
		2.	"Good Moral Character" 290
		3.	Residency 291
		4.	Training Course...291
	B.	Issuing Authorities' Mandatory Written Policy.......................292
	C.	Application Process and Fees...293
	D.	License Revocation and Moving Out of the Jurisdiction.......294
	E.	License Restrictions 295
	F.	Form of Physical License 295
	G.	License Amendments 295
VII.	EXEMPTIONS FOR ACTIVE & RETIRED PEACE OFFICERS..296
	A.	Concealed and Loaded Restrictions 296
		1.	Current Law Enforcement Officers................................296
			a. California Peace Officers......................................296
			b. Current Reserve Peace Officers 297
			c. Other Current Officers 297
			d. Current Federal and Out-of-State Officers 298
		2.	Retired Law Enforcement 298
			a. Retired California Peace Officers 299
			b. Retired Reserve California Peace Officers............301
			c. Retired Federal Peace Officers 301
	B.	Law Enforcement Officers Safety Act (LEOSA/H.R. 218) 302
		1.	QLEO Definition and ID Requirements 302
		2.	QRLEO Definition and ID Requirements.......................303

3. LEOSA and the California Department of Justice 306
4. Limits on LEOSA and the Types of Firearms One May Carry 306
5. LEOSA and Reserve Officers (Active and Retired) 307

VIII. TRANSPORTATION OF FIREARMS IN PUBLIC TRANSPORTATION OR ACROSS STATE LINES 308
   A. Transporting Firearms on Airplanes 308
   B. Transporting on a Bus or Other Public Transportation 310
   C. Transporting Firearms Across State Lines 310

IX. SUGGESTIONS ON HOW TO CARRY FIREARMS IN COMPLIANCE WITH CALIFORNIA FIREARMS LAWS 313

X. CARRY EXEMPTIONS TABLE 314

CHAPTER 8: PLACES WHERE FIREARM POSSESSION IS PROHIBITED AND FIREARM USE IS RESTRICTED 337

I. FIREARM POSSESSION IN GOVERNMENT BUILDINGS 338
   A. Federal Law 338
   B. California Law 338

II. FIREARM POSSESSION IN "SCHOOL ZONES" 340
   A. Federal Law 341
   B. California Law 342
   C. California and Federal Discharge Restrictions 344

III. AMMUNITION & WEAPON POSSESSION ON "SCHOOL GROUNDS" 344

IV. FIREARM POSSESSION IN AIRPORTS, ON AIRPLANES, AND ON COMMON CARRIERS 346
   A. Possession in Airport "Sterile Areas" 346
      1. Federal Law 346
      2. California Law 347
   B. Possession on Commercial Airplanes 348
   C. Possession on Amtrak Trains 348
   D. Possession on Greyhound Buses 349
   E. Possession on All Other Common Carriers 349
   F. Possession in Harbors & Ports 349
   G. Possession in "Sterile Area" of Public Transportation Facility 350

V. FIREARM POSSESSION IN PARKS, FORESTS, AND REFUGES 351

A. Federal Lands..351
   1. National Parks and Wildlife Refuges............................351
   2. National Forests..352
   3. Bureau of Land Management (BLM) and Other Federally Protected Areas..352
   4. United States Army Corps of Engineers (USACE) Managed Land..353
B. California State Lands..353
   1. Other Parks...355

VI. FIREARM POSSESSION IN UNITED STATES AND INTERNATIONAL WATERS..355
VII. FIREARM POSSESSION AT PROTEST EVENTS......................357
VIII. FIREARM POSSESSION AND POLITICIANS...........................357
IX. OTHER RESTRICTED PLACES UNDER CALIFORNIA LAW...358
   A. Gun Shows...358
   B. Polling Places...358
   C. Playgrounds and Youth Centers....................................359
X. RESTRICTING FIREARM POSSESSION BY PRIVATE BUSINESSES...359
XI. GENERAL FIREARM DISCHARGE RESTRICTIONS.................360
XII. SHOOTING RANGE USE RESTRICTIONS................................362
XIII. SUGGESTIONS FOR SHOOTING IN PUBLIC...........................362

CHAPTER 9: REGULATION OF "ASSAULT WEAPONS" AND .50 BMG RIFLES..365
I. "ASSAULT WEAPON" DEFINED...366
   A. Category 1 "Assault Weapons"......................................366
   B. Category 2 "Assault Weapons"......................................366
   C. Category 3 "Assault Weapons"......................................370
      1. A Brief History..370
      2. Category 3 Rifles..371
      3. Category 3 Pistols..372
      4. Category 3 Shotguns...373
      5. "Other" Category 3 Firearms That Are Not Rifles, Pistols, or Shotguns..374
         a. DOJ's Regulatory Definitions Applicable to Category 3 "Assault Weapons"..............................376
   D. Making Firearms That Would Otherwise Be Classified as

        "Assault Weapons" Compliant with California Law 384
           1. Aftermarket Parts 385
           2. Compliant Features 385
      E. Possessing the Parts of an "Assault Weapon" 386
II. .50 BMG RIFLES 387
III. "ASSAULT WEAPON" AND .50 BMG RIFLE USE
RESTRICTIONS 388
      A. Civil Compromise for Illegally Possessing an "Assault
Weapon" or .50 BMG Rifle 389
      B. Infraction for First Violation of Possessing an "Assault
Weapon" 390
IV. EXCEPTIONS TO "ASSAULT WEAPON" AND .50 BMG
RIFLE LAWS 390
A. Law Enforcement and Other Government Agencies 390
      B. Peace Officers and Federal Law Enforcement Acquiring
"Assault Weapons" and .50 BMG Rifles 391
      C. Carrying "Assault Weapons" Under the Law
Enforcement Officer Safety Act (LEOSA) 391
      D. Estate Executor and Inheritance 392
      E. Loaning and Returning an "Assault Weapon" or .50
BMG Rifle 392
      F. Nonresident Possession at Match or Competition 393
      G. California Department of Justice Permits 393
      H. "Licensed Gun Dealer" Exceptions 395
           1. Service or Repair 395
           2. Other Special Allowances 395
V. ACQUIRING NEW "ASSAULT WEAPONS" OR .50 BMG
RIFLES 396
      A. Registration ((with the exception of newly classified
"other" firearms). 396
           1. Post-Registration Modification of "Bullet Buttons"
of Registered Assault Weapons Is Prohibited 398
           2. Voluntary Deregistration 398
      B. Alternatives to Registration 399
VI. MOVING INTO CALIFORNIA WITH AN "ASSAULT
WEAPON" OR .50 BMG RIFLE 399
VII. LAWFULLY USING "ASSAULT WEAPONS" AND .50 BMG
RIFLES 399
      A. Transporting Registered "Assault Weapons" and .50

BMG Rifles..400
VIII. WHAT TO DO IF YOU THINK YOU HAVE AN "ASSAULT WEAPON" OR .50 BMG RIFLE THAT YOU AREN'T SURE IS LEGAL 400
    A. Determine if It Is an "Assault Weapon" or .50 BMG Rifle 400
    B. Determine if Your "Assault Weapon" or .50 BMG Rifle Was Registered 401
    C. If Your "Assault Weapon" or .50 BMG Rifle Is Unregistered 401
IX. "ASSAULT WEAPONS" LISTED BY NAME.............................401
    A. Combined Listing of Category 1 and Category 2 "Assault Weapons" 401

CHAPTER 10: OTHER HEAVILY REGULATED FIREARMS AND DEVICES 407

I. "MACHINEGUNS"...407
    A. Prohibitions 409
    B. California Exceptions to "Machinegun" Restrictions............409
        1. Law Enforcement and Military...........................410
        2. Permits to Possess, Manufacture, and Transport 410
    C. Licenses to Sell "Machineguns" 411
    D. "Bump Stocks" in the Context of Machinegun Restrictions . 411
        1. Bump Stocks Under Federal Law 411
        2. Bump Stocks Under California Law 411
II. "DESTRUCTIVE DEVICES"..412
    A. Permits..415
    B. Exceptions for Peace Officers, Firefighters, and Military.....416
    C. 37mm Flare Launchers v. Grenade Launchers and 22mm Grenade Launchers v. Flash Suppressors/Muzzle Brakes 416
    D. Cannons 417
III. "GENERALLY PROHIBITED WEAPONS" 418
    A. "Cane Gun"..420
    B. "Wallet Gun"..420
    C. "Undetectable Firearm"..420
    D. Firearms Not "Immediately Recognizable" as Firearms 421
    E. "Camouflaging Firearm Container" 422
    F. "Multiburst Trigger Activator"..................................422
    G. "Short-Barreled Shotguns" and "Short-Barreled Rifles".......424

1. "Short-Barreled Shotguns" 424
2. "Short-Barreled Rifles" 426
3. Possession of Parts Constituting "Short-Barreled Shotguns/Rifles"..428
4. Pistol Stabilizing Braces 429

H. "Zip Gun" 431
I. "Unconventional Pistol"...432
J. "Large-Capacity Magazine" and "Large-Capacity Magazine Conversion Kits"...432
1. Definition 432
2. *Duncan v. Becerra* and California's Attempt to Ban "Possession" of "Large-Capacity" Magazines 435
3. Restricted Activity for "Large-Capacity Magazines" 436
4. Restricted Activity for "Large-Capacity Magazine Conversion Kits"...437
5. Local Restrictions on "Large-Capacity Magazines".......439

IV. EXCEPTIONS TO CALIFORNIA LAW FOR "GENERALLY PROHIBITED WEAPONS," "LARGE-CAPACITY MAGAZINE CONVERSION KITS," AND THE BAN ON "LARGE-CAPACITY MAGAZINE" POSSESSION..442
A. "Antique Firearms"..443
B. "Curios or Relics"..443
C. "Any Other Weapons" 443
D. Historical Society, Museum, or Institutional Collection 443
E. Media or Entertainment Events 444
F. People Who Sell Items to Historical Societies, Museums, Institutional Collections, or Entertainment Events 444
G. Law Enforcement Firearm Purchases and Those Who Sell to Law Enforcement...444
H. Transporting Most "Generally Prohibited Weapons" to Law Enforcement..445
I. Forensic Laboratory..445

V. ADDITIONAL CALIFORNIA LAW EXCEPTIONS FOR "LARGE-CAPACITY MAGAZINE" AND "LARGE-CAPACITY MAGAZINE CONVERSION KIT" RESTRICTIONS.....................446
A. Law Enforcement Agencies 446
B. Use During a Basic Training Course Prescribed by the Commission on Peace Officer Standards and Training........446
C. Peace Officers 447
1. Federal Law Enforcement 448

		2. Honorably Retired Sworn Peace Officers & Federal Law Enforcement Officers 448
	D.	Dealer Acquisition 449
	E.	Loans Between Individuals.. 449
	F.	Dealer or Gunsmith Loan for Maintenance/Repair 449
	G.	Importing or Selling Between Out-of-State Clients With a Permit 449
	H.	Entities Operating An Armored Vehicle Business 450
	I.	Manufacturing "Large-Capacity Magazines" by Law Enforcement 450
	J.	Entertainment Industry Props 451
	K.	Purchase by Special Weapons Permit Holder 451
	L.	Receipt or Disposition by Trustees, Executors, or Administrators 451
	M.	Finding and Delivering "Large-Capacity Magazines" to Law Enforcement 451
	N.	Possessing the "Large-Capacity Magazine" Solely for Use with a Firearm that Is Lawfully-Obtained Prior to 2000 that Is Incompatible with Magazines Holding 10 or Fewer Rounds 452
VI.	ADDITIONAL EXCEPTIONS TO CALIFORNIA LAW FOR RESTRICTIONS ON "SHORT-BARRELED SHOTGUNS/RIFLES" 452	
	A.	Law Enforcement Agencies 452
	B.	Permit Authorization 453
VII.	"SILENCERS"/"SOUND SUPPRESSORS" 453	
VIII.	OBLITERATED OR COVERED SERIAL NUMBERS 455	
IX.	"UNSAFE" HANDGUNS 457	
	A.	"Microstamping" 459
		1. "Smart Gun" Technology 461
	B.	Exceptions to the "Unsafe" Handgun Roster Requirement 461
		1. Law Enforcement and Military 461
		2. Purchase of a State-Issued Handgun to Spouse or Domestic Partner of a Peace Officer Who Died in the Line of Duty 462
		3. Private Party, Spousal, Operation of Law, Etc. Transfers 462
		4. Certain Peace Officers from Specified Agencies/Departments 462

	5.	Testing and Prototypes 466
	6.	"Curios or Relics" 466
	7.	Repairs 466
	8.	Pistols Used as Props and Loans to Consultant-Evaluators 466
	9.	Certain Handguns Exempt From the Roster Requirement 466
X.	AMMUNITION RESTRICTIONS 468
	A.	Ammunition With "Flechette Darts" and "Explosive Agents" 468
	B.	Armor-Piercing Handgun Ammunition 469
	1.	The Attempt to Ban "Green Tip" Ammunition 470
	C.	Tracer Ammunition 472
	D.	Lead-Based Ammunition Used in Certain Hunting Applications 472
	1.	General Exceptions to the Lead Ammunition Restrictions 473
		a. Possession of Handguns for Self-Defense 473
		b. Temporary Exception for "Calibers" that Are Commercially Unavailable in Non-lead Due to Federal "Armor Piercing Ammunition" Restrictions 473
		c. Law Enforcement Engaged in Official Duties Exception 474
	2. Penalties for Violating Lead Ammunition Restriction 474
XI.	OTHER REGULATED DEVICES 474
	A.	BB Guns 474
	B.	Toy Guns a.k.a. "Imitation Firearms" 475
	C.	"Tear Gas," "Less Lethal Weapons," and "Stun Guns" 478
	1.	"Tear Gas," Pepper Spray, and Mace 478
	2.	"Less Lethal Weapons" 480
	3.	"Stun Guns" 481
	D.	"Blowguns" 481
	E.	3D-Printed Guns 482
	F.	Sniperscopes (Night Vision Scopes) and Laser Scopes or Laser Pointers 482
XII.	NATIONAL FIREARMS ACT – FIREARM POSSESSION 484
	A.	"Any Other Weapon" Defined 484

		B. Transferring NFA Firearms 485
XIII.	EXPLOSIVES 486	
	A. "Fireworks" and "Explosives" 486	
	B. Ambiguity Concerning the Amount of Black Powder a Person Can Possess 486	
	C. Binary Exploding Targets 488	
XIV.	IGNORANCE OF THE LAW IS NO EXCUSE 488	

INDEX **489**

ABOUT THE AUTHORS **521**

TABLES

CHAPTER 2: THE CALIFORNIA REGULATORY ENVIRONMENT

Table 2.1 Examples of Cities with Restrictive Anti-Gun Ordinances 11

CHAPTER 4: WHO CAN OWN AND POSSESS FIREARMS AND AMMUNITION

Table 4.1 Summary of Restrictions for Minors Possessing Firearms and Ammunition 69
Table 4.2 Violent Crimes Resulting in a Lifetime Restriction in California 73
Table 4.3 Conduct Resulting in a Lifetime Restriction in California 75
Table 4.4 Conduct Resulting in a Ten-Year Restriction in California 75
Table 4.5 Juvenile Offenses 85
Table 4.6 Summary of California Criminal Convictions Resulting in the Loss of Firearm Rights 87
Table 4.7 Summary of Drug Prohibitions 94
Table 4.8 Mental Health Restrictions 101
Table 4.9 Restraining Order Restrictions 107
Table 4.10 A Quick Wrap Up on Other Federal Firearm Possession Restrictions 115

CHAPTER 5: HOW TO OBTAIN FIREARMS AND AMMUNITION

Table 5.1 Identification Requirements 125
Table 5.2 Firearm Safety Certificate Exemptions 138
Table 5.3 Proof of Residency Requirement: An Additional Requirement when Purchasing Handguns in California 153
Table 5.4 Quick Guide: The Process and Required Materials Needed to Purchase a Firearm from a Licensed Firearms Dealer in California 154
Table 5.5 Private Party Transfers 157

Table 5.6	Interstate Firearms Purchases and Transfers	163
Table 5.7	Exemptions to California's Restriction on Out-of-State Transfers	164
Table 5.8	Loan Exemptions	170
Table 5.9	Exemptions to Licensed Vendor Requirement for Firearm Precursor Parts Sales	201
Table 5.10	Exemptions to Electronic Approval Requirement for Firearm Precursor Parts Sales	204
Table 5.11	Exemptions to Restrictions on Bringing Firearm Precursor Parts into California	205
Table 5.12	Registration Deadlines for Individuals	215
Table 5.13	California's FIrearm Storage Laws	224
Table 5.14	California's Firearm Storage Laws	230
Table 5.15	Exemptions to California's Ammunition Vendor & Face-to-Face Requirements	235
able 5.16	Exemptions to California's Restrictions on Bringing or Transporting Ammunition into California	237

CHAPTER 6: CARRYING FIREARMS OPENLY, CONCEALED, AND/OR LOADED

Table 6.1	Carrying Concealed Handguns	244
Table 6.2	Carrying Loaded Firearms	246
Table 6.3	The Different Ways "Loaded" is Defined in California	247
Table 6.4	Openly Carrying Unloaded Handguns	252
Table 6.5	Carrying "Firearms That Are not Handguns"	254

CHAPTER 7: FIREARM CARRY RESTRICTION EXEMPTIONS AND TRANSPORTING FIREARMS

Table 7.1	Conditional Exemptions for Carrying Concealed Handguns	274
Table 7.2	"Other Exemptions" for Carrying Concealed Handguns	276
Table 7.3	Exemptions for Carrying Loaded Firearms	277
Table 7.4	Exemptions to the Restriction on Openly Carrying Handguns in Public	278

Table 7.5	Exemption to Restriction on Openly Carrying Handguns on Your Person in Public	279
Table 7.6	Other Exemptions to the Restriction on Carrying "Firearms That Are not Handguns"	282
Table 7.7	Quick Tips for Transporting Your Firearm Using Public and Private Transportation	309
Table 7.8	Carry Exemptions Table	314

CHAPTER 9: REGULATION OF "ASSAULT WEAPONS" AND .50 BMG RIFLES

Table 9.1	Quick Review of Registration Deadlines for Assault Weapons and .50 BMG Rifles	397
Table 9.2	Combined Listing of Category 1 and Category 2 "Assault Weapons"	401

ABBREVIATIONS USED THROUGHOUT THIS BOOK

Numerous laws from various sources are discussed, quoted, or paraphrased throughout this book. Additionally, common firearm language is discussed as well. Important laws or language will be fully listed when discussed for the first time in each chapter but then will be subsequently abbreviated. Below is a list of commonly used terms and their corresponding abbreviations that are consistently used throughout the book:

Armed Prohibited Persons System	APPS
Assault Weapon Identification Guide	AWIG
Assault Weapons Control Act	AWCA
Assembly Bill	AB
Attorney General	AG
Automated Firearms System	AFS
Bureau of Alcohol, Tobacco, Firearms, and Explosives	ATF
Bureau of Land Management	BLM
California Business and Professions Code	Cal. Bus. & Prof. Code
California Civil Code	Cal. Civ. Code
California Code of Civil Procedure	Cal. Civ. Proc. Code
California Code of Regulations	Cal. Code Regs.
California Department of Justice	DOJ
California Elections Code	Cal. Elections Code
California Family Code	Cal. Fam. Code
California Fish and Game Code	Cal. Fish & Game Code
California Government Code	Cal. Gov't Code
California Health and Safety Code	Cal. Health & Saf. Code
California Law Revision Commission	CLRC
California Penal Code	P.C.
California Rifle and Pistol Association	CRPA
California Vehicle Code	Cal. Veh. Code
California Welfare and Institutions Code	Cal. Welf. & Inst. Code
Carry Concealed Weapon	CCW
Certificate of Eligibility	COE
Code of Federal Regulations	C.F.R.
Code of Public Resources	C. Pub. Res.
Dangerous Weapons Control Act	DWCA

Dealer's Record of Sale	DROS
Entertainment Firearms Permit	EFP
Environmental Protection Agency	EPA
Exclusive Economic Zone	EEZ
Federal Aviation Administration	FAA
Federal Bureau of Investigation	FBI
Federal Firearms Licensee	FFL
Firearm Owners' Protection Act	FOPA
Firearm Safety Certificate	FSC
Gun Control Act	GCA
Handgun Safety Certificate	HSC
Immigration and Nationality Act	INA
Law Enforcement Gun Release	LEGR
Law Enforcement Gun Release - Firearms Eligibility Clearance Letter	LEGR Letter
Law Enforcement Officer Safety Act	LEOSA
Misdemeanor Crime of Domestic Violence	MCDV
National Firearms Act	NFA
National Instant Criminal Background Check System	NICS
National Rifle Association	NRA
National Shooting Sports Foundation	NSSF
The Office of Administrative Law	OAL
Peace Officer Standards and Training	POST
Personal Firearms Eligibility Check Application	PFEC
Post-Traumatic Stress Disorder	PTSD
Private Party Transfer	PPT
Qualified Law Enforcement Officer	QLEO
Qualified Retired Law Enforcement Officer	QRLEO
Senate Bill	SB
Transportation Security Administration	TSA
Unique Serial Number Application	USNA
United Nations Convention on the Law of the Sea	UNCLOS
United States	U.S.
United States Code	U.S.C.
United States Department of Justice	U.S. DOJ

ACKNOWLEDGMENTS

I am particularly grateful to Matthew Cubeiro, Tiffany Cheuvront, Grace Wu, and Alexander Frank for their work on this edition. Matt provided considerable content and information for this edition. Tiffany provided guidance on content and marketing. Grace and Alex reviewed content and piloted this book through the drafting, production, and publication process. I would also like to thank previous contributors to past editions: Joseph Silvoso, Ben Machida, Sean Brady, Jessica Hawari, and Tamara Rider.

I also thank the Michel & Associates, P.C. staffers, attorneys and law clerks who work or worked for Michel & Associates, P.C., or have contributed to the firm's body of firearms law knowledge and resources over the years. These contributors include Lavinia Antemie, Anna Barvir, Joshua Dale, Scott Franklin, Glenn McRoberts, Clint Monfort, Konstadinos Moros, Claudia Nuñez, W. Lee Smith, Haydee Villegas-Aguilar, and many others.

I also owe thanks to the firearm, constitutional, and other lawyers throughout the country who have mentored, counseled, employed, worked for, or worked with me over the years. These include Eric Archer, Jim Baker, Mark Barnes, Chris Chiafullo, Paul Clement, Bruce Colodny, Chris Conte, Jason Davis, John Eastman, Eric Epstein, John Frazer, Steve Halbrook, David Hardy, Irwin Nowick, , Judge Eleanor Hunter, Burt Jacobson, Don Kates, Larry Keane, Don Kilmer, David Kopel, David Lehman, Judge J.D. Lord, John Machtinger, Erin Murphy, Pat O'Malley, Al Peacock, James René, Judge Jesse Rodriguez, and Guy Smith.

I am particularly grateful to civil rights activists and leaders George Barr, Sheriff Tom Bosenko, Tom Boyer, Chris Chang, Clayton Cramer, Paul Dougherty, Jim Erdman, Joel Friedman, Roy Griffin, Hayden Heal, Steve Helsley, Dwight Van Horn, Ed Hunt, John Lott, Tanya Metaksa, Sam Parades, Paul Payne, Senator H.L. Richardson (ret.), Kim Rhode, Rick Travis, Jerry Upholt, Norm Vroman, Gene Wolberg, Ed Worley, and Sheriff Donny Youngblood for their support and insight over the years. And all the individual plaintiffs in the various lawsuits who volunteered to stand up for all of our self-defense civil rights deserve special thanks.

Activist and Bloomfield Press publisher Alan Korwin and Tiger Lilly Enterprises publishing consultant Penny Callmeyer also deserve special mention for their patience and help in making this book happen.

Cooperation and information has been gratefully received from the California Department of Justice Firearms Bureau, the Bureau of Alcohol, Tobacco, Firearms, and Explosives, Los Angeles District Attorney Steve Cooley (ret.) and the Los Angeles County District Attorney's Office, the Los Angeles County Public Defender's Office, officers with the Long Beach and Sacramento Police Departments, Redondo Beach City Attorney Mike Webb and the Redondo Beach City Attorney's Office, San Francisco Public Defender Jeff Adachi and the San Francisco Public Defender's Office, and Turner's Outdoors, Inc. Vice President of Operations Bill Ortiz.

My wife Sydne and my sons Colton and Dawson have also been particularly patient with me.

Last, but certainly not least, I thank my clients the National Rifle Association of America and the California Rifle & Pistol Association, Incorporated for the meaningful, challenging, and fulfilling legal work that those associations have allowed me to perform on behalf of NRA and CRPA members for over twenty-five years, and for the knowledge base that legal work created, much of which was put to use in writing this book.

A SUMMARY OF THE PAST YEAR AND WHAT'S NEW IN THE EIGHTH EDITION

MILLIONS OF NEW GUN OWNERS RESPOND TO DANGEROUS TIMES

2020 was a challenging year for all Americans. The spread of COVID-19 at the start of the year caused substantial disruptions to local businesses and individuals alike, the effects of which are still being felt today. Such disruptions were exasperated by various levels of response from local health officials, none of which have been uniform. Many American's lost their jobs and countless small businesses have been forced to permanently close.

With the future uncertain, the circumstances created a powder keg for civil unrest. The powder was sparked with the death of George Floyd at the hands of a Minneapolis Police Officer. In the months following, what may have started as protests for reform appears to many to have escalated into looting and rioting fueled by an overall anti-American agenda—demonizing most American traditions, and especially anyone who exercises their rights of self-defense and those protected under the Second Amendment in opposition.

Whatever the ultimate agenda may be, it appears to have backfired tremendously in the context of attacking the Second Amendment. Previously-held records for nearly every metric used to track firearm purchases have been broken—including the number of first-time gun buyers.

Of those new gun owners, many have had their previously-held notions about the process of buying a gun shattered after experiencing the reality of the process and the many hurdles and red tape that politicians and the mainstream media often ignore or suggest don't exist. Whether those lessons in the reality of gun control will cause these same individuals to think twice about taking the word of those who criticize gun ownership and diminish the Second Amendment right in general remains to be seen.

GUN STORES FIGHT BACK AGAINST COVID CLOSURES

CRPA was instrumental in ensuring that California gun owners could continue to lawfully exercise their Second Amendment rights and buy guns during these difficult times. In response to COVID-19, several anti-gun jurisdictions ordered firearm-related businesses closed. CRPA worked tirelessly with local officials and law enforcement to educate them on the essential services these businesses provide to their communities, such as facilitating private party firearm transfers and ensuring a prospective purchaser is not prohibited under state or federal laws from owning or possessing firearms.

With the support of many local firearm businesses, but in large part due to the support of the Turner's Outdoorsman stores, CRPA filed several lawsuits challenging local orders that refused to recognize gun stores and ranges as "essential" and shut them down just when folks needed access to self-defense tools most. Thanks in large part to these efforts, all firearm businesses in California were eventually reopened, and are once again open for business. Now they just need the inventory to meet demand.

THE LEGISLATURE ADVANCED ITS ANTI-GUN OWNER AGENDA

Although California's government was partially shut down in response to COVID-19, several new firearm laws were still passed by the Legislature. This Eighth Edition will discuss all the bills affecting gun owners signed into law in 2020. Unless specifically noted otherwise, these laws take effect on January 1, 2021. Summaries of each can be found in the "New Laws for 2021" section. For the Eighth Edition, we have revised, updated, and expanded the Seventh Edition to reflect the changes these new laws will make over the coming years. Don't rely on the 2020 edition in 2021! The legal landscape of California gun laws changes fast!

Of the laws signed by Governor Gavin Newsom for 2020, notable among these are SB 118 and AB 2847. SB 118 classifies certain firearms that cannot meet the legal definition of a rifle, pistol, or shotgun as "assault weapons," while also establishing a registration period for such firearms already lawfully possessed by California gun owners. AB 2847 revises the definition of an "unsafe handgun" as applied to California's microstamping requirement, while also implementing procedures for the removal of handguns currently listed on California's roster that lack microstamping.

AND DOJ DID TOO

In addition to new laws, several regulatory changes were made by the California Department of Justice ("DOJ"). Perhaps most significant among these was the increase in DROS fees from $19 to $31.19. Other changes include amendments to the Unique Serial Number Application Process for home-built firearms, amendments to the ammo vendor licensing regulations requiring COEs for all vendors, and formal rulemaking implementing federally compliant ID requirements for firearm and ammunition background checks.

SECOND AMENDMENT LAWSUITS SEE WINS

2020 also marked significant developments for firearm-related litigation, including several cases challenging California's arbitrary and ineffective gun laws.

On the national level, the United States Supreme Court was presented an opportunity to clearly define the legal standard applicable to Second Amendment related litigation in a lawsuit titled *New York State Rifle & Pistol Association, Inc., ("NYSRPA") v. City of New York, New York*. The lawsuit challenged the City's prohibition against residents transporting a handgun to any place outside city limits, even if the handgun is unloaded and in a locked container. But before oral arguments could start, the City repealed the restriction. As a result, the Supreme Court in April issued a decision holding the case moot, thereby once again failing to establish a clear legal framework for Second Amendment challenges.

Shortly before this book's publication, Supreme Court Justice Ruth Bader Ginsburg died on September 18, 2020, due to complications from metastatic pancreas cancer. Appointed to the Court by former President Bill Clinton in 1993, Justice Ginsburg routinely voted in support of state and federal anti-gun laws, thereby attempting to relegate the Second Amendment to second-hand status next to other rights enshrined by the Constitution. Should President Donald Trump succeed in filling her seat on the Court with a Justice who will instead uphold the Second Amendment, we can expect a dramatic shift in firearm-related litigation in the coming years.

Meanwhile, in California, CRPA-supported lawsuits challenging Proposition 63 and other anti-gun California laws resulted in significant victories.

On April 23, the United States District Court for the Southern District of California issued an order granting a preliminary injunction against California's recently implemented ammunition sales restrictions in the CRPA-supported lawsuit *Rhode v. Becerra*. As a result, California gun owners were once again able to purchase ammunition without the red tape and California's disastrous database errors that made it impossible for hundreds of thousands of law-abiding citizens to purchase ammunition. But just one day later, the Ninth Circuit issued a stay on the preliminary injunction, thereby allowing California to once again enforce its arbitrary and ineffective transfer restrictions. At the time of this book's publication, oral arguments have been scheduled for November 9, 2020. A decision by the Ninth Circuit is expected in the months following.

On August 14, a three-judge panel of the Ninth Circuit issued its opinion in the CRPA-supported lawsuit *Duncan v. Becerra*. The decision struck down as unconstitutional California's statewide prohibitions on magazines capable of holding more than 10 rounds. In doing so, the Ninth Circuit upheld the 2019 decision from the United States District Court in San Diego that resulted in hundreds of thousands—*if not millions*—of magazines being lawfully purchased by California gun owners in what is now commonly known as "Freedom Week." California's Attorney General has since petitioned the Ninth Circuit to rehear the case by a larger

11-judge "en banc" panel. On August 28, the Ninth Circuit ordered CRPA and the other Plaintiffs to file a response to that petition by September 18. At the time of this book's publication, California is prohibited from enforcing restrictions against "possession" of so-called "large-capacity magazines" while the case is litigated on appeal. In other words, individuals may continue to use and possess such magazines that were lawfully acquired.

Several other CRPA-supported lawsuits continue to work their way through the Courts. *Rupp v. Becerra*, which challenges all of California's "assault weapon" restrictions, has already undergone oral arguments on October 8, 2020. *Villanueva v. Becerra*, which is related to Rupp in that it challenges DOJ's regulations regarding "assault weapons," has been fully briefed and is awaiting oral arguments. And *Flanagan v. Becerra*, which challenges California open and concealed carry restrictions, has been fully briefed but stayed pending a decision in *Young v. State of Hawaii*. Be sure to subscribe to CRPA email alerts to keep informed on these cases as well as other Second Amendment litigation in California and throughout the nation.

Looking ahead, filling the vacancy on the Supreme Court left by the late Justice Ginsburg is sure to have a tremendous impact on current and future Second Amendment litigation.

NEW LAWS FOR 2021

All of the new and amended laws below will take effect on January 1, 2021, unless otherwise noted.

AB: Assembly Bill
SB: Senate Bill

AB 12. Gun Violence Restraining Orders — Chapter 4
Amends, Repeals, and Adds P.C. §§ 18109, 18120, 18160, 18170, 18175, 18180, 18185, 18190, & 18197

Current California law allows law enforcement and immediate family to file a petition for a "gun violence restraining order" ("GVRO"), which if issued, can last for a period of up to one year. This bill extends the duration of a GVRO for up to 5 years. This bill authorizes a person subject to a GVRO to submit one written request per year during the effective period of the order for a hearing to terminate the order.

Date When Duration of GVROs Can be Extended to 5   September 1, 2020
Years and When Person Subject to GVRO Can Submit
One Request per Year for Hearing to Terminate GVRO

AB 61. Gun Violence Restraining Orders — Chapter 4
Amends, Repeals, and Adds P.C. §§ 18150, 18170, & 18190

Current California law allows law enforcement and immediate family to file a petition for a "gun violence restraining order" ("GVRO"), which if issued, can last for a period of up to one year. This bill allows employers, coworkers, and employees or teachers of a secondary or postsecondary school that the subject has attended in the last six months to also file a petition for a GVRO, subject to additional requirements.

Date When Employers, Coworkers, and Employees or   September 1, 2020
Teachers of a Secondary or Postsecondary School Can Also
Petition for a GVRO Against Someone, Subject to
Certain Requirements

AB 1493. Voluntary Surrender of Firearm Rights — Chapter 4
Amends P.C. §§ 18115 & 18175

Under current California law, gun violence restraining orders (GVROS) are issued against a person after notice and a hearing and the court finds that there is clear and convincing evidence to issue the GVRO. A GVRO prohibits the subject of the petition from having in their custody or control, or owning, purchasing, possessing, or receiving, a firearm or ammunition for a duration of one year, subject to earlier termination or renewal by the court.

This bill, starting September 1, 2020, allows those individuals facing a GVRO to voluntarily file a form with the court relinquishing their firearm rights for the duration specified on the petition, or if not stated, for one year from the date of the proposed hearing on the GVRO. Filing the form may prevent the subject from appearing before the court.

Date Persons Facing GVROs Can File a Voluntary Surrender of Firearm Rights Form with the Court — September 1, 2020

AB 2617. Out-of-State Gun Violence Restraining Orders — Chapter 4
Amends P.C. §§ 18140, 18205

This bill amends California's prohibition against anyone subject to a Gun Violence Restraining Order ("GVRO") to also apply for any "valid order issued by an out-of-state jurisdiction that is similar or equivalent to a" GVRO in California.

The bill also requires any law enforcement officer who files a petition for a Gun Violence Restraining Order ("GVRO") to file a copy of the order with the court as soon as practicable "but not later than three court days after the order is issued.

AB 2699. Law Enforcement Exceptions to California's Handgun Roster — Chapter 10
Amends P.C. §§ 11106, 25555, 26379, 28230, 32000.

This bill expands the list of government agencies that may obtain handguns that do not comply with the Unsafe Handgun Act (i.e. "off roster" handguns). And for existing exceptions applicable to specified agencies and their officers, the bill imposes new requirements for those officers to be exempt. In connection with both changes, the bill also requires DOJ to establish a system of tracking purchases made through these exceptions.

AB 2847. Changes to California's "Unsafe Handgun" Restrictions — Chapter 10
Amends P.C. § 31910.

This bill revises the definition of an "unsafe handgun" as applied to California's microstamping requirement, while also implementing procedures for the removal of handguns currently listed on California's approved handgun roster that lack microstamping. As a result of this bill, California will only require microstamping on one or more places of the interior surface of a pistol (previously two or more) as a condition of being listed on California's approved handgun roster. But for every newly listed handgun, three handguns lacking microstamping will be removed (selected in reverse order of the date they were added to the roster, beginning with the handgun added on the earliest date).

SB 118. "Other" Firearms Now Classified as "Assault Weapons"/Precursor Parts — Chapter 9
Amends P.C. §§ 16532, 18010, 30400, 30405, 30406, 30412, 30414, 30442, 30445, 30447, 30448, 30450, 30452, 30454, 30456, 30470, 30485, 30515, 30685, 30900, & 30955.

As of September 1, 2020, this bill classifies certain "other" type firearms (ones that do not meet the legal definition of a rifle, pistol, or shotgun) as "assault weapons. Individuals who previously lawfully owned such firearms must now register them with DOJ as "assault weapons" or otherwise modify their firearm by January 1, 2022.

In addition to the above, this bill also expedites the implementation of California's "precursor part" restrictions enacted by AB 879 in 2019.

Effective date of certain "other" firearms now classified as "assault weapons September 1, 2020

Registration Deadline January 1, 2022

Precursor Part Restriction Implementation (New Date) July 1, 2022

SB 723. Outstanding Warrants — Chapters 3 & 4
Amends P.C. §§ 29800 & 29805

This bill clarifies that, regarding California's prohibition against persons with outstanding warrants, actual knowledge of the existence of the warrant is required to be liable for a violation.

AB 2061. DOJ Inspections of Ammunition Vendors and Gun Shows
Amends P.C. §§ 27310 & 30345

This bill provides statutory authority for DOJ to conduct inspections of licensed ammunition vendors at their place of business, as well as any firearm dealer, ammunition vendor, or manufacturer participating in a gun show.

AB 2632. Civil Fines for Firearm Dealer Violations
Amends P.C. § 26800

This bill will, beginning July 1, 2022, impose civil fines between $1,000-$3,000 for any breach of a prohibition or requirement that subjects a California licensed firearms dealer's license to forfeiture.

Effective Date: July 1, 2022

CHAPTER 1:
INTRODUCTION

I. GUN SAFETY IS YOUR RESPONSIBILITY

Firearm ownership, possession, and use are individual rights that carry extraordinary responsibilities, both morally and legally. Possessing and using firearms demands that the owner accept the highest level of responsibility. Depending on your individual circumstances, accepting that personal responsibility may require you to do more than the law demands to avoid accidents.

The overwhelming majority of gun owners are extremely responsible. Gun accidents claim far fewer lives than most people are led to believe. In the last reporting year, 74 children under age 14 died from gun accidents.[1] With over 90 million adults owning a gun and over 60 million children under age 14 living in the United States, the improper use of guns causes astoundingly few accidental deaths. Meanwhile, thousands more tragically die from car accidents, residential fires, bathtub drownings, accidental poisonings, and household hazards.[2] In fact, homes where gun accidents occur usually are not typical homes. In such homes, alcoholism and criminal histories are common, as is a disproportionate involvement in automobile accidents and driver's license suspensions. All of this reflects individual irresponsibility in homes where accidents happen.

Guns are neither safe nor unsafe by themselves. Accidents involving guns generally result from one of two causes: ignorance and carelessness. Having knowledge, skill, and a positive attitude are necessary to eliminate both. To that end, when gun owners learn and practice responsible gun ownership and follow NRA's three simple rules, guns are safe. These rules include: (1) **ALWAYS** keep the gun point-

---

[1] To find statistical information on the number of children who died as a result of a gun accident, see *Fatal Injury Reports, 1999-2016, National, Regional, and States (Restricted)*, CENTERS FOR DISEASE CONTROL AND PREVENTION, NAT'L CENTER FOR INJURY (last updated Feb. 19, 2017), https://webappa.cdc.gov/sasweb/ncipc/mortrate.html (last visited Sept. 9, 2020).

[2] For example, in 2016, motor vehicle accidents resulted in 1,455 deaths of children under 14 years old, versus just 74 unintentional firearms related deaths during that same year. *Fatal Injury Reports, 1999-2016, National, Regional, and States (Restricted)*, CENTERS FOR DISEASE CONTROL AND PREVENTION, NAT'L CENTER FOR INJURY (last updated Feb. 19, 2017), https://webappa.cdc.gov/sasweb/ncipc/mortrate.html (last visited Sept. 9, 2020).

ed in a safe direction; (2) **ALWAYS** keep your finger off the trigger until ready to shoot; and, (3) **ALWAYS** keep the gun unloaded until ready to use.[3]

The gun-ban lobby typically distorts facts and resists efforts to promote real gun-safety instruction or offer gun owners more opportunities to learn. They fear that merely mentioning a firearm in an educational context would tacitly endorse the concept that firearms have social utility. But firearms do have social utility both as self-defense tools and for their crime deterrent effect.[4] Firearms are used at least four times more often to prevent a crime than to commit one.[5] Nonetheless, instead of education, gun-ban lobbyists have pushed one-size-fits-all legislation such as mechanical lock and storage mandates that, while potentially one part of an individualized safety system, often are inappropriate or create a false sense of security that can actually increase carelessness and accidents.

Thanks to the efforts of over 40,000 certified gun-safety instructors who teach gun safety to law enforcement and civilians across the country, as well as the award-winning, time-proven, and law enforcement-endorsed safety programs being used nationally, firearm accident rates from 2014 onwards are lower than they have ever been previously recorded.[6] To do your part, you can learn those guidelines, live by them, and teach them to others. Taking classes in firearms handling is an excellent way to do this. Free materials concerning firearm safety are available in almost every gun store and from the National Rifle Association, National Shooting Sports Foundation, and the California Rifle and Pistol Association websites.

II. HOW TO USE THIS BOOK

Along with your responsibility to know and follow safety procedures, you also have increasing legal responsibilities. The goal of this book is to educate you about California's complex firearms laws so that you can avoid inadvertently violating them, as well as to educate those tasked with enforcing those laws so that they can avoid causing innocent people unnecessary legal problems.

This book discusses how to legally buy, own, transport, and possess firearms, and how to get firearms or firearm ownership rights back if they are taken away. This book also explores, explains, and summarizes how the major firearms laws

---

[3] *See* National Rifle Association of America, *Gun Safety Rules* (Brochure) (Apr. 2013).

[4] *See* Gary Kleck, *What Do CDC's Surveys Say About the Frequency of Defensive Gun Uses?* (July 11, 2018), *available at* https://ssrn.com/abstract=3194685 (last visited Sept. 9, 2020).

[5] In 2011, the Bureau of Justice reported around 478,400 crimes committed with a firearm, compared to estimates of 2.1-2.5 million defensive gun uses. Gary Kleck & Marc Gertz, *Armed Resistance to Crime: The Prevalence and Nature of Self-Defense with a Gun*, 86 J. CRIM. L. & CRIMINOLOGY 150, 167 (1995); MICHAEL PLANTY & JENNIFER L. TRUMAN, U.S. DEPT. OF JUSTICE, FIREARM VIOLENCE, 1993-2011 1 (2013).

[6] *Fatal Injury Reports, 1999-2014, National, Regional, and States (Restricted)*, CENTERS FOR DISEASE CONTROL AND PREVENTION, NAT'L CENTER FOR INJURY (last updated Feb. 19, 2017), https://webappa.cdc.gov/sasweb/ncipc/mortrate.html (last visited Sept. 9, 2020).

affect firearm owners in California and particularly warns about legal "traps" into which California firearm owners often unintentionally fall.

While reading this book, keep in mind that the exact language from many code[7] sections and court decisions have been shortened and/or paraphrased to highlight the point being made. Please note that all code sections referenced in this book are to the 2020 editions unless otherwise indicated. For exact statutory language, and when analyzing the cited cases, the particular statute and/or specific case(s) can and should be consulted directly. It's fairly easy to find these resources online. The California Legislative Counsel maintains all California codes on its website at www.leginfo.ca.gov. Case opinions of the California Supreme Court and Courts of Appeal are available on the Judicial Branch of California website at www.courts.ca.gov/opinions.

Because this book is intended for a wide audience, including firearm owners, firearm consumers, law enforcement, and lawyers, exact legal "Bluebook" citation format is not used.[8] For example, "*id*" and "*supra*," (terms used by lawyers to denote preceding or subsequent authority), do not appear in this book. But, *general* Bluebook citation format is utilized for consistency. For the exact and proper legal citations, please refer to the specific case, statute, or website in which you are interested.

A. The Materials Posted at www.CalGunLawsBook.com and www.crpa.org Complement This Book

More detailed legal memoranda elaborating on particular subjects covered in each chapter of this book and additional helpful materials are posted at www.CalGunLawsBook.com. This website complements this book and vice versa.

If you have firearms law questions, or would like to make suggestions for topics to be included in upcoming editions, email gunlawquestion@calgunlaws.com. To receive blog articles and email news bulletins on cutting-edge self-defense issues, civil rights issues, cases, court rulings, and other legal developments, subscribe to receive these bulletins from www.CalGunLawsBook.com and www.crpa.org.

B. Symbols Used Throughout This Book

Throughout this book I use the following symbols to bring your attention to certain information:

---

[7] "A code is a set of books containing all of the statutes in force in a given jurisdiction, organized by subject matter." THE BLUEBOOK: A UNIFORM SYSTEM OF CITATION 15 (Columbia Law Review Ass'n et al. eds., 19th ed. 2010).

[8] The Bluebook is a style guide for legal citation in the United States that is used by law students, lawyers, scholars, judges and other legal professionals.

This "New Law" symbol indicates an important change in the law. Since many new laws will take effect in 2020, it is imperative for you to understand the changes that these new laws make and how they may affect you.

 This "Caution" symbol points out notable information and potentially troublesome gray areas that you should pay particular attention to as you are reading this book.

 This "California Gun Laws" symbol indicates that a reference has been made to the www.CalGunLawsBook.com website or to the www.crpa.org website, where you can find updates and supplemental materials that complement this book.

III. HOW TO READ LAWS AND DETERMINE WHETHER THEY APPLY

A. Federal Laws, State Laws, and Local Laws

This book covers both federal and state firearms laws. Local laws, however, are mostly beyond the scope of this book. Federal law is made up of the "United States Constitution, federal statutes and regulations, U.S. treatises, and federal [case] law," *i.e.*, court opinions.[9] State law consists of the "state's constitution, statutes, regulations," and state court law cases.[10] Local laws are statutes or ordinances that are applicable to a particular locality rather than the entire state.[11] This book discusses both California and federal law under the main topic or heading, pointing out where most people run into problems with law enforcement. Even though this book does not discuss every local law in California, you are always obligated to comply with federal, state, and also local law.

B. Statutory Interpretation Techniques

Regardless of whether you or a court is examining a federal or state law, the following rules governing statutory interpretation apply.

As the United States Supreme Court explained, "in interpreting a statute a court should always turn first to one, cardinal canon before all others . . . courts must presume that a legislature says in a statute what it means and means

---
[9] BLACK'S LAW DICTIONARY 645 (8th. ed. 2004).
[10] BLACK'S LAW DICTIONARY 1444 (8th. ed. 2004).
[11] BLACK'S LAW DICTIONARY 957 (8th. ed. 2004).

in a statute what it says there .... When the words of a statute are unambiguous, then, this first canon is also the last: 'judicial inquiry is complete.'"[12] "Congress is presumed to act intentionally and purposely when it includes language in one section but omits it in another."[13]

If a statute's plain language is ambiguous, courts then look to the legislature's intent and give it "a reasonable and common sense interpretation consistent with the apparent purpose, which will result in wise policy rather than mischief and absurdity."[14] If necessary, courts will break down the words of the statute and compare their placement within the statute as a whole. Courts will also consider its context, purpose, evils to be remedied, other legislation, and public policy.[15] For example, in *People v. Squier*, the California Court of Appeal said that "[t]he rule of strict interpretation of penal statutes does not apply in California" and "where two interpretations of a penal statute are possible, that construction which favors the defendant is preferred unless such a construction is contrary to public interest, sound sense, and wise policy."[16] Therefore, according to the rule of lenity, when a statute is susceptible to two reasonable interpretations, the court should prefer the interpretation that most favors a defendant. In reality, the rule rarely works to a defendant's advantage.

Courts are also permitted to review secondary sources like legal treatises and law review articles to see what experts in a particular field say about the statute. These secondary sources are not binding, however, and serve merely as persuasive authority.

C. Determining Which Statute Controls When There Are Duplicate Laws for the Same Crime

Although it does not happen often, sometimes duplicate laws are passed that criminalize the same conduct. For example, in 2016, the California Legislature passed Assembly Bill (AB) 1695, making it a crime to falsely report that a firearm has been lost or stolen to a law enforcement agency.[17] Yet, that same year the voters passed Proposition (Prop.) 63, which also made it a crime to falsely report that a firearm has been lost or stolen to a law enforcement agency.[18] Interestingly, instead of simply amending or adding the same Penal Code statutes, AB 1695 amended P.C. section 148.5, making it a misdemeanor to falsely report the theft or loss of a firearm,

---

[12] *Conn. Nat'l Bank v. Germain*, 503 U.S. 249, 253-54 (1992) (internal citations omitted).
[13] *Estate of Bell v. Comm'r*, 928 F.2d 901, 904 (9th Cir. 1991).
[14] 7 B.E. WITKIN, SUMMARY OF CAL. LAW, CONST. LAW § 115 (10th ed. 2012).
[15] *See* 7 B.E. WITKIN, SUMMARY OF CAL. LAW, CONST. LAW § 115 (10th ed. 2012).
[16] *People v. Squier*, 15 Cal. App. 4th 235, 241 (1993).
[17] AB 1695, 2015-2016 Leg., Reg. Sess (Cal. 2016), *available at* https://leginfo.legislature.ca.gov/faces/billNavClient.xhtml?bill_id=201520160AB1695 (last visited Sept. 9, 2020).
[18] FULL TEXT OF PROPOSITION 63, CALIFORNIA ATTORNEY GENERAL, *available at* https://www.oag.ca.gov/system/files/initiatives/pdfs/15-0098%20(Firearms)_0.pdf (last visited Sept. 9, 2020).

and Prop. 63 added P.C. section 25275 to the Penal Code, making it an infraction to falsely report the theft or loss of a firearm.

Currently, case law is silent as to whether two statutes condemning the same crime can coexist. But, dicta[19] from some cases suggests that they can, and their duplication is merely a "housekeeping" issue for the Legislature to eventually clean up by removing one of the duplicate statutes.[20] For example, the Legislature did this with Penal Code (P.C.) section 29805 by using AB 785 to reconcile the two different versions of P.C. section 29805 implemented by Prop. 63 and the Legislature.

That said, just because two duplicative criminal statutes may be able to coexist together, it does not mean that a person can be punished under both statutes. For instance, notice that while both AB 1695 and Prop. 63 prohibit the same type of conduct, the punishments between these statutes are different: one treats the crime as a misdemeanor, while the other treats it as an infraction.

Although nothing expressly prevents a person from being charged and convicted of the same crime under two different statutes, California law does prohibit multiple punishments for a single physical act that violates different provisions of law.[21] In fact, P.C. section 654 provides in relevant part:

> An act or omission that is punishable in different ways by different provisions of law shall be punished under the provision that provides for the longest term of imprisonment, but in no case shall the act or omission be punished under more than one provision.[22]

In other words, although a person can be charged with and convicted of a violation of both P.C. section 148.5 and P.C. section 25275 for falsely reporting that a firearm has been lost or stolen, they can only be punished under the statute that carries the harsher sentence, which in this case would be the misdemeanor under P.C. section 148.5.

---

[19] Dictum (the single form of dicta) is "[a] statement of opinion or belief considered authoritative because of the dignity of the person making it." BLACK'S LAW DICTIONARY 485 (8th ed. 2004). Dicta is merely persuasive and not binding authority.

[20] *See Weiner v. City of San Diego*, 229 Cal. App. 3d 1203, 1208 n. 3 (1991), *superseded by statute on other grounds by Morgan v. Beaumont Police Department*, 246 Cal. App. 4th 144, 159 (2016) (stating "[a]lthough the Legislature by enacting those two identical sections in 1987 may have added more to the Vehicle Code than intended, it is an accepted maxim of jurisprudence 'superfluity does not vitiate.'"); *see also Landeros v. Flood*, 17 Cal. 3d 399, 407, 414 (1976) (stating "[t]here is nothing to prevent the Legislature from imposing a reporting requirement on physicians in two separate statutes, even if their coverage apparently overlaps.").

[21] P.C. § 654.

[22] P.C. § 654.

D. How to Read Court Opinions

When a dispute results in a lawsuit, the court's rulings will usually be issued through an "opinion." These court opinions can be issued by either trial or appellate court judges.[23]

When reading a court opinion, the first thing to look at is the case name or caption. This will identify the parties to the case. The party bringing the lawsuit is the plaintiff. The one defending against the lawsuit is the defendant. If the case is a criminal case, the state or federal prosecutor will bring a lawsuit on behalf of the government. The plaintiff in a criminal case is typically the "United States" or the "People of the State of California."

After the case name, you will see a legal "citation." This tells you where you can locate the actual opinion of the case. Many court opinions are now available for free online. The case citation can tell you which court rendered the decision and when the opinion was rendered. For example, *District of Columbia v. Heller*, the 2008 United States Supreme Court case that determined there is an individual right to keep and bear arms for self-defense, is cited as *District of Columbia v. Heller*, 554 U.S. 570 (2008). The citation of "554" is the volume of the United States Reports, "U.S." is the abbreviation of the United States Reports, and "570" is the page number where this opinion begins. The final "2008" represents the year in which the opinion was rendered.

Reading court opinions helps determine how laws will be interpreted and applied to different sets of facts. The United States has a "common law" system whereby, in addition to state and federal laws, courts look to previously decided cases to aid in making their judgments. Under this "common law" system, some court decisions are considered binding legal "precedent," which means that lower courts must defer to the higher courts' prior interpretation of the law.

Since not all cases are factually the same, lawyers either try to distinguish their facts from the facts that formed the basis of any earlier adverse court opinion(s) so the court does not adopt that opinion as its rationale, or the lawyers try to show why the earlier court opinion(s) should be legal "precedent" that the court should follow and adopt. This can be a difficult task. It is one of the reasons why seeking legal advice is so important.

IV. HOW TO JUDGE A LAWYER

If you ever need a lawyer, regardless of whether it is an attorney with experience in firearms law or an attorney in another practice area, it is important that you properly evaluate the attorney before you retain him or her for your case. There are

---

[23] For a more substantive analysis on how to read court opinions, see Orin S. Kerr, *How to Read a Legal Opinion: A Guide for New Law Students*, 11 GREEN BAG 2D 51 (2007), *available at* http://www.volokh.com/files/howtoreadv2.pdf (last visited Sept. 9, 2020).

a lot of bad lawyers out there. Meaningful factors to consider when evaluating an attorney are years of experience, number of cases actually tried to a jury, practice area(s), specializations, and competence in the particular area in which you need assistance.

There is a lot of helpful information about lawyers on the internet. But do not be fooled by slick internet marketing techniques, inflated website "ratings," and meaningless "awards." These days, a lawyer's reputation can be manipulated online. Just because the attorney claims to be "the best attorney" in a particular area, shows up first on a Google or Yahoo! search, or has a high rating on some forums does not necessarily mean that attorney is the right or best one for you. There are ways attorneys can manipulate their marketing profiles and endorsements to appear accomplished in a particular field when, actually, they either refer those cases to other attorneys or are themselves novice attorneys.

For more guidance on how to evaluate and select an attorney who is right for you, see the "How to Judge a Lawyer" memorandum on the www.CalGunLawsBook.com website.

CHAPTER 2:
THE CALIFORNIA REGULATORY ENVIRONMENT

This book provides a practical guide to California and federal laws regulating firearms. But that area of law is continually evolving because of two Supreme Court decisions that addressed the meaning and application of the Second Amendment to the United States Constitution. This chapter addresses some of the recent developments in Second Amendment jurisprudence and provides a constitutional context for reading the laws discussed in this book. This chapter also addresses some of the other legal doctrines that limit the expansion of laws that restrict your right to self-defense.

So, if you just want to get a question answered about whether a law applies to a situation, you can skip this chapter. But if you are interested in how the Second Amendment may change the legal playing field in the future and how your life, your children's lives, notions of freedom, and perhaps the very way our government interacts with citizens may be changed by the way the Second Amendment is interpreted and applied by courts in the future, read on.

As a society, we are at a turning point. The country is diametrically divided ideologically to perhaps a greater extent than almost any other time in our history, except during the Civil War. It is an understatement to say that the issue is important to us all.

I. THE UGLY PROCESS OF GUN LAW POLITICS

A. The Legislative Process

The California State Legislature is currently controlled by a liberal-Democratic majority and has been for years. Control is unlikely to shift in the foreseeable future unless the people of California take to the polls and make a change. As the party in control, the Democrats shape the agenda and will not allow anything to pass that might make Republicans look good.

Although technically any legislator can author a bill on any subject, when it comes to gun control laws there are certain Democrat legislators who lead the gun ban movement amongst their colleagues. Depending on the demographics of a legislator's district, gun control can translate to press coverage, and press coverage translates to name recognition. Having name recognition is critical to getting elected or reelected and many times is much more valuable to a candidate than the protection of your rights. When a group like the National Rifle Association (NRA) is pulled into the debate, it can actually serve the purposes of an anti-gun legislator because it increases the level of conflict for the media to cover as was seen in 2016 when then Lieutenant Governor Gavin Newsom and Senate President Pro Tempore De León feuded over their competing gun-control measures.[1]

A comprehensive treatment of the California legislative process, and just how corrupt it is, is beyond the scope of this book. But for the purposes of this chapter, suffice it to say that legislators often vote for or against a bill for reasons having nothing to do with its merits and frequently do not read the bills they are voting on. For more information on California's legislative process, refer to "California's Legislature" published by the Legislative Counsel of California, available at www.leginfo.ca.gov/califleg.html.

Over the years, I have had multiple private conversations with anti-gun politicians who were candid enough to admit that their agenda was to ban all civilian gun ownership, or at least civilian ownership of handguns. This undisclosed agenda makes it tough to debate the merits of specific gun laws. I once lobbied a Los Angeles City Councilman to vote against a ban on affordable self-defense handguns that anti-gun politicians demonized by calling "Saturday Night Specials." I pointed out that by the way the proposed ordinance defined that term, the Glock handguns used by the LAPD would be deemed "junk guns." The politician replied that it did not matter since all they really wanted to do was take another step toward banning all handguns. At a luncheon with another anti-gun politician, I established that a ban on .50 caliber target rifles was unnecessary since these rifles were never used in crime. The politician, who had not known this, justified her position by arguing that it was important to "make people *feel* safe." That one floored me. Do we really want our legislators to make us *feel* safe? Particularly, do we want to be fooled into *feeling* safe if we are not *actually* safe? This strikes me as a patronizing approach to governing, one that keeps placated citizens blissfully ignorant of reality while politicians get credit for passing complicated "feel good" laws that do nothing except, too often, turn good people into accidental criminals.

Unfortunately, the reality is that firearm laws are rarely based on technical knowledge, rational principle, or a genuine need for regulation. Rather, politics drives the process, not logic. A retired California Department of Justice (DOJ) official has explained that when he met with the authors of significant gun legislation,

---

[1] Jeremy B. White, *Newsom Camp Calls de León Gun Change 'Shockingly, Sickeningly Cynical,'* THE SACRAMENTO BEE (June 24, 2016), *available at* http://www.sacbee.com/news/politics-government/capitol-alert/article85899487.html (last visited Aug. 23, 2020).

they displayed a level of ignorance about firearms which shows they do not even understand what their proposed laws do. For example, the legislator who authored the "Unsafe Handgun Act" had to ask the DOJ official, "Where is the barrel?"

For an eye-opening account from a retired Sacramento politician about how laws are created and made, read "What Makes You Think We Read the Bills?" by California State Senator H.L. Richardson (ret.). Senator Richardson deserves special recognition because he founded Gun Owners of California and sponsored California's preemption statute, which prohibits local governments from over-regulating firearms.

B. Local Laws

Despite being prohibited from over-regulating firearms, local governments across the state have nonetheless been heavily lobbied by local and national anti-gun groups into passing their own firearms regulations. Cities that are notoriously anti-gun, such as Los Angeles, San Francisco, Oakland, and Sunnyvale have all passed local ordinances that either expand on or are similar to state laws. For instance, localities have adopted firearm storage laws that regulate how gun owners must store their firearms when at home and have banned the possession of so-called "large-capacity magazines." And these cities are not alone. Below are some examples of cities that have adopted ordinances restricting firearm storage, possession, or usage[2]:

Table 2.1

Mandatory Lock Storage	
City of Belvedere	City of San Diego
City of Berkeley	City of Saratoga
City of Los Angeles	City of Sunnyvale
City of Moraga	City of Tiburon
City of Oakland	County of Los Angeles
City of Palm Springs	County of Moraga
City of San Jose[3]	County of San Diego
City of Santa Cruz	County of San Francisco
City of San Francisco	

Mandatory Lost/Stolen Reporting	
City of Belvedere	City of San Jose
City of Los Angeles	City of Santa Cruz
City of Morgan Hill	City of Saratoga
City of San Diego	City of Sunnyvale
City of San Francisco	City of Tiburon

---

[2] Please note this list is not comprehensive and is subject to change. Take care that you seek out and read your local ordinance, as they can vary widely depending on the jurisdiction.

[3] Does not apply at home, however.

Prohibiting Possession of Firearm and/or Ammunition on Public Property[3]

City of Albany
City of Anaheim
City of Antioch
City of Bakersfield
City of Baldwin Park
City of Berkley
City of Calimesa
City of Calistoga
City of Campbell
City of Carlsbad
City of Chino
City of Chula Vista
City of Claremont
City of Clovis
City of Colma
City of Commerce
City of Concord
City of Corona
City of Costa Mesa
City of Covina
City of Culver City
City of Daly City
City of Diamond Bar
City of Dunsmuir
City of El Cajon
City of El Monte
City of Elk Grove
City of Fairmont
City of Fremont
City of Fresno
City of Fullerton
City of Garden Grove
City of Glendale
City of Glendora
City of Hercules
City of Hermosa Beach
City of Hollister
City of Huntington Beach
City of Imperial Beach
City of Inglewood
City of Irvine
City of Irwindale
City of Jurupa Valley
City of La Canada Flintridge
City of La Puente
City of Lancaster
City of Long Beach
City of Los Angeles
City of Los Gatos
City of Madera
City of Menlo Park
City of Merced
City of Mission Viejo
City of Modesto
City of Monrovia
City of Moreno Valley
City of Murrieta
City of Norwalk
City of Oakland
City of Oceanside
City of Ontario
City of Orange
City of Orinda
City of Palo Alto
City of Pasadena
City of Pleasanton
City of Pomona
City of Redding
City of Reedley
City of Rialto
City of Rolling Hills Estates
City of Roseville
City of Sacramento
City of Salinas
City of San Carlos
City of San Diego
City of San Francisco
City of San Jose
City of San Mateo
City of San Rafael
City of Santa Ana
City of Santa Clara
City of Santa Clarita
City of Santa Monica
City of Scotts Valley
City of Simi Valley
City of Solana Beach
City of South Gate
City of South Pasadena
City of Stockton
City of Temecula
City of Vacaville
City of Vallejo
City of Victorville
City of Vista
City of Walnut Creek
City of West Covina
City of Whitter
City of Yountville
County of Alameda
County of Fresno
County of Los Angeles
County of Marin
County of Monterey
County of Orange
County of Riverside
County of Sacramento
County of San Benito
County of San Bernardino
County of San Diego
County of San Francisco
County of San Joaquin
County of San Mateo
County of Santa Barbara
County of Santa Clara
County of Santa Cruz
County of Stanislaus
County of Ventura

Public Gatherings with Firearm Limitations

City of San Francisco

> **Ban on the Possession of Magazines Capable of Holding More Than 10 Rounds**
>
> City of Los Angeles
> City of Morgan Hill
> City of San Francisco
> City of Sunnyvale

The NRA and CRPA, through their Local Ordinance Project (LOP), has worked to stem the creeping tide of local gun control ordinances in California. Over the years, the NRA and CRPA have actively monitored and opposed attempts to restrict Second Amendment rights at the city and county level. But, the NRA and CRPA cannot be everywhere. With over 58 counties and 482 municipalities in California, the NRA and CRPA need your help. Whenever you hear that a gun control proposal is coming to your town, please notify the NRA or the CRPA immediately.

C. How the Initiative Process Works

The ballot initiative process in California was enacted in the early 1900's as a way of providing voters a more direct voice by allowing them to consider laws for the state.[5] Citizens can propose new statutes or constitutional amendments to be placed on a ballot for direct vote by the people. To qualify for a ballot, proponents must gather enough signatures (generally 5% of registered voters from the last gubernatorial election, or 8% if the initiative would change the state constitution). Signature gathering is a costly and time-consuming process. Since 2000, nearly two billion dollars have been spent on signature gathering efforts. Unfortunately, most signature gatherers are paid for each individual signature they gather and have little understanding of the issues they are promoting.

All ballot initiatives must be submitted to the Attorney General and go through a 30-day public comment period. The Attorney General will assign a title and explanation that the Secretary of State will publish to signature gatherers and the public. Many times, attorneys challenge the ballot initiatives before they even get to the publishing stage as being unconstitutional or otherwise unenforceable.

In general, if the ballot initiative is published and receives a majority of the vote from registered voters in the state, it will become effective the day following the elections. The Legislature can propose to amend or repeal the law only through a popular vote, although the courts can rule that a ballot initiative or portions of the ballot initiative are invalid or unconstitutional. Because most voters support being

---

[4] Note: different jurisdictions limit firearms and ammunition on different types of property. Please check with your local jurisdiction regarding these ordinances.

[5] California Election Code sections 9000 through 9015 govern the ballot initiative process.

able to have a say in new laws, it is unlikely that changes to the ballot initiative process will be made in the foreseeable future.

D. The Gun Ban Lobby's "Feel Good" Laws

Anti-gun groups spend millions of dollars on public relations consultants and efforts to demonize guns, exaggerate their dangers, make it politically incorrect to choose to own one, and "spin" pending legislation to appeal to legislators and unsophisticated constituents.[6] Common platitudes include "talk concept, not content," meaning do not get into a debate about the actual language of a bill or what it actually does. Bills often do much more than their emotionally appealing title would reveal. But gun ban lobbyists focus on the seemingly benign concepts of a bill, like some notion of public safety, often "for the children." If they can be pulled into a discussion of what the specific language of a bill actually does, they argue, "don't let the perfect be the enemy of the good." This, to me, is another way of saying "close enough for government work."

Regardless, the gun ban lobby has been quite successful in getting most of their anti-gun-owner agenda passed in California, and they have not stopped pushing for more restrictive laws. But despite their efforts, polls show an increasing recognition and appreciation of the right to choose to own a gun to defend yourself or your loved ones.[7]

Perhaps in recognition of this trend and what appears to be a disturbing new approach, the gun ban lobby has been pushing laws that actually compel otherwise law-abiding gun owners to report themselves to the police, which forces gun owners into a position where they should decline to cooperate.

For example, several cities passed ordinances that require gun owners to report the theft or loss of their firearms within 48 hours[8] and Prop. 63 enacted this on a statewide level. The gun ban lobby claims these laws help prevent unlawful "straw sales," and stop persons engaged in illegal firearm transfers from falsely claiming that a "crime gun" traced to the owner is "stolen" or "lost" when in fact the firearm was supplied to a criminal. But they often further victimize crime victims and *frustrate* police investigations. For example, if you do not report the loss or theft of a gun and you are then contacted by police who have recovered the gun at a crime scene, you face possible criminal prosecution for failing to report the missing gun. Most gun owners would ordinarily be happy to assist the police with their investi-

---

[6] An article concerning this issue and a link to the "anti-gun playbook," entitled "Preventing Gun Violence Through Effective Messaging," can be found at https://www.nraila.org/articles/20130809/anti-gunners-message-guide-emphasizes-emotion-over-logic and http://www.calgunlawsbook.com/links/ (last visited Aug. 23, 2020).

[7] *See* Gallup Poll Social Series: Crime, October 2013; *see also Growing Public Support for Gun Rights*, Pew Research Center, December 10, 2014.

[8] A state-wide version of this law, SB 299 (authored by Senator Mark DeSaulnier), was proposed in 2013, only to be vetoed by Governor Brown.

gation, but the misdirection of police focus in this situation ultimately delays the police in getting the information they need to investigate the crime.

Ronald Reagan was right when he said, "There are two things the public should never watch being made, sausage and laws." Lawmaking in this state is not pretty. Gun-law-making is especially ugly.

E. Law Enforcement's Overaggressive Enforcement

Aside from indecipherable laws and laws making criminals out of crime victims, federal, state, and local law enforcement authorities are continuing their stepped-up efforts to conduct "stings" at gun shows (both inside and outside of California) and against licensed gun dealers, particularly throughout California and in neighboring states. Rare or "almost legal" guns are sometimes offered at "too good to be true" prices in order to seduce the "stingee." The Police also monitor internet message boards, *Shotgun News*, Gun List USA, Gunbroker.com, and other trade magazines, and even run fake ads themselves. Suspects who fall for these "stings" typically have their businesses and residences searched and all of their firearms seized. Meanwhile, DOJ continues to aggressively enforce the "Armed Prohibited Persons System" (APPS) program by going after, in some cases, non-violent felons and misdemeanants whose only conviction was years in the past and who are often unaware that they are prohibited from possessing firearms.

While many of the efforts of these agencies are laudable, far too often the people being arrested are not violent felons. They typically have no prior criminal record and are solid citizens who did not know they were violating the law. Some police agencies simply go for the "easy meat" to bolster their prosecution and gun seizure statistics, regardless of whether violent crime is actually reduced as a result.

Every violation of the law, however inadvertent, is politicized and ultimately used by the gun ban lobby to advance its cultural and political war against civilian firearm ownership in general, and to urge closure of gun stores or an end to gun shows in particular. Sadly, caution must increasingly be exercised before cooperating with authorities. Your attempt at cooperation could easily lead to making an incriminating admission that results in criminal charges for an inadvertent violation. If you are approached about a possibly illegal transaction, remember: do not equivocate – refuse to participate!

F. The Pro-Gun Lobby

There are a number of pro-Second Amendment groups working in Sacramento, including the NRA, CRPA, National Shooting Sports Foundation, and Gun Owners of California. The NRA, the CRPA, and the Gun Owners of California have full-time lobbyists in the California Capital.

The NRA and CRPA deserve special mention because I have had the privilege of representing them for many years.

1. The National Rifle Association and The California Rifle & Pistol Association

Dismayed by the lack of marksmanship shown by their troops, Union veterans Col. William C. Church and Gen. George Wingate formed the National Rifle Association in 1871. That makes it the oldest civil rights organization in the country. In response to repeated attacks on Second Amendment rights, the NRA formed the Legislative Affairs Division in 1934. While the NRA did not lobby directly at first, it did mail out legislative facts and analyses to members whereby they could take action on their own. In 1975, recognizing the critical need for political defense of the Second Amendment, the NRA formed the Institute for Legislative Action (ILA). Meanwhile, the NRA has continued its commitment to training, education, and marksmanship.

While widely recognized today as a major political force and as America's foremost defender of Second Amendment rights, the NRA has, since its inception, been the premier firearms education organization in the world. But the NRA's successes would not be possible without the tireless efforts and countless hours of service its nearly six million members give to champion Second Amendment rights and support NRA programs. As former Clinton spokesman George Stephanopoulos said, "Let me make one small vote for the NRA. They're good citizens. They call their congressmen. They write. They vote. They contribute. And they get what they want over time."[9]

As mentioned, the NRA employs a much-needed lobbyist in Sacramento. But given California's politics, the NRA's power in Washington, D.C., does not translate to the same extent in Sacramento.

Founded in 1875, the California Rifle & Pistol Association is the official state affiliate of the NRA. The CRPA is dedicated to protecting firearm freedoms and promoting shooting sports solely in California. CRPA's full-time lobbyist in Sacramento also fights adverse firearm legislation and works to promote laws that protect your right to choose to own a gun to protect yourself and your family. The CRPA Foundation is the 501(c)(3) sibling of the CRPA and funds some of the Second Amendment litigation and other litigation in which I am often involved.

As you read this book, I hope your education of the problems with California's gun laws will cause you to consider getting involved in California's political process, which means joining these associations, showing up on election day, and generally staying informed about efforts to restrict your right to own a gun for sport or to defend yourself and your family.

---

[9] *About Us*, NATIONAL RIFLE ASSOCIATION (NRA), http://www.nra.org/aboutus.aspx (last visited Aug. 23, 2020).

G. Gun Violence Research

In 2016, the California Legislature passed Assembly Bill (AB) 1602, which, among other things, establishes a center for research on gun violence that will be administered by the University of California, Davis. In 2017, the Legislature passed Senate Bill (SB) 536, which requires DOJ to give information about gun violence restraining orders to this research center.[10] This center is tasked with studying the effectiveness of existing laws and policies intended to reduce firearm violence.[11] Although in theory politically neutral research would be helpful in determining what kind of laws could encourage the safe and responsible use of firearms and reduce the number of firearm related deaths, history has shown that government-funded research into gun violence tends to be politically biased.

A long time ago, Congress used to fund research into gun violence through the Center for Disease Control and Prevention's (CDC). During the late '80s and early '90s, the CDC was not shy about their bias against gun ownership and that their intentions in publishing these studies were to convince citizens that firearms should be banned altogether. In a 1989 issue of the Journal of the American Medical Association, Dr. Patrick O'Carroll, the acting section head of the Division on Injury Control at the CDC, was quoted as saying, "We're going . . . to systematically build a case that owning firearms causes deaths. [] . . . We're doing the most we can do, given the political realities."[12] Dr. O'Carroll later contended that he was misquoted in the journal. But, his predecessor Dr. Mark Rosenberg reiterated this sentiment in the Washington Post when he explained that, "We need to revolutionize the way we look at guns, like what we did with cigarettes. It used to be that smoking was a glamour symbol – cool, sexy, macho. Now it is dirty, deadly – and banned."[13]

By the early '90s, the CDC's plan to convince people through science that firearm ownership should be banned was well underway. In 1993, the New England Journal of Medicine released a study by Dr. Arthur Kellermann – an epidemiologist, physician, outspoken gun-control advocate, and recipient of 1.7 million dollars in grant money from the CDC – entitled *Gun Ownership as a Risk Factor for Homicide in the Home*.[14] In this study, Dr. Kellermann concluded that people who

---

[10] DOJ can even give information identifying specific individuals to this research center, provided that information identifying specific individuals is not revealed or used for anything other than research or statistical activities and will not be reported in publications. SB 536, 2016-2017, Leg. Counsel's Digest (Cal. 2017), *available at* https://www.leginfo.legislature.ca.gov/faces/billNavClient.xhtml?bill_id=201720180SB536 (last visited Aug. 23, 2020). Nothing in this bill prevents the researchers from skewing or misapplying the information to forward their cause.

[11] *See* AB 1602, 2015-2016, Leg. Counsel's Digest (Cal. 2016), *available at* http://www.leginfo.legislature.ca.gov/faces/billNavClient.xhtml?bill_id=201520160AB1602 (last visited Aug. 23, 2020).

[12] Marsha F. Goldsmith, *Epidemiologist Aim at New Target: Health Risk of Handgun Proliferation*, 261(5) J. OF THE AMERICAN MED. ASSOC. 675, 676 (1989).

[13] William Raspberry, *Sick People With Guns*, WASHINGTON POST (Oct. 19, 1994), *available at* https://www.washingtonpost.com/archive/opinions/1994/10/19/sick-people-with-guns/6c7f2bd2-fa57-4d69-b927-5ceb4fa43cf4/ (July 11, 2017) (last visited Aug. 23, 2020).

[14] Arthur K. Kellermann, et al., *Gun Ownership as a Risk Factor for Homicide in the Home*, 329 NEW ENGLAND J. OF MED. 1084 (1993), *available at* http://www.nejm.org/doi/full/10.1056/NEJM199310073291506#t=article (July 11, 2017) (last visited Aug. 23, 2020).

kept guns in their homes were 2.7 times more likely to be victims of a homicide as people who don't keep firearms in their homes.[15] This statistic is still cited by gun control activists to this day, despite multiple studies proving the flawed research methods of this study.[16]

In fact, subsequent studies have shown quite different results than those found by Dr. Kellerman and other publicly funded studies through the CDC. For example, research conducted by Dr. Gary Kleck, a Florida State University criminologist; Professor Gary Mauser, an urban studies expert at Simon Fraser University; Professors James D. Wright and Peter H. Rossi, sociologists at University of Massachusetts, and Dr. John Lott, who formerly taught at the University of Chicago, raised serious questions about the results of Dr. Kellermann's work and generally affirmed the social utility of firearms.[17]

Because of the clear bias against gun ownership, Congress decided to defund these programs. In 1996, it passed the 1996 Omnibus Consolidated Appropriations Bill. This bill included language that prevented the CDC from using tax-payer money to fund advocacy science, specifically stating that "none of the funds made available for injury prevention and control at the [CDC} may be used to advocate or promote gun control."[18]

Despite this defunding, the gun-ban lobby has continued to fund a number of studies to further support gun control. Recently, the continual bias of the CDC was spotlighted in 2018 when it was revealed that the CDC did not release data showing that more people used guns in defense situations than previously thought.[19] Also, there have been a number of studies conducted by Doctor Garen Wintemute of the University of California, Davis. Dr. Wintemute has been a long-time advocate of restricting the right to keep and bear arms and has received thousands of dollars from the gun-control movements financier, the Joyce Foundation. His studies often argue that more gun-control would lead to less crime and gun violence.

---

[15] Arthur K. Kellermann, et al., *Gun Ownership as a Risk Factor for Homicide in the Home*, 329 NEW ENGLAND J. OF MED. 1084 (1993), *available at* http://www.nejm.org/doi/full/10.1056/NEJM199310073291506#t=article (July 11, 2017) (last visited Aug. 23, 2020).

[16] *See* Don B Kates, et al., *Public Health Pot Shots: How the CDC Succumbed to the Gun Epidemic*, REASON (Apr. 2007), *available at* http://reason.com/archives/1997/04/01/public-health-pot-shots (last visited Aug. 23, 2020).

[17] Gary Kleck, *What Are the Risks and Benefits of Keeping a Gun in the Home?* JAMA (Aug. 5, 1998), *available at* http://www.guncite.com/kleckjama01.html (last visited Oct. 9, 2019); Gary Mauser and Don B Kates, *Would Banning Firearms Reduce Murder and Suicide? A Review of International and Some Domestic Evidence*, 30(2) HARV. J. LAW & POLICY 649 (2007), *available at* https://americangunfacts.com/pdf/Vol30_No2_KatesMauseronline.pdf (last visited Aug. 23, 2020); James D. Wright and Peter Rossi, *Gun Control Research- Wright and Rossi Department of Justice Study: Deterrent Effect of Armed Citizens upon Criminal Behavior?* http://www.leg.state.co.us/clics/clics2012a/commsumm.nsf/b4a3962433b52fa787256e5f00670a71/5de089825c00843e872579b80079912d/%24FILE/SenState0305AttachB.pdf (last visited Aug. 23, 2020); John R Lott, MORE GUNS, LESS CRIME: UNDERSTANDING CRIME AND GUN CONTROL LAW (3d ed. 2010).

[18] Pub. L. No. 104-208, 110 Stat. 3009 (1996), *available at* https://www.gpo.gov/fdsys/pkg/PLAW-104publ208/pdf/PLAW-104publ208.pdf (last visited Aug. 23, 2020).

[19] *See* Gary Kleck, *What Do CDC's Surveys Say About the Frequency of Defensive Gun Uses?* (July 11, 2018), available at https://ssrn.com/abstract=3194685 (last visited Oct. 4, 2019).

Having received thousands of dollars from anti-gun groups to conduct his research, Dr. Wintemute is far from being an impartial researcher. Nonetheless, the University of California has chosen him to lead up the University of California Firearm Violence Research Center at Davis.[20]

II. THE RIGHT TO KEEP AND BEAR ARMS AND TO SELF-DEFENSE

A. The United States and California Constitutions

The Second Amendment provides, "A well regulated Militia, being necessary to the security of a free State, the right of the people to keep and bear Arms, shall not be infringed."[21]

In 2008, the U.S. Supreme Court confirmed in *District of Columbia v. Heller* that the Second Amendment protects an *individual's* right to keep and bear arms for self-defense – contrary to gun control advocates' claims for decades that the Second Amendment only provides collective rights for state militias.[22]

In 2010, in *McDonald v. Chicago*,[23] the Supreme Court confirmed that an *individual's* right to keep and bear arms is fundamental and is thus "incorporated" into the Bill of Rights through the 14th Amendment. This means that federal, state, and local governments cannot infringe upon your Second Amendment right to keep and bear arms and to self-defense.

After these decisions came down, hundreds of cases raised the Second Amendment as an issue, and hundreds of courts have addressed the scope of the Second Amendment's protections. Unfortunately, the issue was most often raised as a defense in criminal cases, where the chances of success are decreased by court overcrowding and by lawyers who are insufficiently prepared to properly present such novel and complicated issues to the court.

Even in the few civil cases challenging firearms regulations, or that would serve as precedent to challenge some of California's ill-conceived laws, the lawyers bringing the claims are often inexperienced and lack the resources needed to do the job competently. The NRA and the CRPA, along with several other Second Amendment advocacy groups, have brought a few dozen cases, with mixed success. Those cases, and others that have yet to be filed, are making their way inexorably toward the Supreme Court.

---

[20] Zusha Elinson, *Doctor to Run New Gun-Violence Research Center in California*, THE WALL STREET JOURNAL (Aug. 21, 2016), *available at* https://www.wsj.com/articles/doctor-to-run-new-gun-violence-research-center-in-california-1472667927 (last visited Aug. 23, 2020).

[21] U.S. CONST. amend. II.

[22] *District of Columbia v. Heller*, 554 U.S. 570, 592-93 (2008).

[23] *McDonald v. Chicago*, 561 U.S. 742 (2010).

Since the *Heller* and *McDonald* decisions, several petitions have been filed with the Supreme Court asking them to address cases raising Second Amendment related issues. Though the high court has expressed some heightened interest in hearing a Second Amendment case, it has so far rejected all Second Amendment related petitions.

The high court will inevitably have to address the foundational issues that have been raised regarding the scope and application of *Heller* and *McDonald,* and subsequently will have to address the additional issues that will inevitably arise in cases brought thereafter. But this will be a dynamic and rapidly changing legal landscape.

Most states have their own version of the Second Amendment right to keep and bear arms in their respective constitutions.[24] California, however, does not.

It has been argued though that one provision of the California constitution *does* implicate the right to self-defense: "All people are by nature free and independent and have inalienable rights. Among these are enjoying and defending life and liberty, acquiring, possessing, and protecting property, and pursuing and obtaining safety, happiness, and privacy."[25] Unfortunately, the California Supreme Court has rejected this notion.[26]

B. Primary Issues Being Addressed in Current Second Amendment Litigation

Laws regulating firearms typically fall into one of three categories: (1) laws that regulate where and how firearms can be possessed, (2) laws regulating how to acquire firearms and which types of firearms or firearm accessories can be acquired and possessed, and (3) laws regulating whether certain people can possess firearms.

In a Second Amendment case, the judge must first decide whether the individual conduct being legislatively restricted implicates the Second Amendment at all. In some cases, this initial inquiry should be relatively simple.

For instance, a case regarding the possession of a handgun in the home for self-defense clearly concerns conduct protected by the Second Amendment. Such was the very conduct at issue in *District of Columbia v. Heller*, and the Supreme Court ruled 5-4 that Mr. Heller did have a Second Amendment right to own a handgun for self-defense.

But how about possessing a rifle or shotgun in the home for self-defense? What about air guns? Knives, clubs, swords, or bows? Electronic devices such as tasers? Or chemical self-defense sprays? Is carrying a handgun outside the home for self-defense within the scope of the right? What about possession in gun-free zones? What rights do we have to possess a firearm for things other than self-defense, like

---

[24] *See* Eugene Volokh, *State Constitutional Right to Keep and Bear Arms*, 11 TEX. REV. L. & POL. 191-952 (2006).
[25] CAL. CONST. art. I, § 1.
[26] *Kasler v. Lockyer*, 23 Cal. 4th 472, 481 (2000) ("If plaintiffs are implying that a right to bear arms is one of the rights recognized in the California Constitution's declaration of rights, they are simply wrong.").

target shooting, hunting, or collecting? What kinds of people can have their Second Amendment rights taken away and for how long? Felons? Yes. Forever? Not so clear. What about people with misdemeanor convictions? Which convictions should be prohibiting? For how long? Some would say that a person with any type of criminal conviction should be prohibited from possessing firearms forever.

Each of these questions regarding the scope of the Second Amendment remains unanswered. But cases raising these questions are making their way through the various federal circuit courts, and the Supreme Court will eventually and inevitably be compelled to consider the issues. Stay current on these developments through www.crpa.org.

Once an activity is acknowledged as being within the scope of a constitutional right, does that mean that any restrictions on the right are invalid? Definitely not. Courts use various tests, or "standards of review," to determine if a law is unconstitutional. The three most commonly used of these tests are "strict scrutiny,"[27] "intermediate scrutiny,"[28] and "rational basis review."[29] As its name suggests, strict scrutiny is the most rigorous of the three standards, and most laws subjected to it will be struck down. Rational basis, at the other end of the spectrum, is the least rigorous. Under it, only the most egregious laws will be invalidated because the government can posit almost any reasonable justification for the law. Because constitutional rights are so important, rational basis is rarely used when a law infringes on them. Intermediate scrutiny lies somewhere in the middle, giving the courts great discretion to either uphold or overturn a law. Which test a court utilizes depends on various factors, including the nature of the right at issue. The important question currently before the courts is which test should be applied in Second Amendment rights cases.

Before *Heller* acknowledged the importance of the rights protected by the Second Amendment, many courts upheld all firearm laws because they believed that the Second Amendment did not protect ordinary citizens. Under rational basis review, even a firearm ban would be upheld because the government could posit a "rational" belief that preventing ordinary citizens from having firearms would reduce firearm misuse.

After *Heller*, lower courts have struggled to determine exactly what standard to apply when reviewing laws that impact Second Amendment rights. Aside from explicitly rejecting the aforementioned rational basis review, the *Heller* Court did not formally declare which standard of review should apply. So lower courts have

---

[27] Strict scrutiny requires that a law "be narrowly tailored to promote a compelling Government interest, and if a less restrictive alternative would serve the Government's purpose, the legislature must use that alternative." *See U.S. v. Playboy Entertainment Group, Inc.* 529 U.S. 803, 804 (2000).

[28] Intermediate scrutiny requires that the law be "substantially related" to an "important government interest." *Clark v. Jeter,* 486 U.S. 456, 461 (1988).

[29] Rational basis review requires that the law be "rationally related" to a "legitimate government interest" offered as its justification. *City of New Orleans v. Dukes,* 427 U.S. 297, 303 (1976).

been crafting their own analyses by drawing inferences from *Heller's* reasoning. Of course, many judges have taken very different approaches.

Most courts will review the law to see if the conduct being challenged is within the scope of the Second Amendment right, as that right was understood when the Bill of Rights was drafted. If the conduct being challenged does affect that right, courts will then determine which level of heightened scrutiny[30] to apply based on a number of factors.[31] Many courts, for instance, look to (1) whether a restriction touches upon conduct at the "core" of the Second Amendment and (2) how severely it burdens that conduct. This analysis has often led courts to select intermediate scrutiny—despite the Second Amendment being considered a fundamental right.

In addition, some courts have found that when a statute or regulation causes Second Amendment rights to be *destroyed*, rather than merely burdened, it is appropriate to strike the law down without determining which level of heightened scrutiny to apply.[32] That is the approach *Heller* took in striking down a total denial of the ordinary citizen's right to keep arms.[33]

The scope of the Second Amendment's protection and the means by which the courts will uphold the right are, and will likely continue to be, defined through litigation. Certain cases and examples are therefore highlighted throughout this book to help you understand the different ways firearms laws are being interpreted and applied. These lawsuits encompass a variety of issues, ranging from what types of firearms are constitutionally protected to defining what constitutes a "sensitive place" where firearms may lawfully be prohibited.

Again, to stay updated on the status of Second Amendment litigation and other firearm-related litigation and issues, sign up for free alerts at www.crpa.org.

III. THE PREEMPTION DOCTRINE

A. Federal Preemption Doctrine

Setting California's constitution and politicians aside, it is helpful to address federal and state law preemption before diving into California's firearms laws and their various nuances.

---

[30] The U.S. Supreme Court expressly explicitly rejected the rational basis standard for evaluating Second Amendment claims. "If all that was required to overcome the right to keep and bear arms was a rational basis, the Second Amendment would be redundant with the separate constitutional prohibitions on irrational laws, and would have no effect." *District of Columbia v. Heller*, 554 U.S. 570, 629 n. 27 (2008).

[31] *See, e.g., United States v. Chovan*, 735 F.3d 1127, 1138 (9th Cir. 2013); *see, e.g., Ezell v. City of Chicago*, 651 F.3d 684, 703 (7th Cir. 2011).

[32] *See, e.g., Wrenn v. District of Columbia*, 864 F.3d 650, 664-66 (D.C. Cir. 2017); *see, e.g., Peruta v. County of San Diego*, 742 F.3d 1144, 1175 (9th Cir. 2014); *see, e.g., Moore v. Madigan*, 702 F.3d 933, 941-42 (7th Cir. 2012); *see, e.g., Palmer v. District of Columbia*, 59 F. Supp. 3d 173, 182-83 (D.C. Cir. 2014).

[33] *District of Columbia v. Heller*, 554 U.S. 570, 628-29 (2008).

The concept of federal preemption is found in the Supremacy Clause of the United States Constitution:

> This Constitution, and the Laws of the United States which shall be made in Pursuance thereof; and all Treaties made, or which shall be made, under the Authority of the United States, shall be the supreme Law of the Land; and the Judges in every State shall be bound thereby, any Thing in the Constitution or Laws of any State to the Contrary notwithstanding.[34]

The Supremacy Clause means that if a conflict exists between state and federal law, "the federal law controls and the state law is invalidated because federal law is supreme."[35]

Because federal law can preempt California law in many ways, this book addresses both state and federal firearms laws, though the emphasis is on California law.

B. California Preemption Doctrine

Just as federal law can supersede (or preempt) conflicting state laws, state laws can likewise preempt conflicting local (*i.e.*, city and county) laws.

The California Constitution explicitly notes that a county or city must take care not to fall "in conflict with general laws."[36] Courts have long interpreted this as a limitation on local government's ability to interfere with the proper operation of state law through local legislation. In doing so, courts have looked into whether a local ordinance "*duplicates, contradicts, or enters an area fully occupied* by general law, either expressly or by legislative implication."[37]

Often, California's statutory scheme preempts local firearms laws by fully occupying the field, either expressly or implicitly,[38] or as is the case with Prop 63[39], they can expressly provide that local governments are preempted from enacting further measures.[40] Where state laws expressly preempt local laws, the preemptive effect is generally clear. But, sometimes the law does not expressly state whether local laws are preempted, or the scope of the preemptive effect is unclear. In these circumstances, California's implied preemption doctrine may be implicated. This doctrine

---

[34] U.S. Const. art. VI, cl. 2.

[35] Erwin Chemerinsky, Constitutional Law Principles and Policies 376 (Erwin Chemerinsky et al. eds., 2d ed. 2002). *See also Gade v. Nat'l Solid Wastes Mgmt. Ass'n*, 505 U.S. 88, 108 (1992) (stating "any state law, however clearly within a State's acknowledged power, which interferes with or is contrary to federal law, must yield") (citation and internal quotation marks omitted).

[36] Cal. Const. art. XI, § 7.

[37] *Sherwin-Williams Co. v. City of Los Angeles*, 4 Cal. 4th 893, 897 (1993) (emphasis added)(citation and internal quotation marks omitted).

[38] For example, in *Fiscal v. City and County of San Francisco*, the California Court of Appeal held that a San Francisco ordinance which totally prohibited the possession and sale of handguns within the city was preempted by state law. *See Fiscal v. City and County of San Francisco*, 158 Cal. App. 4th 895 (2008).

[39] *See* Full Text of Proposition 63, Office of the Attorney General, *available at* https://www.oag.ca.gov/system/files/initiatives/pdfs/15-0098%20(Firearms)_0.pdf (last visited Aug. 23, 2020).

[40] *See Viva! Intern. Voice for Animals v. Adidas Promotional Retail Operations, Inc.*, 41 Cal. 4th 929 (2007).

allows for a law to be preempted if the state demonstrates an intent to preempt local regulation. The state's intent can be ascertained by considering whether:

(1) the subject matter has been so fully and completely covered by general law as to clearly indicate that it has become exclusively a matter of state concern; (2) the subject matter has been partially covered by general law couched in such terms as to indicate clearly that a paramount state concern will not tolerate further or additional local action; or (3) the subject matter has been partially covered by general law, and the subject is of such a nature that the adverse effect of a local ordinance on the transient citizens of the state outweighs the possible benefit to the municipality.[41]

What local laws are preempted by California's legal scheme is unclear. But it is clear that localities cannot ban firearms outright, require their registration, or require licenses to own them.

The gun ban lobby has tried to limit the preemption doctrine as it applies to regulating firearms. For example, in 2013, the gun ban lobby pushed legislation that would have created an exception to California's preemption of firearms laws for the City of Oakland, permitting Oakland to enact laws concerning firearms that are more restrictive than state laws. Thankfully, Governor Brown vetoed the legislation, commenting, "[t]he State of California has among the strictest gun laws in the country. Allowing individual cities to enact their own more restrictive firearms regulations will sow confusion and uncertainty."[42]

Governor Brown is absolutely right. Residents of the city would have had to stay updated with any new city ordinances in addition to state law. The legislation was proposed under the guise that it would help to reduce gun violence in the city, but the city is already ill-equipped to enforce state gun laws and local laws. Had the legislation been signed into law, law enforcement efforts would have likely been diverted to implement and maintain further licensing and registration databases to track law-abiding gun owners. This legislation would have opened the door for other localities to request special exemptions from California state preemption for firearms laws. If such exemptions were approved, this would have led to a patchwork of local laws governing firearms throughout the state.

For years, the preemption doctrine prevented local governments from creating firearm laws that were more restrictive than state laws.[43] But, in 2013, an ill-conceived lawsuit brought the effect of the preemption doctrine into question.[44] Since then, the gun-ban lobby has shifted gears and is now using new tactics to limit

---

[41] *In re Hubbard*, 62 Cal. 2d 119, 128 (1964), *overruled in part by Bishop v. City of San Jose*, 1 Cal.3d 56 (1969).

[42] Letter from Edmund G. Brown, Governor of California, to the Members of the California State Assembly (Oct. 11, 2013), *available at* http://gov.ca.gov/docs/AB_180_2013_Veto_Message.pdf (last visited Aug. 23, 2020)..

[43] For example, in *Fiscal v. City and County of San Francisco*, the California Court of Appeal held that the state law preempted a San Francisco ordnance that prohibited the possession and sale of handguns within the city. *See Fiscal v. City and Cnty of San Francisco*, 158 Cal. App. 4th 895 (2008).

[44] *See Calguns Foundation, Inc. v. Cnty of San Mateo*, 218 Cal. App. 4th 661 (2013).

the preemption doctrine and get their anti-gun agenda passed in California. For instance, the gun-ban lobby has begun to take pieces of anti-gun legislation that failed to pass out of the California Legislature and push them in cities that are highly sympathetic to their cause, such as Sunnyvale, San Francisco, and Los Angeles.

Although the question of whether these local ordinances violate the preemption doctrine is outside of the scope of this book, it should be noted that the firearms laws passed in Sunnyvale, San Francisco, and Los Angeles[45] have created a minefield for gun owners who reside in or are traveling through these cities. Because each of these local laws is more restrictive than state law, any gun owner traveling through or residing in these cities must ensure that they know, understand, and comply with the cities' firearms laws.

For a more in-depth analysis of California's preemption doctrine, see the law review article I co-authored: *Local Gun Bans in California: A Futile Exercise.*[46]

IV. THE CALIFORNIA LEGAL SCHEME

A. The Dangerous Weapons Control Act (DWCA)

California's Penal Code (P.C.) sections 16000 *et seq.* are collectively referred to as the Dangerous Weapons Control Act (DWCA), the reorganization of which is further discussed below. These Penal Code sections are home to most of California's firearms laws. But some firearms laws are also found in the California Fish and Game Code (Cal. Fish & Game Code), California Welfare and Institutions Code (Cal. Welf. & Inst. Code), California Vehicle Code (Cal. Veh. Code), California Business and Professions Code (Cal. Bus. & Prof. Code), California Health and Safety Code (Cal. Health & Saf. Code), California Government Code (Cal. Gov't Code), California Code of Regulations (Cal. Code Regs.), California Family Code (Cal. Fam. Code), and other parts of the Penal Code. California is somewhat unique in that some municipal governments have also passed extensive local gun control ordinances.

Of course, federal firearms laws also apply in California and are contained in federal statutes and regulations.

---

[45] Sunnyvale, San Francisco, and Los Angeles have all enacted ordinances that prohibit the possession of "large-capacity magazines" within their respective city limits. See Chapter 10. As of the date of publication, it remains to be seen whether the new restrictions on "large-capacity magazines" that were enacted by Prop. 63 and Senate Bill 1446 preempt these local ordinances. San Francisco also has enacted ordinances that require residents to keep their handguns in locked containers or use trigger locks when storing the firearm inside their homes. See Chapter 5.

[46] Don B. Kates & C.D. Michel, *Local Gun Bans in California: A Futile Exercise*, 41 U.S.F. L. REV. 333 (2007).

B. Confusion Runs Rampant

There are hundreds of federal laws and regulations covering firearms. California state statutes regulating the manufacture, distribution, sale, possession, and use of firearms now number over 800! That does not include administrative regulations, local ordinances, or the California DOJ's "Bureau of Firearms" written and unwritten policies. As former California Attorney General Dan Lungren once noted, thanks to politicians, California firearms laws are now as complex as the state's byzantine environmental and tax laws.[47] And the politicians are not backing off. Unfortunately, unlike corporations with lawyers on retainer to answer legal questions and ensure compliance with the environmental and tax laws, gun owners don't typically have expert lawyers on retainer to advise them on what the increasingly complex gun laws require.

Unsurprisingly, all the overlapping and constantly changing rules have led to rampant confusion among California gun owners. As a result, inadvertent gun law violations by well-intentioned good people have become increasingly common. And in the politicized environment of California firearms laws, the consequences of even an inadvertent violation can be severe.

Because firearms are so extensively regulated, even those tasked with enforcing them are often confused about what the laws require. This confusion also commonly extends to those who choose to own a gun for work, hunting, sport, or defense of themselves and their families.

In commenting on a proposed anti-gun bill in September of 2004, former Governor Arnold Schwarzenegger acknowledged:

> Such ambiguity in the law invites arbitrary enforcement and judicial review.... Before a government exercises its power to take away one's liberty, it should be clear to every person what actions will cause them to forfeit their freedom. Instead of adding to the lengthy and complex area of firearm laws, a reorganization of the current laws should be undertaken to ensure that statutes that impose criminal penalties are easily understandable.[48]

Judges are equally confused. California Court of Appeal Justice William Bedsworth, writing about firearms law said it best: "At first blush, the statutes seem impenetrable. Reading them is hard, writing about them arduous, reading about them probably downright painful. The [complexity] makes for tough sledding. As

---

[47] *See, e.g.,* Carl Ingram, *Assault Weapons Ban Called Unenforceable,* L.A. TIMES, June 25, 1991, *available at* http://articles.latimes.com/1991-06-25/news/mn-1267_1_assault-weapon (last visited Oct. 2, 2019).

[48] Letter from Arnold Schwarzenegger, Governor of California, to the Members of the California State Senate (Sept. 20, 2014), *available at* ftp://leginfo.public.ca.gov/pub/03-04/bill/sen/sb_1101-1150/sb_1140_vt_20040920.html (last visited Aug. 23, 2020).

Alfred North Whitehead wrote of rationalism, the effort is, itself, 'an adventure in the clarification of thought.'"[49]

The California Assault Weapons Control Act (AWCA) is perhaps the most complicated of all California firearms laws, and the consequences for violation are severe. Not only do ordinary citizens find it difficult – if not impossible – to determine whether a semiautomatic firearm should be considered an "assault weapon," trained law enforcement officers, prosecutors, and judges have a similar difficulty.

The author of the legislation requiring the Attorney General to produce the Assault Weapon Identification Guide (AWIG) recognized this difficulty:

> I am writing to request your signature on SB 2444 which would enable law enforcement personnel in the field the means to be able to recognize what actually is or is not an "assault weapon," as defined under state law.... Unfortunately, a great many law enforcement officers who deal directly with the public are not experts in specific firearms identification.... There are numerous makes and models of civilian military-looking semi-automatic firearms which are not listed by California as "assault weapons" but which are very similar in external appearance. This situation sets the stage for honest law-enforcement mistakes resulting in unjustified confiscations of non-assault weapon firearms. Such mistakes, although innocently made, could easily result in unnecessary, time consuming, and costly legal actions both for law enforcement and for the lawful firearms owners affected.[50]

C. 2012 Reorganization of the Dangerous Weapons Control Act

To improve the California Penal Code's organization and understandability, and in recognition of the tremendous confusion surrounding the interpretation and enforcement of California firearms laws, the Dangerous Weapons Recodification Act of 2010 was adopted. Under this recodification, the California Law Revision Commission (CLRC) completely renumbered the DWCA, as well as parts of some other California codes, to "improve the organization and accessibility of the deadly weapons statutes, without making any change to criminal liability under those statutes."[51]

---

[49] *Rash v. Lungen*, 59 Cal. App. 4th 1233, 1235 (1997) (quoting Whitehead, Process and Reality (1929) pt. I, ch. 1, § 3).

[50] *See Harrott v. Cnty. of Kings*, 25 Cal. 4th 1138, 1147 n.4 (2001) (citing Letter from Don Rogers, United States Senator, to George Deukmejian, Governor of California (Aug. 23, 1990)).

[51] *Nonsubstantive Reorganization of Deadly Weapons Statutes*, 38 CAL. L. REVISION COMM'N REPORTS 217, 219 (2009) (citing letter from Pamela L. Hemminger, Chairwoman, California Law Revision Commission, to Arnold Schwarzenegger, Governor of California), *available at* http://clrc.ca.gov/pub/Printed-Reports/Pub233.pdf (last visited Aug. 23, 2020).

The Dangerous Weapons Recodification Act was adopted pursuant to Assembly Concurrent Resolution 73 in 2006,[52] which directed the CLRC, a neutral body of legal experts, to study, report on, and prepare recommended legislation to simplify and reorganize the portions of the Penal Code relating to the control of deadly weapons, without making any substantive change to the scope of criminal liability under those provisions.

The author of Assembly Concurrent Resolution 73 said:

> In addition to the criminal storage laws, *many other provisions of the Penal Code are very confusing. In particular, the laws relating to the transfers of firearms are lengthy, with numerous cross-references, highly fact-specific exemptions, and complex provisions.* For example, Penal Code Section 12078 is 5,880 words long and occupies eleven pages if printed in a 12-point font with conventional margins. The section has cross-references to many scattered sections of other firearms provisions, some of them hundreds of sections away. *The firearms laws occupy over 100 pages of an unannotated version of the Penal Code when printed in dual column in tiny print. These areas of the law are not for legal experts only. Firearms owners, licensed dealers, and law enforcement need to be able to interpret these provisions in order to comply with the law and avoid criminal liability. Ambiguity and confusion do not promote the public policy goals that those laws were designated to accomplish.*[53]

The CLRC completed their task on time in 2009, and the Dangerous Weapons Recodification Act was adopted in 2010. It took effect on January 1, 2012.

To assist persons using those laws, I have posted a disposition table on www.CalGunLawsBook.com showing where each provision was relocated. Visit the site for that and additional information on the reorganization.

D. "Gray Areas" and Test Cases

Despite my best efforts to explain the firearms laws in California, there are some unanswered questions, as is the case with most any legal scheme as convoluted as California's. I may have my own personal beliefs as to how law enforcement would likely interpret these laws. My purpose in addressing these legal "gray areas" is not to provide my position on what the law actually is or should be, nor to persuade or dissuade you from deciding to engage in activities falling in a "gray area" category. But, as an attorney, I believe part of my obligation is to make you aware of the uncertainty about what some of the laws allow and that there are potential risks associated with certain activities. I will let you decide what makes sense for your

---

[52] *See* 2006 Cal. Stat. 7397-98.

[53] *Analysis of ACR 73*, CAL. SEN. RULES COMM., OFFICE OF SENATE FLOOR ANALYSES (S. 2004-2005 Reg. Sess.), ftp://www.leginfo.ca.gov/pub/05-06/bill/asm/ab_0051-0100/acr_73_cfa_20060822_195816_sen_floor.html (last visited Aug. 23, 2020) (emphasis added).

personal situation. When these legal "gray areas" arise in the book, I have tried to indicate them as such and remind the reader of the admonition in this chapter.

Some people choose to push the legal "envelope" by engaging in activities that would fall in these legal "gray areas." And some even insist that certain activities are not "gray" at all, but are clearly legal, and that their interpretation precludes law enforcement from causing you any legal problems. This overly academic mindset is driven by wishful thinking, a misunderstanding of the context of California firearms law, and the practically oriented judicial system in which they are typically applied. When in doubt, if possible, ask a qualified attorney before engaging in legally questionable activity.

And be very careful about relying on the opinions of internet-pseudo-lawyers for answers to your firearms law-related questions. As one court elegantly explained:

> Beware of the dangers of the Internet. It makes semiautomatic assault weapon kits available at the click of a mouse. Furthermore, it would appear to provide guidance on assembling the weapon, as well as suggestions for avoiding criminal convictions arising out of the possession of the parts, their assembly, and even the possession of the completed weapons. But woe betides the consumer who trusts every schematic espoused on the Internet.[54]

E. Government Bias in Applying Gun Laws

In order to protect themselves from criminal or civil liability, people cannot just count on logic or reasonableness alone in deciphering California's firearms laws. If that were the case, there would be little need for this book; at least, it would be much shorter.

In my many years of handling thousands of criminal and civil matters involving firearms, it is my experience that some law enforcement officers, many prosecutors, and most California courts are unsympathetic toward civilian firearm ownership. They have repeatedly gone, and likely will continue to go, out of their way to interpret a questionable practice as unlawful. This is the case even if a technical reading of a statute or regulation suggests the practice is legal. Once your defense depends on parsing the language of statutes and/or explaining technical discrepancies, you are fighting an uphill battle. And the cost of taking on that proverbial "hill" can often be significant. I do not need to warn you that lawyers cost money.

A prime example of the troublesome nature of interpreting firearms laws is the fact that the preeminent case from the U.S. Supreme Court interpreting the Second Amendment right to keep and bear arms as an individual right, *District of Columbia v. Heller*, was decided by a vote of 5-4. That means four justices in the country's highest court disagree that there is even an individual right to firearm

---

[54] *People v. Nguyen*, 212 Cal. App. 4th 1311, 1315 (2013).

possession. The same vote count was repeated in the following Supreme Court ruling on whether the Second Amendment applied to the states and local governments in *McDonald v. Chicago*. And despite this promise from the Supreme Court's *Heller* and *McDonald* decisions, many courts and politicians still remain opposed to fundamental Second Amendment rights and resistant to the Supreme Court's pronouncements.

Unfortunately, *what the law says and what authorities and courts do are not always an exact match*. You must remember that each legal case is different and may lack prior court precedents. A decision to prosecute a case and what charges are brought may involve a degree of discretion from the authorities involved. Sometimes, there is no plain or clear-cut answer upon which you can rely. Abuses, ignorance, carelessness, human frailties, and plain fate subject you to legal risks, which can be exacerbated when firearms are involved. Take nothing for granted, recognize that legal risk is attached to everything you do with a firearm, and unless you are ready to be a test case or have a life and death need, my recommendation is that you err on the side of compliance.

My law firm has been fighting and will continue to fight bad gun laws in courthouses every day, and we have no shortage of test cases and unfortunate gun owners.

CHAPTER 3:
WHAT IS LEGALLY CONSIDERED A "FIREARM" AND "AMMUNITION"?

What is a firearm? What is ammunition? These may seem like dumb questions because you may already have an idea of what a "firearm" and "ammunition" are. But for regulatory purposes, the legal definitions of a "firearm" and "ammunition" can be tricky to apply. Under the law, the term "firearm" includes more than just what we informally call "guns." For example, under California law, flare *guns* might be considered "firearms," while BB *guns* may not. And sometimes only *part* of a firearm is enough to constitute a "firearm" under the law. There are also differences between federal and state law definitions of "firearm" and "ammunition," and even different definitions of those terms *within* those federal and state laws. Misconstruing these definitions causes legal trouble for firearm owners. And in the highly politicized legal environment of gun control laws, the consequences of even an innocent mistake can be severe.

Understanding these legal terms will help you avoid problems with things like flare guns, tear gas guns, certain air and BB guns, and other types of "guns" that might be regulated as "firearms." Knowing how these definitions apply will also help you understand this book's later discussion about restrictions on firearm and ammunition possession and provide you the information you need to lawfully acquire "firearms" and "ammunition."

I. "FIREARM" DEFINITIONS

A. Federal Law "Firearm" Definitions

Federal law defines the term "firearm" in both the federal Gun Control Act (GCA)[1] and the National Firearms Act (NFA),[2] the two Acts that are most relevant to gun owners.

---
[1] Gun Control Act of 1968, codified at 18 U.S.C. §§ 921-931.
[2] National Firearms Act, codified at 26 U.S.C. §§ 5801-5872.

On the one hand, the GCA regulates "firearms" generally with respect to transfers and restricts who can possess them. On the other hand, the NFA defines the term "firearm" by specifically listing highly restricted items in one category (some of which are not "guns"), making it easier to explain the detailed requirements to lawfully possess, import, and transfer those items.

1. The Gun Control Act

The GCA defines a "firearm" as:

(1) Any weapon (including a starter gun) which will or is designed to or may readily be converted to expel a projectile by the action of an explosive; *or*

(2) The frame or receiver of any such weapon;[3] *or*

(3) Any firearm muffler or firearm silencer;[4] *or*

(4) Any destructive device.[5]

An "antique firearm" is not considered a "firearm" for purposes of the GCA.[6] The definition of an "antique firearm" is discussed later in this chapter.

2. The National Firearms Act

Under the NFA, the term "firearm" means:

(1) A shotgun with a barrel or barrels of less than 18 inches in length; *or*

(2) A weapon made from a shotgun if such weapon as modified has an overall length of less than 26 inches or a barrel or barrels of less than 18 inches in length; *or*

(3) A rifle with a barrel or barrels of less than 16 inches in length; *or*

(4) A weapon made from a rifle if such weapon as modified, has an overall length of less than 26 inches or a barrel or barrels of less than 16 inches in length; *or*

(5) "Any other weapon" as defined in subsection (e) of 26 U.S.C. section 5845; *or*

(6) A machinegun;[7] *or*

(7) A silencer as defined in 18 U.S.C. section 921; *or*

(8) A destructive device.[8]

---

[3] See Section I(A)(3) in this Chapter.

[4] The definitions for "silencer" and "destructive device" are the same under the GCA and the NFA. *See* 18 U.S.C. § 921; 26 U.S.C. § 5845(a), (f). Although "firearm muffler" is not defined in the NFA, the Code of Federal Regulations provides a definition for "muffler," which is the same as the GCA's definition. 27 C.F.R. 479.11. These definitions are discussed in Chapter 10.

[5] 18 U.S.C. § 921(a)(3). See Chapter 10.

[6] 18 U.S.C. § 921(a)(3).

[7] Discussed in Chapter 10.

[8] 26 U.S.C. § 5845(a). The definitions and restrictions on "short-barreled shotguns," "short-barreled rifles," "any other weapons," "machineguns," "silencers," and "destructive devices" are discussed in further detail in Chapter 9.

Similar to the GCA, the NFA's definition of "firearm" also excludes "antique firearms." But the NFA's definition for "antique firearm" is slightly different from the GCA's definition (explained below).

As the GCA and the NFA are two separate acts, you should keep in mind that although your firearm may fit within the definition of an "antique firearm" under the GCA, it might not be considered one under the NFA because its definition encompasses fewer firearms.[9]

Also, keep in mind that the "firearms" located in the NFA are considered "firearms" under the GCA. Not all "firearms" under the GCA are considered to be "firearms" under the NFA, however. Consequently, the requirements for the GCA apply to NFA "firearms," in addition to all of the other restrictions and requirements located in the NFA.

Moreover, the definition of a "firearm" under the NFA excludes any device (other than a machinegun or destructive device) that the Secretary of Treasury finds is "primarily a collector's item" and thus unlikely to be used as a weapon.[10]

As mentioned, the NFA's definition of "firearm" simply lists several highly restricted items. These restrictions came about as a result of the NFA's passage in the 1930s, when the government sought to curtail gangland violence by restricting weapons generally associated with gangs in that era, like fully-automatic "Tommy guns" and grenades. Though the government wanted a comprehensive legal scheme to deal with these items, it did not ban them at the time because it believed doing so would violate the Second Amendment.[11] Instead, the government heavily taxed possession and transfer of these items and required that they be registered to assure the tax was paid if they were ever transferred again.[12] Paying a $200 tax was highly cost-prohibitive in the 1930s, but nowadays, that amount is small in comparison to the high costs of the firearms and devices covered in the NFA. The specific characteristics of these "firearms," along with their respective restrictions, are further discussed in Chapter 10.

The Bureau of Alcohol, Tobacco, Firearms, and Explosives (ATF) opines that an item may lose its "firearm" status under the NFA if it is modified in a way that permanently removes the characteristics that make it an NFA firearm or that completely destroys the item.[13]

---

[9] *See* 18 U.S.C. § 921(a)(16); 26 U.S.C. § 5845(g).

[10] 26 U.S.C. § 5845(a).

[11] *See generally, National Firearms Act of (1934)-Further Readings*, http://law.jrank.org/pages/8725/National-Firearms-Act-1934.html (last visited Aug. 23, 2020).

[12] *Firearms-National Firearms Act (NFA)*, U.S. DEPT. OF JUSTICE, BUREAU OF ALCOHOL, TOBACCO, FIREARMS AND EXPLOSIVES, https://www.atf.gov/file/58251/download (last visited Aug. 23, 2020).

[13] *See* U.S. DEPT. OF JUSTICE, BUREAU OF ALCOHOL, TOBACCO, FIREARMS, AND EXPLOSIVES, ATF NATIONAL FIREARMS ACT HANDBOOK 21-22 (rev. Apr. 2009), *available at* http://www.atf.gov/files/publications/download/p/atf-p-5320-8/atf-p-5320-8.pdf (last visited Aug. 23, 2020).

3. What Is a Frame or Receiver Under Federal Law?

Unfortunately, the terms "frame" and "receiver" are not defined within the federal code. They are defined in the Code of Federal Regulations[14] (C.F.R.). Specifically, for purposes of the GCA and the NFA, a "firearm frame or receiver" is defined as "[t]hat part of a firearm which provides the housing for the hammer, bolt or breechblock, and firing mechanism, and which is usually threaded at its forward position to receive the barrel."[15]

Notice that it is unclear which part of a two-part receiver (*i.e.*, those made of an upper and lower receiver) would be considered the firearm's "frame or receiver" for purposes of federal law. Take for example a receiver for an AR-15 semiautomatic rifle, which is made up of both an upper and a lower receiver. Although the upper receiver contains the housing for the bolt and is threaded at its forward position to receive a barrel, it is not considered the "firearm"; the lower receiver is. But according to the definition mentioned above, an AR-15 lower receiver should not be considered a "receiver" for purposes of federal law because it does not house *all* of the components mentioned in the federal definition.

Recognizing this ambiguity, the ATF attempts to clarify which part of a two-part receiver is considered to be the "receiver" for certain firearms. But, these classifications are very arbitrary and they seem to be made without any rhyme or reason. For example, even though an AR-15 lower receiver clearly does not fit within the definition of a "firearm frame or receiver" for purposes of federal law, the ATF still considers it to be the "receiver" of the firearm. In contrast, the ATF considers the upper receiver of an FN Herstal ("FN"), FNC, FN FAL, and FN SCAR to be "receivers" for purposes of federal law.[16]

Similar to the two-part receivers, some semiautomatic firearms and machineguns incorporate a "split" or "hinged" design so that the main portion of the weapon can be separated into upper and lower sections. For purposes of these firearms, the ATF has also attempted to classify which part (*i.e.*, the upper or lower section) is considered to be the "receiver" for purposes of the NFA.[17] But once again, there is no rhyme or reason as to how the ATF made these decisions. For example, the ATF considers the right-side plate of a Browning M1917 to be the "receiver" of the firearm, but considers the upper section of an Armalite AR-10 to be the 80% "receiver."

---

[14] The Code of Federal Regulations is a compilation of rules adopted by federal agencies in furtherance of implementing federal laws enacted by Congress.

[15] 27 C.F.R. § 478.11 (relating to the regulations for the GCA); 27 C.F.R. § 479.11 (relating to the regulations for the NFA).

[16] *See* ATF Rul. 2008-1.

[17] For a list of specific models that incorporate the "split" or "hinged" design, and what portion of those "machineguns" are considered to be the "receiver," see the National Firearms Handbook at https://www.atf.gov/file/58196/download (last visited Aug. 23, 2020).

4. Are Precursor (80%) Receivers "Firearms"?

Incomplete receivers, which are commonly but inaccurately referred to as "80%[18] receivers" or "80% side plates," are generally not considered to be "firearms" because they have not yet been machined into complete functional receivers.

Although there are no laws or regulations that explain when a precursor receiver is complete enough to be considered a "firearm," the ATF has issued letters to 80% receiver manufactures explaining what features cannot be present on a precursor receiver in order for it to not be considered a "firearm." For "80% AR receivers," ATF takes the position that no work can be done to the "fire control cavity" that houses the trigger, no drilling into the receiver for the hammer and trigger pins, and no drilling for the safety.[19] Once work has been started in those areas, then the ATF considers the receiver to be a "firearm" for purposes of federal law.

5. Are Non-Functioning Firearms "Firearms"?

Some "paperweights" (i.e., firearms that no longer function) may be considered "fire- arms" under federal law. For instance, machineguns that appear to have been destroyed so that they are essentially "paperweight firearms" may still be considered "machineguns"[20] if they can be "readily restored to shoot" automatically. In other words, if you possess a machinegun that was poorly "demilled" (i.e., rendered non-operational) or was not destroyed in accordance with an ATF-approved method of destruction,[21] it may still be considered a "machinegun" under federal law. Or, you may be in possession of a broken firearm, but the receiver is intact. As discussed before, frames/receivers can be considered "firearms" by themselves.

B. California Law "Firearm" Definitions

California Penal Code (P.C.) section 16520(a) generally defines the term "firearm" as it is used within other California statutes: "'[F]irearm' means any device, designed to be used as a weapon, from which is expelled through a barrel, a projectile

---

[18] In 2014, the ATF went even further with its position on "80% AR receivers" stating that 80% receivers that have material that extends "past the exterior walls of the casting, indicating the approximate location of the holes to be drilled for the selector, hammer, and trigger pins" were considered to be "firearms" for purposes of federal law. Moreover, the ATF has also taken the position that 80% receivers that have so-called "indexing" (i.e., different colored material that outlines where to drill the fire control cavity) are "firearms" for purposes of federal law. A company tried to challenge ATF's stance on when an 80% receiver is considered a "firearm," but it was ultimately unsuccessful. *See In re Ares Armor , 206/208 N. Freeman St., Oceanside* (9th Cir. 2017) 687 Fed.Appx. 622.

[19] The "80%" denotes how close the firearm is to being a complete firearm, though this is more of an estimate since it is impossible to say what percentage of work remains for a given firearm, which can vary based on experience, available tools, etc.

[20] For the definitions of a "machinegun," see Chapter 10.

[21] To learn more about the ATF-approved method to destroy a "machinegun," see ATF Rul. 2003-1, ATF Rul. 2003-2, ATF Rul. 2003-3, ATF Rule 2003-4, and the *ATF Guidebook-Importation & Verification of Firearms, Ammunition, and Implements of War*, BUREAU OF ALCOHOL, TOBACCO, FIREARMS, AND EXPLOSIVES, *available at* https://www.atf.gov/file/61771/download (last visited Aug. 23, 2020).

by the force of an explosion or other form of combustion."

This definition of "firearm," from Penal Code section 16520(*a*), does not include a bare frame or receiver. But the definition of "firearm" in P.C. section 16520(b), which is applicable only to certain code sections,[22] does include the frame or receiver. This means that when the P.C. section 16520(b) definition applies, the frame or receiver is considered a "firearm" all by itself, even though it cannot function as a firearm without additional parts.

Example of a receiver from a pistol

1. History of California's "Firearm" Definition

To understand the reasoning behind P.C. section 16520 and why some code sections treat frames and receivers as "firearms" while others do not, you need to understand the definition's history and how it developed from former P.C. section 12001.

Before 1969, P.C. section 12001 defined a "firearm" as a "'pistol,' 'revolver,' and 'firearm capable of being concealed upon the person' . . . [including] any device, designed to be used as a weapon, from which is expelled a projectile by the force of any explosion, or other form of combustion, and which has a barrel less than 12 inches in length."[23] Believe it or not, rifles and shotguns were not regulated as "firearms" for purposes of firearm transfers or for the restrictions on prohibited persons at the time.

In 1968, a California court said that if a firearm was unable to fire because its firing pin was broken and another firing pin was unavailable to make the firearm work, the other parts alone were insufficient to be considered a "firearm."[24] In other words, a firearm that was missing a piece of equipment necessary to make it fire (like a firing pin) was *not* considered a "firearm" until the missing piece was replaced.[25] This meant that if someone did not technically possess a functioning "firearm," he or she could not be convicted of feloniously possessing a firearm.

To avoid this result, a broader "firearm" definition was subsequently added to the Penal Code in 1969, but it only applied to certain statutes.[26] This broader definition of "firearm" included frames and receivers – which are not functional firearms by themselves.

---

[22] See Section I(B)(2) of this chapter, for a more detailed discussion on when the definition of "firearm" that includes frames and receivers applies.

[23] *See People v. Thompson*, 72 Cal. App. 3d 1, 4 (1977) (quoting P.C. § 12001 (1968)).

[24] *People v. Jackson*, 266 Cal. App. 2d 341, 349 (1968), *superseded by statute/rule as stated in People v. Nelums*, 31 Cal. 3d 355 (1982).

[25] *People v. Jackson*, 266 Cal. App. 2d 341, 349 (1968), *superseded by statute/rule as stated in People v. Nelums*, 31 Cal. 3d 355 (1982).

[26] *See* P.C. § 12001(1970).

2. When Is a Frame or Receiver Considered a "Firearm"?

The definition of a "firearm" is codified in P.C. section 16520. Although P.C. section 16520(b) sets forth a broader "firearm" definition, which includes frames and receivers, that definition should only apply in certain contexts, usually relating to transfers and illegal possession.[27]

The rationale behind certain firearm *parts* being considered "firearms" themselves presumably is to prevent "prohibited persons"[28] from having access to the operating parts of a firearm, which, when put together, could make a functional firearm. By defining "firearm" to include frames or receivers and regulating them as functional firearms, California law ensures that no one can lawfully sell or transfer these essential parts to those prohibited people.[29] It also closes a loophole for prohibited persons who might try to avoid criminal liability by keeping their firearms disassembled.

3. What Is a Frame or Receiver Under California Law?

Similar to federal law, the terms "frame" and "receiver" are also not defined in the Penal Code. The new "bullet button assault weapon" and "ghost gun" regulations that DOJ adopted in 2017 and 2018, however, define them for purposes of "assault weapon" and "ghost gun" registration, respectively. The "bullet button" regulations define "receiver" as "the basic unit of a firearm which houses the firing and breech mechanisms and to which the barrel and stock are assembled."[30] The "ghost gun" regulations define "receiver" as "the basic unit of a firearm that is a long gun" and that "will generally house the firing and breech mechanisms to which the barrel

---

[27] P.C. § 16520(b). This definition applies to the following provisions: P.C. sections 16550 (Firearm transaction records); 16730 ("Infrequent" firearm transactions); 16960 ("Operation of law" transfers); 16990 (Taking firearm title or possession by "operation of law"); 17070 (Definition of "responsible adult"); 17310 (Definition of "used firearm"); 26500-26588 (License requirements to sell, lease, or transfer and exceptions; sales, leases, or transfers of firearms by licensees; loans of firearms by licensees to specific persons; sales, delivers, and transfers of firearms by licensees to certain persons within and outside the state); 26600-27140 (Exceptions for sale, lease, or transfer to law enforcement; license to sell, lease, or transfer firearms at retail; grounds for forfeiture of license, exception extending waiting period for delivery of a firearm; exceptions for law enforcement for sale, delivery, transfer, or loan of firearm; other exceptions); 27400-28000 (Exceptions for law enforcement at gun shows or events, and crimes relating to firearm transfer); 28100 (Electronic and telephonic transfer register or record); 28400-28415 (Exceptions for law enforcement record keeping, background checks, and fees for firearm sale, lease, or transfer); 29010-29150 (License requirements for firearm manufacturer, licensing process, and prohibitions and requirements applicable to licensed manufacturers); 29180 (Manufacture or assembly of a firearm and serial number requirements); 29610-29750 (Illegal firearm and ammunition possession by minors and exemptions from those restrictions; also punishments for minors violating those restrictions); 29800-29905 (Firearm access prohibitions; exemptions from prohibitions and petitions for relief; and persons convicted of violent offense); 30150-30165 (Exceptions for law enforcement firearm eligibility checks); 31615 (Handgun Safety Certificate requirement); 31705-31830 (Exceptions for sale, delivery, or transfer from the Firearm Safety Certificate requirement); 34355-34370 (Exceptions for the sale, delivery or transfer to authorized law enforcement representatives for ballistics identification system); and California Welfare and Institutions Code (Cal. Welf. & Inst. Code) sections 8100, 8101, 8103 (Mental health restriction prohibitions). *See* P.C. § 16520.

[28] "Prohibited persons" are individuals who are prohibited from possessing firearms. This is further discussed in Chapter 4.

[29] *See* P.C. §§ 26500-26588, 26700.

[30] CAL. CODE REGS. tit. 11, § 5471(aa).

and stock are assembled."[31] In both cases, these definitions are limited in their application, meaning they do not apply to other areas of California firearm laws. That said, courts have also provided some guidance as to what the definition of the term "receiver" is. Courts have defined a "receiver" as "the metal frame in which the action[32] of a firearm is fitted and to which the breech end of the barrel is attached."[33]

Although not defined by statute or court, the term "frame" is defined by the DOJ's new "assault weapon" regulations as "the receiver of a pistol" for purposes of "assault weapon" registration.[34] For purposes of registering self-manufactured firearms, it is defined as "the basic unit of a firearm that is a handgun."[35] Also, it is defined within California's unofficial jury instructions (CALJIC). Under these jury instructions, the term "frame" is defined as "the basic unit of a handgun which serves as a mounting for the barrel and operating parts for the gun."[36] Although these jury instructions are not binding on the courts and are merely persuasive authority, they nonetheless provide some guidance on what the term "frame" may mean for purposes of California law.

4. Are Non-functioning Firearms "Firearms"?

Under California law, "paperweights" may be considered "firearms" under most "use" of firearm offenses[37] and sentencing enhancements,[38] as long as the paperweight still looks like or appears to be a functioning firearm.[39] This is because these statutes focus on the effect that a firearm (whether functional or not) can have on the victim of the crime. As explained by the California Court of Appeal:

> The victim [of crime like robbery, burglary, assault, or rape] is placed in fear and cannot be expected to inquire into the condition of the gun [when being threatened]. The danger remains that the reaction by the victim or some third person to the appearance of the gun will cause harm to befall someone.... [the "use" of firearm offenses in P.C. section 12022.5] appl[y] even if the evidence conclusively proves that the firearm was inoperable,

---

[31] Cal. Code Regs. tit. 11, § 5507(p).

[32] An "action" is defined in DOJ's new regulations as "the working mechanism of a semiautomatic firearm, which is the combination of the receiver or frame and breech bolt together with the other parts of the mechanism by which a firearm is loaded fired and unloaded." Cal. Code Regs. tit. 11, § 5471(b).

[33] *People v. Arnold*, 145 Cal. App. 4th 1408, 1414 (2006) (citing *Harrott v. Cnty. of Kings*, 25 Cal. 4th 1138, 1147 n. 6 (2001)).

[34] Cal. Code Regs. tit. 11, § 5471(u).

[35] Cal. Code Regs. tit. 11, § 5507(l).

[36] CALJIC No. 12.48.

[37] *See* P.C. § 12022.5.

[38] *See* P.C. § 12022.53.

[39] *See People v. Nelums*, 31 Cal. 3d 355, 359 (1982) (In Bank). The term "paperweight" would also include any antique firearms that no longer function.

so long as there is evidence of a gun designed to shoot and which gives the appearance of shooting capability.[40]

In other words, as long as the "paperweight" was once designed to shoot and reasonably appears that it can still shoot, then, even if it can't shoot, it may still be considered a "firearm" under certain California Penal Code sections.

As stated above, remember that, under California law, machineguns that appear to have been destroyed so that they are essentially "paperweight firearms" may still be considered "machineguns."[41] California has not taken a position as to the extent a machinegun must be "de-milled," although it may be assumed that DOJ or law enforcement may turn to the ATF analysis and federal regulations for guidance.

5. Are Precursor (80%) Receivers "Firearms" Under California Law?

California takes no position on when a precursor receiver becomes a firearm. But California law enforcement will likely turn to the ATF's position for guidance (see above). For firearm manufacturing (P.C. sections 29010-29150), however, the term "firearm" includes "the unfinished frame or receiver of a weapon that can be readily converted to the functional condition of a finished frame or receiver."[42]

California imposes specific serialization requirements before you can lawfully complete a precursor receiver and turn it into a functional receiver. To learn more about these requirements, see Chapter 5.

II. FIREARM SUBGROUP DEFINITIONS

Certain items meeting the general "firearm" definition are further classified based on their characteristics and have more specific definitions under California law, the GCA, and the NFA. The most common of these groups are handguns, rifles, and shotguns. But even these groups are further divided into subgroups with more specific definitions, as explained in Chapters 9 and 10. Proper classification of a firearm is crucial to understanding which regulations apply to it. It can mean the difference between conduct being perfectly legal or a crime.

A. "Handguns"

Under the GCA a "handgun" is:

(1) A firearm which has a short stock and is designed to be held and fired by

---

[40] *People v. Jackson*, 92 Cal. App. 3d 899, 903 (1979) (internal quotes and citations omitted); *People v. Nelums*, 31 Cal. 3d 355, 359 (1982) (en banc).
[41] For the definitions of a "machinegun," see Chapter 10.
[42] P.C. § 16520(g).

the use of a single hand; *and*

(2) Any combination of parts from which such a "firearm" as described in (1) can be assembled.[43]

The federal Code of Regulations defines "handgun" as:

(1) Any firearm which has a short stock and is designed to be held and fired by the use of a single hand; *and*

(2) Any combination of parts from which a firearm described in paragraph (a) can be assembled.[44]

Under California law, a "handgun" is "any pistol, revolver, or firearm capable of being concealed upon the person."[45] The terms "firearm capable of being concealed upon the person," "pistol," and "revolver" are further defined as:

[A]ny device designed to be used as a weapon, from which is expelled a projectile by the force of any explosion, or other form of combustion, and that has a barrel less than 16 inches in length. These terms also include any device that has a barrel 16 inches or more in length which is designed to be interchanged with a barrel less than 16 inches in length.[46]

1. Pistols

Glock 9 mm Semiautomatic Pistol

Under federal law, both the GCA and the NFA do not define the term "pistol." The Code of Federal Regulations does, however. Specifically, the Code of Federal Regulations defines the term "pistol" as "[a] weapon originally designed, made, and intended to fire a projectile (bullet) from one or more barrels when held in one hand, and having (a) a chamber(s) as an integral part(s) of, or permanently aligned with, the bore(s); and (b) a short stock designed to be gripped by one hand

---

[43] 18 U.S.C. § 921(a)(29). The NFA does not define "handgun." *See* 26 U.S.C. § 5845. But the NFA regulations do define "pistol" and "revolver." A "pistol" is defined as "[a] weapon originally designed, made, and intended to fire a projectile (bullet) from one or more barrels when held in one hand, and having (a) a chamber(s) as an integral part(s) of, or permanently aligned with, the bore(s); and (b) a short stock designed to be gripped by one hand and at an angle to and extending below the line of the bore(s)." 27 C.F.R. § 479.11. And a "rifle" is defined as "[a] weapon designed or redesigned, made or remade, and intended to be fired from the shoulder and designed or redesigned and made or remade to use the energy of the explosive in a fixed cartridge to fire only a single projectile through a rifled bore for each single pull of the trigger, and shall include any such weapon which may be readily restored to fire a fixed cartridge." 27 C.F.R. § 479.11.

[44] 27 C.F.R. § 478.11.

[45] P.C. § 16640(a).

[46] P.C. § 16530(a).

and at an angle to and extending below the line of the bore(s)."[47] This definition is applicable to the regulations for the GCA and NFA.[48]

Under California law, a "pistol" means the following for purposes of "assault weapon" registration:

> [A]ny device designed to be used as a weapon, from which a projectile is expelled by the force of any explosion, or other form of combustion, and that has a barrel less than 16 inches in length. This definition includes AR-15 style pistols with pistol buffer tubes attached. Pistol buffer tubes typically have smooth metal with no guide on the bottom for rifle stocks to be attached, and they sometimes have a foam pad on the end of the tube farthest from the receiver.[49]

A "semiautomatic pistol" is "a pistol with an operating mode that uses the energy of the explosive in a fixed cartridge to extract a fired cartridge and chamber a fresh cartridge with each single pull of the trigger."[50] But, this definition is only applicable to the "unsafe handgun" and "handgun testing laws" under P.C. sections 16900 and 31910.

Oddly, the "unsafe handgun" and "handgun testing" laws also regulate other varieties of "pistols" and "revolvers," but these terms are not defined in the Penal Code. The California Code of Regulations (Cal. Code Regs.), however, does define "pistol" as "a handgun in which the chamber is part of the barrel. A pistol can either be semiautomatic or non-semiautomatic, but not fully automatic."[51] This definition also only applies to the "unsafe handgun" and "handgun testing" laws.

2. Revolvers

Neither the GCA nor the NFA defines the term "revolver." The Code of Federal Regulations does. Specifically, the Code of Federal Regulations defines the term "revolver" as "[a] projectile weapon, of the pistol type, having a breechloading chambered cylinder so arranged that the cocking of the hammer or movement of the trigger rotates it and brings the next cartridge in line with the barrel for firing."[52] This definition is applicable to the regulations for both the GCA and the NFA.[53]

Ruger & Co.
Speed Six Revolver

---

[47] 27 C.F.R. §§ 478.11, 479.11.
[48] 27 C.F.R. §§ 478.11, 479.11.
[49] CAL. CODE REGS. tit. 11, § 5471(y).
[50] P.C. § 17140.
[51] CAL. CODE REGS. tit. 11, § 4049(p).
[52] 27 C.F.R. §§ 478.11, 479.11.
[53] 27 C.F.R. §§ 478.11, 479.11.

While the California Penal Code does not provide a general definition for "revolver," it is defined in the California Code of Regulations as "a handgun with a cylinder having several chambers so arranged as to rotate around an axis and be discharged successively by the same firing mechanism through a common barrel."[54] This definition of "revolver" applies to the "unsafe handgun" and "handgun testing" laws.[55]

B. "Rifles," "Shotguns,"[56] and "Long Guns"[57]

1. Rifles

The GCA's and NFA's definitions for "rifle" are practically identical. Under the GCA, a "rifle" is defined as "a weapon designed or redesigned, made or remade, and intended to be fired from the shoulder and designed or redesigned and made or remade to use the energy of an explosive to fire only a single projectile through a rifled bore for each single pull of the trigger."[58]

On the other hand, the NFA and the Code of Federal Regulations defines a "rifle" as "a weapon designed or redesigned, made or remade, and intended to be fired from the shoulder and designed or redesigned and made or remade to use the energy of the explosive *in a fixed cartridge* to fire only a single projectile through a rifled bore for each single pull of the trigger, and shall include any such weapon which may be readily restored to fire a *fixed cartridge*."[59] Notice that the difference between the NFA and the GCA's definition of a "rifle" is that the NFA's definition contains the "in a fixed cartridge" qualifier, but the GCA does not.[60]

Unlike federal law, California law does not provide a general definition for the term "rifle." It does define the term "rifle" in the context of "short-barreled rifles" as being "a weapon designed or redesigned, made or remade, and intended to be fired from the shoulder and designed or redesigned and made or remade to use the energy of the explosive in a fixed cartridge to fire only a single projectile through a rifled bore for each single pull of the trigger."[61] An identical definition for the term "rifle" is used in the context of DOJ's "ghost guns" regulations implemented in 2018.[62]

---

[54] Cal. Code Regs. tit. 11, § 4049(t).
[55] See Chapter 10.
[56] Shotguns and rifles are commonly referred to collectively as "long guns," and will be referred to in this way throughout this book when the distinction is not relevant.
[57] When the phrase "long guns" is used in this book, unless it is with respect to the Firearm Safety Certificate (discussed further in Chapter 5), it means "long guns" in general and not as specifically defined in P.C. section 16865.
[58] 18 U.S.C. § 921(a)(7).
[59] 26 U.S.C. § 5845(c) (emphasis added); 27 C.F.R. § 479.11.
[60] See 18 U.S.C. § 921(a)(7); 26 U.S.C. § 5845(c). But, 27 C.F.R. section 478.11 does use the language "in a fixed metallic cartridge" in its definition of "rifle." But this definition is only applicable to the Code of Federal Regulations.
[61] P.C. § 17090.
[62] Cal. Code Regs. tit. 11, § 5507(r).

Also, California law provides a definition for "rifle" in the context of the new "bullet button assault weapon" registration scheme. Per DOJ's new regulations:

"Rifle" means a weapon designed or redesigned, made or remade, and intended to be fired from the shoulder and designed or redesigned and made or remade to use the energy of the explosive in a fixed cartridge to fire only a single projectile through a rifled bore for each single pull of the trigger.[63]

2. Shotguns

Again, the GCA's and NFA's "shotgun" definitions are practically identical. The GCA defines a "shotgun" as "a weapon designed or redesigned, made or remade, and intended to be fired from the shoulder and designed or redesigned and made or remade to use the energy of an explosive to fire through a smooth bore either a number of ball shot or a single projectile for each single pull of the trigger."[64]

On the other hand, the NFA and the Code of Federal Regulations defines a "shotgun" as "a weapon designed or redesigned, made or remade, and intended to be fired from the shoulder and designed or redesigned and made or remade to use the energy of the explosive in a *fixed shotgun shell* to fire through a smooth bore either a number of projectiles (ball shot) or a single projectile for each pull of the trigger, and shall include any such weapon which may be readily restored to fire a *fixed shotgun shell*."[65] Notice that similar to its definition for the term "rifle," the NFA's definition of a "shotgun" contains the "in a fixed shotgun shell" qualifier, while the GCA does not.[66]

California law also does not provide a general definition for "shotgun." It does, however, define "shotgun" in the context of "short-barreled shotguns" as being "a weapon designed or redesigned, made or remade, and intended to be fired from the shoulder and designed or redesigned and made or remade to use the energy of the explosive in a fixed shotgun shell to fire through a smooth bore either a number of projectiles (ball shot) or a single projectile for each pull of the trigger."[67]

3. Long Guns

The Penal Code defines a "long gun" as "any firearm that is not a handgun or machinegun."[68] All "rifles" and "shotguns" are encompassed under the "long gun" definition.

---

[63] Cal. Code Regs. tit. 11, § 5471(ee).
[64] 18 U.S.C. § 921(a)(5).
[65] 26 U.S.C. § 5845(d) (emphasis added); 27 C.F.R. § 479.11.
[66] *See* 18 U.S.C. § 921(a)(5); 26 U.S.C. § 5845(d). But, 27 C.F.R. section 478.11 does define shotgun using the phrase "in a fixed shotgun shell." But once again, this definition is only applicable to the Code of Federal Regulations and not the GCA.
[67] P.C. § 17190.
[68] P.C. § 16865.

Examples of "Long Guns"

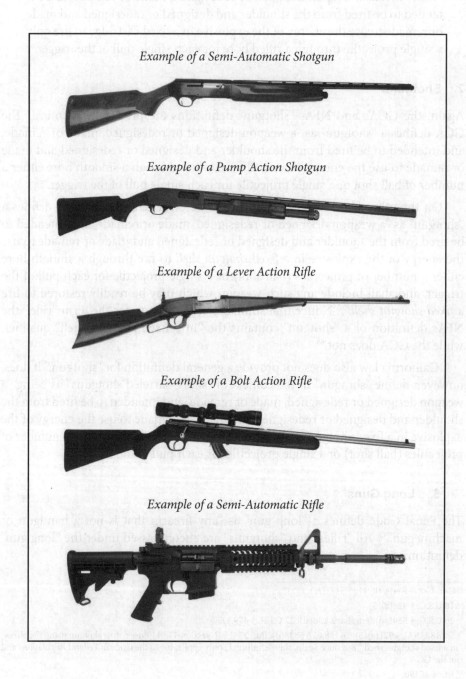

C. Other "Firearms"

Like receivers, certain other items do not fit neatly into the "handgun," "rifle," or "shotgun" categories but still meet the legal definition of, and are treated as, "firearms." For example, a stockless firearm of legal length that shoots shotgun shells (like the Mossberg 500) is not a "shotgun" because it does not have a stock, and therefore it cannot be fired from the shoulder. It is also not a "short-barreled shotgun" because of its length. Nevertheless, it would still be considered a "firearm" because it is a "device, designed to be used as a weapon, from which is expelled through a barrel, a projectile by the force of an explosion or other form of combustion."[69]

"Machineguns" and the NFA's "any other weapon" categories are also firearm subgroups with specific definitions, which are further discussed in Chapter 10. Moreover, modifying a "handgun," "rifle," or "shotgun" may cause it to move from one category to another, or fall outside of one of these categories.

There are sometimes issues regarding whether an item actually meets the applicable "firearm" definition, which is important in determining whether the item is regulated under California and/or federal law, as discussed below.

D. Definition of "Weapon"

An element included in all the above "firearm" definitions is that, in order for something to be a "firearm," it must first be considered a "weapon." Unfortunately, the term "weapon"[70] is not actually defined in the California Penal Code or federal code. Nonetheless, courts have provided some guidance on what a "weapon" is.

Federal courts have defined a "weapon" as "an instrument of offense or defense."[71] Similarly, California courts have instructed that the term "weapon" can "be broadly defined as an instrument of offensive or defensive combat."[72]

Certain items, such as standard firearms, dirks, and daggers, unquestionably meet the definition of a "weapon" and are considered to be "weapons per se."[73] But when an item's uses for "combat" are uncertain or untraditional, such as pen guns (discussed in Section III), it is not always clear as to whether these items actually meet the definition of a "weapon."

For an item to be considered a "weapon," California courts have held that the person who possessed the item must have known that the object was a "weapon,"

---

[69] P.C. § 16520(a).

[70] This issue rears its head again in Chapter 10 concerning "destructive devices." In order to be a "destructive device," an item must be a "weapon." P.C. § 16460.

[71] STEPHEN P. HALBROOK, FIREARMS LAW DESKBOOK 601 (West 2013-2014 ed. 2013) (italics added). *See also United States v. Dalpiaz*, 527 F.2d 548, 551 (6th Cir. 1975) (holding that a "ground burst projectile simulator" that was designed for military training purposes was not a "destructive device" because it was meant to be used for training troops, not for use as a "weapon.").

[72] 63 CAL. JUR. 3d *Weapons* § 1 (citing Am. Jur. 2d, Weapons and Firearms § 1).

[73] The phrase "per se" means "[o]n, in , or by itself; standing alone, without reference to additional facts." Per Se, BLACK'S LAW DICTIONARY (10th ed. 2014).

may be used as a weapon, or they must have possessed the object "as a weapon." The prosecution can prove that a person had knowledge of an item's uses through circumstantial evidence.[74]

When an item is not a "weapon per se," but an instrument of ordinary innocent uses, the prosecution must prove that the person actually possessed the item as a weapon in order for the item to be considered a "weapon."[75] In other words, the prosecution must show that the person "would use the object for a dangerous, not harmless, purpose."[76]

In short, although no set legal definition for "weapon" exists, there are items, such as certain standard firearms, that are likely to be considered "weapons per se." Items that do not fall within the "weapons per se" category are characterized by considering the person's knowledge of the item's uses or the person's actual or intended use of the item as a weapon to determine whether the item is legally considered a "weapon."[77]

E. "Antique Firearms"

Because items meeting the definition of "antique firearm" are not regulated as "firearms" for most purposes, understanding the federal and California defintions for "antique firearm" is useful.

1. Federal Law Definitions

a. The Gun Control Act

As mentioned above, the GCA's "firearm" definition does not include "antique firearms."[78] An "antique firearm" under the GCA is defined as:

(1) Any firearm (including any firearm with a matchlock, flintlock, percussion cap, or similar type of ignition system) manufactured in or before 1898; *or*

(2) Any replica of any firearm described in (1) if such replica:

---

[74] The prosecution does not need to prove that the defendant knew there was a law against possessing the item, nor that the defendant intended to break or violate the law; it must prove that the defendant knew of the item's uses. *People v. King*, 38 Cal. 4th 617, 627 (2006). Evidence is circumstantial when it is "based on inference and not on personal knowledge or observation." EVIDENCE, BLACK'S LAW DICTIONARY (10th ed. 2014).

[75] *People v. Fannin*, 91 Cal. App. 4th 1399, 1400 (2001). In *Fannin*, the California Court of Appeal considered whether a bicycle chain with a lock at the end was a "slungshot," which is a prohibited weapon under the Penal Code. The court held that "if the object is not a weapon per se, but an instrument with ordinary innocent uses, the prosecution must prove that the object was possessed as a weapon." *People v. Fannin*, 91 Cal. App. 4th 1399, 1404 (2001); *see also People v. Grubb*, 63 Cal. 2d 614, 621 (1965) (possession of modified baseball bat) (superseded by statute).

[76] *People v. Fannin*, 91 Cal. App. 4th 1399, 1403 (2001).

[77] See discussion on pen guns, coyote catchers, and potato guns in Section III of this Chapter for application of this rule.

[78] 18 U.S.C. § 921(a)(3).

(a) Is not designed or redesigned for using rimfire or conventional centerfire fixed ammunition; *or*

b) Uses rimfire or conventional centerfire fixed ammunition which is no longer manufactured in the United States and which is not readily available in the ordinary channels of commercial trade;[79] *or*

(3) Any muzzle-loading rifle, muzzle-loading shotgun, or muzzle-loading pistol, which is designed to use black powder, or a black powder substitute, and which cannot use fixed ammunition, but does not include any weapon which incorporates a firearm frame or receiver, any firearm which is converted into a muzzle-loading weapon, or any muzzle-loading weapon which can be readily converted to fire fixed ammunition by replacing the barrel, bolt, breechblock, or any combination thereof.[80]

Items not meeting any of these definitions are regulated as "firearms" under the GCA.[81]

Since "antique firearms" are excluded from the GCA's "firearm" definition, the GCA requirements and restrictions (discussed in Chapters 4 and 5) do not apply to those items meeting the "antique firearm" definition.

---

[79] With almost anything available on the internet, previously rare rimfire and centerfire cartridges have become more easily available. So the question of what ammunition is "not readily available" in subsection (3) becomes obscured. For further analysis of this issue, *see* C.D. Michel, *Gun Ammo Googling: Does Internet Access to Rare Ammunition Calibers Limit the Availability of "Replicas" to Qualify as "Antique Firearms?,"* available at http://www.calgunlaws.com/wp-content/uploads/2012/07/Gun-Anno-Googling.pdf (last visited Aug. 23, 2020). The ATF also discusses this issue in the NFA Handbook: "[c]oncerning ammunition availability, it is important to note that a specific type of fixed ammunition that has been out of production for many years may again become available due to increasing interest in older firearms. Therefore, the classification of a specific NFA firearm as an antique can change if ammunition for the weapon becomes readily available in the ordinary channels of commercial trade." U.S. Dept. Of Justice, Bureau of Alcohol, Tobacco, Firearms, and Explosives, ATF National Firearms Act Handbook 20 (rev. Apr. 2009), *available at* http://www.atf.gov/files/publications/download/p/atf-p-5320-8/atf-p-5320-8.pdf (last visited Aug. 23, 2020).

[80] 18 U.S.C. § 921(a)(16)(C).

[81] Additionally the ATF maintains a list – which it warns is *not* exhaustive and frequently changes – of certain weapons that load from the muzzle that it considers to be "firearms" under the GCA, which includes:

(1) Savage Model 10ML (early, 1st version).
(2) Mossberg 500 shotgun with muzzle loading barrel.
(3) Remington 870 shotgun with muzzle loading barrel.
(4) Mauser 98 rifle with muzzle loading barrel.
(5) SKS rifle with muzzle loading barrel.
(6) RPB sM10 pistol with muzzle loading barrel.
(7) H&R/New England Firearm Huntsman.
(8) Thompson Center Encore/Contender.
(9) Rossi .50 muzzle loading rifle.

Top 10 Frequently Asked Questions and Answers, U.S. Dept. of Justice, Bureau of Alcohol Tobacco, Firearms, and Explosives, https://www.atf.gov/file/61721/download (last visited Aug. 23, 2020).

The above GCA "antique firearm" definition does not apply to California's "firearm" restrictions for prohibited persons, meaning an "antique firearm" is considered a "firearm" for purposes of California's restrictions for prohibited persons. Consequently, a person prohibited from possessing firearms under California law cannot possess "antique firearms" either.[82] But, the above GCA "antique firearm" definition does apply to California's firearm transfer laws (discussed in Chapters 4 and 5).[83]

b. The National Firearms Act

The NFA has a slightly different definition for "antique firearms" than the GCA, which includes:

> [A]ny firearm not designed or redesigned for using rim fire or conventional center fire ignition with fixed ammunition and manufactured in or before 1898 (including any matchlock, flintlock, percussion cap, or similar type of ignition system or replica thereof, whether actually manufactured before or after the year 1898) and also any firearm using fixed ammunition manufactured in or before 1898, for which ammunition is no longer manufactured in the United States and is not readily available in the ordinary channels of commercial trade.[84]

The main difference between the GCA's and the NFA's definitions is that the NFA does not expressly include muzzle-loading firearms that use black powder and that cannot use fixed ammunition, although these firearms appear to fall within the

---

[82] See P.C. § 16520.

[83] See 18 U.S.C. § 921(a)(3), (16); P.C. § 16170(b). As used in the following California provisions, the term "firearm" does not include an unloaded "antique firearm": P.C. sections 16550 (Firearm transaction records); 16730(a), (c) ("Infrequent" firearm transactions); 16960 (Operation of law transfers); 17310 ("Used Firearm"); 26350-26391 (Open carry of unloaded handgun laws and exemptions); 26400-26405 (Open carry of unloaded "firearm that is not a handgun" laws and exemptions); 26500-26588 (License requirements to sell, lease, transfer, or loan firearms and exemptions); 26700-26915 (License to sell, lease, or transfer firearms at retail and grounds for forfeiture of license); 27510 (Sale, supply, delivery, or giving possession of handgun or semiautomatic centerfire rifle by licensed person to minor or young adult); 27530 (Sale or transfer of handgun requirements); 27540 (Delivery of firearm by dealer requirements); 27545 (Sale, loan, or transfer of firearm through licensed firearms dealer); 27555-27570 (Sale, delivery, or transfer of firearm by licensee, verification number required; review of centralized lists of firearm dealers, licensees, and manufacturers; bringing a handgun, firearm, or curio or relic into the state and requirements; and punishments, statutes of limitations, and exceptions); 29010-29150 (Licensing requirements for manufacturing firearms; issuance, forfeiture, and conditions of license to manufacture firearms); 25135 (Requirements for storing firearms when living with a prohibited person). P.C. § 16520(d). NOTE: Outside of these provisions, an "antique firearm" is still considered to be a "firearm" under California law.

[84] 26 U.S.C. § 5845(g).

definition regardless. A similar analysis applies to silencers that attach to muzzle-loading rifles. We discuss why this is important in Chapter 10.

2. California Law Definition

"Antique firearm" is defined in different contexts under California law. For firearm transactions and under DOJ's new "ghost guns" regulations, "antique firearm" means the same as it does in the federal GCA, provided in the section above.[85]

For "generally prohibited weapons,"[86] "antique firearm" means:

(1) Any firearm not designed or redesigned for using rimfire or conventional centerfire ignition with fixed ammunition and manufactured in or before 1898. This includes any matchlock, flintlock, percussion cap, or similar type of ignition system; *or*

(2) Replicas of any of the firearms discussed above, whether actually manufactured before or after the year 1898; *or*

(3) Any firearm using fixed ammunition manufactured in or before 1898, for which ammunition is no longer manufactured in the United States and is not readily available in the ordinary channels of commercial trade.[87]

Example of a Matchlock Musket *Example of a Percussion Cap Rifle*

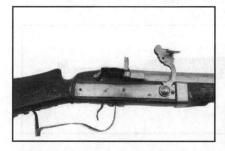

Finally, as it relates to "assault weapons" and .50 BMG rifles, the term "antique firearm" means "any firearm manufactured before January 1, 1899."[88]

F. "Curios or Relics"

"Curios or relics" are defined in the Code of Federal Regulations as firearms "of special interest to collectors by reason of some quality other than is associated with

---

[85] *See* 18 U.S.C. § 921(a)(16) (stating the GCA's definition of "antique firearm"); P.C. § 16170(b); CAL. CODE REGS. tit. 11, § 5507(a). See also Chapter 5 for "antique firearm" transactions.
[86] Discussed in Chapter 10.
[87] P.C. § 16170(c).
[88] P.C. § 16170(a). See also Chapter 9.

firearms intended for sporting use or as offensive or defensive weapons."[89] To be "curios or relics," firearms must either be:

(1) Manufactured at least 50 years before the current date, but not including replicas thereof; *or*

(2) Certified by the curator of a municipal, State, or Federal museum which exhibits firearms to be curios or relics of museum interest; *or*

(3) Any other firearms that derive a substantial part of their monetary value from the fact that they are novel, rare, bizarre, or because of their association with some historical figure, period, or event. Proof of qualification of a particular firearm under this category may be established by evidence of present value and evidence that like firearms are not available except as collector's items, or that the value of like firearms available in ordinary commercial channels is substantially less.[90]

This definition is the same under both California and federal law.[91]

The ATF has opined that a "receiver" is not a "curio or relic" item, and that a firearm must be in its original configuration to qualify as a "curio or relic." But, minor alterations to a "curio or relic" firearm, such as adding scope mounts or sling swivels, are not likely to change its "curio or relic" status.[92]

Example of a "Curio or Relic":
An M1 Carbine

III. IS THAT THING CONSIDERED A "FIREARM"?

Due Process requires each element of the pertinent "firearm" definition to be proven beyond a reasonable doubt to a jury for a person to be convicted of a "firearm" violation.[93] Whether an item meets the applicable "firearm" definition is sometimes unclear. For example, toy guns, pellet guns, and BB guns are not considered "fire-

---

[89] 27 C.F.R. § 478.11.

[90] 27 C.F.R. § 478.11.

[91] P.C. § 17705(a); 27 C.F.R. § 478.11; Cal. Code Regs. tit. 11, § 5507(i).

[92] ATF Rul. 85-10 (1985); *see Firearms Curios or Relics List*, U.S. Dept. of Justice, Bureau of Alcohol Tobacco, Firearms, and Explosives 52 (rev. Dec. 2007), *available at* https://www.atf.gov/firearms/docs/guide/firearms-curios-or-relics-list-1972-2007-atf-p-530011/download (last visited Aug. 23, 2020).

[93] *See Medley v. Runnels*, 506 F.3d 857, 863-64 (9th Cir. 2007).

arms" "because, instead of explosion or other combustion, they use the force of air pressure, gas pressure, or spring action to expel a projectile."[94]

The "projectile" does not need to be traditional ammunition either. One court found a crude device made by a prison inmate – consisting of a tube sealed at one end packed with around 30 match heads with a hole to light them – to be a "firearm" even though no projectiles were found with it.[95] An officer testified that such devices are often used to shoot melted or broken plastic and tinfoil balls.[96] Another court found taser "barbs" that make contact with the target to be "projectiles" within the "firearm" definition.[97] That same court, in holding that a taser *is* a "firearm,"[98] also found the plastic, squared chambers holding the barbs to be "barrels" because "there appears no reason logically or semantically to insist that a gun's barrel must be made of metal or that it be cylindrical."[99]

In another example, a defendant was charged with unlawfully possessing an "unconventional pistol," which, as explained in Chapter 10, is an illegal "firearm." The defendant had a tear gas pen gun designed for launching flares or tear gas canisters – not firing ammunition – though it was shown that ammunition *could be* fired from it (with a likelihood of explosion and causing injury to the shooter). Because ammunition *could* be fired from it, there was an issue about whether it was actually "*designed* to be used as a weapon." The state needed to prove that the pen gun was "designed" to be used as a weapon in order to prove it was a "firearm" and that the owner *knew* it could be used in this way.

There was also an issue as to whether the tear gas pen gun even had a "barrel" through which a projectile was expelled because the tear gas canisters and flares were designed to screw on to the end of it.[100]

A. Bang Sticks/Shark Killers

Sometimes an item that would not generally be referred to as a firearm still meets the legal definition of one. A relatively common example is a "bang stick" – a shaft or pole carried by divers with a "power head" (a device containing a cartridge that has a fixed firing pin) attached at the end that discharges the cartridge when thrust forcefully in a linear motion, usually toward a shark. No trigger or sophisticated mechanics are involved, and it looks more like a boat antenna than a typical firearm.

---

[94] *People v. Law*, 195 Cal. App. 4th 976, 983 (2011) (citing *People v. Monjaras*, 164 Cal. App. 4th 1432, 1435 (2008)).
[95] *People v. Talkington*, 140 Cal. App. 3d 557 (1983).
[96] *People v. Talkington*, 140 Cal. App. 3d 557, 560 (1983).
[97] *People v. Heffner*, 70 Cal. App. 3d 643, 652 (1977).
[98] *People v. Heffner*, 70 Cal. App. 3d 643, 648-49 (1977). As an aside, older model tasers used primers to launch the barbs while modern tasers use compressed air, and thus are not considered "firearms."
[99] *People v. Heffner*, 70 Cal. App. 3d 643, 648-49 (1977) (noting that the taser in question discharged the barbs using combustion).
[100] I litigated this case in Ventura County and ultimately obtained a dismissal of charges for the defendant, but that does not mean the same result is guaranteed for everyone.

But since it is a device designed to be a weapon (albeit against sharks and although blanks can be used just as effectively), and its projectile is still expelled by explosive force, the only real question is whether the "power head" where the cartridge is contained constitutes a "barrel." Though it is unclear, it is arguably a barrel because the cartridge is fully contained and even set back from the opening of the "power head" – especially since a court has considered tasers to have a barrel – likely making a "bang stick" a "firearm" under California law and subject to all applicable restrictions.

B. Coyote Booby Traps

Sometimes, even when the item may technically meet the "firearm" definition, courts will conclude the item is *not* one. For example, a Colorado court decided a "coyote getter" – a device with a hollow tube of light metal, crimped at one end and a spring-loaded firing pin that propels cyanide into a coyote's mouth when it pulls on the bait – was not a "firearm" under the NFA because it lacked practical use as a weapon and because the ATF's expert refused to fire one using live ammunition.[101]

C. Potato Guns a.k.a. "Spud Guns"

A potato gun or "spud gun" is a device that, as its name implies, shoots potatoes, typically using some form of flammable aerosol or liquid. The flammable material is stored in the device that is attached to the barrel, and the potato (or piece of potato) is crammed into the barrel. A well-built potato gun can shoot a potato 100 yards or more.

Since a potato gun is a device that expels a projectile through a barrel by combustive force, the question of whether it is a "firearm" turns on whether it is a "weapon." As explained above, no exact legal definition exists for the term "weapon." But, given the above "weapon" definition and its subsequent analysis, it seems unlikely that a potato gun would be considered a "weapon" unless it was intentionally used as one. An argument could be made, however, that a person need only know that it *could* be used to injure or kill for it to be considered a "weapon."

If potato guns *are* considered "weapons," a question also exists as to whether these devices are illegal "destructive devices" under state and/or federal law (see Chapter 10).

In California, these devices may be considered a launching device for a bomb, grenade, explosive missile, or similar device – though they usually cannot shoot

---

[101] *United States v. Brady*, 710 F. Supp. 290, 292-93 (D. Colo. 1989). In *Brady*, the court noted that the expert would not fire the coyote getter using live ammunition because it was possible that the getter would explode. *United States v. Brady*, 710 F. Supp. 290, 292 (D. Colo. 1989). The court concluded that the getter was not considered "any other weapon" under the federal law definition of a firearm because "[r]esearch ha[d] found no cases in which a court or administrative agency found that a device which was likely to explode if used with normal ammunition was any other weapon." *United States v. Brady*, 710 F. Supp. 290, 293 (D. Colo. 1989).

anything as dense as a bomb or grenade. And some designs or building materials are so flimsy that launching anything heavier than a potato may result in catastrophic failure. Nevertheless, criminal cases have been and will continue to be filed alleging potato guns are "firearms," "destructive devices," or "zip guns" (see Chapter 10).

Under federal law, a potato gun can be considered an illegal "destructive device" that expels a projectile by explosive force with a barrel diameter of more than half an inch. And even if it is not considered a "firearm," it may still meet the definition of some other prohibited item.

It is strongly advised you proceed cautiously before deciding to make a potato gun because of the confusion about their legality.

D. Flare Guns with Metal Inserts

Flare guns, or signal launchers, may be considered "firearms" depending on their construction. Certain flare guns are 12-gauge and fire flares that are specifically designed for these guns. These flare guns are often made of plastic and cannot withstand the pressure of standard ammunition being discharged from them (and certainly not the pressure created by a 12-gauge shotgun shell). For most purposes, these flare guns do not meet the definition of a "firearm" under state or federal law because they are considered signaling devices, not "weapons."[102]

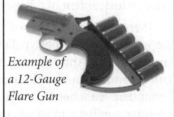

Example of a 12-Gauge Flare Gun

But, there are metal inserts available to the general public that can be used to modify flare guns to discharge certain calibers of conventional ammunition, thereby potentially turning them into "firearms." These metal inserts are typically designed to allow shotguns of varying gauges to fire conventional ammunition (including smaller gauge shotgun shells), but they can also be used to modify flare guns. In a shotgun, the metal insert is slid into the shotgun barrel through the breech with a round of ammunition inserted within it. The breech is closed and the shotgun can fire the single cartridge. To reload, the shooter reopens the breech and removes the insert and the expended ammunition case from the insert. The shooter then reloads another round into the insert and the entire insert is placed back inside the shotgun.

---

[102] For very limited purposes, California laws treat rockets, rocket propelled projectile launchers, and similar devices containing an explosive or incendiary material as "firearms" whether or not the device is designed for emergency or stress signaling purposes. P.C. § 16520(c). This is mostly a concern relating to carrying a concealed handgun or a loaded firearm, as discussed in Chapter 6.

The same metal insert can usually be inserted into a 12-gauge flare gun with only minor modification to the flare gun required. The metal insert, in theory, reinforces the flimsy plastic flare gun and allows it to discharge certain calibers of conventional ammunition, including shotgun shells. When the metal insert is placed inside the flare gun, the flare gun becomes a "weapon" and is therefore considered a "firearm" under California and federal law.[103]

Under federal law, the ATF opines[104] that these metal inserts are considered part of the "any other weapons"[105] category when inserted into or possessed with flare guns.[106] The ATF also notes that four out of the four flare guns they tested using these metal inserts suffered "catastrophic failure" as a result.[107]

E. 37mm Flare Launchers

37mm flare launchers may be considered "weapons" under federal law, depending on whether you possess certain kinds of ammunition with the flare launcher. Generally, a 37mm flare launcher by itself is not considered to be a "weapon" because it is not an instrument of offensive or defensive combat.

There are certain types of "anti-personnel" ammunition that contain materials like wood pellets, rubber pellets or balls, or beanbags that can be used in 37mm flare launchers. And the ATF has opined that, when a person possesses both this "anti-personnel" ammunition and a 37mm flare launcher at the same time, then the 37mm flare launcher becomes a "weapon" because it can be used for offensive or defensive combat and would therefore be regulated under federal law as "destructive devices" (see Chapter 10).[108]

In the past, certain California law enforcement agencies tried to classify all 37mm flare launchers as "destructive devices" under California law because somewhere there exists a 37mm grenade that can be launched from the launcher.

---

[103] *See* 18 U.S.C. § 921(a)(4). See also P.C. section 16520(a) and possibly subdivision (c) as well.

[104] *Flare Insert – Any Other Weapon*, U.S. Dept. of Justice, Bureau of Alcohol, Tobacco, Firearms and Explosives (May 4, 2006), http://www.atf.gov/press/releases/2006/05/050406-openletter-nfa-flare-inserts.html (last visited Aug. 23, 2020).

[105] "Any other weapon" "means any weapon or device capable of being concealed on the person from which a shot can be discharged through the energy of an explosive, a pistol or revolver having a barrel with a smooth bore designed or redesigned to fire a fixed shotgun shell, weapons with combination shotgun and rifle barrels 12 inches or more, less than 18 inches in length, from which only a single discharge can be made from either barrel without manual reloading, and shall include any such weapon which may be readily restored to fire. Such term shall not include a pistol or a revolver having a rifled bore, or rifled bores, or weapons designed, made, or intended to be fired from the shoulder and not capable of firing fixed ammunition." 26 U.S.C. § 5845(e). These are discussed in Chapter 10.

[106] Consequently, metal inserts inserted into or possessed with flare guns must be registered as required by federal law to avoid violating 26 U.S.C. section 5861(d).

[107] *Flare Insert – Any Other Weapon*, U.S. Dept. of Justice, Bureau of Alcohol, Tobacco, Firearms and Explosives (May 4, 2006), http://www.atf.gov/press/releases/2006/05/050406-openletter-nfa-flare-inserts.html (last visited Aug. 23, 2020).

[108] ATF Rul. 95-3 (1995). *See also* 18 U.S.C. § 921(a)(4); 26 U.S.C. § 5845(f).

F. Explosive-Powered Nail Guns

Not all devices that use a combustive force to operate are considered "firearms." Certain nail guns, often referred to as "powder-actuated nail guns," use powder as an explosive charge to drive nails into hard surfaces like stone, concrete, or steel. These devices are commonly available at hardware stores and over the internet.

Because nail guns are not instruments of offensive or defensive combat, they are not considered "weapons" and are therefore not regulated by California or federal law.

G. Items Meeting the "Firearm" Definition, but Expressly Exempted

Even if something you possess is considered contraband by law enforcement because they claim it is a "firearm," it may still be exempt from certain restrictions based on the *type* of "firearm" it is. For example, as explained above, "antique firearms" are usually exempt from certain restrictions, and firearms considered "curios or relics" may be as well.

You are responsible for knowing whether the device you own is a "firearm" and which restrictions do and do not apply to it. The examples listed are just some of the considerations courts make in determining whether something is a "firearm."

IV. "AMMUNITION"

A. Federal Law "Ammunition" Definition

For purposes of the GCA, "ammunition" is "ammunition or cartridge cases, primers, bullets, or propellent powder designed for use in any firearm."[109] Also, the Code of Federal Regulations defines "ammunition" as "[a]mmunition or cartridge cases, primers, bullets, or propellant powder designed for use in any firearm other than an antique firearm. The term [does] not include (a) any shotgun shot or pellet not designed for use as the single, complete projectile load for one shotgun hull or casing, nor (b) any unloaded, non-metallic shotgun hull or casing not having a primer."[110]

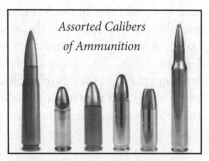

Assorted Calibers of Ammunition

---

[109] 18 U.S.C. § 921(a)(17)(A). This definition also applies to those federally prohibited from possessing firearms and ammunition as discussed in Chapter 4.
[110] 27 C.F.R. § 478.11.

Although the NFA does not provide a definition for "ammunition," the Code of Federal Regulations defines the term as "[a]mmunition or cartridge cases, primers, bullets, or propellent powder designed for use in any firearm other than an antique firearm."[111]

Interestingly, for purpose of the restrictions on juveniles, the GCA expressly restricts juveniles from possessing "ammunition that is suitable for use only in a handgun."[112] The GCA and the Code of Federal Regulations do not provide a definition for this phrase, however.

B. California Law "Ammunition" Definitions

The word "ammunition" is undefined throughout most of the Penal Code, but it is given a specific definition in certain sections.[113] Pay close attention because these specific definitions often include items you would not commonly consider "ammunition."

For those prohibited from possessing firearms and "ammunition" (see Chapter 4) and the restrictions on ammunition purchases by and on behalf of a prohibited person created by Proposition 63 and Senate Bill (SB) 1235, "ammunition" includes, but is not limited to, "any bullet, cartridge, magazine, clip, speed loader, autoloader, or projectile capable of being fired from a firearm with a deadly consequence. 'Ammunition' does not include blanks."[114] In other words, mere components of ammunition like bullets and ammunition-feeding devices like magazines are themselves considered "ammunition" in this context.[115]

Now you may be wondering why the legislature chose to include both the terms "bullet" and "cartridge" within the above definition of "ammunition." The legislature likely did one of two things in writing this definition. Either they meant to prohibit the possession of the projectile and complete "live" cartridges (*i.e.*, the bullet, powder, primer, and case), which would explain the use of the terms "bullet," "cartridge," and "*projectile* capable of being fired from a firearm with a deadly consequence." Or, they didn't realize that a "bullet" and "cartridge" are not synonymous terms and inadvertently included a single part of a cartridge (the bullet) in the definition while meaning a complete round. Given my past experience with the

---

[111] 27 C.F.R. § 478.11. For purposes of this definition, it does not include any shotgun shot or pellet not designed for use as the single, complete projectile load for one shotgun hull or casing, nor any unloaded, non-metallic shotgun hull or casing not having a primer. *Id.*

[112] 18 U.S.C. § 922(x)(2)(B).

[113] *See* P.C. § 16150.

[114] P.C. § 16150(b).

[115] Since July 1, 2020, the law expressly states that the term "ammunition" includes "ammunition-feeding device." This is because California enacted SB 746 into law in 2018. See SB 746, 2018-2019 Leg., Reg. Sess. (Cal. 2018), *available at* https://leginfo.legislature.ca.gov/faces/billTextClient.xhtml?bill_id=201720180SB746 (last visited Aug. 23, 2020).

legislature and their general lack of understanding of firearm parlance, I would say that the latter is probably what happened.

In any event, I strongly caution against possessing ammunition (live or otherwise) or any component of ammunition if you are prohibited from possessing ammunition.

The term "ammunition" is also defined for purposes of the restrictions on ammunition vendors and all of the restrictions relating to acquiring ammunition from an ammunition vendor, face-to-face requirements, and importation of ammunition contained in Proposition 63 and SB 1235 (see Chapter 4). The term "ammunition" will be defined for purposes of these restrictions as "one or more loaded cartridges consisting of a primerdcase, propellant, and with one or more projectiles. 'Ammunition' does not include blanks."[116] This does not include the mere components of ammunition like the projectile, primer, case, or powder when we are talking about the restrictions and requirements for "ammunition" transferred through an ammunition vendor. Therefore, it is important to always be mindful what definition applies to you.

The Penal Code also provides a definition for the term "handgun ammunition." "Handgun ammunition" means ammunition principally for use in handguns, even if it can be used in some rifles.[117] "Handgun ammunition" does *not* include ammunition for "antique firearms" or blanks.[118]

1. Deactivated Ammunition

Although California regulates certain types of ammunition (see Chapter 9) and who can possess ammunition generally (see Chapter 3), it does not prohibit the possession, importation, sale, attempted sale, or transportation of any deactivated ammunition, *i.e.*, ammunition for which the propellant has been removed and the primer has been permanently deactivated.[119]

Because California does not prohibit the possession of deactivated ammunition, a person who is prohibited from possessing firearms and ammunition under California law can possess deactivated ammunition. But if you are prohibited from

---

[116] P.C. § 16150(a).

[117] P.C. § 16650(a), *held unconstitutionally vague by Parker v. State of California*, 221 Cal. App. 4th 340 (2013). The standard "principally for use in a handgun" has been found in at least one context to be unconstitutionally vague because it is impossible to know whether any given cartridge is used more often in a handgun or a rifle, and for this reason, most ammunition vendors ask the purchaser what type of firearm the ammunition will be used in to meet this standard. *See Parker v. State of California*, 221 Cal. App. 4th 340 (2013). I litigated this case. In December 2016, the California Supreme Court dismissed its review of a Court of Appeal opinion affirming the trial court's order on the finding of vagueness. The Court of Appeal's decision is now the final opinion in the case, and Plaintiffs sought their attorneys' fees against the State. In September of 2019, Plaintiffs received $433,860.20 from the State in attorneys' fees. You can keep up to date on this case by visiting www.crpa.org.

[118] P.C. § 16650(b)(1)-(2), *held unconstitutionally vague by Parker v. State of California*, 221 Cal. App. 4th 340 (2013).

[119] P.C. § 30335.

possessing firearms and ammunition, you should be cautious in choosing to possess these items. When law enforcement officers stumble across a piece of deactivated ammunition, like a deactivated artillery shell, they often arrest the person for possessing "ammunition" or classify these objects as "destructive devices," despite the fact they no longer carry propellant and the primer has been otherwise made permanently deactivated. Although they are likely wrong on this matter, it may be safer to not possess deactivated ammunition if you are prohibited from possessing firearms and ammunition under either California or federal law.

C. "Ammunition" Parts

California does not generally regulate the possession of ammunition parts,[120] other than for those persons prohibited from possessing firearms and ammunition. But it does regulate possessing ammunition *powder*. So reloaders beware.

Even though smokeless powder does not technically explode, it is still considered an "explosive" in California because an "explosive" includes, but is not limited to, the following:

(1) "[A]ny substance, or combination of substances, the primary or common purpose of which is detonation or rapid combustion, and which is capable of a relatively instantaneous or rapid release of gas and heat, or any substance, the primary purpose of which, when combined with others, is to form a substance capable of a relatively instantaneous or rapid release of gas and heat"; *or*

(2) Any "explosive" as defined in 18 U.S.C. section 841 and published per 27 Code Fed. Regs. section 555.23; *or*

(3) "Dynamite, nitroglycerine, picric acid, lead azide, fulminate of mercury, *black powder, smokeless powder*, propellant explosives, detonating primers, blasting caps, or commercial boosters";[121] *or*

(4) Certain substances classified by the Department of Transportation;[122] *or*

(5) Any material designated by the Fire Marshal pursuant to regulations in accordance with Department of Transportation standards.[123]

The term "explosive" does "not include any destructive device, [or] ammunition or small arms primers manufactured for use in shotguns, rifles, and pistols."[124]

---

[120] But note that California does regulate the possession of certain prohibited ammunition parts. For example, it would likely be illegal to possess the parts of tracer ammunition because tracer ammunition is considered to be a "destructive device" under California law. See P.C. § 18720. To learn more about destructive devices, see Chapter 9.

[121] P.C. § 16510(a) (emphasis added).

[122] P.C. § 16510(b), (c), (e).

[123] P.C. § 16510(d).

[124] P.C. § 16510(f). "Destructive devices" are discussed in Chapter 9.

Examples of Ammunition Parts

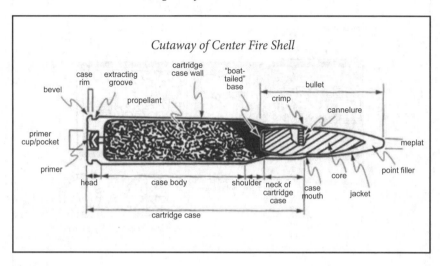

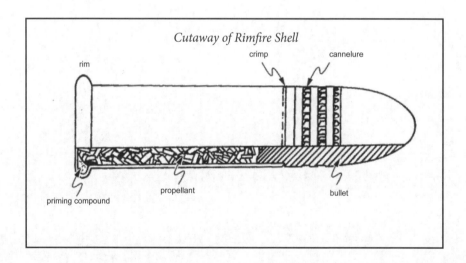

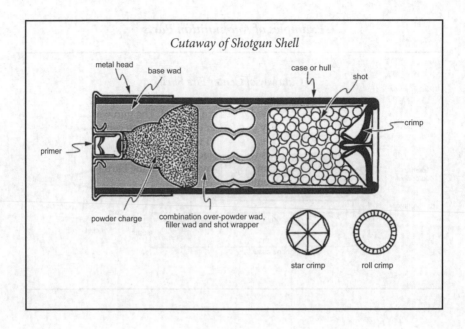

CHAPTER 4:
WHO CAN OWN AND POSSESS FIREARMS AND AMMUNITION?

Both California and federal law restrict certain classes of people from owning and/or possessing firearms, ammunition, and related items.[1] Aside from age restrictions, there are several situations where your right to own and/or possess firearms can be restricted, either temporarily or permanently. For example, you may be prohibited from owning or possessing a firearm because of a criminal conviction, restraining order, or mental health commitment.

How long you may be prohibited depends on which class you are in, the specific situation, and the applicable state and/or federal law. It is possible, for example, for you to be restricted under *both* state and federal law, or under only one of them. The restriction may also be temporary under one set of laws but last a lifetime under the other.

One general distinction between California and federal firearm restrictions is that California law bars prohibited persons[2] from owning firearms,[3] while federal law does not ban firearm *ownership* but rather *possession* (and certain other activities).[4] As explained below, this distinction can significantly impact the activities in which a prohibited person may lawfully participate.

---

[1] What constitutes a "firearm" or "ammunition" is different under California and federal law (see Chapter 3). All firearm restrictions listed in this chapter also include "ammunition" unless specifically stated otherwise.

[2] "Prohibited person" as used in this book means an individual who is subject to one or more legal restrictions relating to the person's legal ability to own and/or possess firearms, ammunition, and related items. But, if a corporation gets convicted of a crime, it too can be prohibited. This is especially problematic if the corporation has a federal contract to manufacture firearms.

[3] The California firearm and ammunition prohibition generally restricts owning, purchasing, receiving, and possessing firearms, or having firearms under your custody or control. *See* P.C. §§ 29800, 29805, 29815, 29820, 29825, 29900, 30305; CAL. WELF. & INST. CODE §§ 8100, 8103. A person with California firearm and ammunition prohibitions is precluded from all of these activities. In the interests of brevity, this book only mentions the prohibition on "possessing" firearms, but remember that all of these activities are also precluded for a person prohibited from "possessing" firearms *and ammunition*. And remember that "ammunition" includes ammunition components, clips, and magazines, as discussed in Chapter 3.

[4] 18 U.S.C. section 922(g) makes it illegal for those with a firearm restriction "to ship or transport in interstate or foreign commerce, or possess in or affecting commerce, any firearm or ammunition; or to receive any firearm or ammunition which has been shipped or transported in interstate or foreign commerce." See 18 U.S.C. section

I. WHAT DOES "POSSESSION" MEAN?

Most state and federal violations occur when a prohibited person is found in "possession" of a firearm. Determining whether you "possess" a firearm, however, is not always easy. There are two kinds of legal possession: "actual possession" and "constructive possession."

"Actual possession" means that you knowingly have direct physical control of an object.[5] For example, you may have "actual possession" of an object in your hands, clothes, purse, bag, or other container. Knowingly having the object for even a limited time and purpose can constitute "actual possession."[6]

"Constructive possession" means that you knowingly have control of, or have *the right to* control the object, either directly or through another person.[7] More than one person can possess the same object at the same time.[8] Whether you can direct the object's movement and whether it would be reasonable to think you have such control are factors in determining if you have "constructive possession."[9] But you must also, in fact, *know* that you have this control over the object to be legally considered to constructively "possess" it.[10]

The idea of "possession" can be problematic if you live with someone who owns firearms (*e.g.*, a family member or roommate) or if you transfer your firearms to someone with whom you live. For instance, although your spouse can legally keep their firearms inside the home during your probationary period (provided that you do not have any access to them), doing so can still be very problematic because it is very easy for a prosecutor to claim that you had access to firearms that are kept inside your home – especially, if you still have a key or know the combination to the gun safe where your firearms arekept. Because of this risk, you should strongly consider removing any firearms in your residence while you are prohibited from possessing them. And if you live with someone who refuses to remove their firearms and ammunition from your home, then you may want to consider living at a different place until you are no longer prohibited. Although this may sound extreme, it is the best way to ensure that you are not found to be in "possession" of any firearms or ammunition while you are prohibited.

922(n) for restrictions on shipment, transportation, and acquisition, discussed at the end of this chapter. Once again, in the interest of brevity, this book only mentions the prohibition on "possessing" firearms, but remember all of these activities are precluded under federal law for a person prohibited from "possessing" firearms *and ammunition*.

[5] *People v. Scott*, 45 Cal. 4th 743, 748 (2009) (citing CALJIC No. 1.24).

[6] *People v. Neese*, 272 Cal. App. 2d 235, 244-45 (1969).

[7] *See Henderson v. United States*, 135 S. Ct. 1780, 1784 (2015); *see also People v. Neese*, 272 Cal. App. 2d 235, 244-47 (1969); *see also People v. Rogers*, 5 Cal. 3d 129, 134 (1971).

[8] *See People v. Azevedo*, 161 Cal. App. 3d 235, 243 (1984), *overruled on other grounds by People v. King*, 38 Cal. 4th 617 (2006) (holding knowledge of a weapon's prohibited character is a necessary element that the prosecution must prove); *see also* CALCRIM No. 2510.

[9] *Armstrong v. Superior Court*, 217 Cal. App. 3d 535, 539 (1990); *see also People v. Scott*, 45 Cal. 4th 743, 757 (2009).

[10] CALJIC No. 1.24.

If you have police or probation officers coming to your residence for any reason, you should seriously consider whether you are in "possession" of any firearms or ammunition. And if you are prohibited and still have firearms inside your home that belong to you, then you should call an attorney experienced in firearms law to discuss how to dispose of them.

II. WHAT DOES "OWN" MEAN?

While the California Penal Code (P.C.) doesn't define what it means to "own" a firearm, the California Civil Code (Cal. Civ. Code) states that "ownership of a thing is the right of one or more persons to possess and use it to the exclusion of others."[11] The California Civil Code also states that all inanimate things, such as property, "which are capable of appropriation or of manual delivery," can be owned.[12]

Since firearms are personal property that can be appropriated or manually delivered, they may be "owned." Therefore, to "own" a firearm, you only need to have *the right to* possess or use it.[13] You don't necessarily need to be in possession of it.

III. DETERMINING WHEN FIREARM POSSESSION PROHIBITIONS APPLY DURING FIREARM PURCHASES

California is a "point of contact" state, meaning the California Department of Justice (DOJ) conducts the background check to determine your eligibility to purchase or receive firearms when you try to buy a firearm, rather than the Federal Bureau of Investigation (FBI). When conducting background checks, DOJ looks for criminal convictions, restraining orders, and mental health records. They access the Federal National Instant Criminal Background Check System (NICS) in addition to other state databases.[14] If your background information doesn't meet any of the firearm restriction criteria explained below, your name is not "flagged." On the other hand, if you have a criminal conviction, are subject to a restraining order, or had a mental health commitment, DOJ will investigate further to determine if you are subject to a firearm restriction.[15]

---

[11] CAL. CIV. CODE § 654.

[12] CAL. CIV. CODE § 655.

[13] *See, e.g., People v. Kozlowski*, 96 Cal. App. 4th 853, 866 (2002) (explaining that "[t]he right to own property implies the right to possess or use a thing to the exclusion of others.").

[14] DOJ also accesses the California Department of Motor Vehicles database, the Automated Firearm System, the Automated Criminal History System, the Wanted Persons System, Mental Health Firearms Prohibition System, and the California Restraining and Protective Orders System. Both state and federal agencies now face penalties for not accurately reporting already required disqualifying records of persons prohibited from receiving or possessing a firearm to the NICS. Consolidated Appropriations Act, 2018, H.R. 1625 115th Cong. (2017).

[15] For example, convictions for felonies, offenses designated as "violent" under P.C. section 29905, and misdemeanor crimes of domestic violence will prohibit you from possessing a firearm for life. Other offenses, such as

It isn't unusual for DOJ to determine that a person is subject to a firearm restriction, even when they may have allowed the person to purchase firearms in the past without incident. Although nothing may have changed since your last firearm purchase (*i.e.*, you have not been convicted of a crime, committed to a mental institution, and are not subject to a restraining order), DOJ may have discovered some information that has caused them to believe you are subject to a firearm restriction. If DOJ believes that you are subject to a firearm restriction, you should consider yourself to be prohibited from owning and possessing firearms until you resolve the issue.[16]

This would also apply to ammunition and, commencing July 1, 2022, firearm precursor parts (discussed in detail in Chapter 5). Unless an exception applies, ammunition vendors can only transfer or sell ammunition to a person if DOJ verifies that he or she is authorized to purchase ammunition.[17] If the purchaser is prohibited from possessing firearms, then DOJ considers the purchaser to be prohibited from acquiring or possessing ammunition.[18] Similarly, if DOJ finds that a person is prohibited from acquiring ammunition, then DOJ would probably consider him or her to be prohibited from possessing firearms. In the event DOJ is unable to ascertain a person's eligibility, DOJ will reject the transfer. Identical restrictions regarding the sale or transfer of firearm precursor parts are set to take effect on July 1, 2022.[19]

IV. CALIFORNIA'S ARMED PROHIBITED PERSON SYSTEM (APPS) AND FIREARM DENIALS REPORTED TO LAW ENFORCEMENT

As of 2006, if you fall under one of the categories of persons prohibited from possessing firearms under California or federal law, your name is entered into the Automated Criminal History System. Once that happens, DOJ is required to check if you possess or own any firearms, including registered "assault weapons" or .50 BMG rifles.[20] If it is discovered that you have firearms, your name and informa-

---

those misdemeanor convictions listed within P.C. section 29805, will prohibit you from possessing firearms for a ten-year period.

[16] To find out more about how to resolve the issue, or if you want to know what can be done if you are incorrectly considered prohibited from purchasing or owning firearm by DOJ, read *Gun Owner's Guide to Restoring Your Rights* (tentative title), a book by Coldaw Publishing that will be available for purchase on Amazon soon.

[17] P.C. §30352(c)-(d). Prior to July 1, 2019, ammunition vendors were able to transfer ammunition without a background check, so long as (1) the person is of age and (2) the ammunition vendor knows, or should know, that the person is not prohibited from possessing ammunition. P.C. § 30306.

[18] P.C. § 30370(b).

[19] As soon as the new ammunition background check laws became operative, DOJ released a press statement in which it announced that it had made roughly a dozen arrests of prohibited peoples in possession of firearms because they failed the background check. *See* "DOJ Special Agents Continue Work to Keep Californians Safe During COVID-19," California Department of Justice, Office of the Attorney General, https://oag.ca.gov/news/press-releases/attorney-general-becerra-announces-recent-firearms-operations-seizure-ghost-guns (May 19, 2020).

[20] P.C. § 30005(a).

tion will be placed on a list accessible to law enforcement via the Armed Prohibited Persons System (APPS).[21] DOJ is required to perform an initial review of any person who is added to this list within seven days of the person being added to the APPS list.[22]

Since 2012, money collected from Dealer's Record of Sale (DROS) fees can be used to pay for the APPS program, allowing law enforcement to go after more people on the APPS list.[23] In 2013, the California Legislature passed Senate Bill (SB) 140, which authorized DOJ to *raid all monies* in the "DROS Account" to further fund the APPS program.[24] Consequently, there has been a rise in law enforcement visiting and arresting people who have firearms registered in their name and have a record of a potentially prohibiting event.

Not content on just raiding the DROS Account to fund a failed program, in 2016, the California Legislature passed another bill (SB 826) to further fund the APPS program. This time, however, the California Legislature decided to take 5 million dollars from the Firearm Safety and Enforcement Special Fund and give it to DOJ so that they can contract with local law enforcement agencies to reduce the backlog of individuals who are in APPS.[25]

If you are prohibited from possessing firearms and ammunition but still possess or have firearms registered in your name, you should speak with an attorney experienced in firearms law and transfer them as soon as possible, as discussed in the following section. If you are prohibited and no longer possess firearms or ammunition, but nonetheless still have firearms registered in your name, you may be able to remove your name from the APPS system by submitting a "Notice of No Longer in Possession" form with DOJ. You can obtain a copy of this form at: https://oag.ca.gov/sites/all/files/agweb/pdfs/firearms/forms/bof-4546-nlip-09-2016.pdf. DOJ currently requires proof that you no longer possess the firearm before removing the registration.

If you are denied a firearm through a firearm purchase or transfer, DOJ is required to report the denial to local law enforcement.[26] Increased enforcement of prohibited person laws may prompt law enforcement to look into the matter further to

---

[21] The funding for this program is discussed in Chapter 5. Details regarding the program and how law enforcement utilizes it will be discussed in the upcoming book by Coldaw Publishing, which will center on firearms seizure, surrender, and return.

[22] P.C. § 30020. In addition to having a strict time frame to investigate individuals who have been added to this list, DOJ will also be required to periodically reassess whether they can complete review of APPS matches more efficiently. P.C. § 30020.

[23] P.C. § 28225.

[24] The NRA is currently challenging the appropriation of these funds as an invalid tax in *Gentry v. Becerra*. The Court recently entered an order that will be incorporated into a forthcoming final judgment upholding the DROS fee as a legitimate regulatory fee. Plaintiffs argue that the Court's finding contradicts established law regarding regulatory fees. Plaintiffs started the appeal process by filing a notice of appeal on June 4, 2019. The matter is still pending.

[25] AB 826, 2015-2016 Leg., Reg. Sess. (Cal. 2016), *available at* https://leginfo.legislature.ca.gov/faces/billNavClient.xhtml?bill_id=201520160SB826 (last visited Oct. 3, 2020).

[26] P.C. § 28220(b).

determine if the denied purchaser possesses other firearms or whether to file criminal charges for lying on the DROS form.[27]

V. FIREARM AND AMMUNITION POSSESSION RESTRICTIONS FOR MINORS (UNDER AGE 18)

To understand the law as applied to minors, it is first important to understand the distinction between restrictions on selling, loaning, and transferring firearms or ammunition to a minor[28] (where punishment for violations applies to the person making the transfer), and the restrictions against minors possessing firearms or ammunition (where punishment for violations applies to the minor). Parents and guardians should understand the law both as it applies to themselves, and to their children.

In this section, we will discuss restrictions against minors possessing firearms and ammunition. Restrictions regarding sales, loans, and transfers to minors by adults are discussed later in Chapter 5.

A. Rifles and Shotguns

Neither California nor federal law prohibits a minor from possessing rifles or shotguns, generally. But as discussed in greater detail in Chapter 5, California law does restrict the transfer of a firearm (including rifles and shotguns) to a minor – subject to some limited exceptions. So unless an exception applies, the law prevents minors from possessing firearms.[29]

B. Handguns

Under federal law, juveniles are prohibited from *possessing* handguns unless they meet an exception (see below). Federal law also prohibits the transfer of handguns to minors except in certain situations.[30]

---

[27] Providing false information either on the DROS form or the federal 4473 form is illegal. If you think you may be prohibited from owning or possessing firearms under state or federal law, you should fill out a Personal Firearms Eligibility Check (PFEC) form (discussed at the end of this chapter) instead of attempting to purchase a firearm to determine your eligibility.

[28] Although the Penal Code uses the term "juveniles" for those persons under the age of 18, we will refer to them as "minors" throughout the book.

[29] Transferring (meaning giving ownership to) rifles or shotguns to minors is limited to either the parents or grandparents giving the child these firearms. P.C. § 27945(a)-(b). But, there are laws that may prevent the transfer of a long gun to a minor. See discussion in Chapter 5. In addition, note that there are additional restrictions and exemptions on loaning firearms to minors. See Chapter 5.

[30] For more information relating to the laws for transferring firearms to minors see Chapter 5.

In California, individuals under age 18 may not generally *possess* handguns[31] unless they are actively engaged in, or are going directly to or from, a "lawful activity"[32] that involves using a handgun, and are either:

(1) With their parent or legal guardian; *or*

(2) With a "responsible adult"[33] and have prior *written* consent from their parent or legal guardian; *or*

(3) At least age 16 with prior *written* consent from their parent or legal guardian; *or*

(4) On lands owned or lawfully possessed by their parent or legal guardian and possess the parent or legal guardian's prior *written* consent.[34]

This handgun restriction also applies to "antique" handguns because "antique firearms" are still considered "firearms" for purposes of minors' possession of firearms.[35] So minors must satisfy one of the above exceptions when possessing an "antique" handgun.

C. Ammunition

Under federal law, minors are generally prohibited from *possessing* ammunition that can only be used in a handgun,[36] unless they meet an exception (see below).

Under California law, minors are generally prohibited from possessing any kind of live ammunition, unless the following conditions are met:

(1) The minor has *written* consent from his or her parent or legal guardian; *or*

(2) The minor is with his or her parent or legal guardian; *or*

(3) The minor is "actively engaged in, or [is] going to or from, a lawful, recreational sport, including, but not limited to, competitive shooting, or agricultural, ranching, or hunting activity, the nature of which involves the use of a firearm."[37]

---

[31] P.C. § 29610.

[32] *I.e.*, "a lawful recreational sport, including, but not limited to, competitive shooting, or agricultural, ranching, or hunting activity, or a motion picture, television, or video production, or entertainment of theatrical event" P.C. § 29615.

[33] "Responsible adult" means someone "at least age 21 who is not prohibited by state or federal law from possessing, receiving, owning, or purchasing a firearm." P.C. § 17070.

[34] P.C. §§ 29610, 29615.

[35] Under the definition of "firearms," "antique firearms" are not considered firearms for the following listed Penal Code sections: 16130, 16370(a), (c), 16400, 16550, 16620, 16810, 16960, 17110, 17310, 26500-26588 (inclusive), 26700-26915 (inclusive), 27510, 27540, 27545, 28100, and 31615. But the Code section prohibiting minors from possessing handguns is not one of these.

[36] 18 U.S.C. § 922(x)(2). Enforcement of this law is very difficult because there really is no such thing as ammunition "suitable for use only in a handgun." Some non-handguns can safely discharge virtually any cartridge in existence. Regardless, this is a non-issue in California as minors are generally prohibited from possessing any kind of ammunition, unless certain criteria are met as explained below.

[37] P.C. § 29655.

Minors who violate this provision can be charged with a crime.[38] When giving written permission to a minor to possess firearms, don't forget to mention that the minor can possess both firearms *and ammunition*. Also, make sure that the minor knows that they must retain that permission on their person while they possess the firearm.

Because of these ammunition restrictions for minors, ammunition sellers often ask to see identification to determine a purchaser's age, regardless of how old the individual appears.

D. Exemption to Federal Restriction on Handguns and "Handgun Ammunition"

Although minors are generally prohibited from possessing handguns and from possessing ammunition that can only be used in a handgun, both those restrictions do not apply if the *handgun* and/or *ammunition is possessed temporarily* and *all* of the following are satisfied:

(1) The handgun is only possessed while engaged in the following activities (including transportation directly between the point of transfer to the place where these activities take place so long as the handgun is unloaded and in a locked container):

   (a) In the course of employment; *or*

   (b) In the course of ranching or farming related to activities at the juvenile's residence (or on property used for ranching or farming at which the juvenile, with the permission of the property owner or lessee, is performing activities related to the operation of the farm or ranch); *or*

   (c) Target practice; *or*

   (d) Hunting; *or*

   (e) A course of instruction in the safe and lawful use of a handgun;

AND

(2) The minor's parent or guardian is not prohibited from possessing firearms by federal, state, or local law and the parent provides prior *written* consent (however, a minor with a prohibited parent or guardian may use a handgun for the ranching or farming related activities discussed above so long as he or she obtains *written* permission from the prohibited parent and is under the direction of an adult who is not prohibited by federal, state or local law from possessing a firearm);

AND

---

[38] P.C. § 29700.

(3) The minor has the prior written consent of his or her parent or guardian and such written consent is in the minor's possession at all times the handgun is possessed by the minor;

AND

(4) All state and local laws are complied with.[39]

The federal handgun and ammunition restrictions mentioned above also do not apply to minors in the following situations:

(1) The minor is a member of the Armed Forces of the United States or the National Guard who possesses or is armed with a handgun in the line of duty; *or*

(2) Transfer by inheritance of title (but not possession) of a handgun and/or ammunition to a minor[40]; *or*

(3) The minor takes possession of the handgun and/or ammunition in defense of himself or herself, or other persons, against an intruder into the residence of the minor or a residence in which the minor is an invited guest.[41]

Table 4.1

SUMMARY OF RESTRICTIONS FOR MINORS POSSESSING AMMUNITION		FIREARMS &
TYPE OF FIREARM	**CALIFORNIA LAW**	**FEDERAL LAW**
Shotguns & Rifles	California law does not regulate the possession of rifles or shotguns by minors.	Federal law does not regulate the possession of rifles or shotguns by minors, unless they meet one of the other firearm prohibitions explained in the sections below.
Handguns	Handgun possession is allowed if the minor is actively engaged in, or is going directly to or from, a lawful activity that involves using a handgun, and the minor has met the requirements enumerated in Section (V)(B).	Handgun possession is allowed if the minor possesses the handgun temporarily and has met the requirements enumerated in Section (V)(B).

---

[39] 18 U.S.C. § 922(x)(3).

[40] Meanwhile, as stated above, California law generally restricts minors from possessing handguns and/or ammunition (see P.C. sections 29650, 29610, 29615, 29655). So, it appears that, in California, minors can inherit ownership of a handgun but are restricted when it comes to possession of a handgun. But with California's restrictions on transferring handguns to minors (see Chapter 5 and P.C. section 27505), it is uncertain how all of this would work.

| Ammunition | Minors cannot possess any kind of live ammunition unless the conditions enumerated in Section (V)(C) are met. | Minors are prohibited from possessing ammunition that can *only* be used in handguns, unless the ammunition is possessed temporarily and all the requirements enumerated in Section (V)(C) are met. |

VI. CRIMINAL CONVICTIONS RESULTING IN LOSS OF FIREARM POSSESSION RIGHTS

Felony and certain misdemeanor convictions cause most firearm restrictions. You can also be prohibited from possessing firearms under certain probation terms. California and federal law sometimes differ as to which convictions trigger restrictions, and to what extent. It is crucial that you and your attorney know what restrictions, if any, apply to any criminal conviction you receive so that you know how to comply with them.

Generally, California restrictions based on criminal convictions are set out in P.C. sections 29800-29875, and 29900-29905.[44] The federal prohibitions are listed in 18 U.S.C. section 922(g). If you are facing criminal charges that may result in firearm restrictions and you currently own firearms, know that some courts have held that a person "has been convicted of a felony" when a verdict is entered or a plea bargain is entered into, while others have required that a final sentence be entered.[45]

A. Federal Restrictions for Certain State or Federal Convictions

While California firearm restrictions focus on the *type* of offense you were convicted of, federal law, for the most part, focuses on the type of *sentence* you *could* have received with your conviction (except when it comes to "misdemeanor crimes of domestic violence" (MCDV), see Section VI(F)).

Specifically, if your conviction under either state or federal law was for a crime *punishable* by imprisonment for more than one year, federal law prohibits you from possessing any firearm or ammunition for life.[46] Whether you have been convicted

---

[41] For a list of state prohibiting charges and situations: see *Firearms Prohibiting Categories*, CAL. DEPT. OF JUSTICE, BUREAU OF FIREARMS, http://oag.ca.gov/sites/all/files/pdfs/firearms/forms/prohibcatmisd.pdf (last visited Oct. 3, 2020). The Bureau of Alcohol, Tobacco, Firearms, and Explosives (ATF) also lists persons who are federally prohibited from shipping, transporting, receiving, or possessing firearms online. *Identify Prohibited Persons*, U.S. DEPT. OF JUSTICE, BUREAU OF ALCOHOL, TOBACCO, FIREARMS AND EXPLOSIVES, HTTPS://WWW.ATF.GOV/FIREARMS/IDENTIFY-PROHIBITED-PERSONS (last visited Oct. 3, 2020).

[45] *People v. Rogers*, 57 Cal. 4th 296, 345 (2013) (stating, "for the purpose of determining if the defendant had acquired the status of a person convicted of a felony, one is 'convicted' when a verdict is entered").

[46] 18 U.S.C. § 922(g)(1). It is not necessary that you actually receive such a sentence.

of a "crime punishable by imprisonment for a term exceeding one year" is determined according to the jurisdiction where you were prosecuted,[47] but does not include any:

(1) Federal or state offenses pertaining to antitrust violations, unfair trade practices, restraints of trade, or other similar offenses relating to the regulation of business practices; *or*

(2) State offenses classified by the laws of the State as a misdemeanor and punishable by a term of imprisonment of two years or less; *or*

(3) Convictions that have been expunged, set aside or for which you have been pardoned or had your civil rights restored unless the pardon, expungement, or restoration of civil rights expressly provided for firearm restrictions.[48]

Because the maximum sentence for any California *felony* conviction always exceeds one year, you are prohibited from owning and possessing firearms under federal law for *any* California felony conviction. But because a California *misdemeanor* conviction is only punishable by a year or less in jail, you are not federally prohibited for any such conviction[49] unless it is for an MCDV (discussed below). Federal firearm prohibitions extend to all 50 states and territories.[50]

B. California Restrictions for Felony Convictions

In California, anyone who has been convicted of a felony under California law, federal law, or another state or country's law,[51] may not own, purchase, receive, or possess firearms or ammunition.[52]

This California prohibition does *not* apply to felony convictions under federal law *unless*:

(1) The conviction was for an offense that would only result in felony punishment under California law; *or*

(2) You were sentenced to a federal correctional facility for more than 30 days and/or were fined more than $1,000.[53]

---

[47] *United States v. Marks*, 379 379 F.3d 1114, 1117 (9th Cir. 2004).

[48] 18 U.S.C. § 921(a)(20).

[49] P.C. § 19.2

[50] *See* 18 U.S.C. § 922(g)(9). There is a limited exception to the firearm and ammunition restrictions under federal law. Except for persons prohibited from possessing firearms for an MCDV, the federal restrictions do "not apply with respect to the transportation, shipment, receipt, possession, or importation of any firearm or ammunition imported for, sold or shipped to, or issued for the use of, the United States or any department or agency thereof or any State or any department, agency, or political subdivision thereof." 18 U.S.C. § 925(a)(1).

[51] Other countries do not possess the same Due Process rights as the U.S. So, under California law, you can be prohibited from possessing firearms and ammunition if you are convicted of a felony in a court in another country that does not provide you with similar Due Process rights.

[52] *See* P.C. § 29800(a)(1).

[53] P.C. § 29800(c)(2).

C. California Lifetime Restrictions Following Convictions of P.C. Section 273.5 and Certain "Violent Crimes"

California prohibits people from owning or possessing firearms for life if they are convicted on or after January 1, 2019 of a misdemeanor violation of P.C. section 273.5 (willful infliction of corporal injury upon a spouse, cohabitant, or other specified person).[54] Any person found to have violated this lifetime restriction faces a potential misdemeanor or felony conviction (commonly known as a "wobbler") and/or a $1000 fine.[55]

Individuals convicted of a misdemeanor violation of P.C. section 273.5 prior to January 1, 2019, may still be subject to a 10-year restriction under California law (discussed in more detail below). But violations of P.C. section 273.5 are typically considered misdemeanor crimes of domestic violence to which a federal lifetime firearm restriction applies (also discussed in more detail below).

California also restricts firearm possession for certain "violent crime" convictions regardless of whether the conviction is a misdemeanor or felony.[56] These "violent crimes" include, but are not limited to, murder, attempted murder, mayhem, rape, and assault with a deadly weapon or force likely to produce great bodily injury.[57] Though most "violent crimes" are felonies – convictions which would carry a firearm prohibition anyway – some can be charged as misdemeanors.[58] Being convicted of any of these "violent crimes," whether a felony or misdemeanor and whether the conviction was inside or outside of California, will result in a lifetime firearm prohibition in California.[59]

If you were convicted of one of these "violent crimes," you may be prosecuted for a felony if you possess a firearm thereafter.[60] And even if probation was granted, or the imposition or execution of your sentence was suspended, you are still likely to be sentenced to a minimum of six months in jail for possessing a firearm.[61]

Being convicted of any of the following "violent crimes" results in a lifetime restriction in California[62]:

---

[54] P.C. § 29805(b). *See also* AB 3129, 2017-2018 Leg., Reg. Sess. (Cal. 2018), *available at* http://leginfo.legislature.ca.gov/faces/billTextClient.xhtml?bill_id=201720180AB3129 (last visited Oct. 3, 2020).

[55] P.C. § 29805(b).

[56] *See* P.C. §§ 29900, 29905.

[57] A full list of "violent crimes" is given in P.C. section 29905 and below.

[58] *People v. Sanchez*, 211 Cal. App. 3d 477, 483 (1989) (the defendant's conviction for a "violent offense" prohibited him from possessing firearms without regard to the misdemeanor status of the conviction). So, both felonies and misdemeanor convictions can be prohibiting offenses under P.C. section 29900.

[59] *People v. Jaffe*, 19 Cal. Rptr. 3d 689, 698-99 (2004), *rev. granted and opinion superseded*, 105 P.3d 115 (Cal. 2005).

[60] *See* P.C. § 29900(a)(1).

[61] P.C. § 29900(a)(3).

[62] *See* P.C. § 29900(a)(1).

Table 4.2

PenalCodeSection	Violent Crimes Resulting in a Lifetime Firearms Restriction in California
P.C. § 29905(a)(1)	Murder or voluntary manslaughter
P.C. § 29905(a)(2)	Mayhem
P.C. § 29905(a)(3)	Rape
P.C. § 29905(a)(4)	Sodomy by force, violence, duress, menace, or threat of bodily harm
P.C. § 29905(a)(5)	Oral copulation by force, violence, duress, menace, or threat of great bodily harm
P.C. § 29905(a)(6)	Lewd acts on a child under the age of 14 years
P.C. § 29905(a)(7)	Any felony punishable by death or imprisonment in the state prison for life
P.C. § 29905(a)(8)	Any other felony in which the defendant inflicts great bodily injury on any person, other than an accomplice, that has been charged and proven, or any felony in which the defendant uses a firearm which use has been charged and proven
P.C. § 29905(a)(9)	Attempted murder
P.C. § 29905(a)(10)	Assault with intent to commit rape or robbery
P.C. § 29905(a)(11)	Assault with a deadly weapon or instrument on a peace officer
P.C. § 29905(a)(12)	Assault by a life prisoner on a non-inmate
P.C. § 29905(a)(13)	Assault with a deadly weapon by an inmate
P.C. § 29905(a)(14)	Arson
P.C. § 29905(a)(15)	Exploding a destructive device or any explosive with intent to injure
P.C. § 29905(a)(16)	Exploding a destructive device or any explosive causing great bodily injury
P.C. § 29905(a)(17)	Exploding a destructive device or any explosive with intent to murder
P.C. § 29905(a)(18)	Robbery
P.C. § 29905(a)(19)	Kidnapping
P.C. § 29905(a)(20)	Taking of a hostage by an inmate of a state prison
P.C. § 29905(a)(21)	Attempt to commit a felony punishable by death or imprisonment in the state prison for life
P.C. § 29905(a)(22)	Any felony in which the defendant personally used a dangerous or deadly weapon.
P.C. § 29905(a)(23)	Escape from a state prison by use of force or violence
P.C. § 29905(a)(24)	Assault with a deadly weapon or force likely to produce great bodily injury
P.C. § 29905(a)(25)	Any felony violation of P.C. section 186.22 (offenses relating to participation in criminal street gang)

PENAL CODE SECTION	VIOLENT CRIMES RESULTING IN A LIFETIME FIREARMS RESTRICTION IN CALIFORNIA
P.C. § 29905(a)(27)	Carjacking
P.C. § 29905(b)	Any attempt to commit a crime listed above other than an assault

D. California Convictions of Offenses Listed in Penal Code Section 23515(a), (b), and (d), or Two or More Convictions Under Penal Code Section 417(a)(2) Resulting in a Lifetime Restriction

As outlined in the chart below, individuals who are convicted of an offense listed in P.C. section 23515(a), (b), or (d); or who have two or more convictions under Penal Code section 417(a)(2) are subject to a lifetime restriction on owning, purchasing, receiving, and possessing any firearm.[63] A violation of this restriction is a felony.[64] A conviction for any one of the following offenses (misdemeanor or felony) results in a lifetime restriction from possessing firearms[65]:

Table 4.3

PENAL CODE SECTION	CONDUCT RESULTING IN A LIFETIME FIREARMS RESTRICTION IN CALIFORNIA
P.C. § 23515(a)	A violation of P.C. section 245(a)(2)-(3) (assault with a firearm or machinegun) or P.C. section 245(d) (assault with a firearm on a peace officer or firefighter)
P.C. § 23515(b)	A violation of P.C. section 246 (maliciously and willfully discharging a firearm at an inhabited dwelling house, occupied building, occupied motor vehicle, occupied aircraft, inhabited housecar, or inhabited camper)
P.C. § 23515(c)	A violation of P.C. section 417(a)(2) (brandishing a firearm in threatening manner during a fight or quarrel) if the person has two or more convictions for violating P.C. section 417(a)(2)
P.C. § 23515(d)	Two or more convictions of P.C. section 417(c) (brandishing a firearm in threatening manner in the presence of a peace officer)

---

[63] P.C. § 29800.
[64] P.C. § 29800.
[65] P.C. §§ 23515(a), (b), (d); 29800.

E. California Restrictions for Certain Misdemeanor Convictions

If a California misdemeanor conviction results in a firearm restriction, it *usually* lasts ten years, but some have lifetime prohibitions as discussed above. For your reference, comprehensive lists of the types of misdemeanor convictions that result in firearm restrictions are included below.

1. Misdemeanor Convictions Resulting in a Ten-Year Restriction

Individuals owning, purchasing, receiving, or possessing any firearm within ten years of being convicted of any of the below listed misdemeanors may be prosecuted for a public offense, punishable by imprisonment in a county jail not exceeding one year, or in the state prison, punishable by a fine not exceeding one thousand dollars ($1,000), or by both imprisonment and fine.[66]

A conviction for any one of the following misdemeanors will result in a ten-year restriction[67]:

Table 4.4

STATUTE	CONDUCT RESULTING IN A TEN-YEAR FIREARMS RESTRICTION IN CALIFORNIA
P.C. § 71	Threatening officers or employees of a public or private school, or any public officer or employee
P.C. § 76	Threatening certain public officers, appointees, judges, staff, or their immediate family members, with the intent and apparent ability to carry out the threat
P.C. § 136.1	Intimidating witnesses or victims
P.C. § 136.5	Possessing a deadly weapon with the intent to intimidate a witness
P.C. § 140	Threatening witnesses, victims, or informants
P.C. § 148(d)	Attempting to remove or take a firearm from a public officer or peace officer or from the public or peace officer's immediate presence
P.C. § 148.5(f)	Falsely reporting that a firearm has been lost or stolen
P.C. § 171b	Unauthorized possession of a weapon in a courtroom, courthouse, or court building, or at a public meeting

---

[66] P.C. § 29805.
[67] *See* P.C. § 29805.

Statute	Conduct Resulting in a Ten-Year Firearms Restriction in California
P.C. § 171c(a)(1)	Bringing or possessing loaded firearms in the State Capitol, any legislative offices, any office of the Governor or other constitutional officer, any hearing room in which any committee of the Senate or Assembly is conducting a hearing, or upon the State Capitol grounds
P.C. § 171d	Bringing or possessing loaded firearms in the Governor's Mansion or residence of other constitutional officers
P.C. § 186.28	Supplying, selling or giving firearm possession to anyone to participate in criminal street gangs
P.C. §§ 240, 241	Assault
P.C. §§ 242, 243	Battery
P.C. § 243.4	Sexual battery
P.C. § 244.5	Assault with a stun gun or less lethal weapon
P.C. § 245	Assault with a deadly weapon other than a firearm, or with force likely to produce great bodily injury
P.C. § 245.5	Assault with a deadly weapon or instrument by any means likely to produce great bodily injury, or with a stun gun or taser, on school employees engaged in performing their duties
P.C. § 246.3	Discharging a firearm or BB device in a grossly negligent manner
P.C. § 247	Shooting at an unoccupied aircraft, motor vehicle, or uninhabited building or dwelling house
P.C. § 273.5	Inflicting corporal injury on a spouse or significant other Note: misdemeanor convictions of P.C. § 273.5 post January 1, 2019, result in a lifetime firearm restriction under California law. See P.C. § 29805(b).
P.C. § 273.6	Willfully violating a domestic restraining or protective order
P.C. § 417	Drawing, exhibiting, or using a deadly weapon other than a firearm
P.C. § 417.6	Inflicting serious bodily injury as a result of brandishing
P.C. § 422	Threatening to commit a crime that will result in death or great bodily injury to another person
P.C. § 422.6	Using force or threat of force to interfere with victim's civil rights because of victim's actual or perceived characteristics (e.g., race, religion, etc.) or knowingly defacing, damaging, or destroying victim's property for purposes of intimidating or interfering with victim's civil rights because of victim's actual or perceived characteristics

Statute	Conduct Resulting in a Ten-Year Firearms Restriction in California
P.C. § 490.2	Petty theft of a firearm (only if convicted between November 5, 2014 and November 9, 2016)[67]
P.C. § 626.9	Bringing or possessing firearms in or upon public schools or grounds
P.C. § 646.9	Stalking
P.C. § 830.95	Wearing of peace officer uniform while picketing or at other informational activities
P.C. § 17500	Possessing a deadly weapon to intentionally commit an assault
P.C. § 17510	Carrying a firearm or deadly weapon while engaged in labor-related picketing
P.C. § 25100	Criminal storage of firearm accessible to child
P.C. § 25135	Criminal storage of firearm accessible to prohibited person
P.C. § 25200	Criminal storage of firearm accessed by child or prohibited person and carried off-premises
P.C. § 25300	Carrying a firearm in a public place or street while masked
P.C. § 25800	Armed criminal action -carrying a loaded firearm with intent to commit a felony
P.C. § 26100(b) or (d)	Driver of any vehicle who knowingly allows another person to discharge a firearm from the vehicle, or anyone who willfully and maliciously discharges a firearm from a motor vehicle themselves
P.C. § 27510	Firearms dealer who sells, transfers, or gives firearms to someone underage, or a person or corporation who sells any concealable firearm to a minor
P.C. § 27590(c)	Various violations involving the sale and transfer of firearms
P.C. § 30315	Possessing ammunition designed to penetrate metal or armor
P.C. § 32625	Unauthorized machinegun possession/transportation or conversion of a firearm into a machinegun
Cal. Welf. & Inst. Code § 871.5	Bringing or sending contraband into or possession within juvenile hall (The contraband must be a firearm for this restriction)
Cal. Welf. & Inst. Code § 1001.5	Bringing or sending contraband into grounds in possession of Youth Authority institutionsa (The contraband must be a firearm for purposes of this restriction)

STATUTE	CONDUCT RESULTING IN A TEN-YEAR FIREARMS RESTRICTION IN CALIFORNIA
CAL. WELF. & INST. CODE § 8100	Purchasing, possessing, or receiving a firearm or deadly weapon while receiving in-patient treatment for a mental disorder, or by someone who has threatened serious physical violence to a licensed psychotherapist against an identifiable victim by someone has communicated a threat of violence to a psychotherapist against an identifiable victim.
CAL. WELF. & INST. CODE § 8101	Providing a firearm or deadly weapon to someone described in California Welfare and Institutions Code (Cal. Welf. & Inst. Code) sections 8100 or 8103
CAL. WELF. & INST. CODE § 8103	Purchasing, possessing, or receiving a firearm or deadly weapon by someone adjudicated as a mentally disordered sex offender, incompetent to stand trial, not guilty by reason of insanity, or placed under conservatorship, and those prohibited from possessing firearms following Cal. Welf. & Inst. Code sections 5150, 5250, 5260, or 5270.15 commitments

Despite the very specific code sections listed above, one California court ruled that certain related code sections also carry a firearm restriction upon conviction. In one case, a minor was convicted of P.C. section 243.6 (battery on a school official), and the court decided that because the *definition* of battery (P.C. section 242) and the offense of battery (P.C. section 243) were prohibiting offenses, a conviction for P.C. section 243.6 should also be a prohibiting offense even though it is not on the list.[69] Therefore, the minor was considered prohibited.

There is also some ambiguity as to whether a misdemeanor conviction for assault with a deadly weapon *other than* a firearm (P.C. section 245(a)(1)) would result in either a ten-year or lifetime prohibition. The uncertainty of which prohibition

---

[68] Currently, P.C. section 490.2 (petty theft) does not cover firearms. The section specifically says, "[t]his section shall not apply to theft of a firearm." This was added as a result of Prop. 63. Between November 5, 2014 (the date that P.C. section 490.2 was added to the Penal Code by Prop. 47) and November 9, 2016 (the date when Prop. 63 laws became effective), the theft of a firearm valuing less than $950 (i.e., petty theft of a firearm) was considered to be a misdemeanor. Before that time, the theft of a firearm was a felony (and of course ,a firearm prohibiting offense). But because the Legislature wanted to make the theft of a firearm a prohibiting offense, it added the misdemeanor petty theft of a firearm to offenses listed in P.C. section 29805 that carry a 10-year restriction. But Prop. 63 modified P.C. section 490.2 and made it so that a person could not be convicted of petty theft for stealing a firearm. And Prop. 63 failed to change section 29805. Therefore, a person could have only been convicted for petty theft by stealing a firearm between November 5, 2014 and November 9, 2016. Currently, the theft of a firearm is considered grand theft (P.C. section 487) and punishable as a felony (P.C. section 489(a)).

[69] *In re David S.*, 133 Cal. App. 4th 1160, 1163-68 (2005).

would apply in this context was created by dicta[70] written by the California Court of Appeal in *Rash v. Lungren*.[71]

In *Rash*, the California Court of Appeal was faced with the question of whether a person with a prior conviction under P.C. section 245(a)(2) (assault with a *firearm*) fell under the lifetime or ten-year prohibitions under former P.C. sections 12021 (currently codified at P.C. section 29800) (lifetime prohibitions) and 12021.1 (currently codified at P.C. section 29805).[72] While the court quickly concluded that any conviction (felony or misdemeanor) under any of the P.C. section 245 offenses involving the use of a firearm would result in a permanent prohibition, it also ruled that the ten-year prohibition "is reserved for those with misdemeanor convictions under section 245, subdivision (a)(1) (assaults with deadly weapons *other than* firearms) . . . ."[73]

The court continued to distinguish the two prohibitions and explained that the lifetime prohibition is only applicable to those who are convicted of either a felony or misdemeanor assault *with* a firearm, while the ten-year prohibition is only applicable to those who have a misdemeanor conviction of assault with a weapon *other than* a firearm under P.C. section 245(a)(1).[74] So, the court seemed to suggest that if you have a prior conviction under P.C. section 245(a)(1), you would only be subject to the ten-year prohibition.

This distinction, however, is odd given that P.C. section 29905, which lists the "violent crimes" that are subject to lifetime prohibitions under P.C. section 29900, specifically lists assault with a deadly weapon as a "violent crime."[75] This would arguably include any of the offenses listed in P.C. section 245, including subdivision (a)(1). Therefore, it seems that if you received a misdemeanor conviction for assault with a deadly weapon other than a firearm under P.C. section 245(a)(1), you would still be subject to the lifetime prohibition on owning, purchasing, receiving, or possessing firearms because it would still be considered a "violent crime."[76] But given the court's decision in *Rash*, there is clearly uncertainty as to which prohibition would apply.

Beware: the California Legislature periodically attempts to expand the list of misdemeanor convictions that result in firearm restrictions. In 2016, the Califor-

---

[70] Dictum (the single form of dicta) is "[a] statement of opinion or belief considered authoritative because of the dignity of the person making it." BLACK'S LAW DICTIONARY 485 (8th ed. 2004). Dicta is merely persuasive and not binding authority; it is legal reasoning in an opinion that does not drive the outcome of the legal opinion.

[71] *Rash v. Lungren*, 59 Cal. App. 4th 1233 (1997).

[72] *Rash v. Lungren*, 59 Cal. App. 4th 1233, 1234, 1235 (1997).

[73] *Rash v. Lungren*, 59 Cal. App. 4th 1233, 1238-39 (1997).

[74] *See Rash v. Lungren*, 59 Cal. App. 4th 1233 n.8 (1997) ("The Legislature has, thus, chosen to differentiate between convictions involving the use, or lack of use, of a firearm – at least in cases involving assaults with deadly weapons . . . . In view of the expressed legislative concern about increasing violent gun use, the distinction drawn . . . between offenses meriting a permanent prohibition as opposed to a ten-year restriction is certainly one that they were entitled to draw.").

[75] P.C. §§ 29900; 29905(24).

[76] *See* P.C. §§ 29900; 29905(24).

nia Legislature expanded the list when it passed AB 1695. In 2017, the California Legislature expanded the list again when it passed AB 785 and added P.C. section 422.6 (interference with another person's civil rights) to the list. While you may not currently be prohibited form possessing firearms due to a misdemeanor conviction, the laws can change.

Your period of prohibition could start years after your conviction. For example, those who were convicted of misdemeanor violations of P.C. section 422.6 will be prohibited from possessing firearms as of January 1, 2018. The length of the prohibition will be 10 years from the date of the convictions. So, a person who was convicted on January 1, 2010 of a misdemeanor violation of P.C. section 422.6 will be prohibited from possessing firearms pursuant to P.C. section 29805 on January 1, 2018, and the prohibition will end on January 1, 2020. There is no mechanism to provide notice to persons who will be prohibited from possessing firearms to let them know that they will be prohibited as of January 1, 2018.

There is a mechanism to restore firearm rights for people who become prohibited from possessing firearms after their date of conviction because the Legislature added their offenses to the list of misdemeanor convictions resulting in ten-year restriction. This mechanism will be discussed in detail in an upcoming book by Coldaw Publishing, tentatively titled *Gun Owner's Guide to Restoring Your Gun Rights*.

2. Misdemeanor Conviction Resulting in a Five-Year Restriction

Any person who has been convicted of a misdemeanor under P.C. section 18205 (possessing a firearm or ammunition—which includes "magazines"[77]—while a "gun violence restraining order" is in effect) will be prohibited from having in his or her custody or control, owning, purchasing, possessing, or receiving, or attempting to purchase or receive, a firearm or ammunition for five years, beginning the date the gun violence restraining order expires.[78]

F. Federal Restrictions for a Misdemeanor Crime of Domestic Violence (MCDV)

An MCDV occurs when someone is convicted of an offense that has, as an element,[79] the use or attempted use of physical force or the threatened use of a deadly weapon, and the accused either:

(1) Is "a current or former spouse, parent, or guardian of the victim"; *or*

(2) "[S]hares a child in common" with the victim; *or*

---

[77] P.C. § 18100(b).

[78] P.C. § 18205.

[79] *See United States v. Hayes*, 555 U.S. 415, 422 (2009) (defining an element as "[a] constituent part of a claim that must be proved for the claim to succeed"). For example, one of the elements of speeding is that the prosecutor must prove that the defendant was going faster than the speed limit. The requirement that the offense has, as an element, the use or attempted use of physical force is discussed below.

(3) Is living, or has lived, "with the victim as a spouse, parent, or guardian"; *or*

(4) Is "similarly situated to a spouse, parent, or guardian of the victim."[80]

An MCDV is a misdemeanor offense under federal, state, and tribal law,[81] but it triggers a lifetime ban under federal law.[82] You are not considered to be "convicted" of an MCDV unless you: (1) were represented by counsel or waived your right to be represented by counsel, *and* (2) if entitled to a jury trial, you either tried the case, waived your right to have the case tried by a jury by entering a guilty plea, or waived your right to a jury trial by some other way.[83] That being said, it is highly unlikely that a California judge would allow your guilty or no contest plea without attorney representation or a jury trial, unless you properly waived your rights to both first.

Determining whether an offense under California law meets the definition of an MCDV usually boils down to three issues: (1) the type of offense that was committed, (2) the nature of the relationship between the defendant and the victim, and (3) whether the conviction was legally removed from the defendant's record in order to restore firearm rights.

1. California Offenses that May Be a Misdemeanor Crime of Domestic Violence

Two Penal Code sections are typically considered "domestic violence" statutes: P.C. sections 273.5 and 243(e).[84] But, as discussed below, other California crimes can be considered "domestic violence" crimes to which the federal MCDV lifetime firearm restriction applies.[85]

a. Injuring a Spouse, Cohabitant, Fiancé, Etc.

A violation of P.C. section 273.5 – injuring a former or current spouse or cohabitant, the father or mother of one's child, or a fiancé or someone with whom a person has or had an engagement or dating relationship[86] – may meet the definition of an MCDV under federal law. DOJ (which does the background checks on firearm purchases) considers a P.C. section 273.5 conviction to be an MCDV automati-

---

[80] 18 U.S.C. § 921(a)(33)(A)(ii). *See also United States v. Hayes*, 555 U.S. 415 (2009). Although a crime must have, as an element, the use or attempted use of force or the threatened use of deadly weapon in order to fall under the definition of an MCDV, the relationship status of the victim does not have to be a defining element of the predicate offense. *United States v. Hayes*, 555 U.S. 415, 429 (2009).

[81] 18 U.S.C. § 921(a)(33)(A)(i).

[82] *See* 18 U.S.C. § 922(g)(9).

[83] 18 U.S.C. § 921(a)(33)(B)(i).

[84] Remember, almost all of the Penal Code sections (with the exception of P.C. section 415) discussed here carry a ten-year firearm restriction under California law. You should be mindful of this while reading this section, as well as the possibility that the conviction may also result in a federal firearm restriction.

[85] 18 U.S.C. § 922(g)(9). Under P.C. section 29805, a section 243 misdemeanor conviction or a P.C. section 273.5 misdemeanor conviction (if convicted prior to January 1, 2019) results in a ten-year California firearm restriction.

[86] "'Dating relationship' means frequent, intimate associations primarily characterized by the expectation of affectional or sexual involvement independent of financial considerations." P.C. § 243(f)(10).

cally. But DOJ may be wrong, especially if the conviction occurred after January 1, 2014.[87] A P.C. section 273.5 violation can *only* be committed against a spouse or former spouse, cohabitant,[88] mother or father of one's child, or a fiancé or someone with whom a person has or had an engagement or dating relationship. But, some of these relationships might not be the type of relationship that triggers an MCDV firearm restriction under federal law (see section above).

P.C. section 273.5 can only be violated when there is a corporal injury resulting in a "traumatic condition."[89] A "traumatic condition" means a condition of the body, such as a wound, or external or internal injury, including, but not limited to, injury as a result of strangulation or suffocation, whether of a minor or serious nature, caused by a *physical force*. For purposes of this definition, "strangulation" and "suffocation" include impeding the normal breathing or circulation of the blood of a person by applying pressure on the throat or neck.[90] While a P.C. section 273.5 violation rests on the type of injury the victim received, an MCDV only requires that a certain level of force is met. A P.C. section 273.5 violation has been determined to involve the "use, attempted use, or threatened use of physical force against the person of another" by a federal court trying to determine whether it is a "crime of violence" under federal sentencing enhancements.[91] Under the court's analysis, a P.C. section 273.5 violation was considered to require physical force because it requires the use of force resulting in a "traumatic condition." This same analysis can be extended to whether a P.C. section 273.5 conviction is an MCDV, and it is very likely that this analysis would be used by a court.

b. Battery Against a Spouse, Cohabitant, Fiancé, Etc.

A conviction under P.C. section 243(e) does not necessarily result in a federal MCDV firearm restriction, but it may. You can be charged under P.C. section 243(e) if you commit a battery and the victim is a spouse, someone you are cohabiting with, someone who is the parent of your child, a former spouse, fiancé, or someone you are or were dating.[92]

Note that a fiancé or someone you are or were dating or engaged to be married does not necessarily meet the definition of a victim under the federal MCDV

---

[87] In 2014, the categories of relationships under P.C. section 273.5 were expanded to include former fiancés, as well as current and former dating relationships. AB 16, 2013-2014 Leg. Reg. Sess. (Cal. 2013) *available at* http://leginfo.legislature.ca.gov/faces/billNavClient.xhtml?bill_id=201320140AB16 (last visited Oct. 3, 2020). These relationships might not be the type of relationship that meets the definition of a MCDV under federal law.

[88] *See People v. Holifield*, 205 Cal. App. 3d 993, 999-1000 (1999) (providing that for purposes of P.C. section 273.5, the term "cohabiting" means "something more than a platonic, rooming-house arrangement . . . [it] means an unrelated man and woman living together in a substantial relationship – one manifested, minimally, by permanence and sexual or amorous intimacy").

[89] P.C. § 273.5(a).

[90] P.C. § 273.5(d). "Traumatic condition" includes bruising. *United States v. Hall*, 419 F.3d 980, 986 (9th Cir. 2005); *People v. Beasley*, 105 Cal. App. 4th 1078, 1085-86 (2003).

[91] *United States v. Laurico-Yeno*, 590 F.3d 818 (9th Cir. 2010).

[92] P.C. § 243(e).

statute.⁹³ This means that if you are convicted of a P.C. section 243(e) battery where the victim is one of these individuals, you may not have a federal lifetime firearm restriction under 18 U.S.C. section 922(g)(9) because it may not be considered an MCDV. The facts of your relationship need to be further analyzed to determine if the "victim" in your case meets the definition of a person that triggers the restriction.

In 2014, the United States Supreme Court held in *United States v. Castleman* that the element of "physical force" is satisfied by the degree of force that supports a common-law battery conviction – namely, offensive touching.⁹⁴ In other words, both P.C. section 243(e) and P.C. section 242 have as an element the "use of physical force" because both crimes require an amount of force either greater than or equal to an offensive touching.

Prior to 2014, there was some ambiguity as to whether a conviction under P.C. section 243(e) or P.C. section 242 qualified as an MCDV because courts were split as to whether an offense that could be violated by a simple touching (such as P.C. section 242) met the required "physical force" element to be an MCDV. For instance, in 2013, the California Court of Appeal held in *Shirey v. Los Angeles County Civil Service Commission* that a person convicted of battery is not automatically considered prohibited from possessing firearms under federal law for an MCDV.⁹⁵ As the court explained, under P.C. section 242, a battery can be committed by simply touching the victim. Therefore, when the law requires the "use of physical force" as an element, some type of *force* must be used. Simple touching is not enough. As a result, the court concluded that a battery conviction does not automatically result in a federal firearm restriction.

But, shortly after the decision in *Shirey* was published, another California Court of Appeal reached an opposite conclusion. In *James v. State*, the court determined that a misdemeanor P.C. section 242 conviction *does* meet the definition of an MCDV (provided that the relationship between the defendant an the victim is one falling under the requirement for an MCDV).⁹⁶ The court concluded that a P.C. section 242 violation, regardless of the amount of force actually used in the underlying offense, is considered an MCDV.

James was ultimately appealed to the California Supreme Court. But, because the U.S. Supreme Court had granted certiorari in *Castleman*, the California Supreme Court deferred review. After the U.S. Supreme Court issued its opinion on March 26, 2014, the California Supreme Court transferred the case back down to the California Court of Appeal with directions to vacate the decision and reconsider the case in light of the decision in *Castleman*. But, on review, the California

---

⁹³ *See* 18 U.S.C. § 921(a)(33)(A).

⁹⁴ *United States v. Castleman*, 134 S. Ct. 1405, 1413 (2014).

⁹⁵ *Shirey v. Los Angeles Cnty. Civil Serv. Comn'n*, 216 Cal. App. 4th 1 (2013). It was undisputed that the relationship between the defendant and the victim in *Shirey* met the relationship requirement of an MCDV.

⁹⁶ *James v. State*, No. F065003 (Cal Ct. App. Sept. 24, 2013), *available at* http://caselaw.findlaw.com/ca-court-of-appeal/1645252.html (last visited Oct. 3, 2020).

Court of Appeal again concluded that a misdemeanor P.C. section 242 conviction does meet the definition of an MCDV because P.C. section 242 has, as an element, the "use of physical force."[97]

Although neither *James* nor *Castleman* expressly overturned the decision in *Shirey*, given both the U.S. Supreme Court's decision in *Castleman* and the California Court of Appeal's subsequent decision in *James*, it seems to be a forgone conclusion that a conviction under P.C. section 242 categorically meets the "physical force" requirement needed to be an MCDV.

2. Other California Crimes That May Be Considered a Misdemeanor Crime of Domestic Violence

Other California crimes that may be considered an MCDV include assault (P.C. section 240); battery (P.C. section 242); assault with a deadly weapon or force likely to produce great bodily injury (P.C. section 245); and fighting, noise, and offensive words (P.C. section 415).

To determine whether a misdemeanor conviction qualifies as an MCDV under federal law, DOJ will first consider the initial charges. If necessary, DOJ will review the court file or plea form for additional facts to determine the nature of the relationship between the convicted person and the victim. Defense attorneys will often try to "plea down" a domestic violence charge to something milder than a P.C. section 273.5 conviction (such as a P.C. section 242, 243(e), or 415(1)). But beware before doing this because DOJ will look at the initial charge of P.C. section 273.5, and if you have pled to a P.C. section 242 or P.C. section 415, DOJ may still believe that you were automatically convicted of an MCDV. This is because DOJ will assume that, if the person was originally charged with a P.C. section 273.5, there are sufficient facts to believe the person had a relationship with the victim that satisfies the relationship requirement for an MCDV. This assumption may not be accurate, or DOJ may lack the information to determine that the person is prohibited from possessing firearms for an MCDV restriction. Nevertheless, DOJ may declare that the person is prohibited from receiving firearms until he or she can prove otherwise to their satisfaction.

If you are facing criminal charges, be sure to discuss the possible ramifications of a conviction with your attorney. If your attorney cannot give you answers, or you are concerned that your attorney does not know these answers, you should seek assistance from other counsel.

G. Juvenile Offenses

Certain juvenile offenses may lead to firearm restrictions that prohibit possession of firearms until the age of 30. For a juvenile offense to lead to those restrictions, the juvenile must have been:

(1) Alleged to have committed an offense listed in Table 4.5; *and*

---

[97] *James v. State*, 229 Cal. App. 4th 130, 141 (2014).

(2) "[S]ubsequently adjudged a ward of the juvenile court" because the juvenile committed that offense.[98]

A violation of this firearm restriction is punishable by imprisonment in a county jail or state prison not exceeding one year, by a fine not exceeding one thousand dollars ($1,000), or by both that imprisonment and fine. The following juvenile offenses may lead to these firearm restrictions[99]:

Table 4.5

STATUTE	JUVENILE OFFENSE
CAL. WELF. & INST. CODE § 707(b)(1)	Murder
CAL. WELF. & INST. CODE § 707(b)(2)	Arson as provided in P.C. section 451(a) or (b)
CAL. WELF. & INST. CODE § 707(b)(3)	Robbery
CAL. WELF. & INST. CODE § 707(b)(4)	Rape with force, violence, or threat of great bodily harm
CAL. WELF. & INST. CODE § 707(b)(5)	Sodomy by force, violence, duress, menace, or threat of great bodily harm
CAL. WELF. & INST. CODE § 707(b)(6)	A lewd or lascivious act as provided in P.C. section 288(b)
CAL. WELF. & INST. CODE § 707(b)(7)	Oral copulation by force, violence, duress, menace, or threat of great bodily harm
CAL. WELF. & INST. CODE § 707(b)(8)	An act of sexual penetration when the act is accomplished against the victim's will by means of force, violence, duress, menace, or fear of immediate and unlawful bodily injury on the victim or another person
CAL. WELF. & INST. CODE § 707(b)(9)	Kidnapping for ransom
CAL. WELF. & INST. CODE § 707(b)(10)	Kidnapping for purposes of robbery
CAL. WELF. & INST. CODE § 707(b)(11)	Kidnapping with bodily harm
CAL. WELF. & INST. CODE § 707(b)(12)	Attempted murder
CAL. WELF. & INST. CODE § 707(b)(13)	Assault with a firearm or destructive device
CAL. WELF. & INST. CODE § 707(b)(14)	Assault by any means of force likely to produce great bodily injury
CAL. WELF. & INST. CODE § 707(b)(15)	Discharge of a firearm into an inhabited or occupied building

---

[98] P.C. § 29820(a).
[99] *See* P.C. § 29820.

Statute	Juvenile Offense
Cal. Welf. & Inst. Code § 707(b)(16)	An offense described in P.C. section 1203.09
Cal. Welf. & Inst. Code § 707(b)(17)	An offense described in P.C. section 12022.5 or 12022.53
Cal. Welf. & Inst. Code § 707(b)(18)	A felony offense in which the minor personally used a weapon described in any provision listed in P.C. section 16590
Cal. Welf. & Inst. Code § 707(b)(19)	A felony offense described in P.C. section 136.1 or 137
Cal. Welf. & Inst. Code § 707(b)(20)	Manufacturing, compounding, or selling one-half ounce or more of a salt or solution of a controlled substance specified in Cal. Health & Saf. Code section 11055(e)
Cal. Welf. & Inst. Code § 707(b)(21)	A violent felony, as defined in P.C. section 667.5(c), which also would constitute a felony violation of P.C. section 186.22(b)
Cal. Welf. & Inst. Code § 707(b)(22)	Escape, by the use of force or violence, from a county juvenile hall, home, ranch, camp, or forestry camp in violation of P.C. section 871(b) if great bodily injury is intentionally inflicted upon an employee of the juvenile facility during the commission of the escape
Cal. Welf. & Inst. Code § 707(b)(23)	Torture as described in P.C. sections 206 and 206.1
Cal. Welf. & Inst. Code § 707(b)(24)	Aggravated mayhem, as described in P.C. section 205
Cal. Welf. & Inst. Code § 707(b)(25)	Carjacking, as described in P.C. section 215, while armed with a dangerous or deadly weapon
Cal. Welf. & Inst. Code § 707(b)(26)	Kidnapping for purposes of sexual assault, as punishable in P.C. section 209(b)
Cal. Welf. & Inst. Code § 707(b)(27)	Kidnapping as punishable in P.C. section 209.5
Cal. Welf. & Inst. Code § 707(b)(28)	Willfully and maliciously discharging a firearm from a motor vehicle at another person other than an occupant of a motor vehicle
Cal. Welf. & Inst. Code § 707(b)(29)	Igniting or exploding destructive device or explosive with intent to commit murder
Cal. Welf. & Inst. Code § 707(b)(30)	Voluntary manslaughter, as described in P.C. Section 192(a)
P.C. § 25400(a)	Carrying a concealed firearm
P.C. § 29805	Any offense enumerated in P.C. section 29805 (see Table 4.4)
P.C. § 25850	Carrying a loaded firearm in public
P.C. § 25400	Carrying a concealed firearm
P.C. § 26100 (a)	Permitting loaded firearm in motor vehicle

STATUTE	JUVENILE OFFENSE
P.C. § 1203.073	Felony convictions for controlled substances violations involving cocaine, cocaine base, methamphetamine, phencyclidine, or heroin

H. Persons on Probation or Parole

In some cases, courts may prohibit someone convicted of a crime from owning and possessing firearms or "deadly or dangerous weapons"[100] even if the law itself does not require it (commonly referred to as "weapons conditions"). This generally occurs when a firearm restriction is created as a probation condition.[101] This type of restriction may last for the entire length of the probation period. Those who violate their probation condition, in addition to being charged with the crime of a prohibited person in possession of a firearm and with a violation of a court order (which a probation condition is), will have to deal with a probation or parole violation reopening their previous case and exposing them to an additional sentence on the original charges.[102]

Under the Full Faith and Credit Clause of the U.S. Constitution, these probation conditions, like orders issued in restraining orders, travel across state lines.[103]

Table 4.6

SUMMARY OF CALIFORNIA CRIMINAL CONVICTIONS RESULTING IN THE LOSS OF FIREARMS RIGHTS[100]	
CALIFORNIA LAW	FEDERAL LAW
FELONY: Felony convictions will result in a lifetime restriction on owning, purchasing, receiving, and possessing firearms.	Conviction of a crime (with some exceptions) that is punishable by imprisonment for more than one year will result in a lifetime restriction on receiving or possessing firearms.

---

[100] Probation conditions prohibiting a person from possessing "dangerous or deadly weapons" or from possessing a "replica firearm" are neither unconstitutionally vague nor overbroad. *People v. Hall*, 236 Cal. App. 4th 1124 (2015); *People v. Forrest*, 237 Cal. App. 4th 1074 (2015).

[101] P.C. § 29815.

[102] *See* P.C. § 1203.2(c).

[103] JUD. COUNCIL OF CAL., ADMIN. OFFICE OF THE COURTS, JUDGES GUIDE TO DOMESTIC VIOLENCE CASES: FIREARMS AND FULL FAITH AND CREDIT (rev. 2014), *available at* http://www2.courtinfo.ca.gov/protem/pubs/firearms.pdf (last visited Oct. 3, 2020).

[104] Even after being convicted, you may be restricted from possessing and owning firearms and other "deadly or dangerous weapons" because of a condition of your parole or probation.

MISDEMEANOR	Conviction of a misdemeanor violation of P.C. section 273.5 (willful infliction of corporal injury upon a spouse, cohabitant, or other specified person) on or after January 1, 2019, as well as convictions of any of the crimes listed in Tables 4.2 and 4.3 will result in a lifetime restriction on owning, purchasing, receiving, and possessing firearms. Convictions of any of the misdemeanors listed in Table 4.4 will result in a ten-year restriction on owning, purchasing, receiving, and possessing firearms.	Conviction of a Misdemeanor Crime of Domestic Violence (MCDV) will result in a lifetime restriction on purchasing, receiving, or possessing firearms.
JUVENILE	Firearm possession is prohibited until age 30 if the juvenile is alleged to have committed any offense listed in Table 4.5 and is declared "a ward of the juvenile court" because the juvenile committed that offense.	There are no additional restrictions than those explained in Section VII.

I. Notice Required

In order to ensure that individuals who have been convicted of an offense listed in P.C. section 29800 or 29805 understand that they are prohibited from owning and possessing firearms, California law requires courts to notify these individuals of their firearm prohibition and provide the person with a "Prohibited Persons Relinquishment Form".[105] Using this form, the individual must then name a designee and grant the designee power of attorney for the purpose of transferring or disposing of any firearms.[106] The designee must then either: 1) Surrender the firearms to the control of a local law enforcement agency; 2) Sell the firearms to a licensed firearms dealer; or, 3) Transfer the firearms for storage to a firearms dealer.[107] But note that a court's failure to provide this notice is not a defense to subsequently being prosecuted for possessing firearms while prohibited.[108]

---

[105] P.C. § 29810(a)(2). A copy of this form can be obtained online at https://www.courts.ca.gov/documents/bof1022.pdf
[106] P.C. § 29810(a)(3).
[107] P.C. § 29810(a)(3).
[108] P.C. § 29810(b). Courts often failed to give this notice, although they are getting better at providing it.

J. Unlawful Detainer Actions

City attorneys and city prosecutors may initiate eviction proceedings against tenants for committing nuisance violations involving an "unlawful weapons and ammunition purpose."[109] For purposes of this law, a nuisance violation involving "unlawful weapons or ammunition purpose" is defined as the illegal use, manufacturing, causing to be manufactured, importation, possession, possession for sale, sale, furnishing, or the giving away of any:

(1) Firearm;[110] or

(2) Ammunition;[111] or

(3) "Assault Weapon";[112] or

(4) .50 BMG Rifle;[113] or

(5) Tear gas weapon.[114]

Anytime a person is arrested for any of the above violations, or has a warrant issued against hem for any of the above violations, the city attorney or prosecutor is allowed to bring an unlawful detainer proceeding to evict the person from his or her residence, even if the person has not been convicted of the offense.

VII. APPLICATION OF EX POST FACTO PROHIBITIONS ON FIREARM POSSESSION

The list of crimes carrying firearm restrictions has changed over time, with new crimes being added to the list. As a result, many people have been convicted of crimes that did not result in firearm restrictions at the time of conviction, but California and federal courts have permitted the legislature to retroactively apply firearm restrictions to convictions that originally did not carry those restrictions.[115]

In other words, it does not matter if you were convicted of an offense *before* the legislature added a firearm restriction to it because you are *now* in a class of persons the legislature has decided to prohibit from possessing firearms. Therefore, you can be prosecuted for possessing a firearm based on your previous conviction[116] even though the conviction occurred before the restriction was added to the code.

---

[109] CAL. CIV. CODE § 3485; AB 2310, 2013-2014, Leg. Counsel's Digest (Cal. 2014) *available at* http://leginfo.legislature.ca.gov/faces/billNavClient.xhtml?bill_id=201320140AB2310# (last visited Oct. 3, 2020).

[110] As defined in P.C. section 16520(a).

[111] As defined in P.C. sections 16150(b), 16650, 16660.

[112] As defined in P.C. sections 30510, 30515.

[113] As defined in P.C. section 30530.

[114] P.C. § 3485. Tear gas weapons are defined in P.C. section 17250.

[115] *United States v. Wilhelm*, 65 Fed. App'x. 619, 620 (9th Cir. 2003); *People v. Mesce*, 52 Cal. App. 4th 618, 622-26 (1997); *Helmer v. Miller*, 19 Cal. App. 4th 1565, 1570-71 (1993).

[116] *United States v. Collins*, 61 F.3d 1379, 1382-83 (9th Cir. 1995).

A. The Effect of a California Conviction in Other States

Generally, firearm restrictions under California law resulting from California convictions only apply while you are in California. That means that you may be able to lawfully possess firearms in another state, despite the fact that you are subject to a California restriction.[117] But be careful. Although you may not be subject to a California firearm restriction in another state, you may still be prohibited from possessing firearms because the state may treat your California conviction as if it occurred within the state, thereby subjecting you to a firearm prohibition under that state's laws. Or, you might discover that you are subject to a federal restriction. Because of this potential danger, you should always check the state's laws to determine whether your conviction restricts you there *before* possessing any firearms within that state.[118]

Some states have their own procedures for restoring firearm rights that were restricted due to offenses that occurred in a different state, while other states require that the conviction be addressed in the state where it occurred. Contacting an attorney in your new state is best to determine if the conviction can be addressed there. But, if nothing can be done there, you should discuss what can be done to restore your firearms rights with a California attorney. But, as discussed below, California has limited options for vacating convictions or restoring firearm rights under federal law.

To be clear, California felony convictions prohibit firearm possession in all 50 states under federal law (because a California felony is punishable by more than one year in state prison). This means that California felony convictions prohibit firearm possession under federal law no matter where the person resides.[119] Similarly, an MCDV conviction carries a lifetime prohibition under federal law.[120]

VIII. POSSESSING A FIREARM WHILE BEING A "FUGITIVE FROM JUSTICE" AND THE CALIFORNIA RESTRICTION FOR POSSESSING A FIREARM WHILE HAVING AN OUTSTANDING WARRANT FOR CERTAIN OFFENSE

A. Federal Law for Firearm Prohibitions Based on "Fugitive from Justice" Status

---

[117] *People v. Laino*, 32 Cal. 4th 878, 889 (2004); *Williams v. North Carolina*, 317 U.S. 287, 296 (1942).

[118] Whether you are prohibited from possessing firearms in any state may be unclear from a plain reading of the law. If you have been convicted of a misdemeanor anywhere, it is a good idea to check with an attorney practicing in the state where you plan to travel while possessing a firearm to find out whether your conviction means you are restricted from possessing or owning firearms in that state.

[119] 18 U.S.C. § 922(g)(1).

[120] 18 U.S.C. § 922(g)(9).

Federal law prohibits a "fugitive from justice" from possessing firearms.[121] A "fugitive from justice" is someone who (1) has fled the state; (2) has done so to avoid prosecution for a crime or to avoid giving testimony in a criminal proceeding, and (3) is subject to a current or imminent criminal prosecution or testimonial obligation.[122] In addition, many courts have held that in order to be a "fugitive from justice," a person must "*purposefully*" flee the state when "*knowing* that charges are pending."[123]

Hence, individuals charged with being a "fugitive from justice" in possession of a firearm can defend themselves in court (preferably with the help of an experienced criminal defense attorney) by showing that they were unaware of the charges pending against them.[124] Along the same lines, they can argue that they did not intend to flee for purposes of avoiding prosecution or an appearance in court.

B. California Law for Firearm Prohibitions Based on an Outstanding Warrant for a Felony or for Certain Misdemeanors

The passage of AB 103 into law on June 27, 2017 caused California's firearm prohibitions to also attach when a person merely has an "outstanding warrant" for a felony or for those certain misdemeanors in P.C. sections 29800 and 29805; criminal proceedings need not reach the point of conviction for the firearm prohibition to attach.[125] Presumably, the California Legislature wanted to make a law to mirror the federal restriction against "fugitives from justice," which, as stated in the previous section, prohibits fugitives from justice from receiving and possessing firearms.[126] They failed horribly.

California lawmakers apparently thought that certain persons who simply have an outstanding warrant against them are "fugitives" who should be prohibited from possessing firearms under federal law. But whereas the federal "fugitive from justice" *knows* that he or she is fleeing the state because of criminal proceedings, his California counterpart has no idea that there is an outstanding warrant issued for his arrest, because law enforcement can obtain an arrest warrant from a judge without giving any notice to the person to be arrested. Many Californians don't know that there is an outstanding warrant issued against them, much less that this means that they are now prohibited from owning and/or possessing firearms and

---

[121] 18 U.S.C. §§ 921 (a)(15), 922(g)(2).

[122] 27 C.F.R. § 478.11; *see also* 18 U.S.C. 921(a)(15); *see also* Letter from Robin A. Stark-Nutter, Section Chief, NICS Section of the Federal Bureau of Investigation, to CJIS Systems Officer and State Points of Contact (Feb. 15, 2017), *available at* https://www.documentcloud.org/documents/3493269-Fugitive-From-Justice-Guidance-State.html (last visited Oct. 3, 2020).

[123] *See United States v. Spillane*, 913 F.2d 1079 (4th Cir. 1990) (emphasis added); *see also United States v. Durcan*, 539 F.2d 29 (9th Cir.1976).

[124] *See United States v. Spillane*, 913 F.2d 1079 (4th Cir. 1990); *see also United States v. Durcan*, 539 F.2d 29 (9th Cir.1976).

[125] P.C. §§ 29800, 29805; AB 103, 2017-2018 Leg., Reg. Sess. (Cal. 2017), *available at* https://leginfo.legislature.ca.gov/faces/billCompareClient.xhtml?bill_id=201720180AB103 (last visited Oct. 3, 2020).

[126] 18 U.S.C. § 921 (a)(15), 922(g)(2).

ammunition. Subsequent amendments to California's restriction have since clarified that the individual must at least have knowledge of the outstanding warrant for the restriction to apply.[127]

A person charged for the crime of possessing a firearm when prohibited from doing so because of an outstanding warrant can get their charge dismissed if it is proven that he or she did not have knowledge of the outstanding warrant. But even if the case is dismissed, the defendant will have suffered the stressful experience of being pulled into the criminal justice system, defending himself, and paying thousands of dollars to hire a criminal defense attorney to make the affirmative defense for him. In other words, this is not a perfect cure to the "notice" problems generated by AB 103. Depending on the facts and circumstances of a case, it might be possible to file a due process violation claim against the government.

IX. DRUG ADDICTION FIREARM POSSESSION PROHIBITIONS

Illegal drug use may also result in firearm restrictions under federal and California law.[128] The rationale for these restrictions is that individuals who are addicted to narcotics "present a clear and present danger to society" because addicts are often forced to purchase drugs through criminal acts or corruption.[129]

A. Federal Restrictions for Drug Addiction and Use

Anyone who is considered an "unlawful user" of any "controlled substance"[130] is prohibited under federal law from possessing firearms. The "controlled substances" that fall under this prohibition do not just include narcotics, but also marijuana.[131]

The ATF has defined an "unlawful user" or an addict of a "controlled substance" as:

> A person who uses a controlled substance and has lost the power of self-control with reference to the use of controlled substance; and any person who is a current user of a controlled substance in a manner other than as prescribed by a licensed physician.[132]

Although it seems like this definition of "unlawful user" would exclude users of medical marijuana if it was prescribed to them by a licensed physician, the ATF has

---

[127] *See* SB 112 (2017) and SB 723 (2020); *see also* P.C. § 29851 (repealed starting on January 1, 2021).

[128] Although these drug addiction prohibitions rarely arise, the government might begin to prohibit people who have had prior drug convictions on their records under these restrictions because the Charleston Church Shooting suspect was purportedly addicted to a narcotic known as Suboxone.

[129] *People v. Washington*, 237 Cal. App. 2d 59, 66 (1965).

[130] The term "controlled substance" is defined in 21 U.S.C. section 802(6).

[131] 18 U.S.C. § 922(g)(3).

[132] 27 C.F.R. § 478.11.

expressly stated that users of medical marijuana are still considered to be "unlawful users of or addicted to controlled substances.[133] On September 21, 2011, the ATF issued an "Open Letter to All Federal Firearms Licensees" stating:

> [A]ny person who uses or is addicted to marijuana, regardless of whether his or her State has passed legislation authorizing marijuana use for medicinal purposes, is an unlawful user of or addicted to a controlled substance, and is prohibited by Federal law from possessing firearms or ammunition. Such persons should answer "yes" to question 11.e. on ATF Form 4473 . . . and you may not transfer firearms or ammunition to them. Further, if you are aware that the potential transferee is in possession of a card authorizing the possession and use of marijuana under State law, then you have "reasonable cause to believe" that the person is an unlawful user of a controlled substance. As such, you may not transfer firearms or ammunition to the person, even if the person answered "no" to question 11.e. on ATF Form 4473.[134]

Title 27 of the Code of Federal Regulations (C.F.R.) section 478.11 also guides the determination of whether someone is an "unlawful user" of a "controlled substance." Some courts have held that the government must show a defendant's "pattern, and recency, of drug use . . . or that the . . . use was sufficiently consistent, prolonged and close in time to . . . possession" of a firearm.[135] This can be as simple as using drugs while possessing a firearm.[136]

Although the Open Letter does not carry the force of the law, several courts have supported this view and the letter itself is indicative of how the government would prosecute these cases.[137] As such, users of medical marijuana should be aware that they are likely prohibited under federal law and that a federal firearms licensee cannot sell a firearm to an individual if they know or have reason to believe that they use medical marijuana. We have heard a number of stories where individuals have used a medical marijuana card as a second form of identification when attempting to purchases a firearm. These individuals are often upset when the dealer refuses to transfer or sell any firearms to them. But, as explained above, any person who uses marijuana for medical purposes is still prohibited for purposes of federal law.

---

[133] *Open Letter to All Federal Firearms Licensees*, U.S. DEPT. OF JUSTICE, BUREAU OF ALCOHOL, TOBACCO, FIREARMS AND EXPLOSIVES, http://www.atf.gov/files/press/releases/2011/09/092611-atf-open-letter-to-all-ffls-marijuana-for-medicinal-purposes.pdf (last visited Oct. 3, 2020).

[134] *Open Letter to All Federal Firearms Licensees*, U.S. DEPT. OF JUSTICE, BUREAU OF ALCOHOL, TOBACCO, FIREARMS AND EXPLOSIVES, http://www.atf.gov/files/press/releases/2011/09/092611-atf-open-letter-to-all-ffls-marijuana-for-medicinal-purposes.pdf (last visited Oct. 3, 2020).

[135] *United States v. Williams*, 216 F. Supp. 2d 568, 575 (E.D. Va. 2002) (internal quotations omitted).

[136] *United States v. Oleson*, 310 F.3d 1085, 1089-90 (8th Cir. 2002); *United States v. Herrera*, 313 F.3d 882, 885 (5th Cir. 2002).

[137] *See, e.g., Wilson v. Lynch*, 835F. 3d 1083 (9th Cir. 2016) (holding that banning gun sales to people who hold medical marijuana cards does not violate their Second Amendment rights); *see also United States v. Harvey*, 794 F. Supp. 2d 1103, 1105-06 (S.D. Cal. 2011) (providing that Schedule I drugs like marijuana cannot be lawfully prescribed because other federally defined prescription drug "schedules" intentionally omit Schedule I drugs). Several U.S. Supreme Court and California cases purportedly support this position.

Because of its sharp stance on medical marijuana users, it is also likely that the ATF would also consider any person who uses marijuana for recreational purposes as an "unlawful user" or an "addict" of a "controlled substance." This is especially important to note given the recent passage of Proposition 64 (i.e., the "Control, Regulate and Tax Adult Use of Marijuana Act"). Prop. 64, which was passed during the November 2016 election, legalizes the recreational use of marijuana in California for individuals who are 21 years old or older.[138] Any person who uses marijuana, even if they are doing so legally under Prop. 64, will still be considered an "unlawful user" or "addicted" to a "controlled substance" and will be prohibited from possessing firearms and ammunition under federal law.

B. California Restrictions for Drug Addiction

If you are considered addicted to narcotic drugs, you are also prohibited from possessing firearms under California law.[139] Narcotic drugs are specifically defined under the Cal. Health & Saf. Code and include opium and cocaine.[140] Marijuana is not included in the California law definition of narcotic drugs. Users, and even marijuana addicts, are thus not per se prohibited from owning or receiving firearms under California law.

Table 4.7

SUMMARY OF DRUG PROHIBITIONS	
CALIFORNIA LAW	**FEDERAL LAW**
If you are considered addicted to narcotic drugs, you are prohibited from possessing firearms. This does not include marijuana use.	If you are an "unlawful user" or "addict" of any "controlled substance," including marijuana, you are prohibited from possessing firearms.

---

[138] FULL TEXT OF PROPOSITION 64, OFFICE OF THE ATTORNEY GENERAL, *available at* https://www.oag.ca.gov/system/files/initiatives/pdfs/15-0103%20(Marijuana)_1.pdf (last visited Oct. 3, 2020). DOJ appears to be denying firearm purchases for people with recent drug-related convictions. It remains to be seen how DOJ knows a person is currently "addicted" to narcotics based on a past conviction. This is a recent development we are currently keeping an eye on for purposes of potential challenges.

[139] P.C. § 29800(a). It is illegal under California law to be in possession of a loaded, operable firearm and in possession of any amount of a substance "containing cocaine base, a substance containing cocaine, a substance containing heroin, a substance containing methamphetamine, a crystalline substance containing phencyclidine, a liquid substance containing phencyclidine, plant material containing phencyclidine, or a hand-rolled cigarette treated with phencyclidine . . . ." CAL. HEALTH & SAF. CODE § 11370.1(a). It is also illegal to be under the influence of certain controlled substances and be in the immediate personal possession of a loaded, operable firearm. CAL. HEALTH & SAF. CODE § 11550(e). For purposes of CAL. HEALTH & SAF. CODE section 11370.1(a), the firearm need only be "available for immediate offensive or defensive use." For section 11550(e), immediate personal possession includes the interior passenger compartment of a motor vehicle.

[140] CAL. HEALTH & SAF. CODE § 11019.

X. MENTAL HEALTH RELATED FIREARM RESTRICTIONS

Under California law, if a person is found to suffer from certain mental health conditions, they are also prohibited from owning and possessing firearms and deadly weapons.[141] "Deadly weapon," as used here and in Cal. Welf. & Inst. Code sections 8101, 8102, and 8103, means possessing or carrying any concealed weapon that is prohibited by P.C. section 16590 (*i.e.*, "generally prohibited weapons").[142] Law enforcement officers often believe the term "deadly weapon" includes all weapons (*e.g.*, bows, BB guns, knives) and ammunition, and incorrectly confiscate or charge the individual for violating the law as a result.

The availability of relief from mental health firearm restrictions depends on the nature of the mental health restriction. For example, individuals are prohibited from owning and possessing firearms and deadly weapons while they are admitted (either with or without their consent) to a facility to receive inpatient treatment and are deemed by the health professional primarily responsible for the patient's treatment as a danger to themselves or others, as specified in Cal. Welf. & Inst. Code sections 5150, 5250, or 5300.[143] There is no "inpatient" prohibition once they are discharged from the facility, but they may still be prohibited for any of the reasons below.[144]

My office continues to have an increased number of calls concerning mental health restrictions. These calls typically had to do with one of three issues: (1) posttraumatic stress disorder (commonly referred to as "PTSD"), (2) individuals voluntarily seeking, or who have sought in the past, the help of psychiatrists for issues like depression or anxiety, and (3) prescription medication to deal with a mental health issue like depression, anxiety, etc.

Unless you meet one of the criteria set forth below, you should *not* be considered prohibited from owning and possessing firearms under California or federal law for a mental health restriction. If you still do not know for certain whether you may lawfully own and possess firearms after you read the information below, you should file a "Personal Firearms Eligibility Check" (PFEC), which is discussed at the end of this chapter.

There are a lot of rumors and bad information surrounding mental health restrictions. Most of these are based on misstatements of the law, bad reporting and/or investigation by the media, and internet rumors or the like. Make certain that you obtain information from reputable sources, not just what "some guy" heard at his local firearm dealer's store.

---

[141] CAL. WELF. & INST. CODE §§ 8100, 8103.

[142] CAL. WELF. & INST. CODE § 8100(e). "Generally prohibited weapons" are listed and discussed in Chapter 10.

[143] CAL. WELF. & INST. CODE § 8100(a). "Danger to self," as used in subdivision (a), means one who has made a serious threat of, or attempted, suicide with the use of a firearm or other deadly weapon. CAL. WELF. & INST. CODE § 8100(f).

[144] CAL. WELF. & INST. CODE § 8100(a).

A. Federal Mental Health Restrictions

Federal law prohibits those "adjudicated as a mental defective or who ha[ve] been committed to a mental institution" from owning or possessing firearms for life.[145] In order to determine whether these prohibitions apply to you, you must first understand the meaning of "adjudicated as a mental defective" and "committed to a mental institution."

No federal statute defines "adjudicated as a mental defective" or "committed to a mental institution." Meanwhile, the Code of Federal Regulations provides that an individual is adjudicated as a mental defective if a court, board, commission, or other lawful authority determines that, as a result of marked subnormal intelligence, mental illness, incompetency, condition, or disease, the individual is either a danger to him or herself or to others or lacks the mental capacity to contract or manage his or her own affairs.[146] The Code of Federal Regulations definition also includes individuals found insane by a court in a criminal case as well as individuals found incompetent to stand trial or found not guilty by reason of lack of mental responsibility under articles 50a and 72b of the Uniform Code of Military Justice, 10 U.S.C. sections 850a, 876b.[147]

The Code of Federal Regulations defines "committed to a mental institution" as:

> A formal commitment of a person to a mental institution by a court, board, commission, or other lawful authority. The term includes a commitment to a mental institution involuntarily. The term includes commitment for mental defectiveness or mental illness. It also includes commitments for other reasons, such as for drug use. The term does not include a person in a mental institution for observation or a voluntary admission to a mental institution.[148]

---

[145] 18 U.S.C. § 922(g)(4).
[146] 27 C.F.R. § 478.11.
[147] 27 C.F.R. § 478.11. In 2015, ATF proposed a new regulation that expands the scope of the statutory term "adjudicated as a mental defective." This regulation expands the language relating to findings of insanity by a court and persons incompetent to stand trial to include those persons found not guilty by reason of insanity, mental disease or defect, or lack of mental responsibility by a court in a criminal case; those found guilty but mentally ill by a court in a criminal case in a jurisdiction that provides for such a finding; and those persons found incompetent to stand trial by a court in a criminal case. The term does not include any person adjudicated by a department or agency of the Federal Government, if any of the conditions of section 101(c)(1) of the NICS Improvement Amendments Act of 2007 apply; or any person who has been adjudicated and subsequently received relief under 18 U.S.C. section 925(c) or under a program authorized by 18 U.S.C. section 101(c)(2) or section 105(a) of the NICS Improvement Amendments Act of 2007. See Amended Definition of "Adjudicated as a Mental Defective" and "Committed to a Mental Institution," 79 Fed. Reg. 774 (proposed Jan. 3, 2014) (to be codified at 27 C.F.R. pt. 478). As of the date of publication, the ATF has yet to finalize this regulation. To keep up to date with information on this regulation, visit www.crpa.org.
[148] 27 C.F.R. § 478.11. This definition is subject to change just like "adjudicated as a mental defective." The proposed definition states: a formal commitment of a person to a mental institution by a court, board, commission, or other lawful authority. The term includes an involuntary commitment to a mental institution for inpatient or outpatient treatment. The term includes an involuntary commitment for mental defectiveness, i.e., mental illness, to a mental institution. It also includes a commitment to a mental institution for other reasons, such as for drug use. The term does not include a person in a mental institution solely for observation or evaluation, a voluntary admission to a mental institution, or voluntary outpatient treatment. The term shall not include any person so committed by a

1. California Commitments Resulting in Federal Restrictions

Under federal law, someone who has been committed to a mental health institution for mental defectiveness, illness, or drug use, is prohibited for life from owning and possessing firearms. Whether someone has been "committed to a mental health institution" is a question of federal law and it is often guided by state law.[149] A commitment under Cal. Welf. & Inst. Code section 5150 will not result in a federal firearm restriction, but according to DOJ and the FBI, a Cal. Welf. & Inst. Code section 5250 commitment does. While California allows a one-time application with the court to restore firearm rights for an intensive treatment commitment,[150] this has no effect on the *federal* restriction.

B. Dangerous Inpatients

Individuals who are admitted to a facility and are receiving inpatient treatment and, in the opinion of the attending health professional who is primarily responsible for their treatment of a mental disorder, who are a danger to themselves or to others, as specified by Cal. Welf. & Inst. Code section 5150, 5250, or 5300, are prohibited from possessing, having under their control, purchasing, receiving, or attempting to purchase or receive any firearms or deadly weapons, even though they have consented to the treatment.[151] But, they are not subject to *this* prohibition after they have been discharged from the facility.[152] They may still be prohibited for another reason (discussed below).

C. Communicating Threats to a Psychotherapist

If an individual communicates "a serious threat of physical violence against a reasonably identifiable victim or victims" to a licensed psychotherapist, they are prohibited form possessing firearms and deadly weapons for a period of five years starting from the date the psychotherapist reports the threat to a local law enforcement agency.[153]

DOJ is required to mail a notice of the restriction to the restricted person who may thereafter request a hearing to restore his or her firearm rights during the restriction period.[154] Upon petition to the court, the state has the burden of showing

---

department or agency of the Federal Government, if any of the conditions of section 101(c)(1) of the NICS Improvement Act of 2007 apply, or any person who has received relief from disabilities under a program authorized by section 101(c)(2) or section 105(a) of that Act or under 18 U.S.C. section 925(c). But, as of the date of publication, the ATF has yet to finalize this regulation.

[149] *United States v. Whiton*, 48 F.3d 356, 358 (8th Cir. 1995).
[150] CAL. WELF. & INST. CODE § 8103(g)(4).
[151] CAL. WELF. & INST. CODE § 8100(a).
[152] CAL. WELF. & INST. CODE § 8100(a).
[153] CAL. WELF. & INST. CODE § 8100(b)(1).
[154] CAL. WELF. & INST. CODE § 8100(b)(2).

that the person would not be likely to use firearms in a safe and lawful manner. If the state fails to make such a showing, the five-year prohibition will not apply.[155]

D. Mental Disorders, Illnesses, or Disordered Sex Offenders

Individuals who "ha[ve] been adjudicated by a court of any state . . . to be a danger to others . . . [because] of a mental disorder or mental illness, or who ha[ve] been adjudicated to be a mentally disordered sex offender" are prohibited from possessing, purchasing, or attempting to purchase or receive, or having in his or her possession firearms or deadly weapons.[156] Firearm rights may be restored, however, if the same court that adjudicated the mental illness or disorder issues a certificate, either at or after that person's release from treatment, stating the person is now safe to possess a firearm or any other deadly weapon.[157]

This rights restoration mechanism is only available as long as the person has not been adjudicated (again) to be a danger to others as a result of a mental disorder or illness before asking for this certificate.[158]

E. Not Guilty by Reason of Insanity

Individuals found not guilty of any crime by reason of insanity[159] cannot purchase or receive, or attempt to purchase or receive, or have under their control any firearm or other deadly weapon.[160] Certain serious offenses have a lifetime firearm restriction without any available relief.[161] For all other less serious convictions where individuals are found not guilty by reason of insanity, firearm rights may be restored if the court finds they have recovered their sanity.[162]

F. Incompetent to Stand Trial

Individuals found to be mentally incompetent to stand trial[163] are likewise prohibited from purchasing or possessing firearms unless their competence to stand trial is restored by the committing court.[164]

---

[155] CAL. WELF. & INST. CODE § 8100(b)(3).
[156] CAL. WELF. & INST. CODE § 8103(a)(1).
[157] CAL. WELF. & INST. CODE § 8103(a)(1).
[158] CAL. WELF. & INST. CODE § 8103(a)(1).
[159] Pursuant to P.C. section 1026 or any other state or the U.S.
[160] CAL. WELF. & INST. CODE § 8103(b)-(c); see also P.C. § 1026.
[161] CAL. WELF. & INST. CODE § 8103(b)(1). Refer directly to Cal. Welf. & Inst. Code section 8103(b)(1) for a list of offenses.
[162] CAL. WELF. & INST. CODE § 8103(c)(1). See P.C. section 1026.2 for recovering sanity.
[163] Pursuant to P.C. section 1370 or 1370.1 or the law of any other state or the U.S.
[164] CAL. WELF. & INST. CODE § 8103(d)(1).

G. Individuals Under Conservatorship

Individuals placed under conservatorship because they are gravely disabled by a mental disorder or chronic alcoholism cannot possess a firearm or deadly weapon while under the conservatorship if, at the time the conservatorship was ordered, the court found that possession of a firearm or deadly weapon by the individual would present a danger to the individual or others.

In this situation, courts must notify the individual placed under conservatorship of the firearm restriction. The firearm restriction can last the duration of the conservatorship or be lifted by the court if it finds that the individual no longer presents a danger to the individual or others.[165]

H. Dangerous or Gravely Disabled Persons

Individuals taken into custody under Cal. Welf. & Inst. Code section 5150 because they are a danger to themselves or others, assessed under Cal. Welf. & Inst. Code section 5151, are admitted to a designated facility and may not possess a firearm or deadly weapon for five years after they are released from the facility.[166] A "5150 commitment" usually occurs after a peace officer or medical health care professional determines the individual is a danger to themselves or others. Often, calls to a suicide hotline or calls by concerned family members prompt law enforcement to investigate and bring individuals in on a "5150 commitment."

Under current California law, the facility is required to notify the individual that he or she is "prohibited from owning, possessing, controlling, receiving, or purchasing any firearm for a period of five years" before or at the time of discharge from the facility.[167] But beginning, if the individual has been admitted to a facility on a 5150 hold one or more times within a period of one year preceding the most recent admittance, the facility is required to notify the individual that he or she is "prohibited from owning, possessing, controlling, receiving, or purchasing any firearm" for life.[168] Failure by the facility, however, to provide notice will not necessarily prevent prosecution of the individual for possessing firearms.

Individuals must also be notified of their right to request a hearing to restore their firearm rights.[169]

People often think they have a limited time to request a hearing to restore firearm rights. But failure to request a hearing upon discharge does not preclude the individual from requesting one later. Current California law specifically states that a person prohibited as a result of a 5150 commitment may make a "single request

---

[165] CAL. WELF. & INST. CODE § 8103(e).

[166] CAL. WELF. & INST. CODE § 8103(f)(1).

[167] CAL. WELF. & INST. CODE § 8103(f)(3).

[168] CAL. WELF. & INST. CODE § 8103(f)(3).

[169] CAL. WELF. & INST. CODE § 8103(f)(3). The procedure for restoring firearm rights after a 5150 commitment is governed by Cal. Welf. & Inst. Code section 8103(f)(4)-(9).

for a hearing *at any time* during the five-year period."[170] And, individuals subject to a lifetime firearm prohibition as a result of more than one 5150 commitment in a given year, are entitled to file subsequent petitions every five years.[171]

I. Those Committed to Intensive Treatment

Individuals that undergo intensive treatment under Cal. Welf. & Inst. Code sections 5250, 5260, or 5270.15 cannot possess any firearm or deadly weapon for five years.[172] Lifting this state restriction is similar to restoring firearm rights for someone with a 5150 commitment. But these restrictions require the *individual* to prove that the firearm(s) will be used in a safe and lawful manner.[173] What's more, they may only make a one-time application with the court to restore firearm rights.[174]

---

[170] CAL. WELF. & INST. CODE § 8103(f)(4) (emphasis added).
[171] CAL. WELF. & INST. CODE § 8103(f)(10).
[172] CAL. WELF. & INST. CODE § 8103(g)(1). Restoring rights for state restrictions is governed by Cal. Welf. & Inst. Code section 8103(g)(3)-(4). You are also subject to a federal lifetime ban.
[173] CAL. WELF. & INST. CODE § 8103(g)(4).
[174] CAL. WELF. & INST. CODE § 8103(g)(4).

Table 4.8

MENTAL HEALTH RESTRICTIONS	
FIVE-YEAR RESTRICTION	**RESTRICTION UNTIL RIGHTS ARE RESTORED BY THE COURT**
Under California law, an individual is prohibited from purchasing and possessing firearms and dangerous weapons for a five-year period under any of the following situations: (1) The individual communicates "a serious threat of physical violence against a reasonably identifiable" victim(s) to a licensed psychotherapist; *or* (2) The individual is detained under Cal. Welf. & Inst. Code 5150, receives a mental evaluation, and is admitted to a designated facility. The five-year prohibition starts after the individual is released from such facility; *or* (3) The individual undergoes intensive treatment under Cal. Welf. & Inst. Code sections 5250, 5260, or 5270.5.	Under California law, an individual is prohibited from purchasing and possessing firearms and dangerous weapons until his or her rights are restored by a court under any of the following situations: (1) The individual is adjudicated by a court to be a danger to others because of a mental disorder or illness, or if the individual is adjudicated a mentally disordered sex offender; *or* (2) The individual is found not guilty of any crime by reason of insanity for certain offenses; *or* (3) The individual is found mentally incompetent to stand trial; *or* (4) The individual is placed under conservatorship because he or she is gravely disabled by a mental disorder or chronic alcoholism and the court took his or her firearm rights away when placed under conservatorship. (5) The individual has more than one 5150 commitment within a one-year period. This results in a lifetime firearm prohibition unless a court grants the individual's request for an order permitting him or her to own, possess, control, receive, or purchase a firearm.

XI. RESTRAINING ORDERS AND FIREARM POSSESSION RESTRICTIONS

A. Federal Domestic Violence Restraining Orders

Unlike the broad California firearm restrictions for restraining orders, discussed below, the federal restrictions are very narrow. Under federal law, individuals are prohibited from receiving and possessing firearms if they are subject to a court order that:

(1) Was issued after a hearing where they received actual notice, and had an opportunity to participate; *and*

(2) Restrains them from harassing, stalking, or threatening an intimate partner or child of such intimate partner or person, or engaging in other conduct that would put an intimate partner in reasonable fear of bodily injury to the partner or the child; *and*

(3) Either includes a finding that they represent a credible threat to the physical safety of an intimate partner or child; or by its terms specifically prohibits the use, attempted use, *or* threatened use of physical force that would reasonably be expected to cause bodily injury against the intimate partner or child.[175]

This means that, unlike California's restraining order restrictions that can take effect without notice of the hearing (*i.e.*, a temporary restraining order or emergency protective order), the federal restriction requires notice and an opportunity to participate.[176] Also, to trigger the federal restriction the specific type of conduct in (2) must be prohibited.

A court has discretion in issuing a restraining order to determine which types of conduct the restrained person should not do. The court can order a person not to contact or come within (for example) 100 yards of the protected individual and their residence. This narrow type of order should not result in a federal restriction. But, in a lot of cases, especially those relating to domestic violence, courts "rubber stamp" probation terms that result in a federal firearm restriction.

---

[175] 18 U.S.C. § 922(g)(8).

[176] 18 U.S.C. § 922(g)(8)(A). For example, a protective order signed without either notice of a hearing and the ability to present evidence is not considered one where the defendant received actual notice. Accordingly, it is not within the scope of 18 U.S.C. section 922(g)(8). *United States v. Spruill*, 292 F.3d 207, 215-20 (5th Cir. 2002). Because the defendant must "receive actual notice," some temporary restraining order issued under California law would not result in a federal restriction if they are issued ex parte, *i.e.*, they can be issued without giving the defendant notice or a hearing. *See, e.g.*, CAL. CIV. PROC. CODE § 527.6 (civil harassment protective orders), 527.8 (workplace violence protective orders), 527.85 (private postsecondary educational institution protective orders); CAL. PENAL CODE § 646.91 (emergency protective orders obtained ex parte enjoining specified behavior); CAL. FAM. CODE § 6218(c) (domestic violence protective orders); CAL. WELF. & INST. CODE § 15657.03(c) (elder and dependent adult abuse protective orders).

B. California Law Restrictions

Under California law, if you are subject to a restraining order, temporary restraining order, or court order under any of the following code sections, you are prohibited from owning, purchasing, receiving, possessing, or attempting to purchase and receive firearms:

(1) California Code of Civil Procedure (Cal. Civ. Proc. Code) section 527.6 (civil harassment temporary restraining order or injunction);[177] *or*

(2) Cal. Civ. Proc. Code section 527.8 (employers seeking a temporary restraining order or an injunction for an employee who has suffered unlawful violence or credible threat of violence); *or*

(3) Cal. Civ. Proc. Code section 527.85 (schools seeking temporary restraining orders or injunctions for students who have suffered off-campus credible threats of violence); *or*

(4) California Family Code (Cal. Fam. Code) section 6218 (protective orders issued in accordance with Cal. Fam. Code sections 6320, 6321, and 6322); *or*

(5) P.C. sections 136.2[178] and 646.91 (court orders against victim and/or witness intimidation and orders protecting against stalking); *or*

(6) Cal. Welf. & Inst. Code section 15657.03 (protective order in response to elder or dependent adult abuse);[179] *or*

(7) Cal. Welf. & Inst. Code section 213.5, 304, 362.4, and 726.5 (juvenile protective orders);[180] *or*

---

[177] When a court issues a temporary civil harassment restraining order, the court may also issue, on a showing of good cause, a restraining order instructing the restrained person to stay away and refrain from taking or harming an animal owned, possessed, leased, kept, held by, or that resides in the house of the person protected by the restraining order. CAL. CIV. PROC. CODE § 527.6 Any person subject to this order is prohibited from owning and possessing firearms and ammunition. CAL. CIV. PROC. CODE § 527.6.

[178] Under P.C. section 136.2, a court must consider issuing a protective order, which can last for up to ten years, in any case in which a criminal defendant has been convicted of a crime involving "domestic violence" as defined in P.C. section 13700 or in Cal. Fam. Code 6211; a violation of P.C. sections 261, 261.5, or 262; or any other crime that requires the defendant register under P.C. section 290(c). P.C. § 136.2(i)(1). "Domestic violence," for the purposes of this code section, has two different meanings "abuse committed against an adult or minor who is a spouse, former spouse, cohabitant, former cohabitant, or person with whom the suspect had a child or is having or has had a dating or engagement relationship" or "abuse perpetuated against . . . a spouse or former spouse; a cohabitant or former cohabitant, as defined in [Cal Fam. Code section 6209]; a person with whom the respondent has had a child, where the presumption applies that the male is the father of the child of the female parent under the Uniform Parentage Act (Part 3 (commencing with Section 7600) of Division 12); a child of a party or a child who is subject to an action under the Uniform Parentage Act, where the presumption applies that the male parent is the father of the child to be protected; [and] any other person related by consanguinity or affinity within the second degree. P.C. § 13700; CAL. FAM. CODE § 6211.

[179] P.C. § 29825(a)-(b).

[180] There seems to be some ambiguity as to whether a juvenile protective order issued under Cal. Welf. & Inst. Code section 213.5 results in a firearm prohibition. This is because Cal. Welf. & Inst. Code section 213.5 does not explicitly provide that a person who is subject to a restraining order under that code section is prohibited from owning and possessing firearms. *See* CAL. WELF. & INST. CODE § 213.5. Despite this ambiguity, however, the Judicial Council form for juvenile protective orders issued under section 215.3 still contains boiler plate language that states that any person subject to a juvenile protective order – even those issued under section 213.5 – is prohibited

(8) P.C. section 18205 ("gun violence restraining orders" and, effective Jan. 1, 2021, a similar order issued by an out-of-state jurisdiction[181]); or

(9) Any other valid order issued by an out-of-state jurisdiction that is similar or equivalent to a temporary restraining order, injunction, or protective order that includes a prohibition from owning or possessing a firearm.[182]

In instances where a temporary restraining order is issued, and regardless of whether the court ultimately issues a permanent restraining order, you are prohibited from possessing firearms until the temporary order ends or expires. You are also prohibited from possessing ammunition clips, magazines, and the like (as discussed in this Chapter). If you knowingly violate this term of the restraining order, you can be held criminally liable.[183]

Individuals served with a restraining order are required to sell their firearms and ammunition, store them with an FFL, or turn them in to law enforcement.[184] Generally, this must be done within 24 hours of being served with the restraining order[185] (or it must be done *immediately* if requested by law enforcement after service of a restraining order under Cal. Fam. Code section 6218 or a temporary "gun violence restraining order").[186] Regardless of which option the restrained person chooses to surrender the firearm, he or she must file a receipt with the court within 48 hours of being served with the restraining order that proves the firearms and ammunition were either surrendered, sold, or transferred to an FFL for storage.[187] A copy of this receipt must also be filed within 48 hours with the law enforcement agency that served the restraining order if a "gun violence restraining order" is at issue.[188]

In addition, note that in certain cases, the court may grant exemptions from the relinquishment requirement of most of the previously-mentioned restraining orders,[189] for a particular firearm. The mechanism to obtain these exemptions is explained in Coldaw Publishing's next book, which will be on firearm surrender, seizure, and return.

---

from owning and possessing firearms. *See* Restraining Order-Juvenile (Form JV-255), *available at* http://www.courts.ca.gov/documents/jv255.pdf (last visited Oct. 3, 2020). As such, if you receive a juvenile protective order, you should play it on the safe side and consider yourself to be prohibited for the duration of the protective order.

[181] The out-of-state order "must be issued upon a showing by clear and convincing evidence that the person poses a significant danger of causing personal injury to themselves or another because of owning or possessing a firearm or ammunition." P.C. § 18205(b) (effective Jan. 1, 2021).

[182] P.C. § 29825.

[183] P.C. §§ 29825(a)-(b), 18205.

[184] P.C. § 29825(d). These requirements and their exceptions are specifically discussed in Coldaw Publishing's upcoming book, which will be on firearm surrender, seizure and return.

[185] *See* Cal. Civ. Proc. Code § 527.9(a); *see also* Cal. Fam. Code § 6389(c)(2); *see also* P.C. §§ 18120(b)(2), 29825(d).

[186] *See* Cal. Fam. Code § 6389(c)(2); *see also* P.C. § 18120(b)(2).

[187] Cal. Civ. Proc. Code § 527.9(b); Cal. Fam. Code § 6389(c)(2); P.C. §§ 18120(b)(2), 29825(d).

[188] P.C. § 18120(b)(2).

[189] Cal. Civ. Proc. Code § 527.9(f); Cal. Fam. Code § 6389(h). This exemption does not exist for "gun violence restraining orders."

1. "Gun Violence Restraining Orders"[190]

If you are subject to a "gun violence restraining order" ("GVRO"), you are prohibited from having in your custody or control, owning, purchasing, possessing, or receiving firearms,[191] ammunition,[192] or magazines[193] while the restraining order is in effect.[194]

GVROs were created by AB 1014,[195] which was passed by the California Legislature in 2014 in response to the Isla Vista shootings in Santa Barbara, California. Law enforcement officers, "immediate family members,"[196] employers, coworkers[197], and employees or teachers[198] of a secondary or postsecondary school attended by the subject in the last six months may seek a temporary or permanent GVRO to to prevent a person, whom they believe is a danger to themselves or another, from owning and possessing firearms and ammunition.[199] If granted, a temporary GVRO can last for up to 21 days and can be extended for up to five years after notice and a hearing.[200]

As a practical matter, allowing all of these people to seek a GVRO leaves the process open to rampant abuse. For example, a disgruntled roommate could seek a

---

[190] This section will only cover the "gun violence restraining order" insofar as it relates to firearm restrictions. For a more detailed analysis of "gun violence restraining orders," please visit www.CalGunLawsBook.com.

[191] The term "firearm" for purposes of GVROs means "a device, designed to be used as a weapon, from which is expelled through a barrel, a projectile by the force of an explosion or other form of combustion." P.C. § 16520(a). The term does not seem to include frames or receivers. See P.C. § 16520(b). But, this was likely an oversight by the California Legislature. If you are subject to a GVRO, you should err on the side of caution and remove any frames or receivers from your immediate possession and control until you are no longer subject to the restraining order.

[192] For the purposes of GVROs, the term "ammunition" is not defined. See P.C. §§ 16150, 18120. Therefore, it is hard to tell whether the term "ammunition" would also include bullets, cartridges, magazines, clips, speed loaders, autoloaders. But, if you are subject to a GVRO, I strongly suggest you err on the side of caution and also remove all of these items from your immediate possession and control until you are no longer subject to the restraining order.

[193] As that term is defined in P.C. § 16890. P.C. § 18100(b).

[194] P.C. § 18120(a). In 2019, California adopted AB 164, which prohibits persons subject to a restraining order, temporary or otherwise, issued in any out-of-state jurisdiction from possessing firearms or ammunition. See AB 164, 2019-2020, Leg. Counsel's Digest (Cal. 2019) available at https://leginfo.legislature.ca.gov/faces/billNavClient.xhtml?bill_id=201920200AB164 (last visited Oct. 3, 2020).

[195] See AB 1014, 2013-2014, Leg. Counsel's Digest (Cal. 2014) available at https://leginfo.legislature.ca.gov/faces/billNavClient.xhtml?bill_id=201320140AB1014# (last visited Oct. 3, 2020).

[196] An "immediate family member" is defined as "any spouse, whether by marriage or not, domestic partner, parent, child, any person related by consanguinity or affinity within the second degree, or any other person who regularly resides in the household, or who, within the prior six months, regularly resided in the household."P.C. § 422.4(b)(3). nder this definition, not only could your spouse, parents, or children request a GVRO, but also your roommates, long-term house guests, and even your in-laws.

[197] Coworkers must have substantial and regular interactions with the person and approval of their employer.

[198] The employee or teacher must have approval of a school administrator or a school administration staff member with a supervisorial role. P.C. §§ 18150, 18170, 1819.

[199] P.C. §§ 18150, 18170, 1819. During the first two years of its existence, the GVRO has been used sparingly; from 2016 to 2018, California courts issued fewer than 200 GVROs. In response, supporters like Los Angeles City Attorney Mike Feuer are cur- rently trying to increase the usage of GVROs. See Marisa Gerber, 2016 State Law that Could Curb Gun Violence Is Rarely Invoked, L.A. Times (Sept. 19, 2018), available at http://www.latimes.com/local/lanow/la-me-gun-violence- restraining-order-law-20180919-story.html (last visited Oct. 3, 2020).

[200] P.C. § 18175. Note that a "temporary emergency gun violence restraining order" generally lasts only 21 days. Courts automatically hold a hearing within 21 days from the expiration of the 21-day period to determine if an extended GVRO should be issued after notice and hearing. P.C. § 18148.

GVRO against you as a form of retaliation, or an ex-wife could potentially request the order to gain an advantage in another lawsuit.

The potential for abuse is exacerbated by the fact that the evidentiary standard for obtaining a temporary GVRO is very low.[201] In fact, under this law, a court can issue an emergency GVRO to a law enforcement officer if it simply finds that there is a reasonable cause to believe that an individual will cause personal injury to himself, herself, or to another, and that there are no other less restrictive alternatives available.[202] Similarly, a court can also issue a temporary GVRO to an "immediate family member," employer, coworker, or employee or teacher of a secondary or postsecondary school that the subject attended within the last six months if it finds that there is a *substantial likelihood*[203] that the individual will cause personal injury to himself, herself, or to another, and that there are no other less restrictive alternatives available.[204]

To make matters worse, a court can issue a temporary GVRO without providing prior notice or a hearing to the individual, and without providing them with a mental health or medical evaluation to ensure that he or she is actually a danger to himself or herself, or to another. And, temporary emergency GVROs can be both requested and issued orally,[205] and courts will compulsorily hold a hearing after the expiration of a temporary GVRO to determine if a more permanent GVRO should be issued after notice and hearing.[206]

Given these issues, the GVRO process can easily be abused by law enforcement officers,[207] "immediate family members," employers, coworkers, or employees or teachers of a secondary or postsecondary school that the subject attended within the last six months to temporarily deprive a person of the right to own and possess firearms and ammunition.

That said, California law does make it illegal to file a frivolous request for a GVRO. Specifically, under this bill, it is a misdemeanor for a person to file a petition for a "gun violence restraining order" knowing that the information in the petition is false, or if the petition was filed with the intent to harass.[208] If you believe

---

[201] *See* P.C. §§ 18125(a), 18150(b), 18155(b), 18175(a)-(b).

[202] P.C. § 18125(a).

[203] The evidentiary standard for a "substantial likelihood" is never defined, which makes it unclear as to what exactly this standard would be.

[204] P.C. § 18150(b).

[205] P.C. §§ 18140, 18145. AB 2526 requires officers to sign a declaration under penalty of perjury reciting the oral statements provided to the court and memorialize the order on paper and serve the restrained person if they can reasonably be located. *See* AB 2526, 2017-2018 Leg., Reg. Sess. (Cal. 2018), *available at* https://leginfo.legislature.ca.gov/faces/billCompareClient.xhtml?bill_id=201720180AB2526 (last visited Oct. 3, 2019).

[206] P.C. § 18148.

207 Assembly Bill 339 (2019) presumably seeks to curb some of that abuse by requiring municipal police departments and county sheriff's departments, the Department of the California Highway Patrol, and the University of California and California State University Police Departments to develop and adopt written policies and standards regarding the use of GVROs. *See* AB 339, 2019-2020, Leg. Counsel's Digest (Cal. 2019) *available at* https://leginfo.legislature.ca.gov/faces/billCompareClient.xhtml?bill_id=201920200AB339 (last visited Oct. 6, 2019).

[208] P.C. § 18200(b).

that someone has frivolously requested a GVRO against you, you should immediately contact an attorney experienced in firearms law.[209]

Table 4.9

RESTRAINING ORDER RESTRICTIONS
FEDERAL LAW
If you are subject to a court order that meets the requirements listed in subsection (A) above, you are prohibited from receiving and possessing firearms for the duration of the order.
CALIFORNIA LAW
If you are subject to a restraining order, temporary restraining order, or court order under any of the code sections listed in subsection (B) above, you are prohibited from owning, purchasing, receiving, or possessing firearms while you are subject to the restraining order (as well as ammunition or magazines if you are subject to a GVRO).
Remember: If you are served with a restraining order, you are required to sell or store your firearms with an FFL, or turn them in to law enforcement.

2. **Voluntary Surrender of Firearm Rights for Individuals Facing GVRO**

In 2019, California adopted AB 1493, which, allows those individuals facing a GVRO to file a form with the court relinquishing their firearm rights for the duration specified on the petition, or if not stated, for one year from the date of the proposed hearing on the GVRO.[210] If that form is filed, then the court shall issue the GVRO without the individual having to appear at any hearing.[211] While there does not appear to be any advantage in filing this form, one possible reason would be to avoid having to make an appearance in court. Depending on the individual, this could be highly preferable to making an appearance. In any event, it is strongly encouraged that you seek assistance of counsel before filing such as this form.

---

[209] If you would like to learn more about GVROs, you can purchase an informational booklet on the topic from the California Rifle & Pistol Association at www.crpa.org.

[210] P.C. § 18175(d)(1).

[211] P.C. § 18175(d)(1). All firearms, ammunition, and magazines must be surrendered within 48 hours of filing the form relinquishing firearm rights. See P.C. § 18175(d)(3).

XII. EXCEPTIONS FOR PROHIBITED PERSONS POSSESSING FIREARMS

A. Self-Defense

If you are subject to one of the prohibitions discussed above, you may be able to possess a firearm for self-defense or defense of others under very limited circumstances. Specifically, if you are subject to a prohibition under federal law (or a prohibition that falls under both California and federal law), then you may be able to possess a firearm without violating 18 U.S.C. section 922(g) if you are:

(1) Are under an unlawful and present threat of death or serious bodily injury; *and*

(2) Did not recklessly place yourself in a situation where you would be forced to engage in criminal conduct; *and*

(3) Had no reasonable legal alterative to possessing the firearm or avoiding the threatened harm; *and*

(4) Can show that there was a direct causal relationship between the criminal action and the avoidance of the threatened harm.[212]

On the other hand, if you are subject to a prohibition under California law, you may be able to possess a firearm in self-defense or defense of others without violating P.C. section 29800 when:

(1) You "reasonably believe" you or someone else was "in *imminent* danger of suffering great bodily injury"; *and*

(2) You reasonably believe that the immediate use of force was necessary to defend against that danger; *and*

(3) *A firearm must have become available to you without planning or preparation on your part; and*

(4) You only possess the firearm temporarily, meaning no longer than what was necessary or reasonably appeared to be necessary for self-defense; *and*

(5) There are no other means of avoiding the danger or injury; *and*

(6) Using the firearm was reasonable under the circumstances.[213]

---

[212] *See United States v. Mooney*, 497 F.3d 397, 406 (4th Cir. 2007); *see also United States v. Leahy*, 437 F.3d 401, 409 (1st Cir. 2007) (*citing Dixon v. United States*, 548 U.S. 1, 4 n.2 (2006)); *United States v. Deleveaux*, 205 F.3d 1292, 1297 (11th Cir. 2000); *United States v. Gomez*, 92 F.3d 770, 774-75 (9th Cir. 1996); *United States v. Paolello*, 951 F.2d 537, 540–41 (3d Cir. 1991), *holding modified by Government of Virgin Islands v. Lewis*, 54 V.I. 882, 620 F.3d 359 (3d Cir. 2010); *United States v. Vigil*, 743 F.2d 751, 756 (10th Cir. 1984); *United States v. Panter*, 688 F.2d 268, 271 (5th Cir. 1982); *United States. v. Agard*, 605 F.2d 665, 667 (2d Cir. 1979).

[213] *See* CALCRIM No. 2514 (emphasis added).

The California Supreme Court created this limited defense to P.C. section 29800 in *People v. King*. In that case, Mr. King, a person prohibited from possessing firearms, was attending a birthday party when a fight broke out between an uninvited guest and another person at the party.[214] As the two men fought outside the apartment, several of the uninvited guest's friends swarmed the balcony to break up the fight. Their efforts were unsuccessful.[215] As the fighting raged on, the apartment owner shut the balcony door so that the remaining people inside the apartment would be somewhat safe.[216] Angered by the fact that they were locked out of the apartment, the people on the balcony began beating on the door and threatening to break it open.[217] Then, one of the men on the balcony grabbed a double hibachi grill and threw it through a window into the dining area of the apartment where Mr. King and his paraplegic friend were seated.[218] The grill struck Mr. King and showered glass over him and his paraplegic friend, and shards of the glass got stuck in Mr. King's eye.[219]

After washing the glass out of his eyes, Mr. King noticed that his disabled friend was having difficulty fleeing the area because the wheels of his wheelchair had locked up.[220] So, Mr. King helped wheel his friend into a neighboring bedroom where many of the partygoers were hiding and attempting to call the police.[221] Mr. King then went outside to confront the men.[222]

As Mr. King was stepping outside, one of the partygoers hiding inside the apartment pulled out a handgun from her purse and handed to Mr. King.[223] He then stepped outside and fired several shots into the air to disperse the crowd.[224] Although the men fighting outside initially retreated, they then regrouped and again began to run toward the apartment door.[225] Mr. King then fired shots over their heads, wounding one of the men out on the balcony.[226] After the police arrived, Mr. King was arrested and charged with two counts of assault with a deadly weapon, as well as being a felon in possession of a firearm.[227]

In analyzing Mr. King's case, the California Supreme Court noted that the legislature did not intend to deny prohibited persons the right to use a firearm to

---

[214] *People v. King*, 22 Cal. 3d 12, 16 (1978).
[215] *People v. King*, 22 Cal. 3d 12, 16-17 (1978).
[216] *People v. King*, 22 Cal. 3d 12, 16-17 (1978).
[217] *People v. King*, 22 Cal. 3d 12, 16-17 (1978).
[218] *People v. King*, 22 Cal. 3d 12, 18 (1978).
[219] *People v. King*, 22 Cal. 3d 12, 18 (1978).
[220] *People v. King*, 22 Cal. 3d 12, 18 (1978).
[221] *People v. King*, 22 Cal. 3d 12, 18 (1978).
[222] *People v. King*, 22 Cal. 3d 12, 18 (1978).
[223] *People v. King*, 22 Cal. 3d 12, 18 (1978).
[224] *People v. King*, 22 Cal. 3d 12, 18 (1978).
[225] *People v. King*, 22 Cal. 3d 12, 18 (1978).
[226] *People v. King*, 22 Cal. 3d 12, 18 (1978).
[227] *People v. King*, 22 Cal. 3d 12, 18-19 (1978).

defend themselves or others in emergency situations.[228] As the Court explained, the laws governing self-defense date back to 1872 (the year the Penal Code was first enacted), and the code sections for justifiable homicide can be traced back to 1850[229] (the year California became the 31st state). The court identified that there was a conflict between the laws for self-defense and the laws that prohibit a person from possessing handguns.[230]

In resolving this conflict, the Court recognized that "the prohibition of [P.C.] section 12021 [now P.C. sections 29800-29825] was . . . intended only to prohibit members of the affected classes from arming themselves with concealable firearms or having such weapons in their custody or control in circumstances other than those in which the right to use deadly force in self-defense exists or reasonably appears to exist."[231]

This means that when prohibited persons are, or believe themselves or others to be, in immediate danger of great bodily harm, and as long as the firearm was made available to them without their preconceived intent or participation, they may temporarily possess a firearm for no longer than necessary to use it in self-defense without violating P.C. section 29800.

Finally, as in all cases where deadly force is used or threatened in self-defense, using a firearm must be reasonable under the circumstances and may be resorted to only if no other alternative means are available. In the case of felons defending themselves, such alternatives may include having to retreat in situations that non-prohibited persons would not be required to do so.[232]

B. Momentary Possession

Prohibited persons may also be able to momentarily possess a firearm under California law in order to abandon, dispose of, or destroy it as long as the prohibited person:

(1) Possessed the firearm for a momentary or transitory period; *and*

(2) Possessed the firearm in order to abandon, dispose of, or destroy it[233]; *and*

(3) Did not intend to prevent law enforcement officials from seizing the firearm.[234]

---

[228] *People v. King*, 22 Cal. 3d 12, 15 (1978).

[229] *People v. King*, 22 Cal. 3d 12, 22-23 (1978). Indeed, the laws governing self-defense are some of the oldest on the books.

[230] *People v. King*, 22 Cal. 3d 12, 23 (1978). The firearm restriction for felons was only limited to handguns at the time of the *King* case.

[231] *People v. King*, 22 Cal. 3d 12, 24 (1978).

[232] *People v. King*, 22 Cal. 3d 12, 23 (1978).

[233] For example, the prohibited person may legally transfer any firearm, ammunition feeding device, or ammunition to a firearms dealer or an ammunition vendor for storage during the prohibition if the prohibition will expire on a specific ascertainable date. *See generally* P.C. § 29830.

[234] CALCRIM No. 2510; *People v. Hurtado*, 47 Cal. App. 4th 805, 813-14 (1996).

But, note that this exception is very limited. For example, in *People v. Hurtado*, a felon, who was prohibited from possessing firearms, was given a loaded firearm that his girlfriend's eleven-year-old son had found outside on the ground.[235] Even though the felon intended to eventually dispose of the gun, he still had it in his possession three days later when the police stopped him for a traffic violation.[236]

On appeal, the California Court of Appeal held that the "momentary possession" defense extended to situations where a felon possess a firearm to abandon, dispose of, or destroy the firearm.[237] As the court explained, "Firearms . . . are admittedly dangerous items; [but] it is the retention of these items, rather than the brief possession for disposal . . . which poses the danger which is criminalized by the relevant statutes."[238] But, because the felon possessed the firearm for at least two full days, during which it was loaded and free to use in any way he saw fit, the court held that his possession was not momentary or temporary in any sense.[239] Therefore, the felon was not entitled to a "momentary possession" defense.

Nonetheless, a prohibited person can momentarily possess a firearm to abandon, dispose of, or destroy it as long as they are not doing so to prevent law enforcement from seizing the firearm.

C. Justifiable Possession

A prohibited person may also be able to possess a firearm under California law if he or she can prove that their possession was justified. In order to prove that their possession was justified, he or she must be able to show that they:

(1) Found the firearm or took it from a person who was committing a crime against them; *and*

(2) Possessed the firearm no longer than was necessary to deliver or transport the firearm to a law enforcement agency so that the agency can dispose of the weapon or to a licensed firearms dealer for storage pursuant to P.C. section 29830.[240]

Moreover, if the prohibited person plans on transporting the firearm to a law enforcement agency or licensed firearms dealer, they must give prior notice to the agency or dealer that they will be transporting the firearm to them for disposal or storage.[241]

---

[235] *People v. Hurtado*, 47 Cal. App. 4th 805, 808-9 (1996).
[236] *People v. Hurtado*, 47 Cal. App. 4th 805, 808-9 (1996).
[237] *People v. Hurtado*, 47 Cal. App. 4th 805, 814 (1996).
[238] *People v. Hurtado*, 47 Cal. App. 4th 805, 813 (1996).
[239] *People v. Hurtado*, 47 Cal. App. 4th 805, 814 (1996).
[240] P.C. § 29850; CALCRIM No. 2510.
[241] P.C. § 29850; CALCRIM No. 2510.

XIII. OTHER FEDERAL LAW FIREARM POSSESSION RESTRICTIONS

A. Aliens

Unless an exception is met, federal law also prohibits "aliens" who are in the U.S. illegally or who have been admitted to the U.S. under a nonimmigrant visa[242] from receiving and possessing firearms.[243] An "alien" is anyone who is not a U.S. citizen or national;[244] however, the phrase "alien[s] illegally or unlawfully in the United States" refers to "[a]liens who are unlawfully in the United States [and] are not in valid immigrant, nonimmigrant, or parole status."[245] The term includes any alien:

(1) Who unlawfully entered the U.S. without inspection and authorization by an immigration officer and who have not been paroled into the U.S. under section 212(d)(5) of the Immigration and Nationality Act (INA); *or*

(2) Who are nonimmigrants and whose authorized period of stay has expired or who have violated the terms of the nonimmigrant category in which they were admitted; *or*

(3) Paroled under INA section 212(d)(5) whose authorized parole period has expired or whose parole status has been terminated; *or*

(4) Under an order of deportation, exclusion, or removal, or under an order to depart the U.S. voluntarily, whether or not they have left the U.S.[246]

Certain aliens lawfully admitted to the U.S. and who hold a nonimmigrant visa[247] may be exempt from this general federal prohibition if they are:

(1) Admitted to the U.S. for lawful hunting or sporting purposes or in possession of a hunting license or permit lawfully issued in the U.S.; *or*

(2) An official representative of a foreign government who is either:

    (a) Accredited to the U.S. Government or the Government's mission to an international organization having its headquarters in the U.S.; *or*

---

[242] As defined in the Immigration and Nationality Act, 8 U.S.C. section 1011(a)(26).

[243] 18 U.S.C. § 922(g)(5)(B). In 2015, the Seventh Circuit Court of Appeals held that "aliens" may receive Second Amendment protections if they can show that they have come within the territory of the United States and developed a substantial connection with the country. *United States v. Meza-Rodriguez*, No. 14-3271, 2015 WL 4939943, at *7 (7th Cir. Aug. 20, 2015). This case makes it clear that the "Second-Amendment right to bear arms is no second-class entitlement," and even those who are not lawfully in the United States may still receive Second Amendment protections under certain circumstances. *United States v. Meza-Rodriguez*, No. 14-3271, 2015 WL 4939943, at *7 (7th Cir. Aug. 20, 2015). The United States Supreme Court denied certiorari in April of 2016.

[244] 18 U.S.C. § 922(y)(1)(A); 8 U.S.C. § 1101(a)(3).

[245] 27 C.F.R. § 478.11.

[246] 27 C.F.R. § 478.11.

[247] 27 C.F.R. § 478.11 (a nonimmigrant visa is a "visa properly issued to an alien as an eligible nonimmigrant by a competent officer as provided in the Immigration and Nationality Act, 8 U.S.C. section 1101 et seq.").

(b) En route to or from another country to which that alien is accredited; *or*

(3) An official of a foreign government or distinguished foreign visitor who has been so designated by the Department of State; *or*

(4) A foreign law enforcement officer of a friendly foreign government entering the U.S. on official law enforcement business.[248]

An exemption is also extended to those aliens admitted to the U.S. holding a nonimmigrant visa if they have been issued a waiver to possess firearms.[249]

Even if a person has been admitted to the U.S. *without* a nonimmigrant visa, that person might still be eligible to possess firearms. On July 9, 2012, the ATF enacted a change to the Code of Federal Regulations allowing certain aliens without visas to lawfully possess and acquire firearms.[250] This change occurred because the U.S. allows citizens of a number of other countries entry into the U.S. without a visa, and these individuals were considered prohibited from possessing firearms because they did not possess a visa.[251] For instance, it was common for Canadian visitors who entered the U.S. to hunt, and because these visitors were permitted entry without a visa, their possession of firearms within the U.S. prior to this change in the interpretation of the law was illegal.

Now "[n]onimmigrant aliens lawfully admitted to the U.S. without a visa, pursuant either to the Visa Waiver Program or other exemptions from visa requirements, will not be prohibited from shipping, transporting, receiving, or possessing firearms or ammunition. The regulations will also no longer proscribe the sale or other disposition of firearms or ammunition to such nonimmigrant aliens."[252]

---

[248] 18 U.S.C. § 922(y)(2). A lawfully issued hunting license or permit includes those issued by a state, local government, or Indian tribe federally recognized by the Bureau of Indian Affairs. *See Questions and Answers - Revised ATF F4473* (Apr. 2012 ed.), U.S. Dept. of Justice, Bureau of Alcohol, Tobacco, Firearms and Explosives, https://www.atf.gov/file/61841/download (last visited Oct. 3, 2020).

[249] 18 U.S.C. § 922(y)(3).

[250] Firearms Disabilities for Certain Nonimmigrant Aliens, 77 Fed. Reg. 33625-01 (June 7, 2012) (effective July 9, 2012 and codified as 27 C.F.R. §§ 478.32, 478.44, 478.45, 478.99, 478.120, and 478.124). The ATF's previous position was that only aliens holding nonimmigrant visas who met an exception to the firearm restriction could possess and acquire firearms. See Implementation of Public Law 105-277, Omnibus Consolidated and Emergency Supplemental Appropriations Act, 1999, Relating to Firearms Disabilities for Nonimmigrant Aliens, and Requirement for Import Permit for Nonimmigrant Aliens Bringing Firearms and Ammunition Into the United States, 67 Fed. Reg. 5422 (Feb. 5, 2002).

[251] Citizens of 36 participating countries may enter the United States under the Visa Waiver Program. Visa Waiver Program (VWP), U.S. Dept. of State, https://travel.state.gov/content/travel/en/us-visas/tourism-visit/visa-waiver-program.html (last visited Oct. 3, 2020). Certain residents of Canada and Bermuda may also enter the United States without a visa, but under a different exception. Citizens of Canada and Bermuda, U.S. Dept. of State, http://travel.state.gov/content/visas/english/visit/canada-bermuda.html (last visited Oct. 3, 2020).

[252] Firearms Disabilities for Certain Nonimmigrant Aliens, 77 Fed. Reg. 33625-01, 33627 (June 7, 2012) (effective July 9, 2012 and codified as 27 C.F.R. §§ 478.32, 478.44, 478.45, 478.99, 478.120, and 478.124).

B. Dishonorable Discharge From the Armed Forces

Individuals who have been dishonorably discharged or dismissed by a general court martial from the armed forces are likewise prohibited from possessing and receiving firearms.[253] Those who are merely "separated" from service in the armed forces because of any other discharge are not prohibited (*e.g.*, a "bad conduct" discharge does not qualify).[254] But, the "separation" from the armed forces may stem from a criminal conviction. In that case, the restrictions on firearms for criminal convictions may apply.

C. Renouncing United States Citizenship

If you renounce your U.S. citizenship, you are also prohibited from receiving and possessing firearms.[255] To be prohibited under this law, you must have renounced your U.S. citizenship before either:

(1) A diplomatic or consular officer of the U.S. in a foreign state under 8 U.S.C. section 1481(a)(5); *or*

(2) An officer designated by the U.S. Attorney General when the U.S. is in a state of war under 8 U.S.C. section 1481(a)(6).[256]

Your citizenship has not been renounced if the renunciation has been reversed by an administrative or judicial appeal.[257]

D. Federal Restrictions Against Indicted Persons Receiving Firearms

If you are "under indictment for a crime punishable by imprisonment for a term . . . [of more than] one year[258] . . . [you cannot] ship or transport in interstate or foreign commerce any firearm or ammunition or receive any firearm or ammunition which has been shipped or transported in interstate or foreign commerce."[259]

Federal law, however, does not prohibit *possessing* firearms or ammunition during this time; you simply cannot acquire new firearms or remove ones you already own from the state.

---

[253] 18 U.S.C. § 922(g)(6); see also 27 C.F.R. § 478.11.
[254] *See* 27 C.F.R. § 478.11.
[255] 18 U.S.C. § 922(g)(7).
[256] 27 C.F.R. § 478.11.
[257] 27 C.F.R. § 478.11.
[258] This does not include any federal or state offenses regarding antitrust violations, unfair trade practices, restraints of trade, or similar offenses relating to business practices regulation, and any state misdemeanors punishable by imprisonment for two or less years. 18 U.S.C. § 921(a)(20).
[259] 18 U.S.C. § 922(n).

Table 4.10

A QUICK WRAP UP ON OTHER FEDERAL FIREARM POSSESSION RESTRICTIONS
The following individuals are prohibited from *receiving* and *possessing* firearms or ammunition under federal law: ✓ Fugitives from justice (as stated previously in the Chapter) ✓ Aliens who are illegally or unlawfully in the U.S. ✓ Aliens who have been admitted to the U.S. under a nonimmigrant visa, unless they meet an exemption listed in 18 U.S.C. section 922(y)(2) ✓ Individuals who have been dishonorably discharged or dismissed by a general court martial from the armed forces ✓ Individuals who have renounced their U.S. citizenship **The following individuals are prohibited only from *receiving* firearms or ammunition under federal law:** ✓ Individuals who are under indictment for a crime punishable by imprisonment for a term of more than one year

XIV. DEALER'S RECORD OF SALE (DROS) DELAYS

Even though an arrest should not stop a person from acquiring a firearm, beginning in early 2012, there were instances of firearm transaction *delays* for individuals with arrests and rejected and/or dismissed cases. Further, as a result of (what appears to be) a change in policy at DOJ, individuals with felony arrests and cases were denied firearms in some instances. If a person has an arrest, criminal case, or conviction on his or her record and attempts to purchase a firearm, the DOJ analyst conducting the background check investigates to determine whether the case resulted in a conviction, and if so, whether the conviction is prohibiting.

In the past, DOJ analysts were giving "approved" responses for firearm transactions where there might have been an arrest or criminal case but there was no confirmation of a prohibiting conviction. Now, DOJ analysts have been giving a "delay" response when they cannot find conclusive proof that an arrest or charge is not firearm prohibiting. This may happen, for example, if a person has a criminal arrest from 1976 for grand theft auto and the case was later rejected by the District Attorney's office and not filed. Nevertheless, the arrest remains on the person's record. Consequently, when that person attempts to purchase a firearm, he or she gets a "delayed" response because often the reason for the rejection was never recorded (in this case, the decision not to prosecute). In some cases, firearm transactions for individuals whose cases were dismissed were delayed because the dismissal was not entered into the person's criminal history - the history simply reflects an arrest, a (sometimes felony) criminal charge, and nothing else.

This problem became a pandemic, and countless individuals who previously were able to acquire firearms found themselves "delayed." This problem was compounded by the fact that once DOJ found a possible prohibiting event with no disposition, they threw their arms in the air and allowed the individual to remain delayed indefinitely. DOJ, that is when they could be reached, often informed individuals that it is their responsibility to track down their own criminal records and prove that they are not prohibited in order for DOJ to release their firearm(s).

As with the example above, in many cases, the individual's records are 20-30 years old and often no longer exist. It is not unusual for law enforcement agencies to destroy records five years after the case is adjudicated and for courts (depending on the jurisdiction) to destroy closed case files. The delayed individual is often left with no option other than to prove to DOJ that he or she is not prohibited.

This problem prompted the Legislature to take action. As discussed in Chapter 5, these DROS delays should last no more than 30 days, and if DOJ cannot make a determination concerning a person's eligibility at the end of this period, the firearm dealer may release the firearm.[260]

But, this "fix" may prove to have some downside. For example, if you have an arrest from years ago and cannot show a favorable result in the case, you may see a 30-day delay every time you try to purchase or transfer a firearm. While this is better than no firearm being released at all, it is still unacceptable.

The Legislature's current stance is to tacitly approve this unacceptable delay. In October 2017, the Legislature passed SB 393, which allows certain individuals, who are suffering an arrest that did not result in a conviction, to petition the court to have their arrests sealed.[261] Sealing the arrest records would mean that the arrest is deemed not to have occurred and that, outside of a few exceptions, the petitioner is released from all penalties and disabilities resulting from the arrest.[262] But, buried in this law is the statement that the sealing of the arrest "does *not* affect the petitioner's authorization to own, possess, or have in his or her custody or control any firearm . . . if the arrest would otherwise affect this authorization[.]"[263] But arrests currently *do* "otherwise affect [a person's] authorization" to own, possess, or have firearms because DOJ uses arrests to delay the release of a firearm if DOJ cannot determine how the case ended. DOJ does this even though, under California law, arrests do not result in firearm restrictions; convictions do. So, the sealing of an arrest, not to mention any arrest by itself, will still continue to affect (i.e., delay) a person's authorization to own, possess, or have firearms. It seems the Legislature carved out a special exception to allow DOJ to keep doing what it has been doing

---

[260] *See* P.C. § 28220.

[261] SB 393, 2016-2017 Leg., Reg. Sess. (Cal. 2017), *available at* https://leginfo.legislature.ca.gov/faces/billTextClient.xhtml?bill_id=201720180SB393 (last visited Oct. 3, 2020); *see* P.C. §§ 851.91, 851.92.

[262] *See* P.C. § 851.92.

[263] P.C. § 851.91(e)(2)(B)(iii) (emphasis added).

in delaying people due to arrests alone. DOJ still persists in using arrests for DROS delays.

XV. ACQUIRING YOUR CRIMINAL RECORDS AND DETERMINING YOUR ELIGIBILITY TO POSSESS FIREARMS

A. Obtaining Your Criminal History

If you have problems acquiring a firearm, you should request a copy of your criminal history from DOJ or the FBI to confirm its accuracy as these are usually the records DOJ uses to deny or delay your firearm transaction. Your criminal history can be obtained from the Attorney General's Office by completing the instructions at the Attorney General's website at: https://oag.ca.gov/fingerprints/record-review. Once you receive a copy of your criminal history and believe it to be inaccurate or incomplete (which is fairly common), DOJ provides a form to request that DOJ correct your criminal record. On this form, you should provide any and all information that you are able to obtain about the inaccuracy or incompleteness of the record, including court records for your case, if accessible. You should also attempt to track down the records from any prior criminal cases and use them as support in your request to correct your record.

You may likewise request your criminal history summary from the FBI, which is strongly recommended if you are currently living outside of California or have a past arrest or criminal case outside of California. The instructions for how you may request your criminal history from the FBI are located at: http://www.fbi.gov/about-us/cjis/criminal-history-summary-checkscriminal-history-summary-checks. This website also provides links for how you can challenge the accuracy of your criminal history summary.

B. Determining Your Firearm Eligibility

If you don't know whether you can legally possess or purchase firearms in California, *do not attempt to purchase a firearm*. If you reside in California, you should instead submit a PFEC to DOJ. This form can be downloaded at: https://oag.ca.gov/sites/all/files/agweb/pdfs/firearms/forms/pdf/pfecapp.pdf. DOJ will let you know whether you are eligible to possess firearms. If you are ineligible, you can contact them to find out why.

If you think you may be restricted or you find yourself restricted from owning or possessing firearms, you will need to check both California and federal law and obtain copies of specific court and/or medical records relating to your situation to determine the specific nature of your restriction and whether there is a way to restore your rights.[264]

---

[264] Detailed explanations on how to obtain the needed records, how to determine your firearm eligibility, and (if applicable) how to determine the nature of your restriction and restore your firearm rights can be found in the tentatively-titled book *Gun Owner's Guide to Restoring Your Gun Rights*. This book will be published by Coldaw Publishing and made available for purchase on Amazon soon.

CHAPTER 5:
OBTAINING FIREARMS AND AMMUNITION

The information in this chapter assumes you are eligible to own, possess, and receive firearms under state and federal law. Questions about possessing firearms and ammunition by minors and those with rights restrictions are covered in Chapter 4.

In California, *almost all* firearm ownership transfers, whether money is exchanged or not, must be processed through a licensed firearms dealer. A dealer is commonly referred to as a Federal Firearms Licensee (FFL).[1] As the name suggests, a federal firearms license is required to be a lawful firearms dealer.

The easiest, and in most cases the *only*, way to lawfully obtain a firearm in California is through a properly licensed FFL with a California firearms dealer's license. Most FFLs operate from a retail storefront, but it is not unlawful (unless prohibited by local zoning laws) for FFLs to operate in a non-retail setting like their home. These individuals are sometimes called "kitchen-table" FFLs. Although they are legal under federal and state law, if you decide to obtain a firearm through a "kitchen-table" FFL, make sure that the person you are purchasing from is actually an FFL[2] (if the transaction requires one) and that you are complying with all applicable laws. With the exception of antique firearms,[3] the absence of paperwork is a serious red flag about the legality of the transfer and the operations of the seller.

---

[1] Federal licenses are required for those engaged in business as a firearms dealer (gunsmithing), manufacturer, or importer. There is a separate license for "curio or relic" *collectors*. For purposes of this book, FFL will mean firearm "dealers" (unless specified otherwise) who possess both a Federal Firearms License to engage in the business of dealing in firearms (a Type 01 license) and a California firearms dealer's license. "FFL," in general parlance, is often used to refer to both the licensee and the license. In other words, a person must have an "FFL" in order to be an "FFL."

[2] Under California law, when neither party to the transaction is a licensed firearms dealer, they are required to complete the sale, loan, or transfer of the firearm through an FFL, unless they meet one of the exceptions outlined later in this Chapter. P.C. § 27545. If neither party to the transaction is a licensed firearms dealer, both the seller/transferor and the buyer/transferee can be prosecuted if they complete the firearm transaction without going through an FFL. P.C. § 27590; see also Opinion No. 10-504, 93 Ops. Cal. Atty. Gen. 54 (2013), *available at* https://oag.ca.gov/system/files/opinions/pdfs/10-504.pdf (last visited Oct. 10, 2020). This is true even if the seller/transferor or buyer/transferee didn't know that the other person was unlicensed. *See People v. Vaughn*, 230 Cal. App. 4th 332, 333 (2014). So, always make sure to ask whether the person you plan on purchasing from, selling to, or transferring a firearm to is an FFL or that an exception to this requirement actually applies.

[3] Discussed later in this Chapter.

The California Penal Code (P.C.) refers to a dealer in firearms as a "licensee" or a "dealer." In order to qualify as a licensee or dealer in California, certain additional state-issued (and sometimes even local government) permits and licenses are required.

To legally operate as a firearms dealer under California law, a "dealer" must *minimally* have *all* of the following[4]:

(1) A valid Federal Firearms License; *and*

(2) A valid Seller's Permit issued by the State Board of Equalization; *and*

(3) A Certificate of Eligibility (COE) issued by the California Department of Justice (DOJ); *and*

(4) Any regulatory business license(s) required by local government;[5] *and*

(5) If required by the local authority, a local firearms license (or if no such license is required, a letter from the city or county confirming no such license is required);[6] *and*

(6) Be listed in DOJ's Centralized List of Firearms Dealers.[7]

I. PURCHASING FIREARMS FROM A LICENSED DEALER

A. Sale Requirements for All Firearms (Both Handguns and Long Guns)

1. Federal Form 4473 Requirements

Federal law requires you to fill out a federal form, Form 4473, for any firearm (as defined under the Gun Control Act (GCA)) *transferred* to you by an FFL.[8] In most cases, only a single Form 4473 is required regardless of how many firearms are included in the transaction.[9]

---

[4] *See* P.C. § 26700.

[5] Local regulation of FFLs has become increasingly popular among California cities and counties. For example, in 2013, the city of Pleasant Hill caused a stir when it passed a slate of regulations requiring, among other things, that local firearm businesses obtain a local firearm business permit, carry minimum liability insurance, and implement various security measures. Pleasant Hill's law also severely limited the number of locations where a new firearm business may open and operate.

[6] P.C. § 26705(c)(3).

[7] P.C. § 26715.

[8] 27 C.F.R. § 478.124(a). This does not apply to certain loans from an FFL or the return of firearms after repairs by the FFL.

[9] If more than one semiautomatic rifle with a caliber greater than .22 (including .223/5.56) capable of accepting a "detachable magazine" is transferred to the same person within a five-day period, the FFL must additionally complete Form 3310.4. *See* ATF E-Form 3310.12, U.S. Dept. of Justice, Bureau of Alcohol, Tobacco, Firearms, and Explosives, http://www.atf.gov/files/forms/download/atf-f-3310-4.pdf (last visited Oct. 10, 2020). For firearm transaction reporting purposes, a "detachable magazine" includes a rifle with a "bullet button" (discussed in Chapter 9). *See Q&As for the Report of Multiple Sate or Other Disposition of Certain Rifles*, U.S. Dept.

On Form 4473, you must provide information such as your name, gender, address, birth date, place of birth, height, weight, ethnicity, state of residence, and any factors affecting your eligibility to possess firearms.[10] The FFL will fill out information about the specific firearm(s) being purchased and identify the store (if applicable) and his or her FFL number.[11] FFLs are legally required to maintain all 4473 forms on their premises for 20 years.[12] Those forms must be made available for inspection for law enforcement and legal compliance purposes.[13]

Beware: it is generally illegal to provide false information on a Form 4473.[14] So, always make sure that you provide correct information on the form. If you have any questions about how to properly fill out or answer any questions on a Form 4473, contact an attorney who is experienced in firearms law. Do not rely on any "advice" from the dealer when you are trying to decide how to fill out the form. Dealers are not trained attorneys, and their advice may open you to criminal prosecution.

Full-time paid peace officers[15] are not required to fill out Form 4473 if they certify, on agency letterhead with an authorized signature, that they will use the firearm for official duties and a record check shows they have no misdemeanor crime of domestic violence (MCDV) convictions.[16]

2. California Dealer's Record of Sale (DROS) Form

In addition to the federal form, California requires a dealer to fill out a Dealer's Record of Sale (DROS) form electronically. Your personal information is obtained by the FFL by swiping your driver license or ID card though the dealer's magnetic strip reader.[17] The information required on the DROS form includes firearm type (*i.e.*, the make, model, serial number, etc.); transaction type (*i.e.*, dealer sale, private party transfer (PPT), pawn/consignment, or loan); waiting period requirement exemptions, if any (see below); and your name, address, birth date, etc.

Always check to make sure that the information on the form is correct and accurate before submitting it. It is a crime under California law to provide false

---

OF JUSTICE, BUREAU OF ALCOHOL, TOBACCO, FIREARMS, AND EXPLOSIVES, https://www.atf.gov/files/firearms/industry/080911-qa-multiple-rifles.pdf (last visited Oct. 10, 2020). Likewise, if the transaction involves more than one handgun to the same person within a five-day period, the FFL must additionally complete Form 3310.4. 27 C.F.R. § 478.126a. This is generally not a concern for California FFLs, unless the customer is exempt from the "one handgun per month" rule or the FFL is facilitating a transfer of multiple handguns between two private parties. As an aside, the District Court for the District of Columbia upheld the ATF's multiple-firearm reporting requirement. See *Nat'l Shooting Sports Found., Inc. v. Jones*, 840 F. Supp. 2d 310 (D.D.C. 2012).

[10] ATF E-Form 3310.4, U.S. DEPT. OF JUSTICE, BUREAU OF ALCOHOL, TOBACCO, FIREARMS, AND EXPLOSIVES, https://www.atf.gov/file/61426/download (last visited Oct. 10, 2020).

[11] For further details about the transferee and FFL's obligations regarding Form 4473, see 27 C.F.R. sections 478.11 and 478.124(c).

[12] 27 C.F.R. § 478.129(b).

[13] 18 U.S.C. § 923(g).

[14] 18 U.S.C. §§ 922(a)(6); 924(a)(1)(A).

[15] As defined in P.C. sections 830-832.9.

[16] 27 C.F.R. § 478.134. Because no Form 4473 is filled out, dealers who conduct this transaction must keep the letter for their records and note in their books how this firearm was transferred. 27 C.F.R. § 478.134(c).

[17] P.C. § 28180.

information on a DROS form.[18] If you are unsure as to whether you are eligible to possess firearms, you should run a Personal Firearms Eligibility Check (see Chapter 3) or contact an attorney experienced with firearms law *before* you attempt to obtain a firearm through an FFL.

After filling out the information on a DROS form, the FFL must take your right thumbprint unless you qualify for an exception.[19] The FFL is required to keep a copy of the DROS form on file for at least three years and make it available for peace officer, DOJ, or ATF inspection.[20]

The FFL is also required to give you a copy of your DROS form at the time of delivery of the firearm.[21] Although you are not required to keep your copy of the DROS it is strongly suggested you retain a copy for your records in the event your firearm is lost, stolen, or proof of ownership is requested.

Unlike federal law, where you can just fill out one 4473 Form for all firearms purchased at the same time, a separate DROS form is required for each firearm transferred.[22] Formerly, this requirement applied only to handguns, and the transfer of multiple long guns required only a single DROS form.[23] But, California law now requires the submission of a separate form for every firearm transfer, even in a single transaction, for both handguns and long guns.[24]

3. Proof of Identity, Age, and Address

You must present clear evidence of your identity and age to a firearms dealer before he or she can release a firearm to you.[25]

Under federal law, an FFL is prohibited from delivering a *handgun* to anyone under age 21 or any firearm to anyone under age 18.[26] California law, however, is more restrictive with regards to dealer transactions following the enactment of SB 1100 in 2018 and SB 61 in 2019. Since January 1, 2019, California licensed firearm dealers have been prohibited from selling, supplying, delivering, or giving possession or control of any firearm (whether it be a handgun, rifle, shotgun, or otherwise) to any person under the age of 21.[27] While there are exceptions, SB 61 further

---

[18] P.C. § 28250.
[19] P.C. § 28160(b). The requirements for handguns apply to all firearms.
[20] P.C. § 28215(c).
[21] P.C. §§ 28210(e), 28215(e). This new requirement was created by AB 538 (2013).
[22] P.C. § 28170(d).
[23] P.C. § 28160 (2013).
[24] P.C. § 28170(d).
[25] 18 U.S.C. §§ 922(t)(1)(C), 1028(d)(3); 27 C.F.R. §§ 478.11, 478.124(c)(3)(i); P.C. §§ 26815(c), 27540(c).
[26] Also, federal law prohibits dealers from selling a firearm that is neither a "rifle" nor a "shotgun" (*e.g.*, a frame/receiver) to anyone under age 21 (18 U.S.C. § 922(b)(1), (x)). See Chapter 3 for definitions and examples. It is not unusual for persons reaching the age of 18 to attempt to purchase a receiver to build their own rifle, , but federal law requires a dealer to deny such a purchase.
[27] P.C. § 27510(a); *see also* SB 1100, 2017-2018 Leg., Reg. Sess. (Cal. 2018), *available at* https://leginfo.legislature.ca.gov/faces/billTextClient.xhtml?bill_id=201720180SB1100 (last visited Oct. 10, 2020); SB 61, 2019-

limits those exceptions to apply to sales or transfers of firearms that are not handguns or semiautomatic centerfire rifles.[28] Specifically, a California licensed firearms dealer may sell, supply, deliver, or give possession or control of a firearm that is *not a handgun or a semiautomatic centerfire rifle* to a person over the age of 18 but under 21 who either:

(1) Possesses a valid, unexpired hunting license issued by the Department of Fish and Wildlife; or,

(2) Provides proper identification of being an honorably discharged member of the United States Armed Forces, the National Guard, the Air National Guard, or the active reserve components of the United States.[29]

For a California licensed firearms dealer to sell, supply, deliver, or give possession or control of a semiautomatic centerfire rifle to a person over the age of 18 but under 21, the person must:

(1) Be an active peace officer, as described in P.C. sections 830-832.9, authorized to carry a firearm in the course and scope of their employment;

(2) Be an active federal officer or law enforcement agent who is authorized to carry a firearm in the course and scope of employment;

(3) IBe a reserve peace officer, as defined in P.C. section 832.6, who is authorized to carry a firearm in the course and scope of employment; or,

(4) Provide proper identification of active membership in the United States Armed Forces, the National Guard, the Air National Guard, or active reserve components of the United States.[30]

a. Federal Identification Requirements

In most situations, a California driver license or California ID card will suffice for the identification requirements under federal law.[31] But federal law requires that you present a valid government-issued "identification document" that has your name, picture, date of birth, and residence address.[32] The address on your ID is important because a dealer can only transfer a firearm to someone residing in the same state as the dealer's place of business.[33] This requirement (and consequently, the address requirement), however, shall not apply to the sale or delivery of any *rifle*

2020 Leg., Reg. Sess. (Cal. 2020), *available at* http://leginfo.legislature.ca.gov/faces/billTextClient.xhtml?bill_id=201920200SB61 (last visited Oct. 10, 2020).

[28] P.C. § 27510(b).

[29] P.C. § 27510(b)(1-2). For purposes of these exceptions, "proper identification" includes an Armed Forced Identification Card or other written documentation certifying that the individual is an honorably discharged member. P.C. § 27510(b)(2).

[30] P.C. § 27510(b)(3)(A-D). For purposes of these exceptions, "proper identification" includes an Armed Forced Identification Card or other written documentation certifying that the individual is an active member. P.C. § 27510(b)(3)(D).

[31] Federal law makes it illegal in most cases for an FFL to transfer a firearm directly to a person who does not reside in the FFL's state of residence. 18 U.S.C. § 922(a)(2).

[32] 27 C.F.R. §§ 478.11; 478.124.

[33] 18 U.S.C. § 922(b)(3).

or *shotgun* to a resident residing in another state than the one which the dealer's place of business is located if (1) the person receiving the gun meets in person with the person transferring the gun to accomplish the transfer, and (2) the sale, delivery, and receipt fully comply with the legal conditions of sale in both such states.[34]

It is not unusual for a person to move and for his or her driver license to reflect their *old* address, or for a person to use a P.O. Box or police station address on their ID rather than a residential address. The address on your ID is important because a dealer can only transfer a firearm to someone residing in the same state as the dealer's place of business.[35]

But beware: failing to provide the address where you reside is a violation of federal law. Under federal law, not only must you complete a 4473 form (discussed further below), but you must also do so truthfully.

According to the Bureau of Alcohol, Tobacco, Firearms, and Explosives (ATF), federal law allows a purchaser to use a combination of *government-issued* documents[36] to satisfy the federal identification requirement.[37] So you could still acquire a firearm if, for example, you have your valid California driver license (to satisfy the California identification requirement) with a P.O. Box listed as your address and a voter registration card with your actual residence address (to satisfy the federal identification requirement).

For those who have a confidential or hidden address, you can obtain a government-issued document that contains your actual residence address by requesting a full ten-year driving record report from the California Department of Motor Vehicles (DMV). In order to obtain your ten-year driving record, you will need to go in person to the DMV and request your record. This report should reflect your confidential address, which you can use as proof of residency to satisfy the federal identification requirement.

b. California Identification Requirements

Under California law, clear evidence of your identity and age must be shown with either a valid California driver license or a valid California identification (ID) card issued by the DMV.[38] If your license has expired or is suspended, your firearm

---

[34] 18 U.S.C. § 922(b)(3).

[35] 18 U.S.C. § 922(b)(3).

[36] Documents include those which are "made or issued by or under the authority of the United States Government, a State, political subdivision of a State, a foreign government, political subdivision of a foreign government, an international governmental or an international quasi-governmental organization which, when completed with information concerning a particular individual, is of a type intended or commonly accepted for the purpose of identification of individuals." 27 C.F.R. § 478.11.

[37] ATF Rul. 2001-5 (Dec. 31, 2001) ("Examples of documents that may be accepted to supplement information on a driver license or other identification document include a vehicle registration, a recreation identification card, a fishing or hunting license, a voter identification card, or a tax bill. However, the document in question must be valid and must have been issued by a government agency.").

[38] P.C. § 16400. California requires additional documentation to show "proof of residency" for the purchase of handguns (discussed in Subsection (B)(2) below). Although the California identification requirement requires that you have a valid California driver license or California ID card, they do not need to reflect your current ad-

transaction will not be approved. There are additional identification and proof of residence requirements imposed when purchasing a handgun. These are discussed later in this chapter

Table 5.1

IDENTIFICATION REQUIREMENTS[38]
FEDERAL LAW
You must present a government-issued document (such as a California driver license or ID). The government-issued identification document must contain the following: (1) Your name; *and* (2) Your current residence address; *and* (3) Your date of birth; *and* (4) A photograph of you. In order to meet this identification requirement, federal law allows you to use a *combination* of government-issued documents. Therefore, if your current government-issued identification does not contain your current address, you may present another government-issued document (like a voter registration card) that contains your current address.
CALIFORNIA LAW
You must have clear evidence of your identity and age in order to purchase a firearm. This means you must present a *valid* California driver license or *valid* California ID, issued by the California DMV. If you are a member of the military stationed in California, your Military Identification and permanent duty station orders will satisfy the California ID requirement.

c. REAL IDs, Non-REAL IDs, and AB 60

In 2005, the United States Congress enacted the REAL ID Act, which, among other provisions, requires federally compliant identification (i.e., REAL ID) to board any airplane, enter any military base, or enter any federal facility beginning October 1, 2020.[40] In the years following the adoption of this law, it was unclear if it would also apply to the purchase of a firearm. ATF issued a newsletter in 2012 clarifying that non-REAL IDs could continue to be used to purchase firearms. But then California enacted Assembly Bill No. 60 ("AB 60") in 2013, which required the DMV to issue identification to individuals who could not provide proof of their lawful presence in the United States. This created a problem when it was discovered that identification issued pursuant to AB 60 was identical to that issued to lawful U.S. residents.

---

dress. In fact, the information required on the Dealer's Record of Sale (DROS) form is your "local address," and if your current address is temporary, then you need to provide your permanent address. You do not need to provide additional documentation to prove your permanent address. P.C. § 28160. California law does not define these terms "temporary" or "permanent." Federal law, however, does require you to provide documentation to prove your place of residence.

[39] All of the tables within this book are paraphrases of the law and are not a complete summary of each subject area. Please review the corresponding sections within this chapter for a more in-depth discussion of each topic and for the applicable statutes and/or case law that is paraphrased within the tables.

[40] REAL ID Act of 2005, H.R. 418, 109th Cong.

Further compounding the confusion was DOJ's unsupported position that non-REAL IDs could not be used to purchase firearms in California—despite ATF's clear position otherwise. CRPA, with the support of NRA, challenged DOJ's opinion, and eventually received clarification from DOJ that it would accept non-REAL IDs for purposes of firearm purchases. But in 2019, DOJ proposed and adopted an "emergency" regulation in connection with California's new ammunition sales restrictions that took effect on July 1, 2019.[41] Formal regulations have since been implemented as of April 27, 2020.[42]

Examples of a REAL ID (left) versus a non-REAL ID (right)[43]

Pursuant to DOJ's new regulation, a person undergoing an "eligibility check"[43] using an ID with the notation "FEDERAL LIMITS APPLY" must also submit "proof of lawful presence in the United States" using one of the following documents:

(1) A valid, unexpired U.S. passport or passport card;

(2) A certified copy of a U.S. birth certificate;

(3) A Certification of Birth Abroad (FS-545);

(4) A Certification of Report of Birth (DS-1350);

---

[41] Readers should note that DOJ's regulations are being challenged in connection with CRPA's *Rhode v. Becerra* lawsuit. As of the date of this book's publication, The United States District Court for the Southern District of California issued an order granting a preliminary injunction, but that order was stayed pending an appeal to the Ninth Circuit. The case has since been fully briefed and is awaiting oral arguments.

[42] *See* Cal. Code. Regs., tit. 11, §§ 4002, 4142, 4045.1, 5478.

[43] Defined as a background check based on any application or report for which an applicant is required to submit a ID so that DOJ may determine the applicant's eligibility to possess a firearm or ammunition under state or federal law. Cal. Code Regs. tit. 11, § 4045.1.

(5) A Consular Report of Birth Abroad of a Citizen of the United States of America (FS-240);

(6) A valid, unexpired foreign passport with valid U.S. immigrant visa and approved Record of Arrival/Departure (I-94) form;

(7) A certified copy of a birth certificate from a U.S. Territory;

(8) A Certificate of Naturalization or U.S. Citizenship; or,

(9) A valid, unexpired Permanent Resident Card.[44]

If, however, the person's name as it appears on the federal non-compliant identification also differs from the proof of lawful presence document presented, the applicant must also submit one of the following certified documents:

(1) An adoption document that contains the legal name of the applicant as a result of the adoption;

(2) A name change document that contains the applicant's legal name both before and, as a result of, the name change;

(3) A marriage certificate;

(4) A dissolution of marriage document that contains the legal name of the applicant as a result of the court action;

(5) A certificate, declaration, or registration document verifying the formation of a domestic partnership; or,

(6) A dissolution of domestic partnership document that contains the legal name of the applicant as a result of the court action.[45]

i. Eligibility Checks Submitted Via Paper Format

For eligibility checks in connection with a paper application submitted to DOJ, the above listed documents (if required) must be submitted along with the application. Paper applications subject to this requirement include:

(1) Certificate of Eligibility ("COE") applications;

(2) New Resident Report of Firearm Ownership;

(3) Firearm Ownership Report;

(4) Curio or Relic Firearm Report;

(5) Collector In-State Acquisition of Curio or Relic Long Gun Report;

(6) Report of Operation of Law or Intra-Familial Firearm Transaction; or,

(7) Dangerous Weapon License/Permit Applications (including renewal applications).

---

[44] CAL. CODE REGS. tit. 11, § 4045.1(b).
[45] CAL. CODE REGS. tit. 11, § 4045.1(c).

ii. Eligibility Checks Submitted Via Electronic Format

For eligibility checks in connection with an electronic application submitted to DOJ through the California Firearms Application Reporting System ("CFARS"), the above listed documents (if required) must be submitted along with the applications by uploading them to CFARS as prompted during the application or reporting process. CFARS applications subject to this requirement include:

(1) Certificate of Eligibility ("COE") applications;

(2) Unique Serial Number Applications;

(3) New Resident Report of Firearm Ownership;

(4) Firearm Ownership Report;

(5) Curio or Relic Firearm Report;

(6) Collector In-State Acquisition of Curio or Relic Long Gun Report;

(7) Report of Operation of Law or Intra-Familial Firearm Transaction.[46]

iii. DROS Transactions (Firearms and Ammunition Purchases)

DOJ's regulation also includes instructions for California licensed firearm dealers and/or ammunition vendors when processing a transaction through the DROS Entry System ("DES"). In such cases, the dealer and/or vendor must examine the applicant's ID.[47] If the ID is federally non-compliant with the notation "FEDERAL LIMITS APPLY," the dealer and/or vendor must require the applicant to provide the required supplemental documentation listed above (as necessary) which will be copied by the dealer and/or vendor.[48] These copies will be kept with the dealer and/or vendor pursuant to their record keeping requirements.[49]

iv. Other Eligibility Check Applications

Lastly, DOJ's regulation also contemplates applications or reports submitted to other agencies that include fingerprint data used by DOJ to determine the applicant's eligibility to possess a firearm or ammunition under state or federal law. These applications include:

(1) Peace officer applicants, custodial officers, or transportation officers, pursuant to P.C. section 832.15;

(2) Peace officers, pursuant to P.C. section 832.16;

(3) Applicants for admission to a basic course of training certified by the Commission on Peace Officer Standards and Training that includes the carrying and use of firearms, pursuant to P.C. section 13511.5; or,

---

[46] Cal. Code Regs. tit. 11, § 4045.1(e).
[47] Cal. Code Regs. tit. 11, § 4045.1(f).
[48] Cal. Code Regs. tit. 11, § 4045.1(f).
[49] Cal. Code Regs. tit. 11, § 4045.1(f).

(4) Applicants for an explosives permit, pursuant to Health & Safety Code section 12101.[50]

In connection with these applications, the processing agency must require the applicant to provide the required supplemental documentation listed above (as necessary) if the applicant presents a federally non-compliant ID with the notation "FEDERAL LIMITS APPLY."[51] The agency must keep a copy of the required documents as part of the permanent record of the application, which DOJ may request a copy of at a future date.[52]

d. Special Circumstances

i. Members of the Military Stationed in California

Although California law limits the accepted forms of identification (*i.e.*, California driver licenses and DMV identification cards), DOJ also accepts military identification and permanent duty station orders as proof of identification.[53]

These same documents satisfy the ID and proof of residency requirements under federal law as well. Section 921(b) of the GCA provides that "a member of the Armed Forces on active duty is a resident of the State in which his permanent duty station is located."[54] The purchaser's official orders showing that his or her permanent duty station is within the state where the FFL's premises are located suffice to establish the purchaser's residence for GCA purposes. "In combination with a military identification card, such orders will satisfy the Brady Act's requirement for an identification document, even though the purchaser may actually reside in a home that is not located on the military base."[55]

ii. Non-Citizens (Aliens)

As explained in Chapter 4, federal law generally prohibits aliens who are unlawfully in the U.S., as well as those who are lawfully in the country via a "nonimmigrant visa" or who are not required to have a visa, from possessing and, of course, acquiring firearms. There are exceptions, however.[56]

---

[50] CAL. CODE REGS. tit. 11, § 4045.1(g).
[51] CAL. CODE REGS. tit. 11, § 4045.1(g).
[52] CAL. CODE REGS. tit. 11, § 4045.1(g).
[53] *Frequently Asked Questions*, CAL. DEPT. OF JUSTICE, OFFICE OF THE ATTORNEY GENERAL, http://oag.ca.gov/firearms/pubfaqs (last visited Oct. 10, 2020) (The answer to question 3 states, "[a]s part of the DROS process, the buyer must present 'clear evidence of identity and age' which is defined as a valid, non-expired California driver license or ID card issued by the Department of Motor Vehicles. A military identification accompanied by permanent duty station orders indicating a posting in California is also acceptable.").
[54] 18 U.S.C. § 921(b).
[55] ATF Rul. 2001-5 (Dec. 31, 2001).
[56] 18 U.S.C. § 922(g)(5)(A),(B). See Chapter 4 for a detailed discussion on who is an "alien" and when an alien is prohibited from possessing and receiving firearms. An alien who is not prohibited may purchase a firearm provided he or she can meet the requirements in this chapter. Often aliens "just visiting" the United States will not possess the proper identification required under federal or California law.

For those aliens who may lawfully acquire a firearm in the U.S., state and federal laws relating to the acquisition of firearms still apply. The alien must therefore possess a California driver license or ID[57] to meet the state requirements. In addition, the individual must "reside" in a state to meet the federal requirement because, though there are a few exceptions, federal law generally restricts people from receiving firearms outside of the state in which they reside (this is discussed in much more detail in the next subsection).[58]

Previously, there was a 90-day residency requirement before aliens could acquire firearms; however, the U.S. DOJ amended the law to remove this requirement. Aliens, when acquiring firearms, must also provide their alien number or admission number on the 4473 form.[59]

iii. Dual Residency

Federal law recognizes "dual residency," *i.e.*, when a person maintains a home in two states and resides in one or the other for certain periods of the year.[60] This means that if you are a resident of California and can establish residency in another state, you can purchase firearms in the other state during the time you reside there, presumably even if the firearms would be illegal in California.

For example, what if you live in California but also have a home in Arkansas where you spend your summers, and you want to purchase a firearm in Arkansas? First, you must determine where you actually "reside" under the law. According to federal law, an individual resides in a state if he or she is present in a state with the intention of making a home in that state.[61] The ATF determines residency by looking at where the individual resides, so if the individual has multiple homes in multiple states, he or she will be considered a resident of each state, respectively, for the portion of the year he or she resides there.[62]

In most instances, you must be a resident of the state in which you are acquiring a firearm.[63] To prove residency, you need to provide valid ID as required by federal law and the laws of that state concerning firearm transactions (if the state has any). For example, if you want to purchase a firearm in Arkansas directly from an FFL licensed in that state, you need to be an Arkansas resident.[64] If you aren't, you need

---

[57] P.C. §§ 26815(c), 27540(c).

[58] 18 U.S.C. § 922(a)(3).

[59] 27 C.F.R. § 478.124(c)(1).

[60] 27 C.F.R. § 478.11 (see definition for "state of residence"). For example, if you maintain a home in state X and then travel to state Y on a hunting trip, you do not become a state Y resident because of such a trip. On the other hand, if you maintain a home in state X and a home in state Y and reside in state X during the week and summer months and state Y for weekends and the rest of the year, you are a state X resident when you are in state X, and you are a state Y resident when you are in state Y.

[61] 27 C.F.R. § 478.11.

[62] 27 C.F.R. § 478.11.

[63] 18 U.S.C. § 922(a)(3), (b)(3).

[64] This requirement is subject to a federal exemption for rifles and shotguns (discussed below) that does not apply to a person who only resides in California.

to have the firearm sent to an FFL in the state you reside.[65] But, subject to a few very limited and narrow exceptions, you cannot send or bring firearms into California that are illegal to possess here, even if you obtained them legally in another state.

Moreover, you cannot send or bring a firearm that you lawfully purchased or otherwise obtained on or after January 1, 2015, from another state into California, unless the firearm is first delivered to an FFL in California, or you meet one of the few exceptions (discussed in Section IV(C) of this Chapter).[66] This means that all the pertinent California requirements (*i.e.*, ten-day wait, DROS, etc.) must be satisfied before you can lawfully receive the firearm in California.

e. Dealer Record of Sales Fees

Only one DROS fee can be charged for a single transaction, regardless of whether the second or subsequent firearms are transferred.[67] Individuals must also pay a $1 Firearm Safety Fee and a $5 Firearm Safety and Enforcement Fee.[68] As of January 1, 2020, the current DROS fee is $31.19 following the adoption of a DOJ regulation implementing AB 1669.[69]

4. Background Checks

The information collected on Federal Form 4473 and the DROS form is used to check your background and eligibility to possess, own, and receive firearms. Both California and federal law require FFLs to perform background checks for all firearm transfers.[70] Recall from Chapter 4 that California is a "point of contact" state, meaning that the California DOJ conducts the background checks for all firearm purchases in California and determines whether a person is eligible to possess firearms.[71]

---

[65] 18 U.S.C. § 922(a)(3), (b)(3).

[66] P.C. § 27560(a).

[67] P.C. § 28240(b). "[T]he DROS fee is $19 for one or more firearms (handguns, rifles, shotguns) transferred at the same time to the same transferee." CAL. CODE REGS. tit. 11, § 4001.

[68] P.C. §§ 23690, 28225, 28240, 28300; CAL. CODE REGS. tit. 11, § 4001. In 2016, the California Legislature passed Senate Bill (SB) 843, giving DOJ the authority to increase the $1 Firearm Safety Testing fee and the $5 Safety and Enforcement fee at a rate not to exceed any increase in the California Consumer Price Index and the reasonable costs of regulation to DOJ. But, as of the date of publication, DOJ has yet to promulgate any regulations to increase these fees.

[69] CAL. CODE REGS. tit. 11, § 4001.

[70] 27 C.F.R. § 478.124; P.C. § 28215. Eligibility requirements are discussed in Chapter 4, and procedures for appealing DOJ's denial of allowing your firearm transfer to proceed will be discussed in an upcoming publication by Coldaw Publishing tentatively titled *Gun Owner's Guide to Restoring Your Gun Rights*. This publication will be available for purchase on Amazon soon.

[71] Although DOJ has been tasked with performing all background checks for firearm purchases, it has consistently dropped the ball on performing background checks and has had numerous problems properly identifying people who are prohibited from owning and possessing firearms. In 2015, the California State Auditor released a report that chastised DOJ for failing to fully implement certain recommendations that the State Auditor made in 2013 when it discovered that the Armed Prohibited Person System (APPS) had trouble identifying individuals who should be prohibited from possessing firearms due to a mental health commitment because DOJ had not taken any steps to ensure that mental health facilities and courts were properly reporting these incidents. *See* California State Auditor, *Follow-up—California Department of Justice: Delays in Fully Implementing Recommendations Prevent it From Accurately and Promptly Identifying All Armed Persons with Mental Illness, Resulting in Continued Risk*

5. Registration at Time of Purchase

Before January 1, 2014, only handgun transfers were registered, and California law prohibited DOJ from keeping records relating to transfers of long guns from a dealer.[72] As of January 1, 2014, all firearms acquired from a licensed firearms dealer in California are registered to the transferee.[73] DOJ takes the information collected by the mandatory DROS form, which includes the purchaser's personal identifying information and the firearm's make, model, serial number, etc., and it enters that information into its Automated Firearm System (AFS), thereby generating a firearm transaction record in the purchaser's name.[74]

Because of the amount of paperwork and information gathered, it is not unusual for those who went through the DROS process to believe their long gun was recorded prior to January 1, 2014. But, aside from documents kept by the dealer and the purchaser, no transaction records on long gun transfers were kept by the government. A disturbingly large number of Californians also mistakenly believe that the DROS process was the same one required to register "assault weapons." But that is also not the case. Because they filled out the long gun purchase paperwork, people are still discovering that firearms they thought were registered as "assault weapons" are not registered as such, and in the case of long guns purchased before January 1, 2014, they are not, in fact, recorded at all.

a. Voluntary Registration

You may, however, voluntarily record ownership any lawfully owned firearm by submitting a "Firearm Ownership Record" form to DOJ.[75] This form is available on DOJ Bureau of Firearms' website. Though not legally required, having this record on file with DOJ may help your firearm be returned to you if it is ever seized, lost, or stolen.[76] Doing so can also safeguard against a felony. For example, an individual charged for carrying a handgun illegally concealed or loaded that is recorded in AFS would not result in a felony, because a recorded firearm carried illegally is, in most situations, only a misdemeanor (discussed in Chapter 6).

 Contrary to advice proffered by a number of websites a few years ago, the use of the voluntary form is not a way to bypass the requirement that most transactions of firearms must be done through an FFL.

---

to Public Safety (July 2015), available at https://www.auditor.ca.gov/pdfs/reports/2015-504.pdf (last visited Oct. 10, 2020). The State Auditor also reported that DOJ had incorrectly found that certain individuals were prohibited from possessing firearms because the APPS unit did not review all pertinent information when processing background checks, and that DOJ has not been (and will not be) able to review the backlog cases where a person might be a prohibited person in possession of a firearm. See California State Auditor, Follow-up—California Department of Justice: Delays in Fully Implementing Recommendations Prevent it From Accurately and Promptly Identifying All Armed Per-sons with Mental Illness, Resulting in Continued Risk to Public Safety (July 2015), available at https://www.auditor.ca.gov/pdfs/reports/2015-504.pdf (last visited Oct. 10, 2020).

[72] P.C. §§ 11106(a)-(b), 28210(c)(3) (2013).

[73] P.C. § 11106(b).

[74] P.C. §§ 28155, 28160, 28215(d).

[75] The processing fee for filing a Firearm Ownership Record form is $19. Cal. Code Regs. tit. 11, § 4002.

[76] Frequently Asked Questions, Cal. Dept. Of Justice, Office of the Attorney General, http://ag.ca.gov/firearms/pubfaqs.php/forms/pdf/index.php#26 (last visited Oct. 10, 2020).

Even though handguns acquired in California from a licensed firearm dealer should be recorded, this is often not the case. The AFS has holes you can pilot the U.S.S. Missouri through. Individuals who have large collections may find it amusing to request their AFS records.[77] These lists are often filled with inaccuracies, including firearms that were transferred years ago through a dealer, firearms the individual never purchased, as well as incorrect serial numbers and/or make/model designations.

b. Confusion Regarding the AFS Record Requirement for All Firearms After January 1, 2014

There was some confusion relating to the change in California law that occurred on January 1, 2014. The law did not create a requirement to register firearms acquired/purchased before January 1, 2014. Rather, the new law only affects firearms transferred through an FFL and firearms you either import into this state as a "personal firearm importer" or received without going through a dealer[78] *after* January 1, 2014. Firearms you transferred (via an exemption to the dealer requirement where the recipient didn't need to record the acquisition of the firearm) or imported (prior to January 1, 2014, the general AFS recprd requirement of firearms brought into the state only applied to handguns and "personal *handgun* importers") prior to January 1, 2014, that did not need to be recorded, still do not need to be recorded.

6. Waiting Period

Under California law, you must wait ten days (ten 24-hour periods) from when your DROS form is submitted until you may lawfully receive any firearm transferred through an FFL.[79] If you clear the background check (assuming all other requirements are satisfied), the FFL may transfer the firearm to you after the ten days.[80]

The following people and transfers are exempt from this ten-day waiting period:

(1) Properly identified full-time paid peace officers authorized by their employer to carry firearms for their confirmed duties;[81] *and*

---

[77] You can request a list of firearms registered in your name by filling out and submitting an "Automated Firearms System (AFS) Request for Firearms Records" form. You may download the form at https://oag.ca.gov/sites/all/files/agweb/pdfs/firearms/forms/AFSPrivateCitizen.pdf (last visited Oct. 10, 2020). The form will need to be notarized and include a photocopy of a valid identification card (driver license, military ID, etc.).

[78] This transfer must have been made pursuant to an exception to the requirement that all private party transfers (PPTs) be conducted through a dealer (see below for the requirement and exceptions to that requirement).

[79] P.C. § 26815(a). A lawsuit was filed to challenge the 10-day wait as applied to current gun owners. In December 2016, the 9th Circuit issued its decision upholding the 10-day wait as applied to current gun owners. *Silvester v. Harris*, 843 F.3d 816 (9th Cir. 2016). Plaintiffs petitioned the Ninth Circuit to rehear the case, but that petition was denied on April 4, 2017. Plaintiffs petitioned the United States Supreme Court for review, but the Supreme Court declined to review the case. *Silvester v. Becerra*, 138 S.Ct. 945 (2018).

[80] P.C. § 26815(a).

[81] P.C. §§ 26950, 27650.

(2) Firearm deliveries, sales, or transfers to DOJ-issued special weapons permit holders;[82] *and*

(3) Persons with ATF-issued "curio or relic" collector's licenses who have a valid DOJ-issued COE when purchasing "curio or relic" firearms;[83] *and*

(4) FFLs delivering firearms to another FFL, or an FFL transferring a firearm from store inventory to the FFL's personal collection (subject to additional ATF and California requirements).[84]

Additionally, you have 30 days from the date your DROS was submitted to pick up your firearm from the FFL. Otherwise, federal law voids your background check, and you will be required to go through the entire process again, fees and everything.[85]

Also, your firearm transaction could be delayed up to 30 days if the FFL sends your information to DOJ and one of the following occur:

(1) You were taken into custody and placed in a facility for mental health treatment or evaluation and may be a person described in section 8100 or 8103 of the California Welfare and Institutions Code (Cal. Welf. & Inst. Code), and DOJ cannot actually determine whether you are prohibited; *or*

(2) You were arrested for, or charged with, a crime that would make you, if convicted, a person who is prohibited by state or federal law from possessing firearms, and DOJ is unable to determine whether you were convicted of that offense; *or*

(3) You may be a person who has purchased a handgun in the last 30 days, and DOJ is unable to determine whether you are or not.[86]

If DOJ cannot figure out whether or not you are prohibited based on the foregoing, it is required to notify the dealer (presumably before the end of the ten-day wait)[87] and let the dealer know there is a delay in the transaction. The dealer is then required to provide you with information for contacting DOJ regarding the delay.

---

[82] P.C. §§ 26965, 27665. The permits include those issued per P.C. sections 33300 (short-barreled rifle and shotgun permittees), 32650 (machinegun, "assault weapons," and .50 BMG permits), 32700 (permits to sell machineguns), and 18900 (permits for destructive devices).

[83] P.C. §§ 26970, 27670, 27820. Acquiring antique and "curio or relic" firearms is discussed later in this chapter. "Curio or relic" firearms are defined in Chapter 3.

[84] P.C. §§ 26960, 27660.

[85] *See* 27 C.F.R. § 478.102(c).

[86] P.C. § 28220(f)(1)(A).

[87] A regulation that was implemented in now prohibits a dealer from releasing a firearm unless the dealer receives an "Approved" from DOJ. Under these regulations, if DOJ had no response, even after the end of the 10-day wait, arguably the dealer could not release the firearm. CAL. CODE REGS tit. 11, § 4230.

DOJ is also required to send you notice by mail regarding the delay and the process for obtaining the criminal or mental health information DOJ has on file.[88] If during the 30-day delay DOJ is able to determine your eligibility, they are required to notify the dealer accordingly.[89] If at the end of the 30 days DOJ is unable to determine your eligibility, they are required to notify the dealer and the dealer *may* immediately transfer the firearm to you.[90] Make a special note of the word "may," because this is not a requirement. A dealer may release the firearm but doesn't have to.

This legislative change appears to be in response to problems with the processing of a number of firearm transactions. As discussed in Chapter 4, some firearm transactions were taking longer than ten days when DOJ could not determine whether a person was prohibited. These cases often involved individuals who had an arrest or criminal charge on their record with no disposition of the case available to DOJ. In some cases, the delay became indefinite. As a result, the legislature implemented the 30-day delay limit.

7. Required Locking Devices and Warnings

Federal law also requires licensed importers, manufacturers, and dealers to provide a "secure gun storage or safety device"[91] when delivering a *handgun* to anyone who is not another FFL or otherwise exempt.[92]

California requires all firearms transferred by an FFL, including Private Party Transfers (PPTs) (discussed in Section II below) or those manufactured in California, be accompanied by an approved "firearm safety device"[93] and warning language or labels upon delivery.[94] The safety device must be one of those listed on the

---

[88] P.C. § 28220(f)(1)(B).

[89] P.C. § 28220(f)(3)(A)-(B).

[90] P.C. § 28220(f)(4).

[91] Defined in 18 U.S.C. section 921(a)(34) as either a device that is designed to prevent the firearm from being operated without first deactivating the device; a device incorporated into the firearm's design to prevent the firearm from being operated by anyone without access to the device; or a safe, gun safe, gun case, lock box, or other device designed to be, or that can be, used to store a firearm and that is designed to only be unlocked with a key, combination, etc.

[92] 18 U.S.C. § 922(z)(1)-(2). Exceptions include: transfer to or by the U.S., a state, its departments, agencies, or subdivisions, or law enforcement officers employed by any of these entities; transfer to a rail police officer for law enforcement purposes; transfer of a "curio or relic" to a licensed collector; and transfer whereby the secure gun storage device is unavailable due to theft, casualty, loss, consumer sales, back orders, etc., beyond FFL control, and where the FFL delivers a secure gun storage or safety device within ten days after the transfer.

[93] P.C. § 23635(a). A "firearm safety device" means a device other than a gun safe that locks and is designed to prevent children and unauthorized users from firing a firearm. The device may be installed on a firearm, incorporated into the design of the firearm, or prevent access to the firearm. P.C. § 16540.

[94] P.C. § 23640. When a firearm is sold or transferred within California, the packaging and any descriptive material must bear a warning label (in both English and Spanish) that states that firearms should be handled responsibly and be securely stored to prevent access by children and other unauthorized users, that information on firearm laws can be found at the California Attorney General's website, and that a firearm owner may face criminal prosecution for failing to abide by California's firearm laws. As of June 1, 2020, the warning label must also include language that references the national suicide prevention lifeline.

"Roster of Firearm Safety Devices Certified for Sale" and identified as appropriate for the specific firearm.[95]

This safety device requirement does not apply if:

(1) You own a gun safe that meets certain standards[96] and you present an original receipt for it or proof of owning the gun safe as authorized by the AG;[97] or

(2) You purchase an approved safety device no more than 30 days before you take possession of the firearm; you present the approved safety device to the FFL when picking up the firearm; you present an original receipt to the FFL showing the safety device's purchase date, name, and the model number;[98] or

(3) You buy an "antique firearm";[99] or

(4) You are employed as a salaried full-time peace officer.[100]

Examples of "Firearm Safety Devices"

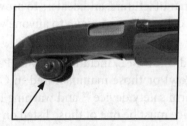

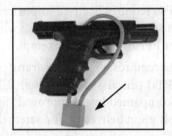

Example of a trigger lock on a shotgun   Example of a cable lock

Note that federal safety device requirement (see above) is different from California's in both its scope and exceptions because, unlike California law, the federal requirement only applies to handguns. FFLs should be careful to make sure a locking device meets both state and federal requirements. For the general public, however, the most important distinction is that federal law does not recognize California's gun-safe affidavit exception when the transfer involves *handguns*. So, despite California law, a gun-safe affidavit is only valid when the transfer involves a *long gun*.

---

[95] P.C. § 23635(a). The entire Roster is found on DOJ's website. *Roster of Firearm Safety Devices Certified for Sale,* CAL. DEPT. OF JUSTICE, OFFICE OF THE ATTORNEY GENERAL, http://oag.ca.gov/firearms/fsdcertlist (last visited Oct. 10, 2020).

[96] P.C. § 23650(a)(3).

[97] P.C. § 23635(b)(2). But, this safe-affidavit exception is not recognized for *handgun* transfers under federal law.

[98] P.C. § 23635(c).

[99] P.C. § 23630. Discussed in Chapter 3.

[100] P.C. § 23630.

8. Firearm Safety Certificate

Anyone purchasing a firearm (handgun or long gun) must present a valid Firearm Safety Certificate (FSC) to the licensed firearms dealer to show that he or she has passed a written "Firearm Safety" test, unless they fall under an exception (see subsection below). The FSC requirement replaced the former Handgun Safety Certificate (HSC) requirement that was in place prior to January 1, 2015. Under that requirement, handgun purchasers were required to show an HSC to the dealer, showing that he or she passed a written "Handgun Safety" test. In 2013, however, the California Legislature passed a bill Senate Bill (SB) 683, which expanded these requirements and its exemptions to apply to all firearm purchases.

To obtain an FSC, the individual wishing to purchase the firearm must pass a written "Firearm Safety" test administered by a DOJ Certified Instructor. Most FFLs or their employees are FSC Certified Instructors who can administer the written test in their store, even on the same day as your purchase. The test includes thirty multiple-choice questions and costs up to $25 ($15 of which goes to DOJ, and the rest goes to the instructor).[101] You must correctly answer at least 75% of the questions in order to get the FSC. That means that you must answer, at least, twenty-three of the thirty questions correctly to pass the "Firearm Safety" test.[102]

After passing the test, the FSC is only good for five years.[103] If you lose or completely destroy your FSC, you can get a duplicate certificate by asking the instructor who issued the test to you for one, proving your identity, and paying up to $15.[104] To be clear, an FSC is only necessary to receive a firearm (handgun or long gun). It is not necessary, however, to *possess* one.

a. "Firearm Safety" Certificate Exemptions

The following people, property, and transactions are exempt from the FSC requirement:

---

[101] P.C. § 31650(b).

[102] P.C. § 31645(a). Do not be concerned about passing this test. It is relatively straightforward, and the FFL has materials to review before taking it. The dealer should have copies or you can study up online at: http://oag.ca.gov/sites/all/files/agweb/pdfs/firearms/forms/hscsg.pdf (last visited Oct. 10, 2020). If English is not your first language, you are entitled to a translator if you need one. P.C. § 31640(b). But the translator cannot help you answer the questions.

[103] *Frequently Asked Questions*, CAL. DEPT. OF JUSTICE, OFFICE OF THE ATTORNEY GENERAL, https://oag.ca.gov/firearms/fscpfaqs (last visited Oct. 10, 2020).

[104] P.C. § 31660.

Table 5.2

Penal Code Section	Exemption
P.C. § 31700(a)(1)	Active or honorably retired peace officers as defined in Chapter 4.5 of Title 3 of Part 2 of the Penal Code (commencing with P.C. section 830)
P.C. § 31700(a)(2)	Active or honorably retired federal officers or law enforcement agents
P.C. § 31700(a)(3)	Reserve peace officers as defined in P.C. section 832.6
P.C. § 31700(a)(4)	Anyone who has successfully completed the peace officer training course in P.C. section 832
P.C. § 31700(a)(5)	California FFLs acting in the scope of their duties as an FFL
P.C. § 31700(a)(6)	Licensed collectors who are acquiring or being loaned a firearm that is a "curio or relic" and who have a COE issued by DOJ under P.C. section 26710
P.C. § 31700(a)(7)	Firearm owners who are having their firearms returned to them. But this exemption shall not apply to the return of that firearm to that person, if the person has requested the firearm and is eligible to receive it.
P.C. § 31700(a)(8)	Family members of peace officers or deputy sheriffs killed in the line of duty who receive a firearm under Cal. Gov't Code section 50081
P.C. § 31700(a)(9)	Anyone with a valid carry license (i.e., a license issued under P.C. section 26150 and 26155)
P.C. § 31700(a)(10)	Active or honorably retired members of the U.S. Armed Forces, National Guard, Air National Guard, or the U.S. active reserve
P.C. § 31700(a)(11)	Anyone authorized to carry loaded firearms in the scope of their employment under P.C. section 26025 and 26030(a)-(c); such as patrol special police, animal control officers, zookeepers, harbor police officers, guards, messengers, private investigators, and private patrol officers; and DOJ-issued special weapons permit holders
P.C. § 31700(a)(12)	Anyone who holds a special weapons permit issued under P.C. sections 32650 (for machinegun manufacturing) or 33300 (for short-barreled rifle/shotguns), 18900 through 18910 (for destructive devices), or 32700 through 32720 (for machinegun sales)

Penal Code Section	Exemption
P.C. § 31700(b)(1)-(6)	Those who take possession of firearms by operation of law in a representative capacity, such as an executor, personal representative, or administrator of an estate, a secured creditor or employee who possess it as collateral, a levying officer, a receiver, a bankruptcy trustee, or an assignee for the benefit of creditors.
P.C. § 31700(b)(7)-(13)	Those who take possession of firearms by operation of law in a representative capacity, such as a trustee of a trust, a person acting pursuant to the person's power of attorney, a limited or general conservator appoint by a court, a guardian ad litem, a special administrator, or a guardian appointed by a court.
P.C. § 31700(c)	Any person who has been issued a valid hunting license that is unexpired or that was issued for the hunting season immediately preceding the calendar year in which the person is takes title or possession of the long gun. This exception does not apply to handgun purchases
P.C. § 31700(d)	A person who takes possession of a firearm for purposes of delivering the firearm to a law enforcement agency pursuant to P.C. section 27922.
P.C. § 31700(e)	A person being loaned a firearm pursuant to P.C. sections 27882 or 27883.
P.C. § 31705	The sale, delivery, or transfer of firearms made to an authorized law enforcement representative of any city, county, city and county, or state, or of the federal government, for exclusive use by the governmental agency if, prior to the sale, delivery, or transfer of these firearms, written authorization[103] from the head of the agency authorizing the transaction is presented to the person from whom the purchase, delivery, or transfer is being made
P.C. § 31740	The sale, delivery, or transfer of firearms between or to importers and licensed firearm manufacturers
P.C. § 31830	The loan of an unloaded firearm to a consultant-evaluator by a person licensed under P.C. sections 26700-26915 (i.e., a California-licensed firearms dealer), if the loan does not exceed 45 days from the date of delivery

Penal Code Section	Exemption
P.C. § 31710	Loans of firearms by law enforcement agencies to peace officers if the following conditions are satisfied: (1) The loan is made by an authorized law enforcement representative of a city, county, or city and county, or of the state or federal government; *and* (2) The loan is made to a peace officer employed by that agency and authorized to carry a firearm; *and* (3) The loan is made for the carrying and use of that firearm by that peace officer in the course and scope of the officer's duties
P.C. § 31715	The sale, delivery, or transfer of a firearm by a law enforcement agency to a peace officer pursuant to Cal. Pub. Contract Code section 10334
P.C. § 31720	The sale, delivery, or transfer of a firearm by a law enforcement agency to a retiring peace officer who is authorized to carry a firearm under Chapter 5 (commencing with P.C. section 26300) of Division 5
P.C. § 31725	The sale, delivery or transfer of a firearm if both of the following are satisfied: (1) The sale, delivery, or transfer is to an authorized representative of a city, city and county, county, or state government, or of the federal government, and is for the governmental entity; *and* (2) The entity is acquiring the weapon as part of an authorized, voluntary program in which the entity is buying or receiving weapons from private individuals

Penal Code Section	Exemption
P.C. § 31730	The sale, delivery, loan, or transfer of a firearm by an authorized law enforcement representative of a city, county, city and county, or state, or of the federal government, to any public or private nonprofit historical society, museum, or institutional collection, or the purchase or receipt of that firearm by that public or private nonprofit historical society, museum, or institutional collection, if: (1) The entity receiving the firearm is open to the public; *and* (2) The firearm prior to delivery is deactivated or rendered inoperable; *and* (3) The firearm is not subject to P.C. sections 18000, 18005, 34000, 34005, 34010, or Division 4 (commencing with P.C. section 18250) of Title 2 (governing firearm surrender or forfeiture because it was used in a crime and/or not claimed by law enforcement); *and* (4) The firearm is not prohibited by other provisions of law from being sold, delivered, or transferred to the public at large
P.C. § 31745	The sale, delivery, or transfer of a handgun to an FFL, where the FFL is receiving the handgun in the course and scope of his or her activities as a person licensed under P.C. sections 26700-26915

Penal Code Section	Exemption
P.C. § 31735	The sale, delivery, loan, or transfer of a firearm made by a person other than a representative of an authorized law enforcement agency to any public or private nonprofit historical society, museum, or institutional collection, if all of the following conditions are met: (1) The entity receiving the firearm is open to the public; *and* (2) The firearm is deactivated or rendered inoperable prior to delivery; *and* (3) The firearm is not a type prohibited from being sold, delivered, or transferred to the public; *and* (4) Prior to delivery, the entity receiving the firearm submits a written statement to the person selling, loaning, or transferring the firearm stating that the firearm will not be restored to operating condition, and will either remain with that entity, or if subsequently disposed of, will be transferred in accordance with the applicable provisions listed in P.C. section 16575 and, if applicable, with P.C. section 31615
P.C. § 31750	The loan of a firearm if the following conditions are met: (1) The person loaning the firearm is at all times within the presence of the person being loaned the firearm; *and* (2) The loan is for a lawful purpose; *and* (3) The loan does not exceed three days in duration; *and* (4) The individual receiving the firearm is not prohibited by state or federal law from possessing, receiving, owning, or purchasing a firearm; *and* (5) The person loaning the firearm is 18 years of age or older; *and* (6) The person receiving the firearm is 18 years of age or older
P.C. § 31755	The delivery of a firearm to a gunsmith for service or repair, or to the return of the firearm to its owner by the gunsmith, or to the delivery of a firearm by a gunsmith to a person licensed under Chapter 44 (commencing P.C. section 921) of Title 18 of the United States Code (i.e., a firearms manufacturer, importer, or dealer licensed under federal law) for service or repair and the return of the firearm to the gunsmith

Penal Code Section	Exemption
P.C. § 31760	The sale, delivery, or transfer of firearms if all the following requirements are satisfied: (1) The sale, delivery, or transfer is made by a person who resides in California; *and* (2) The sale, delivery, or transfer is made to a person who resides outside this state is an FFL; *and* (3) The sale, delivery, or transfer is in accordance with Chapter 44 (commencing P.C. section 921) of Title 18 of the United States Code and the regulations thereto (i.e., the requirements for firearms transfer under federal law)
P.C. § 31765	The loan of a firearm to a person 18 years of age or older for the purpose of target shooting at targets if the loan occurs on the premises of a target facility that holds a business or regulatory license, or on the premises of any club or organization organized for the purpose of practice shooting at targets upon established ranges, whether public or private, if the firearm is at all times kept within the premises of the target range or on the premises of the club or organization
P.C. § 31770	The delivery, transfer, or return of firearms made pursuant to any of the following: (1) P.C. sections 18000 and 18005 (stating the manner a weapon or instrument should be confiscated and destroyed); *and* (2) Division 4 (commencing with Section 18250) of Title 2 (governing seizure of firearm or other deadly weapon at scene of domestic violence); *and* (3) Chapter 2 (commencing with Section 33850) of Division 11 (governing the return or transfer of firearm in custody or control of a court or law enforcement agency); *and* (4) P.C. sections 34005 (providing alternatives to destruction of firearms) and 34010 (requiring law enforcement retaining custody of, or destroying, a firearm to notify DOJ of the retention or destruction)
P.C. § 31780	The sale, delivery, transfer of unloaded firearms by an FFL to an FFL outside of California

Penal Code Section	Exemption
P.C. § 31785	The sale, delivery, or transfer of unloaded firearms to a wholesaler if the firearms are being returned to the wholesaler and are intended as merchandise in the wholesaler's business
P.C. § 31790	The sale, delivery, or transfer of a firearm if all the following are met: (1) The firearms are unloaded; *and* (2) The sale, delivery, or transfer is made by one FFL to another FFL, upon proof of compliance with the requirements of P.C. section 27555 (which governs the California Firearms Licensee Check System); *and* (3) The firearms are intended as merchandise in the receiving FFL's business
P.C. § 31800	The loan of an unloaded firearm by an FFL who also operates a target facility that holds a business or regulatory license on the premises of the building designated in the license or whose building designated in the license is on the premises of any club or organization organized for the purposes of practicing shooting at targets upon established ranges, whether public or private, to a person at that target facility or that club or organization, if the firearm is at all times kept within the premises of the target range or on the premises of the club or organization
P.C. § 31805	The sale, delivery, or transfer of unloaded firearms to a wholesaler as merchandise in the wholesaler's business by a manufacturer or importer licensed to engage in that business under federal law, or by another wholesaler, if the sale, delivery, or transfer is made in accordance with federal law

Penal Code Section	Exemption
P.C. § 31815	The loan of a firearm if all of the following requirements are satisfied: (1) The loan is "infrequent"[105]; *and* (2) The firearm is unloaded; *and* (3) The loan is made by a person who is neither a dealer nor an FFL; *and* (4) The loan is made to a person 18 years of age or older; *and* (5) The loan is for use solely as a prop in a motion picture, television, video, theatrical, or other entertainment production event
P.C. § 31835	The delivery, sale, or transfer of a firearm when made by authorized law enforcement representatives for cities, counties, cities and counties, or of the state or federal government, if all of the following conditions are met: (1) The sale, delivery, or transfer is made to one of the persons or entities identified in P.C. section 26620(a); *and* (2) The sale, delivery, or transfer is not subject to the procedures set forth in P.C. sections 18000 (surrendering weapons to authorities), 18005 (offer of surrendered weapons for sale at public auction, stolen weapons, weapons used in manner constituting nuisance without knowledge of owner, destruction of surrendered weapons), 34000 (firearms no longer needed as exhibits in criminal actions or proceedings, firearms that are unclaimed or abandoned property, sale or destruction), or 34005 (alternatives to destruction of firearms); *and* (3) The sale, delivery, or transfer of the firearm follows the procedures set forth in P.C. section 26620 (i.e., the receiving agency registers the firearm in the Automated Firearms System).

---

[105] "Infrequent" means less than 6 firearm transactions per calendar year, regardless of the type of firearm, and no more than 50 total firearms in total. P.C. § 16730.

Penal Code Section	Exemption
P.C. § 31810	The FSC requirement does not apply to or affect the following: (1) The loan of a firearm to a minor by the minor's parent or legal guardian, provided that both of the following conditions are met: 　(a) The minor is being loaned the firearm for the purpose of engaging in a lawful, recreational sport, including but not limited to, competitive shooting, or agricultural, ranching, or hunting activity or hunting education, or a motion picture, television, or video production, or entertainment or theatrical event, the nature of which involves the use of a firearm; *and* 　(b) The duration of the loan does not exceed the amount of time that is reasonably necessary to engage in the activity. (2) The loan of a firearm to a minor by a person who is not the minor's parent or legal guardian, provided all the following conditions are met: 　(a) The minor is accompanied by the minor's parent or legal guardian when the loan is made, or the minor has the written consent of his or her parent or legal guardian, which is presented at the time of the loan, or earlier; *and* 　(b) The minor is being loaned the firearm for a lawful, recreational sport, including, but not limited to, competitive shooting, or agricultural, ranching, or hunting activity or hunting education, or a motion picture, television, or video production, or entertainment or theatrical event, the nature of which involves the use of a firearm; *and* 　(c) The duration of the loan does not exceed the time that is reasonably necessary to engage in the activity; *and* 　(d) The duration of the loan does not, in any event, exceed ten days.

Penal Code Section	Exemption
P.C. § 31820	The loan of a firearm if all the following requirements are satisfied: (1) The firearm is unloaded; *and* (2) The loan is made by a person who is not a dealer but is an FFL; *and* (3) The loan is made to a person who possesses a valid entertainment firearms permit issued under Chapter 2 (commencing with Section 29500) of Division 8; *and* (4) The firearm is loaned solely as a prop in a motion picture, television, video, theatrical, or other entertainment production event; *and* (5) The person loaned the firearm retains a photocopy of the entertainment firearms permit as proof of compliance with these requirements
P.C. § 31825	The loan of a firearm if all the following requirements are satisfied: (1) The firearm is unloaded; *and* (2) The loan is made by a dealer; *and* (3) The loan is made to a person who possesses a valid firearms permit issued in accordance with Chapter 2 (commencing with P.C. section 29500) of Division 8; *and* (4) The firearm is loaned solely for use as a prop in a motion picture, television, video, theatrical, or other entertainment event; *and* (5) The dealer must retains a copy of the entertainment firearms permit as proof of compliance with this requirement

b. **Firearm Safe-Handling Demonstration**

Anyone acquiring a firearm (long gun or handgun) must perform a safe-handling demonstration in front of a DOJ Certified Instructor before receiving the firearm.[106] For example, if you are receiving a pump action long gun, you must demonstrate, among other things, that you can safely open the ejection port, visually and physically inspect the chamber to ensure the firearm is unloaded, that you can remove the firearm safety device, and engage the safety.[107] The dealer may assist you during

---

[106] P.C. §§ 26850, 26860.

[107] *Firearm Safety Certificate, Manual*, CAL. DEPT. OF JUSTICE, OFFICE OF THE ATTORNEY GENERAL (Jan. 2015), *available at* https://oag.ca.gov/sites/all/files/agweb/pdfs/firearms/forms/hscman.pdf (last visited Oct. 10, 2020).

the demonstration if needed. Anyone who is exempt from the FSC requirement is also exempt from the safe-handling demonstration (see subsection above).

As many gun owners may remember, prior to January 1, 2015, only those who were purchasing handguns were required to perform a safe-handling demonstration. But, this all changed when the California Legislature passed Assembly Bill (AB) 683.[108]

Under this bill, DOJ was required to adopt regulations before January 1, 2015, that establish FSC regulations and a long gun safe-handling demonstration requirement that included, at a minimum, the loading and unloading of the long gun.[109] When January 1, 2015, rolled around, DOJ had not promulgated or established any kind of regulations for the long gun safe-handling demonstration, despite the fact that they were required to do so under the law. Instead, DOJ attempted to underhandedly create an FSC and safe-handling program by sending a letter to firearm dealers outlining the new procedures that added additional requirements on DOJ Certified Instructors that did not exist before. For example, under the temporary regulations Certified Instructors are required to obtain a COE, have access to a personal computer, printer, and email; and only allow Instructors to accept payments from major credit cards. As a result, the California Rifle & Pistol Association, FFLGuard, and several individual gun owners and firearm instructors sued DOJ in *Belemjian v. Harris*.[110]

Ultimately, this lawsuit pushed DOJ to promulgate temporary emergency regulations for the FSC and safe-handling demonstration requirement. As a result, the lawsuit was dismissed.[111] But, DOJ was still required to create an adopt permanent regulations for the FSC and safe-handling demonstration program.

After promulgating permanent regulations, pro-gun groups and concerned citizens submitted public comments to voice their opinions about some of the burdensome and unworkable requirements contained in the FSC regulations. But DOJ ignored the hundreds of public comments it received and chose not to change anything about its regulations. On March 23, 2016, the Office of Administrative finally approved DOJ's permanent regulations. These regulations can now be found at Cal. Code Regs. tit. 11, sections 4250-4259.

---

[108] *See* AB 683, 2013-2014, Leg. Counsel's Digest (Cal. 2014), *available at* http://leginfo.legislature.ca.gov/faces/billNavClient.xhtml?bill_id=201320140SB683 (last visited Oct. 10, 2020).

[109] P.C. § 26860(b).

[110] *See* Verified Complaint for Declaratory and Injunctive Relief and Petition for Writ of Mandate, *Belemjian v. Harris*, No. 15 CECG00029 (Cal. Super. Ct. Jan. 6, 2015), *available at* http://michellawyers.com/wp-content/uploads/2015/01/Complaint.pdf (last visited Oct. 10, 2020).

[111] *See* Judgement of Dismissal, *Belemjian v. Harris*, No. 15 CECG 00029 (Cal. Super. Ct. Jan. 6, 2015), *available at* http://michellawyers.com/wp-content/uploads/2015/01/Belemjian_Judgment-of-Dismissal-After-Sustaining-of-Demurrer-to-Firsts-Amended-Complaint-Without-Leave-to-Amend.pdf (last visited Oct. 10, 2020).

B. Additional Purchase Requirements[112]

1. Only One Firearm Purchase Every 30 Days

Until July 1, 2021, you are not allowed to purchase, or even apply to purchase, more than one handgun within any 30-day period.[113]

There are exceptions to this restriction. Specifically, the following people, agencies, and facilities are exempt from the one handgun every 30-day restriction:

(1) Any law enforcement agency;

(2) Any agency duly authorized to perform law enforcement duties;

(3) Any state or local correctional facility;

(4) Any private security company licensed to do business in California;

(5) Any person who is properly identified as a full-time paid peace officer,[114] who is authorized to, and does, carry a firearm during the course and scope of his or her employment as a peace officer;

(6) Any motion picture, television, or video production company or entertainment or theatrical company whose production by its nature involves the use of a firearm;

(7) Any person who may claim an exemption to the waiting period under P.C. section 27600-27620 (exceptions relating to law enforcement), P.C. section 27650-27670 (exceptions only to waiting period), or P.C. section 27700-27750 (exceptions to the restrictions on delivery of a firearm);

(8) Any transaction conducted through a licensed firearm dealer under P.C. section 28050-28070 (private party transfers);

(9) Any person who is licensed as a collector under 18 U.S.C. 921-931 and the regulations issued pursuant thereto, and who has a current COE issued by DOJ under P.C. section 26700-26725;

(10) The exchange of a handgun where the dealer purchased the firearm from the person seeking the exchange within the 30-day period immediately preceding the date of exchange or replacement;

(11) The replacement of a handgun when the person's handgun was lost or stolen, and the person reported that firearm lost or stolen prior to the completion of the application to purchase to any local law enforcement agency of the city, county, or city and county, in which the person resides;

---

[112] See Chapters 9 and 10 for restrictions on which handguns an FFL can lawfully sell in California.
[113] P.C. § 27535(a).
[114] As defined in P.C. sections 830-832.9.

(12) The return of any handgun to its owner; *and,*

(13) A community college that is certified by the Commission on Peace Officer Standards and Training (POST) to present the law enforcement academy basic course or other commission-certified law enforcement training.[115]

This restriction does *not* apply to intra-familial transfers or operation of law transfers, and it does not apply to PPTs (discussed below).

But due to the enactment of SB 61 in 2019, the above restriction and listed exceptions will change on July 1, 2021, to prohibit Californians from purchasing more than one handgun *or semiautomatic centerfire rifle* (no longer just handguns) within any 30-day period.[116] Only the following are exempt from this restriction:

(1) Any law enforcement agency;

(2) Any agency duly authorized to perform law enforcement duties;

(3) Any state or local correctional facility;

(4) Any private security company licensed to do business in California;

(5) Any person who is properly identified as a full-time paid peace officer authorized to, and does, carry a firearm during the course and scope of his or her employment as a peace officer;

(6) Any motion picture, television, or video production company or entertainment or theatrical company whose production by its nature involves the use of a firearm;

(7) Any person who may claim an exemption to the waiting period under P.C. section 27600-27620 (exceptions relating to law enforcement), P.C. section 27650-27670 (exceptions only to waiting period), or P.C. section 27700-27750 (exceptions to the restrictions on delivery of a firearm);

(8) Any transaction conducted through a licensed firearm dealer under P.C. section 28050-28070 (private party transfers);

(9) Any person who is licensed as a collector under 18 U.S.C. 921-931 and the regulations issued pursuant thereto, and who has a current COE issued by DOJ under P.C. section 26700-26725;

(10) The exchange of a handgun or semiautomatic centerfire rifle where the dealer purchased that firearm from the person seeking the exchange within the 30-day period immediately preceding the date of exchange or replacement;

(11) (The replacement of a handgun or semiautomatic centerfire rifle when the person's firearm was lost or stolen, and the person reported that firearm

---

[115] P.C. § 27535(b).
[116] P.C. § 27535(a).

lost or stolen prior to the completion of the application to purchase the replacement;

(12) The return of any handgun or semiautomatic centerfire rifle to its owner; and, *and,*

(13) A community college that is certified by the Commission on Peace Officer Standards and Training (POST) to present the law enforcement academy basic course or other commission-certified law enforcement training.[117]

First-time violators who apply to purchase more than one handgun (or semi-automatic centerfire rifle on or after July 1, 2021) within any 30-day period may be fined up to $50.[118] A second violation can be punished with a fine up to $100, and a third violation is a misdemeanor.[119]

2. Proof of Residency

In addition to providing proof of your identification and age to obtain a *handgun*, under California law, you must also provide documentation that you are a California resident.[120] The address that is considered your "residence" is not explained in the Penal Code. But, California Government Code (Cal. Gov't Code) section 244 sheds some light on what may be considered your place of "residence" in California.

In determining your place of residence, the following criteria apply:

(1) It is the place where one remains when not called elsewhere for labor or other special or temporary purpose, and to which he or she returns in seasons of repose.

(2) There can only be one residence.

(3) A residence cannot be lost until another is gained.

(4) The residence of the parent with whom an unmarried minor child maintains his or her place of abode is the residence of such unmarried minor child.

(5) The residence of an unmarried minor who has a parent living cannot be changed by his or her own act.

(6) The residence can be changed only by the union of act and intent.

(7) A married person shall have the right to retain his or her legal residence in the State of California notwithstanding the legal residence or domicile of his or her spouse.[121]

Under California law, you can prove residency by using one of the documents listed in Table 5.3, such as

---

[117] P.C. § 27535(b)(1-13) (effective July 1, 2021).
[118] P.C. § 27590(e)(1).
[119] P.C. § 27590(e)(2), (e)(3).
[120] P.C. § 26845.
[121] Cal. Gov't Code § 244.

(1) A utility bill from the last three months;

(2) A residential lease;

(3) A property deed; *or,*

(4) Military permanent duty station orders showing assignment within this state, or other residency evidence allowed by DOJ.[122]

Each of these documents, except for military permanent duty station orders,[123] must meet certain requirements under the California Code of Regulations (Cal. Code Regs.) before they can be accepted.[124]

Issues have occurred with people being unable to make this documentary showing; for example, those living at a place where their name is not on any deed, lease, or utility bill. If you find yourself in this situation, contact a lawyer with experience in firearms law.

---

[122] CAL. CODE REGS. tit. 11, § 4045; P.C. § 26845.

[123] Although the California Code of Regulations outlines the requirements for utility bills, residential leases, and property deeds, they do not outline requirements for when a person's military permanent duty station orders can be accepted as proof of residency in California. *See* CAL. CODE REGS. tit. 11, § 4045. Therefore, it is unclear as to when a person's military permanent duty station orders would be sufficient to prove residency. For example, is there a specific date or time frame that the permanent duty station orders must have been issued in order for it to be acceptable? This question remains unanswered by the Penal Code and the California Code of Regulations. But, it would appear military permanent duty station orders showing assignment in California are sufficient to meet the residency requirement, regardless of when they were issued.

[124] A list of acceptable forms for "Proof of Residency" can be found at: https://oag.ca.gov/firearms/dlrfaqs#13G (last visited Oct. 10, 2020).

Table 5.3

PROOF OF RESIDENCY REQUIREMENT
AN ADDITIONAL REQUIREMENT WHEN PURCHASING HANDGUNS IN CALIFORNIA

In addition to providing proof of your identity, you must also provide documentation that you are a California resident if you are attempting to purchase a handgun in California. Any of the following documents will be accepted to show proof of residency[125]:

Utility Bill: A utility bill is a statement of charges for providing direct services to your residence. This includes either a physical connection (*i.e.*, a landline telephone, water, gas connection, etc.) or a telemetric connection (*i.e.*, satellite TV, or radio broadcast service bill) to a non-mobile, fixed antenna reception device. The utility bill must state the following in order to fulfill the proof of residency requirements:

(1) A date that is within three months of the current date; *and*
(2) Either your current residential address as declared on the DROS form or your address (or change of address) as it appears on (or attached to) your California driver license or California ID.

Residential Lease: A Residential Lease is either a signed and dated contract by which a tenant agrees to pay some amount or provides other consideration for the right to occupy a residence for a specified period of time, or a rental agreement signed and dated, in which the tenant agrees to pay some amount or provide other consideration at fixed intervals for the right to occupy a residence. The lease must state the following:

(1) Your name; *and*
(2) Either your current residential address as declared on the DROS form or your address (or change of address) as it appears on (or attached to) your California driver license or California ID.

Property Deed: A property deed is a valid deed of trust for your current residence that identifies you as the grantee of trust, or a valid Certificate of Title issued by a licensed title insurance company that identifies you as a title holder to your property of current residence. The property deed must state the following:

(1) Your name; *and*
(2) Either your current residential address as declared on the DROS form or your address (or change of address) as it appears on (or attached to) your California driver license or California ID.

Other Evidence of Residency: DOJ may accept other forms of proof of residence. This includes a valid peace officer credential issued by a California law enforcement agency to an active, reserve, or retired peace officer. This other proof of residency also includes a current government-issued license, permit, or registration (other than a California driver license or ID) that has a specific expiration date or period of validity. The license, permit, or registration must include the following:

(1) Your name; *and*
(2) Either your current residential address as declared on the DROS form or your address (or change of address) as it appears on (or attached to) your California driver license or California ID.

---

[125] *See* CAL. CODE REGS. tit. 11, § 4045.

Table 5.4

QUICK GUIDE: THE PROCESS AND REQUIRED MATERIALS TO PURCHASE A FIREARM FROM A LICENSED FIREARMS DEALER IN CALIFORNIA & CONDUCT PRIVATE PARTY TRANSFERS

PURCHASING FIREARMS (HANDGUNS & LONG GUNS)

The following is a quick checklist of the process and sale requirements that must be met before you can purchase a firearm (handgun or long gun) from a licensed dealer in California (see above for the specific requirements of each):

> **BEWARE!**
>
> Federal law requires that you bring a valid *government-issued* "identification document" that has your name, picture, date of birth, and *current* home address.
>
> If your identification, such as your California driver license, does not reflect your current home address, then it will not meet the identification requirement and an additional government-issued document is required.
>
> Remember, not providing your current home address and providing a false address is a violation of federal law.

✓ **Identification, Age, and Address**: In order to purchase a firearm, you must have some form of valid identification that presents clear evidence of your identity, age, and address. This requires you to have a California driver license or California identification card. Military identification accompanied by permanent duty station orders indicating a posting in California will suffice.

✓ **Complete Federal Form 4473**: This form is required when any firearm is *transferred* to you by an FFL. If you are a *full-time paid peace officer*, however, then you are not required to fill out this form if you certify, on agency letterhead with an authorized signature, that a records check shows you do not have a misdemeanor domestic violence conviction and will use the firearm for official duties. A single form can be used for all firearms purchased at the same time.

✓ **Complete a Dealer's Record of Sales (DROS) Form**: California law also requires a completed DROS form. As of January 1, 2014, the information required on the form for all firearms includes (1) firearm type; (2) transaction type; (3) waiting period requirement exemptions; (4) and your name, address, birth date, etc. Your thumbprint must also be taken and, as of January 1, 2014, the FFL is required to give you a copy of the DROS form at the time the firearm is delivered to you.[126] A separate DROS form is required for each firearm transferred.

✓ **Ten-Day Waiting Period**: You must wait ten days (meaning ten 24-hour periods) from when your DROS form is submitted until you may lawfully receive any firearm transferred from an FFL. But, certain people are exempt from the ten-day waiting period. See Section I(A)(6) of this Chapter for a list of people who are exempt.

✓ **Receive Required Lock Device and Warnings**: California law requires that all firearms transferred by an FFL be accompanied by an approved "firearm safety device" (with certain exceptions). Federal law requires a safety device for handguns delivered by a dealer. California law also requires warning language or labels upon delivery.

✓ **Firearm Safety Requirement**: Anyone purchasing a firearm must present a Firearm Safety Certificate (FSC) to the dealer, and anyone acquiring a firearm must perform a safe handling demonstration before receiving a firearm from a licensed firearm dealer. There are exceptions to this requirement.

✓ **Firearm Safe Handling Demonstration**: Before receiving your firearm, California law requires you to perform a safe handling demonstration in front of a DOJ Certified Instructor. If you are physically unable to perform the demonstration, you may be exempt from the demonstration requirement if you have a letter from your physician stating you are physically unable to perform it.

---

[126] P.C. §§ 26840, 26860, 31615.

> **QUICK GUIDE: THE PROCESS AND REQUIRED MATERIALS TO PURCHASE A FIREARM FROM A LICENSED FIREARMS DEALER IN CALIFORNIA & CONDUCT PRIVATE PARTY TRANSFERS**
>
> **ADDITIONAL REQUIREMENTS FOR PURCHASING HANDGUNS**
>
> There are additional requirements that you must meet if you intend on purchasing a handgun from a licensed firearms dealer in California:
>
> ✓ **Proof of Residency**: In addition to providing proof of your identification and age, you must also provide documentation that you are a California resident. See Section I(B)(2) of this Chapter for information on how to determine where "your place of residence" is located.
>
> > **BEWARE!**
> >
> > You are not allowed to purchase, or even apply to purchase, more than one handgun from a dealer within a *30-day waiting period* in California. First-time violators who apply to purchase more than one handgun within this waiting period may be fined up to $50, a second violation may result in a fine up to $100, and a third violation is a misdemeanor.
> >
> > There are exceptions to this restriction, however. See Section (I)(B)(2) of this Chapter for the specific exceptions.

II. PRIVATE PARTY FIREARM TRANSFERS

A PPT occurs when firearms are transferred between two private parties, neither of whom is a California-licensed firearms dealer.[127] Both California and federal law have different requirements for *interstate* and *intrastate* PPTs and for handguns versus long guns. With few exceptions, PPTs must be processed by an FFL.[128] Not using an FFL for a PPT is a misdemeanor, and you can be prosecuted for a felony if the firearm is a handgun.[129] FFLs are *required* to process PPTs upon request unless the FFL does *not* sell, transfer, or keep a handgun inventory.[130] In other words, an FFL can choose not to process PPTs involving handguns if they do not actually sell handguns. But, an FFL must process non-handgun PPTs.

Most of the same requirements for FFL transfers to individual buyers also apply to a PPT. A 4473 and DROS forms are still required, but the DROS form must include both the transferee's *and* the transferor's information.[131] Also, an FSC and safe handling demonstration will be required as discussed above.[132] If the firearm is a handgun, the transferee must also show proof of California residency. The handgun must also have a locking device when the FFL delivers it to the transferee, or the transferee must meet one of the exceptions to the locking device requirement

---

[127] You should be aware that an FFL that is *not* licensed *in California* pursuant to P.C. section 26700 is treated like a normal person and not a "dealer" for the purpose of these transfers.

[128] Under California law, years ago transfers by individuals did not need to go through a licensed firearms dealer and no record of the transaction needed to be retained. Through 1990, handguns could still be transferred between two individuals who resided in California, provided that the individuals personally knew each other, and long guns could be freely transferred between residents of California. Provided that the firearm is not illegal for you to possess currently, there is no requirement that you register your firearm or go back through a licensed firearms dealer.

[129] P.C. §§ 27545, 27590(c)(5).

[130] P.C. § 28065.

[131] *See* P.C. § 28060(c). The transferor's information is required in case the transferee is prohibited from acquiring firearms. DOJ can conduct a background check on the transferor to determine if returning the firearm is legal.

[132] P.C. § 26860.

(discussed above).Finally, PPTs are exempt from the "one per month" limitation.[133] This means you can *buy* as many handguns or semiautomatic centerfire rifles as you want in a month if you do so through a PPT. But, this does *not* mean you can *transfer* as many handguns or semiautomatic centerfire firearms as you want in a month. If you are not an FFL, you may not make "frequent" transactions or engage in the business" of dealing firearms. This is explained in detail below.

In addition to the DROS and other transfer fees, an FFL may charge a fee to process a PPT, but it cannot be more than $10 per firearm.[134]

If during the ten-day waiting period it is discovered you are prohibited from possessing firearms, the FFL can return the firearm to the transferor before the waiting period expires, unless the FFL determines the transferor is also prohibited. If this happens, the FFL must deliver the firearm to the sheriff or police chief who will dispose of the firearm accordingly.[135] Recently, however, law enforcement agencies refused to accept these firearms, not realizing that state law requires the FFL to surrender the firearms when this happens.

Lastly, the FFL is required to provide the seller and purchaser in the PPT a copy of the DROS form with the personal information of the other party redacted (*i.e.*, blacked out or removed).[136]

---

[133] P.C. § 27535(b).
[134] P.C. § 28055.
[135] P.C. § 28050(d).
[136] P.C. §§ 28210(e)-(f), 28215(e)-(f).

Table 5.5

Private Party Firearm Transfers
What is a Private Party Transfer?
A private party transfer (PPT) occurs when firearms are transferred between two *private* individuals, neither of whom is a licensed California firearms dealer.
Checklist for a Private Party Transfer

- ✓ **Almost All PPTs Must Be Conducted Through a Federal Firearms Licensee (FFL):** Under California law a PPT must be conducted through an FFL. The seller or transferor of the firearm must deliver the firearm to the FFL who will retain the firearm for the duration of the transfer. After the transaction is complete and the ten-day waiting period has passed, the FFL will deliver the firearm to the buyer or transferee.

> **REMEMBER**
> PPTs are exempt from the "one handgun per month" limitation. This means you can *buy* as many handguns as you want if done through a PPT. But, you cannot *transfer or sell* as many handguns or firearms as you want, as there are limits under California and federal law.

- ✓ **DROS Form:** Under California law both the *seller or transferor* and the *buyer or transferee* of a PPT must provide their information in the DROS form (in contrast, with non-PPTs, the seller/transferor need not provide information). As of January 1, 2014, the dealer is required to provide the seller or transferor and the buyer or transferee this form (with the other parties' personal information redacted) when the firearm is delivered.

- ✓ **Federal Form 4473:** The transferee or buyer must also complete a federal Form 4473 with all the necessary information.

- ✓ **Handgun and Firearm Safety Certificates:** If you are purchasing a handgun, or one is being transferred to you, then you must have an FSC.

- ✓ **Perform Safe Handling Demonstration**: Unless you meet an exception to the requirement you must perform a safe handling demonstration.

- ✓ **Ten-Day Waiting Period:** You must wait ten days (meaning ten 24-hour periods) from when your DROS Form is submitted until you may lawfully receive any firearm transferred from a PPT.

- ✓ **Locking Device and Warnings**: When the FFL delivers to the purchaser or transferee a handgun, the handgun must be accompanied by a locking device and warning language or labels. As for other firearms, they need to be accompanied by a locking device or other exception to the lock requirement when the FFL delivers them to you. For more information, see Section I of this Chapter.

- ✓ **Additional Proof of Residency (Handguns Only):** If you have purchased a handgun or it is being transferred to you in a PPT, you are still required to show proof to the FFL that you are a resident of the state.

III. DEALER LICENSE REQUIREMENTS AND SELLING YOUR FIREARMS

A. Federal Law

Federal law has a different definition of what it means to be a dealer of firearms. Under federal law, it is unlawful for any person[137] "except a licensed importer, licensed manufacturer, or licensed *dealer*, to *engage in the business* of importing, manufacturing, or dealing in firearms, or in the course of such business to ship, transport, or receive any firearm in interstate or foreign commerce."[138]

Both the GCA and the Code of Federal Regulations (C.F.R.) define a "dealer" as:

(1) Any person *engaged in the business* of selling firearms at *wholesale or retail; or*

(2) Any person engaged in the business of repairing firearms or of making or fitting special barrels, stocks, or trigger mechanisms to firearms; *or*

(3) Any person who is a pawnbroker.[139]

The Code of Federal Regulations defines a person "engaged in the business" as:

[A] person who devotes time, attention, and labor to dealing in firearms as a regular course of trade or business *with the principal objective of livelihood and profit* through the repetitive purchase and resale of firearms, but such term shall not include a person who makes occasional sales, exchanges, or purchases of firearms for the enhancement of a personal collection or for a hobby, or who sells all or part of his personal collection of firearms.[140]

The phrase "with the principal objective of livelihood and profit" means that the underlying intent of the sale or disposition of firearms is predominantly one of obtaining livelihood and pecuniary gain, as opposed to other reasons, such as

---

[137] Under the GCA, the term "person" includes "any individual, corporation, company, association, firm, partnership, society, or joint stock company." 18 U.S.C. § 921(a)(1).

[138] 18 U.S.C. § 922(a)(1)(A) (emphasis added). "The term 'interstate or foreign commerce' includes commerce between any place in a State and any place outside of that State, or within any possession of the United States (not including the Canal Zone) or the District of Columbia, but such term does not include commerce between places within the same State but through any place outside of that State. The term 'State' includes the District of Columbia, the Commonwealth of Puerto Rico, and the possessions of the United States (not including the Canal Zone)." 18 U.S.C. § 921(a)(2).

[139] 18 U.S.C. § 921(a)(11); 27 C.F.R. § 478.11. 18 U.S.C. section 921(a)(11) also defines a "licensed dealer" as anyone licensed under the provisions of 18 U.S.C. section 921.

[140] 18 U.S.C. § 921(a)(21)(C) (emphasis added).

improving or liquidating a personal firearms collection. The Code of Federal Regulations notes that proof of profit is not required for anyone engaged in the "regular and repetitive purchase and disposition of firearms for criminal purposes or terrorism."[141] Additionally, the Code of Federal Regulations states that you may be considered a dealer even if you engage in these activities on a part-time basis.

It is not unusual for people to believe they are fully complying with the law when they comply only with California's dealer's license requirements. But you must comply with both state and federal laws! Buying and selling *a few* firearms over the course of a year (while complying with both state and federal transfer requirements) might be legal under state and federal law. But conducting multiple transactions, buying and selling a number of firearms, and/or buying and immediately selling a recently purchased firearm may be an indication that you are *dealing* in firearms under federal law. *Dealing* in firearms without the proper licenses has some serious consequences.[142]

If you decide you do not want to possess a firearm anymore, there are some things to consider. Remember you must abide by the requirements discussed in the book relating to PPTs, interstate sales, transfers that don't need to go through a dealer, and laws relating to prohibited persons. The simplest option may be selling your firearm to a licensed firearms dealer.

B. California Law

In most cases, firearm transfers by anyone without an FFL must be "infrequent," even when the transfers are all processed through an FFL.[143] Following the adoption of SB 376 in 2019, the term "infrequent" is defined as the following:

(1) The person conducts less than six transactions per calendar year; and,

(2) The person sells, leases, or transfers no more than 50 total firearms per calendar year.[144]

As used in this definition, the term "transaction" is defined to mean a single sale, lease, or transfer of any number of firearms.[145]

---

[141] 18 U.S.C. § 921(a)(22).

[142] For example, in 2015, former Sacramento County Sheriff's Deputy Ryan McGowan was found guilty of engaging in the business of dealing in firearms without a license when he used his position as a sheriff's deputy to purchase "off-roster" handguns (see Chapter 10) and resold them at inflated prices to private individuals in California. See Jury Returns Guilty Verdict for Former Sacramento County Sheriff's Deputy and Federal Firearms Licensee in Firearm Straw-Buyer Scheme, Dep't of Justice, U.S. Attorney's Office, Eastern District of California (June 11, 2015), *available at* https://www.justice.gov/usao-edca/pr/jury-returns-guilty-verdicts-former-sacramento-county-sheriff-s-deputy-and-federal (last visit Oct. 10, 2020).

[143] P.C. §§ 26500, 26520.

[144] P.C. § 16730(a).

[145] P.C. § 16730(b).

A "calendar year" begins January 1 and ends December 31.[146] By ending in December rather than *any* twelve-month period, use of the term "calendar year" in this context is significant. It means you can lawfully make all five of your handgun transactions for the year in December and still make up to another five the following January, only a month later, so long as you do not make any other transfers until the following January. Again, the ATF may be very interested in your activities in this situation and may want to ask you a few questions to determine whether you were dealing in firearms.

1. Exceptions

You can transfer as many unloaded "antique firearms" as often as you want without violating the law. Just make sure they are actually "antique firearms" (see Chapter 3). A "Gun Show Trader"[147] may transfer up to 75 used[148] non-handguns in a *calendar* year spanning a total of 12 total gun shows (or similar events). And no more than 15 can be transferred during any given event.[149] But be mindful of federal requirements, law enforcement from both state and federal agencies attend gun shows in undercover capacities and try to entice gun owner to forego the California and federal requirements for gun sales (see Chapter 2).

IV. INTERSTATE FIREARM PURCHASES AND TRANSFERS

A. Transfers From Out-of-State Dealers

California residents can purchase firearms from out-of-state FFLs as long as the transfer would be lawful in California (*e.g.,* the firearm cannot be an "assault weapon" or an "unsafe handgun").[150] But, there are certain restrictions.

Under federal law, an FFL may transfer *rifles or shotguns* over the counter to an out-of-state resident if both states' laws and requirements are satisfied.[151] Yet, given California's mandatory ten-day wait on all firearm transactions and the DROS process, an out-of-state dealer cannot abide by California's stringent transfer requirements. Therefore, barring limited exception to the federal requirement or dual residency, almost all firearms a California resident acquires from outside of California must be passed through a California FFL.

---

[146] BLACK'S LAW DICTIONARY 217 (8th ed. 2004).
[147] A non-California FFL with a COE.
[148] "Used" means the firearm has been previously sold at retail and is more than three years old. P.C. § 17310.
[149] P.C. §§ 26500(a), 26525(a).
[150] 18 U.S.C. § 922(b)(2); 27 C.F.R. § 478.99(b). Firearms that are illegal to possess or have restrictions on transfer in California are discussed in Chapters 9 and 10.
[151] 18 U.S.C. § 922(b)(3).

In addition, given California's requirement that all firearms purchasers have a valid California DMV-issued ID (see above), it is also difficult for out-of-state residents to purchase long guns in California, even though it is legal for them to do so under federal law.

Your "state of residence" is the state where you are present and where you also intend to make your home, and that you can be a "resident" of more than one state.[152] The ATF has explained that:

> An individual resides in a State if he or she is present in a State with the intention of making a home in that State. Ownership of a home or land within a given State is not sufficient, by itself, to establish a State of residence. However, ownership of a home or land within a particular State is not required to establish presence and intent to make a home in that State. Furthermore, temporary travel, such as short term stays, vacations, or other transient acts in a State are not sufficient to establish a State of residence because the individual demonstrates no intention of making a home in that State.[153]

Under federal law, an out-of-state FFL cannot transfer a firearm directly to you if the firearm you are purchasing is *not a rifle or a shotgun* (*i.e.*, a lawful handgun or other non-long gun). Instead, to lawfully transfer the firearm to you, the out-of-state FFL must ship the firearm to an FFL in California, who must then process the transfer in accordance with California law (*i.e.*, the ten-day wait, DROS, etc.) before the firearm can finally be delivered to you.[154]

California law also provides that an out-of-state FFL cannot transfer a firearm directly to you unless an exception applies.[155] Unlike the federal restriction, the California restriction applies to all firearm purchases (*i.e.*, handguns *and* long guns).[156] That means, in order to lawfully transfer a firearm to you under California law, an out-of-state FFL must ship the firearm to an FFL in California, who must then process the transfer in accordance with California law before the firearm can be transferred to you.

Never assume that because you are in compliance with California law, your concerns are over. You must also comply with *federal law* (and vice versa). For example, a number of the exceptions to the California law allow you to acquire firearms pursuant to a permit, or because they are specific firearms regulated by certain statutes. But, under federal law, you are still required to transfer the firearm

---

[152] 27 C.F.R. § 478.11.

[153] ATF Rul. 2010-6 (Nov. 10, 2010).

[154] 18 U.S.C. §§ 922(a)(3), 922(b)(3). In 2015, this requirement was ruled unconstitutional under the Second Amendment by a federal court in Texas. See *Mance v. Holder*, 4:25-cv-539-O (N.D. Tx. Feb. 11, 2015). But this judgment was reversed and vacated by the Fifth Circuit in *Mance v. Sessions*, 896 F.3d 699 (5th Cir. 2018). The United States Supreme Court rejected Plaintiffs' petition for certiorari on June 15, 2020.

[155] P.C. § 27585.

[156] P.C. § 27585.

through a dealer, and, in certain situations relating to NFA "firearms," seek ATF approval before receiving the firearm in California.

Also remember that "dual residents," *i.e.*, those who can establish residency in more than one state, are residents of the state that they are currently "residing" in (see Section I(A)(3)(c)(iii) of this Chapter).

B. Interstate Private Party Transfers

Federal law requires PPTs between residents of different states to take place through an FFL in the *recipient's* home state.[157] Regardless of whether an out-of-state transfer is from an FFL or an individual, the California FFL can charge a service fee for any amount they want, so determine what your FFL charges ahead of time. Bear in mind that this federal restriction includes transfers between family members, so a father living in Missouri cannot give a son living in California a firearm without the transfer going through an FFL in California.

There are some exceptions to this requirement. For instance, a non-licensee can transport into or receive in their state of residence, any firearm that they obtained through bequest or intestate succession.[158] In other words, if you inherit a firearm from a resident of another state by bequest or intestate succession (regardless of whether you are a family member of the person who passed away), federal law allows you to take that firearm in the other state and transport it back into California without using an FFL.[159] But note, under California law, you can only bypass the need for an FFL if you inherit the firearm from an immediate family member.[160] This assumes that the firearm is lawful for you to possess in California in the first place and there are also exceptions for firearms transferred to government and military agencies.[161] Restrictions (or lack thereof) on interstate ammunition sales are discussed below.

Under the new DROS Entry System (DES), California appears to allow PPTs from an individual who doesn't reside in California to a Californian. Previously, under the old DROS system (prior to January 1, 2014), FFLs were only able to input information on California residents into the DROS system. Currently, the DES accepts identification from individuals who reside outside the state of California as transferors in a PPT. If, as discussed above, a transaction in a PPT is denied because the recipient is prohibited from receiving and possessing firearms, California law requires the immediate return of the firearm to the transferor.[162] Presumably, this return would require the California FFL to send the firearm to an FFL in the transferor's home state, who would then return the firearm. Despite this DOJ still

---

[157] 18 U.S.C. § 922(g)(3), (b)(3).
[158] 18 U.S.C. § 922(a)(3), 27 C.F.R. §§ 478.29; 478.30.
[159] 18 U.S.C. § 922(a)(3); 27 C.F.R. § 478.30(a).
[160] P.C. § 27875. Discussed below.
[161] *See* 18 U.S.C. § 925(a).
[162] P.C. § 28050(d).

prohibits PPTs from an out-of-state individual even when that person is physically in California and at the FFL. Dealers are required to treat this transaction as if the dealer purchased the firearm and is selling it to the PPT recipient (therefore restrictions like "unsafe handgun," discussed in Chapter 10, apply).

Table 5.6

INTERSTATE FIREARMS PURCHASES AND TRANSFERS
TRANSFERS FROM OUT-OF-STATE DEALERS
General Rule: A California resident can purchase a firearm from an out-of-state FFL as long as the transfer would be lawful in California (*e.g.*, the firearm cannot be an "assault weapon" or "unsafe handgun").
Restrictions: There are certain restrictions on purchasing firearms from out-of-state dealers.   ✓ **Restrictions on Firearms That Are Not Rifles or Shotguns**: Under federal law, an out-of-state FFL cannot transfer a firearm that is not a rifle or a shotgun directly to you. Instead, the firearm must be shipped to a California FFL who will then process the transfer according to California law. This means all pertinent California regulation requirements will be applied to the transfer (see Table 5.4 for these requirements).   ✓ **Restrictions on Rifles or Shotguns**: An out-of-state FFL could transfer California-legal rifles or shotguns to you if *both* states' laws are complied with. Because an out-of-state FFL cannot comply with California's requirements, this exception does not apply to California residents.
INTERSTATE PRIVATE PARTY TRANSFERS (PPTS)
Federal Rules: Federal law requires PPTs between residents of different states to take place through an FFL in the *recipient's* home state. For information on the federal laws concerning the shipping or mailing of firearms, read this section.
California Rules: California law appears to require both parties to be present at a PPT. But, this requirement remains contested. DOJ will require the dealer to treat this transfer as a dealer sale to the recipient of the firearm.

1. Shipping Firearms

There are federal laws governing the shipment of firearms that you must comply with when shipping firearms. Long guns may be mailed through the USPS or a private carrier, as long as they are unloaded and comply with any other rules of the carrier.[163] Of course, you should not send firearms into a state where their possession and/or importation is illegal unless there is an exception that applies to you and/or the recipient.

For handguns, the laws differ depending on who is shipping the firearm. If you are not a licensed manufacturer of firearms, an FFL, or an authorized agent of the federal or state government, you can only ship handguns via a common or contract carrier[164] (such as FedEx or UPS). Additionally, you can only send handguns to:

---

[163] *Mailability Requirements for Firearms*, USPS, http://pe.usps.com/text/pub52/pub52c4_009.htm#ep308518 (last visited Oct. 10, 2020); *Shipping Firearms*, UPS, http://www.ups.com/content/us/en/resources/ship/packaging/guidelines/firearms.html (last visited Oct. 10, 2020).There are special requirements for shipping most NFA firearms (defined in Chapter 10) across state lines that are not addressed here.

[164] *See* 18 U.S.C. § 1715 (prohibiting handguns from being sent using the USPS).

(1) Yourself in another state where you intend to hunt or engage in any other lawful activity, so long as the package is sent in the care of another person in the state, and upon reaching its destination, persons other than the owner do not open the package or take possession of the firearm;[165] *or*

(2) An FFL for repair or any other lawful purpose (and the FFL may return it to you without transferring through an FFL in your state of residence).[166]

Finally, federal law requires a non-licensee to provide *written* notice to the common carrier that the package contains a firearm.[167] If you have a federal firearm license, handguns may be shipped via USPS so long as you comply with their procedures.[168] Be sure to confirm the policies and procedures for shipping firearms with the private carrier, since they may change unexpectedly.

C. Exemptions to California's Restriction on Out-of-State Transfers

As explained above, California law generally prohibits individuals from importing, bringing, or transporting into California, any firearms that he or she purchased after January 1, 2015, from outside of the state, unless the firearm is first transferred through an FFL.[169] But, there are a limited number of exceptions to this restriction (note that the federal restrictions still apply). Specifically, the following people, firearms, and transactions are exempt from this restriction:

Table 5.7

PENAL CODE SECTION	EXEMPTION
P.C. § 27585(b)(1)	A licensed collector who is subject to and complies with P.C. Section 27565[170]
P.C. § 27585(b)(2)	A dealer, if the dealer is acting in the course and scope of his or her activities as a dealer
P.C. § 27585(b)(3)	A wholesaler, if the wholesaler is acting in the course and scope of his or her activities as a wholesaler

---

[165] *Top 10 Frequently Asked Firearms Questions and Answers*, U.S. DEPT. OF JUSTICE, BUREAU OF ALCOHOL, TOBACCO, FIREARMS AND EXPLOSIVES, https://www.atf.gov/files/firearms/industry/0501-firearms-top-10-qas.pdf (last visited Oct. 10, 2020).

[166] 18 U.S.C. § 922(a).

[167] 18 U.S.C. § 922(e).

[168] See the USPS website or your local post office for a list of requirements. *Mailability Requirements for Firearms*, USPS, http://pe.usps.com/text/pub52/pub52c4_009.htm#ep308518 (last visited Oct. 10, 2020).

[169] P.C. § 27585.

[170] Relating to the registration of curio or relic firearm(s) when a curio or relic collector brings these firearm(s) acquired outside of the state into California, which is discussed in this chapter.

Penal Code Section	Exemption
P.C. § 27585(b)(8)	A person who is on the centralized list of exempted federal firearms licensees (FFLs) under P.C. section 28450 if the person is acting within the course and scope of his or her activities as a licensee
P.C. § 27585(b)(4)	A person licensed as an importer of firearms or ammunition or licensed as a manufacturer of firearms or ammunition, in accordance with 18 U.S.C. sections 921-931 and their regulations, if the importer or manufacturer is acting in the course and scope of his or her activities as a licensed importer or manufacturer.
P.C. § 27585(b)(5)	A "personal firearms importer"[171] who is subject to and complies with P.C. section 27560.
P.C. §§ 27585(b)(6), 27875(b)	A person who complies with P.C. section 27875(b)[172], provided the following criteria are met: (1) The person acquires ownership of the firearm from an immediate family member by bequest or intestate succession; *and* (2) The person has obtained a valid FSC, except that in the case of a handgun, a valid unexpired HSC may be used; *and* (3) The receipt of any firearm by the individual by bequest or intestate succession is infrequent as defined in P.C. section 16730; *and* (4) Within 30 days of that person taking possession of the firearm and importing, bringing, or transporting it into the state, the person must submit a report to DOJ, in a manner prescribed by the department, that includes information concerning the individual taking possession of the firearm, how title was obtained and from whom, and a description of the firearm in question.
P.C. § 27585(b)(12)	A firearm regulated pursuant to Article 2 (commencing with Section 33300) of Chapter 8 of Division 10 acquired by a person who holds a permit issued pursuant to Section 33300,[173] if that person is acting within the course and scope of his or her activities as a licensee and in accordance with the terms and conditions of the permit.

---

[171] "Personal firearm importers" are defined and discussed later in this Chapter.

[172] As amended by AB 1609. AB 1609, 2013-2014, Leg. Counsel's Digest (Cal. 2014), *available at* https://leginfo.legislature.ca.gov/faces/billNavClient.xhtml?bill_id=201320140AB1609 (last visited Oct. 10, 2019).

[173] Referring to "short-barreled rifles" and "short-barreled shotguns" and the permits required to possess them.

Penal Code Section	Exemption
P.C. § 27585(b)(10)	A firearm regulated pursuant to Chapter 2 (commencing with P.C. section 30500) of Division 10 acquired by a person who holds a permit issued pursuant to Section 31005,[174] if that person is acting within the course and scope of his or her activities as a licensee and in accordance with the terms and conditions of the permit.
P.C. §§ 27585(b)(7), 27920(d)	A person who imports the firearm into this country pursuant to the provisions of 18 U.S.C. section 925(a)(4),[175] and meets the following criteria: (1) The person is not subject to the requirements of P.C. section 27560 (imposing requirements on a personal firearm importer upon bringing a firearm into the state); *and* (2) The firearm is not a firearm that is prohibited by any provision listed in P.C. section 16590 (*i.e.*, a "generally prohibited weapon"); *and* (3) The firearm is not an "assault weapon"; *and* (4) The firearm is not a machinegun; *and* (5) The firearm is not a .50 BMG rifle; *and* (6) The firearm is not a "destructive device"; *and* (7) The person is 18 years of age or older; *and* (8) Within 30 days of taking possession of the firearm and importing, bringing, or transporting it into this state, the person must submit a report to DOJ, in a manner described by the department, that includes information concerning the individual taking possession of the firearm, how title was obtained and from whom, and a description of the firearm in question[176]
P.C. § 27585(b)(11)	A firearm regulated pursuant to Chapter 6 (commencing with Section 32610) of Division 10 acquired by a person who holds a permit issued pursuant to Section 32650,[177] if that person is acting within the course and scope of his or her activities as a licensee and in accordance with the terms and conditions of the permit

---

[174] Referring to "assault weapons" and .50 BMG rifles and the permits a person may acquire to lawfully possess, import, make, transport and/or sell these devices under California law, discussed in Chapter 9.

[175] This provision of federal law allows certain members of the United States Armed Forces to bring certain firearms into the United States.

[176] This requirement appears to be at odds with the rule governing military members who are active law enforcement and bring their own firearms into the state. Under P.C. section 17000, members of the Armed Forces do not need to register their personal firearms until they are discharged from active service in California. This new law requires active military members to register their firearms acquired from overseas using this rather obscure federal law.

[177] Referring to "machineguns" and the permits required for possession, manufacture, or transportation of "machineguns" under California law. "Machineguns" are discussed in Chapter 10.

Penal Code Section	Exemption
P.C. § 27585(b)(9)	A firearm regulated pursuant to Chapter 1 (commencing with Section 18710) of Division 5 of Title 2 acquired by a person who holds a permit issued pursuant to Article 3 (commencing with Section 18900) of Chapter 1 of Division 5 of Title 2,[178] if that person is acting within the course and scope of his or her activities as a licensee and in accordance with the terms and conditions of the permit
P.C. §§ 27585(b)(7), 27920(c)	A person who acquired ownership of the firearm by bequest or intestate succession as a surviving spouse or as the surviving registered domestic partner of the decedent who owned that firearm, and meets the following criteria: (1) If acquisition of the firearm has occurred within California, the receipt of the firearm by the surviving spouse or registered domestic partner would be exempt from the provisions of P.C. section 27545 (i.e., requiring the sale, loan, or transfer of firearm to be completed through a licensed dealer) by virtue of P.C. section 16990(h) (i.e., taking title or possession of a firearm by operation of law); *and* (2) Within 30 days of taking possession of the firearm and importing, bringing, or transporting it into this state, the person must submit a report to DOJ, in a manner described by the department, that includes information concerning the individual taking possession of the firearm, how title was obtained and from whom, and a description of the firearm in question; *and* (3) The person obtained a valid FSC, except that in case of a handgun, a valid unexpired HSC may be used

---

[178] Referring to "destructive devices" and permits issued allowing a person to lawfully possess, manufacture, transport, import, and/or sell a destructive device under California law, as discussed in Chapter 10.

PENAL CODE SECTION	EXEMPTION
P.C. §§ 27585(b)(7), 27920(b)	A person who acquired ownership of a firearm as as an executor, a personal representative, a trustee, or an administrator of an estate, and he or she meets the following criteria: (1) If the firearm has been acquired in California, the receipt of the firearm by the executor or administrator would be exempt from the provisions of P.C. section 27545 (i.e., requiring the sale, loan, or transfer of firearm to be completed through a licensed dealer); *and* (2) Within 30 days of taking possession of the firearm and importing, bringing, or transporting it into California, the executor or administer must submit a report to DOJ, in a manner proscribed by the department, that includes information concerning himself or herself, *i.e.*, the individual taking possession of the firearm, how title was obtained and from whom, and a description of the firearm in question; *and* (3) If the executor, personal representative, trustee, or administrator of an estate subsequently acquires ownership of that firearm in an individual capacity, prior to transferring ownership to himself or herself, he or she shall obtain a valid FSC, except that in the case of a handgun, a valid unexpired HSC may be used; *and* (4) The executor, personal representative, trustee, or administrator of an estate is 18 years of age or older
P.C. §§ 27585(b)(14)	The importation, transportation, or bringing of a firearm into the state by a person who meets any of the following criteria: (1) The person is listed in the registry set forth in P.C. section 11106 as the owner of the firearm; (2) The person has been issued documentation by DOJ pursuant to subdivision (b) of P.C. section 11106 that indicates the person is listed in the centralized registry as owning that firearm; (3) The person has a copy of a Dealer's Record of Sale that shows that the person received that firearm from the dealer listed in that Dealer's Record of Sale and is listed as the owner of the firearm; or, (4) If the firearm is a handgun, the person has a license to carry that handgun under P.C. sections 26150-26225 and the person is licensed to carry that handgun.

Penal Code Section	Exemption
P.C. § 27585(b)(13)	The importation of a firearm into the state, bringing a firearm into the state, or transportation of a firearm into the state, that is regulated by any of the following statutes, if the acquisition of that firearm occurred outside of California and is conducted in accordance with the applicable provisions of the following statutes: (1) Chapter 1 (commencing with P.C. section 18710) of Division 5 of Title 2, relating to "destructive devices" and explosives; *and* (2) P.C. section 24410, relating to cane guns; *and* (3) P.C. section 24510, relating to "firearms that are not immediately recognizable as firearms;" *and* (4) P.C. sections 24610 and 24680, relating to "undetectable firearms;" *and* (5) P.C. section 24710, relating to wallet guns; *and* (6) Chapter 2 (commencing with P.C. section 30500) of Division 10, relating to "assault weapons;"[179] *and* (7) P.C. section 31500, relating to unconventional pistols; *and* (8) P.C. sections 33215 and 33225, inclusive, relating to "short-barreled rifles" and "short-barreled shotguns"; *and* (9) Chapter 6 (commencing with P.C. section 32160) of Division 10, relating to machineguns; *and* (10) P.C. section 33600, relating to zip guns and the exemption in Chapter 1 (commencing with P.C. section 17700) of Division 2 of Title 2, as they relate to zip guns.
P.C. § 27585(b)(15)	A licensed common carrier or an authorized agent or employee of a licensed common carrier, when acting in the course and scope of duties incident to the delivery of or receipt of that firearm in accordance with federal law.

V. LOANING FIREARMS TO ADULTS

Under federal law, you may temporarily loan or rent a firearm to an out-of-state resident who is not prohibited from possessing firearms[180] for lawful sporting pur-

---

[179] Oddly, .50 BMG rifles are not mentioned here despite the fact that they are regulated in this Chapter of the Penal Code.
[180] *See* Chapter 4.

poses if you do not know, or have reasonable cause to believe, that the person is prohibited from receiving or possessing firearms.[181]

But in California, a firearm can only be infrequently loaned between any of the following individuals, as long as the loan does not exceed 30 days (with few exceptions):

(1) Spouses or registered domestic partners; *or*

(2) Any parent, child, siblings, grandparent, or grandchild, whether related by consanguinity, adoption, or step relation.[182]

In addition, the person being loaned the firearm must have a valid FSC (or in the case of a handgun, a valid and unexpired HSC).[183]

Under this new exception, the person being loaned the firearm must have a valid FSC. If the firearm being loaned in a handgun, then the person being loaned the firearm can also use an unexpired HSC.[184] And if the firearm being loaned is a handgun, it must be registered to the person making the loan as provided in P.C. section 11106.[185] But there are some exceptions that gun owners can use to loan a firearm to another person without having to go through a licensed firearms dealer, with several of them added by SB 172 in 2019. These exceptions include:

Table 5.8

PENAL CODE SECTION	EXEMPTION
P.C. §§ 26625, 27970	An individual can loan a firearm to another person without going through a licensed firearms dealer if both of the following conditions are met: (1) The person receiving the firearm is enrolled in the course of basic training prescribed by the Commission on Peace Officer Standards and Training, or in any other course certified by the Commission; *and* (2) The loan is for purposes of participation in the course.

---

[181] 18 U.S.C. § 922(b)(3).
[182] P.C. § 27880.
[183] P.C. § 27880(e).
[184] P.C. § 27880(e).
[185] P.C. § 27880(f).

Penal Code Section	Exemption
P.C. § 27881	An individual can loan a firearm to another on the lender's private property if all the following conditions are met: (1) If the firearm being loaned is a handgun, the handgun is registered to the person making the loan pursuant to Section 11106; (2) The loan occurs within the lender's place of residence or other real property, except for property that is zoned for commercial, retail, or industrial activity; (3) The individual receiving the firearm is not prohibited by state or federal law from possessing, receiving, owning, or purchasing a firearm; (4) The individual receiving the firearm is 18 years of age or older; *and* (5) The firearm does not leave the real property upon which the loan occurs.

P.C. § 27882	A licensed firearms dealer need not be utilized to process a temporary transfer of a firearm for purposes of suicide prevention if all the following conditions are met:
	(1) The firearm is voluntarily and temporarily transferred to another person who is 18 years of age or older for safekeeping to prevent it from being accessed or used to attempt suicide by the transferor or another person that may gain access to it in the transferor's household;
	(2) The transferee does not use the firearm for any purpose and, except when transporting the firearm to the transferee's residence or when returning it to the transferor, keeps the firearm unloaded and secured in the transferee's residence in one of the following ways:
	  (a) Secured in a locked container;
	  (b) Disabled by a firearm safety device;
	  (c) Secured within a locked gun safe; or,
	  (d) Locked within a locking device as described in P.C. section 16860 that has rendered the firearm inoperable;
	AND
	(3) The duration of the loan is limited to that amount of time reasonably necessary to prevent the harm described in paragraph (1).[186]

---

[186] If the firearm cannot be returned to the owner because the owner has become prohibited, the person in possession must deliver the firearm to a law enforcement agency "without delay." P.C. § 27882(b).

Penal Code Section	Exemption

P.C. § 27883	An individual may loan a firearm to another for purposes of storage if all the following requirements are met:
	(1) The firearm being loaned is registered to the person making the loan pursuant to P.C. section 11106;
	(2) The firearm being loaned is stored in the receiver's place of residence or in an enclosed structure on the receiver's private property, which is not zoned for commercial, retail, or industrial activity;
	(3) The firearm at all times stays within the receiver's place of residence or in an enclosed structure on the receiver's private property, which is not zoned for commercial, retail, or industrial activity;
	(4) The individual receiving the firearm is not prohibited by state or federal law from possessing, receiving, owning, or purchasing a firearm;
	(5) The individual receiving the firearm is 18 years of age or older;
	(6) At least one of the following applies:
	  (a) The firearm is maintained within a locked container;
	  (b) The firearm is disabled by a firearm safety device;
	  (c) The firearm is maintained within a locked gun safe; or
	  (d) The firearm is locked within a locking device, as defined in Section 16860, which ahs rendered the firearm inoperable.
	(7) The loan does not exceed 120 days in duration;
	(8) The loan is made without consideration;
	(9) There is a written document in a format prescribed by DOJ that explains the obligations imposed by this section that is signed by both the party loaning the firearm for storage and the person receiving the firearm; *and*
	(10) Both parties to the loan have signed copies of the written document.[187]

---

[187] What's more, California's FSC requirement does not apply to a temporary transfer made pursuant to this section. P.C. § 31700(d).

Penal Code Section	Exemption
P.C. § 27885	An individual who is 18 years of age or older can loan a firearm to another person who is 18 years of age or older without going through a licensed firearms dealer provided the following conditions are met: (1) The person loaning the firearm is at all times within the presence of the person being loaned the firearm; *and* (2) The loan is for a lawful purpose; *and* (3) The loan does not exceed three days in duration; *and* (4) The individual receiving the firearm is not prohibited by state or federal law from possessing, receiving, owning, or purchasing a firearm.
P.C. §§ 27910, 31765	An individual can loan a firearm to a person 18 years of age or older for the purposes of target shooting without going through a licensed firearms dealer, as long as: (1) The loan occurs on the premises of a target facility that holds a business or regulatory license; or on the premises of any club or organization organized for the purposes of practicing shooting at targets upon established ranges, whether public or private; *and* (2) The firearm is at all times kept within the premises of the target range or on the premises of the club or organization.
P.C. § 27950	An individual can loan a long gun to a licensed hunter without going through a licensed firearms dealer, as long as the loan does not exceed the duration of the hunting season for which the firearm is to be used.
P.C. § 27955	An individual can loan a firearm to another person 18 years of age or older without going through a licensed firearms dealer, provided all the following are satisfied: (1) The loan is "infrequent"; *and* (2) The firearm is unloaded; *and* (3) The loan is made by a person who is neither a dealer nor a federal firearms licensee pursuant to Chapter 44 (commencing with 18 U.S.C. section 921) of Title 18 of the United States Code; *and* (4) The loan is for use solely as a prop in a motion picture, television, video, theatrical, or other entertainment production or event.

Penal Code Section	Exemption
P.C. § 27955	A federal firearms licensee can loan a firearm to a person who possess a valid entertainment firearms permit issued under Chapter 2 (commencing with P.C. section 29500) of Division 8 of the Penal Code without going through a licensed firearms dealer, as long as the following conditions are met: (1) The firearm is unloaded; *and* (2) The firearm is loaned for use solely as a prop in a motion picture, television, video, theatrical, or other entertainment production or event; *and* (3) The person loaning the firearm retains a photocopy of the entertainment firearm permit as proof of compliance with this requirement.
P.C. § 27966	An individual can loan, sell, or transfer a firearm to a collector licensed under Chapter 44 of Title 18 of the United States Code, and the regulations issued thereto without going through a licensed firearms dealer provided that: (1) The loan, sale, or transfer is "infrequent;" *and* (2) The firearm is not a handgun; *and* (3) The firearm is a curio or relic; *and* (4) The person receiving the firearm has a current certificate of eligibility issued in accordance with P.C. section 267410; *and* (5) Within 30 days of taking possession of the firearm, the person to whom it is transferred must forward by prepaid mail, or deliver in person to the Department of Justice, a report that includes information concerning the individual taking possession of the firearm, how title was obtained and form whom, and a description of the firearm in question.

In addition to the exceptions above, there are also exceptions for loans to historical societies. Specifically, an authorized law enforcement representative of a city, county, city and county, or state, or the federal government can sell, deliver, loan, or transfer a firearm to any public or private nonprofit historical society, museum, or institutional collection without going through a licensed firearms dealer if all the following conditions are met:

(1) The entity receiving the firearm is open to the public; *and*
(2) The firearm is deactivated or rendered inoperable prior to delivery; *and*
(3) The firearm is not subject to any of the following:

(a) P.C. section 18000 (dealing with the surrender of nuisance weapon to law enforcement) or P.C. section 18005 (offering surrendered weapons for sale at public auction, return of stolen weapons and weapons used in a manner constituting a nuisance without knowledge of owner, destruction of surrendered weapons); *or*

(b) P.C. section 18250-18275 (firearms seized at a domestic violence incident); *or*

(c) P.C. section 34000 (Sale or destruction of firearms no longer needed as exhibits in criminal actions or proceedings, and firearms that are unclaimed or abandoned); *or*

(d) P.C. section 34005 (alternatives to destruction of firearms and parts) or P.C. section 30410 (notice of retention or destruction of firearms); *or*

(4) The firearm is not prohibited by other provisions of law from being sold, delivered, or transferred; *and*

(5) Prior to delivery, the entity receiving the firearm submits a written statement to the law enforcement representative stating that the firearm will not be restored to operating condition, and will either remain with that entity, or if subsequently disposed of, will be transferred in accordance with the applicable provisions listed in P.C. section 16575 (referencing the 2012 renumbering of firearm Code sections and how the new sections are continuations of these sections) and, if applicable with P.C. section 31615 (prohibition on purchase or receipt of, or sale, delivery, loan, or transfer of a firearm to a person lacking a valid safety certificate); *and*

(6) Within ten days of the date the firearm is sold, loaned, delivered, or transferred to that entity, all of the following information is reported to DOJ:

(a) The name of the government entity delivering the firearm; *and*

(b) The make, model, serial number, and other identifying characteristics of the firearm; *and*

(c) The name of the person authorized by the entity to take possession of the firearm.[188]

Any person other than a representative of an authorized law enforcement agency may also sell, deliver, loan, or transfer a firearm to any public or private nonprofit historical society, museum, or institutional collection without going through a licensed firearms dealer if all the following conditions are met:

(1) The entity receiving the firearm is open to the public; *and*

(2) The firearm is deactivated or rendered inoperable prior to delivery; *and*

---

[188] P.C. § 27855.

(3) The firearm is not a type of prohibited from being sold, delivered, or transferred to the public; *and*

(4) Prior to delivery, the entity receiving the firearm submits a written statement to the person selling, loaning, or transferring the firearm stating that the firearm will not be restored to operating condition, and will either remain with that entity, or if subsequently disposed of, will be transferred in accordance with the applicable provisions listed in P.C. section 16575 and, if applicable, with P.C. section 31615; *and*

(5) If title to the firearm is being transferred to the public or private nonprofit historical society, museum, or institutional collection, then the designated representative of that entity shall, within 30 days of taking possession of that firearm, forward by prepaid mail or deliver in person to DOJ, a single report signed by both parties to the transaction, which include all of the following information:

  (a) Information identifying the person representing the public or private historical society, museum, or institutional collection; *and*

  (b) Information on how title was obtained and from whom; *and*

  (c) A description of the firearm in question; *and*

  (d) A copy of the written statement referred to in (4), above.[189]

VI. TRANSFERRING AND LOANING FIREARMS TO YOUNG PEOPLE

A. Dealer Sales

1. Federal Law

Federal law prohibits firearm dealers from selling firearms to anyone under the age of 18, and handguns may only be sold to those who are who are 21 or over.[190] And federal law only allows the sale of rifles and shotguns to those between ages 18 and 21.[191]

Although federal law allows a person to buy "complete" rifles and shotguns from an FFL once he or she turns 18, frames and receivers (see Chapter 3) cannot be purchased until the purchaser reaches age 21. Federal law specifies that only "rifles" and "shotguns" can be purchased by 18 to 21-year-olds, and the ATF interprets this rule to mean "complete" firearms.[192]

---

[189] P.C. § 27860.
[190] *See* 18 U.S.C. § 922(b)(1).
[191] 18 U.S.C. § 922(b)(1), (x)(1).
[192] *Open Letter to All Federal Firearms Licensees*, U.S. Dept. of Justice, Bureau of Alcohol, Tobacco, Firearms and Explosives (Jul. 7, 2009), *available at* http://www.atf.gov/files/press/releases/2009/07/070709-openlet-

2. California Law

As noted above, California law is more restrictive than federal law by generally prohibiting California licensed firearm dealers from selling, supplying, delivering, or giving possession or control of a firearm to anyone under the age of 21.[193] But that restriction does not apply to non-licensed individuals, such as "immediate family" (defined below) that may still give a firearm (regardless of type) to a person between the ages of 18-21 years of age via an intra-family transfer exception.[194]

B. Those Under Age 18

With the exception of "assault weapons" and .50 BMG rifles, neither California nor federal law regulates rifle or shotgun *possession* by minors specifically. But, firearm *transfers* to a minor are heavily regulated.

Under federal law, it is unlawful for anyone to knowingly transfer a handgun or "ammunition that is suitable for use only in a handgun"[195] to a minor. But it is legal to *temporarily* loan a handgun or such ammunition to a minor if:

(1) The handgun and ammunition are possessed and used by the minor in the course of employment, ranching, farming (with consent of the rancher or farmer), target practice, hunting, or in a firearm training course; *and*

(2) The minor's parent, who is not a prohibited person, provides written consent for the minor to possess the handgun or ammunition (subject to transportation and farming exceptions); *and*

(3) The minor keeps the written consent at all times while possessing the handgun or ammunition; *and*

(4) The minor's use is in accordance with State and local law.[196]

A minor may also inherit *title* to a handgun or ammunition, but *not* possession.[197]

1. Loans and Transfers to Minors

Under California law, parents, legal guardians, or grandparents (with the express permission of parents) may *loan or transfer* a non-handgun to their minor children subject to specific requirements.

---

ter-ffl-gca.pdf (last visited Oct. 10, 2020); *see* 18 U.S.C. § 922(b)(1); *see also ATF Form 4473 - Firearm Transaction Record*, U.S. Dept. of Justice, Bureau of Alcohol, Tobacco, Firearms and Explosives, http://www.atf.gov/files/forms/download/atf-f-4473-1.pdf (last visited Oct. 10, 2020).

[193] P.C. § 27510(a).
[194] P.C. § 27875.
[195] 18 U.S.C. § 922(x)(1).
[196] For exact wording of this statute, refer to 18 U.S.C. section 922(x)(3) and/or Chapter 4.
[197] 18 U.S.C. § 922(x)(3)(C).

Before addressing these requirements, however, a discussion regarding the difference between a "loan" and simple "use" of a firearm is warranted. It seems the authors of California's restrictions have failed to grasp the distinction.

In the context of California firearms law, the term "loan" is not expressly defined. But as commonly understood, the act of loaning necessarily implies the exclusive use and control of that firearm (temporary or otherwise) by a person who does not own the firearm. In other words, the owner is not necessarily physically present to maintain control over the firearm.

The act of "loaning," therefore, seems to differ from situations where the owner is present and merely allowing another to use their firearm, such as while at a shooting range for recreational purposes.[198]

The distinction may be trivial and perhaps insignificant. But California law appears to recognize the distinction in certain contexts. For example, it is a crime to knowingly "give possession or control" of a firearm to a person who is prohibited from owning or possessing firearms.[199] And as discussed above, California licensed firearm dealers are generally prohibited from "giving possession or control" of a firearm to anyone under the age of 21.

The use of the phrase giving "possession or control" as opposed to "loan" clearly implies these restrictions are more comprehensive in their application. Such haphazard use of and lack of express definitions for these terms result in confusion and misunderstanding by gun owners. That lack of precision is all too typical in California firearm legislation and regulations. A legal background, or a lawyer on retainer, shouldn't be necessary to comprehend what constitutes lawful conduct, particularly when it comes to the exercise of a constitutional right.

Despite CRPA's attempts to clarify this, California law provides exceptions for the *loan* but not *use* of a firearm by a minor in accordance with P.C. section 27505. Specifically, nothing in the law addresses the act of an adult (parent, guardian, or otherwise) simply allowing a minor to use or otherwise handle a firearm in a manner that might not legally constitute a "loan." Assuming there is a difference, it is therefore unclear to what degree, if any, California law regulates such activity.

The actual drafters of California's laws on this topic have expressly assured CRPA that this statute does not limit or otherwise prevent youth shooting activities. Nevertheless, to ensure gun owners do not inadvertently run afoul of California's restrictions, careful adherence to P.C. section 27505's requirements are advisable—regardless if actually loaning the firearm or otherwise.

---

[198] On a related note, California law provides an exception to the dealer processing requirement for the loan of a firearm to a person 18 years of age or older for the purposes of target shooting on the premises of a target facility subject to specific requirements. P.C. § 27910.
[199] P.C. § 27500.

Penal Code section 27505 outlines the specific requirements for the loan or transfer a long gun to a minor. As applied to handguns, however, one may only "loan" the handgun to a minor. These requirements are outlined below.

Permissible Loans or Transfers of Long Guns to Minors:

- The transfer or loan of a long gun, to a minor by the minor's parent or legal guardian.
- The transfer or loan of a long gun to a minor by a grandparent who is not the legal guardian, if done with the express permission of the minor's parent or legal guardian.
- The loan of a long gun to a minor with the express permission of the minor's parent or legal guardian if the loan does not exceed 30 days and is for a lawful purpose.[200]

Permissible Loans (But Not Transfers) of Handguns to Minors:

- The loan of a handgun to a minor by their parent or legal guardian is allowed if both of the following are true:

    (1) The minor is being loaned the firearm for the purposes of engaging in a lawful, recreational sport, which includes, but is not limited to, competitive shooting, hunting, or theatrical event, the nature of which involves the use of a firearm; and,

    (2) The duration of the loan does not exceed the amount of time reasonably necessary to engage in such activity.[201]

- The loan of a handgun to a minor by a person who is not the minor's parent or legal guardian is allowed if all the following are true

    (1) The minor is accompanied by the minor's parent or legal guardian, or has the written consent of the parent or legal guardian which is presented at the time of the loan or earlier;

    (2) The minor is being loaned the firearm for purposes of engaging in a lawful, recreation sport which involves the use of a firearm;

    (3) The duration of the loan does not exceed the amount of time reasonably necessary to engage in such activity; and,

    (4) The duration of the loan does not, in any event, exceed 10 days.[202]

---

[200] P.C. § 27505(b)(2-4).
[201] P.C. § 27505(b)(5).
[202] P.C. § 27505(b)(6).

As applied to the above, "antique firearms" are generally not considered "firearms," even though they are considered firearms for purposes of minors possessing handguns.[203] What this means is that a crime will be committed the moment a minor takes *unlawful* possession of a handgun from you (e.g., when the minor doesn't have parental or guardian permission), even though California says that no crime was committed by the act of loaning an "antique" handgun to the minor.

Keep in mind that the exceptions above only apply to the *loan* or *transfer* of a firearm to a minor; it does not exempt the minor from the restrictions on the *possession* of firearms. In other words, in order for the minor to lawfully possess a firearm that is loaned or transferred to them, they must also meet one of the exceptions outlined in Chapter 4.

VII. EXCEPTIONS TO TRANSFERRING FIREARMS THROUGH A FEDERAL FIREARMS LICENSEE IN CALIFORNIA

A. Federal Law

Federal law does not generally regulate firearm transfers between two individuals who reside in the same state. But, federal law does prohibit you from transferring a firearm to a person that you know or have reasonable cause to believe is prohibited from possessing firearms.[204] And remember that if you are not an FFL, you may only transfer firearms "infrequently" under California and cannot "engage in the business" of dealing firearms under federal law (see Section III).

B. California Law

1. Intra-Family Transactions

Under California law, using an FFL is *not* required for *infrequent*[205] transfers of firearms that are generally lawful to possess in California to an "immediate family" member, whether transferred by gift, bequest, intestate succession (*i.e.*, inheritance from someone who passed away without a will), or other means.

"Immediate family" is a parent-child and/or grandparent-grandchild relationship.[206] This means that siblings, aunts, cousins, etc., are not allowed to directly transfer firearms to each other without using an FFL.

---

[203] *See* P.C. §§ 16170(b), 27505(b)(1), 27510.
[204] 18 U.S.C. § 922(d).
[205] P.C. § 16730(a).
[206] P.C. § 16720.

To transfer firearms through an intra-family transaction, the transferring party does not need to do anything, but the receiving party must:

(1) Give DOJ a completed "Report of Operation of Law or Intra-Familial Firearm Transaction" form within 30 days of receiving the firearm; *and*

(2) Have an FSC; *and*

(3) Be at least age 18.[207]

After January 1, 2015, if the transfer only involves one or more handguns, the transferee may take possession of the handgun(s) with a valid HSC or FSC; in all other situations (meaning transfers involving handguns and long guns or just long guns), the recipient must possess an FSC.[208]

a. Change in Law for Long Guns

Before January 1, 2014, an intra-family transfer involving a long gun that was otherwise legal to transfer in California[209] didn't require any paperwork.[210] The only restriction was that the recipient be lawfully eligible to possess firearms. There was no minimum age requirement for the recipient when long guns were transferred from a parent, but if a grandparent was transferring a gun to a minor, then the minor's parent or guardian must have given express permission.[211]

As of January 1, 2014, immediate family members may still transfer non-handguns if the party taking possession registers the long gun using the "Report of Operation of Law or Intra-Familial Firearm Transaction" form and the person receiving the firearm is over the age of 18.[212]

On January 1, 2014, however, a conflict in the law arose with regard to transferring non-handguns to minors. While the Penal Code allows for the transfer of a non-handgun to a minor by a parent/guardian or grandparent with the parent/guardian's permission,[213] P.C. section 27875 requires that the recipient of a transfer of non-handguns between immediate family members be over the age of 18. The requirements of section 27875 would apply to parent-to-child and grandparent-to-grandchild transfers. It is not clear how this conflict should be resolved. This being said, if a transfer was done prior to January 1, 2014, no documentation or registra-

---

[207] P.C. § 27875.

[208] P.C. § 27875(a)(4). Subject to the person being exempt from this requirement.

[209] If you inherit an "assault weapon" or .50 BMG rifle, and the firearm wasn't otherwise registered to you separately as an "assault weapon" or .50 BMG rifle as discussed in Chapter 10, you have 90 days for "assault weapons" or 180 days for .50 BMG rifles to make the weapon permanently inoperable, sell it to an approved FFL, get a Dangerous Weapons Permit from DOJ, or remove the firearm from California. P.C. §§ 30925 ("assault weapons"); 30930, 30935 (.50 BMG rifles); 27875 (inheritance of firearms). California law is unclear on what you should do if you inherit machineguns, destructive devices, or other highly regulated firearms (although such inheritance is highly unlikely to happen in California). It is strongly advised you contact an attorney experienced in firearms law to assist you.

[210] P.C. § 27870 (2013). Per AB 809, starting in 2014, long gun transfers between immediate family members will also need to be registered like handguns. See below.

[211] P.C. § 27505(b)(2)-(3).

[212] A $19 processing fee will be charged for filing this form. CAL. CODE REGS. tit. 11, § 4002.

[213] *See* P.C. § 27505(b)(2)-(3).

tion needed to be generated. After January 1, 2015, transfers of all firearms will both need to be reported to DOJ and the transferee will need to possess an FSC.[214] An FSC cannot be issued to anyone under the age of 18.[215]

2. Transfers Between Spouses or Domestic Partners

Under California law, firearm transfers between spouses and domestic partners must go through an FFL unless the transferring spouse "transmutes" his or her interest in the firearm to the recipient spouse or domestic partner.[216] A "transmutation" occurs when, during marriage, a spouse shows an express intent, in a signed writing, to change ownership of his or her property.[217] This means that one spouse's separate property can be transmuted (change classification) into the community property of both spouses or into the separate property of the other spouse.[218]

To "transmute" a firearm, the spouse should create a document stating that he or she wishes to make the firearm transfer or that the transferring spouse is releasing his or her separate or community property interest in the firearm, and that the receiving spouse is taking the property as his or her sole and separate property. Both parties should sign and date the document and keep a copy. Additionally, all of the above requirements for "intra-familial transfers" also apply to transmutations of firearms between spouses. This means that the recipient spouse must register the firearms, with DOJ and possess an HSC if the transfer involves a handgun.[219] After January 1, 2015, the spouse receiving the firearm must possess an FSC unless the transfer only involves handguns, in which case a valid HSC will suffice.[220]

a. Firearms and Divorce

California uses the community property method to divide marital possessions at divorce or termination of a registered domestic partnership.[221] Generally speaking, when property (such as a firearm) is acquired by either spouse during the marriage, it is considered community property (*i.e.*, the property belonging to the spouses jointly, barring some other exception).[222] When a marriage is dissolved, the community property is usually divided equally between the spouses.[223] If any firearms are considered community property at divorce, a court may give the firearms to one spouse and compensate the other spouse with other similarly valued community

---

[214] P.C. § 27875.
[215] P.C. § 31625(b) (2015).
[216] P.C. § 27920(b).
[217] Cal. Fam. Code § 852(a).
[218] Cal. Fam. Code § 850.
[219] P.C. § 27920(b).
[220] P.C. § 27920(b)(2).
[221] Cal. Fam. Code § 297.5(a).
[222] Cal. Fam. Code § 760. Property acquired by a spouse either before or during marriage by "gift, bequest, devise or descent" is the separate property of that spouse, not community property. Cal. Fam. Code § 770(a).
[223] Cal. Fam. Code § 2550.

assets to accomplish an equal division of the community estate.[224] Alternatively, a court could order a sale of all community property that cannot be divided and distribute the proceeds equally between the spouses.[225]

As discussed above, when handguns are acquired from a firearms dealer, they are registered to the individual who purchases them. Long guns purchased after January 1, 2014, are likewise registered to the purchaser when acquired from a firearms dealer. Currently, under California law, there is no way to jointly register firearms[226] with the exception of "assault weapons" and .50 BMG rifles that were registered to the possessor(s) as required by California law (see discussion in Chapter 8). Consequently, if firearms were purchased by one spouse and were awarded to the other spouse after a divorce, the firearms would technically need to be transferred in the manner discussed above. When going through a divorce, your family law attorney should consult an attorney familiar with firearms law because dividing community property that involves firearms is often not a simple task.

3. "Operation of Law" Transfers Other Than Transfers Between Spouses Involving Transmutation of Property

The requirement to use a dealer to facilitate firearm transfers does not apply to a person who takes title or possession of a firearm by "operation of law," provided that the person is not prohibited by state or federal law from possessing, receiving, owning, or purchasing a firearm.[227] "[T]he phrase 'a person taking title or possession of a firearm by operation of law' includes, but is not limited to, any one of the following instances in which an individual receives title to, or possession of, a firearm"[228]:

(1) The executor, personal representative, or administrator of an estate, if the estate includes a firearm;

(2) A secured creditor or an agent or employee of a secured creditor when a firearm is possessed as collateral for, or as a result of, a default under a security agreement under the Commercial Code; *and*

(3) A levying officer;[229]

(4) A receiver performing the functions of a receiver, if the receivership estate includes a firearm;

(5) A trustee in a bankruptcy performing the duties of a trustee, if the bankruptcy estate includes a firearm;

---

[224] CAL. FAM. CODE §§ 2550-2552.

[225] *In re Marriage of Cream*, 13 Cal. App. 4th 81 (1993).

[226] The California Legislature attempted to change this in 2016 when it passed SB 1332. SB 1332, 2015-2016 Leg., Reg. Sess (2016), *available at* https://leginfo.legislature.ca.gov/faces/billNavClient.xhtml?bill_id=201520160SB1332 (last visited Oct. 10, 2020). But, Governor Brown vetoed the bill.

[227] P.C. § 27920(a).

[228] P.C. §16990 (subdivisions (k) through (s).

[229] As defined in California Code of Civil Procedure sections 481.140, 511.060, or 680.260.

(6) An assignee for the benefit of creditors performing the functions of an assignee, if the assignment includes a firearm;

(7) A transmutation of property between spouses; [230]

(8) The transfer of a firearm by a law enforcement agency to the person who found the firearm where the delivery is to the person as the finder of the firearm;[231]

(9) A firearm received by a family of a police officer or deputy sheriff from a local agency;[232]

(10) The trustee of a trust that includes a firearm and that was part of a will that created the trust;

(11) A person acting pursuant to the person's power of attorney;[233]

(12) A limited or general conservator appoint by a court;[234]

(13) A guardian ad litem appoint by a court; [235]

(14) A trustee of a trust that includes a firearm that is under court supervision;

(15) A special administrator appointed by a court;[236] *and*,

(16) A guardian appointed by a court.[237]

Additionally, the dealer-processing requirement does not apply to operation of law transfers when the person who takes possession of a firearm in a representative capacity subsequently transfers ownership of the firearm to themselves in an individual capacity, so long as they possess a valid Firearm Safety Certificate, or in the case of a handgun, a valid Handgun Safety Certificate.[238]

Furthermore, depending on which "operation of law" transfer is at issue, there are some other criteria that must be met before the transaction can be exempt from California's requirement to transfer firearms through a federal firearms licensee. For instance, if the person taking title or possession is an executor or administrator of an estate, a secured creditor or agent/employee of a secured creditor when the firearm is possessed as collateral, a receiver, a trustee in bankruptcy, or an assignee for the benefit of creditors, then he or she must, within 30 days, report the transfer to DOJ by using a *Report of Law or Intra-Familial Firearm Transaction* form.[239]

---

[230] As provided in California Family Code section 850.

[231] As provided in California Article 1 (commencing with Section 2080) of Chapter 4 of Title 6 of Part 4 of Division 3 of the California Civil Code.

[232] As provided in Government Code section 50081.

[233] In accordance with Division 4.5 (commencing with Section 4000) of the Probate Code.

[234] Who was appointed pursuant to the Probate Code or Welfare and Institutions Code.

[235] Pursuant to Section 372 of the Code of Civil Procedure.

[236] Pursuant to Section 8540 of the Probate Code.

[237] Pursuant to Section 1500 of the Probate Code.

[238] P.C. § 27925.

[239] P.C. § 27920(a)(1). The *Report of Law or Intra-Familial Firearm Transaction* form can be accessed at https://oag.ca.gov/sites/all/files/agweb/pdfs/firearms/forms/oplaw.pdf. You can also submit this form to DOJ through

If the person taking title or possession of the firearm is receiving the firearm pursuant to a transmutation of property under Family Code section 850 or is receiving the firearm as a surviving spouse pursuant to Probate Code sections 13500 through 13506, then the person must:

(1) Within 30 days, report the transfer to DOJ by using a *Report of Law or Intra-Familial Firearm Transaction* form; *and*

(2) Possess a valid firearm safety certificate or, in the case of a handgun, a valid handgun safety certificate.[240]

Where the person receiving title or possession of the firearm is receiving the firearm from a law enforcement agency as the finder of the firearm (i.e., the firearm is delivered pursuant to Civil Code sections 2080 through 2080.10), then that person must present proof to the law enforcement agency that he or she possesses a valid Firearm Safety Certificate or, in the case of a handgun, a valid Handgun Safety Certificate.

4. Gun Trusts

A "gun trust" is a legal trust that is specifically created to acquire, hold ownership to, and facilitate the transfer of firearms. A legal "trust" is any arrangement by which property is transferred by a person (i.e., the "settlor") with the intention that it be held and administered by another person (i.e., the "trustee") for the benefit of a third party (i.e., the "beneficiary"). In other words, a trust is basically just a legal relationship that holds assets for the benefit of another. Trusts are generally considered advantageous because they can help people avoid certain estate taxes and avoid the public forum of a probate court.

When people speak of "gun trusts" in California, they usually mean one of two things: (1) trusts that are specifically created to hold ownership to and acquire firearms regulated by the National Firearms Act of 1934 (NFA), or (2) trusts that are created to hold ownership to and facilitate the transfer of other types of firearms (e.g., legal to own handguns and long guns) that are lawful to possess in California.

a. NFA Trusts

As stated in more detail in Chapter 10, the NFA[241] regulates the manufacture, importation, possession, and transfer of certain highly restricted firearms, including "machineguns," "short-barreled rifles," "short-barreled shotguns," "silencers," destructive devices, "and "any other weapons." These items are often referred to as "NFA firearms," and they are subject to strict federal registration, transfer, and tax requirements.

CRIS, which can be accessed at https://cfars.doj.ca.gov/login.do;jsessionid=ZiceNrwzku1-gSNUEdlUWvXW.cfars_worker01.

[240] P.C. § 27920(a)(2).
[241] 26 U.S.C. §§ 5801-5872.

NFA trusts are increasingly popular in some states because they allow multiple individuals to possess the same NFA firearms and they make it easier for future trustees and beneficiaries to deal with an estate containing NFA firearms. But, despite their popularity in other states, NFA trusts are practically irrelevant to most California gun owners. This is because it is generally illegal under California law for individuals to purchase and possess NFA firearms, unless the individual has obtained a "dangerous weapons" permit—something that is virtually impossible to obtain unless, in most cases, the individual can demonstrate that he or she already has a law enforcement customer, military, or entertainment industry base and is obtaining the permit to sell NFA firearms to these entities.[242]

Because most Californians generally cannot possess NFA firearms in California, NFA trusts will not be discussed in further detail in this book. Readers are warned: be careful when selecting attorneys who profess that they are experienced with gun trusts, especially the attorneys who do not reside in California and who offer a way for you and your family to keep regulated firearms in California for years to come without registration. While these attorneys may be apt in using gun trusts to acquire NFA firearms, that does not mean that they understand the complexities of California law. Often, attorneys who encourage gun owners to establish gun trusts in California misstate California law or do not fully understand it.

b. Non-NFA Gun Trusts in California

Before placing a legally-owned firearm into trust, you must understand that the California and federal law heavily regulating the possession and transfer of firearms, as violation of any of these laws can result in criminal liability.

i. California Firearm Transfer Laws in the Context of Gun Trusts

Understand that when a firearm is placed in trust, ownership over that firearm must be transferred to a trustee and, eventually, to the beneficiary(ies) of the trust.[243] And California law generally prevents one firearm from being transferred to more than one person; DROS forms and laws covering firearm transfers refer to only a single recipient.[244]

Also, each time ownership over the firearm is transferred to another person, the transfer itself must be conducted in accordance with California and federal law. So, assuming that the trustee is not also the settlor (in which case no transfer would occur because ownership over the firearm is not being given to a third party), then the firearm must be lawfully transferred from the settlor to the trustee. Assuming that the trustee and/or settlor are not licensed firearms dealers, then this transfer

---

[242] *See* P.C. § 32650.

[243] Although the settlor can be the trustee of a trust, the settlor cannot be the beneficiary of a trust.

[244] *See* P.C. §§ 27500-27590, 28050-28070, 28100, 28160; *see also* CAL. CODE REGS., tit. 11, § 4210; *see also Dealer's Record of Sales (DROS) Worksheet,* BOF 929, CALIFORNIA DEPARTMENT OF JUSTICE, BUREAU OF FIREARMS (2014), *available at* https://des.doj.ca.gov/forms/DROS_Worksheet_BOF-929.pdf (last visited Oct. 10, 2020).

would likely be considered a private party transfer (PPT) under California law.[245] Analogously, if the trust documents state that the firearms are to be distributed to the beneficiary at a certain time and if neither the settlor nor the beneficiary is a licensed firearm dealer, the firearm must once again be lawfully transferred from the trustee to the beneficiary pursuant to the laws governing PPTs. All PPTs in California (regardless of whether money is exchanged) must be processed through a licensed firearms dealer unless the transfer meets one of the few exceptions.[246] A violation of this rule is a crime, punishable as a misdemeanor or a felony depending on the type of firearm involved in the transfer.[247]

Prior to 2020, it was unclear if the "operation of law" exception to the dealer requirements allowed trustees to take possession of a firearm without having to go through a dealer. But this law has since been amended to expressly contemplate trustees and other similarly situated individuals (see the more detailed discussion in the "Taking Title by Operation of Law" subsection below).[248]

When the settlor and trustee reside in different states and a transfer through a dealer must occur, remember that federal law requires firearms to be transferred through an FFL in the recipient's home state.[249] While there is an exception for bequest and intestate succession, it is likely that a trust does not fall within that exception.

California law seems to state that both parties in a PPT must appear before the licensed firearms dealer. Given that most current gun owners (*i.e.*, the settlors) will likely want to retain ownership over their firearms,[250] this requirement could cause some difficulty due to the fact that upon death, the original owners cannot appear before a licensed firearm dealer in order to transfer the firearm. Because of this ambiguity, it may be best to ensure that each transfer of the firearm (*e.g.*, from settlor to transferee, transferee to successive transferee, and transferee to beneficiary) is done via PPT or meets one of the exceptions explained below, or otherwise occurs before the original gun owner (settlor) is deceased.

---

[245] See Section II of this Chapter for a more in-depth discussion on private party transfers.
[246] *See* P.C. §§ 16730, 27545.
[247] P.C. §§ 27545, 27590(c)-(d).
[248] AB 1292, 2018-2019, Leg., Reg. Sess. (Cal. 2019), *available at* https://leginfo.legislature.ca.gov/faces/billCompareClient.xhtml?bill_id=201920200AB1292 (last visited Oct. 10, 2020).
[249] 18. U.S.C. § 922(a)(5).
[250] Current owners can retain ownership over their firearms by naming themselves as the initial trustee or by creating a trust that does not come into effect until after the settler dies.

ii. Relevant Exceptions to Having to Process Firearm Transfers Through a Licensed Firearms Dealer, As Applied to Non-NFA Gun Trusts

Intra-Familial Transfers

As stated previously in this Chapter, "*infrequent*"[251] transfers of firearms between members of the same "immediate family"[252]— whether transferred by gift, bequest, intestate succession (i.e., inheritance from someone who passed away without a will), or by other means from one individual to another —do not need to be processed through a licensed firearms dealer.[253]

Transfers of Firearms Between Spouses

The California Penal Code is silent as to whether spouses or domestic partners can jointly register a firearm. Currently, when a firearm is purchased from a licensed firearms dealer, the firearm is registered to the individual who purchased the firearm, meaning that only one spouse or domestic partner can be the registered owner of the firearm.

Despite the fact that the California Penal Code does not state that spouses or domestic partners can jointly register a firearm, California law allows spouses and domestic partners to transfer firearms between each other without using a licensed firearms dealer if the transferring spouse "transmutes" his or her separate interest in the firearm to the receipt spouse or domestic partner (i.e., to community property or to the recipient's separate property).[254] A "transmutation" occurs when, during a marriage, a spouse or domestic partner shows an express intent, in a signed writing, to change ownership of his or her property.[255] In other words, one spouse's or domestic partner's separate party can be changed into the community property of both spouses or vice versa.[256]

Under California law, a transmutation is considered an "operation of law" transfer.[257] And, as explained below in further detail, "operation of law" transfers can be conducted without using a licensed firearms dealer as long certain conditions are met. Therefore, a spouse may be able to transfer a firearm that was purchased as separate property without using a licensed firearms dealer if he or she transmutes it into community property or into the separate property of the receiving spouse. In theory, this means that spouses should be able to jointly register a firearm, but this theory has been untested.

---

[251] Beginning January 1, 2020, "infrequently" means less than 6 firearm transactions per calendar year, regardless of the type of firearm, and no more than 50 total firearms in total. P.C. § 16730(a).

[252] "Immediate family" means a parent-child and/or grandparent-grandchild relationship. P.C. § 16720. Hence, under California law, siblings, aunts, uncles, cousins, and other distant family members are not allowed to directly transfer firearms to each other without going through a firearms dealer.

[253] P.C. § 27875.

[254] P.C. § 27920(b).

[255] CAL. FAM. CODE § 852(a).

[256] CAL. FAM. CODE § 850.

[257] P.C. § 16990.

Taking Title by Operation of Law

As explained above in the subsection discussing "operation of law" transfers, a firearm can be transferred to an individual without going through a licensed firearms dealer if the person receiving the firearm is taking possession of the firearm by "operation of law," so long as the person is not prohibited by state or federal law from possessing, receiving, owning, or purchasing a firearm. For this exemption to apply when the beneficiary is receiving the firearm pursuant to a transmutation of property under California Family Code section 850[258] (e.g., when spouses sign a trust in which they agree that the firearm is the settlor's separate property and that it shall be transmuted to the other spouse's separate property), then the beneficiary must:

(1) File the *Report of Law or Intra-Familial Firearm Transaction* form within 30 days, *and*

(2) Possess a valid firearm safety certificate or, in the case of a handgun, a valid handgun safety certificate.[259]

Recently in 2019, California law was amended to expressly contemplate trustees who take possession of a firearm pursuant to "a trust that includes a firearm and that was part of a will that created the trust," as well as other similar situated individuals.[260] Prior to this amendment it was unclear whether a transfer from a settlor to a trustee would fit within this exception. That said, DOJ has yet to provide any official guidance regarding these recent amendments.

Transfers of Long Guns to Minors by Immediate Family Members

Another exception to the dealer processing requirement that is likely applicable to certain estate transfers is the transfer of firearms, other than handguns, to a minor by the minor's parent or legal guardian, or by the minor's grandparent with the permission of the minor's parent or legal guardian (discussed previously in this Chapter).[261]

Keep in mind that minors are still generally prohibited under California law from possessing live ammunition[262] and from possessing a pistol, revolver, or other firearm capable of being concealed upon the person.[263] There are a number of exceptions to this restriction, but they generally require the presence or permission of the minor's parents during a lawful activity, and only if such activities involve the use of a firearm.[264]

---

[258] I.e., transmuting community property to separate property of spouse, transmuting separate property of spouse to community property, or transmuting separate property of one spouse to separate property of the other spouse.

[259] P.C. § 27920(a)(2).

[260] AB 1292, 2018-2019, Leg., Reg. Sess. (Cal. 2019), *available* at https://leginfo.legislature.ca.gov/faces/billCompareClient.xhtml?bill_id=201920200AB1292 (last visited Oct. 10, 2020). Assembly Bill No. 1292. It should also be noted that California's general requirement requiring a license to sell, lease, or transfer a firearm does not apply to the delivery or transfer of a firearm to a licensed firearm dealer by the trustee of a trust provided the trust is not of the type describe in either subdivision (k) or (p) of Penal Code section 16990 and the trustee is acting within the course and scope of their duties as the trustee of that trust. P.C. § 26589 (added by AB 1292 in 2019).

[261] P.C. § 27945(a-b).

[262] P.C. § 29650.

[263] P.C. § 29610.

[264] P.C. §§ 29615, 29655.

So, if the firearm being transferred is a handgun, only title of the firearm can be transferred through a trust to a minor.[265] The parent or legal guardian will be required to maintain possession of the handgun until the minor reaches eighteen years of age.

"Antique Firearms"

As stated in sections III and VI above, "antique firearms" can be transferred between private parties without having to go through a licensed firearms dealer, provided that the recipient is eligible under California law and the "antique" is not illegal to possess.

iii. Limitation of Non-NFA Gun Trusts: Firearms Cannot be Shared Amongst Trustees, So California Laws on Firearm Loaning Must be Followed if Trustees Want to "Share" Firearms

While NFA trusts allow the trustees to possess and use the NFA firearms that have been acquired by, or placed in, the trust, this benefit does not exist when a settlor transfers ordinary firearms into a trust in California. This is because the firearm must be transferred to a specific trustee, not to the trust as a legal entity.

Because the firearm must be registered to a specific trustee, the only way to share a firearm amongst other trustees (or any other person who is not prohibited from possessing firearms for that matter) would be to loan or transfer the firearm. But there are only certain situations where a firearm can be lawfully loaned, and they are explained in sections V and VI above.

iv. Limitations of Non-NFA Gun Trusts as Applied to "Assault Weapons"/.50 BMG Rifles and "Large-Capacity Magazines"

Along with complying with California's strict transfer requirements, individuals who intend on placing any lawfully owned "assault weapons" or "large-capacity magazines" in trust need to understand and comply with California's restrictions on the transfer and possession of those devices.

"Assault Weapons" and .50 BMG Rifles

Some individuals have marketed gun trusts as a way to possess, hand down, or transfer "assault weapons" to other individuals or family members in California. What these marketers fail to mention, or mention later in fine print, is that California law does not allow a person inheriting an "assault weapon" to keep it in California, unless

---

[265] This is because the federal handgun and ammunition restrictions do not apply when a minor inherits title of a handgun and/or ammunition. 18 U.S.C. § 922(x)(3). Meanwhile, as stated above, California law generally restricts minors from possessing handguns and/or ammunition (see P.C. sections 29650, 29610, 29615, 29655). So, it appears that, in California, minors can inherit ownership of a handgun but are restricted when it comes to possession of a handgun. But with California's restrictions on transferring handguns to minors (see P.C. section 27505), it is uncertain how all of this would work.

the firearm is already registered to him or her.²⁶⁶ In other words, unless the "assault weapon" is jointly registered to you and the other people in your family, the "assault weapon" cannot be transferred through a gun trust (or any other process) to other people in California and still be possessed within the state.

If the person inheriting the "assault weapon" is not a registered owner, then the person in possession of the "assault weapon" and the registered owner can be charged with a crime for illegally transferring an "assault weapon" (unless another exception applies). Consequently, a person acquiring a firearm meeting the definition of an "assault weapon" (in its "assault weapon" configuration) through a gun trust or any other type of transfer will not be able to possess the firearm in California.

In this respect, a "gun trust" only acts as an inheritance vehicle requiring the new owner to take and possess the "assault weapon" outside of California. But this is nothing novel. Nothing under California law prohibits the inheritance of an "assault weapon" by bequest or intestate succession (we discuss inheritance of "assault weapons" in Chapter 9). As a result, the benefits of a gun trust are dubious when it comes to "assault weapons."

"Large-Capacity Magazines"

Under California law, it is generally illegal to manufacture or cause to be manufactured, import, keep for sale, offer or expose for sale, give, lend, buy, or receive a "large-capacity magazine."²⁶⁷ Therefore, "large-capacity magazines" cannot be placed in trust without violating California law because the magazine would need to be transferred to a trustee or beneficiary at some point in time. And the potential ban on the possession of "large-capacity magazines" makes this even more problematic.

5. Transfers to Those with an Entertainment Firearm Permit (EFP)

Under California and federal law, people who possess an Entertainment Firearm Permit (EFP) are exempt from several firearm transfer requirements for up to one year from the time they were issued the EFP, including the federal background check and the DROS.²⁶⁸ Authorized EFP holders may possess firearms for props in motion picture, television, video, theatrical, or other entertainment productions.²⁶⁹

---

²⁶⁶ *See* P.C. § 30915. Joint registration of "assault weapons" and .50 BMG rifles, and ways to modify an "assault weapon," are discussed in Chapter 9.

²⁶⁷ P.C. § 32310.

²⁶⁸ P.C. §§ 27960, 29530. The National Instant Criminal Background Check System (NICS) exemption provided by the California Entertainment Firearms Permit (EFP) is a qualifying alternative to the background check requirements for up to one year from the issue date. To check the status of the EFP as an acceptable alternative to NICS, see *Permanent Brady Permit Chart*, U.S. DEPT. OF JUSTICE, BUREAU OF ALCOHOL, TOBACCO, FIREARMS AND EXPLOSIVES, https://www.atf.gov/rules-and-regulations/permanent-brady-permit-chart (last visited Oct. 10, 2020).

²⁶⁹ P.C. § 27960(a)(4). For other exemptions provided to EFP holders see P.C. sections 27960(a), 27810(a)(3), 31820(a); see also *Entertainment Firearms Permit Application*, CAL. DEPT. OF JUSTICE, OFFICE OF THE ATTORNEY

6. Acquiring Antiques and "Curio or Relic" Firearms

California laws about "antiques" and "curio or relic" firearms are complex. These are two different classes of firearms, and they accordingly have different state and federal requirements.

a. Antique Firearms

As discussed in Chapter 3, "antique firearms" are not generally considered "firearms"[270] for the state and federal laws governing firearm transfers.[271] This means that "antique firearms" can be bought outside of your state of residence, purchased from an FFL or any retailer without filling out a federal Form 4473 or DROS, or transferred between private parties without going through an FFL.

But, as discussed in Chapter 4, because someone prohibited from possessing firearms in California is also prohibited from possessing "antique firearms," it is illegal to give one to someone knowing he or she is prohibited from possessing firearms.[272] Likewise, it is unlawful to transfer an "antique firearm" that is a "handgun" to a minor.[273]

b. "Curio or Relic" Firearms

Since both California and the ATF define a "curio or relic" firearm the same way (see Chapter 3), if the ATF considers a firearm a "curio or relic," then so does California. The regulations of "curio or relic" transfers, however, differ between California and federal law.

"Curio or relic" firearms are associated with a Type 03 FFL, which is commonly known as a "collector's license."[274] The federal privileges conferred by this license extend *only* to transactions involving weapons classified as "curio or relic" firearms for personal collection purposes. This means a person with a collector's license is still subject to general federal firearm transfer regulations when purchasing non-"curio or relic" firearms and cannot be "engaged in the business"[275] of selling even "curio or relic" firearms without a separate *dealer's* license (*i.e.*, Type 01 FFL).[276] Additionally, Type 03 FFLs must still comply with state laws, meaning they are not

---

GENERAL, http://oag.ca.gov/sites/all/files/pdfs/firearms/forms/efpapp.pdf (last visited Oct. 10, 2020).

[270] P.C. § 16170(b); 18 U.S.C. § 921(a)(3).

[271] For example, "antique firearms" are not "firearms" for dealer licensing requirements, sales or loans between private parties, firearm safety device requirements, or HSCs. *See* P.C. §§ 16620; 16730(a), (c); 16960; 17310; 26500-26588 (inclusive); 16130; 16400; 16550; 16810; 17110; 26700-26915 (inclusive); 27510; 27540; 27545; 28100; 31615.

[272] P.C. § 27500(a).

[273] P.C. § 27505(a)-(b)(1).

[274] 18 U.S.C. § 921(a)(13); 27 C.F.R. § 478.41(c)-(d).

[275] 18 U.S.C. § 921(a)(21).

[276] 18 U.S.C. §§ 922(a), 923(b); 27 C.F.R. §§ 478.41(c)-(d), 478.93. To obtain a collector's license, submit ATF Form 7CR, Application for License (Collector of Curios or Relics). 27 C.F.R. § 478.47.

exempt from transfer or possession restrictions on certain firearms, even "curio or relic" firearms, if not allowed under state law.[277]

The general advantages of a collector's license are that it exempts you from the federal background check requirement[278] and allows you to purchase "curio or relic" firearms from FFLs from other states.[279] Individuals who do *not* possess a collector's license may acquire "curio or relic" *long guns* in a state where they are not a resident as long as:

(1) The rifle/shotgun is acquired from a federally licensed importer, manufacturer, dealer, or collector; *and*

(2) The purchaser meets with the licensee at the licensee's premises to accomplish the transfer, sale, and delivery; *and*

(3) A background check is conducted, and a federal Form 4473 is filled out when the firearm is transferred by the importer, manufacturer, or dealer; *and*

(4) The *conditions of sale in both parties' states* are satisfied.[280]

The option to acquire "curio or relic" long guns out of state is effectively not available to a California-only resident. This is because the out-of-state seller cannot comply with California's transfer requirements. Prior to January 1, 2014, there was an exception that could have applied if the out-of-state seller was a collector and *not* a Type 01 FFL. This is because the transfer of some "curio or relic" long guns (those over 50 years old) *from* a collector did not have to go through a Type 01 FFL if transferred in California. Therefore, they were not subject to California's general transfer requirements (whereas they would be if the seller were a Type 01 FFL). So, such a transfer satisfied federal law requirements that both states' laws are complied with (assuming that is also the case for the other state).

There are additional federal requirements and restrictions for those with a collector's license, including record-keeping requirements of their "curio or relic" transactions, which are beyond the scope of this book but which you need to be aware of before you engage in such transactions.[281]

Before January 1, 2014, a California resident could transfer or buy a "curio or relic" *long gun* from another California resident without going through an FFL as long as the rifle or shotgun was 50 years or older.[282] After January 1, 2014, this type

---

[277] 18 U.S.C. § 922(b)(2); 27 C.F.R. § 478.99(b)(2).

[278] 18 U.S.C. § 922(t)(1). This does not mean that you may possess a "curio or relic" firearm if you are prohibited from possessing firearms in general, just that you do not have to undergo a background check to get one. Likewise, it does not allow you to transfer "curio or relic" firearms to prohibited persons. 27 C.F.R. § 478.32(d).

[279] 18 U.S.C. § 922(a)(2); 27 C.F.R. § 478.41(c)-(d).

[280] 27 C.F.R. § 478.96(c)(1).

[281] For general information on "curio or relic" licenses, related federal laws, and the list of "curio or relic" firearms, see *Firearms Curios or Relics List*, U.S. DEPT. OF JUSTICE, BUREAU OF ALCOHOL, TOBACCO, FIREARMS AND EXPLOSIVES, http://www.atf.gov/publications/firearms/curios-relics/index.html (last visited Oct. 10, 2020).

[282] *Information Bulletin No. 98-24-BCIA Curio and Relic Long Guns and 30-day Firearms Delivery Requirements*, CAL. DEPT. OF JUSTICE, OFFICE OF THE ATTORNEY GENERAL, http://oag.ca.gov/sites/all/files/pdfs/firearms/infobuls/9824.pdf (last visited Oct. 10, 2020). If you cannot confirm the rifle or shotgun is at least 50 years old, do

of transfer was no longer possible for the general public. But a Type 03 FFL with a COE can infrequently *acquire* "curio or relic" long guns from regular citizens provided the Type 03 FFL holder registers the firearm with DOJ. And beginning January 1, 2020, the requirement that the Type 03 FFL's acquisition be "infrequent" restriction will no longer apply.[283] "Curio or relic" handguns must be transferred through an FFL just like modern ones, even if the purchaser is a Type 03 FFL.

An FFL must transfer any "curio or relic" firearm the same way as a non-"curio or relic" modern firearm even if it is being transferred to a Type 03 FFL. There are a few exceptions, however.

Specifically, in California, a Type 03 FFL who holds a COE is exempt from California's ten-day waiting period when buying a "curio or relic" firearm, even if it's *less than* 50 years old.[284] And, as explained above, these FFLs are also exempt from California's general requirements for handgun transfers, such as transferees having an FSC, the need to perform the safe-handling demonstration, and the one handgun per month restriction if the handgun is a "curio or relic."[285] Additionally, firearms listed as "curio or relic" handguns need not pass the safety and functionality tests required to be on the DOJ's Roster of handguns that FFLs can sell in California.[286]

DOJ previously held a position that Type 03 FFLs who hold a COE were only exempt from the one-handgun-per-30-calendar-day restriction when acquiring "curio or relic" handguns. But following a recent lawsuit, licensed collectors with a valid COE can now purchase more than one handgun in a 30-day period, even if the handgun is not a curio/relic.[287] DOJ has since notified California licensed firearm dealers of this change through the DROS Entry System ("DES").[288]

When a Type 03 FFL obtains *any firearm* from out of state,[289] it must register it with DOJ within five days of transporting the firearm into California.[290] This requirement previously only applied to handguns.

---

not purchase it without going through an FFL. As discussed above, you cannot engage in the business of dealing firearms without a license and you must be eligible to possess firearms. P.C. § 27965.

[283] P.C. § 27966(c).

[284] P.C. §§ 26970(a), 27670(a).

[285] P.C. §§ 27535(b)(9), 26970(a), 27670(a).

[286] P.C. § 32000(b)(3). Discussed in Chapter 10.

[287] *Doe v. Becerra*, 20 Cal.App.5th 330 (2018).

[288] DOJ issued an "Important Notice" to California licensed firearm dealers through DES advising them of the change and the procedures by which dealers could process such sales. A copy of this notice is available online at http://michellawyers.com/wp-content/uploads/2018/05/Bulletin-Name-50-Important-Ntc-re-1-30-Exemptions-for-03-FFL-w.a-COE-posted-5-29-18.pdf. Interestingly, these procedures created additional problems as applied to the required 10-day waiting period. Specifically, while exempt from the 10-day waiting period when purchasing a curio/relic firearm, Type 03 FFLs with COEs are not exempt from the waiting period when purchasing modern firearms. Nevertheless, the procedures adopted by DOJ inadvertently allows dealers to release a firearm to a Type 03 FFL with a valid COE prior to the expiration of the 10-day waiting period, even if the firearm is not a curio/relic. At the time of this book's publication, the problem has not yet been corrected.

[289] Type 03 FFLs from California can obtain a "curio or relic" handgun while outside of the state and bring it back, provided they comply with the California registration requirements for "curio or relic" collectors. 18 U.S.C. § 922(a)(3); P.C. § 27565.

[290] P.C. § 27565(b). Use Form FD 4100A, which is available on the DOJ website, and pay a $19 processing fee per handgun. Cal. Code Regs. tit. 11, § 4002. Before January 1, 2014, this requirement only applied to "curio or relic"

Certain firearms meeting the "curio or relic" definition may still have possession and transfer restrictions (*e.g.*, "machineguns" or destructive devices). Make sure the firearm is legal to possess federally and in California, and then, no matter what the firearm's age, consult the ATF "Firearms Curio and Relic List." Also, consult California's firearms laws and regulations to make sure the firearm does not fall under California's "assault weapons" ban. While that ban does not include certain "antique firearms,"[291] it can include "curio or relic" firearms, even popular ones like some M1A1 carbines. "Curio or relic" firearms are, however, exempt from California's ban on .50 BMG rifles that are not already "assault weapons."[292]

7. Auction of Non-Handguns

Since January 1, 2020, the dealer processing requirement does not apply to the "loan" of a non-handgun at an auction, raffle, or similar event by a nonprofit corporation if all the following conditions are met:

(1) The firearm at all times remains on the premises where the auction, raffle, or similar event occurs;

(2) The firearm is to be auctioned, raffled, or otherwise sold for the benefit of that nonprofit public benefit or mutual benefit corporation; and,

(3) The firearm, when sold or otherwise transferred, is delivered to a person licensed under P.C. sections 26700-26915, for sale or other transfer to the person who purchased or otherwise acquired ownership of the firearm.[293]

Likewise, donating a non-handgun through a PPT to a nonprofit for sale at such an auction or raffle does not need to go through an FFL if delivered to the nonprofit immediately before or during the auction.[294]

As applied here, a California firearm dealers license is not required for the delivery, sale, or transfer of an unloaded firearm that is not a handgun if both of the following conditions are met:

(1) The delivery, sale, or transfer is made by a nonprofit public benefit or mutual benefit corporation, including a local chapter of the same nonprofit corporation, organized pursuant to the Corporations Code; and,

(2) The sale or other transfer of ownership of that firearm is to occur as part of an auction, raffle, or similar event conducted by that nonprofit public benefit or mutual benefit corporation organized pursuant to the Corporations Code.[295]

---

handguns.

[291] The exception to the "assault weapon" ban for antique firearms only applies to firearms manufactured before January 1, 1899. P.C. § 16170(a).

[292] P.C. § 30530(b). Definition of "curio or relic" is located in Chapter 3.

[293] P.C. § 27900. Although the exception has been changed from applying to "infrequent" sales or transfers to simply "loans," in practice, this change appears to have little, if any, effect.

[294] P.C. §§ 27900(a), 27905.

[295] P.C. § 26581.

8. "Gun Buybacks"

A number of the restrictions on transferring firearms are suspended if you transfer your firearms to a state, local, or federal government entity, so long as the transfer is for the governmental entity, and the entity is acquiring the firearm "as part of an authorized, voluntary program in which the entity is buying or receiving weapons from private individuals."[296] These events are known as "gun buybacks."

At a gun buyback, government entities will often exchange money (for example, a prepaid credit or gift card) for firearms. The buyback events are often advertised as "no questions asked" opportunities where the public can turn in their firearms. With the hopes that a large number of firearms will be taken in, the promoters of these events usually claim that the firearms turned in will not be investigated and that no background check will be run on them. Herein lies one huge problem with these types of events. The "no questions asked" policy gives criminals the opportunity to turn in firearms either used in crimes (like homicides) or stolen from lawful owners. Not only can criminals get rid of the evidence of a crime, but they also get paid for it. The lawful firearm owner who had his or her firearm stolen will *never* see that firearm again.

Another problem with gun buyback events is that people usually do not realize that turning their firearms over does not *unregister* the firearm. This can cause huge problems for people down the road, especially if they later become prohibited from possessing firearms and are flagged in the Armed Prohibited Person System (APPS) or are required to surrender their firearms because they still have a firearm registered in their name. And because these gun buyback programs are "no questions asked," it can be very difficult to prove to law enforcement that you are no longer in possession of the firearm because you will likely not be given a receipt showing that you turned the firearm into a government agency. Therefore, it may be nearly impossible to prove that you no longer possess the firearm.

For legitimate firearm owners who turn in their firearms, gun buybacks provide a different concern. For instance, in some cases, the money the gun buyback agency is offering for the firearm is less than what the firearm is worth. Gun buybacks treat junk guns and valuable antiques equally. People often do not know the true value of their firearms, and there are often more cost-effective ways to lawfully dispose of your firearms if you no longer want or need them. For example, firearms dealers and certain nonprofit organizations may be willing to accept your firearm (and potentially provide you more money for the firearm than the buyback will).

I strongly suggest contacting a local gun shop to see if they are interested in buying the firearm or offering your firearm to a nonprofit for a potential tax write-off before giving a firearm to a gun buyback.

---

[296] P.C. §§ 27850, 31725.

9. Other Limited Exceptions

In 2019, AB 1292 amended the law so that the dealer transfer requirement does not apply to a person who takes possession of a firearm and subsequently delivers that firearm to a law enforcement agency, provided the following requirements are satisfied:

(1) The person found the firearm or took the firearm from a person who was committing a crime against them;

(2) The person taking possession subsequently delivers the firearm to a law enforcement agency; *and*

(3) The person gives prior notice to the law enforcement agency that the person is transporting the firearm to the agency for disposition.[297]

Also in 2019, California adopted SB 172, which among its many other provisions included new exceptions to the requirement that firearms be transferred through a California licensed firearms dealer. These include loans occurring on the lender's private property, temporary transfers for purposes of suicide prevention, and temporary loans for purposes of storage on another's private property. Specific requirements for each of these new exceptions are listed in Table 5.8.

VIII. BUILDING YOUR OWN FIREARM

Another way to obtain a firearm is by making one or assembling one from parts. This practice can be lawful under both California and federal law.

Federal law prohibits the "manufacturing" of firearms without a license, but only considers those who are "engaged in the business" of making firearms (*i.e.*, those who devote time, attention, and labor to doing so as a regular course of business) to be "manufacturers" who need a license.[298] This means that making a firearm for personal use does not require a license under federal or California law as long as you do not build an item that is prohibited to possess or make under California or federal law (see Chapters 9 and 10).[299]

Exempting licensed manufacturers with government permission and those fixing lawfully acquired firearms,[300] federal law prohibits assembling a semiautomatic rifle or any shotgun using more than ten "imported parts"[301] if the assembled fire-

---

[297] P.C. § 27922 (added by AB 1292 in 2019). It should also be noted that California's general requirement requiring a license to sell, lease, or transfer a firearm does not apply to transfers made to law enforcement agencies pursuant to Penal Code section 27922. See P.C. § 26582 (added by AB 1292 in 2019).

[298] 18 U.S.C. §§ 921(a)(10), (a)(21), 923(a)(1).

[299] Though there are other prohibited items, the main concern is to avoid inadvertently building an "assault weapon" (Chapter 9).

[300] 27 C.F.R. § 478.39(b).

[301] 27 C.F.R. § 478.39(a). "Imported parts" are: (1) frames, receivers, receiver castings, forgings, or stampings; (2) barrels; (3) barrel extensions; (4) mounting blocks (trunions); (5) muzzle attachments; (6) bolts; (7) bolt carriers; (8) operating rods; (9) gas pistons; (10) trigger housings; (11) triggers; (12) hammers; (13) sears; (14) disconnectors; (15) buttstocks; (16) pistol grips; (17) forearms, handguards; (18) magazine bodies; (19) followers; and (20) floor plates. 27 C.F.R. § 478.39(c).

arm is prohibited from being imported[302] on the basis that it is not "particularly suitable for or readily adaptable to sporting purposes."[303]

Also, unless you make a "firearm" as defined under the National Firearm Act (NFA), which would require a tax payment and ATF approval,[304] there isn't a federal requirement that you register a firearm assembled for personal use.

Prior to 2016, California did not require people to register a firearm assembled for personal use. This all changed on July 22, 2016, though, when Governor Brown signed Assembly Bill (AB) 857 into law. This bill requires individuals who plan on assembling or manufacturing a firearm after July 1, 2018 to obtain a serial number or identification mark from DOJ before actually assembling or manufacturing the firearm.[305] This bill also requires any person who owns a firearm that does not bear a serial number assigned to it after July 1, 2018 to apply for and obtain a serial number before January 1, 2019.[306] This bill and the new requirements will be explained in further detail below.

But, before delving into these requirements, let's first discuss some of the ways that people have built personal firearms.

A. Ways to Build Your Own Firearm

1. Creating a Firearm from a Prefabricated Frame or Receiver

First, you can purchase a finished "frame" or "receiver"[307] and then assemble it with additional parts to complete the firearm. With the exception of what California law defines as a "firearm precursor part" (discussed below), state and federal laws generally do not prohibit or otherwise restrict acquiring firearm parts. But because California laws consider a "frame" or a "receiver" to be a "firearm,"[308] you have to get the frame or receiver through an FFL just like any other firearm or meet one of the exceptions. As mentioned above, you also must be at least age 21 to purchase a receiver.

The 3D printed parts of "The Liberator"

---

[302] 18 U.S.C. § 925(d)(3); 26 U.S.C. § 5845(a).
[303] 18 U.S.C. §§ 922(r), 925(d)(3); 27 C.F.R. § 478.39(a).
[304] *See* 26 U.S.C. § 5822.
[305] AB 857, 2015-2016, Leg., Reg. Sess. (Cal. 2016), *available at* https://leginfo.legislature.ca.gov/faces/billNavClient.xhtml?bill_id=201520160AB857 (last visited Oct. 10, 2020). *See* P.C. § 29180-29183.
[306] *See* P.C. § 29180.
[307] A "receiver" is "[t]he basic unit of a firearm which houses the firing mechanism and to which the barrel and stock are assembled. In revolvers, pistols and break-open firearms, it is called the frame." Nat'l Shooting Sports Found., The Writer's Guide to Firearms & Ammunition 15 (Jan. 2012 ed.), *available at* http://www.nssf.org/share/pdf/writers_guide.pdf (last visited Oct. 10, 2020).
[308] 18 U.S.C. § 921(a)(3)(B); P.C. § 16520(b). See Chapter 3.

This process is not covered under the "ghost gun"[309] bill requirements discussed below.

In 2019, California adopted AB 879, creating a "first of its kind of law" by requiring the sale of "firearm precursor parts" to be conducted by or processed through a licensed "firearm precursor part vendor." And the implementation of this new law has been expedited following the adoption of SB 118 in 2020. For those familiar with California's new laws regulating ammunition sales as a result of Proposition 63 and SB 1235, many of the provisions applicable to "firearm precursor parts" are nearly identical to the ammunition sales restrictions. Per the language of AB 879, the term "firearm precursor part" includes either:

(1) An unfinished receiver, including both a single part receiver and multiple part receiver, such as a receiver in an AR-10 or AR-15 style firearm; or,

(2) An unfinished handgun frame.[310]

For purposes of AB 879, an "unfinished receiver" includes "a receiver tube, a molded or shaped polymer frame or receiver, a metallic casting, a metallic forging, and a receiver flat, such as a Kalashnikov-style weapons system, Kalashnikov-style receiver channel, or a Browning-style receiver side plate."[311] Despite this definition, it is unclear exactly what items will be restricted pursuant to AB 879. And while the legislature has mandated DOJ to provide written guidance and pictorial diagrams, it remains to be seen if DOJ will be able to provide the necessary guidance in a manner that is not unconstitutionally vague.[312]

a. Requirement that Firearm Precursor Part Sales Be Conducted Through a Licensed Precursor Part Vendor

Beginning July 1, 2022, the sale of a firearm precursor part by any party must be conducted by or processed through a licensed firearm precursor part vendor.[313] For purposes of this requirement, both California licensed firearm dealers and ammunition vendors are automatically deemed licensed precursor part vendors) This includes when firearm precursor parts are sold between two private parties, neither of whom is a licensed firearm precursor part vendor. Anyone selling more than one firearm precursor part in a 30-day period needs to obtain a firearm precursor part vendor license.[314]

Like PPTs, any time a non-licensed individual wishes to sell a firearm precursor part to another non-licensed party, they must first take the part to a licensed ven-

---

[309] The term "ghost gun" is a made-up term that generally refers to a firearm that does not have a serial number or a homemade gun, like one created using a 3D printer.

[310] P.C. § 16531(a)(1-2).

[311] P.C. § 16531(a)(1). What's more, firearm precursor parts that can only be used on "antique firearms" as defined under subdivision (c) of P.C. section 16170 are not firearm precursor parts for purposes of these restrictions. P.C. § 16531(c).

[312] See P.C. § 16531(b).

[313] P.C. § 30412(a)(1).

[314] P.C. § 30442(a).

dor who will then process the transaction in accordance with California law.[315] If the vendor cannot deliver the part to the purchaser because he or she is prohibited or is otherwise unable to obtain the required DOJ-authorization beginning July 1, 2022 (discussed below), the vendor must return the part to the seller.[316]

In addition to charging any other applicable fees allowed by California law, vendors may charge the individual purchasing the firearm precursor part in a private transaction an administrative fee to process the transaction in an amount to be set by DOJ.[317] As of the time of publication, DOJ has yet to adopt the necessary regulations regarding this fee.

Failing to conduct a firearm precursor part sale through a licensed vendor is punishable as a misdemeanor.[318]

b. Face-to-Face Transaction Requirement

Commencing July 1, 2022, firearm precursor part sales, deliveries, and transfers of ownership must occur in a face-to-face transaction with the seller, deliverer, or transferor.[319] That means that anytime you plan on selling or transferring a firearm precursor part to another private party, you must be physically in front of the other party when conducting the transfer or sale. You cannot mail or otherwise send the part to another person.

California law still allows individuals to purchase firearm precursor parts over the internet or by other means of remote ordering. The law specifies that firearm precursor parts "may be purchased or acquired over the internet, or through other means of remote ordering, if a licensed firearm precursor part vendor":

(1) Initially receives the firearm precursor part; and

(2) Processes the transaction in compliance with Penal Code sections 30412 and 30442 through 30456.[320]

The background check and record-keeping requirements (discussed below) do not go into effect until July 1, 2022.[321] And DOJ has yet to propose the necessary regulations implementing those requirements. But given the substantial similarity between AB 879 and California's ammunition sales restrictions, it is anticipated that the regulations for AB 879 will be similar, if not identical.

---

[315] P.C. § 30412(a)(2).
[316] P.C. § 30412(a)(2).
[317] P.C. § 30412(a)(2).
[318] P.C. § 30412(e).
[319] P.C. § 30412(b).
[320] P.C. § 30412(b).
[321] P.C. §§ 30452(a), 30470(a).

Selling, delivering, or transferring a firearm precursor part in violation of the above face-to-face transfer requirements is punishable as a misdemeanor.[322]

c. **Exceptions to the Requirement that Firearm Precursor Part Sales Must Be Conducted Through a Licensed Firearm Precursor Part Vendor and Face-to-Face Requirement**

Both the requirement that the sale of firearm precursor parts must be conducted by or through a licensed firearms dealer, and the requirement that any firearm precursor part sold, delivered, or transferred to another party must be conducted in a face-to-face transaction, do not apply to the following individuals:

Table 5.9

Penal Code Section	Exemption
P.C. § 30412(c)(1)	An authorized law enforcement representative of a city, county, city and county, or state or federal government, if the sale, delivery, or transfer is for exclusive use by that governmental agency and, prior to the sale, delivery, or transfer of the firearm precursor part, written authorization from the head of the agency employing the purchaser or transferee is obtained, identifying the employee as an individual authorized to conduct the transaction, and authorizing the transaction for the exclusive use of the agency employing the individual.
P.C. § 30312(c)(2)	A sworn peace officer, as defined in P.C. sections 830-832.9, or sworn federal law enforcement office, who is authorized to carry a firearm in the course and scope of the officer's duties.
P.C. § 30312(c)(3)	An importer or manufacturer of ammunition or firearms who is licensed to engage in business under 18 U.S.C. sections 921-931 and the regulations issued pursuant thereto.
P.C. § 30312(c)(4)	A person who is on the centralized list of exempted federal firearms licensees maintained by DOJ under P.C. sections 28450-28490.
P.C. § 30312(c)(5)	A person whose licensed premises are outside this state and who is licensed as a dealer or collector of firearms under 18 U.S.C. sections 921-931.

---

[322] P..C. § 30412(e).

PENAL CODE SECTION	EXEMPTION
P.C. § 30312(c)(6)	A person who is licensed as a collector of firearms under 18 U.S.C. sections 921-931 and the regulations issued pursuant thereto, whose licensed premises are within this sate and who also has a current COE.
P.C. § 30312(c)(7)	A firearm precursor part vendor.
P.C. § 30312(c)(8)	An authorized representative of a city, county, city and county, or state or federal government, if the firearm precursor part is obtained as part of an authorized, voluntary program in which the governmental entity is buying or receiving firearm precursor parts from private individuals.

Astute observers will note several exceptions to California's ammunition sales restrictions are missing from the above table of exceptions to AB 879's restrictions. As written, the law does ***not*** exempt transfers of firearm precursor parts between spouses, registered domestic partners, or "immediate family members," nor does it exempt transfers to persons enrolled in the basic training academy for peace officers or consultant-evaluators.

d. Recording of Firearm Precursor Part Purchaser or Transferee Information

Beginning July 1, 2022, firearm precursor part vendors cannot sell or transfer ownership of any firearm precursor part without, at the time of delivering the part to the purchaser or transferee, first recording and submitting the following information to DOJ:

(1) The date of the sale or other transfer;

(2) The purchaser's or transferee's driver's license or other identification number and the sate in which it was issued;

(3) The brand, type, and amount of firearm precursor parts sold or otherwise transferred;

(4) The purchaser's or transferee's full name and signature;

(5) The name of the salesperson who processed the sale or other transaction;

(6) The purchaser's or transferee's full residential address and telephone number; and,

(7) The purchaser's or transferee's date of birth.[323]

---

[323] P. C. § 30452(a)(1)(A-G).

e. Persons Prohibited from Possessing Firearm Precursor Parts

Beginning July 1, 2022, anyone who supplies, delivers, sells, or gives possession or control of a firearm precursor part to anyone who that person knows or using reasonable care should know is prohibited from owning, possessing, or having under custody or control a firearm precursor part is guilty of a misdemeanor.[325] AB 879 prohibits individuals who are prohibited from owning or possessing a firearm from also possessing a firearm precursor part.[326] And beginning July 1, 2022, it is a misdemeanor to:

(1) Sell a firearm precursor part to a person under 21 years of age; or,

(2) Supply, deliver, or give possession of a firearm precursor part to a minor who the person, corporation, or dealer knows, or using reasonable care should have known, is prohibited from possessing a firearm or ammunition at that time.[327]

f. Authorization to Purchase Firearm Precursor Parts

Beginning July 1, 2022, DOJ will electronically approve the purchase or transfer of a firearm precursor part through a vendor at the time of purchase of transfer prior to the purchaser or transferee taking possession.[328] Only the following people will be authorized to purchase a firearm precursor part:

(1) A purchaser or transferee whose information matches an entry in the Automated Firearms System ("AFS") and who is eligible to possess firearm precursor parts;

(2) A purchaser or transferee who has a current certificate of eligibility issued by DOJ; or,

(3) A purchaser or transferee who is not prohibited from purchasing or possessing firearm precursor parts in a single firearm precursor part transaction or purchase made pursuant to subdivision (c) of Penal Code section 30470.[329]

DOJ is required to develop a procedure in which a person who is not prohibited from purchasing or possessing a firearm precursor part may be approved for a single firearm precursor part transaction or purchase . But it is highly likely this procedure will be similar or identical to the procedure used by DOJ for "Basic Am-

---

[324] P.C. § 30454.
[325] P.C. § 30406.
[326] P.C. § 30405.
[327] P.C. § 30400.
[328] P.C. § 30470(a).
[329] P.C. § 30470(a)(1-3).

munition Eligibility Checks" under section 4303, Title 11, of the California Code of Regulations.

There are exceptions to the electronic approval requirement. Specifically, the restriction outlined above does not apply to the sale or other transfer of ownership of firearm precursor parts by a firearm precursor part vendor to any of the following (if properly identified):

Table 5.10

PENAL CODE SECTION	EXEMPTION
P.C. § 30452(e)(1)	A firearm precursor part vendor.
P.C. § 30452(e)(2)	A person who is on the centralized list of exempted federal firearm licensees maintained by DOJ under P.C. sections 28450-28490.
P.C. § 30452(e)(3)	A gunsmith.
P.C. § 30452(e)(4)	A wholesaler.
P.C. § 30452(e)(5)	A manufacturer or importer of firearms or ammunition licensed under 18 U.S.C. sections 921-931 and the regulations issued thereto.
P.C. § 30452(e)(6)	An authorized law enforcement representative of a city, county, city and county, or state or federal government, if the sale or other transfer of ownership is for exclusive use by that governmental agency, and, prior to the sale, delivery, or transfer of the firearm precursor part, written authorization from the head of the agency authorizing the transaction is presented to the person from whom the purchase, delivery, or transfer is being made.[330]
P.C. § 30452(e)(7)	A properly identified sworn peace officer or federal law enforcement officer who is authorized to carry a firearm in the course and scope of the officer's duties.[331]

---

[330] For the purposes of this exception, "proper written authorization" is defined as "verifiable written certification from the head of the agency by which the purchaser, transferee, or person otherwise acquiring ownership is employed, identifying the employee as an individual authorized to conduct the transaction, and authorizing the transaction for the exclusive use of the agency by which that individual is employed." P.C. § 30452(e)(6).

[331] For the purposes of this exception, "proper identification" is defined as "verifiable written certification from the head of the agency by which the purchaser or transferee is employed, identifying the purchaser or transferee as a full-time paid peace officer who is authorized to carry a firearm in the course and scope of the officer's duties." P.C. § 30452(e)(7)(B)(i). The certification must be delivered to the vendor at the time of purchase or transfer and the

g. Restriction Against Bringing Firearm Precursor Parts into California

Beginning July 1, 2022, California residents are prohibited from transporting into California a firearm precursor part that was purchased or otherwise obtained from outside California unless they first have the firearm precursor part delivered to a licensed firearm precursor part vendor for delivery.[332] A violation of this provision is a misdemeanor.[333] The exceptions to this restriction are as follows:

Table 5.11

PENAL CODE SECTION	EXEMPTION
P.C. § 30414(b)(1)	A firearm precursor part vendor.
P.C. § 30414(b)(2)	A sworn peace officer, as defined in P.C. sections 830-832.9, or sworn federal law enforcement officer who is authorized to carry a firearm in the course and scope of the officer's duties.
P.C. § 30414(b)(3)	An importer or manufacturer of ammunition or firearms who is licensed to engage in business pursuant to 18 U.S.C. sections 921-931 and the regulations issued pursuant thereto.
P.C. § 30414(b)(4)	A person who is on the centralized list of exempted federal firearms licensees maintained by DOJ under P.C. sections 28450-28490.
P.C. § 30414(b)(5)	A person who is licensed as a collector of firearms under 18 U.S.C. sections 921-931 and the regulations issued thereto, whose licensed premises are within California and who has a current COE.
P.C. § 30414(b)(6)	A licensed common carrier or an authorized agent or employee of a licensed common carrier, when acting in the course and scope of duties incident to the delivery of or receipt of that firearm in accordance with federal law. (Note: it appears this exception was poorly drafted by using the word "firearm" instead of "firearm precursor part.")

---

purchaser or transferee must provide bona fide evidence of identity to verify that they are the person authorized in the certification. P.C. § 30452(e)(7)(B)(ii). Vendors must keep the certification with the record of sale and submit the certification to DOJ. P.C. § 30452(e)(7)(B)(iii).

[332] P.C. § 30414.
[333] P.C. § 30414(c).

2. Creating a Firearm From an 80% Receiver

The second way is to machine a firearm either from completely raw materials or partially finished materials. Making a firearm from partially finished materials is more popular, as it takes less skill. Generally, you start with an incomplete receiver commonly referred to as an "80% receiver" or "80% side plate."

The "80%" denotes how close the receiver is to being a complete firearm – though this is more of an estimate since it is impossible to say what percentage of work remains for a given firearm, which can vary based on experience, available tools, etc.

The ATF has issued letters to 80% receiver manufactures explaining what features cannot be present on an 80% receiver in order for it to not be considered a "firearm." For "80% AR receivers," the ATF has taken the position that no work can be done to the "fire control cavity" and trigger, no drilling into the receiver for the hammer and trigger pins, and no drilling for the safety.[334] Once work has been started in those areas, the ATF considers the receiver to be a "firearm" for purposes of federal law.

3. "Build Parties"

A number of firearm enthusiasts are participating in activities called "build parties." There are two different types of activities associated with this term.

The first are get-togethers organized around finishing an 80% firearm frame or receiver. Usually, the machines needed for these jobs (typically a drill press or manual mill) are expensive and not something found in every garage. Consequently, groups of firearm enthusiasts form "build parties" where they convene at the machine owner's home and finish their 80% receivers together, usually under the oversight of someone experienced in finishing the receiver. Provided nothing created is illegal to own and no money changes hands, there should be nothing troubling about this practice under state or federal law.

"Build party" is also used to describe a type of activity that is more problematic. This activity usually involves a situation where either money exchanges hands for assistance with completing the 80% receiver, machinery is rented, and/or a computer numerical control machine (CNC machine) is used. A CNC machine is an automatic machine that will perform milling based on instructions from a programmable code. Once programed, the machine can perform its program over and over again (for example, finishing 80% receivers). Some companies and organizations have offered to sell 80% receivers and an opportunity to finish the purchased

---

[334] In 2014, the ATF went even further with its position on the "80% AR receiver" stating that 80% receivers that have material that extends "past the exterior walls of the casting, indicating the approximate location of the holes to be drilled for the selector, hammer, and trigger pins" were considered to be "firearms" for purposes of federal law. Moreover, the ATF has also taken the position that 80% receivers that have so-called "indexing," *i.e.*, different colored material that outlines where to drill the fire control cavity, are "firearms" for purposes of federal law.

80% receiver with their machinery. Other businesses are offering an opportunity for people to use their CNC machine for the purpose of finishing 80% receivers.

These practices are problematic, and the ATF has determined that any businesses/individuals engaging in these practices are engaged in the business of manufacturing firearms under federal law.[335] Engaging in the business of manufacturing requires a license, bookkeeping, special engraving, and all of the other requirements associated with manufacturing and transferring firearms.

4 3D Printing

In May 2013, there was a lot of press about 3D-printed handguns. In August 2013, there were reports of a 3D-printed .22 caliber rifle, and in November 2013 a company created a 3D-printed 1911 handgun.[336] While the process of making a firearm for personal use is generally lawful, 3D-printed firearms do have some additional concerns.

There are many processes that can be classified as "3D printing." The general concept is usually the same. An object or device is either designed or scanned in three dimensions, and the data is fed into a computer. The data from the computer is then sent to the 3D printer. Similar to how a computer tells a conventional printer to print out a document, the computer tells the 3D printer how to construct the three-dimensional object.

The 3D printer adds layer upon layer of the material to create the object. The material used depends on the machine and process. Currently, there is no process to create a single object that has moving parts, but existing technology allows the printer to create all of the individual parts of an object comprised of moving parts. While the process cannot make a whole firearm, it can make each of the parts for a firearm, which can then be assembled. For instance, now available for purchase is a computer-numerically-controlled (or CNC) mill that can complete an 80% receiver for you. Most 3D printers use some form of plastic or polymer, though there are more expensive 3D printers that work with metal, such as the one used to create a metal 1911 handgun. To make a firearm, the material must be strong enough to stand up to the stress of being fired. If made solely from plastic or polymer, a "printed" firearm could theoretically be undetectable to airport metal detectors.

Part of the concern when 3D-printed firearms were first discussed was that they might not be able to be detected by airport security. Since these firearms may be considered an "undetectable firearm,"[337] "zip gun"[338] or "an unconventional pistol,"[339]

---

[335] ATF Rul. 2015-1 (2015). Manufacturing a firearm without a valid license is a violation of 18 U.S.C. section 922(a)(1)(A).
[336] Solid Concepts Manufactures First 3D-Printed Metal Pistol, Gizmag (Nov. 8, 2013), http://www.gizmag.com/worlds-first-3d-printed-gun/29702/ (last visited Oct. 10, 2020).
[337] 18 U.S.C. § 922(p); P.C. §§ 24610, 17280.
[338] P.C. §§ 17360, 33600.
[339] P.C. §§ 17270, 31500 (this depends on whether or not the barrel is rifled).

exercise caution in possessing them as these types of firearms are illegal under federal and California law. The legality of 3D-printed firearms is discussed in greater detail in Chapter 10.

B. Registration Requirements for Manufacturing or Assembling Your Own Firearm

Although Governor Jerry Brown vetoed prior legislation regarding "ghost guns" in 2014,[340] he signed AB 857 on July 22, 2016. In short, AB 857 generally requires individuals to (1) obtain a unique serial number from DOJ for firearms they own that do not have identifying marks and for the firearms that they plan to create after July 1, 2018; (2) engrave that unique serial number into the firearm; and (3) notify DOJ that they completed that engraving.[341] The deadline to apply for a unique serial number was January 1, 2019 for firearms completed prior to July 1, 2018.[342]

And with the adoption of SB 746, new residents moving into California after January 1, 2019 with home-built firearms lacking a unique serial number must also apply to DOJ for a serial number within 60 days of arrival using this same process.[343]

AB 857 required DOJ to adopt regulations governing how a person can apply for and obtain a unique serial number. Those regulations have since been implemented and have been in effect since July 1, 2018.[344] And as of January 28, 2020, amendments to those regulations have also been adopted. Under these regulations, all applications for DOJ-approved serial numbers must be submitted electronically using DOJ's California Firearms Application Reporting System ("CFARS"), which can be accessed at https://cfars.doj.ca.gov/.[345] DOJ has also created a "Unique Serial Number Application" page on their website that provides additional information about the process of submitting applications.[346]

1. Submitting Applications for a DOJ-Approved Serial Number

Submitting applications for a DOJ-approved serial number through CFARS requires individuals to create a CFARS account (if they do not have one already).[347] The application requires individuals to provide their full name, residence, email, telephone number, date of birth, gender, military ID number (if applicable), California Driver's License or ID number, U.S. citizenship status, place of birth, country

---

[340] *See* SB 808, 2013-2014 Leg., Reg. Sess. (Cal. 2014), *available at* https://leginfo.legislature.ca.gov/faces/billNavClient.xhtml?bill_id=201320140SB808 (last visited Oct. 10, 2020).

[341] *See generallly* P.C. § 29810.

[342] Cal. Code Regs. tit. 11, § 5510(a).

[343] P.C. § 29180(e).

[344] Cal. Code Regs. tit. 11, §§ 5505-5522.

[345] Cal. Code Regs. tit. 11, § 5511.

[346] *See Unique Serial Number Application*, Attorney General, State of California Department of Justice, https://oag.ca.gov/firearms/usna (last visited Oct. 10, 2020).

[347] Cal. Code Regs. tit. 11, § 5512.

of citizenship, and alien registration or I-94 number (if applicable).[348] All of this information will be used to conduct the required background check.

Regarding applications for DOJ-approved serial numbers, applicants must provide a description of the firearm for which the serial number is being sought.[349] This includes the date manufacture/assembly will be complete (or for a person moving into California, the date the firearm was previously completed), the firearm type, caliber, color, barrel length, unit of measurement, type of material used (aluminum, steel, plastic, or other), whether the firearm is a frame or receiver only, and any additional identification marks.[350] If the applicant specifies the firearm is a "single shot" pistol, the applicant will also need to specify whether the pistol is a "bolt action" or "break top" design.[351] What's more, if the applicant specifies that the receiver is made from material "other" than aluminum, steel, or polymer plastic, the applicant must provide a brief explanation of the type of material used.[352] Should DOJ deem it necessary, it may request additional information such as digital images "to confirm that an applicant is compliant with state firearm laws," which if not received within 30 calendar days of the request, will result in the rejection of the application.[353] Due to the enactment of both Senate Bill 1100 and Senate Bill 746 in 2018, all applicants must be at least 21 years old if their application for a unique serial number is submitted on or after February 1, 2019.[354] Regardless of the applicant's age, they must have a valid Firearms Safety Certificate or Handgun Safety Certificate.[355]

The total initial application fee is $35, which is comprised of $20 for the required firearms eligibility check and $15 for the issuance of one unique serial number for a firearm.[356] This fee must be paid online by debit or credit card at the time the application is submitted through CFARS.[357] If you have more than one firearm to include with your application, it will cost an additional $15 per firearm.[358] There is no limit to the number of firearms that can be included on an application.

---

[348] CAL. CODE REGS. tit. 11, § 5513(a)(1).

[349] Note that both the Penal Code and DOJ's regulations prohibit individuals from manufacturing or assembling certain firearms pursuant to these provisions. Such firearms include "generally prohibited" firearms (such as cane guns, short-barreled rifles/shotguns, etc.), "assault weapons," machine guns, .50 BMG rifles, and destructive devices. See P.C. § 29182(e); CAL. CODE REGS. tit. 11, § 5506. What's more, following the enactment of SB 746, the Penal Code has been amended to also state that the manufacture or assembly of an "unsafe handgun" as defined in Penal Code section 31910 is likewise prohibited. See P.C. § 29182(e)(2).

[350] CAL. CODE REGS. tit. 11, § 5513(a)(2).

[351] CAL. CODE REGS. tit. 11, § 5513(a)(2)(A).

[352] CAL. CODE REGS. tit. 11, § 5513(a)(2)(B).

[353] CAL. CODE REGS. tit. 11, § 5513(b).

[354] For applications submitted prior to February 1, 2019, applicants must be at least 18 years old, provided the application is for a firearm that is not a handgun. See P.C. § 29182(b). And note that DOJ currently has in place "emergency" regulations that implement the changes made to the Penal Code under Senate Bill 1100 and/or Senate Bill 746. See CAL. CODE REGS. tit. 11, § 5513(a)(1)(A).

[355] CAL. CODE REGS. tit. 11, § 5513(a)(3).

[356] CAL. CODE REGS. tit. 11, § 5514(a).

[357] CAL. CODE REGS. tit. 11, § 5514(b).

[358] CAL. CODE REGS. tit. 11, § 5514(a).

Once the application has been submitted along with all appropriate fees, DOJ will grant or deny the application within 15 calendar days.[359] Individuals should be aware, however, that DOJ will not process an application where no disposition can be generated for the applicant's criminal history. In other words, if DOJ cannot determine whether you are prohibited from owning or possessing firearms, DOJ will deny your application for a unique serial number.[360] If you are unsure whether you will pass a background check, you can submit a Personal Firearms Eligibility Check ("PFEC") application prior to submitting your application for a DOJ-approved serial number.[361]

2. Engraving the Unique Serial Number and Required Digital Images

Should the applicant pass the required background check, DOJ will inform the applicant via CFARS and assign each firearm associated with the application a unique[362] serial number.[363]

To engrave the firearm, individuals may either: 1) contact a Type 07 FFL (manufacturer) to apply the unique serial number; 2) seek the assistance of an unlicensed individual or business so long as the applicant never leaves the firearm unattended with them; or, 3) personally apply the unique serial number.[364] Regardless of the method chosen, the serial number must be engraved, cast, stamped, or otherwise permanently placed in a conspicuous location on the receiver or frame of the firearm in a manner not susceptible of being readily obliterated, altered, or removed.[365] And the engraving, casting, or stamping of the serial number shall be to a minimum depth of .003 inches and in a print no smaller than 1/16 of an inch.[366] Certain additional information must also be engraved, cast, or stamped on the frame, receiver, or barrel of the firearm, including:

(1) The model of the firearm, if such designation has been made;

(2) The caliber or gauge of the firearm;

(3) The manufacturer's first and last name as provided to DOJ for recording purposes, when applicable; and,

---

[359] Cal. Code Regs. tit. 11, § 5517.

[360] This appears to be a policy position DOJ has taken regarding individuals who may result in an "undetermined" status following the required background check. But this policy position is unsupported by any law or regulation regarding the "ghost gun" serialization requirements.

[361] See BOF 116 (rev. 09/2016): Personal Firearms Eligibility Check Application, California Department of Justice, Bureau of Firearms, https://oag.ca.gov/sites/all/files/agweb/pdfs/firearms/forms/pfecapp.pdf (last visited Sept. 30, 2019).

[362] So for applications requesting multiple serial numbers for multiple different firearms, DOJ will assign each firearm a distinct serial number that will differ from all other serial numbers received by the applicant. Cal. Code Regs. tit. 11, § 5515(b).

[363] Cal. Code Regs. tit. 11, § 5515(a).

[364] Cal. Code Regs. tit. 11, § 5520(a)(1). Be aware that businesses, including Type 07 FFLs, are under no obligation to perform this work.

[365] Cal. Code Regs. tit. 11, § 5520(a)(2)(A).

[366] Cal. Code Regs. tit. 11, § 5520(a)(2)(A).

(4) The city and state (or recognized abbreviation thereof) where the manufacturer made the firearm.[367]

Upon completion of the above engraving requirements, applicants must then upload a total of four clear digital images depicting the firearm and its newly engraved serial number to CFARS. These images include:

(1) A close-up of the unique serial number and additional information located on the receiver or frame of the firearm;

(2) The entire firearm encompassing the following:

    (a) For long guns, the end of the barrel to the end of the stock.

    (b) For handguns, the point furthest from the end of the barrel to the opposite end of the handgun.

    (c) For receivers/frames only, the entire firearm;

(3) The left side of the receiver/frame; and,

(4) The right side of the receiver/frame.[368]

3. Deadlines to Engrave and Upload Required Digital Images

Per DOJ regulations, applicants whose firearms were completed prior to July 1, 2018, have 10 calendar days after receipt of the issued serial number to engrave, cast, stamp, or otherwise permanently place the issued serial number in a conspicuous location on the receiver or frame of the firearm and then upload the required digital images to CFARS.[369] For the purposes of this requirement, the date of receipt is considered to be the date on the email containing the electronic notice telling the applicant to log into CFARS.[370] Failure to engrave the firearm and upload the required images within the 10-day deadline will invalidate the issued serial number and will require re-submission of an application.[371]

Applicants who manufacture or assemble a firearm after July 1, 2018 have 30 days after receipt of the issued serial number to (1) manufacture or assemble the firearm,[372] (2) engrave the firearm with the issued serial number, and (3) upload the required digital images to CFARS.[373] But the issued serial number must be engraved, cast, stamped, or otherwise permanently placed in a conspicuous location on the receiver or frame of the firearm within 10 calendar days of manufacturing

---

[367] CAL. CODE REGS. tit. 11, § 5520(a)(2)(B).

[368] CAL. CODE REGS. tit. 11, § 5521.

[369] CAL. CODE REGS. tit. 11, § 5518(b)(1).

[370] CAL. CODE REGS. tit. 11, § 5518(b)(1)

[371] Remember that applications for firearms completed prior to July 1, 2018 must be submitted before January 1, 2019. If your application for such a firearm is rejected or incomplete for any reason after January 1, 2019, the firearm will fail to comply with the law. CAL. CODE REGS. tit. 11, § 5518(b)(1)(B).

[372] Applicants must wait until after they receive the unique serial number to begin manufacturing or assembling the firearm. CAL. CODE REGS. tit. 11, § 5518(b)(2)(A).

[373] CAL. CODE REGS. tit. 11, § 5518(b)(2).

or assembling the firearm.[374] In other words, you should finishing manufacturing the firearm no later than 20 days after being issued a unique serial number in order to allow for a full 10-day window to complete the engraving process and submit the required digital images before the 30-day window closes.[375] Failure to manufacture, assemble, engrave, or upload photographs of the firearm before the 30-day period closes will necessitate reapplication for a new unique serial number.[376] Furthermore, if you want to modify the firearm during the 30-day period after DOJ issues the unique serial number, you may do so as long as you record the changes in CFARS when reporting the firearm and upload photographs that reflect the final version of the firearm reflecting the changes.[377]

4. Firearms Exempt from AB 857's Serialization Requirements

Both AB 857 and DOJ's regulations provide for certain, limited exceptions to the above serialization requirements. Pursuant to P.C. section 29181 and DOJ's regulations, the following types of firearms are exempt from the above requirements:

(1) A firearm that has a serial number assigned to it under P.C. section 23910 (assignment of a new firearm identification number or mark when original number or mark is missing or obliterated) or 18 U.S.C. sections 921-931 (assignment of a serial number on each firearm imported or manufactured by a licensed importer or manufacturer);

(2) A firearm made or assembled prior to December 16, 1968, that is not a handgun;

(3) A firearm entered into the centralized registry under P.C. section 11106 prior to July 1, 2018, as being owned by a specific individual or entity if a distinguishing number or identification mark has been assigned to that firearm by virtue of DOJ accepting entry of the firearm into the centralized registry[378];

(4) A firearm that has a serial number assigned to it under the NFA and the regulations issued pursuant thereto; *or*

(5) A firearm that is a "curio or relic" or "antique," as those terms are defined in 27 C.F.R. section 479.11.[379]

---

[374] CAL. CODE REGS. tit. 11, § 5518(b)(2)(B).

[375] *See* CAL. CODE REGS. tit. 11, § 5518(b)(2)(B).

[376] CAL. CODE REGS. tit. 11, § 5518(b)(2)(C).

[377] CAL. CODE REGS. tit. 11, § 5522.

[378] Theoretically, this exception should apply to a person who engraved their own identification mark and subsequently voluntarily registered their firearm with DOJ in accordance with P.C. section 28000 before July 1, 2018. This is because once the firearm has been voluntarily registered, it will (or at least should) be entered into the centralized registry set forth in P.C. section 11106.

[379] 27 C.F.R. section 479.11 does not actually define the term "curio or relic." DOJ recognized this error and, as a result, adopted a definition that aligns with the correct federal citation. See 27 C.F.R. section 478.11

But regardless of the above, any firearm manufactured on or before 1898 is a "curio or relic" firearm. This is because any firearm that is at least 50 years old satisfies the federal definition of a "curio or relic" firearm.[380] As a result, several of the above exemptions for AB 857 are superfluous, including the limited exception for long guns manufactured prior to December 16, 1968.[381]

IX. COMING INTO CALIFORNIA WITH FIREARMS

A. Visiting California

If you are coming into California to visit or establish residency and are bringing firearms, ammunition, or magazines, your first order of business is to determine if these items are legal for you to possess or import into California. You can do this by reviewing Chapters 9 and 10 of this book and the DOJ Bureau of Firearms' website. If you lawfully possess items out of state that are illegal to possess in California, you will need to get the applicable permits or licenses or meet one of the exceptions mentioned in the corresponding chapters *before* bringing them into California. Also, make sure that you familiarize yourself with California's transportation and storage requirements before you bring your firearms into the state.

B. Moving Into California

In addition to the restrictions when just visiting California, if you come to the state as a new resident wanting to possess a firearm here that you previously manufactured out of state, you must do a number of things if that firearm does not have a unique serial number or mark of identification. You must first apply to DOJ for a unique serial number within 60 days of your arrival in California.[382] And you must then follow the same engraving and photograph-submission procedures outlined in the preceding sections of this book.[383]

---

[380] *See* 27 C.F.R. section 478.11.

[381] DOJ confirmed this point in response to public comments regarding their regulations, stating "[f]irearms without a serial number made by a company before the Gun Control Act would not be subject to these regulations. Such firearms meet the definition of a curio or relic because they were manufactured at least 50 years prior to January 1, 2019." See DOJ's response to public comment #33 as included in their "Final Statement of Reasons" for their AB 857 regulations, available online at https://oag.ca.gov/sites/all/files/agweb/pdfs/firearms/regs/usna-fsor-a-b.pdf (last visited Oct. 10, 2020).

[382] P.C. § 29180(e).

[383] *See* P.C. § 29180(e).

Further, if you meet the definition of a "personal firearm importer," you will have to report ownership of your firearms[384] with DOJ or sell or transfer them within 60 days of bringing them into California.[385]

You are considered a "personal firearm importer" if you are over 18 years of age, own a firearm, and meet all of the following:

(1) You are not licensed pursuant to P.C. sections 26700 to 26915, inclusive (i.e., you are not a California-licensed firearms dealer);

(2) You are not a licensed firearms manufacturer or importer;[386]

(3) You own the firearm;

(4) You acquired the firearm outside of California;

(5) For handguns, you moved into this state on or after January 1, 1998, and for all firearms, you moved into California on or after January 1, 2014, as a resident[387] of this state;

(6) You intend to possess the handgun within this state on or after January 1, 1998, or firearm within this state on or after January 1, 2014;

(7) The firearm was delivered to you by a person who is not licensed as a California firearms dealer;[388]

(8) While a California resident, you did not previously report ownership of that firearm to DOJ with information about you and a description of the firearm;

(9) The firearm is not prohibited by any of P.C. section 16590's provisions (i.e., it is not a "generally prohibited weapon"); *and,*

(10) The firearm is not an "assault weapon," .50 BMG rifle, destructive device, or "machine gun."[389]

People are often concerned that they have not properly reported ownership of their firearm after the 60-day requirement has lapsed. In the past, DOJ has allowed late handgun registration, but this could change in the future.

---

[384] Before January 1, 2014, this requirement only related to handguns and most of the requirements above for "personal firearm importers" applied to these "personal handgun importers."

[385] P.C. § 27560. In order to register your firearm, you must fill out a "New Resident Report of Firearm Ownership" form (BF 4010A) and pay the requisite $19 processing fee. CAL. CODE REGS. tit. 11, § 4002.

[386] 18 U.S.C. § 921.

[387] You are a resident of California if California is your true, fixed, and permanent home and principal residence to which you intend to return whenever you are absent. P.C. § 17000(b)(1); CAL. VEH. CODE § 12505. For military members, residency is established when you are discharged from active service in California. P.C. § 17000(b)(2).

[388] The person must be licensed per P.C. sections 26700 to 26915, inclusive i.e., the person is a California-licensed firearms dealer) and must have delivered the firearm as set forth in P.C. sections 27540 and P.C. sections 26700-26915, inclusive (governing dealers' requirements in delivery of firearm, such as abiding by the 10-day wait, and dealers' licensing requirements).

[389] P.C. § 17000.

Table 5.12

Registration Deadlines for Individuals	
Type of Transfer	Registration Deadline
Transfers through a licensed firearms dealer, including Private Party Transfers (P.C. § 28155, 28160, 28215(d))	Since the 1990s, handguns transferred through a licensed dealer are required to be reported once the DROS is filed. Effective January 1, 2014, any firearm transferred through a licensed dealer is automatically reported once the DROS is filed.
Individuals bringing a handgun into the state who are considered "personal handgun importers" (P.C. §§ 17000, 27560)	Effective January 1, 1989, must be reported to DOJ within 60 days of bringing a handgun into the state.
Individuals bringing any firearm into the state who are considered a "personal firearm importer" (P.C. § 27560)	Effective January 1, 2014, must be reported to DOJ within 60 days of bringing any firearm into the state.
Transfers of any firearms by gift, bequest, intestate succession between members of the same immediate family who both reside in the state of California (P.C. § 27875)	Effective January 1, 1995, must be reported to DOJ within 30 days of taking possession.
Transfer of a firearm from one spouse to another via transmutation who both reside in California (P.C. §§ 16990(g), 27920)	Effective January 1, 1993, must be reported to DOJ within 30 days of taking possession.
Transfer, or importation into California, of "curio or relic" *long guns* to a licensed collector of "curio or relic" firearms with a COE (P.C. § 27966)	Effective January 1, 2014, must be reported to DOJ within 30 days of taking possession.
Transfer of "curio or relic" handguns from out of state to a licensed collector of "curios or relics" (P.C. §§ 27590, 27565(b))	Effective January 1, 1998, must be reported within five days of transporting a firearm into California.

X. FIREARM STORAGE

Although both California and federal law require that a "safety device" accompany your firearm purchase in certain circumstances, neither set of laws requires that you actually use one while storing it. In fact, there is no general California or federal law specifically requiring you to store firearms in any particular manner. But, some cities have local firearm-storage requirements.

Even if your city does not have such requirements, you may nonetheless be prosecuted for criminally storing a firearm in certain situations.

A. Criminal Storage in the First, Second, and Third Degree for Loaded Firearms

Historically, you could only be criminally prosecuted in situations where children gained access to your firearms. But, with the passage of SB 363 in 2013, criminal liability has been expanded to cover situations where others gain possession of your firearms. Specifically, you may be prosecuted if you store a firearm in a place under your custody or control in a way that a person prohibited from possessing firearms under state or federal law may gain access to it and cause tragic results (as discussed below).[390] This would be considered "criminal storage of a firearm" in the first degree or second degree.[391] And beginning January 1, 2020, these restrictions apply regardless if the firearm is loaded or unloaded.[392]

You can be charged with "criminal storage of a firearm" in the first degree if you keep a firearm (loaded or unloaded) anywhere under your custody or control where you know, or reasonably should know, a child or a person prohibited from possessing firearms under state or federal law is likely to gain unpermitted access to it, a child or prohibited person does get access to it, and death or great bodily injury occurs as a result.[393]

Though it is a lesser offense, you may also be prosecuted if a child or prohibited person who accesses your firearm either injures, "brandishes" it or carries it to a public place.[394] This is "criminal storage of a firearm" in the second degree.

You may be prosecuted for a misdemeanor if you negligently store or leave a loaded firearm (and beginning January 1, 2020, any unloaded firearm) in a location where you know, or reasonably should know, that a child is likely to gain access to the firearm. This is considered "criminal storage of a firearm" in the third degree.[395] To violate this law, there is no requirement that the child harm someone

---

[390] P.C. § 25100.
[391] P.C. § 25100(a-b).
[392] P.C. § 25100.
[393] P.C. § 25100(a).
[394] P.C. § 25100(b)(3).
[395] P.C. § 25100(c).

or take the firearm to a public place. It is important to note that this crime may be committed even if the child does not actually gain possession of the firearm.

You are not liable under these laws if you took reasonable action to secure the firearm against access by the child, or your conduct falls under any of the exceptions discussed below.

One important criticism of this law, and something that you should be vigilant of, is the fact that the law seems to leave open a large amount of discretion for law enforcement to determine what constitutes negligent storage. Where the person who allegedly stored a firearm in violation of P.C. section 25100 is the parent or guardian of a child injured or killed, California law gives prosecutors express discretion to bring or not bring charges. It suggests charges should only be brought where the parent acted in a grossly negligent manner or where other "egregious circumstances" exist. But it is best to avoid tragedy and reliance on a prosecutor's mercy by properly storing your firearms whenever children are present.

B. Storage of Firearms

Prior to 2020, you could have been prosecuted for a misdemeanor if you keep a handgun, whether loaded or unloaded, anywhere under your custody or control and know, or reasonably should know, that a child or prohibited person is likely to gain unpermitted access to it, and a child or prohibited person does gain access to it and thereafter carries it off-premises.[396] As of January 1, 2020, this restriction applies to any firearm (no longer just handguns).[397] And any person who is convicted on or after January 1, 2020, of a misdemeanor violation of P.C. sections 25100, 25135, or 25200 is prohibited from owning or possessing firearms for a period of 10 years.[398]

Moreover, is also a misdemeanor, with a possible steeper maximum fine ($5,000 vs. $1,000), if the child or prohibited person takes any firearm to a preschool, elementary, middle, or high school, or to any school-sponsored event, activity, or performance, whether it occurs on school grounds or not.[399]

C. Exceptions to Criminal Storage in the First, Second, and Third Degree and Storage of Firearms

You should not be prosecuted under the laws discussed above for criminally storing a loaded firearm or if a child or prohibited person carries a firearm off-premises if:

(1) The child obtained the firearm as a result of an illegal entry to your premises by any person;

---

[396] P.C. § 25200(a).
[397] P.C. § 25200(a).
[398] P.C. § 29805(c).
[399] P.C. § 25200(b).

(2) The firearm is kept in a locked container or place a reasonable person would believe is secure;

(3) The firearm is carried on you or is so close in proximity to you that you can easily obtain and use it as if it were actually carried on you;

(4) The firearm has a locking device that has made the firearm inoperable;

(5) You are a peace officer or National Guard or military member, and the child obtains the firearm during, or incidental to, the performance of your duties;

(6) The child obtains, or obtains and discharges, the firearm in self-defense or in defense of another person; *or,*

(7) Based on objective facts and circumstances, it would be unreasonable to expect a child to be present on your premises.[400]

D. Residing With a Person Who Is Prohibited from Possessing, Receiving, Owning, or Purchasing Firearms

There are restrictions on firearm storage if you reside with someone who is prohibited from possessing, receiving, owning, or purchasing firearms under state or federal law.[401] If you live with such a person, you cannot keep a firearm in the residence[402] unless the firearm is:

(1) Kept within a locked container, locked gun safe, or locked trunk, or it is locked with a locking device;

(2) Disabled by a firearm safety device; *or,*

(3) Carried on you or is so close in proximity to you that you can easily obtain and use it as if it were actually carried on you.[403]

Disturbingly, this law requires that you keep your firearms locked up if you live with *anyone* who cannot purchase a firearm. As discussed above, minors cannot purchase firearms, so it seems that your firearms must be secured as described above if you live with a minor.

These restrictions do apply to ammunition. Remember that a person with a California firearm prohibition is prohibited from "possessing" firearms and ammunition. And remember that "ammunition" includes clips, magazines, and speed loaders as well, as discussed in Chapter 3.

---

[400] P.C. §§ 25105, 25205.
[401] P.C. § 25135.
[402] For purposes of this restriction, a "residence" is "any structure intended or used for human habitation, including, but not limited to, houses, condominiums, rooms, motels, time-shares, and recreational or other vehicles where human habitation occurs." P.C. § 17060.
[403] P.C. § 25135.

There have also been attempts in California to enact laws requiring firearms to be locked at all times when the owner is not home, even if they are in a locked home where no one is present. These attempts have so far been unsuccessful. Firearm-storage laws represent an evolving area of firearms law with some localities attempting to place further restrictions on their residents regarding firearms storage.[404]

E. Storage of Handgun in Unattended Vehicle

In response to a string of incidents where individuals stole firearms from unattended law enforcement vehicles and used them to commit heinous crimes, the Legislature enacted a new law in 2016 (which has been subsequently amended in both 2017 and 2018) that governs the storage of handguns in unattended vehicles (SB 869, SB 497, and SB 1382).[405] Under these bills, any person (including any peace officer or honorably retired peace officer) who leaves a handgun in an unattended "vehicle" must:

(1) Lock the handgun in the vehicle's trunk;

(2) Lock the handgun in a "locked container"[406] and place the container out of plain view;

(3) Lock the handgun in a "locked container" that is permanently affixed to the vehicle's interior and not in plain view; *or,*

(4) Lock the handgun in a locked toolbox or utility box.[407]

As originally enacted, a "peace officer"[408] was only exempt from this restriction "during circumstances requiring immediate aid or action that are within the course

---

[404] The City and County of San Francisco, for example, maintains one of the most restrictive firearm-storage laws in the country. San Francisco Police Code section 4512 requires handguns to be kept in a locked container or disabled with a trigger lock *at all times* when not under the control of a peace officer or on the person of an adult over 18. I challenged San Francisco's requirement on behalf of the NRA in *Jackson v. City and County of San Francisco*, No. C09-cv-02143 (N.D. Cal. filed May 15, 2009). In that lawsuit, we argued that the San Francisco's firearm storage laws infringed on the Second Amendment. After the Ninth Circuit Court of Appeals upheld the constitutionality of San Francisco's storage laws, we petitioned the United States Supreme for a writ of certiorari. Although the Supreme Court ultimately denied cert, two Supreme Court Justices, Justice Thomas, and Justice Scalia, dissented from the denial of certiorari arguing that the court should have granted review as "San Francisco's law burdens the core of the Second Amendment right." *Jackson v. City and Cnty. of San Francisco*, 134 S. Ct. 2799, 2801 (2015). In 2015, the Los Angeles City Council also approved a measure that may require residents to lock up or disable their handguns with trigger locks when the handgun is not being carried or within arm's reach inside their home. See Emily Alpert Reyes, *L.A. to Require that Stored Handguns be Locked up or Disabled*, L.A. TIMES (Oct. 27, 2015), available at http://www.latimes.com/local/lanow/la-me-ln-gun-storage-20151027-story.html (last visited Oct. 10, 2020). In addition, San Jose is pursuing a similar mandatory locked-storage ordinance.

[405] SB 1382, 2017-2018 Leg., Reg. Sess. (Cal. 2018), *available at* https://leginfo.legislature.ca.gov/faces/billTextClient.xhtml?bill_id=201720180SB1382 (last visited Oct. 10, 2020).

[406] "Locked container" means a secure container that is fully enclosed and locked by a padlock, keylock, combination lock, or similar locking device. The term "locked container" does not include the utility or glove compartment of a motor vehicle. P.C. § 25140(d)(1)(A).

[407] P.C. § 25612.

[408] P.C. § 25140(d)(1)(C).

of his or her official duties."[409] But the Legislature later amended the law to allow peace officers to lock a handgun out of plain view within the center utility console of an unattended motor vehicle if (1) that vehicle is not equipped with a trunk and (2) he or she is unable to otherwise comply with the requirements listed above.[410]

Failing to abide by these requirements for storing handguns in an unattended vehicle is an infraction, punishable as a fine not to exceed one thousand dollars.[411]

A vehicle is considered "unattended" when "a person who is lawfully carrying or transporting a handgun in a vehicle is not within close enough proximity to the vehicle to reasonably prevent unauthorized access to the vehicle or its contents."[412] And a locked container will be considered to be in "plain view" when it can be seen "by peering through the windows of the vehicle, including windows that are tinted, with or without illumination."[413]

The "trunk" of a vehicle is defined for purposes of this section as "the fully enclosed and locked main storage or luggage compartment of a vehicle that is not accessible from the passenger compartment."[414] But it does not include the "rear of a hatchback, station wagon, or sport utility vehicle, any compartment which has a window, or a toolbox or utility box attached to the bed of a pickup truck."[415] People with vehicles lacking a "trunk" must use alternative means of securing a handgun pursuant to the above requirements.

Individuals may also secure the handgun in a "locked toolbox or utility box," which is defined as a "fully enclosed container that is permanently affixed to the bed of a pickup truck or vehicle that does not contain a trunk, and is locked by a padlock, keylock, combination lock, or other similar locking device."[416] Though this greatly increases the available options to those with vehicles lacking a "trunk," be aware that the container must be "permanently affixed" to the vehicle. What exactly is required for the container to be considered "permanently affixed" remains unclear.

Gun owners should know that some local ordinances may also be more restrictive, for this law "does not supersede any local ordinance that regulates the storage of handguns in unattended vehicles if the ordinance was in effect before September 26, 2016."[417] That being said, this law does not apply to "the transportation of unloaded firearms by a person operating a licensed common carrier or an authorized

---

[409] P.C. § 25140(e).
[410] P.C. § 25140(b).
[411] P.C. § 25140(c).
[412] P.C. § 25140(d)(2).
[413] P.C. § 25140(d)(3).
[414] P.C. § 25140(d)(1)(D).
[415] P.C. § 25140(d)(1)(D).
[416] P.C. § 25140(d)(1)(B).
[417] P.C. § 25140(f).

agent or employee thereof when the firearms are transported in conformance with applicable or federal laws."[418]

1. Storage of Lawfully-Obtained "Unsafe" Handgun in Unattended Vehicle by Certain Law Enforcement Officers

As explained more fully in Chapter 10, "unsafe" handguns are handguns that are not listed on DOJ's Roster of Handguns Certified for Sale (Roster). Generally, California residents cannot acquire "unsafe" handguns unless they meet one of the exceptions listed in P.C. section 32000 (and discussed in detail in Chapter 10).[419] Individuals that meet one of those exceptions can lawfully obtain an "unsafe" handgun. One of those exceptions is located in P.C. section 32000(b)(6), and it applies to the purchase of an "unsafe" handgun by sworn members of certain law enforcement entities[420] who have satisfactorily completed the firearms portion of a training course prescribed by the Commission on Peace Officer Standards and Training.[421]

If an individual obtained an "unsafe" handgun pursuant to the specific exception stated in P.C. section 32000(b)(6), he or she must do one of the following when leaving their "unsafe" handgun unattended[422] in a vehicle[423]:

(1) Lock the "unsafe handgun" in the vehicle's trunk,

(2) Lock the "unsafe handgun" in a "locked container"[424] and place the container out of plain view; *or*

---

[418] P.C. § 25645.

[419] P.C. § 32000.

[420] The applicable law enforcement entities are: A) The Department of Parks and Recreation; (B) The Department of Alcoholic Beverage Control; (C) The Division of Investigation of the Department of Consumer Affairs; (D) The Department of Motor Vehicles; (E) The Fraud Division of the Department of Insurance; (F) The State Department of State Hospitals; (G) The Department of Fish and Wildlife; (H) The State Department of Developmental Services; (I) The Department of Forestry and Fire Protection; (J) A county probation department; (K) The Los Angeles World Airports, as defined in Section 830.15; (L) A K-12 public school district for use by a school police officer, as described in Section 830.32; (M) A municipal water district for use by a park ranger, as described in Section 830.34; (N) A county for use by a welfare fraud investigator or inspector, as described in Section 830.35; (O) A county for use by the coroner or the deputy coroner, as described in Section 830.35; (P) The Supreme Court and the courts of appeal for use by marshals of the Supreme Court and bailiffs of the courts of appeal, and coordinators of security for the judicial branch, as described in Section 830.36; (Q) A fire department or fire protection agency of a county, city, city and county, district, or the state for use by either (i) A member of an arson-investigating unit, regularly paid and employed in that capacity pursuant to Section 830.37 or (ii) A member other than a member of an arson-investigating unit, regularly paid and employed in that capacity pursuant to Section 830.37; (R) The University of California Police Department, or the California State University Police Departments, as described in Section 830.2; (S) A California Community College police department, as described in Section 830.32. P.C. § 32000(b)(6); and (T) A harbor or port district or other entity employing peace officers described in Section 830.33(b), the San Diego Unified Port District Harbor Police, and the Harbor Department of the City of Los Angeles."

[421] P.C. § 32000(b)(6).

[422] A vehicle is considered to be "'unattended' when a person who is lawfully carrying or transporting a handgun in the vehicle is not within close proximity to the vehicle to reasonably prevent unauthorized access to the vehicle or its contents." P.C. § 32000(c)(2)(C)(ii).

[423] A "'vehicle' is a device by which any person or property may be propelled, moved, or drawn upon a highway, excepting a device moved exclusively by human power or used exclusively upon stationary rails or tracks." CAL. VEH. CODE § 670; P.C. § 32000(c)(2)(C)(i).

[424] The term "locked container" is defined in Chapter 7.

(3) Lock the "unsafe handgun" in a "locked container" that is permanently affixed to the vehicle's interior and not in plain view.[425]

This restriction does not apply to a peace officer during circumstances requiring immediate aid or action that are within the course of his or her official duties.[426]

As explained in Chapter 7, a "locked container" does not include a vehicle's "utility or glove compartment," even if it is locked.[427] So, you cannot store an "unsafe handgun" in the utility or glove compartment when leaving your vehicle unattended.

Failing to properly store an "unsafe handgun" in an unattended vehicle as explained above is an infraction, punishable by a fine not exceeding a thousand dollars.[428]

F. Local Storage Laws

Along with the state's restrictions on firearm storage, a number of cities, including Los Angeles,[429] Oakland,[430] San Francisco,[431] Santa Cruz,[432] Palm Springs,[433] Sunnyvale,[434] and Tiburon[435] have also passed their own local ordinance that regulate how gun owners must store firearms inside their homes. In general, these ordinances prohibit individuals from keeping their handguns and/or long guns inside their homes unless they are stored in a locked container or disabled with a trigger lock.

As explained in the Introduction of this book, we will not address local restrictions in detail for the purpose of this book. Still, it is always important to check your local laws to make sure that you are lawfully storing your firearm inside your home.

---

[425] P.C. § 32000(c)(2).
[426] P.C. § 32000(c)(2)(E).
[427] P.C. § 25610(a)(1).
[428] P.C. § 32000(c)(2)(B).
[429] LA., CAL. MUN. CODE § 55.21.
[430] OAKLAND, CAL. MUN. CODE § 9.39.040.
[431] S.F., CA. MUN. CODE § 4512.
[432] SANTA CRUZ, CA. MUN. CODE § 9.29.020.
[433] PALM SPRINGS, CA. MUN. CODE § 11.16.045.
[434] SUNNYVALE, CA. MUN. CODE § 9.44.040.
[435] TIBURON, CA. MUN. CODE § 32-30.

G. Community Care Facilities, Residential Care Facilities, Residential Care Facilities for the Elderly, Family Care Homes, and Day Care Centers

Under California law, the California Department of Social Services must issue a civil penalty of $500 per day to any "community care facility,"[436] "residential care facility,"[437] "residential care facility for the elderly",[438] "family day care home,"[439] or "day care center"[440] that has firearms or ammunition accessible, and $100 for each day the violation continues after the citation is issued.[441]

Gun owners should also be aware that in 2019 California adopted SB 172, which in addition to the changes made to California's negligent storage provisions, also adds several new provisions to California's Health and Safety Code dubbed the "Keep Our Seniors Safe Act."[442] These new laws implement specific firearm storage requirements for residential care facilities for the elderly, residential care facilities for persons with chronic life-threatening illness, and community care facilities for adults that are licensed by the State Department of Social Services, Community Care Licensing Division.[443] DOJ is required to promulgate regulations implementing these new requirements,[444] and until doing so, may implement and administer the new laws through the issuance of written directives that are exempt from California's typical rulemaking requirements. At the time of this book's publication, DOJ has yet to promulgate any regulations or issue any written directives regarding

---

[436] A "community care facility" is defined as "any facility, place, or building that is maintained and operated to provide nonmedical residential care, day treatment, adult day care, or foster family agency services for children, adults, or children and adults, including, but not limited to, the physically handicapped, mentally impaired, incompetent persons, and abused or neglected children, and includes" "residential facilities," "adult day pro-grams," "therapeutic day services facilities," "foster family agencies;" "small family homes;" "social rehabilitation facilities;" and "community treatment facilities." CAL. HEALTH & SAF. CODE § 1502.

[437] A "residential care facility" is "a residential care facility for persons with chronic, life-threatening illness who are 18 years of age or older or are emancipated minors, and for family units." CAL. HEALTH & SAF. CODE § 1568.01.

[438] A "residential care facility for the elderly" is "a housing arrangement chosen voluntarily by persons 60 years of age or over, or their authorized representative, where varying levels and intensities of care and supervision, protective supervision, or personal care are provided, based upon their varying needs, as determined in order to be admitted and to remain in the facility." CAL. HEALTH & SAF. CODE § 1569.2.

[439] A "family day care home" is "a home that regularly provides care, protection, and supervision for 14 or fewer children, in the provider's own home, for periods of less than 24 hours per day, while the parents or guardians are away, and is either a large family day care home or a small family day care home." CAL. HEALTH & SAF. CODE § 1596.78.

[440] A "day care center" is "any child day care facility other than a family day care home, and includes infant centers, preschools, extended day care facilities, and school age child care centers." CAL. HEALTH & SAF. CODE § 1596.76.

[441] CAL. HEALTH & SAF. CODE §§ 1548(c)(5) ("community care facilities"), 1568.0822(c)(5) ("residential care facilities"), 1569.49(c)(5) ("residential care facilities for the elderly"), 1596.99(c)(5) ("day care centers"), 1597.58(c)(5) ("family day care homes).

[442] CAL. HEALTH & SAF. CODE § 1569.280.

[443] For instance, they require these facilities to accept, retain, and centrally store their clients' firearm and/or ammunition and ensure that they f are stored unloaded in a locked safe that is separate from where the ammunition is locked up. CAL. HEALTH & SAF. CODE §§ 1567.92, 1568.097, 1569.282. In addition, the residents of these care facilities may not bring certain types of firearms with them to these facilities. *See* CAL. HEALTH & SAF. CODE §§ 1567.93, 1568.098, 1569.283.

[444] *See* CAL. HEALTH & SAF. CODE § 1568.095(b-c).

these new laws. Consult with an experienced firearms law attorney should you have questions regarding these new requirements in the interim.

Table 5.13

CALIFORNIA'S FIREARM STORAGE LAWS	
STORAGE OF A HANDGUN AND ANY FIREARM (P.C. § 25200)	
You may be guilty of a misdemeanor punishable by imprisonment in county jail not exceeding one year, by a fine not exceeding $1,000, or by both if: (1) You keep *a handgun*, loaded or unloaded, within any premises under your custody or control; *and* (2) You know or reasonably should know that a child is likely to gain access to the handgun without the permission of the child's parent or legal guardian, or that a prohibited person is likely to gain access to it; *and* (3) The child or prohibited person obtains access to the handgun and carries it off-premises.	You may be guilty of a misdemeanor punishable by imprisonment in a county jail not exceeding one year, by fine not exceeding $5,000, or by both if: (1) You keep *any firearm* within any premises under your custody or control; *and* (2) You know or reasonably should know that a child is likely to gain access to the firearm without the permission of the child's parent or legal guardian, or that a prohibited person is likely to gain access to it; *and* (3) The child or prohibited person carries the firearm off-premises to any public or private school, elementary school, middle school, high school, or to any school-sponsored event, activity, or performance, whether occurring on school grounds or elsewhere.

California's Firearm Storage Laws

Criminal Storage of Firearms (P.C. § 25100)

Criminal Storage of a Firearm in the 1st Degree	Criminal Storage of a Firearm in the 2nd Degree	Criminal Storage of a Firearm in the 3rd Degree
You may be guilty of criminal storage of a firearm in the 1st degree if: (1) You keep a *loaded firearm* within any premises that are under your custody or control; *and* (2) You know or reasonably should know that a child is likely to access the firearm without the permission of the child's parent or legal guardian, or that a person prohibited from possessing a firearm or deadly weapon is likely to gain access to the firearm; *and* (3) The child or prohibited person gains access to the firearm or deadly weapon and causes death or great bodily injury to themselves or any other person.	You may be guilty of criminal storage of a firearm in the 2nd degree if: (1) You keep any *loaded firearm* within any premises that are under your custody and control; *and* (2) You know or reasonably should know that a child is likely to gain access to the firearm without the permission of the child's parent or legal guardian, or that a person prohibited from possessing a firearm or deadly weapon is likely to gain access to the firearm; *and* (3) The child or prohibited person obtains access to the firearm and causes injury, other than great bodily injury, to themselves or any other person, or carries the firearm to a public place in violation of P.C. section 417.	You may be guilty of criminal storage of a firearm in the 3rd degree if: (1) You keep any *loaded firearm* within any premises that are under your custody or control; *and* (2) Negligently store or leave a *loaded firearm* in a location where the person knows, or reasonably should know, that a child is likely to gain access to the firearm without the permission of the child's parent or legal guardian, unless you take reasonable action to secure the firearm against access by the child.

Storage of a Firearm While Residing with a Prohibited Person (P.C. § 25135)

If you live with a person prohibited from possessing, receiving, owning, or purchasing firearms under state or federal law, you cannot keep a firearm in the residence unless the firearm is either:

(1) Kept within a locked container, locked gun safe, or locked trunk, or it is locked with a locking device; *or*
(2) Disabled by a firearm safety device; *or*
(3) Carried on you or is so close in proximity to you that you can easily obtain and use it as if it were actually carried on you.

Though not restricted in section 25135, remember that the prohibited person cannot have access to both firearms *and ammunition*. And "ammunition" includes clips, magazines, and speed loaders as well, as discussed in Chapter 3.

XI. FALSE REPORTS OF LOST OR STOLEN FIREARMS

Since January 1, 2017, it is a misdemeanor under California law to report to any peace officer listed in P.C. sections 830-832.9 or an employee who is assigned to accept reports from citizens, either directly or by telephone, and who is employed by a state or local law enforcement agency which is designated in P.C. section 830.1, 830.2, 8303(e), 830.31, 830.32, 830.33, 830.34, 830.35, 830.36, 830.37, or 830.4 that a firearm has been lost or stolen, knowing that the report is false.[445]

Oddly, Proposition 63 (Prop. 63) also makes it a crime as of November 9, 2016, to report to a local law enforcement agency that a firearm has been lost or stolen, knowing that the report was false.[446] Filing a false report is an infraction, punishable by a fine of $250 for the first offense, and by a fine of $1,000 for a second or subsequent offense.[447]

But filling a false police report has always been illegal pursuant to Penal Code section 148.5, which states that it is a misdemeanor. Therefore, Prop. 63 actually made it less of a violation to falsely report a stolen firearm.

XII. REPORTING LOST OR STOLEN FIREARMS

Since July 1, 2017, any person who discovers that they lost a firearm, or found out that their firearm was stolen, must report the theft or loss to a local law enforcement in the jurisdiction where the theft or loss occurred within five days of the time that he or she knew, or reasonably should have known, that the firearm was lost or stolen.[448]

Despite this general requirement, certain people, organizations, and firearms are exempt from the reporting requirement. Specifically, the following people, organizations, and firearms are exempt:

(1) Antique firearms;[449]

(2) Any law enforcement agency or peace officer acting within the scope of his or her employment or official duties if he or she reports the loss or theft to his or her employing agency;

(3) Any United States marshal or member of the Armed Forces of the United States or the National Guard, while engaged in his or her official duties; *and*

---

[445] P.C. § 148.5(f).
[446] P.C. § 25275, Office of the Attorney General, Full Text of Proposition 63, *available at* https://www.oag.ca.gov/system/files/initiatives/pdfs/15-0098%20(Firearms)_0.pdf (last visited Oct. 10, 2020).
[447] P.C. § 25275.
[448] P.C. § 25250.
[449] As defined in P.C. §16170. See Chapter 3.

(4) Any person who is licensed under 18 U.S.C. sections 921-931 (i.e., a federally licensed manufacturer, importer, or dealer) and the regulations issued pursuant thereto, and who reports the theft or loss in accordance with 18 U.S.C. section 923(g)(6) (i.e., loss reporting requirement that states that the theft or loss must be reported to the Attorney General and to the appropriate local authorities within 48 hours after the theft or loss is discovered), or its successor provision, and the applicable regulations issued thereto; *and,*

(5) Any person whose firearm was lost or stolen prior to July 1, 2017.[450]

Any person who fails to report a lost or stolen firearm is guilty of an infraction, punishable by fine of $100.[451] Subsequent violations of this general restriction can be punished more severely, as a second violation can be punishable with a fine of $1,000 and the third can be punishable by imprisonment in a county jail for up to six months and/or a $1,000 fine.[452]

When reporting a firearm lost or stolen, you must report the make, model, and serial number of the firearm, if known, and provide "any additional relevant information required by the local law enforcement agency taking the report."[453] It is unclear what "any additional relevant information" law enforcement agencies may require. But, there may be serious Fifth Amendment concerns if they request information that may subject you to criminal liability for failing to properly report a lost or stolen firearm under this new law.

If you fail to report that your firearm is lost or has been stolen before the end of the five day window, contact an attorney who is experienced in firearms law immediately to discuss your options.

XIII. ACQUIRING AMMUNITION

Prior to 2016, there were very few restrictions on acquiring ammunition or ammunition components. The main restrictions at the time generally prevented prohibited persons from receiving ammunition.[454] But this all changed with the passage Senate Bill (SB) 1235 and Prop. 63 in 2016.

At the time of this book's publication, CRPA, with the support of NRA, filed a lawsuit titled *Rhode v. Becerra*, challenging SB 1235 and Prop 63's restrictions as a violation of the Second Amendment and Commerce Clause of the United States Constitution. On April 23, 2020, the United States District Court for the Southern District of California issued an order granting a preliminary injunction prohibit-

---

[450] P.C. §§ 25250(c), 25255.
[451] P.C. § 25265.
[452] P.C. § 25265.
[453] P.C. § 25270.
[454] See Chapter 4 for more on individuals restricted from possessing ammunition.

ing further enforcement of California's ammunition transfer restrictions while the lawsuit was pending. But the following day, the Ninth Circuit issued a stay of the District Court's order. As a result, California's ammunition transfer restrictions remain in effect for now. Be sure to visit CRPA's website for any new information regarding the *Rhode* lawsuit and California's ammunition transfer restrictions.

A. Ammunition Sales & Transfers

As of July 1, 2019, SB 1235 and Prop 63's ammunition sales restrictions are in full effect. In addition to the legislative changes, DOJ has adopted regulations regarding the background check requirements. Some of these regulations, however, are inconsistent with SB 1235 and Prop 63's statutory language. What's more, DOJ has adopted several policy positions that are not expressly addressed in either the statutes or regulations which have only come to light due to *Rhode*. And as discussed in more detail below, some of those policy positions actually conflict with California law.

1. Requirement that Ammunition Sales Must Be Conducted Through a Licensed Ammunition Vendor

In general, "ammunition"[455] sales must be conducted by or processed through a licensed "ammunition vendor" (California-licensed firearms dealers are automatically considered "ammunition vendors").[456] This includes the sale of ammunition between two private parties, neither of whom is a licensed ammunition vendor.[457] And anyone selling more than 500 rounds of ammunition in 30 days needs to obtain an ammunition vendor license regardless.[458]

Like PPTs of firearms (see above), anytime a non-licensed individual sells ammunition to another non-licensed party, they will need to first take that ammunition to a licensed vendor, who will then process the transaction in accordance with the law and deliver it to the purchaser. If the ammunition vendor cannot deliver the ammunition to the purchaser because he or she is prohibited from owning and/ or possessing ammunition, the ammunition vendor must return the ammunition back to the seller.[459]

In addition to charging any other applicable fees allowed by California law, an ammunition vendor can charge the individual purchasing the ammunition an

---

[455] The term "ammunition" is defined in Chapter 3.

[456] P.C. § 30312(a)(1). Violations of this restriction are a misdemeanor. P.C. § 30312(d). For purposes of this restriction, a licensed "ammunition vendor" is defined as either "a firearms dealer licensed pursuant to Sections 26700 to 26915, inclusive" or "any person, firm, corporation, or other business enterprise that holds a current ammunition vendor license issued pursuant to [Penal Code section] 30385." P.C. § 16151. And following the adoption of amendments to DOJ's existing regulations, ammunition vendors must maintain an active Certificate of Eligibility or risk invalidating their license. CAL. CODE REGS. tit. 11, § 4261 (d).

[457] P.C. § 30312(a)(2).

[458] P.C. § 30342.

[459] P.C. § 30312(a)(2).

administrative fee to process the ammunition sale.⁴⁶⁰ DOJ regulations state that if the purchaser is present for "immediate delivery" of the ammunition, vendors may only charge a $5 fee for processing the transfer.⁴⁶¹ But if the purchaser is not immediately present, the vendor may then charge an additional storage fee as agreed upon with the purchaser prior to the vendor receiving the ammunition.⁴⁶² It is unclear what storage fees, if any, can be charged absent a prior agreement between the vendor and the purchaser. And given the delays some individuals are experiencing in obtaining the necessary electronic approval from DOJ (discussed in more detail below), it is possible some customers may be forced to wait hours, even days, before the transfer can be completed. In such circumstances, no prior agreement between the vendor and the purchaser may exist.

What's more, even though the language of the law suggests ammunition vendors are required to process private party ammunition transactions, DOJ has instructed vendors that they may nevertheless refuse to process these transactions.

2. Face-to-Face Transaction Requirement

In addition to the vendor processing requirement discussed above, ammunitions sales, deliveries, and transfers of ownership must occur in a face-to-face transaction with the seller, deliverer or transferor.⁴⁶³ That means that anytime you plan on selling or transferring ammunition to another private party, you must actually be physically in front of the other party when conducting the transfer or sale. You cannot mail or otherwise send ammunition to another person.

California law still allows individuals to purchase ammunition over the internet or by other means of remote ordering.⁴⁶⁴ The law specifies that "ammunition may be purchased or acquired over the Internet or through other means of remote ordering if a licensed ammunition vendor":

(1) Initially receives the ammunition; *and,*

(2) Processes the transaction in compliance with

(a) P.C. section 30312 [law requiring ammunition sales to be conducted by and through licensed ammunition vendors] and

(b) P.C. sections 30342 through 30369 [i.e., California's background check and record-keeping requirements].⁴⁶⁵

---

⁴⁶⁰ P.C. § 30312(a)(2).
⁴⁶¹ CAL. CODE REGS. tit. 11, § 4263(a).
⁴⁶² CAL. CODE REGS. tit. 11, § 4263(b).
⁴⁶³ P.C. § 30312(b).
⁴⁶⁴ P.C. § 30312(b).
⁴⁶⁵ P.C. § 30312(b) (emphasis added).

Selling, delivering, or transferring ammunition in violation of the above requirements is punishable as a misdemeanor.

3. **Exceptions to the Requirement that Ammunition Sales Must Be Conducted Through a Licensed Ammunition Vendor and Face-to-Face Requirement**

Both the requirement that ammunition sales must be conducted by or through a licensed firearms dealer and the requirement that any ammunition sold, delivered, or transferred to another party must be conducted in a face-to-face transaction do not apply to the following individuals:

Table 5.14

PENAL CODE SECTION	EXEMPTION
P.C. § 30312(c)(1)	An authorized law enforcement representative of a city, county, city and county, or state or federal government, if the sale, delivery, or transfer is for exclusive use by the government agency and, prior to the sale, delivery, or transfer of the ammunition, written authorization from the head of the agency employing the purchaser or transferee is obtained, identifying the employee as an individual authorized to conduct the transaction, and authorizing the transaction for the exclusive use of the agency employing the individual
P.C. § 30312(c)(2)	A sworn peace officer, as defined in P.C. sections 830-832.9, or sworn federal law enforcement officer, who is authorized to carry a firearm in the course and scope of the officer's duties
P.C. § 30312(c)(3)	An importer or manufacturer of ammunition or firearms who is licensed to engage in business under 18 U.S.C. sections 921-931 and the regulations issued pursuant thereto
P.C. § 30312(c)(4)	A person who is on the centralized list of exempted federal firearms licensees maintained by DOJ under P.C. sections 28450-28490
P.C. § 30312(c)(5)	A person whose licensed premises are outside this state and who is licensed as a dealer or collector of firearms under 18 U.S.C. sections 921-931
P.C. § 30312(c)(6)	A person who is licensed as a collector of firearms under 18 U.S.C. sections 921-931 and the regulations issued pursuant thereto, whose licensed premises are within the state and who has a current COE[466]
P.C. § 30312(c)(7)	An ammunition vendor

---

[466] Although the exception for licensed collectors who possess a COE is expressly contemplated in the statute, DOJ indicated in *Rhode* that out-of-state persons cannot ship ammunition directly to such individuals. This position is clearly contrary to California law.

PENAL CODE SECTION	EXEMPTION
P.C. § 30312(c)(8)	A consultant-evaluator
P.C. § 30312(c)(9)	A person who purchases or receives ammunition at a target facility holding a business or other regulatory license, provided that the ammunition is at all times kept within the facility's premises
P.C. § 30312(c)(10)	A person who purchases or receives ammunition from a spouse, registered domestic partner, or "immediate family member"[467]
P.C. § 30312(c)(11)	A person enrolled in the basic training academy for peace officers or any other course certified by the Commission on Peace Officer Standards and Training, an instructor of the academy or course, or a staff member of the academy or entity providing the course, who is purchasing the ammunition for the purpose of participation or use in the course

4. Recording of Ammunition Purchaser or Transferee Information

SB 1235 and Prop 63 require ammunition vendors, at the time of delivering the ammunition to the purchaser or transferee, to record specific information regarding the sale or transfer. This information is transmitted to DOJ upon completion of the transfer and is required to be kept by the vendor for a period of no less than five years.[468]

Although SB 1235 and Prop 63's statutory language states what information is to be collected, DOJ's regulations require additional information depending on the type of background check being processed. That said, DOJ's electronic system for processing ammunition transactions appears to require all information on the electronic form to be entered regardless of the type of background check being processed. The information to be collected by the vendor is as follows:

<u>**Required by SB 1235/Prop 63**</u>

(1) The date of the sale or other transfer;

(2) The purchaser's or transferee's driver's license or other identification number and the state in which it was issued;

(3) The brand, type, and amount of ammunition sold or otherwise transferred;

(4) The purchaser's or transferee's full name and signature[469];

---

[467] An 'immediate family member" means either of the following relationships: (1) parent and child, or (2) grandparent grandchild. P.C. § 16720.

[468] P.C. § 30355.

[469] It is worth noting that all of the required information is submitted electronically through DOJ's DROS Entry System ("DES"). But this system does not allow for a person's signature to be submitted. In response to this issue, DOJ has instructed vendors to collect the purchaser's signature after the transaction has been completed and keep it with the records required to be kept by the vendor.

(5) The name of the salesperson who processed the sale or other transaction;

(6) The purchaser's or transferee's full residential address and telephone number; and,

(7) The purchaser's or transferee's date of birth.[470]

Additional Information Required by DOJ

(8) Gender;

(9) Hair color;

(10) Eye color;

(11) Height;

(12) Weight;

(13) United States Citizenship status;

(14) Federal Alien Registration Number or I-94 (if applicable);

(15) Place of birth;

(16) Alias name(s); and,

(17) Race.[471]

5. Required DOJ Electronic Approval

As a result of SB 1235, Prop 63, and DOJ regulations, ammunition vendors can only sell or transfer ammunition to a person who obtains electronic DOJ approval authorizing the transaction.[472] Per DOJ regulations, this electronic approval can be obtained in one of the following ways:

(1) **Standard Ammunition Eligibility Check (AFS Match)** - A purchaser or transferee is authorized to purchase ammunition if their information matches an entry in the Automated Firearm System ("AFS") and does not match an entry in the Prohibited Armed Persons File.[473]

(2) **Basic Ammunition Eligibility Check (Single Transaction or Purchase)** - A purchaser or transferee is authorized to purchase ammunition if they are not prohibited from purchasing or possessing ammunition following a determination made by DOJ.[474]

---

[470] P.C. § 30352.
[471] Cal. Code Regs. tit. 11, § 4303(c).
[472] P.C. § 30352(c)-(d).
[473] Cal. Code Regs. tit. 11, § 4302.
[474] Cal. Code Regs. tit. 11, § 4303.

(3) **Firearms Eligibility Check** - An individual who is purchasing or transferring a firearm and ammunition in the same transaction who successfully completes the firearms eligibility check.[475]

(4) **COE Verification Process** - A purchaser or transferee is authorized to purchase ammunition if they hold a current Certificate of Eligibility as verified by DOJ.[476]

It is up to the individual to determine which of these four options to use when attempting to purchase ammunition. Selecting either the Standard Ammunition Eligibility Check or COE Verification Process will require a non-refundable $1 fee.[477] Selecting the Basic Ammunition Eligibility Check will require a non-refundable $19 fee.[478] Selecting the Firearms Eligibility Check will not require a fee in addition to that which is already required in connection with the firearm purchase.[479]

Processing times for each of the above options can vary widely. While DOJ initially estimated it would take approximately two minutes to process a Standard Ammunition Eligibility Check and issue the required electronic approval, many individuals have reported that it takes between 10-20 minutes just to prepare the required information. And while some have reported instant approvals upon submitting the information to DOJ, others have reported that it has taken hours for DOJ to issue a response.

a. **Updating AFS Records for Purposes of Obtaining the Required DOJ Electronic Approval**

Individuals who attempt to purchase ammunition pursuant to the Standard Ammunition Eligibility Check (AFS Match) option but are denied because their information does not match an entry in AFS may attempt to "correct" future denials by updating their AFS records. This can generally be accomplished in one of two ways:

(1) Creating a new AFS record, either by purchasing a firearm or reporting the ownership of a firearm to DOJ; or,

(2) Updating existing AFS records on file with DOJ.

While there are multiple ways to report the ownership of a firearm to DOJ for purposes of creating a new AFS record, the most common method is to submit a Firearm Ownership Report form (BOF 4542A) to DOJ. Individuals with questions about doing so should consult with an experienced firearms attorney.

---

[475] CAL. CODE REGS. tit. 11, § 4304.
[476] CAL. CODE REGS. tit. 11, § 4305.
[477] CAL. CODE REGS. tit. 11, §§ 4302(b), 4305(b).
[478] CAL. CODE REGS. tit. 11, § 4303(b).
[479] CAL. CODE REGS. tit. 11, § 4304(b).

To update an existing AFS record, individuals must create an account on DOJ's CFARS website (https://cfars.doj.ca.gov/).[480] Upon logging into CFARS, individuals must then select "Automated Firearms System (AFS) Personal Information Update" and follow the on-screen instructions. Updating an AFS record will require the individual to provide their current personal information in addition to all of the information associated with an existing AFS record.[481]

What may be difficult for some individuals is providing their information as reflected on an existing AFS record. Unless the individual kept records of their firearm transactions, providing this information may be difficult, if not impossible. In such circumstances, the only option is to request a copy of your existing AFS records by submitting a notarized form to DOJ.[482] Individuals have reported that obtaining a copy of their AFS records from DOJ using this method can take 3-4 months on average.

Assuming all of the required information can be provided, any updates to a person's name, date of birth, identification type and/or identification number require the individual to electronically upload documents verifying the change.[483] In addition to uploading a copy of a current California Driver License, California Identification Card, or military identification card with military station orders, individuals must provide the following:

(1) For a change of name, a copy of a marriage license, endorsed court order regarding restoration of a former name, or endorsed court order regarding name change.

(2) For a change of date of birth, a copy of a birth certificate.

(3) For a change of identification type or number, a copy of a new California Driver License, California Identification Card, or out-of-state driver license.[484]

Once all of the required information has been uploaded and submitted, DOJ will either approve or reject the request to update the existing AFS records and notify the individual of the results via email.[485] Any rejection will provide information on how to proceed.[486]

---

[480] CAL. CODE REGS. tit. 11, § 4353(a).

[481] CAL. CODE REGS. TIT. 11, § 4353(c-d). Additional information regarding the AFS update process can be found at https://oag.ca.gov/firearms/afspi.

[482] This form, titled Automated Firearms System (AFS) Request for Firearm Records (BOF 053), can be downloaded on DOJ's website at https://oag.ca.gov/firearms/forms.

[483] CAL. CODE REGS. TIT. 11, § 4353(f).

[484] CAL. CODE REGS. tit. 11, § 4353(f)(1-3).

[485] CAL. CODE REGS. tit. 11, § 4353(i).

[486] CAL. CODE REGS. tit. 11, § 4353(i).

6. Exceptions to the Record Keeping and Electronic Approval Requirements

California's Penal Code expressly provides exceptions to the record keeping requirements, but not to the electronic approval requirements. Nevertheless, DOJ regulations have made clear that these same exceptions apply to the electronic approval requirement. As stated in DOJ's regulations, the following types of identification will properly identify an individual who is exempt from the electronic approval and record keeping requirements:

Table 5.15

Regulation	Exemption
Cal. Code Regs. tit. 11, § 4306(a)(1)	An ammunition vendor who presents a valid ammunition vendor license.
Cal. Code Regs. tit. 11, § 4306(a)(2)	A person who is on the centralized list of exempted federal firearms licensees maintained by DOJ who presents a Department-issued Listing Acknowledgement Letter indicating that the individual is currently on the centralized list of exempted federal firearms licensees.
Cal. Code Regs. tit. 11, § 4306(a)(3)	A gunsmith who presents a valid Type 01 Federal Firearms License.
Cal. Code Regs. tit. 11, § 4306(a)(4)	A wholesaler who presents a valid Type 01 Federal Firearms License.
Cal. Code Regs. tit. 11, § 4306(a)(5)	A manufacturer of firearms who presents a valid Type 07 Federal Firearms License
Cal. Code Regs. tit. 11, § 4306(a)(6)	An importer of firearms or ammunition who presents a valid Type 08 Federal Firearms License.
Cal. Code Regs. tit. 11, § 4306(a)(7)	A manufacturer of ammunition who presents a valid Type 06 Federal Firearms License
Cal. Code Regs. tit. 11, § 4306(a)(8)	An authorized law enforcement representative of a city, county, city and county, or state or federal government who presents written authorization from the head of the agency authorizing the ammunition purchase or transfer, as described in P.C. section 30352(e)(7).

Regulation	Exemption
Cal. Code Regs. tit. 11, § 4306(a)(9)	A properly identified sworn peace officer, as defined in Chapter 4.5 of Title 3 of Part 2 of the Penal Code, who is authorized to carry a firearm in the course and scope of the officer's duties who presents both: 1) A sworn state or local peace officer's credential; and, 2) Verifiable written certification from the head of the agency, as described in P.C. section 30352(e)(8)(B)(i).[487]
Cal. Code Regs. tit. 11, § 4306(a)(10)	A properly identified sworn federal law enforcement officer, who is authorized to carry a firearm in the course and scope of the officer's duties who presents both: 1) A sworn federal law enforcement officer's credential; and, 2) Verifiable written certification from the head of the agency as described in P.C. section 30352(e)(8)(B)(i).[488]

Regardless of these exceptions, ammunition vendors must require the purchaser or transferee to provide a document issued by a federal, state, county, or municipal government, or subdivision or agency thereof (including but not limited to a motor vehicle operator's license, state identification card, identification card issued to a member of the armed forces, or other form of identification) that bears the name, date of birth, description, and picture of the person to verify that the person who is receiving delivery of the ammunition is in fact the same person who is exempted.[489] Once the ammunition vendor has verified that the individual is exempt, the vendor may process an ammunition purchase or transfer without obtaining the required DOJ approval.[490]

Note that when Prop. 63 was passed, only certain sections of SB 1235 went into effect. These sections *did not* include any of the exceptions that would have exempted a number of individuals and organizations, such as hunting clubs, shooting clubs, nonprofit mutual and public benefit corporations organized for recreational shooting and lawful hunting activities, and persons participating in a shooting or

---

[487] Per DOJ's regulation, the verifiable written certification from the head of the agency expires 30 days after issuance for purposes of this exception. Cal. Code Regs. tit. 11, § 4306(a)(9)(B).

[488] Per DOJ's regulation, the verifiable written certification from the head of the agency expires 30 days after issuance for purposes of this exception. Cal. Code Regs. tit. 11, § 4306(a)(10)(B).

[489] Cal. Code Regs. tit. 11, § 4306(c).

[490] Cal. Code Regs. tit. 11, § 4306(d). It should also be noted that for purposes of the exceptions as applied to sworn peace officers or sworn federal law enforcement officers, vendors must keep a photocopy of the front and back of the credential, identification document, and original verifiable written certification from the head of the agency. Vendors must make a copy of these records available to DOJ upon request.

hunting events from the restrictions on ammunition purchases.[491] Had Prop. 63 not passed on November 8, 2016, these organizations would have been exempted from these restrictions. But unfortunately, these organizations were left behind by then-Lt. Gov. Newsom's Prop. 63.

B. Restriction on California Residents Bringing or Transporting Ammunition into California

California residents are generally prohibited from bringing or transporting any ammunition into this state that was purchased or otherwise obtained from outside of the state unless the ammunition is delivered to an ammunition vendor in California.[492] A violation of this provision is a misdemeanor.[493]

There are some exceptions to this general prohibition. Specifically, the following individuals can bring or transport ammunition into the state that was purchased or otherwise obtained outside of California without having to go through an ammunition vendor:

Table 5.16

PENAL CODE SECTION	EXEMPTION
P.C. § 30314(b)(1)	An ammunition vendor
P.C. § 30314(b)(2)	A sworn peace officer, as defined in P.C. sections 830-832.9, or sworn federal law enforcement officer, who is authorized to carry a firearm in the course and scope of the officer's duties
P.C. § 30314(b)(3)	An importer or manufacturer of ammunition or firearms who is licensed to engage in business under 18 U.S.C. sections 921-931 and the regulations issued pursuant thereto
P.C. § 30314(b)(4)	A person who is on the centralized list of exempted federal firearms licensees maintained by DOJ under P.C. sections 28450-28490
P.C. § 30314(b)(5)	A person who is licensed as a collector of firearms under 18 U.S.C. sections 921-931 and the regulations issued thereto, whose licensed premises are within this state, and who has a current certificate of eligibility issued by DOJ under P.C. section 26710
P.C. § 30314(b)(6)	A person who acquired the ammunition from a spouse, registered domestic partner, or "immediate family member"[459]

---

[491] See SB 1235, 2015-2016 Leg., Reg. Sess. (2016), available at https://leginfo.legislature.ca.gov/faces/billNavClient.xhtml?bill_id=201520160SB1235 (last visited Oct. 10, 2020).

[492] P.C. § 30314.

[493] P.C. § 30314(c).

[494] An "immediate family member" refers to a parent-child relationship and a grandparent-grandchild relationship. P.C. § 16720.

CHAPTER 6:
CARRYING FIREARMS OPENLY, CONCEALED, AND/OR LOADED

Violations involving the illegal transportation or possession of firearms are the most common firearm-related criminal offenses. Thousands of people are prosecuted for these violations each year in California. Knowing the restrictions on carrying firearms (discussed in this chapter), the exceptions to these restrictions (discussed in Chapter 7), and places where the possession of firearms is illegal (discussed in Chapter 8) will provide you with a good understanding of the common legal pitfalls involved with firearm ownership. Together, the laws that prohibit carrying firearms openly, concealed, and/or loaded, and their exemptions, create the general framework of California's regulation of firearms outside of the house.

California law generally restricts carrying of concealed "handguns"[1] and the carrying of loaded firearms in most populated areas. And it likewise restricts the open carry of handguns and non-handguns in most populated areas.

To understand when the prohibitions apply, you first need to know how the terms used in the statutes are interpreted and defined. That is the focus of this chapter.[2]

I. WHAT DOES "CARRY" MEAN?

As discussed later in this chapter, the California Penal Code (P.C.) generally prohibits you from carrying firearms "on your person" and "in vehicles" under your control. But what exactly does it mean to "carry" a firearm?

---

[1] "Handgun" means "any pistol, revolver, or firearm capable of being concealed upon the person." P.C. § 16640(a). "Firearm capable of being concealed upon the person," "pistol," and "revolver" include "any device designed to be used as a weapon, from which is expelled a projectile by the force of any explosion, or other form of combustion, and that has a barrel less than 16 inches in length" or that "has a barrel 16 inches or more in length which is designed to be interchanged with a barrel less than 16 inches in length." P.C. § 16530(a).

[2] Note that this chapter assumes that the person possessing the firearm may legally do so and that the firearm itself is legal in California. For exceptions to carrying firearms openly, concealed, or loaded, refer to Chapter 7. For firearms that may be generally prohibited, refer to Chapters 9 and 10.

Although the Penal Code does not provide a specific definition for the term "carry", courts have provided some guidance as to what it means to "carry" a firearm. Specifically, the California Court of Appeal has explained that "[s]peaking generally in the context of statutes concerned with firearms, 'carry' or 'carrying' has been said to be used in the sense of holding or bearing arms."[3]

Moreover, the term "carry" has been construed as to not require actual locomotion, *i.e.*, movement from one place to another.[4] Rather, to be considered "carried" according to the few cases that have discussed the issue, the firearm only needs to be connected with the person or vehicle in such a way that would allow the person or vehicle to carry the firearm if it was in actual locomotion.[5] So, a firearm stowed under the seat of a parked car or on a person sitting in or on a parked car would still be considered "carried," even if the car was not actually moving.

II. WHAT DOES "IN A VEHICLE," "ON," OR "UPON THE PERSON" MEAN?

In the context of a vehicle, courts have held that a person can "carry" a firearm "in a vehicle" even if the firearm is not actually in contact with them. For example, a firearm under the seat of a vehicle is being "carried" by the person controlling the car, even though it may not be in their exclusive possession or control.[6]

Similarly, courts have held that arms can be "carried on the person" even when they are not physically attached to the person's body, such as when a person is carrying a firearm inside a suitcase.[7] But, at least one California appellate court has disagreed with that view.[8]

Specifically, in *People v. Pellecer*, the defendant was leaning on a closed backpack that contained a dagger.[9] The court held that this was not considered "carried upon the person" because "upon the person" means just that, and if the legislature intended that term to include items beyond the body, it could have said so.[10] It

---

[3] *People v. Overturf*, 64 Cal. App. 3d Supp. 1, 6 (1976) (citing *In re Bergen*, 61 Cal. App. 226, 228 (1923)); *see People v. Smith*, 72 Cal. App. 2d Supp. 875, 878 (1946).

[4] *See United States v. Parker*, 919 F. Supp. 2d 1072, 1087 n.6 (2013); *People v. Smith*, 72 Cal. App. 2d Supp. 875, 879 (1946).

[5] *See United States v. Parker*, 919 F. Supp. 2d 1072, 1087 n.6 (2013); *People v. Smith*, 72 Cal. App. 2d Supp. 875, 879 (1946).

[6] *See People v. Davis*, 157 Cal. App. 2d 33, 36 (1958) (defendant found to be "carrying" a concealed revolver under the driver's seat; exclusive possession was not required because the vehicle was under the control and/or direction of the defendant).

[7] *People v. Dunn*, 61 Cal. App. 3d Supp. 12, 14 (1976) (defendant found to be "carrying" a concealed handgun in his locked suitcase when the locked suitcase passed through an airport x-ray machine). It should be noted that this case was from the Appellate Department of the Los Angeles County Superior Court. *Pellecer* was decided by the California Court of Appeal, Second District, Division 1, a higher court located in the same jurisdiction as the *Dunn* court.

[8] *People v. Pellecer*, 215 Cal. App. 4th 508 (2013).

[9] *People v. Pellecer*, 215 Cal. App. 4th 508, 511 (2013).

[10] *People v. Pellecer*, 215 Cal. App. 4th 508, 517 (2013).

should also be noted that although the *Pellecer* court distinguished the phrase "on or about the person" from "on the person," it uses the words "upon" and "on" interchangeably. This could mean two things. First, this could be an oversight by the court, and it meant "upon" when it said "on." But given the frequency it used "on" in place of "upon," that is probably unlikely. The other, more likely, conclusion is that the court considered the two words ("upon" and "on") as interchangeable.

Laws for the four different types of restricted carry, discussed below, use the same language when they discuss a person carrying a firearm illegally. The restriction for carrying concealed says "upon the person,"[11] the restriction for carrying a loaded firearm says "on the person,"[12] and the restriction for open carry of a handgun says "upon his or her person" while the person is outside a vehicle, and that it doesn't matter "whether or not [the handgun is] on his or her person" while the person is inside or on a vehicle.[13] Moreover, the restriction for carrying a firearm that is not a handgun in public says "upon his or her person."[14]

In 2015, the California Court of Appeal chose to not follow the decision in *Pellecer* when it ruled in *People v. Wade* that a person wearing a backpack with a loaded firearm inside is still carrying a firearm "on their person" for purposes of restrictions on carrying loaded firearms.[15] Because this case caused a split between the courts, the California Supreme Court granted review. And on May 9, 2016, the California Supreme Court upheld the decision of the lower court's decision.[16] As the court explained, "[t]he backpack was on his person and, accordingly, anything inside that backpack was also on his person."[17]

III. CONCEALED CARRY LAW

A. Carrying "Concealed"

Unless an exemption applies, you can be found guilty of carrying a concealed *handgun*[18] if you knowingly do any of the following:

(1) Carry any concealed handgun in any vehicle under your control or direction;

(2) Carry any concealed handgun on your person; *or*,

---

[11] P.C. § 25400(a)(2).
[12] P.C. § 25850(a).
[13] P.C. § 26350(a)(1)-(2).
[14] P.C. § 26400(a).
[15] *People v. Wade*, 183 Cal. Rptr. 3d 714, 715 (2015), *superseded by* 63 Cal. 4th 137 (2016).
[16] *People v. Wade*, 63 Cal. 4th 137 (2016).
[17] *People v. Wade*, 63 Cal. 4th 137, 140 (2016).
[18] The term "handgun" in this section includes "rocket[s], rocket propelled projectile launcher[s], or similar device[s] containing any explosive or incendiary material." *See* P.C. §§ 16520(c)(3), 25400.

(3) Cause a handgun to be carried concealed in a vehicle where you are an occupant.[19]

Note that the concealed carry law only applies to handguns, and it applies whether or not the handgun is loaded or unloaded. This means that under California law, a long gun (meaning a shotgun or rifle) is never considered to be "carried concealed." The concealed carry law applies any time a handgun is hidden from view, possibly even if partially hidden.

Carrying concealed is generally charged as a misdemeanor,[20] unless:

(1) You are not in "lawful possession" of the handgun[21] or are generally prohibited from possessing firearms under California law (discussed in Chapter 4);[22]

(2) You have been convicted of a felony or certain firearm-related crimes;[23]

(3) The handgun is stolen, and you knew or had reason to believe it was stolen;[24]

(4) You are an active participant in a criminal street gang;[25] *or*,

(5) You have been convicted of a crime against person or property or of a narcotic or dangerous drug violation.[26]

In those cases, the charge is either a "wobbler" (meaning that it can be charged as a misdemeanor or felony) or a straight felony offense.[27]

Also, if you are unlawfully carrying a concealed handgun that is not registered to you and that handgun is either loaded (definition explained below) or unexpended ammunition for that handgun is in your immediate possession or readily accessible, you can be charged with a felony.[28] If you didn't obtain the handgun through a Federal Firearms Licensee (FFL) or register it with the California Department of Justice (DOJ) yourself, it is probably not registered to you and could be registered to someone else.[29]

---

[19] P.C. § 25400(a).

[20] P.C. § 25400(c)(7).

[21] "Lawful possession" means the person possessing the firearm either lawfully owns it or has permission from the lawful owner or a person who otherwise has apparent authority to possess it. P.C. § 16750(a).

[22] P.C. § 25400(c)(4).

[23] P.C. § 25400(c)(1). The list of firearm-related crimes is in P.C. section 16580.

[24] P.C. § 25400(c)(2).

[25] P.C. § 25400(c)(3). Whether a person is an active participant in a criminal street gang is discussed in subdivision (a) of P.C. section 186.22, under the Street Terrorism Enforcement and Prevention Act (Chapter 11 (commencing with Section 186.20) of Title 7 of Part 1).

[26] P.C. § 25400(c)(5).

[27] P.C. § 25400(c).

[28] P.C. § 25400(c)(6).

[29] If you want to find out which firearms are registered in your name, you can submit an Automated Firearms System (AFS) Request for Firearm Records to DOJ. You can access this form at: http://oag.ca.gov/sites/all/files/pdfs/firearms/forms/AFSPrivateCitizen.pdf (last visited Oct. 9, 2020). *See* Chapter 5.

B. What Does "Concealed" Mean?

The Penal Code does not define "concealed," other than to say a firearm carried openly in a belt-holster is *not* "concealed."[30] Case law provides some guidance in figuring out the definition, however.

At least one court has suggested that a semiautomatic handgun is considered legally "concealed" just by ejecting its magazine and placing the magazine in a nearby location where it is not visible, even if the firearm itself is visible.[31] In *People v. Hale*, the defendant's handgun was on the passenger seat of his car in plain view, and the handgun's magazine, full of ammunition, was underneath the ashtray in the center console.[32] The court concluded that concealing a vital part of a visible weapon in a way that "make[s] the weapon *readily available for use as a firearm*" threatens public order just like concealing the entire firearm would.[33]

It is unclear what other "vital parts" of a visible firearm – aside from a magazine containing ammunition – would render, if concealed, the entire firearm "concealed" for purposes of the concealed restriction. It is also unclear whether a concealed magazine must have ammunition in it to make a visible handgun "readily available for use as a firearm" and thus considered "concealed" under the reasoning of *Hale*. Unless you want to be a test case, you should assume that concealing even an *empty* magazine is prohibited if you are also "carrying" the handgun that uses it. To be safe, you should assume concealing any part of a handgun is prohibited.

The exact definition of "concealed" is not entirely clear. Beyond a few gray areas, like where one's shirt or jacket covers part of a holstered handgun, it is generally obvious whether a firearm is "concealed" as that term is commonly understood, *i.e.*, kept secret, hidden, or out of sight.[34]

---

[30] P.C. § 25400(b).

[31] *People v. Hale*, 43 Cal. App. 3d 353, 356 (1974).

[32] *People v. Hale*, 43 Cal. App. 3d 353, 355 (1974).

[33] *People v. Hale*, 43 Cal. App. 3d 353, 356 (1974) (emphasis added). It should be noted that this case does not specifically deal with California's concealed carry laws but provides an analysis of them that a court may find persuasive.

[34] A concealed weapon is "[a] weapon that is carried by a person but that is not visible by ordinary observation." BLACK'S LAW DICTIONARY 1624 (8th ed. 2009).

Table 6.1

CARRYING CONCEALED HANDGUNS[35]
(P.C. § 25400)

Restriction: You may be guilty of carrying a concealed handgun if you knowingly:

(1) Carry any concealed handgun in any vehicle under your control or direction; *or*
(2) Carry any concealed handgun on your person; *or*
(3) Cause a handgun to be carried concealed in a vehicle where you are an occupant.

Penalty: Carrying a concealed handgun is a misdemeanor, but may be charged as a "wobbler," or even a straight felony, under certain circumstances.

Things to Remember: These restrictions apply regardless of whether the handgun is concealed *on your person*, or *in a vehicle*; or is *loaded or unloaded*; or *where you are* carrying the concealed handgun. Remember, these restrictions apply *everywhere*, unless you are subject to an exemption (discussed in Chapter 7).

IV. LOADED CARRY LAW

A. Loaded Firearm Restrictions

You can be charged with the crime of carrying a loaded firearm if you carry it on your person or in a vehicle "while in any public place or on any public street in an incorporated city or in any public place or on any public street in a prohibited area[36] of unincorporated territory."[37] Even *inoperable* firearms may violate loaded carry laws.[38]

You can be prosecuted for carrying a loaded firearm even if you didn't know that the firearm was loaded. The prosecuting attorney does not have to prove that you knew the firearm was loaded, just that you knew you were carrying a firearm.[39] In the case of *People v. Dillard*, Mr. Dillard was stopped while riding his bicycle and carrying a rifle in its case.[40] The officer examined the rifle and found a round in the chamber and six more in the "cylinder." Mr. Dillard testified that the firearm was his, that he just picked the firearm up from his stepfather's house, and he didn't examine the firearm. The court determined that, in light of the "legislative

---

[35] All of the tables within this book are paraphrases of the law and are not a complete summary of each subject area. Please review the corresponding Sections within this chapter for a more in-depth discussion of each topic and for the applicable statutes and/or case law that is paraphrased within the tables.

[36] As used in this code section, a "prohibited area" is "any place where it is unlawful to discharge a weapon." P.C. § 17030.

[37] P.C. § 25850(a). This includes "rockets" and related devices. P.C. § 16520(c)(4). Pay particular attention to this "prohibited area of an unincorporated territory" language. Even if the area is unincorporated and is not a place where you may lawfully discharge a firearm, carrying a loaded firearm there can be a crime.

[38] *See People v. Taylor*, 151 Cal. App. 3d 432, 437 (1984) (holding that "operability is not an element of possession of a loaded firearm in a public place"). See also Chapter 3 (defining "firearm").

[39] CALCRIM No. 2530.

[40] *People v. Dillard*, 154 Cal. App. 3d 261, 263 (1984).

concern for the public safety as against the presence of armed individuals in public places," the restriction against possessing a loaded firearm in public is a "quintessential public welfare statute" and no actual knowledge that the firearm was loaded must be proven.[41]

California law also authorizes peace officers to examine any firearm carried in any "public place" where the loaded restriction applies to determine whether it is loaded. A refusal of such an inspection is grounds for arrest.[42]

It is also a misdemeanor to permit someone to carry a loaded firearm inside your vehicle in violation of P.C. section 25850(a) or Fish & Game Code section 2006. But, there is a split among the California Courts of Appeal as to whether a person can be prosecuted for allowing another person to carry a loaded firearm in their vehicle if they did not know that the firearm was loaded.[43]

On one hand, the California Court of Appeal, First District held that the prosecution does not need to prove that a person knew that the firearm was loaded.[44] Instead, the prosecutor just needs to show that the person knew that a passenger inside the vehicle was carrying a firearm.[45] As the court explained, if the prosecution was required to show that the defendant knew that the passenger was carrying a loaded firearm, then it would defeat the statute's objective of deterring drive-by shootings and making owners and drivers responsible for the presence of loaded guns in their vehicles.[46]

On the other hand, the California Court of Appeal, Sixth District has expressly rejected the First District's holding and has instead ruled that the prosecution must prove that the person actually knew that the passenger inside their car was carrying a loaded firearm.[47] In rejecting the First District's holding, the Sixth District explained that the First District relied too heavily upon committee reports about unrelated bills in drawing out the Legislature's intent.[48] Instead, the court reasoned that the Legislature intended on limiting the restriction to only those drivers who knew that a passenger was carrying a loaded firearm in a vehicle, as it is not illegal to allow a passenger to carry an unloaded firearm in the vehicle.[49]

Because of this split in opinion, it is always a good idea to be cautious when you know that passengers inside your vehicle are carrying firearms and ensure that their firearms are not loaded.

Like carrying a concealed handgun unlawfully, possessing a loaded firearm in a

---

[41] *People v. Dillard*, 154 Cal. App. 3d 261, 266 (1984).
[42] *See* P.C. § 25850(b).
[43] *Compare People v. Gonzales*, 232 Cal. App. 4th 1449 (2015), with *In re. Ramon A.*, 40 Cal. App. 4th 935 (1995) and *People v. Dillard*, 154 Cal. App. 3d 261 (1984).
[44] *In re. Ramon A.*, 40 Cal. App. 4th 935, 941-42 (1995)
[45] *In re. Ramon A.*, 40 Cal. App. 4th 935, 941-42 (1995)
[46] *In re. Ramon A.*, 40 Cal. App. 4th 935, 941 (1995)
[47] *People v. Gonzales*, 232 Cal. App. 3d 1449, 1463 (2015).
[48] *People v. Gonzales*, 232 Cal. App. 3d 1449, 1462 (2015).
[49] *People v. Gonzales*, 232 Cal. App. 3d 1449, 1462 (2015).

restricted public place unlawfully is also generally a misdemeanor,[50] unless:

(1) You are not in "lawful possession" of the firearm;[51]
(2) You are generally prohibited from possessing firearms under California law (discussed in Chapter 4);[52]
(3) You have been convicted of a felony and certain firearm-related crimes;[53]
(4) The firearm is stolen, and you knew or had reason to believe it was stolen;[54]
(5) You are an active participant in a criminal street gang;[55] or,
(6) You have been convicted of a crime against person or property or of a narcotic or dangerous drug violation.[56]

In those cases, the charge is either a "wobbler" or a straight felony.[57] Also, if it is a "loaded" *handgun*, carrying it "concealed" can be charged as a separate (possibly felony) offense.[58]

Table 6.2

CARRYING LOADED FIREARMS
(P.C. § 25850)

Restrictions: You may be guilty of carrying a loaded firearm if you carry a loaded firearm (openly or concealed) on your person or in a vehicle while you are in or on:

(1) A public place or public street in an *incorporated* city; or
(2) A public place or public street in a *prohibited area* of *unincorporated* territory.

Penalty: Carrying a loaded firearm is a misdemeanor but may be charged as a "wobbler," or even a straight felony, under certain circumstances.

Things to Remember: You should always be cautious when carrying firearms in any "public place" or on any public street. Peace officers may examine any of your firearms to determine if they are loaded if you are carrying them in a "public place" or on a public street, listed above.

---

[50] P.C. § 25850(c)(7).

[51] As defined in P.C. section 16750(b), "lawful possession of the firearm" "means that the person who has possession or custody of the firearm either lawfully acquired and lawfully owns the firearm or has the permission of the lawful owner or person who otherwise has apparent authority to possess or have custody of the firearm. A person who takes a firearm without the permission of the lawful owner or without the permission of a person who has lawful custody of the firearm does not have lawful possession of the firearm."

[52] P.C. § 25850(c)(4). Although juveniles are generally prohibited from possessing firearm under California law (see Chapter 4), they are not automatically subject to felony punishment under P.C. section 25850(c)(4). *See In re. D.D.*, 234 Cal. App. 4th 824, 833 (2015).

[53] P.C. § 25850(c)(1) (crimes made punishable by a provision listed in section 16580).

[54] P.C. § 25850(c)(2).

[55] P.C. § 25850(c)(3). Whether a person is an active participant in a criminal street gang is discussed in P.C. section 186.22(a), under the Street Terrorism Enforcement and Prevention Act (Chapter 11 (commencing with Section 186.20) of Title 7 of Part 1).

[56] P.C. § 25850(c)(5).

[57] P.C. § 25850(c).

[58] *See* P.C. §§ 25400, 25850

B. What Does "Loaded" Mean?

There are different definitions of "loaded" in the Penal Code. Even the Fish & Game Code has its own definition of "loaded" that applies to shotguns and rifles transported while hunting. So, it isn't surprising that people, even law enforcement, get confused about whether a firearm is legally considered "loaded."

Table 6.3[59]

The Different Ways "Loaded" is Defined in California
The General Definition of "Loaded"   (P.C. § 16840(b)(1))
Generally, a firearm is loaded when it has "an unexpended cartridge or shell consisting of a case that holds a charge of powder and a bullet or shot, in, or attached to, the firearm, including, but not limited to, in the firing chamber, magazine, or clip attached in any manner to the firearm." In *People v. Clark*, though, the court held that a shotgun is not "loaded" under this definition if the ammunition is not yet in the firing position, and stored elsewhere.
The Definition of "Loaded" While Committing a Felony or in "Sensitive Places"   (P.C. § 25800(a))
A person possesses a "loaded" firearm if the person simultaneously possesses *both* the firearm and the ammunition to fire it.
The Definition of "Loaded" Under The California Fish & Game Code   (Cal. Fish & Game Code § 2006)
A rifle or shotgun (but not a handgun) is "loaded" if there is a live round, *i.e.*, an unexpended cartridge or shell, *in the firing chamber*.

1. General Definition of "Loaded"

Generally, a firearm is "loaded" when it has "an unexpended cartridge or shell consisting of a case that holds a charge of powder and a bullet or shot, in, or attached in any manner to, the firearm, including, but not limited to, in the firing chamber, magazine, or clip thereof attached to the firearm."[60] This general definition of "loaded" also applies to "any rocket, rocket propelled projectile launcher, or similar device containing any explosive or incendiary material."[61] A muzzle-loader firearm is considered "loaded" "when it is capped or primed and has a powder charge and ball or shot in the barrel or cylinder."[62]

Under the general definition, a firearm must have ammunition in a position from where it can be fired or be "ready for firing." A clear example of when a fire-

---

[59] *People v. Clark*, 45 Cal. App. 4th 1147 (1996).
[60] P.C. § 16840(b)(1).
[61] P.C. § 16520(c).
[62] P.C. § 16840(b)(2). A muzzle-loading firearm is typically a firearm that uses black powder as a propellant, which along with the bullet (ball or shot) is inserted through the muzzle.

arm would be considered "loaded" is where ammunition is placed in the chamber or cylinder. The ammunition is "attached" and is in a position from where it can be fired.[63] But not all scenarios are so clear.

In the case of *People v. Clark*, the police seized a shotgun that didn't have a shell in the firing chamber.[64] Three shells, however, were located in a covered compartment at the rear of the shotgun's stock. The shells could not be fired from their position but would have to be manually inserted into the shotgun's chamber.[65] Mr. Clark was convicted of possession of methamphetamine while armed with a "loaded," operable firearm, but the conviction was reversed on appeal because the shotgun was not "loaded" within the term's "commonly understood meaning."[66] The Court of Appeal reasoned that the phrase "attached to the firearm" applies when "the [ammunition] is placed in a position from which it can be fired" or if it is "ready for firing."[67] Additionally, the court interpreted the statute's legislative intent to *not* "indicate a clear intent to deem a gun 'loaded' when the ammunition . . . is in a storage compartment which is not equivalent to either a magazine or clip *and from which the ammunition cannot be fired*."[68]

Clark's reasoning for why the shotgun was not "loaded" is not necessarily applicable to determining whether a firearm is "loaded" when its uninserted magazine or clip (or speed loader) contains ammunition. The court expressly distinguished a permissible separate storage compartment "from which [ammunition] cannot be fired" from "a magazine or clip" (which likely includes a speed loader).[69] Of course, this language was intended to explain what does *not* constitute "loaded." It is possible – even likely – that such language does *not* mean that a firearm is "loaded" if you have ammunition in a magazine or clip that is ejected from the firearm.

And the fact that a shotgun with ammunition inside its stock, as was the case in *Clark*, is not considered "loaded" further supports the view that a firearm that has neither a round in the chamber nor a magazine inserted into its magazine well is probably not considered "loaded" under this general definition. This likely remains true even if you have a magazine full of ammunition near the firearm, such as in the same locked container, since both scenarios allow the firearm to accept and discharge a round with similar speed. Of course, you should be cautious because this issue remains undecided, and law enforcement could see it another way.

A semiautomatic firearm without a round in the chamber but having a magazine containing ammunition inserted in the magazine well may be (and in practice

---

[63] *People v. Clark*, 45 Cal. App. 4th 1147, 1154 (1996).
[64] *People v. Clark*, 45 Cal. App. 4th 1147, 1152 (1996).
[65] *People v. Clark*, 45 Cal. App. 4th 1147, 1152 (1996).
[66] *People v. Clark*, 45 Cal. App. 4th 1147, 1153 (1996).
[67] *People v. Clark*, 45 Cal. App. 4th 1147, 1154 (1996).
[68] *People v. Clark*, 45 Cal. App. 4th 1147, 1154 (1996) (emphasis added).
[69] *People v. Clark*, 45 Cal. App. 4th 1147, 1154 (1996).

usually is) considered "loaded" even though the firearm is not completely "ready for firing" until a round is cycled into the chamber.

Because of the different definitions of "loaded," you should consider transporting ammunition in a way that it cannot contact the firearm to avoid problems with law enforcement, even though it may not be required by law.

2. "Loaded" While Committing a Felony or in Sensitive Places

The general definition of "loaded" (described above) does not apply when someone is charged with "armed criminal action." "Armed criminal action" occurs when someone "carries" a "loaded" firearm and intends to commit a felony.[70] Here, a firearm is considered "loaded" if the person simultaneously possesses *both* the firearm and the ammunition to fire it.[71] The ammunition does not need to be physically touching the firearm.

An almost identical definition of "loaded" applies to carrying firearms in certain sensitive places like those listed in P.C. sections 171c and 171d, including the California State Capitol building and legislative offices.[72]

3. Fish and Game's Definition of "Loaded"

Under Cal. Fish & Game Code section 2006, a *rifle* or *shotgun*[73] (but not a handgun) is loaded if it has a live round (*i.e.*, an unexpended cartridge or shell) *in the firing chamber*.[74] This means that even if the rifle or shotgun has ammunition in it, like in a magazine, it is still not "loaded" under this definition, unless it has a round in the chamber.

This definition applies to the restriction on loaded rifles and shotguns while "in any vehicle or conveyance or its attachments, which is standing on, along, or is being driven on or along any public highway *or other way open to the public*."[75]

Careful, this does not mean you are exempt from the general prohibition on loaded firearms in public as long as you have a rifle or shotgun and you are in a vehicle on a public highway. For one, you might actually be carrying on a "public street," thereby triggering the general prohibition according to the Attorney General's opinion, as discussed at the end of the Chapter. Secondly, while it is not entirely clear, it appears this section is intended to apply where the general restriction does not. Specifically, it seems to be aimed at hunters who are in or near areas where it is

---

[70] P.C. § 25800(a).
[71] P.C. § 16840(a).
[72] *See, e.g.*, P.C. § 171e. See Chapter 8 for other examples.
[73] See Chapters 3 and 10 for definitions of "rifle" and "shotgun."
[74] *See* CAL. FISH & GAME CODE § 2006(b).
[75] *See* CAL. FISH & GAME CODE § 2006(a) (emphasis added). Note that this section has been interpreted as authorizing law enforcement to inspect rifles and shotguns to determine whether they are "loaded." *See People v. Perez*, 51 Cal. App. 4th 1168 (1996); *People v. Johnson*, 108 Cal. App. 3d 175 (1980).

legal to have a loaded firearm and may be using vehicles to track or transport game. In other words, it is a reminder to eject the round from the chamber when leaving a hunting field or moving to a new one. If you are in a prohibited area, you can still be charged under the general loaded restriction instead, which does not require that a round be chambered to be in violation. But, if the general restriction does not apply, you can still have a loaded handgun without running afoul of Cal. Fish & Game Code section 2006.

V. OPEN CARRY OF HANDGUNS RESTRICTION[76]

You may be guilty of a misdemeanor if you openly[77] carry an unloaded[78] handgun[79] on your person, or inside or on a vehicle, while you are in or on any of the following:

(1) A public place or public street in an incorporated city or city and county;

(2) A public street in a prohibited area of an unincorporated area of a county or city and county; *or,*

(3) A public place in a prohibited area of a county or city and county.[80]

Violating these restrictions is a misdemeanor, generally punishable by up to six months in county jail and/or a maximum $1,000 fine.[81] But you can be sentenced to up to one year in county jail, a maximum $1,000 fine, or both, if you openly carry an unloaded handgun:

(1) Outside of a vehicle;

(2) In a public place or public street in an incorporated city or city and county *or* a public street in a prohibited area of an unincorporated area of a county or city and county;

(3) Have ammunition that can be used with the handgun in your immediate possession; *and,*

---

[76] In response to people protesting California's restrictive firearms laws by publicly carrying unloaded handguns in holsters, the California legislature passed AB 144 amending the Penal Code to make that practice a crime. Prior to January 1, 2012, it was generally legal to publicly carry an unloaded handgun if it was not concealed.

[77] The Penal Code provides that a handgun is carried "openly" when it is not being "carried concealed within the meaning of section 25400." P.C. § 16950. But, as explained above, P.C. section 25400 itself does not define "concealed," other than to say a firearm carried in a belt-holster is *not* "concealed." P.C. § 25400(b). So, what "openly" means, just as with the definition of "concealed," is not entirely clear.

[78] A handgun is "unloaded" if it is not "loaded" within the meaning of P.C. section 16840(b). P.C. § 17295. See discussion above for determining whether a firearm is "loaded."

[79] For this restriction, "rockets" and related devices are *not* covered.

[80] P.C. § 26350(a).

[81] P.C. § 26350(b)(1).

(4) You are not in lawful possession[82] of the handgun.[83]

Each handgun carried in violation of P.C. section 26350(a) is chargeable as a separate offense. For example, if you are openly carrying two unloaded handguns unlawfully at the same time, you can be charged with two separate misdemeanors.

If you are the driver or owner of a motor vehicle and knowingly allow another person "to carry into or bring into" your vehicle (or the vehicle you are driving) a handgun openly carried in violation of P.C. section 26350(a), you are guilty of a misdemeanor.[84] Since the punishment for this violation is not specified, the Penal Code limits the possible punishment to "imprisonment in the county jail not exceeding six months, or by fine not exceeding one thousand dollars ($1,000), or by both."[85]

Note that the question of whether a firearm being openly carried in a "public place" as described in P.C. section 26350(a)(1)(A)-(C) is "loaded" or not is generally only important with respect to what Penal Code statute is being violated. If it is "loaded," you will be charged with violating section 25850(a) (carrying a loaded firearm). If it is "unloaded," you will be charged with violating P.C. section 26350(a) (openly carrying an unloaded handgun). Either activity is generally a criminal act. But, as explained above, the penalties for unlawfully carrying a "loaded" firearm are potentially much more severe than those for unlawfully openly carrying an unloaded handgun.

---

[82] "Lawful possession" means that the person who has possession of the firearm either lawfully acquired and lawfully owns the firearm or has the permission of the lawful owner (or someone who has apparent authority to possess or have custody of the firearm). P.C. § 16750(b). In other words, if you acquired the firearm by stealing it, borrowing it without permission, exceeding California's time limits for a lawful loan, or without going through an FFL (unless acquired prior to that requirement becoming law or you meet an exception thereto), you are *not* in "lawful possession" of the firearm per P.C. section 26350(b)(2).

[83] P.C. § 26350(b)(2).

[84] P.C. § 17512.

[85] P.C. § 19.

Table 6.4

Openly Carrying Unloaded Handguns (P.C. § 26350)
Restrictions: You may be guilty of openly carrying an unloaded handgun if you carry on your person an exposed and unloaded handgun outside of a vehicle or inside or on a vehicle (whether or not the handgun is on your person) while you are in or on any of the following: (1) A public place or public street in an *incorporated* city or city and county; *or* (2) A public street in a *prohibited area* of an *unincorporated* area of a county or city and county; *or* (3) A public place in a *prohibited area* of a county or city and county.
Penalty: Openly carrying an unloaded handgun is a misdemeanor. But you can be sentenced to up to one year in county jail, a maximum $1,000 fine, or both, if the handgun and unexpended ammunition capable of being discharged from that handgun are in your immediate possession and you are not in lawful possession of that handgun. Each handgun carried in violation of this restriction can be charged as a separate offense.
Things to Remember: If you are the driver or owner of a vehicle and you knowingly allow another person to carry or bring into your vehicle (or a vehicle you're driving) a handgun openly carried in violation of the above restrictions, you may be guilty of a misdemeanor.

VI. RESTRICTION ON CARRYING FIREARMS OTHER THAN HANDGUNS

When the ban on the open carry of handguns (Assembly Bill (AB) 144) became law in 2011, a number of individuals protested by carrying their rifles and shotguns in public. Not content to leave the laws alone, and likely upon realizing that the handgun ban didn't include long guns, the California Legislature passed AB 1527 in 2012.

AB 1527 prohibits you from carrying an unloaded "firearm that is not a handgun" when you are outside of a vehicle in an incorporated city, or city and county unless an exception applies.[86] While almost identical to its handgun-restriction counterpart, there are at least two significant differences in the scope of AB 1527.

First, AB 1527 doesn't apply within a vehicle. So, unlike handguns, which generally must be transported in a locked container while in a vehicle and generally cannot be transported openly in a vehicle, there is no requirement that non-handguns be locked up under California law; therefore, non-handguns can be left open and unlocked within a vehicle.[87] Nevertheless, consider transporting your long gun

---

[86] P.C. § 26400.

[87] Note, California generally requires handguns, "assault weapons," and .50 BMG rifles to be transported in a locked container at all times, and federal law additionally requires that all firearms (including long guns) be in a locked container or a locked firearms rack that is in a motor vehicle when in a "school zone." 18 U.S.C. § 922(q)(2)(B). See Chapter 8 for more on school zones.

the same way you do your handgun in order to avoid potential problems with law enforcement.

AB 1527 didn't apply to *unincorporated* areas.

But in 2017, the Legislature passed AB 7, extending the reach of AB 1527 to unincorporated areas, i.e., a public place or a public street in a prohibited area of a county's unincorporated area.[88] This new restriction came into effect on January 1, 2018.

A. "Firearm That Is Not a Handgun"

P.C. section 26400 specifically applies to "firearms that are not handguns." Since the term is phrased in the negative (firearm that is *not* a handgun[89]), it is necessary to look at the definition of "handgun" and work back. Any firearm that doesn't fit under any of the definitions of "handgun" in Chapter 3 will be subject to P.C. section 26400. Generally, such firearms include rifles, shotguns, carbines, and those firearms that fit neither the handgun nor traditional long-gun definitions.

According to P.C. section 16520, an "antique" firearm is not considered a "firearm" for purposes of P.C. section 26400's non-handgun carry restriction. "Antique firearms" are also discussed in Chapter 3, but briefly put, non-handguns made in or before 1898, certain but not all replicas thereof, or certain muzzle-loading firearms using black powder that are incapable of using fixed ammunition are antiques and thus not prohibited from being publicly carried under P.C. section 26400.

B. Penalties for Unlawful Carry of Non-Handguns

Under P.C. section 26400, if you carry an unloaded "firearm that is not a handgun" on your person outside of a vehicle in an incorporated city, or city and county, you are guilty of a misdemeanor. And, you would also be guilty of a misdemeanor under P.C. section 26400 if you carry an unloaded "firearm that is not a handgun" on your person outside of a vehicle in a "public place or a public street in a prohibited area of an unincorporated area of a county."[90] These misdemeanors are punishable by up to six months in county jail, a maximum $1,000 fine, or both, unless you meet one of the applicable exceptions discussed in Chapter 7. You can be sentenced to one year in county jail, a maximum $1,000 fine, or both, if the unloaded "firearm that is not a handgun" and the ammunition for that firearm are in your immediate possession and you are not lawfully in possession of the firearm.[91]

---

[88] AB 7, 2017-2018 Leg. Council's Digest (2017), *available at* https://leginfo.legislature.ca.gov/faces/billCompare-Client.xhtml?bill_id=201720180AB7 (last visited Oct. 9, 2020); *see* P.C. § 26400.

[89] I discuss the definitions of "firearm" and "handgun" in Chapter 3.

[90] P.C. § 26400(a).

[91] P.C. § 26400(a), (b).

Each non-handgun carried unlawfully is chargeable as a separate offense. For example, if you are carrying two unloaded non-handguns unlawfully at the same time, you can be charged with two separate misdemeanors.⁹²

Table 6.5

Carrying "Firearms That Are Not Handguns" (P.C. § 26400)
Restrictions: You may be guilty of carrying an unloaded "firearm that is not a handgun" if you carry upon your person an unloaded "firearm that is not a handgun" outside of a vehicle while in an incorporated city or city and county *or* while in a public place or a public street in a prohibited area of a county's unincorporated area.
Penalty: Openly carrying an unloaded "firearm that is not a handgun" is a misdemeanor. But you can be sentenced to up to one year in county jail, a maximum $1,000 fine, or both, if the unloaded "firearm that is not a handgun" and ammunition for that firearm are in your immediate possession and you are not lawfully in possession of the firearm. Each non-handgun carried unlawfully is chargeable as a separate offense.
Things to Remember: Make sure you understand what a "firearm that is not a handgun" is. This generally includes such firearms as: rifles, shotguns, carbines, and those firearms that fit neither the handgun nor traditional long-gun definitions. But, this may be tricky when you are dealing with "antique firearms" (read Chapter 3 for more detail). Moreover, these provisions do not apply when you are carrying a "firearm that is not a handgun" in your vehicle. Other restrictions may apply, however.

VII. PLACES WHERE CARRY RESTRICTIONS APPLY

As explained above, California has numerous restrictions on carrying firearms, each of which has a slightly different description of where the restriction applies. Some of these distinctions are trivial while others are quite significant.

The concealed carry restriction applies to *handguns* inside vehicles and on your person, regardless of where you are, unless one of the exceptions discussed in Chapter 7 applies. The long-gun carry restriction applies only when outside of a vehicle while in an incorporated city or while in a public place or public street of a prohibited area within a county's unincorporated area.⁹³ The difference between an unincorporated area and an incorporated area is that an unincorporated area is not an official city, but is land that is generally governed by the county in which it lies.⁹⁴

While written somewhat differently, the restriction on carrying a loaded firearm and the one on carrying an unloaded handgun openly apply in the same places,

---

⁹² P.C. § 26400(d).

⁹³ For a list of incorporated cities within each county, visit: http://www.csac.counties.org/cities-within-each-county (last visited Oct. 9, 2020). This list is subject to change.

⁹⁴ This distinction is noteworthy, as demonstrated by the case of *People v. Knight*, 121 Cal. App. 4th 1568, 1573 (2004). In *Knight*, the prosecution failed to establish that the place where the defendant possessed a loaded firearm was in an incorporated city or prohibited area of unincorporated territory.

i.e., in any public place or on any public street in an incorporated city or in a "prohibited area" of unincorporated territory.[95] A "prohibited area" is "any place where it is unlawful to discharge a weapon."[96] This means that neither restriction applies in any part of an unincorporated territory where discharging a firearm is lawful. It is not always easy to determine what these areas are. When in doubt, assume it is a prohibited area to stay out of trouble. The same goes for determining what a "public place" and "public street" are for the purposes of these restrictions.

A. What Does "Public Place" Mean?

Although the Penal Code makes clear that it is generally illegal to carry a firearm, whether loaded or unloaded, in a "public place," it does not provide a definition of a "public place." Consequently, we must look elsewhere for an interpretation of what is considered a "public place." Many sources and laws define "public place" differently. For example, *Black's Law Dictionary*, a dictionary that lawyers use, defines "public place" as "[a]ny location that the local, state, or national government maintains for the use of the public, such as a highway, park, or public building."[97] A California Government Code section governing litter receptacles defines "public place" as "any area that is used or held out for the use of the public," whether publicly or privately owned or operated, not including indoor areas (*i.e.*, enclosed areas covered with a roof and protected from weather).[98]

P.C. section 653.20 (governing prostitution loitering), defines a "public place" as an area "open to the public, or an alley, plaza, park, driveway, or parking lot, or an automobile, whether moving or not, or a building open to the general public, including one which serves food or drink, or provides entertainment, or the doorways and entrances to a building or dwelling, or the grounds enclosing a building or dwelling."[99] P.C. section 647(f) (prohibiting public intoxication), includes an "area outside a home in which a stranger is able to walk without challenge" in its definition of a "public place."[100]

The closest thing to a definition for "public place" with respect to firearms is the one given for "*imitation* firearms," which is any "area open to the public" including streets, sidewalks, bridges, alleys, plazas, parks, driveways, front yards, parking lots, automobiles – whether moving or not – and buildings open to the general public, including those that serve food or drink, or provide entertainment, and the doorways and entrances to buildings or dwellings, including public schools and colleges

---

[95] *See* P.C. §§ 25850(a); 26350(a).
[96] P.C. § 17030.
[97] BLACK'S LAW DICTIONARY 1267 (8th ed. 2004).
[98] CAL. GOV'T CODE § 68055.1(a).
[99] *See* CAL. HEALTH & SAF. CODE § 11530(b) (governing drug activity loitering).
[100] *People v. Cruz*, 44 Cal. 4th 636, 674 (2008); *see People v. Olson*, 18 Cal. App. 3d 592, 598 (1971) (finding that the term "public" refers to areas that are "[c]ommon to all or many; general; open to common use" and "[o]pen to common, or general use, participation, [and] enjoyment.").

or universities.[101] Nonetheless, because this definition was provided for "imitation firearms" and not for real firearms, courts do not have to use this definition.

California courts also attempted to define the term "public place" with mixed results. Ultimately, "[w]hether a particular location is a 'public place' depends upon the facts of the individual case."[102] For example, market parking lots,[103] hospital parking lots,[104] barbershops,[105] and apartment complex driveways[106] can be "public places" due to their open access to the public.

And, as shown at the end of the Chapter, it is still a little uncertain whether every "public road" is a "public place" for purposes of applying California's restrictions on carrying loaded firearms.

But what is known for sure is that an area is *not* a "public place" just because it is exposed to public view. This means that your front yard is not necessarily a public place if it is not "open to common use"[107] or if you exclude the public. This would not be the case, though, with a privately-owned sidewalk where the public has an easement; or with walkways and driveways without fences, gates, etc.,[108] making them easily accessible to anyone, or if the public can access them "without challenge."[109]

In other words, even though your front yard, for instance, might be private property, it is likely a "public place" if the general public can walk across it to gain access to your front door.[110] It would be *unlikely*, however, for that same front yard

---

[101] P.C. § 20170(b).

[102] *See People v. White*, 227 Cal. App. 3d 886, 890-92 (1991) (in determining whether the defendant was in a "public place," the court took into account the fact that he was in his own front yard, the yard was surrounded by a three-and-a-half-foot-tall fence with a gate that could be locked, and the defendant had released his three dogs into the yard).

[103] *See People v. Vega*, 18 Cal. App. 3d 954, 958 (1971) (defendant unlawfully carried a loaded firearm in a "public place" by having a firearm in his vehicle, which was in the parking lot of a market. A "parking lot of a market, being accessible to members of the public having business with the market, is a public place.").

[104] *See People v. Green*, 15 Cal. App. 3d 766, 771 (1971) (providing that "[t]he [hospital] parking lot, being accessible to members of the public having business with the hospital, was a public place").

[105] *In re Zorn*, 59 Cal. 2d 650, 652 (1963) (defendant found to be in public while in a barbershop because "'public' has been defined as '[c]ommon to all or many; general; open to common use,' and '[o]pen to common, or general use, participation, enjoyment, etc.; as, a *public* place, tax, or meeting.'").

[106] *See generally People v. Overturf*, 64 Cal. App. 3d Supp. 1 (1976) (apartment complex manager was properly subject to criminal conviction for "carrying" a firearm onto his driveway).

[107] *See People v. White*, 227 Cal. App. 3d 886, 891-92 (1991) (appellant was *not* in a "public place" when found in his own front yard surrounded by a three-and-a-half-foot-tall fence with a closed but unlocked gate with three dogs in the yard; fence, closed gate, and dogs all provided challenge to public access, and the area was thus not "open to common use").

[108] *People v. Tapia*, 129 Cal. App. 4th 1153, 1160 (2005) (defendant was in a "public place" by standing on a sidewalk in front of his house, though the defendant argued his father owned the property in front of his house up to the curb including the sidewalk; the court held that "a sidewalk on an easement of way which has been granted to a public entity is not private property.").

[109] *People v. Krohn*, 149 Cal. App. 4th 1294, 1298-99 (2007) (defendant was *not* in a "public place" in the courtyard of his apartment complex because the complex was guarded by a fence and an automatically locked gate; the complex's rear parking lot was also guarded by an electric gate, thereby impeding public access to that area).

[110] *See, e.g., People v. Yarbrough*, 169 Cal. App. 4th 303, 318-19 (2008) (upholding a conviction for carrying a loaded firearm in the driveway of a private residence because it was "reasonably accessible to the public without a barrier").

to be considered a "public place" if it were blocked off by a 3½ foot fence with three dogs in the yard (or some other similar deterrent), as this would then be considered a "challenge to public access," even if the gate were unlocked.¹¹¹

B. What Does "Public Street" Mean?

Note that the Penal Code specifically uses the phrase "public street," as opposed to the term "public road" or "public highway," when restricting where you may carry a firearm.¹¹² And, as explained further below, some authorities, like the California Attorney General, thinks that this makes a significant difference.

But, as with the term "public place," the Penal Code does not define the term "public street." So, again, we must look elsewhere for an interpretation of what is considered a "public street." Many sources conflate streets, roads, and highways, but it appears that some sources agree that a "street" is a thoroughfare in a more urban setting whereas a "road" is a thoroughfare in a more rural setting. For example, *Black's Law Dictionary* defines "street" as "[a] *road* or public thoroughfare used for travel in an urban area, including the pavement, shoulders, gutters, curbs, and other areas within the street lines."¹¹³ The same source also appears to characterize "roads" as a kind of street outside of an urban setting. Therefore, a "street" is sometimes understood to be something within a city or municipality, while a "road" is to be found mainly outside of cities or towns:

> Strictly speaking, a 'street' is a public thoroughfare in an urban community such as a city, town, or village, and the term is not ordinarily applicable to roads and highways outside of municipalities. Although a street, in common parlance, is equivalent to a highway, it is usually specifically denominated by its own proper appellation.¹¹⁴

Merriam-Webster Dictionary similarly defines "street" as "a thoroughfare *especially in a city, town, or village* that is wider than an alley or lane and that usually includes sidewalk"¹¹⁵ while it defines "road" as "an open way for vehicles, persons, and animals; *especially one lying outside of an urban district*."¹¹⁶

Despite this distinction, some people may be confused by how the Penal Code states that "public streets" may be found in both incorporated and unincorporated

---

[111] *See, e.g., People v. White*, 227 Cal. App. 3d 886, 892 (1991).

[112] For instance, see the Sections above discussing loaded firearm restrictions under P.C. section 25850, the restriction against carrying an unloaded "firearm that is not a handgun" under P.C. section 26400, and the open carry of an unloaded handgun under P.C. section 26350.

[113] *Street*, BLACK'S LAW DICTIONARY (10th ed. 2014) (emphasis added).

[114] *Street*, BLACK'S LAW DICTIONARY (10th ed. 2014) (citing 39 Am. Jur. 2d Highways, Streets, and Bridges § 8, at 588–89 (1999)).

[115] *Street*, MERRIAM-WEBSTER ONLINE DICTIONARY, https://www.merriam-webster.com/dictionary/street (last visited Oct. 9, 2020) (emphasis added).

[116] *Road*, MERRIAM-WEBSTER ONLINE DICTIONARY, https://www.merriam-webster.com/dictionary/road (last visited Oct. 30, 2017) (emphasis added).

areas. Remember, though, that the difference between an incorporated area and an unincorporated area is that an unincorporated area is not an official city but is land that is generally governed by the county in which it lies.[117] So, the incorporated versus unincorporated distinction does not necessarily conflict with the general distinction between "public street" versus "public road," though it may certainly heighten people's confusion.

The issue of whether you are on a "public street" becomes significant if you are carrying a loaded firearm and want to determine whether you are on a "public street" or "public road." This is because the California Attorney General's Office concluded that California's restrictions on carrying a loaded firearm apply to those on a "public street" but not a "public road" in unincorporated territory that is not otherwise a "prohibited area."[118] The Attorney General's Office argues that because the prohibition on carrying firearms in unincorporated areas is "modified by the. . . concept, 'prohibited area,' mak[ing] 'public streets' synonymous with 'public roads and highways' would leave little meaningful difference between incorporated and unincorporated areas."[119] In reaching its decision, the Attorney General's Office appears to have applied the same reasoning as the above dictionaries.

The main difficulty for consumers and firearms owners is that it is not always easy to tell whether a thoroughfare is a street or a road, or where an incorporated street ends and an unincorporated road begins. Given this uncertainty, it may be better for you to assume that you are indeed in a place where California's restrictions on carrying a loaded firearm applies to you. For one thing, although California Attorney General opinions are afforded great weight, they are not binding on the courts.[120] In other words, a judge might still find that you are prohibited from carrying a loaded firearm even though you are indeed on a "public road." And secondly, the California Attorney General's opinion doesn't say whether or not a "public road or highway" is in fact a "public place" that triggers California's restriction against carrying a loaded firearm. Meanwhile, many California courts have held that "public streets, highways, and sidewalks" are in fact "public places" that trigger these restrictions.[121] This means that courts might be inclined to find that the "public road or highway" you are on is a "public place" that triggers the restrictions on carrying a loaded firearm.

In the end, it is very difficult to determine whether you are in an area that triggers California's restrictions on carrying a loaded firearm. Even prosecutors and law enforcement officers are confused by where exactly these restrictions ap-

---

[117] *See People v. Knight,* 121 Cal. App. 4th 1568, 1573 (2004).

[118] Opinion No. 68-175, 51 Ops. Cal. Atty. Gen. 197 (1968).

[119] Opinion No. 68-175, 51 Ops. Cal. Atty. Gen. 197 (1968).

[120] *See, e.g., Moore v. Panish,* 32 Cal.3d 535 (1982) (finding Attorney General interpretation of statutory provision at issue not persuasive).

[121] *People v. Strider,* 177 Cal. App. 4th 1393, 1401-02 (2009) (emphasis added) (citing *People v. Belanger,* 243 Cal. App.2d 654, 657-659 (1966)).

ply.¹²² When in doubt, you might want to assume that you are in an area triggering these restrictions.

---

[122] *See, e.g., People v. Knight*, 121 Cal.App.4th 1568, 1575-77 (2004) (overturning defendant's conviction for violating California's restriction on carrying loaded firearm after it was determined prosecutor failed to produce any evidence that defendant was carrying in an incorporated city or a prohibited area of an unincorporated territory).

CHAPTER 7:
FIREARM CARRY RESTRICTION EXEMPTIONS AND TRANSPORTING FIREARMS

As discussed in Chapter 6, California law generally prohibits carrying a concealed *handgun* anywhere, whether or not it is loaded,[1] and generally prohibits in most "public places": (1) openly carrying *unloaded* handguns;[2] (2) carrying *unloaded* "firearms that are not handguns" (long guns);[3] and (3) carrying loaded *firearms*.[4] This chapter explains each of the exemptions to these general restrictions.

I. HOW TO USE THIS SECTION

First, determine the type of conduct you would like to engage in. Would you like to carry a concealed handgun or a loaded firearm? How about openly carrying a handgun or "firearm that is not a handgun?" Maybe you would even like to engage in a combination of these activities, such as carrying a concealed and loaded handgun.

Next, determine whether that conduct is restricted under California law, and if so, whether there are any applicable exemptions. For example, you are restricted from carrying an unloaded "firearm that is not a handgun" (*e.g.*, a rifle) outside of a vehicle in an *incorporated* city or in a public place or a public street in a prohibited area of an unincorporated area of a county. If you wish to carry your rifle in an *unincorporated* area where you can discharge firearms, this restriction is not applicable, and therefore you do not need to meet an exemption. But, if the conduct you

---
[1] P.C. § 25400.
[2] P.C. § 26350.
[3] P.C. § 26400.
[4] P.C. § 25850(a). As explained in Chapter 6, the restrictions on carrying "concealed" handguns or "loaded" firearms also apply to "rockets" and related devices, including signal flares. Although the "loaded" carry exceptions discussed in this chapter generally apply to such devices, the "concealed" exceptions do not. It is unlawful to carry a concealed "rocket" or related device, even though such devices are not "firearms." But, if a rocket-launching device is unloaded, you can carry it openly.

wish to engage in is restricted – for example, if you want to carry your rifle openly in an *incorporated* city – then read below for any applicable exemptions.

If you want to engage in a combination of restricted activities, then each activity must meet an exemption. For example, if you are engaging in two kinds of "carrying" (*e.g.*, carrying concealed while carrying loaded) both activities must be covered by an exemption. Some of the most common exemptions are listed in the beginning of this chapter (*e.g.*, carrying in your residence, place of business, when you are in grave danger, and while camping and hunting). The other exemptions are arranged according to the respective carrying activity to which they apply. Carry licenses and special exemptions for current and retired law enforcement are also covered in this chapter.

As you read this chapter, keep in mind that you may still be subject to other restrictions depending on your location even though your conduct may fall under one of the carrying exemptions. For example, even if your conduct fits within one of the carry exemptions below, you may still be restricted from carrying a firearm in a government building (discussed in Chapter 8).

For your convenience, there is a table at the end of this chapter that boils down the varying exemptions to the carry restrictions that are discussed below. This table will help you sift through these exemptions, and hopefully provide you with a simple framework to determine the circumstances in which you may lawfully carry your firearm.

II. EXEMPTIONS TO THE GENERAL CARRY RESTRICTIONS IN NON-PUBLIC PLACES: RESIDENCES, PRIVATE PROPERTY, AND PRIVATE PLACES OF BUSINESS

A. Exemptions for Carrying Loaded Firearms and Openly Carrying Unloaded Handguns

Recall from Chapter 6 that California's restrictions on carrying loaded firearms and openly carrying unloaded handguns only apply in certain "*public places.*" Therefore, you may lawfully carry loaded firearms or openly carry unloaded handguns when you are not in a "public place."[5] In other words, if you are in or on a "non-public" place (*i.e.*, a place that does not fit the definition of "public place" as defined in Chapter 6), you are exempt from the restrictions on carrying loaded firearms

---

[5] Keep in mind, when you are in a place generally accessible by the public, it doesn't necessarily mean that you are illegally carrying a firearm in a "public place" as it is used in the statute. For example, if you are in an unincorporated territory, the restrictions will only apply if you are in a *prohibited area* (see Chapter 6). P.C. §§ 25850, 26350. Therefore, you can carry a loaded firearm or openly carry an unloaded handgun in a public place that is in an unincorporated territory and is not a "prohibited area."

or openly carrying unloaded handguns. These places can include your residence, certain private property, and certain private business locations.

But, if your private property or private business, or portions of your private property or private business, is located in a *"public place,"* then the carry restrictions will apply to these public places and your conduct must fall under one of the exemptions before you can lawfully carry a firearm in or on that private property or private business (discussed further below).

B. Exemptions for Carrying a Concealed Handgun

Unlike the restrictions discussed above, the restrictions on carrying *concealed* handguns are not limited to "public places." These restrictions apply in both "public" and "non-public places." In order to lawfully carry a concealed handgun, you must first meet an exemption.

One exemption to the general concealed carry restriction (and to the open carry of handgun restriction as well) is if you are carrying your concealed handgun in your residence, private property, or private place of business.[6] To meet the requirements of this exemption, you must first be able to establish that you have a "proprietary, possessory, or substantial ownership interest" in the residence, private property, or private place of business in which you wish to carry a concealed firearm or handgun.[7] To have a "possessory interest" in the property you must show two things:

(1) You have the right to exclude others from using it; *and,*

(2) You control activities that occur on it.[8]

If the residence, private property, or private business in which you wish to carry a concealed handgun meets this test and you are over the age of 18, a lawful U.S. citizen or resident, and are not otherwise prohibited by law from possessing firearms,[9] you may lawfully carry a concealed handgun in that place. And if your residence, private property, or private business is located in a "non-public place" then you may also carry the concealed handgun loaded (see above).

C. Exemptions for Carrying "Firearms That Are Not Handguns"

As with the restriction on carrying a concealed handgun, the restriction on carrying "firearms that are not handguns" applies in incorporated areas regardless of whether you are in or on a "public" or "non-public place." It also restricts the car-

---

[6] P.C. § 25605.
[7] *People v. Barela*, 234 Cal. App. 3d Supp. 15, 19-20 (1991).
[8] *People v. Barela*, 234 Cal. App. 3d Supp. 15, 20 (1991) (citing 1989 Cal. Legis. Serv. 2988-89 (West)).
[9] See Chapter 4 for prohibited persons.

rying of non-handguns in public places and public streets in a prohibited area of an unincorporated area of a county. But, there is an exemption to these restrictions when you are carrying such firearms in your residence, private property, or private business.[10] To meet this exemption you must have a "possessory interest" in the property, you must be over the age of 18 and a lawful U.S. citizen or resident, and you must not otherwise be prohibited from possessing firearms.[11]

You may also carry a "firearm that is not a handgun" in or on another person's residence, private property, or private place of business if you have the other person's permission.[12] Keep in mind, though, that the person giving permission must be able to meet the exemption themselves (*i.e.*, they must have a "possessory interest" in the property, be over the age of 18, etc.) in order to give you valid permission to carry your firearm on their property.

III. EXEMPTIONS TO THE GENERAL CARRY RESTRICTIONS IN PUBLIC PLACES

A. Temporary Residences and Campsites

"Temporary residences" and "campsites" in public places are treated differently than permanent residences. California law provides that you may *have* a loaded firearm, if otherwise lawful, while in or on a "temporary residence" or "campsite."[13] Although the law does not define either term, presumably this provision exempts people from the loaded restriction when lawfully residing in non-permanent shelters that are in a "public place" since people can generally *have* a loaded firearm in a non-public place.

But, it is unclear whether you can *carry* a loaded firearm in or on a "temporary residence" or "campsite" without a Carry License (discussed in Section VI) because case law currently distinguishes the terms "carry" and "have."[14] Remember, California law only provides that you may *have* a loaded firearm while you are in or on a "temporary residence" or "campsite", it does not say that you may *carry* one.

---

[10] P.C. § 26405(a).
[11] P.C. §§ 26405(a), 25605.
[12] P.C. § 26405(b).
[13] P.C. § 26055.
[14] *See People v. Overturf*, 64 Cal. App. 3d Supp. 1, 6 (1976) (holding where a statute only says it is lawful to "have" without mentioning "carry," then the statute does not allow "carrying" a loaded firearm). It is unlikely this distinction, to the extent it prohibits carrying a firearm in any manner within a "temporary residence," will be upheld as constitutional in the wake of *Heller* and *McDonald*. Although, it remains legally unsettled. *See* Chapter 2. The confusion surrounding this restriction is compounded when the question turns to the open carry of handguns and the carrying of "firearms that are not handguns." The exemption to the open carry of handguns restriction relevant here is P.C. section 26362, which allows for the open carrying of a handgun to the extent that person may openly *carry* a loaded handgun pursuant to Article 4 (commencing with section 26000) of Chapter 3. The above exemption for loaded carry is included in Article 4. But it appears a person cannot *carry* a loaded handgun and therefore a person couldn't carry a handgun openly. The same is true for the carrying of a "firearm that is not a handgun." P.C. § 26405(f).

It is also unclear whether you can carry a concealed firearm in either place since the exemption to the concealed carry restriction for residences does not expressly mention "temporary residences" or "campsites."[15] Of course, if the "temporary residence" is on private property that you own or lawfully possess, you can carry the firearm however you want.

But the agency or department governing the land you are camping on may have its own rules concerning firearms, so check with them before bringing your firearms on your camping trip.[16]

In 2014, a district court in Idaho held that a tent is akin to a home, meaning an individual has a Second Amendment right to carry a firearm while in his or her tent.[17] In that case, the court struck down an Army Corps of Engineers regulation[18] which barred the possession of a loaded firearm in recreation areas surrounding Corps' dams because it violated the Second Amendment.[19] The court reasoned that "[w]hile often temporary, a tent is more importantly a place – just like a home – where a person withdraws from public view, and seeks privacy and security for himself and perhaps also for his family and/or his property."[20] Therefore, the court held that because an individual has a Second Amendment right to carry a firearm in his or her home, the individual can likewise carry it in his or her tent. Moreover, the court also struck down the Corps' regulation because it prohibited individuals from carrying firearms outside their tents for self-defense purposes.[21] This case was appealed to the Ninth Circuit, but, at the request of both parties, oral arguments have been canceled and the case has been referred to the 9th Circuit's mediation program. As a result, the Army Corps of Engineers is reconsidering its firearms policy, and it will work with the plaintiffs to settle the matter outside of court. While this decision sheds some light on the issue of whether you have a right to carry a firearm in a "temporary residence" like a tent, it remains to be seen how it will be treated by California courts and whether it will impact California's carry restrictions.

B. Business or Other Privately Owned or Possessed Property Open to the Public

You may *carry* an *unloaded* firearm, concealed or openly, in your business if you are age 18 or older, you are a lawful U.S. citizen or resident, and you are not oth-

---

[15] *See* P.C. § 25605(a). There is an exemption for carrying concealed, but that relates only to transporting a firearm (in a locked container) when going to or from a lawful camping activity. P.C. § 25550 (discussed below).
[16] P.C. § 25550(b). *See also* Chapter 8.
[17] *See Morris v. U.S. Army Corps of Engineers*, 990 F. Supp. 2d 1082 (D. Id. 2014).
[18] 36 C.F.R. § 237.13.
[19] *Morris v. U.S. Army Corps of Engineers*, 990 F. Supp. 2d 1082 (D. Id. 2014).
[20] *Morris v. U.S. Army Corps of Engineers*, 990 F. Supp. 2d 1082 (D. Id. 2014).
[21] *Morris v. U.S. Army Corps of Engineers*, 990 F. Supp. 2d 1082 (D. Id. 2014).

erwise prohibited from possessing firearms.[22] But it is unclear whether you can *carry* a *loaded* firearm within your business if it is located in a "public place." This is because the exemption that allows for concealed carry at one's business does not mention the loaded restriction, which applies in "public places."

Individuals engaged in a lawful business (or nonprofit organization) operating from a "public place" where the loaded restriction applies (see Chapter 6 for examples) may nevertheless *have* (as opposed to carry) a loaded firearm in their business if it is for lawful purposes connected with that business, as may their authorized agents or employees.[23] For the reasons discussed above concerning carrying at a "temporary residence" or "campsite," this means you can lawfully *have* a loaded firearm at your business, but you cannot necessarily *carry* a loaded firearm there. The distinction between "having" and "carrying" a firearm is especially blurred if you conduct your business, or reside in, a moving vehicle or boat, as discussed below.

The same exemptions that apply to a firearm lawfully possessed within your place of business generally apply to firearms on your other privately owned or possessed property, which vary depending on whether they are located in a "public place."[24] Moreover, there is arguably stronger Second Amendment protection on private property, depending on the circumstances.

C. Vehicle or Boat as a Residence

While being driven, motor homes are generally treated like "motor vehicles," meaning you must keep your firearm like you would in a vehicle (discussed in Section III(E) of this Chapter). While "camping" in a motor home, it *might* be treated like a "temporary residence" or "campsite," meaning you can *have* a loaded firearm in it.[25] Unfortunately, since "temporary residence" and "campsite" are undefined terms, this is another legal "gray area," so how a motor home is treated for purposes of firearm possession may depend on how you are using it at the time.[26] If you are prosecuted for having a loaded firearm in your motor home, the issue will likely be whether you were at a "temporary residence" or "campsite."

If you are at an established campground with your motor home "hooked up," it should qualify as a "temporary residence" or "campsite" and you should be able to keep your firearms like you would in your home. This means you may *have* a firearm in a motorhome while it is "hooked up." But, it is unclear whether you can *carry* them on your person, especially concealed (as discussed above). Moreover,

---

[22] P.C. §§ 26405(a), 25605(a).
[23] P.C. § 26035.
[24] P.C. §§ 25605(a), 26035.
[25] P.C. § 26055.
[26] *See Garber v. Superior Court*, 184 Cal. App. 4th 724 (2010), *modified by* No. 045632, 2010 Cal. App. Lexis 740 (May 25, 2010) (holding at the time of violating the concealed and loaded restrictions, appellant was not using his mobile home for residential purposes, though it was parked, and thus was not entitled to a "place of residence" defense).

if you pull into a rest stop to sleep for a few hours, you may not qualify for this exemption because it may not be seen as a "temporary residence" or "campsite." Public campgrounds may also impose other firearm restrictions, so check the rules beforehand.

The law is unclear with respect to boats, but it is reasonable to assume that if the boat is designed to be lived on, like a house boat, it should be treated similarly to a motor home. This means if a boat that is designed to be lived on is moored, the same firearms laws that apply to one's residence should apply to the boat. But, if the boat is motoring through "internal waters" like a marina (see Chapter 8), firearms should be kept as if they are being transported in a vehicle (explained below). Licensed fishermen may be exempt from the concealed carry restriction (see Section IV).

Although the concealed and loaded restrictions also apply to rockets and related devices, including signal flares, it is lawful to store a rocket, rocket-propelled projectile launcher, or similar device designed primarily for emergency signaling purposes on a boat.[27]

D. Vehicle or Boat as a Place of Business

If your vehicle is also your place of business, depending on the type of business, you may have a loaded and concealed firearm in your vehicle. In one case, a taxi driver possessed a loaded pistol on the floorboard of his leased taxicab. Although he kept it in the vehicle for self-defense, he did not have a Carry License (discussed below). The court concluded that although he was in his taxi cab, he possessed the firearm in his "place of business" and therefore met an exemption to the concealed and loaded restrictions.[28] On the other hand, another court held that a bounty hunter carrying a loaded and concealed firearm in his glove compartment did *not* meet this exemption because, although he was often in a car for his work, the car itself was not his "place of business."[29]

The same rules about vehicles operating as your "place of business" also presumably apply to boats.

E. Motor Vehicles

A person who is over the age of 18 and is not prohibited from possessing firearms may carry an *unloaded*, concealed handgun inside a motor vehicle that is in a "public place" when it is in an appropriate "locked container" or while being carried *directly* to or from a motor vehicle in such a container "for any lawful purpose."[30]

---

[27] P.C. § 26060.
[28] *People v. Marotta*, 128 Cal. App. 3d Supp. 1 (1981).
[29] *People v. Wooten*, 168 Cal. App. 3d 168 (1985).
[30] P.C. § 25610(a).

1. Locked Container Requirement

Firearm owners most often get in trouble when transporting firearms inside, or to and from, their vehicles in an unlawful manner. The most common mistake that people make is not storing their handguns in a proper "locked container," which is required for the transportation exemption to the concealed carry prohibition to apply.

Example of a hard case

For purposes of this exemption, a "'locked container' means a secure container that is fully enclosed and locked by a padlock, key lock, combination lock, or similar locking device."[31] A "locked container" also includes a lockable trunk of a vehicle but does not include a vehicle's "utility or glove compartment," even if it is locked.[32]

The law does not define "utility compartment." Therefore, handguns should not be transported in a vehicle's center console or in the storage area behind the rear seat in most "hatchback" type automobiles because these areas may not be considered "utility compartments." Also, it is not advised to use the various storage compartments found in today's popular sport utility vehicles. Further, while most of us would consider a cross-bed toolbox in a pickup truck to be the functional equivalent to a vehicle's trunk, particularly if there is no access to the cab of the pickup, it too might be considered a "utility compartment" where a firearm could not be legally stored. To be safe, carry the gun in a locked container inside the tool box because this is still a "gray area."

Even if your vehicle has a trunk, you should still use an appropriate "locked container" (*i.e.*, fully enclosed and locked by a padlock, key lock, combination lock, or similar locking device) that is solely for transporting your handgun. Otherwise, if you need to open the trunk or unlock the container to retrieve a separate item from it, the container could then be considered "unlocked" – arguably violating the concealed and/or open carry restrictions.[33]

Example of a lock to a hard case

Whether you have a handgun in a vehicle, or are carrying one directly to or from a vehicle, hard cases that can be locked, when used correctly, are the best way to be sure you are complying with California law. The law does not specifically require the container to be hard-sided, but you will be more likely to avoid questions or concerns from law enforcement if it is.

For example, you may be able to comply with California law if you transport your handgun inside of a TITAN Gun Vault. A TITAN Gun Vault is a handgun safe that can be installed in the center counsel of a vehicle or under the driver's seat.[34]

---

[31] P.C. § 16850.

[32] P.C. § 25610(a)(1).

[33] P.C. §§ 25400, 26350.

[34] *See* TITAN SECURITY PRODUCT, INC. TITAN GUN SAFE/VAULT (2006), http://ethostactical.com/wp-content/uploads/2017/02/Titan_Gun_Safe_Owners_Manual_Revised_JUL_2016.pdf (last visited Oct. 10, 2020).

This safe utilizes a combination locking mechanism that requires users to push a sequence of buttons in order to open the safe.[35] Given that the TITAN Gun vault is a fully enclosed safe that uses a combination lock, it meets the definition of a "locked container" for purposes of California law. Therefore, a person could comply with the "locked container" requirement if they transported their handgun inside a TITAN Gun Vault, as long as the handgun is kept unloaded.[36]

2. "Lawful Purpose" Requirement

It is unclear what is considered a "lawful purpose" for carrying an unloaded, concealed handgun in a "locked container" inside, and to and from, a motor vehicle. Possibly the term is referring *exclusively* to the locations and activities listed in P.C. sections 25510-25595. For the unloaded-and-locked-transportation exemption to apply, "the course of travel shall include only those deviations between authorized locations as are reasonably necessary under the circumstances."[37] The only "locations" that seem to be "authorized" are those listed in P.C. sections 25510-25595. This means that when you are outside of a vehicle, you are likely only exempt from the concealed carry restriction when transporting an unloaded handgun in a locked container *directly* to or from one of those locations.

To qualify for the exemption to have a concealed handgun when you are *inside* your vehicle, there is some debate over whether you must be directly transporting it to or from one of the locations or activities listed in P.C. sections 25510-25595. But the exemption's plain language supports the interpretation that you *can* keep an *unloaded* handgun in a locked container in a vehicle *at all times*, regardless of your destination.[38] This means you do not need to be on the way to the shooting range, hunting, or any other firearm-related "lawful purpose." You are allowed to leave your *unloaded* handgun in a "locked container" in your vehicle at all times as long as you are not in a prohibited area. This includes when you leave the vehicle "unattended" (see Chapter 5). Although this interpretation appears accurate, this practice is risky because law enforcement officers may be unaware that it is legal or have a different point of view of its legality.

---

[35] *See* TITAN SECURITY PRODUCT, INC. TITAN GUN SAFE/VAULT (2006), http://ethostactical.com/wp-content/uploads/2017/02/Titan_Gun_Safe_Owners_Manual_Revised_JUL_2016.pdf (last visited Oct. 10, 2020).

[36] Some gun owners who have bought and installed TITAN Gun Vaults inside of their vehicles have also attached a TITAN Ammo Box to the gun safe. TITAN Ammo Box is a separate locked container that can be installed on the outside of the TITAN Gun Vault. This device allows you to store you unloaded handgun and magazines in separate storage containers. Because of the close proximity of the ammunition to the handgun, some law enforcement have wrongfully arrested people for carrying "loaded" handguns when magazines and ammunition were kept in the TITAN Ammo Box. Yet, as long as the handgun is kept unloaded inside the gun vault and the ammunition is kept ammo box, then the handgun is likely not considered "loaded" under California law because, when locked in the ammo box, the ammunition is not in a position where it can be fired or where it is "ready for firing." *See People v. Clark*, 45 Cal. App. 4th 1147, 1154 (1996). For more information on when a firearm is considered "loaded," see Chapter 6.

[37] P.C. § 25505.

[38] P.C. § 25610(a). **WARNING:** This is subject to a few limitations including school grounds, P.C. § 626.9, playgrounds and youth centers, P.C. § 626.95, and others (see Chapter 8). This is not an exhaustive list of limitations, however, and you should always be sure to consult local county and city laws.

3. Transporting "Assault Weapons" and .50 BMG Rifles in Motor Vehicles

Generally, a person can transport a lawfully registered "assault weapon" or .50 BMG rifle between:

(1) Their residence, place of business, or other property he or she owns, or on property owned by another with the owner's express permission;

(2) A target range of a public or private club or organization organized for the purpose of practice shooting at targets;

(3) A target range that holds a regulatory or business license for the purpose of practicing shooting at that target range;

(4) A shooting club that is licensed pursuant to the Fish & Game Code;

(5) Any exhibition, display, or educational project that is about firearms and that is sponsored by, conduct under the auspices of, or approved by a law enforcement agency or a nationally recognized entity that fosters proficiency in, or promotes education about, firearms; *and,*

(6) Any licensed firearms dealer who possesses a Dangerous Weapons Permit (DWP), for servicing or repair pursuant to P.C. section 31050 (exemption to restriction on possessing "assault weapon" for service or repair by licensed firearms dealer who possesses a valid DWP).[39]

When being transported between any of the places mentioned above, "assault weapons" and .50 BMG rifles must be transported in a "locked container" or in the locked trunk of the vehicle.[40]

F. Motorcycles and Bicycles

The law is unclear about how unloaded handguns are to be transported on motorcycles or bicycles. While a motorcycle is a "motor vehicle," the exemption requires that the handgun be "within" the vehicle. Generally, that is not possible with a motorcycle. While some motorcycles have lockable luggage boxes, keeping a handgun in one may be problematic. Although keeping a handgun in a lockable luggage box is arguably keeping it "within" a vehicle or in a "locked container," it could alternatively be considered a "utility compartment" because it is accessible and within the driver's reach (though not safely while operating the motorcycle), thereby taking it out of the definition of "locked container."

 Until the law is clearly interpreted, motorcyclists should be particularly careful when transporting firearms in a lockable luggage box of a motorcycle. If you chose to transport firearms while you are on a motorcycle, I suggest you have the unloaded handgun in a separate "locked container" inside the motorcycle's luggage box or a rider's backpack.

---

[39] P.C. § 30945.
[40] P.C. § 30945(g).

CHAPTER 7: FIREARM CARRY RESTRICTION EXEMPTIONS AND TRANSPORTING FIREARMS | 271

These issues are even more important for bicyclists because the exemptions for motor vehicle transportation do not specifically apply to bicycles.[41] Therefore, it is advised that bicyclists comply with the laws for transporting firearms on foot when riding on a bicycle. Generally, these laws require that the handgun be unloaded and in a "locked container" and that the course of travel be to or from the locations and activities listed in P.C. sections 25510-25595, with only reasonably necessary deviations.

As for transporting "firearms that are not handguns," whether on a motorcycle or a bicycle, such firearms must be unloaded and should be "encased" as explained below.

G. Boats

Although the law is unclear, as explained above, it is reasonable to assume boats are treated like motor homes. This means they will probably be treated either like a residence (see Section III(C)) or a vehicle, depending on how the boat is being used at the time.[42]

H. Being in "Grave Danger"

Despite the limitations on carrying loaded firearms in "public places," if you are considered to be in "grave danger," you may fall under an exemption to the carry restrictions.[43]

1. Protected by a Restraining Order

You may lawfully carry a *loaded* firearm *openly* or *concealed* if you reasonably believe you are "in grave danger because of circumstances forming the basis of a current restraining order" issued against someone who has been found to pose a threat to your safety.[44] This is only an affirmative defense to the crime of carrying a loaded firearm openly or concealed. It is a factual consideration for the prosecutor, judge, or jury to determine whether you really were in "grave danger" at the time you were carrying a loaded firearm. But this defense may not apply if there is a mutual restraining order in place against you.[45]

---

[41] P.C. § 25610.
[42] See Chapter 8 for more on firearm possession and use on boats. As previously explained, signal flares, though considered firearms, are exempt on boats. P.C. § 26060.
[43] P.C. § 26045.
[44] P.C. §§ 25600; 26045(b), (d); 26405(d); 26362.
[45] P.C. §§ 25600; 26045(b), (d); 26405(d); 26362.

2. Not Protected by a Restraining Order

If no restraining order exists but you still reasonably believe you or someone else is in "immediate" "grave danger" of being attacked, you are allowed to carry a firearm, loaded or unloaded, *openly*, but *not concealed*.[46] For purposes of this exemption, "immediate" means "the brief interval before and after the local law enforcement agency, when reasonably possible, has been notified of the danger and before the arrival of its assistance."[47]

In other words, it is the brief time between law enforcement being notified of the danger and their arrival. So, this is a rather limited exemption. As with the restraining order exemption, this is only an affirmative defense. And in addition to whether you were in "grave danger," the prosecutor, judge, or jury will determine whether the carrying was done while the danger was "immediate." This exemption does not expressly extend to carrying *unloaded* "firearms that are not handguns."

IV. CARRYING WHILE HUNTING OR FISHING

The laws and regulations surrounding hunting are so numerous and complex that a whole book would be necessary to completely cover this subject. This book does not go into much detail about hunting laws.[48] Nevertheless, because there are specific rules for carrying firearms in connection with hunting, they will be addressed here.

A licensed hunter while engaged in hunting or while transporting a firearm when going to, or returning from, a hunting expedition is exempt from the restrictions on carrying concealed handguns, openly carrying unloaded handguns, and carrying unloaded "firearms that are not handguns."[49] Licensed fishermen who are fishing, or going to or returning from a fishing expedition, are only exempt from the carrying concealed restrictions.[50]

A licensed hunter is exempt from the restriction on openly carrying an unloaded handgun or unloaded "firearm that is not a handgun" while he or she is training a dog for use in hunting (as long as that type of hunting is not prohibited by law) or while transporting the firearm to and from that training.[51] But licensed hunters are not exempt from the restriction carrying a concealed handgun.[52]

Remember from Chapter 6 that the concealed carry restrictions are in force everywhere unless an exemption applies. Meanwhile, restrictions on open carry,

---

[46] P.C. §§ 26045(a), 26362.
[47] P.C. § 26045(c).
[48] If you are interested in the subject, the California Department of Fish and Wildlife provides information on its website at https://www.wildlife.ca.gov/ (last visited Oct. 10, 2020).
[49] P.C. §§ 25640, 26366, 26405(j).
[50] P.C. § 25640.
[51] P.C. §§ 26405(a-f), 26366.5.
[52] P.C. § 26366.5.

loaded carry, and carrying a "firearm that is not a handgun" are generally not in force where hunting – or to a lesser extent fishing – is allowed because these places are generally in unincorporated areas where it is lawful to discharge a firearm (*i.e.*, they are not restricted "public places"). Otherwise, it would not be legal to hunt there in the first place.

This is why there are no provisions generally exempting hunters from the *loaded* firearm restriction. Individuals who are lawfully hunting outside city limits are, by definition, in places where the loaded firearm restriction does not apply in the first place.[53] There is, however, a provision specifically exempting individuals who are hunting within city limits in an area where the city council has not made hunting illegal.[54] Similarly, members of shooting clubs while hunting on the premises of those clubs are exempt from the loaded firearm restriction.[55]

Also, the loaded firearm restriction does not prohibit storing a rocket, rocket-propelled projectile launcher, or similar device designed primarily for emergency signaling purposes on any vessel or aircraft, carrying one in a permitted hunting area, or while traveling to or from a hunting area with a valid California hunting license.[56]

Beware: the exemptions discussed in this section are general ones. The California Fish & Game Code, and its accompanying regulations, contains an enormous number of very specific carry restrictions in very specific areas of the state, mostly state land set aside for hunting or preservation and federal restrictions may apply. For a more detailed discussion on these restrictions, see Chapter 8.

V. ADDITIONAL EXEMPTIONS TO THE GENERAL CARRY RESTRICTIONS

The exemptions discussed above cover the most common persons, places, and activities exempt from the general carry restrictions. There are many others that address more specific scenarios.

A. Exemptions for Carrying Concealed Handguns

The law divides the exemptions for carrying concealed handguns into three categories: Conditional Exemptions,[57] "Other Exemptions" (some of which apply specifically to peace officers),[58] and Peace Officer Exemptions (discussed in Section VI).[59]

---

[53] See Chapter 6.
[54] P.C. § 26040.
[55] P.C. § 26005.
[56] P.C. § 26060.
[57] P.C. §§ 25505-25595.
[58] P.C. §§ 25600-25655.
[59] P.C. §§ 25450-25475.

1. Conditional Exemptions for Carrying Concealed Handguns

Some of the conditional exemptions involve the transportation of handguns while others discuss the transportation and possession of handguns for a specific activity. The Penal Code labels these exemptions "conditional" because they are subject to or dependent on a particular condition. As discussed above, in order to be exempt from the concealed carry restriction while transporting a handgun, it must be "unloaded and kept in a locked container, and the course of travel [should] include only those deviations between authorized locations as are reasonably necessary under the circumstances."[60]

The following are conditionally exempted activities from the concealed carry restriction:

Table 7.1

Statute	Exempted Activity
P.C. § 25510(a)	Possession of a handgun by an authorized participant in a motion picture, television, or video production, or an entertainment event, when the participant lawfully uses the firearm as part of that production or event, or while going directly to or coming directly from the production or event.
P.C. § 25510(b)	Transportation of a handgun by an authorized employee or agent of a supplier of firearms while going directly to or coming directly from a motion picture, television, video production, or entertainment event for the purpose of providing the handgun to an authorized participant to lawfully use as part of that production or event.
P.C. § 25515	Possession of a handgun in a locked container by a member of any club or organization whose purpose is lawfully collecting or displaying firearms while that member is at the organization's meetings, or while going directly to or coming directly from a meeting of the club or organization.
P.C. § 25520	Transportation of a handgun by a participant going directly to or coming directly from a recognized safety or hunter safety class or sporting event involving the handgun.
P.C. § 25525(a)	Transportation of a handgun by a citizen of the U.S. or legal resident over the age of 18 who resides in or is temporarily within California, and who is not prohibited from possessing firearms under California law, when transported directly between the individual's residence, business, or other private property he or she owns or lawfully possesses.
P.C. § 25525(b)	Transportation of a handgun by a citizen of the U.S. or legal resident over the age of 18 who resides in or is temporarily within California, and who is not prohibited from possessing firearms under California law, when going from a place where the individual lawfully received the handgun to his or her residence, business, or other private property he or she owns or lawfully possesses.
P.C. § 25530	Transportation of a handgun by an individual going directly to or coming directly from a fixed place of business or private residence for the purpose of lawfully repairing, transferring, selling, or loaning that handgun.
P.C. § 25535(a)	Transportation of a handgun by an individual going directly to or coming directly from a gun show, swap meet, or similar public event where the public is invited, for the purpose of displaying that a handgun in a lawful manner.

---

[60] P.C. § 25505.

CHAPTER 7: FIREARM CARRY RESTRICTION EXEMPTIONS AND TRANSPORTING FIREARMS | 275

Statute	Exempted Activity
P.C. § 25535(b)	Transportation of a handgun by an individual going directly to or coming directly from a gun show or similar event, as defined under federal law, to lawfully transfer, sell, or loan that handgun to a private party using a Federal Firearms License (FFL).
P.C. § 25540	Transportation of a handgun by an individual going directly to or coming directly from a licensed target range for practicing shooting targets with that handgun.
P.C. § 25545	Transportation of a handgun by an individual going directly to or coming directly from a licensing agency authorized to issue Carry Licenses, when done at the request of the issuing agency so that the agency can determine whether the license should be issued to that individual to carry that firearm.
P.C. § 25550(a)	Transportation of a handgun by an individual going directly to or coming directly from lawful camping activities for purposes of having a handgun available for lawful personal protection while at the campsite.
P.C. § 25555	Transportation of a handgun by an individual for a lawful transfer of that handgun to an immediate family member by gift, bequest, intestate succession, or by operation of law.
P.C. § 25560	Transportation of a handgun by an individual exempt from using an FFL for firearm transfers or registering firearm acquisitions, ownership, or disposal to report that to the California Department of Justice (DOJ) as it relates to the handgun being transported.
P.C. § 25565	Transportation of a handgun by an individual in order to sell, deliver or transfer that handgun to an authorized representative of a city, city and county, or state or federal government that is acquiring the handgun as part of an authorized, voluntary gun buy-back event.
P.C. § 25570	Transportation of a firearm by an individual who finds a firearm in order to deliver the found firearm to the police or restore it to its owner, and if transporting the handgun to a law enforcement agency, the individual gives prior notice to the law enforcement agency that he or she is transporting the handgun there OR Transportation of a firearm by a person who took the firearm from a person committing a crime against them and is transporting it to a law enforcement agency provided the law enforcement agency is given notice.
P.C. § 25575	Transportation of a handgun by an individual in order to comply with the personal handgun importer requirements of P.C. section 27560 as it pertains to that firearm.
P.C. § 25580	Transportation of a lawfully obtained "curio or relic"[61] handgun into California by a federally licensed "curio or relic" collector[62] whose licensed premises in California.
P.C. § 25585	Transportation of a handgun by an individual for the purpose of obtaining an identification number or mark assigned to that handgun from DOJ.
P.C. § 25590	Transportation of a handgun by an individual if done directly between any of the following: (1) A place where that individual may carry that firearm concealed pursuant to an exemption to the concealed carry restriction. (2) A place where that individual may carry that firearm loaded, either pursuant to an exemption to the loaded carry restriction or when that restriction does not apply. (3) A place where that individual may openly carry a firearm pursuant to an exemption to the open carry restriction or when that restriction does not apply.

These transportation provisions do "not prohibit or limit the otherwise lawful carrying or transportation of any handgun in accordance with the provisions listed in [P.C.] Section 16580."[63] As mentioned in Chapter 2, most of the Penal Code sections concerning firearms were renumbered in 2012. P.C. section 16580 explains which newly renumbered sections are continuations of statutes under the previous numbering system. So, the statute quoted directly above referencing section 16580 is a clarification that the legislature did not intend to go beyond its express limitations on transporting firearms that were in place at the time of the renumbering.

2. "Other Exemptions" for Carrying Concealed Handguns

Some of the more commonly utilized "other exemptions," such as carrying while in a home, in a business, and on private property, are discussed above. The "other exemptions" listed below also exclude the following activities and/or persons from the restriction on carrying concealed handguns, even if the handgun is *not* in a "locked container":

Table 7.2

STATUTE	EXEMPTED ACTIVITY
P.C. § 25615	Possession or transportation of unloaded handguns as merchandise by those who are licensed to manufacture, import, wholesale, repair, or deal in firearms (or their agents) while engaged in the lawful course of business.
P.C. § 25620	U.S. military members when on duty or any members of organizations legally allowed to purchase or receive firearms from the U.S. or California.
P.C. § 25625	Military or civil organization members who possess or transport a handgun while parading or transporting to or from the meeting places of these organizations.
P.C. § 25630	Guards or messengers of common carriers, banks, and other financial institutions employed in and about the shipment, transportation, or delivery of valuable items.
P.C. § 25635	Possession and transportation of handguns by members of organizations whose purpose is to practice shooting targets with handguns at established ranges.
P.C. § 25645	Transportation of unloaded handguns by licensed common carriers or their authorized agents or employees, when transported according to federal law.
P.C. § 25655	An individual with a Carry License.

B. Exemptions for Carrying Loaded Firearms

Remember that the crime of carrying a loaded firearm requires that the carrying occurs in a "public place." The following persons, places, and activities are exempt from the general loaded firearm restriction:

---

[61] As defined in 27 C.F.R. section 478.11.
[62] See 18 U.S.C. section 921 and related regulations.
[63] P.C. § 25595.

Table 7.3

Statute	Exemptions
P.C. § 26000	State or U.S. military members engaged in the performance of their duties.
P.C. § 26005	Individuals who are using target ranges for the purpose of practice shooting and members of shooting clubs while hunting on the club's premises.
P.C. § 26010	An individual with a Carry License.
P.C. § 26015	Armored vehicle guards, as defined by the Cal. Bus. & Prof. Code section 7582.1(d), while acting in the course and scope of their employment (1) If hired before January 1, 1977; or (2) If hired on or after January 1, 1977, if they have received a firearms qualification card from the Department of Consumer Affairs.
P.C. § 26020	Honorably retired federal officers or agents of any federal law enforcement agency, including but not limited to the Federal Bureau of Investigation, the United States Secret Service, the United States Customs Services, the Federal Bureau of Alcohol, Tobacco, Firearms, and Explosives, the Federal Bureau of Narcotics, the United States Drug Enforcement Administration, the United States Border Patrol, and any officer or agent of the Internal Revenue Service who was authorized to carry weapons while on duty, who was assigned to duty within the state for a period of at least one year, or who retired from active service in the state, who have approval of the sheriff of the county in which the retiree resides.
P.C. § 26025	Any of the following who have completed a regular course in firearms training approved by the Commission on Peace Officer Standards and Training (POST): (1) Patrol special police officers appointed by the police commission of any city, county, or city and county under the express terms of its charter who also, under the express terms of the charter, are subject to suspension or dismissal after hearing on charges duly filed with the commission after a fair and impartial trial, they are between the ages of 18 and 40, they possess physical qualification proscribed by the Commission, and they are designated by the Commission as the owners of a certain beat or territory; and (2) Certain animal control officers or zookeepers, while acting in the course and scope of their duties; and (3) Persons authorized to carry weapons under California Corporations Code section 14502, while actually engaged in the performance of their duties; and (4) Harbor police officers designated pursuant to California Harbors and Navigation Code section 663.5.
P.C. § 26030	Certain guards, messengers of common carriers, banks, and other financial institutions, private investigators and their employees, uniformed patrol operators, uniformed security guards, and alarm company operators, listed in P.C. section 26030(a)(1)-(10), with a certificate from the Department of Consumer Affairs confirming the person successfully completed the required courses per P.C. section 26030(d). Peace officers generally do not need such a certificate to carry a firearm for off-duty employment purposes per P.C. section 26030(c).
P.C. § 26035	Having a loaded firearm in a lawful business (discussed above).
P.C. § 26040	Carrying a loaded firearm while hunting (discussed above).
P.C. § 26045	Carrying a loaded firearm while in "grave danger" (discussed above).
P.C. § 26050	Individuals making or trying to make a lawful arrest.
P.C. § 26055	Having a loaded firearm at your place of residence, including temporary residences or campsites (discussed above).

STATUTE	EXEMPTIONS
P.C. § 26060	Storing a rocket, rocket-propelled projectile launcher, or similar device, such as a flare gun designed primarily for emergency signaling purposes on any vessel or aircraft, or possessing such a device while in a permitted hunting area or transporting to or from the area while carrying a valid California permit or license to hunt.

C. Exemptions to the Restriction on Openly Carrying Handguns in Public

There are many exemptions to the general ban on openly carrying an unloaded handgun. Some exemptions are to the entire restriction (*i.e.*, carrying both on your person and in/on a vehicle), while other exemptions only apply to carrying handguns on your person.

The following people and activities are exempt from the restriction on openly carrying handguns *in public*:

Table 7.4

STATUTE	EXEMPTION
P.C. § 26362	Individuals who meet the exemptions to carrying *loaded* handguns under P.C. sections 26000-26060 (these are exceptions for carrying a loaded firearm discussed in Table 7.3).
P.C. § 26363	Possession or transportation of handguns as merchandise by those who are licensed to manufacture, import, wholesale, repair, or deal in firearms (or their agents) while lawfully engaged in their business.
P.C. § 26364	Duly authorized military or civil organizations, or members thereof, possessing a handgun while parading or while rehearsing or practicing parading at the organization's meeting place.
P.C. § 26367	Transportation of handguns by licensed common carriers or their authorized agent or employee, when transported according to federal law.
P.C. § 26368	Members of organizations chartered by the U.S. Congress or nonprofit mutual or public benefit corporations meeting the nonprofit tax-exempt organization requirements while on official parade duty, during ceremonial occasions or while rehearsing or practicing for these events.
P.C. § 26370	Individuals in school zones as defined in P.C. section 626.9, provided that their carrying of the firearm meets an exception to the Gun-Free School Zone restriction (P.C. § 626.9). (See Chapter 8).
P.C. § 26371	Individuals acting in accordance with P.C. section 171b exemptions concerning possessing weapons in state or local public buildings/meetings (see Chapter 8).
P.C. § 26372	Individuals making or trying to make a lawful arrest.
P.C. § 26373	When a handgun is being loaned, sold, or transferred according to California law (P.C. sections 27500-27590) or under an exception to the requirement that a firearm must be transferred through a licensed firearm dealer between private parties, as long as the handgun is on private property with the property owner's permission.
P.C. § 26374	Individuals engaged in firearm-related activities, while on business premises licensed to conduct activities related to firearm sales, manufacturing, repairs, transfers, pawning, or use/training.

CHAPTER 7: FIREARM CARRY RESTRICTION EXEMPTIONS AND TRANSPORTING FIREARMS | 279

Statute	Exemption
P.C. § 26375	Authorized employees or agents of a firearm supplier for, or participants in, a motion picture, television, video production, or entertainment event when they lawfully use firearms as part of that production or event.
P.C. § 26378	Individuals summoned and assisting a peace officer in making an arrest or preserving the peace.
P.C. § 26380	Individuals carrying a handgun incident to and during sworn peace officer training as part of a Peace Officer Standards and Training (POST) course.
P.C. § 26381	Individuals carrying incident to and during the training course required to obtain a Carry License (P.C. sections 26150-26225) with permission from the person authorized to issue it.
P.C. § 26382	Individuals carrying incident to and at the request of a sheriff, police chief, or other municipal police department head.
P.C. § 26385	Individuals with permission from the Chief Sergeants at Arms of the State Assembly *and* the State Senate to carry upon the premises of the State Capitol or its grounds, any legislative office, any office of the Governor or other Constitutional officer, or any hearing room in which any committee of the Senate or Assembly is conducting a hearing (pursuant to P.C. section 171c).
P.C. § 26386	Individuals exempt from the restrictions against possessing firearms in state legislative members', constitutional officers', and the Governor's homes mentioned in P.C. section 171d.
P.C. § 26387	Individuals exempt from the restriction against carrying firearms in sterile areas of public transportation facilities in P.C. section 171.7(c)(1)(F).
P.C. § 26388	Individuals lawfully carrying and possessing handguns on publicly owned land if specifically allowed by the land's managing agency.
P.C. § 26389	Individuals carrying an unloaded handgun in a locked trunk of a motor vehicle or a locked container.
P.C. § 26390	Individuals who possess a permit to possess destructive devices, "assault weapons," .50 BMG rifles, machineguns, and/or short-barreled rifles or shotguns, provided the carrying of the handgun is conducted in accordance with the terms and conditions of the permit.
P.C. § 26391	Individuals who are carrying in accordance with the provisions of section 171.5(d) (lawful carry in sterile environment of airport).

The following people are exempt from openly carrying unloaded handguns *on their person*:

Table 7.5

Statute	Exemption
P.C. § 26365	Members of organizations whose purpose is to practice shooting targets with handguns at established ranges.
P.C. § 26369	Individuals at a gun show conducted according to P.C. sections 27200-27245 and 27300-27350.
P.C. § 26376	Individuals carrying a handgun incident to obtaining a DOJ identification number or mark for the handgun according to P.C. section 23910.
P.C. § 26377	Individuals at any established range while using the handgun at the target range.

STATUTE	EXEMPTION
P.C. § 26379	Individuals carrying a handgun incident to any of the following (as outlined in P.C. section 26379): (1) The requirements for registering or transferring a handgun as a personal handgun importer (P.C. section 27560) or registering "curio or relic" handguns by a collector who is bringing them into the state (P.C. section 27565). (2) Reporting handgun acquisition by those exempt from P.C. section 27545's private party transfer requirements or otherwise not required to report handgun acquisition, ownership, or disposition (P.C. section 28000). (3) Firearm transfers to authorized governmental representatives for voluntary gun buy-back programs (P.C. sections 27850, 31725). (4) Handgun transfers between immediate family members (P.C. sections 27870, 27875). (5) Operation of law and other similar types of transfers (P.C. sections 26556, 27915, 27920, 27925, 29810, or 29830).
P.C. § 26383	An individual in a place of business, a place of residence, or on private property, if done with the permission of a person who, by virtue of P.C. section 25605(a), may carry openly an unloaded handgun within that place of business, place of residence, or on that private property that is owned or lawfully possessed by that individual.
P.C. § 26384	Individuals may openly carry an unloaded handgun if all of the following conditions apply: (1) He or she is at an auction, raf or similar event of a nonprofit public benefit or mutual benefit corporation at which firearms are auctioned or otherwise sold to fund the corporation or its local chapters; *and* (2) The handgun is to be auctioned or otherwise sold to benefit that corporation; *and* (3) The handgun is to be delivered by an FFL.
P.C. § 26932	Transportation of a handgun by an individual who finds a firearm in order to deliver the found firearm to the police or restore it to its owner, and if transporting the handgun to a law enforcement agency, the individual gives prior notice to the law enforcement agency that he or she is transporting the handgun there. OR Transportation of a firearm by a person who took the firearm from a person committing a crime against them and is transporting it to a law enforcement agency provided the law enforcement agency is given notice.

There is an argument that the ban against open carry is also inapplicable to antique firearms.[64] So you may be able to openly carry an unloaded, antique handgun in "public places."[65] But due to law enforcement confusion, this practice is not recommended.

---

[64] P.C. § 16520(d). According to P.C. section 16170(b), "antique firearm" has the same meaning as in 18 U.S.C. section 921(a)(16). See Chapter 3.

[65] Pursuant to P.C. section 16520(d)(5), an antique firearm (discussed in Chapter 3) is not a "firearm" for purposes of the sections relating to carrying a handgun openly (Chapter 6 (commencing with P.C. section 26350) of Division 5 of Title 4 of the Penal Code). It would appear that, by including the open carry exemptions, this exception to the definition of "firearm" for antique firearms would allow for the open carry of antique handguns.

D. Exemptions to Restriction on Carrying "Firearms That Are Not Handguns"

There are almost as many exemptions to the restriction on carrying "firearms that are not handguns" as there are for carrying handguns openly in public.[66] Remember from Chapter 6 that the restriction on carrying "firearms that are not handguns" only applies outside of a vehicle, so this restriction does not affect how you may transport your "firearm that is not a handgun" while *inside* a vehicle.[67] The following explains the exemptions to this restriction.

1. "Locked Container" or "Encased"

The most commonly used exemption for the ban on carrying "firearms that are not handguns" is the "locked container" or "encased" exemption. A person may carry an unloaded "firearm that is not a handgun" if it is either:

(1) In a "locked container" (as defined in Section (III)(E)(1));[68] *or*

(2) "Encased";

AND

(3) "It is being transported directly between places where a person is not prohibited from possessing that firearm and the course of travel" and only includes "those deviations between authorized locations as are reasonably necessary under the circumstances."[69]

A firearm is "encased" "when that firearm is enclosed in a case that is expressly made for the purpose of containing a firearm and that is completely zipped, snapped, buckled, tied, or otherwise fastened with no part of that firearm exposed."[70]

The term "encased" poses a huge problem. Its definition, "expressly made for the purpose of containing a firearm," is not as straightforward as it sounds, and there is no clear understanding of what this would be. Is it sufficient that the manufacturer names a box a "firearm case?" Or must a case be approved or recognizable by law enforcement? There are a number of gun cases available that are expressly made for the purposes of containing a firearm, but do not readily appear to be capable of containing a firearm. Would the case require a certain type of material to be used? Could a gun sock suffice? These questions have not been addressed by the courts.

---

[66] All of these exemptions (with some cross-references) are listed in P.C. section 26405.
[67] Note, however, that California generally requires "assault weapons" and .50 BMG rifles to be transported in a locked container at all times. P.C. § 30945(g). Federal law additionally requires that all firearms (including long guns) be in a locked container or a locked firearm rack that is on a motor vehicle when in a "school zone." 18 U.S.C. § 922(q)(2)(B) (see Chapter 8 for more on school zones). And almost all transportation should be done with the firearm unloaded unless you meet an exception to the loaded restriction.
[68] P.C. § 16850.
[69] P.C. § 26405(c).
[70] P.C. § 16505.

2. Other Exemptions to the Restriction on Carrying "Firearms That Are Not Handguns"

The restriction on carrying "firearms that are not handguns" does not apply to, or affect, the carrying of an unloaded "firearm that is not a handgun" in the following situations or by the following individuals:

Table 7.6

STATUTE	EXEMPTION
P.C. § 26405(a)	An Individual within a place of business, a place of residence, or on private real property, if done by a citizen of the U.S. or legal resident over the age of 18 who resides in or is temporarily within California, and who is not prohibited from possessing firearms under California law, may carry a firearm within that place of business, place of residence, or on that private real property owned or lawfully occupied by that individual.
P.C. § 26405(b)	Individuals within a place of business, a place of residence, or on private real property, if done with the permission of a person who is a citizen of the U.S. or legal resident over the age of 18 who resides in or is temporarily within California, and who is not prohibited from possessing firearms under California law, may carry a firearm within that place of residence or on that private real property owned or lawfully occupied by that person.
P.C. § 26405(c)	When the firearm is either in a locked container or encased (discussed above) and it is being transported directly between places where the individual is not prohibited from possessing that firearm, and the course of travel includes only those deviations between authorized locations as are reasonably necessary under the circumstances.
P.C. § 26405(d)	Individuals carrying a "firearm that is not a handgun" while in "grave danger" (discussed above).
P.C. § 26405(e)	A peace officer or an honorably retired peace officer if that officer may carry a concealed firearm pursuant to Article 2 (commencing with P.C. section 25450) of Chapter 2, or a loaded firearm pursuant to Article 3 (commencing with P.C. section 25900) of Chapter 3.
P.C. § 26405(f)	An individual may carry a "firearm that is not a handgun" to the extent that individual may openly carry a loaded "firearm that is not a handgun" pursuant to Article 4 (commencing with P.C. section 26000-26060) of Chapter 3 (exceptions to carrying loaded handguns discussed above).
P.C. § 26405(g)	Merchandise firearms carried by an individual who is engaged in the business of manufacturing, importing, wholesaling, repairing, or dealing in firearms and who is licensed to engage in that business, or the authorized representative or authorized agent of that individual, while engaged in the lawful course of the business.
P.C. § 26405(h)	A duly authorized military or civil organization, or the members thereof, while parading or while rehearsing or practicing parading, when at the meeting place of the organization.
P.C. § 26405(i)	A member of a club or organization organized for the purpose of practicing shooting at targets upon established target ranges, whether public or private, while the members are using "firearms that are not handguns" upon the target ranges or incident to the use of a firearm that is not a handgun at that target range.

Statute	Exemption
P.C. § 26405(j)	A licensed hunter while engaged in hunting or while transporting the firearm when going to or returning from a hunting expedition.
P.C. § 26405(k)	Carrying incident to transporting a handgun[72] by an individual operating a licensed common carrier, or by an authorized agent or employee thereof, when transported in conformance with applicable federal law.
P.C. § 26405(l)	A member of an organization chartered by the Congress of the U.S. or a nonprofit mutual or public benefit corporation organized and recognized as a nonprofit tax-exempt organization by the Internal Revenue Service while on official parade duty or ceremonial occasions of that organization or while rehearsing or practicing for official parade duty or ceremonial occasions.
P.C. § 26405(m)	Individuals within a gun show conducted pursuant to Article 1 (commencing with P.C. section 27200) and Article 2 (commencing with P.C. section 27300) of Chapter 3 of Division 6.
P.C. § 26405(n)	Individuals within a school zone, as defined in P.C. section 626.9, if their carrying of the firearm meets an exception to the Gun-Free School Zone restriction (P.C. § 626.9). (See Chapter 8)
P.C. § 26405(o)	Firearms carried in accordance with the provisions of P.C. section 171b (exemption for carrying a firearm in a state or local public building or public meeting as provided in that section).
P.C. § 26405(p)	Individuals engaged in the act of making or attempting to make a lawful arrest.
P.C. § 26405(q)	Individuals engaged in firearms-related activities while on the premises of a fixed place of business that is licensed to conduct and conducts, as a regular course of its business, activities related to the sale, making, repair, transfer, pawn, or use of firearms, or related to firearms training.
P.C. § 26405(r)	An authorized participant in, or an authorized employee or agent of a supplier of firearms for a motion picture, television, or video production or entertainment event, when the participant lawfully uses that firearm as part of that production or event, as part of rehearsing or practicing for participation in that production or event, or while the participant or authorized employee or agent is at that production or event, or rehearsal or practice for that production or event.
P.C. § 26405(s)	Individuals carrying incident to obtaining an identification number or mark assigned for that firearm from DOJ pursuant to P.C. section 23910.
P.C. § 26405(t)	Individuals using the firearm upon an established public target range.
P.C. § 26405(u)	An individual summoned by a peace officer to help make arrests or preserve the peace, while the individual is actually engaged in assisting that officer.

Table 7.6

Statute	Exemption
P.C. § 26405(v)	An individual carrying incident to any of the following: (1) Complying with P.C. sections 27560 or 27565, as it pertains to that firearm (personal firearm importer and collector bringing curio or relic firearm into California, and registration requirements); *or* (2) P.C. section 28000, as it pertains to that firearm (transfer of firearms by persons not required to use a licensed firearm dealer); *or* (3) P.C. sections 27850 or 31725, as it pertains to that firearm (sale, delivery, or transfer of firearm to government entity as part of an authorized program, and firearm buy-back programs); *or* (4) Complying with P.C. sections 27870 or 27875, as it pertains to that firearm (transfers by immediate family members); *or* (5) Complying with P.C. sections sections 26556, 27915, 27920, 27925, 27966, 29810, or 29830, as it pertains to that firearm (taking title or possession of firearm by operation of law).
P.C. § 26405(w)	Individuals carrying incident to, and in the course and scope of, training of, or by an individual to become a sworn peace officer as part of a course of study approved by the Commission on POST.
P.C. § 26405(x)	Individuals carrying incident to, and in the course and scope of, training of or by an individual to become licensed pursuant to Chapter 4 (commencing with P.C. section 26150) (license to carry concealed) as part of a course of study necessary or authorized by the person authorized to issue the license pursuant to that chapter.
P.C. § 26405(y)	Individuals carrying incident to and at the request of a sheriff, chief, or other head of a municipal police department.
P.C. § 26405(z)	If all of the following conditions are satisfied: (1) The open carrying occurs at an auction, raffle, or similar event of a nonprofit public benefit or mutual benefit corporation at which firearms are auctioned, raffled, or otherwise sold to fund the activities of that corporation or the local chapters of that corporation; *and* (2) The unloaded firearm that is not a handgun is to be auctioned, raffled, or otherwise sold for that nonprofit public benefit or mutual benefit corporation; *and* (3) The unloaded firearm that is not a handgun is to be delivered by a person licensed pursuant to, and operating in accordance with, P.C. sections 26700 to 26915, inclusive.
P.C. § 26405(aa)	Individuals with permission from the Chief Sergeants at Arms of the State Assembly *and* the State Senate to carry upon the premises of the State Capitol or its grounds, any legislative office, any office of the Governor or other Constitutional officer, or any hearing room in which any committee of the Senate or Assembly is conducting a hearing (pursuant to P.C. section 171c).
P.C. § 26405(ab)	Individuals carrying pursuant to P.C. section 171d (exemption for carrying loaded firearm in certain state and federal government buildings).
P.C. § 26405(ac)	Individuals carrying pursuant to P.C. section 171.7(c)(1)(F) (exemption from possessing firearm in sterile area of public transit facility).
P.C. § 26405(ad)	Individuals on publicly owned land, if the possession and use of an unloaded "firearm that is not a handgun" is specifically permitted by the managing agency of the land and the person carrying that firearm is in lawful possession of that firearm.

Statute	Exemption
P.C. § 26405(ae)	Individuals carrying in any of the following ways: (1) The carrying of an unloaded firearm that is not a handgun that is regulated pursuant to Chapter 1 (commencing with P.C. section 18710) of Division 5 of Title 2 (a destructive device) by an individual who holds a permit issued pursuant to Article 3 (commencing with P.C. section 18900) of that chapter, if the carrying of that firearm is conducted in accordance with the terms and conditions of the permit; or (2) The carrying of an unloaded firearm that is not a handgun that is regulated pursuant to Chapter 2 (commencing with Section 30500) of Division 10 ("assault weapon" and .50 BMG rifle) by an individual who holds a permit issued pursuant to P.C. section 31005, if the carrying of that firearm is conducted in accordance with the terms and conditions of the permit; or (3) The carrying of an unloaded firearm that is not a handgun that is regulated pursuant to Chapter 6 (commencing with P.C. section 32610) of Division 10 (machinegun) by an individual who holds a permit issued pursuant to P.C. section 32650, if the carrying of that firearm is conducted in accordance with the terms and conditions of the permit; or (4) The carrying of an unloaded firearm that is not a handgun that is regulated pursuant to Article 2 (commencing with P.C. section 33300) of Chapter 8 of Division 10 (short-barreled shotguns and rifles) by an individual who holds a permit issued pursuant to P.C. section 33300, if the carrying of that firearm is conducted in accordance with the terms and conditions of the permit.
P.C. § 26405(af)	A licensed hunter while engaged in training a dog for the purpose of using the dog in hunting that is not prohibited by law, or while transporting the firearm while going to or returning from that training.
P.C. § 26405(ag)	Individuals carrying pursuant to the provisions of P.C. section 171.5(d) (the exemption from the restriction against possessing firearm in sterile airport environments).
P.C. § 26405(ah)	An individual engaged in the business of manufacturing ammunition and who is licensed to engage in that business, or the authorized representative or authorized agent of that individual, while the firearm is being used in the lawful course and scope of the licensee's activities as an individual licensed pursuant to Chapter 44 (commencing with P.C. section 921) of Title 18 of the United States Code and regulations issued pursuant thereto.
P.C. § 26405(ai)	When on the navigable waters of this state that are held in public trust, if the possession and use of an unloaded "firearm that is not a handgun" is not prohibited by the managing agency thereof, and the person carrying the firearm is in lawful possession of that firearm.
P.C. § 26406	Transportation of a handgun by an individual who finds a firearm in order to deliver the found firearm to the police or restore it to its owner, and if transporting the handgun to a law enforcement agency, the individual gives prior notice to the law enforcement agency that he or she is transporting the handgun there. OR Transportation of a firearm by a person who took the firearm from a person committing a crime against them and is transporting it to a law enforcement agency provided the law enforcement agency is given notice.

VI. LICENSES TO CARRY A LOADED HANDGUN

The average person must obtain a Carry License to be generally exempt from the loaded and concealed (and in some cases open) carry restrictions in public.[71] These licenses may only be issued to you by the police chief or the sheriff in your city or county of residence, although a *sheriff* may issue a temporary Carry License to non-residents if their principal place of employment or business is in that county and they spend a substantial amount of time there.

If you live in an unincorporated county territory, you can only apply for a Carry License with the sheriff of your county. If you live in an incorporated city, you can apply with either your local police department (if you have one) or with your county sheriff. Issuing authorities are required to accept and process all Carry License applications.[72] Chiefs of police have the option to cede their issuing authority to the sheriff of the county, in which case the police chief *must* reject *all* Carry License applications.[73] If that is the case with your city police department, you will have to apply with the sheriff of your county.[74]

In 2015, Governor Brown signed AB 1134 into law, expressly giving county sheriffs the authority to enter into an agreement with a local police chief or other head of municipal police departments to process all applications for licenses, renewals of licenses, or amendments to Carry Licenses.[75] This bill was passed in response to the California Court of Appeal's unpublished decision in *Lu v. County of Los Angeles*. In that case, the court held that Los Angeles County Sheriff's Department did not violate Equal Protection when it delegated its authority to process Carry License applications for residents who live in incorporated cities that are not policed by the Sheriff's Department to the Chief of Police in those cities. As the court explained, Equal Protection was not violated because applicants could still apply for review or reconsideration with the Sheriff if their application was denied.[76]

But note that under AB 1134, it is unclear as to whether the sheriff can still review or reconsider an application for a Carry License if a Chief of Police or other head denies the application. Nonetheless, when applying for a Carry License, you should check with the sheriff of your county to determine whom you will have to send your Carry License application to (*i.e.*, the county sheriff, local chief of police, or other head of a municipal police department).

---

[71] A Carry License is also widely known as a "CCW" (carry concealed weapon). *See* P.C. § 16360. But the trend is to move away from that term because of the negative connotation associated with the phrase "concealed weapon," and because not all licenses are for carrying "concealed" firearms – as some are for *open* carry.

[72] *Salute v. Pitchess*, 61 Cal. App. 3d 557 (1976).

[73] P.C. §§ 26150, 26155.

[74] Some issuing authorities have adopted the policy of requiring applicants to first apply with the other issuing authority. This is likely an unlawful practice and at least one court has ruled it such. *See Lu v. Baca*, No. BC480493 (Ca. Sup. Ct. Jan. 13, 2014), *available at* http://michellawyers.com/wp-content/uploads/2012/08/Ruling-Re-Motion-for-Summary-Judgment.pdf (last visited Oct. 10, 2020).

[75] *See* P.C. § 26450.

[76] *See Vargas v. Cnty. of Los Angeles*, No. B257371, 2015 WL 5786608 (Oct. 5, 2015). Keep in mind, though, that this decision is unpublished, meaning that it is not binding authority on the courts.

The most common type of Carry License (excluding those for law enforcement) only allows you to carry a *concealed* handgun and is valid statewide, unless otherwise specifically limited by the issuing authority.[77] In counties of less than 200,000 residents, the sheriff or police chief may issue you a license to *openly* carry a handgun, but *only* while within that county.[78] A Carry License is typically valid for two years.[79] Temporary Carry Licenses issued by a sheriff to non-residents based on their employment or business in that specific county are valid for 90 days and only within the county where issued.[80]

State law generally allows Carry License holders to take a handgun into normally prohibited places such as state courts, schools, and the state Capitol. There are still places, though, where it is unlawful to possess a firearm even with a Carry License.[81] You are responsible for knowing the restrictions for the area where you travel. The sheriff or police chief who issued your Carry License may restrict you from entering additional places as well.

A. Criteria for Issuance

An issuing authority may only issue you a Carry License if you demonstrate the following:

(1) "Good cause" exists for issuance of the license;

(2) You are of "good moral character";

(3) You are a "resident" of that city or county (or, if you are applying to a sheriff, your principal place of business is in the county and you spend substantial time there); *and,*

(4) You have completed the course of training that the issuing authority requires.[82]

The law does not specify the age a Carry License applicant must be, but presumably the minimum age is 18 years since a minor cannot generally possess a handgun. Nonetheless, most issuing authorities will only issue to persons 21 years of age and over.

Even if you meet all these requirements, an issuing authority may still refuse to issue you a Carry License because the law is currently understood as granting

---

[77] A Carry License exempts you from most loaded carry restrictions. P.C. § 26010.

[78] P.C. §§ 26150(b)(2), 26155(b)(2). Sheriffs or police chiefs may also issue a Carry License to anyone they deputize or appoint as a peace officer. P.C. § 26170. These types of Carry Licenses are generally exempt from the training and fee requirements for such licenses.

[79] P.C. § 26220(a). Certain Carry Licenses for judges, commissioners, and magistrates are valid for up to three years. P.C. § 26220(c). Carry Licenses for custodial officers working for a sheriff or peace officers, per P.C. section 830.6, can be valid for up to four years. P.C. § 26220(d)-(e).

[80] P.C. § 26220(b).

[81] See Chapter 8 for a discussion on such places.

[82] P.C. §§ 26150(a), 26155(a).

the issuing authorities broad discretion to decide whether to issue one.[83] It is quite common for issuing authorities to set their standards so high that most people cannot meet them. Also, issuing authorities may require psychological testing of any initial applicant (but not of renewal applicants unless there is compelling evidence that such testing is necessary), and can deny Carry Licenses to applicants who fail such testing.[84]

1. "Good Cause"

The ability to obtain a Carry License in any given jurisdiction almost always depends on the respective issuing authority's interpretation of what constitutes "good cause." Different jurisdictional interpretations of what constitutes "good cause" have led to wide disparity in whether Carry Licenses are issued in any given jurisdiction.[85] Some issuing agencies simply require the assertion of a desire for self-defense to establish "good cause," while others refuse to issue any licenses at all, no matter what evidence of "good cause" an applicant provides. For policy reasons, these issuing agencies simply do not want civilians to have Carry Licenses.

2. "Good Moral Character"

While issuing authorities conceivably have the same authority to determine whether an applicant is of "good moral character" as they do to determine one's "good cause," this standard has, practically speaking, been of little consequence. This is likely because issuing authorities that do not want to issue many licenses will simply rely on the "good cause" standard to bar an applicant and never reach this standard. Moreover, those with a more liberal "good cause" standard are likely much

---

[83] See *Gifford v. City of Los Angeles*, 88 Cal. App. 4th 801, 805 (2001). Note that this case was decided before *Heller*, where the U.S. Supreme Court recognized an individual Second Amendment right. The constitutionality of this standard is thus dubious and is still being litigated. See Chapter 2. In contrast to *Gifford*, there are the more promising results from *Wrenn v. District of Columbia*, 864 F.3d 650 (D.C. Cir. 2017). On July 25, the D.C. Circuit issued its decision for *Wrenn*, declaring Washington D.C.'s "good reason" requirement for the issuance of a CCW as a violation of the Second Amendment. The Court also issued a permanent injunction prohibiting D.C. from enforcing the requirement. On September 28, the D.C. Circuit denied Washington D.C.'s request for rehearing. In response, the Attorney General for the District of Columbia said that he would not petition the case to the United States Supreme Court. As such, Washington D.C. is now effectively a "shall issue" jurisdiction.

[84] P.C. § 26190(f).

[85] On June 9, 2016, an en banc panel of the Ninth Circuit Court of Appeals held in *Peruta v. County of San Diego* "that there is no Second Amendment right for members of the general public to carry concealed firearms in public." *Peruta v. Cnty. of San Diego*, No. 10-56971 3 (9th Cir. June 9, 2016). As such, the court upheld the constitutionality of the "good cause" requirement under P.C. section 26150 and 26155, which requires citizens to establish some special need in order to obtain a carry license. This decision overturned a previous decision in which a three-judge panel of the Ninth Circuit ruled that the Second Amendment prohibited cities and counties from requiring some special need in order for an applicant for a Carry License to establish "good cause," see *Peruta v. Cnty. of San Diego*, 10-56971, 742 F.3d 1144 (9th Cir. 2014), and that California Attorney General Kamala Harris could not intervene into the case because her petition was untimely and the decision itself did not implicate the constitutionality of any state statute, see *Peruta v. Cnty. of San Diego*, 771 F.3d 570 (9th Cir. 2014). Shortly after the en banc panel's decision, the plaintiff's petitioned the United States Supreme Court for certiorari. On June 26, the Supreme Court issued an order declining to hear the case, but not without a strong dissenting opinion from newly appointed Justice Gorsuch and Justice Thomas, highlighting how the en banc panel improperly declined to answer the core question of the case.

less prone to reject an applicant based on lack of "good moral character" unless there is a legitimate concern.

Nevertheless, some jurisdictions have denied applicants a Carry License if they have an arrest on their record. If you have an arrest, or a criminal conviction, on your record, you may be denied based on that reason alone. Although, as explained above, it is more likely that you would be denied under the "good cause" standard.

3. Residency

What constitutes "residency" for the purposes of qualifying for a Carry License is not very clear. You are obviously a resident of the city and county in which you own or rent a residence that is your exclusive dwelling, meaning you do not spend substantial amounts of time elsewhere. Nevertheless, some issuing authorities reject applicants for lack of residency who are "part-time" residents or who have only resided in the area for a short period of time. The legality of such restrictive residency definitions is unclear and will eventually need to be litigated. If you are denied for lack of residency, you may want to contact an attorney experienced in firearms law to determine what your options are.[86]

4. Training Course

First-time Carry License applicants are required to complete a training course chosen by the sheriff or police chief. As of January 1, 2019, the course must be at least eight hours in length but cannot exceed 16 hours total.[87] And it must include live-fire shooting exercises on a firing range and instruction on firearm safety, firearm handling, shooting technique, and laws regarding the permissible use of a firearm.[88]

---

[86] In 2013, a U.S. district court ruled on a summary judgment motion in which it interpreted the term "residency" as used within P.C. section 26160 to "mean a status akin to 'domiciliary' under California law." *Raulinaitis v. Ventura Cnty. Sheriffs Dept.*, No. 2:13-cv-02605-MAN (C.D. Cal. Filed Dec. 31, 2013) (order denying motion for summary judgment). In other words, under the court's interpretation of the word "residency," county sheriffs may grant Carry Licenses "only to those persons who are physically present within their respective counties to an extent consistent with the concept of 'domicile.'" *Raulinaitis v. Ventura Cnty. Sheriffs Dept.*, No. 2:13-cv-02605-MAN (C.D. Cal. Filed Dec. 31, 2013) (order denying motion for summary judgment). A person's "domicile" under California law is "the one location with which for legal purposes to have the most settled and permanent connection, the place where he intends to remain and to which, whenever he is absent, he has the intention of returning, but which the law may also assign to him constructively...." *Raulinaitis v. Ventura Cnty. Sheriffs Dept.*, No. 2:13-cv-02605-MAN (C.D. Cal. Filed Dec. 31, 2013) (order denying motion for summary judgment) (citing Smith v. Smith, 45 Cal. 2d 235, 239 (1955)). Although this opinion is well written, it is merely persuasive and not binding authority. This interpretation of "residence" is also subject to a Second Amendment challenge. The plaintiff appealed the decision in *Raulinaitis* to the Ninth Circuit. On November 7, 2016, the Ninth Circuit affirmed the district court's summary judgment ruling, holding that the Los Angeles County Sheriff's Department's policies do not violate the Second Amendment "for the same reasons" that the San Diego and Yolo County Sheriff's Department policies at issue in *Peruta* survived a Second Amendment challenge (i.e., that a member of the general public does not have a right under the Second Amendment to carry a concealed firearm in public and a state may impose restrictions, including a showing of good cause, on concealed carry). *Raulinaitis v. Los Angeles County Sheriff's Dept.*, 670 Fed. Appx. 569 (9th Cir. 2016).

[87] P.C. § 26165(a)(2). Prior to 2019, the law just required that the course include instruction on firearm safety and the laws on permissible firearm uses. P.C. § 26165(a)(1).

[88] P.C. § 26165(a).

An applicant must also demonstrate the safe handling of, and shooting proficiency with, each firearm that the applicant is applying to be licensed to carry.[89]

Sheriffs or police chiefs must establish and make available the standards they use for the required live-fire shooting exercises, including the minimum number of rounds to be fired and minimum passing scores from specified firing distances.[90]

To renew a license, applicants must complete a minimum four-hour training course that the sheriff or police chief finds acceptable and that includes live-fire shooting exercises and instruction on firearm safety, firearm handling, shooting technique, and laws regarding the permissible use of a firearm.[91] But if the renewal applicant is certified by the sheriff or police chief as a trainer, that person need not complete the minimum 4-hour training course.[92]

Alternatively, sheriffs or police chiefs may require first-time Carry License applicants to pass a community college course of up to 24 hours that is certified by the Commission on POST,[93] but only if this is required of *all* initial applicants.[94] Requiring this type of course for renewal applicants does not appear to be allowed.

B. Issuing Authorities' Mandatory Written Policy

Issuing authorities *must* publish an official written policy explaining the circumstances under which they consider an applicant to:

(1) Have "good cause" for a Carry License;

(2) Be of "good moral character"; *and,*

(3) Be a "resident" of the respective county or city (or, for sheriffs only, to qualify for a non-resident license based on business activity in the county).

Additionally, this official written policy must explain exactly what firearm training is required by the issuing authority per P.C. section 26165.[95]

A copy of your respective issuing authority's official written policy should be available online or upon request to that agency.

---

[89] P.C. § 26165(a)(3).
[90] P.C. § 26165(b).
[91] P.C. § 26165(d).
[92] P.C. § 26165(d).
[93] Cal. Comm'n on Peace Officer Standards and Training, http://www.post.ca.gov/ (last visited Oct. 10, 2020).
[94] P.C. § 26165(b).
[95] P.C. § 26160 (formerly P.C. § 12050.2). This requirement was the result of an NRA and CRPA sponsored bill, Senate Bill (SB) 610 (2011).

C. Application Process and Fees

Carry License applications must be on a form prescribed by the Attorney General (AG) and must be the same throughout the state.[96] The issuing authority cannot require any additional information beyond what is necessary to complete the standard DOJ application form, except when it is necessary to clarify any information that was provided on the application.[97] Any false statement made on the application is at least a misdemeanor and may be a felony if the false statement is about any of the following:

(1) The denial or revocation of a license, or the denial of an amendment to a license;

(2) A criminal conviction;

(3) A finding of not guilty by reason of insanity;

(4) The use of a controlled substance;

(5) A dishonorable discharge from military service;

(6) A commitment to a mental institution; *or,*

(7) A renunciation of U.S. citizenship.[98]

Generally, along with the standard application, you must also provide two copies of your fingerprints and DOJ's requisite fee ($95), all of which is forwarded to DOJ to conduct your background check.[99]

In addition to the background check fee, you may also be charged a fee for the sheriff or police chief's costs to initially process the application. Prior to 2020, this fee could not exceed $100. But with the adoption of AB 1297 in 2019, local licensing authorities now must charge a fee "equal to the reasonable costs for processing the application for a new license, issuing the license, and enforcing the license" in addition to other associated fees.[100] At this time, it is unclear what each local licensing authority will charge, but it is anticipated the amount will exceed $100.

Only the first 20% of the initial application fee may be collected up front.[101] For a renewal application, you may be charged up to $25 total.[102] If psychological testing is required, the issuing authority may charge an additional fee of up to $150.[103]

---

[96] As of publication, the required form is located online. *See Standard Initial and Renewal Application for License to Carry a Concealed Weapon,* CAL. DEPT. OF JUSTICE, BUREAU OF FIREARMS, https://www.sjpd.org/PDF_Forms/BOF_4012_CCWapplication_112012.pdf (last visited Oct. 10, 2020). No doubt there will be revisions to the form in the future. Make sure your law enforcement agency is using the current form.

[97] P.C. § 26175.

[98] P.C. § 26180.

[99] P.C. § 26185.

[100] P.C. § 29160(b).

[101] P.C. § 26190(b), 26190(c).

[102] P.C. § 26190(c).

[103] P.C. § 26190(f).

It is against the law for the issuing authority to charge a fee relating to the Carry License application process unless it is expressly authorized by P.C. section 26190, as are any conditions requiring the applicant to pay additional money.[104] And requiring liability insurance for a Carry License is specifically prohibited.[105]

Once you complete and submit your initial or renewal Carry License application, you must be given written notice about whether your application is granted or not. This should occur within 90 days of your application being received or 30 days after the sheriff or police chief receives your background check from DOJ, whichever is later.[106] But expect substantial delays during this process.

P.C. section 26202 also requires issuing authorities to provide Carry License applicants *written* notice that either:

(1) "Good cause" exists and the applicant should continue with any training required pursuant to P.C. section 26165; *or,*

(2) The Carry License is denied for lack of "good cause," stating the specific reason why the applicant lacks "good cause" under the issuing authority's written policy (as required by P.C. section 26160).[107]

You cannot be required to pay for any required training course until you have received this written notice.[108] If you are denied a Carry License for something *other than* "good cause," the issuing authority must explain in writing what requirement you did not satisfy, but they do not need to explain the specific reason(s) for the denial. But, nothing precludes such an explanation.

D. License Revocation and Moving Out of the Jurisdiction

The universe of circumstances allowing sheriffs or police chiefs to revoke currently valid Carry Licenses is unclear. But it is clear that they can revoke a Carry License if the license holder becomes a prohibited person.[109] Many issuing authorities will have their revocation policies in writing.

If you change addresses, you must notify the sheriff or police chief of this within 10 days. An address change cannot be the basis for *revoking* the Carry License, even if you move outside of the county in which it was issued. But, if your residence was the basis for the issuance of the license, it will *expire* 90 days after you move from the county of issuance. And if your license is for loaded and exposed carry, it will expire immediately upon your change of residence to another county.[110]

---

[104] P.C. § 26190(g).
[105] P.C. § 26190(g). This restriction was created by SB 610 (2011).
[106] P.C. § 26205.
[107] The specific reason should come from the issuing authority's published policy required under P.C. section 26160. This notice requirement was also part of SB 610 (2011).
[108] P.C. § 26165(d).
[109] P.C. § 26195. See Chapter 5.
[110] P.C. § 26210.

E. License Restrictions

Any type of Carry License may have "reasonable restrictions or conditions" placed on it by the sheriff or police chief including, but not limited to, time, place, manner, and circumstance restrictions. Any such restriction(s) must be indicated on the license itself.[111]

Check with the authorities who have jurisdiction over the place(s) you want to go with your firearm. You should be aware that bringing a firearm to certain places may be a sensitive matter, even if it is legal to carry it there. For example, state court judges regularly prohibit Carry License holders from possessing firearms in their courtrooms even though state law allows it. Be especially careful on federal property where it generally will *not* be legal.

F. Form of Physical License

California law requires an issued Carry License to be laminated and have the license holder's name, occupation, residence and business address, age, height, weight, color of eyes and hair, the reason for desiring the license (*i.e.*, "good cause"), and a description of any handgun carried pursuant to the license with the manufacturer's name, the serial number, and the caliber.[112]

In 2016, Governor Brown signed AB 2510 into law.[113] This bill requires the California Attorney General to develop a uniform Carry License, with uniform information and criteria, that can be used throughout the state.[114]

G. License Amendments

A Carry License holder may request the issuing agency to amend the license in the following ways:

(1) Add or delete a handgun that is allowed to be carried pursuant to the license;

(2) Change permission to carry the handgun from openly to concealed, or from concealed to openly (if allowed in that particular county); *or,*

(3) Change any restrictions or conditions placed on the license by the issuing authority.[115]

---

[111] P.C. § 26200.
[112] P.C. § 26175(i).
[113] AB 2510, 2015-2016 Leg. Council's Digest (2016), *available at* http://leginfo.legislature.ca.gov/faces/billTextClient.xhtml?bill_id=201520160AB2510 (last visited Oct. 10, 2020).
[114] P.C. § 26175.
[115] P.C. § 26215(a).

If the issuing authority amends the license, a new physical license reflecting such amendment(s) will be issued to the license holder.[116] The new physical license does not change the original license's expiration date, meaning the license will still need to be renewed upon expiration as it would if no amendment was made.[117]

Some states honor Carry Licenses issued in another state, but this varies between states. For example, California does not recognize Carry Licenses issued in any other state, even though some states recognize California licenses. But, as discussed below, federal law requires California to allow certain active and retired law enforcement officers to carry within California as long as the requirements outlined in the Law Enforcement Office Safety Act (LEOSA). For more information on Carry License issues, visit www.CalGunLawsBook.com.

VII. EXEMPTIONS FOR ACTIVE & RETIRED PEACE OFFICERS

A. Concealed and Loaded Restrictions

1. Current Law Enforcement Officers

a. California Peace Officers

Current California peace officers are exempt from both the concealed handgun and loaded firearm restrictions.[118] Whether you are considered a "peace officer" for purposes of these exemptions is usually straightforward, but there are cases that are not so clear. This is because the Penal Code sections are oddly worded, providing "[a]ny peace officer, listed in Section 830.1 or 830.2, or subdivision (a) of Section 830.33, whether active or honorably retired" is exempt from the restrictions on carrying concealed or loaded.[119] But the same sections go on to say that "[a]ny other duly appointed peace officer" is also exempt.[120] Based on this wording, it *appears* that *any* person falling under the definition of a "peace officer" is exempt from the restrictions for carrying a firearm concealed and/or loaded.[121]

But the Penal Code treats some "peace officers" differently. For example, persons employed by the Division of Investigation of the Department of Consumer Affairs may carry firearms only if authorized and under the terms and conditions

---

[116] P.C. § 26215(b).

[117] P.C. § 26215(c).

[118] P.C. §§ 25450(a)-(b), 25900(a)-(b). These exceptions can generally be found in P.C. sections 25450-25475 (for carrying concealed) and 25900-29525 (for carrying loaded). While these sections are practically identical there are some minor differences. If you are a peace officer and interested in carrying concealed and/or loaded, you should check both sections to confirm you are in compliance.

[119] P.C. §§ 25450(a), 25900(a). The additional requirements for retired officers are below.

[120] P.C. §§ 25450(b), 25900(b).

[121] "Peace officers" are defined in P.C. sections 830-832.9.

as specified by their employing agency.[122] Despite the fact that a person can be a "peace officer" and be denied by his or her employer the ability to carry a firearm while on-duty, generally a "peace officer's" employer cannot restrict or deny the officer's ability to carry a firearm either loaded or concealed while off-duty.[123] Although, this too is not without limitations. For example, parole officers of the Juvenile Parole Board must receive special permission from the chairperson of the board.[124]

If you do not know whether you fall under this exemption, you should determine whether you are considered a "peace officer" under the Penal Code and if there are any limits on your ability to carry firearms. Members of law enforcement in states neighboring California and members of the National Guard are considered "peace officers" in certain limited contexts and may be able to carry firearms in those limited contexts.[125]

b. Current Reserve Peace Officers

While it seems that active reserve peace officers enjoy these same exemptions,[126] it is unclear if this is the case in practice. Many agencies take the view that reserve officers must obtain a Carry License pursuant to P.C. section 26170 in order to be exempt.

c. Other Current Officers

The following individuals are exempt from the general laws against carrying loaded firearms in public as long as they complete a regular firearms training course approved by the POST Commission:

(1) "Patrol special police officers" appointed by the city or county police who meet the criteria set forth in P.C. section 26025(a)(1)-(4);

(2) Authorized animal control officers and zookeepers compensated by the government in the scope of their duty when authorized by a local ordinance or resolution;

(3) Persons authorized to carry the weapons listed in California Corporations Code section 14502 while actually engaged in duties per that section; *and,*

(4) Harbor police officers.[127]

---

[122] *See* P.C. § 830.3.
[123] *See Orange Cnty. Employees Ass'n v. Cnty. of Orange,* 14 Cal. App. 4th 575 (1993). The AG's office has also issued a number of opinions concerning these issues. *See* Opinion No. 94-1106, 78 Cal. Ops. Atty. Gen. 209 (1995); Opinion No. 89-505, 72 Cal. Ops. Atty. Gen. 167 (1989); Opinion No. 79-1207, 63 Cal. Ops. Atty. Gen. 385 (1980).
[124] P.C. § 830.5.
[125] P.C. §§ 830.39, 830.4.
[126] *See* P.C. §§ 830, 830.6 (declaring reserve officers "peace officers" provided they meet specified criteria set forth in P.C. section 832.6).
[127] P.C. § 26025.

While these individuals are exempt from the general laws against carrying loaded firearms in public, this does *not* mean they are exempt from prohibitions on *concealed* carry.

d. Current Federal and Out-of-State Officers

California law exempts out-of-state and federal peace officers who are "full-time paid" and "carrying out official duties while in California"[128] from the restrictions on carrying concealed and loaded firearms. But virtually all law enforcement officers that satisfy these criteria enjoy these exemptions under *federal* law regardless of whether they meet California's preconditions, as discussed below.

Federal officers meet the definition of a "peace officer" only in a limited capacity, but active officers are exempt from the restrictions on carrying concealed and loaded firearms by statute. California law explicitly states that "[f]ederal criminal investigators and law enforcement officers are *not* California peace officers" but may exercise the powers of arrest of a peace officer in certain situations.[129] As unambiguous as this language is, ambiguities abound because the statute further states "[d]uly authorized federal employees who comply with training requirements set forth in Section 832 *are* peace officers when they are engaged in enforcing applicable state or local laws on property owned or possessed by the United States government, or on any street, sidewalk, or property adjacent thereto, and with the written consent of the sheriff or the chief of police, respectively, in whose jurisdiction the property is situated."[130] Presumably, when a federal criminal investigator or law enforcement officer meets the definition of a "peace officer" as defined above, he or she would be permitted to carry concealed or loaded under the general "peace officer" exemption.

But of course, this being California law, there is an exception to the exemption because national park rangers are *not* peace officers despite having the power to arrest and the powers *of* a peace officer in certain situations and under certain criteria.[131]

2. Retired Law Enforcement

"Honorably retired" California peace officers are also generally exempt from both the concealed handgun and loaded firearm restrictions, but they must meet some

---

[128] P.C. §§ 25450(e), 25900(e). Full-time salaried federal law enforcement officers who are Department of Defense police officers at the Los Angeles Air Force Base may be "exempt from the state law prohibition against carrying concealed, loaded firearms even when they are not on duty." *See* Opinion No. 01-1005, 85 Ops. Cal. Atty. Gen. 68 (2002).

[129] P.C. § 830.8(a) (emphasis added). Federal investigators and law enforcement officers are also required to have been certified by their agency heads as having satisfied the training requirements of P.C. section 832 or the equivalent thereof. Bureau of Land Management (BLM) and U.S. Forest Service officers do not have the power to arrest unless they have written consent of the sheriff or chief of police in whose jurisdiction they are assigned. P.C. § 830.8(a).

[130] P.C. § 830.8(b) (emphasis added).

[131] P.C. § 830.8(c). This exception to the exemption also applies to "Washoe tribal law enforcement officers" under certain circumstances. P.C. § 830.8(e)(1)-(b)(4).

preconditions that current officers do not. An "honorably retired" peace officer includes any peace officer who has qualified for and accepted "a service or disability retirement," but does not include "an officer who has agreed to a service retirement in lieu of termination."[132] This unequivocally includes retired level I reserve officers who have met the requirements stated in Penal Code section 26300(c)(2).[133]

a. Retired California Peace Officers

Any honorably retired peace officer who was authorized to, and did, carry a firearm on the job, or whose position is listed in P.C. section 830.5(c), is generally entitled to be issued an identification certificate by the agency from which the officer retired.[134] In most cases the issuing agency is also required to endorse such certificates for peace officers who honorably retired after January 1, 1981, stating that the retired officer is approved to lawfully carry a concealed and loaded firearm.[135] An unendorsed certificate is generally sufficient authorization for a peace officer who honorably retired prior to 1981 to lawfully carry a concealed and loaded firearm, unless it has been stamped "No CCW privilege" by the agency that issued it after a showing of "good cause" for denying the person's ability to carry.[136]

Current peace officers and those honorably retired peace officers with endorsed identification certificates issued by the agency they retired from are also exempt from both the restrictions on openly carrying unloaded handguns and "firearms that are not handguns" in "public places."[137] Generally, honorably retired peace officers must petition to renew their Carry License certificate every five years with the agency they retired from.[138] Peace officer positions listed in P.C. section 830.5(c), however, must qualify every year to maintain a valid Carry License certificate.[139]

The agency the officer retired from may only deny or revoke a Carry License certificate for "good cause."[140] Although it is unspecified what constitutes "good cause" for denial or revocation, California law provides the following:

(1) Psychological disability;

---

[132] P.C. § 16690.

[133] This unequivocally includes retired level I reserve officers who has met the requirements stated in Penal Code section 26300(c)(2).

[134] P.C. §§ 25455(a), 25905(a); see also P.C. §§ 25450(c)-(d), 25900(c)-(d). The required format of the certificate is provided in P.C. section 25460. The issuing agency may charge a fee necessary to cover its reasonable expenses incurred by issuing the certificate. P.C. § 25455(b). P.C. section 26300 was recently amended by AB 703 (2013) to also allow retired level I reserve officers to obtain a certificate equivalent to a carry license.

[135] P.C. § 26300(b)-(c); see also P.C. § 25455(c). This applies to those officers listed in P.C. sections 830.1, 830.2, or 830.5(c), as well as those officers who were authorized to, and did, carry a firearm during the course and scope of their appointment as peace officers.

[136] P.C. § 26300(a); see also P.C. § 25455(d). This applies only to those officers listed in P.C. sections 830.1, 830.2, or 830.5(c).

[137] P.C. §§ 26361, 26405.

[138] P.C. §§ 25465, 25915.

[139] P.C. §§ 25475(a), 25925(a). These are certain officers and employees of the Department of Corrections and Rehabilitation, including some in that department's Division of Juvenile Justice.

[140] P.C. §§ 25470(a), 25920(a), 26305(d).

(2) "[V]iolating any departmental rule, or state or federal law that, if violated by an officer on active duty, would result in that officer's arrest, suspension, or removal from the agency"; *or,*

(3) Conduct that compromises public safety.[141]

An officer whose Carry License certificate is denied or revoked has 15 days after receiving proper notice of revocation to request a hearing.[142] Failing to request a hearing within that time frame forfeits the officer's right to one.[143]

Any honorably retired peace officer[144] must be issued an identification certificate by the law enforcement agency from which he or she retired.[145] "If the agency from which the officer has retired is no longer providing law enforcement services or the relevant government body is dissolved, the agency that subsequently provides law enforcement services for that jurisdiction shall issue the identification certificate" to that retired peace officer if all the following conditions are met[146]:

(1) The successor agency is in possession of the retired officer's complete personnel records or can otherwise verify the retired officer's honorably retired status;

(2) The retired officer is in compliance with all the requirements of the successor agency for the issuance of a retirement identification card and concealed weapon endorsement;

(3) The issuing agency may charge a fee necessary to cover any reasonable expenses incurred by the agency in issuing certificates pursuant to P.C. sections 25900, 25910, 25925, and 25905;

(4) Any officer, except an officer listed in P.C. sections 830.1, 830.2, 830.33(a), or 830.5(c) who retired prior to January 1, 1981, shall have an endorsement on the identification certificate stating that the issuing agency approves the officer's carrying of a loaded firearm; *and,*

(5) An honorably retired peace officer listed in P.C. sections 830.1, 830.2, 830.33(a), or 830.5(c) who retired prior to January 1, 1981, shall not be required to obtain an endorsement from the issuing agency to carry a loaded firearm.[147]

---

[141] P.C. § 26305(a)-(c).
[142] P.C. § 26312. This notice must be personally served. The hearing is governed by P.C. section 26320.
[143] P.C. §§ 26310, 26312, 26315.
[144] Defined in P.C. section 25900.
[145] P.C. § 25905(a)(1).
[146] P.C. § 25905(a)(2).
[147] P.C. § 25905(a)(2).

b. Retired Reserve California Peace Officers

Like retired full-time peace officers, any honorably retired reserve peace officer who was authorized to, and did, carry a firearm during the course and scope of his or her appointment as a peace officer is generally entitled to an identification certificate with an endorsement from the agency the officer retired from stating that the officer is approved to carry a concealed and loaded firearm, but only if the officer:

(1) Was a level I reserve officer;[148] *and,*

(2) Served in aggregate the minimum amount of time as specified by the officer's agency's policy as a level I reserve officer, provided that the policy shall not set an aggregate term requirement that is less than 10 years or more than 20 years.[149]

If a retired reserve officer meets all of the above requirements, then he or she is entitled to a carry permit.[150] But note that a law enforcement agency has the same discretion to revoke or deny an endorsement issued to such a retired reserve peace officer for "good cause," as it does for a current full-time officer as discussed above.[151]

c. Retired Federal Peace Officers

Unlike retired state peace officers who are generally entitled to a certification exempting them from all the restrictions on carrying handguns in public, honorably retired federal officers or agents are not exempt under California law. Rather, under California law these officers might be able to carry if they apply to the sheriff of the county where they reside for a permit. The sheriff may, but is not required to, issue this permit to a retired federal officer or agent who:

(1) Was authorized to carry weapons while on duty;

(2) Was assigned to duty within California for a period of not less than one year; *or ,*

(3) Is retired from active service in California.[152]

These officers and agents must give the sheriff a certification from the agency from which they retired certifying their service in the state that states the nature of their retirement and indicates the agency's agreement that they should be allowed to carry a loaded firearm.[153]

---

[148] Described in P.C. section 832.6(a)(1).
[149] P.C. § 26300(c).
[150] P.C. § 16990(a).
[151] P.C. §§ 26300(c), 26305.
[152] P.C. §§ 26020(a), 25650(a).
[153] P.C. §§ 26020(b), 25650(b).

This permit is valid for a period not exceeding five years and must be carried by the retired federal officer or agent at all times while carrying a loaded firearm. The permit may be revoked for "good cause."[154]

Even if a retired federal officer or agent cannot obtain such a permit, he or she may still be able to carry under federal law (under the Law Enforcement Officers Safety Act (LEOSA, explained immediately below), albeit in a somewhat more limited fashion than what they would be able to with a permit from their sheriff.

B. Law Enforcement Officers Safety Act (LEOSA/H.R. 218)

LEOSA[155] amended the federal Gun Control Act (GCA) to exempt qualified law enforcement officers (QLEO) and qualified retired law enforcement officers (QRLEO) from most state and local laws prohibiting the carrying of concealed firearms as long as they have the proper photo ID (and certification if needed for QRLEOs) from the law enforcement agency they are currently employed by or separated from. But, LEOSA places limits on the types of firearms[156] a QLEO and QRLEO may carry and on the locations where the exemption applies.

1. QLEO Definition and ID Requirements

An employee of a governmental agency is a QLEO under LEOSA if he or she meets all of the following criteria:

(1) Is authorized by law to engage in or supervise the prevention, detection, investigation, prosecution, or the incarceration of any person for, any violation of law, and has statutory powers of arrest or apprehension;[157] (2) Is authorized by the agency to carry a firearm;

(3) Is not the subject of any disciplinary action by the agency which could result in suspension or loss of police powers;

(4) Meets standards, if any, established by the agency which require the employee to regularly qualify in the use of a firearm;

(5) Is not under the influence of alcohol or another intoxicating or hallucinatory drug or substance; *and,*

---

[154] P.C. §§ 26020(c), 25650(d).

[155] Also known as "H.R. 218," found at 18 U.S.C. sections 926B, 926C.

[156] Machine guns, silencers, and destructive devices are not found under LEOSA. 18 U.S.C. §§ 926B(e), 926C(e). Beyond those limitations, however, "firearm" is not defined.

[157] The apprehension powers must be granted under 10 U.S.C. section 807. "[A] law enforcement officer of the Amtrak Police Department, a law enforcement officer of the Federal Reserve, or a law enforcement or police officer of the executive branch of the Federal Government qualifies as an employee of a governmental agency who is authorized by law to engage in or supervise the prevention, detection, investigation, or prosecution of, or the incarceration of any person for, any violation of law, and has statutory powers of arrest or apprehension . . . ." 18 U.S.C. § 926B(f).

(6) Is not prohibited by federal law from receiving a firearm.[158]

Additionally, QLEOs must carry the proper identification; specifically, "photographic identification issued by the governmental agency for which the individual is employed that identifies the employee as a police officer or law enforcement officer of the agency."[159]

2. QRLEO Definition and ID Requirements

A QRLEO is an individual who:

(1) Is separated in good standing from service with a public agency as a law enforcement officer;[160]

(2) Before such separation, was authorized by law to engage in or supervise the prevention, detection, investigation, prosecution, or the incarceration of any person for, any violation of law, and had statutory powers of arrest or apprehension;[161]

(3) Either:

  (a) Before such separation, served as a law enforcement officer for an aggregate of 10 years or more; *or*,

  (b) Separated from service with such agency after completing any applicable probationary period of such service due to a service-connected disability, as determined by such agency;

  AND

(4) During the most recent 12-month period has met, at the expense of the individual, the standards for qualification in firearms training for active law enforcement officers, as determined by:

  (a) The individual's former agency,

  (b) The State in which the individual resides, *or*,

  (c) If the State has not established such standards, either (1) a law enforcement agency within the State in which the individual resides; or (2) the standards used by a certified firearms instructor that is qualified to conduct a firearms qualification test for active duty officers within that State;

  AND

---

[158] 18 U.S.C. § 926B(c).

[159] 18 U.S.C. § 926B(d).

[160] "[T]he term 'service with a public agency as a law enforcement officer' includes service as a law enforcement officer of the Amtrak Police Department, service as a law enforcement officer of the Federal Reserve, or service as a law enforcement or police officer of the executive branch of the Federal Government." 18 U.S.C. § 926C(e)(2).

[161] The apprehension powers must be granted under 10 U.S.C. section 807(b).

(5) Either:

    (a) Has not been officially found by a qualified medical professional employed by the agency to be unqualified for reasons relating to mental health and as a result of this finding will not be issued the photographic identification for LEOSA; *or,*

    (b) Has not entered into an agreement with the agency from which the individual is separating from service in which the individual acknowledges he or she is not qualified under this section for reasons relating to mental health and for those reasons will not receive or accept the photographic identification for LEOSA;

AND

(6) Is not under the influence of alcohol or another intoxicating or hallucinatory drug or substance; *and,*

(7) Is not prohibited by Federal law from receiving a firearm.[162]

The identification needed for a QRLEO to carry under LEOSA is either:

(1) A photo ID that:

    (a) Is issued by the agency that the individual worked for; *and,*

    (b) Identifies the individual as having been employed as a police officer or law enforcement officer;

AND EITHER OF THE FOLLOWING:

(2) The ID indicates that the individual has not been tested or otherwise found by the agency to meet the active duty standards for qualification in firearms training as established by the agency to carry a firearm of the same type as the concealed firearm less than one year before the date the individual is carrying the concealed firearm;[163] *or,*

(3) The retired officer possesses a certification:

    (a) Issued by:

        (i) The state where the individual resides; *or,*

        (ii) By a certified firearms instructor that is qualified to conduct a firearms qualification test for active duty officers within that State;

    AND

    (b) That indicates the individual has, not less recently than one year before the date the individual is carrying the concealed firearm, been tested or otherwise found by the agency to meet the active duty standards for qualification in firearms training as established by the state or a

---

[162] 18 U.S.C. § 926C(c).
[163] 18 U.S.C. § 926C(d)(1).

certified firearms instructor that is qualified to conduct a firearms qualification test for active duty officers within the state to have met:

(i) The active duty standards for qualification in firearms training, as established by the state, to carry a firearm of the same type as the concealed firearm; or,

(ii) If the state has not established such standards, standards set by any law enforcement agency within the state to carry a firearm of the same type as the concealed firearm.[164]

If you meet the identification requirements from your pervious agency discussed directly above in (1) & (2), you do not need to meet the identification and certification requirements of (1) & (3). In a number of cases, an officer cannot qualify through that officer's former agency, or the agency will not qualify a retired officer so that the officer can meet the requirements of (1) & (2). Consequently, the retired officer will need to have the ID and certification discussed in (1) & (3). Most agencies issue the required identification, but some do not.

LEOSA does not create a right to carry a concealed firearm, nor does it entitle an active or retired law enforcement officer to be issued the ID, or ID and certification, to carry a firearm under LEOSA. There is no requirement under federal law that a law enforcement agency issue the required ID for an officer to carry under LEOSA.[165] But, if an officer qualifies as an eligible officer under LEOSA and possesses the proper ID, or ID and certification, that person should be able to carry firearms under LEOSA without any further permission.

In the case that a QRLEO can obtain the required identification under (1), there is still the matter of the certification in (3). This "certification" requirement is rife with ambiguities.

The first is the uncertainty as to what form the "certification" must be in. Most states do not issue a "certification." Nevertheless, the "certification" can be issued by a "certified" firearms instructor "qualified" to conduct a firearms qualification test for active duty officers within the state. LEOSA creates some ambiguities here as well. There is no definition of what a "certified" firearm instructor is or what it means for the instructor to be "qualified." Apparently, any certified firearms instructor who conducts qualification tests for active duty officers within California will suffice.

The standards a QRLEO is required to meet is ambiguous as well. In addition to states rarely issuing certifications under LEOSA, some states (like California) do not have an established standard for qualification for active duty law enforcement. And as discussed above, if no set standard is established, the standards a QRLEO can qualify under can be from *any* law enforcement agency in the state. In other words, if the qualified instructor conducts qualification tests for an agency with

---

[164] 18 U.S.C. § 926C(d)(2)(A)-(B).

[165] *Johnson v. New York State Dept. of Correctional Servs.*, 709 F. Supp. 2d 178 (N.D.N.Y. 2010).

exceedingly low qualification standards, the instructor can then test and certify a QRLEO using those same standards.¹⁶⁶

3. LEOSA and the California Department of Justice

DOJ apparently still thinks that retired federal law enforcement cannot carry a concealed firearm without a California Carry License. This opinion appears to be based in part on the fact that California has no state standard for "active duty law enforcement." According to DOJ's website:

> Both "qualified law enforcement officers" and "qualified retired law enforcement officers" are required to meet the state's standards for the "training and qualification for active law enforcement officers to carry firearms" under the LEOSA. Penal Code Section 832.3 sets forth the initial and continuing training and testing requirements for peace officers in California. The specific curriculum for the training of peace officers is established by the California Commission on Peace Officer Standards and Training (P.O.S.T.). However, current California law does not set a statewide standard for the training and qualification of active law enforcement officers after graduation from the academy. Standards are established by individual law enforcement agencies for both active and retired officers in those agencies.¹⁶⁷

A close reading of DOJ's website and synopsis of LEOSA reveals the probable cause for confusion. The version of LEOSA that DOJ has on its website is the version of LEOSA from when it was introduced in 2004. At that time, both QLEOs and QRLEOs had to comply with state standards for active law enforcement. But LEOSA has changed since 2004 to include the current language allowing for any state law enforcement standards. Therefore, DOJ's written position is nine years old and inaccurate. Nevertheless, this is DOJ's stated position on its website, and it's the position DOJ takes when asked by representatives of retired federal law enforcement agencies.

This position is likely also incorrect under the current LEOSA. If DOJ changes its position, or its website is updated with additional information, it will be available on www.crpa.org.

4. Limits on LEOSA and the Types of Firearms One May Carry

Although they are exempt from *general* prohibitions on concealed carry, QLEOs and QRLEOs are still subject to state laws restricting firearm possession on state or local government property, installations, buildings, bases, or parks (this restric-

---

¹⁶⁶ Frequently asked LEOSA questions can be found on the NRA's website at: http://www.nraila.org/gun-laws/leosa/leosa-frequently-asked-questions (last visited Oct. 10, 2020).

¹⁶⁷ CAL. DEPT. OF JUSTICE, OFFICE OF THE ATTORNEY GENERAL, SUMMARY OF THE LAW ENFORCEMENT OFFICERS SAFETY ACT (LEOSA) OF 2004, *available at* https://oag.ca.gov/sites/all/files/agweb/pdfs/firearms/forms/leosasummary.pdf (last visited Oct. 10, 2020).

tion would arguably cover places like schools and state courthouse as discussed in Chapter 8), as well as federal laws restricting firearm possession (*e.g.*, in airports, federal courts, and post offices). LEOSA specifies that it does not protect a person in areas a *state* restricts.[168] Consequently, it appears that a person carrying pursuant to LEOSA is exempt from *local* restrictions. You should therefore be familiar with the laws of places you intend to travel with a concealed firearm if you are carrying under LEOSA. LEOSA also doesn't supersede or limit a state's laws that allow private persons or entities to prohibit or restrict the possession of concealed firearms on their property.[169]

When LEOSA uses the term "firearm" it means "firearm" as defined in 18 U.S.C. section 921 (discussed in Chapter 3).[170] The term "firearm" also includes ammunition not expressly prohibited by federal law (like armor piercing handgun ammunition) or subject to provisions of the National Firearms Act (NFA) (like destructive devices).[171] The term "firearm" also does not include "machinegun" (as defined in the NFA) or silencers and destructive devices (as defined in the GCA).[172]

This is a rather odd distinction because states often ban other types of firearms (for instance, "assault weapons"). Still, it would appear that in setting limits to only these types of firearms and devices, Congress intended to allow QLEOs and QR-LEOs to carry other types of firearms that are potentially prohibited by state laws. But I would strongly suggest not attempting to push this apparent hole in the law. You should wait for either clarification by Congress or a court decision. Do not make yourself a test case.

Another area of concern relates to restrictions that certain states have (like California) regarding "large-capacity magazines" (discussed in Chapter 10). There appears to be no allowance for magazines in LEOSA. Consequently, restrictions on magazines would apply unless the officer meets an exemption to those restrictions pursuant to that state's laws. Because of this ambiguity, I suggest an officer wishing to carry pursuant to LEOSA familiarize himself or herself with California's restrictions to "large capacity magazines" and "large capacity magazine conversion kits" (and exemptions thereto) before bringing and possessing the magazines in California.[173]

5. LEOSA and Reserve Officers (Active and Retired)

Despite the restrictions on carrying firearms, exemptions, and special exemptions for law enforcement under California law, if a person meets the requirements for LEOSA and possesses the proper ID, or ID and certification, a person may carry a firearm in California although he or she may not be able to under an express

---

[168] 18 U.S.C. § 926B(b).
[169] 18 U.S.C. §§ 926B(b), 926C(b).
[170] 18 U.S.C. § 926B(e)(1).
[171] 18 U.S.C. § 926B(e)(2).
[172] 18 U.S.C. § 926B(e)(3).
[173] See Chapter 10.

provision of California law. With the exemptions to the restrictions under state law concerning where a person can carry and restrictions imposed by federal law, an individual who qualifies under LEOSA, and is carrying pursuant to LEOSA is protected against most violations of California law and all local laws.[174]

The ability for reserve officers to carry under LEOSA has created a point of contention between some officers and their agencies. Some reserve officers are not receiving the required ID and, thus, are unable to carry under LEOSA. Others are being told they may not carry despite the fact they meet the criteria and ID requirements. As of the publication of this book, this issue is still in contention.

VIII. TRANSPORTATION OF FIREARMS IN PUBLIC TRANSPORTATION OR ACROSS STATE LINES

A. Transporting Firearms on Airplanes

If you plan to transport firearms on an airplane, you must use the ticket counter check-in process and notify the airline that you are transporting a firearm or ammunition. The firearm must be unloaded and transported as *checked* baggage in a locked, hard-sided container that only you have the key or combination to (not even law enforcement should have it). You can and should open the container for them if they request it.[175] The hard-sided, locked container may either be separate from your suitcase or inside it unless the airline tells you otherwise.

These requirements apply equally to disassembled firearms. If you have a frame or receiver, you have a "firearm."

Also, remember that when you are transporting your firearm to the airport and to and from the terminal, you must comply with all of California's transportation laws.

Ammunition[176] must also be transported as *checked* baggage, securely packed in boxes[177] or other packaging specifically designed to carry small amounts of ammunition (*e.g.*, the manufacturer's packaging). You can only transport ammunition for personal use, and the specific amount of ammunition is set by the airlines. Airline policies typically limit you to 11 pounds of ammunition,[178] so if you have a

---

[174] *See* 18 U.S.C. §§ 926A, 926B.

[175] 49 C.F.R. § 1540.111(c). *See also Firearms and Ammunition*, TRANSP. SEC. ADMIN., http://www.tsa.gov/traveler-information/firearms-and-ammunition (last visited Oct. 10, 2020); *Guide to the Interstate Transportation of Firearms*, NRA-ILA, http://www.nraila.org/gun-laws/articles/2010/guide-to-the-interstate-transportation.aspx (last visited Oct. 10, 2020).

[176] For transporting by plane, "ammunition" means: "[a]mmunition consisting of a cartridge case fitted with a center or rim fire primer and containing both a propelling charge and solid projectile(s)." 49 C.F.R. § 173.59.

[177] The TSA recommends the box be made of a fiber (such as cardboard), wood, or metal. *See Firearms and Ammunition*, TRANSPORTATION SECURITY ADMINISTRATION, https://www.tsa.gov/travel/transporting-firearms-and-ammunition (last visited Oct. 10, 2020).

[178] *See Firearms and Ammunition*, AMERICAN AIRLINES, http://www.aa.com/i18n/travelInformation/baggage/firearms.jsp (last visited Oct. 10, 2020).

significant amount, you should call the airline and confirm the acceptable amount and weight of ammunition before arriving at the airport.

Magazines and clips must also be securely boxed.[179] The Transportation Security Administration (TSA) requires ammunition, magazines, and clips be transported in a hard-sided, locked case, even if together with an unloaded firearm, as long as properly packaged.[180] To be allowed on an airplane, the ammunition cannot be designed to shoot from firearms of a caliber larger than 19.1 mm (.75 inches) unless they are shotgun cartridges, in which case *any* gauge is permitted.[181] Additionally, black powder is not considered ammunition but rather an explosive[182] and therefore cannot be transported on a plane.

This means firearms and ammunition must be checked in and out of your possession before you go through the airport's metal detectors (and into a "sterile area" as explained in Chapter 8). All firearms and ammunition are subject to law enforcement inspection within the airport. Because the law does not specify how airlines must transport firearms and ammunition, airline policies may differ as to what containers or locks (or number of locks) are acceptable, how many firearms you may transport at once, or how much ammunition you may transport in a single flight. So, it is best to call the airline in advance to ask about its policy for transporting firearms and ammunition.

The fees airlines may charge for transporting firearms also vary. It is a good idea to print out the airline's written policy from its website, confirm your compliance with it, and bring it with you to the airport in case your compliance is questioned. The TSA warns that failing to follow the proper transport regulations will preclude you from traveling with firearms, ammunition, or firearm parts.

If you are flying to another state, and especially to other countries, know the other state's and/or country's laws about transporting firearms and ammunition, as well as whether your particular firearm or ammunition is legal there. That way you will be in compliance with those laws as soon as you leave the airport.

Although federal law generally protects you from being prosecuted under state laws when transporting an unloaded firearm across state lines between places where it is legal for you to have the firearm, as long as neither the firearm nor any ammunition is "readily accessible" (*e.g.*, in a locked case),[183] people have nevertheless been arrested and prosecuted while doing so. One famous case is that of a man who was traveling by plane from Utah to Pennsylvania. His flight included a layover in New Jersey, a state that requires a state-issued permit to possess a firearm and prohibits possessing hollow-point ammunition in public. The man missed his connecting flight, which caused him to have to take a bus. But he missed the bus when

---

[179] 49 C.F.R. § 175.10(a)(8).

[180] *Firearms and Ammunition*, TRANSPORTATION SECURITY ADMINISTRATION, https://www.tsa.gov/travel/transporting-firearms-and-ammunition (last visited Oct. 10, 2020).

[181] 49 C.F.R. § 173.59.

[182] 49 C.F.R. § 173.59. *See also* 27 C.F.R. section 555.11, excluding black powder from the definition of "ammunition."

[183] 18 U.S.C. § 926A.

he realized his luggage was not on it. The next day after finding his luggage with his firearm, as required by federal law, he told the airline that he had a firearm in his luggage and that it was unloaded and locked. He was then arrested for possessing a firearm without a New Jersey permit and for possessing hollow-point ammunition.

Even though criminal charges were eventually dropped, he spent four days in jail and did not get his firearm or related items back until two years later. He sued the New Jersey officials over the incident but lost. The court held that the general federal immunity for transporting firearms ended once he took possession of his luggage in New Jersey because the firearm was then "readily accessible."[184] The moral of the story is that transporting firearms by plane can be risky, and you should protect yourself by knowing whether a situation like this could potentially arise in your connecting or destination state(s).

The gentleman in New Jersey would not have violated the law had he not taken possession of his luggage, but it is unclear what he should have done instead. The court suggested people in this situation request law enforcement or airport personnel keep their luggage overnight but failed to provide further guidance if law enforcement refuses to do so.

Along with Newark, LaGuardia Airport in New York also reportedly arrests and prosecutes unwitting and blameless "violators" of firearm transport laws, some of whom are not technically committing crimes.

B. Transporting on a Bus or Other Public Transportation

Assuming there is no restriction on having firearms on a specific type of public transportation, the same laws that apply when going directly to or from your vehicle "for any lawful purpose" likely also apply to public transportation. California law does not otherwise expressly address how to lawfully transport firearms on public transportation. But it does regulate where you can possess firearms and ammunition inside public transit facilities (see Chapter 8).

C. Transporting Firearms Across State Lines

Despite state or local laws to the contrary, federal law allows you to transport firearms "for any lawful purpose" by motor vehicle between any states where you may legally possess a firearm. The firearm must be unloaded, and neither the firearm nor any ammunition can be easily or directly accessible from within the vehicle's passenger compartment. If your vehicle does not have a compartment separate from the passenger compartment, the firearm or ammunition must be in a separate locked container other than a "glove compartment or console."[185]

---

[184] *Revell v. Port Auth. of New York, New Jersey*, 598 F.3d 128 (3d Cir. 2010), *cert. denied*, 131 S. Ct. 995 (2011).

[185] 18 U.S.C. § 926A (part of the Firearm Owners' Protection Act (FOPA)).

The NRA's "Guide to the Interstate Transportation of Firearms"[186] lists numerous places with special rules about transporting firearms. Be careful because, like California, some restrict what types of weapons you can possess within the state, have specific laws on how to transport firearms, and may even require you to obtain a license/permit before carrying within the state. So before transporting a firearm through another state, check the state's laws to make sure that you comply with them.[187]

Table 7.7

Quick Tips for Transporting Your Firearms Using Public and Private Transportation
Airplanes
If you plan on transporting firearms or ammunition on an airplane, you should keep these tips in mind:
✓ You must use the ticket counter check-in process and inform the check-in agent that you are transporting a firearm or ammunition. This requirement also applies to disassembled firearms.
✓ The firearm must be unloaded and transported as *checked* baggage in a locked, hard-sided container that only you have the key to, but keep in mind that, if law enforcement at the airport asks you to open the container, you should comply immediately.
✓ Any ammunition should be securely packed in boxes or other packaging specifically designed to carry small amounts of ammunition (*e.g.*, the manufacturer's packaging).
✓ You should also check the airline's website or call them before the flight to confirm any additional rules they may have with respect to transporting firearms. This is especially important when it comes to the amount of ammunition that you may transport on an airline as each airline differs in this respect. The typical limit, however, is 11 pounds of ammunition.
✓ You should also know the laws of any other state (or states if your flight has a layover) so you will be in compliance with them as soon as the airplane lands. And, make sure that you transport your firearms to and from the airport in accordance with state laws.
Amtrak Trains
If you are traveling on Amtrak (see Chapter 8) you should:
✓ Declare to Amtrak your intent to transport a firearm at the time the reservation is made (online reservations for checking firearms are not accepted), or at least 24 hours before departure.
✓ Unload and transport your firearm in a locked, hard-sided container in checked baggage.

---

[186] *See Guide to the Interstate Transportation of Firearms*, NRA-ILA, https://www.nraila.org/articles/20150101/guide-to-the-interstate-transportation (last visited Oct. 10, 2020).

[187] Discussed further in Chapter 9. Under FOPA you will be protected from prosecution if you are merely traveling through a state that prohibits the possession of "assault weapons" and if your firearm meets all the transportation requirements outlined in the law. *See* 18 U.S.C. 926A. But if your destination is a state that prohibits "assault weapons," or you stop in such a state, you will not be protected under the provisions the law. Out of an abundance of caution, however, you should be careful when transporting firearms across state lines.

Quick Tips for Transporting Your Firearms Using Public and Private Transportation
Motor Vehicles
If you are traveling in a motor vehicle and plan on transporting a handgun in it, you should follow these tips:
✓ The handgun must be *unloaded* and in an *appropriate container*. For specifics on what is an *appropriate container*, see Section II above, which outlines the container requirements for concealed handguns.
Buses or Other Public Transportation
If you plan on transporting a firearm or ammunition on a bus or other public transportation system, you should keep the following in mind:
✓ You should check to see if there any restrictions on having firearms or ammunition on that specific type of public transportation system.
✓ If there are no special rules, the laws that apply to the transporting of firearms when going to or from your vehicle "for any lawful purpose" will apply. See Section II above for more details. And, keep in mind that once inside the bus terminal (see Chapter 8).
✓ If you plan on traveling on a Greyhound Bus with your firearms, think again. Greyhound does not allow firearms or ammunition to be transported on their buses (see Chapter 8).
Motorcycles
If you are planning on transporting an unloaded handgun or "firearm that is not a handgun" while you are on a motorcycle, you should make sure the firearm is:
✓ Unloaded.
✓ If it is a handgun, it should be in an appropriate locked container. If it is a "firearm that is not a handgun," it must be "encased."
✓ The definition of a "locked container" here, however, is unclear, as a lockable luggage box on the side of the motorcycle may or may not be considered a "utility compartment." To be safe, you should transport the unloaded handgun in a separate "locked container" inside the motorcycle's luggage box or a rider's backpack.
Bicycles
If you are planning on transporting your firearm while you are riding a bike, you should make sure the firearm is:
✓ Unloaded.
✓ If it is a handgun, it should be in an appropriate locked container. If it is a "firearm that is not a handgun," it must be "encased."
Motor Homes
If you are transporting a firearm in a motor home, you should keep the following in mind:
✓ If the motor home is in motion, it will generally be treated the same as a motor vehicle. See the tips for transporting firearms in motor vehicles in this table.
✓ If you are "camping" in the motor home, it may be treated like a residence. But this is unclear.
✓ Always check the rules posted by public campgrounds beforehand.

Quick Tips for Transporting Your Firearms Using Public and Private Transportation
Boats
If you are transporting a firearm in a boat, you should keep the following in mind: ✓ If a boat is designed to be lived on, it is likely that it will be treated similarly to a motor home. Meaning it will be treated either as a residence or a vehicle depending on how it is used.   ✓ If the boat is moving, the firearm should be kept as if it were being transported via a motor vehicle. See the section above in this table for tips for transporting firearms in motor vehicles.

IX. SUGGESTIONS ON HOW TO CARRY FIREARMS IN COMPLIANCE WITH CALIFORNIA FIREARMS LAWS

People often ask how a person should carry firearms in compliance with California's firearms laws. A lot of different considerations come into play for each situation, such as the reasons for carrying firearms, the person's destination, whether the person has a Carry License, and what areas the person is traveling through, to name a few. Nevertheless, some suggestions are universal, and some of these suggestions go beyond what California law requires. I've had more than my fair share of people who have called while facing serious criminal charges because they transported firearms under a "gray area" of California law, or law enforcement was unaware they were carrying the firearm lawfully because the way the firearm was transported was unusual or appeared to violate California law.

First of all, firearms should be transported unloaded. ALWAYS check (and double check) to see if your firearm is unloaded before packing the firearm in a case to transport it, packing it to take away from a range, etc. Especially if the handgun is the firearm you use for home defense. This being said, not only should the firearm not hold any ammunition, but there should be no ammunition in magazines, clips, speed loaders, etc. Ammunition should be transported in the box it came in (preferably) and in a separate bag or container from the firearm. The magazine should be transported with, but not in, the firearm, and no ammunition should be in the magazine.

All firearms should be transported in a gun case or container. Long guns should be locked up for reasons discussed in Chapter 8 relating to federal gun-free school zone restrictions. Handguns should be in a secure, fully enclosed case (preferably hard-sided) and locked within the case. Lawfully registered "assault weapons" or .50 BMG rifles should likewise be transported in a "locked container" or locked in the trunk of the vehicle.

If you want to put a gun lock or trigger lock on your firearm, that would be even better. Is one required? No, not if you are transporting your firearm lawfully. But it could potentially show law enforcement officers that you did everything, and even more than what's required, to transport your firearms.

The packing of firearms and ammunition should be done in your residence. Then the firearms should be taken to your vehicle for transportation. If you have a vehicle with a trunk, the firearms and ammunition should be transported in the trunk. In vehicles where the entire interior is accessible from the passenger compartment (*e.g.*, hatchback cars, SUVs, trucks), the firearms should be stored as far away as possible from the driver or anyone else occupying the vehicle. Again, this goes beyond the legal requirements for transporting firearms, but the purpose is to go beyond what is required to ease law enforcement's concerns if they happen to come across the firearms.

The course you take to your intended destination (*e.g.*, hunting area, range, dealer/gunsmith) should have as few deviations as possible (*e.g.* stopping for gas or restroom breaks). This means you should not stop to go to work, to go shopping at a mall, or to eat a big meal at a restaurant. If stops are required, make certain that the firearm and containers are not visible or recognizable from outside of the vehicle. And you should certainly make no stops at places where firearm possession is illegal or restricted, *e.g.*, schools and federal buildings (see Chapter 8 for other examples). You must also store any handguns in a "locked container" or locked in the trunk of your vehicle when leaving them in your vehicle unattended (see Chapter 5).

Once you arrive at your intended destination, keep your firearms and ammunition in the containers until you are inside the location and/or until they are needed to be used. Only load your firearms when they are ready to be discharged.

When returning to your place of residence, the above tips apply all over again: make sure the firearms are unloaded; placed in their locked containers, and placed in the vehicle; with no stops, except necessary ones, along the way; and keep the firearms in their cases until inside your residence. If you have to stop make sure that you store your handguns in a "locked container" or in the locked trunk of your care when leaving your vehicle unattended, and that all other firearms and containers are kept out of sight so that they are not visible from outside of the car.

Obviously, each person's individual needs and situations are different. Hopefully, this book sheds some light on California and federal laws, exceptions, and requirements for transporting firearms.

X. CARRY EXEMPTIONS TABLE

After reading this chapter, you probably realized there are numerous – and often convoluted – exemptions to the carry restrictions, which make it difficult to determine when, where, and how you may carry a firearm (*i.e.*, concealed, open, loaded). The following table organizes and consolidates these exemptions to assist you with the difficult chore of determining if any exemptions apply to you.

Before turning to the table, you must first determine the type of conduct you wish to engage in, and whether that conduct is restricted under California law (see Chapter 6). If that conduct is not restricted, you do not need to review this table. But, if that conduct *is* restricted, review the table to see if you fall under any applicable exemptions.

The table is broken down into three main sections: (1) exemptions based on *who* you are; (2) exemptions based on *where* you are; and (3) exemptions based on the *activity* you are engaged in. After determining that the conduct you wish to engage in is restricted, review these sections to see if there is an applicable exemption to your specific situation. Exemptions that apply to certain people because of their occupation, club affiliations, or because they possess certain licenses and/or permits, can be found in the first section entitled, "Exemptions Based on *Who* You Are." Exemptions that apply to certain locations, such as your residence or private place of business, can be found in the second section entitled, "Exemptions Based on *Where* You Are." Exemptions that apply while you engage in or travel to specific activities, such as hunting or target shooting, can be found in the third and final section entitled, "Exemptions Based on The *Activity* You Engage In."

Once you determine the relevant section, locate your specific status or circumstance in the left-hand column of the table. From there, you should follow the row to the right to see if your status or circumstance allows you to carry an unloaded handgun concealed, an unloaded handgun openly, an unloaded "firearm that is not a handgun," and/or a loaded firearm. Beware, some exemptions have additional, important information in the "Notes and Comments" column that you should be aware of and follow to lawfully carry your firearm. These specific exemptions are marked with one or more asterisk (*) that correspond to the information in the "Notes and Comments." Information in the "Notes and Comments" column that is *not* marked with an asterisk applies to each exemption with a "yes."

Remember, if you wish to engage in a combination of restricted activities (*e.g.*, carrying concealed and loaded), each activity must be covered by an exemption. Keep in mind that even though your conduct may fall under an exemption, you can still be subject to other restrictions depending on your location (see Chapter 8). For example, you may still be restricted from carrying a firearm in a government building despite the fact that you would otherwise fall under an exemption.

Finally, although most of the exemptions to the carry restrictions appear in this table, you may not be able to find every circumstance or situation that you are involved in. Also, I make no claims, promises, or guarantees as to the completeness or accuracy of the information in this table, nor do I guarantee that adhering to this table will keep you from being arrested and/or convicted of a crime. This table is solely a guide, and you should refer to the applicable Penal Code sections before carrying a firearm while engaging in any of these activities. If you have any questions or concerns as to whether you can lawfully carry a firearm in a certain situation, you should contact an attorney experienced in firearms law.

Table 7.8

EXEMPTIONS BASED ON WHO YOU ARE

WHO ARE YOU?	DESCRIPTION	CAN YOU CARRY AN UNLOADED HANDGUN CONCEALED?	CAN YOU CARRY AN UNLOADED HANDGUN OPENLY?	CAN YOU CARRY AN UNLOADED "FIREARM THAT IS NOT A HANDGUN"?[189]	CAN YOU CARRY A LOADED FIREARM?	NOTES AND COMMENTS
Carry License Holders	Do you have a valid carry license?	Yes* P.C. § 25655	Yes** P.C. § 26150(b)(2)	No	Yes* P.C. § 26010	*The exemption to the carry concealed restriction is firearm specific, meaning the code section allows you to carry a handgun only if you are licensed to carry that specific handgun. Oddly, the exemption to the loaded restriction allows you to carry "any handgun" so long as you have a valid carry license. **This exemption applies only if you are issued a license under P.C. § 26150(b)(2), i.e., a license to carry a handgun loaded and exposed. But, a sheriff can only issue this license when the population of the county in which you live is less than 200,000 persons according to the most recent federal decennial census, and the license is only effective in the county it was issued in.
Special Permit Holders	Do you have a valid permit to possess destructive devices, "assault weapons," .50 BMG rifles, machineguns, or short-barreled rifles or shotguns, and are you carrying pursuant to the terms and conditions of your permit?	No	Yes P.C. § 26390	Yes P.C. § 26405(ae)	No	These exemptions apply only if the type of firearm (handgun or long gun) you are carrying is a destructive device, assault weapon, .50 BMG rifle, machinegun, or short-barreled rifle. See Chapters 9 & 10 for the definitions of these items.
Active Peace Officers	Are you an active peace officer listed in P.C. §§ 830.1, 830.2, 830.33(a) or any other duly appointed peace officers?	Yes P.C. § 25450(a)-(b)	Yes P.C. § 26361	Yes P.C. § 26405(e)	Yes P.C. § 25900(a)-(b)	You may also be exempted under LEOSA (discussed in Chapter 7, Section (VII)(B)).

[189] For purposes of this category, we are assuming that you are carrying the firearm outside of your vehicle. Remember, the restriction on carrying unloaded "firearms that are not handguns" does not apply when you are carrying the firearm inside of a vehicle.

CHAPTER 7: FIREARM CARRY RESTRICTION EXEMPTIONS AND TRANSPORTING FIREARMS | 315

Retired Peace Officers	Are you an honorably retired peace officer listed in P.C. §§ 830.5(c), 830.1, 830.2, 830.33(a), 832.6(a)(1), or were you authorized to carry a firearm while employed as a peace officer, and in fact did?	Yes P.C. § 25450(a), (c)-(d)	Yes P.C. § 26361	Yes P.C. § 26405(e)	Yes P.C. § 25900(a), (c)-(d)	You may also be exempted under LEOSA (discussed in Chapter 7, Section (VII)(B)).
Active Peace Officers From Another State	Are you a full-time, paid peace officer from another state carrying out official duties in California?	Yes P.C. § 25450(e)	Yes P.C. § 26361	Yes P.C. § 26405(e)	Yes P.C. § 25900(e)	You may also be exempted under LEOSA (discussed in Chapter 7, Section (VII)(B)).
Persons Assisting in an Arrest	Have you been summoned by any of the officers discussed in the three proceeding rows of this table to assist in making an arrest or preserving the peace?	Yes P.C. § 25450(f)	Yes P.C. § 26378	Yes* P.C. § 26405(u)	Yes P.C. § 25900(f)	All of these exemptions apply only *while* you are assisting the officer. *These exemptions apply to any "peace officer" who requests your assistance, not just to the ones discussed in the preceding rows.
Federal Agents	Are you a full-time paid peace officer of the federal government carrying out official duties in California?	Yes P.C. § 25450(e)	Yes P.C. § 26361	Yes P.C. § 26405(e)	Yes P.C. § 25900(e)	You may also be exempted under LEOSA (discussed in Chapter 7, Section (VII)(B)).
Retired Federal Agents	Are you an honorably retired federal officer or agent who was authorized to carry weapons while on duty, who was assigned to duty within California for a period of not less than one year, or who was retired from active service in California and possess a permit from your local sheriff?	Yes P.C. § 25650	Yes P.C. § 26362	Yes P.C. § 26405(f)	Yes P.C. § 26020	You may also be exempted under LEOSA (discussed in Chapter 7, Section (VII)(B)).

Exemptions Based on Who Are You

Who Are You?	Description	Can You Carry an Unloaded Handgun Concealed?	Can You Carry an Unloaded Handgun Openly?	Can You Carry an Unloaded "Firearm That Is Not a Handgun"?	Can You Carry a Loaded Firearm?	Notes and Comments
Guards of Common Carriers or Financial Institutions	Are you a guard or messenger of a common carrier, bank, or other financial institution who is employed to transport money, treasure, bullion, bonds, or other things of value?	Yes P.C. § 25630	Yes* P.C. § 26362	Yes* P.C. § 26405(f)	Yes* P.C. § 26030(a)(1)	In order for any of these exemptions to apply, you must actually be employed and shipping, transporting, or delivering the money, treasure, bullion, bonds or other things of value. *In order to meet these three exemptions, you must be certified by the Department of Consumer Affairs (*i.e.*, complete a course in carrying and using firearms, and the powers of arrest). Peace officers specified in P.C. § 26030(c) do not need the certificate.
Armored Vehicle Guards	Are you an armored vehicle guard employed by an armored contract carrier who, during the course and scope of your employment, carries a deadly weapon (*see* Cal. Bus. & Prof. Code § 7581.1)?	No	Yes P.C. § 26362	Yes P.C. § 26405(f)	Yes P.C. §§ 26015, 26030(a)(2)-(3)	If you were hired *on or after* January 1, 1977, you must have received a firearms qualification card in order to qualify for these exemptions. You must also be acting within the scope of your employment for these exemptions to apply. Peace officers specified in P.C. § 26030(c) do not need the certificate.
Private Investigators	Are you a person who is licensed under the Private Investigators Act or a uniformed employee of a private investigator?	No	Yes P.C. § 26362	Yes P.C. § 26405(f)	Yes P.C. § 26030(a)(4)-(5)	In order to meet any of these exemptions, you must be certified (*i.e.*, complete a course in carrying and using firearms, and the powers of arrest), and you must be acting in the scope of your employment. Peace officers specified in P.C. § 26030(c) do not need the certificate.

Private Patrol Officers	Are you a licensed private patrol officer or a uniformed employee of a private patrol officer?	No	Yes P.C. § 26362	Yes P.C. § 26405(f)	Yes P.C. § 26030(a)(6)-(7)	In order to meet any these exemptions, you must be certified (*i.e.*, complete a course in carrying and using firearms, and the powers of arrest), and you must be acting in the scope of your employment. Peace officers specified in P.C. § 26030(c) do not need the certificate. Alarm company operators must be certified (*i.e.*, complete a course in carrying and using firearms, the powers of arrest and possess an exposed firearm permit), and acting in the scope of employment to meet any these exemptions. Peace officers specified in P.C. § 26030(c) do not need the certificate.
Alarm Company Operators/ Agents	Are you a licensed alarm company operator or uniformed alarm company agent?	No	Yes P.C. § 26362	Yes P.C. § 26405(f)	Yes P.C. § 26030(a)(8), (10)	Uniformed alarm company agents must also be certified (*i.e.*, complete a course in carrying and using firearms, the powers of arrest and possess an exposed firearm permit), and must actually be engaged in preserving the property of their employers, or on duty or en route to or from their residence, place of employment, or a target range to meet these exemptions. Peace officers specified in P.C. § 26030(c) do not need the certificate.

Exemptions Based on Who You Are

Who Are You?	Description	Can You Carry An Unloaded Handgun Concealed?	Can You Carry An Unloaded Handgun Openly?	Can You Carry An Unloaded "Firearm That Is Not A Handgun"?	Can You Carry A Loaded Firearm?	Notes and Comments
Uniformed Security Guards/Night Watch Persons	Are you a night watch person employed by a public agency, a uniformed security guard employed by a public agency, or employed by a lawful business to act as a security guard?	No	Yes P.C. § 26362	Yes P.C. § 26405(f)	Yes P.C. § 26030(a) (9)-(10)	Uniformed security guards and night watch persons employed by *a public agency* must be certified (*i.e.*, complete a course in carrying and using firearms, the powers of arrest and possess an exposed firearm permit) and be acting within the scope of employment to meet any these exemptions. Peace officers specified in P.C. § 26030(c) do not need the certificate. Uniformed security guards employed by *a lawful business* must be certified (*i.e.*, complete a course in carrying and using firearms, the powers of arrest and possess an exposed firearm permit), and must actually be engaged in preserving the property of their employers, or on duty or en route to or from their residence, place of employment, or a target range to meet these exemptions. Peace officers specified in P.C. § 26030(c) do not need the certificate.
Patrol Special Officers	Are you a patrol special officer appointed by the police commissioner who has completed a course in firearms training approved by POST?	No	Yes P.C. § 26362	Yes P.C. § 26405(f)	Yes P.C. § 26025(a)	In order to meet any of these exemptions, the patrol special officer must: (1) be subject to suspension or dismissal after a hearing on charges duly filed with POST after a fair and impartial trial; (2) not be less than 18 years old or more than 40 years old; (3) possess physical qualities prescribed by POST; and (4) have a designated beat or territory.
Animal Control Officers or Zookeepers	Are you an animal control officer or zookeeper who works for a government agency?	No	Yes P.C. § 26362	Yes P.C. § 26405(f)	Yes P.C. § 26025(b)	You can only carry these firearms when acting in the course and scope of your employment, and it must be designated by local ordinance or resolution that you may carry these firearms.
Humane Officers	Are you a humane officer?	No	Yes P.C. § 26362	Yes P.C. § 26405(f)	Yes P.C. § 26025(c)	You can only carry under these exemptions if you are actually engaged in the performance of your duties under Cal. Corp. Code § 14502.

CHAPTER 7: FIREARM CARRY RESTRICTION EXEMPTIONS AND TRANSPORTING FIREARMS | 319

Harbor Police Officers	Are you a harbor police officer designated under Cal. Harbors & Navigation Code § 663.5?	No	Yes P.C. § 26362	Yes P.C. § 26405(f)	Yes P.C. § 26025(d)	N/A
Common Carriers	Are you a person operating a licensed common carrier or an authorized agent or employee of a common carrier transporting a firearm?	Yes P.C. § 25645	Yes P.C. § 26367	Yes* P.C. § 26405(k)	No	In order to meet these exemptions, you must transport the firearm in conformance with applicable federal law. *This exemption states that you are exempted from transporting "handguns." But, the legislature likely meant "firearms that are not handguns."
Lawful Firearms Businesses	Are you a person licensed to engaged in the business of manufacturing, importing, wholesaling, repairing, or dealing in firearms, or an agent or employee of that person?	Yes P.C. § 25615	Yes P.C. § 26363	Yes P.C. § 26405(g)	No	In order to meet any of these exemptions, the firearm must be carried as "merchandise" while you are engaged in the lawful course of business.
Ammunition Manufacturers	Are you engaged in the business of manufacturing ammunition, or an authorized representative or agent of a person who is?	No	No	Yes P.C. § 26405(ah)	No	In order to meet this exemption, you must be licensed to manufacture ammunition under Chapter 44 of Title 18 of the United States Code or employed by such a person. This exemption only applies while you are using the firearm in the lawful course and scope of activities related to the manufacturing of ammunition.
Military Members	Are you a member of the Army, Navy, Air Force, Coast Guard, or Marine Corps of the United States, or National Guard?	Yes* P.C. § 25620	Yes P.C. § 26362	Yes P.C. § 26405(f)	Yes P.C. § 26000	*This exemption specifically requires you to be "on duty" to meet, while the other exemptions only require you to be performing your duties as a military member.

Exemptions Based on Who You Are

Who Are You?	Description	Can You Carry an Unloaded Handgun Concealed?	Can You Carry an Unloaded Handgun Openly?	Can You Carry an Unloaded "Firearm That Is Not A Handgun"?	Can You Carry A Loaded Firearm?	Notes and Comments
Organizations Acquiring Firearms from the Government	Are you an organization that is authorized by law to purchase or receive firearms from the United States or California?	Yes P.C. § 25620	No	No	N/A	
Members of Organizations or Clubs	Are you a member of an organization or club organized for the purpose of shooting targets and are practicing shooting at targets on an established target range?	Yes* P.C. § 25635	Yes** P.C. § 26365	Yes P.C. § 26405(f), (i)	Yes*** P.C. § 26005(a)	*The concealed carry exemption also allows you to transport an unloaded handgun directly to and from an established target range. **This exemption applies only when you are outside of a vehicle. ***While the other exemptions in this section are specific to members of clubs or organizations, the exemption to the loaded restriction is not. This exemption applies to all persons who are using target ranges for the purpose of practice shooting, regardless of whether they are members of a club or organization.

Exemptions Based on Where You Are

Where Are You?	Description	Can You Carry An Unloaded Handgun Concealed?	Can You Carry An Unloaded Handgun Openly?	Can You Carry An Unloaded "Firearm That Is Not A Handgun"?	Can You Carry A Loaded Firearm?	Notes and Comments
Your Residence	Are you at your residence?	Yes* P.C. § 25605(a)	Yes P.C. § 25605	Yes P.C. § 26405(a)	Yes** P.C. § 26055	*You may also transport an unloaded handgun in a locked container directly between your place of residence, place of business, or other privately owned property. P.C. § 25525, 25505. **This exemption provides that you may *have* a loaded firearm at your residence; it does not say that you may *carry* a loaded firearm there.
Your Other Private Property	Are you on your private property that you own or lawfully possess?	Yes* P.C. § 25605(a)	Yes P.C. §§ 25605(a),	Yes P.C. § 26405(a)	Yes** P.C. § 26035	*You may also transport a handgun unloaded in a locked container directly between your place of residence, place of business, or other privately owned property. P.C. § 25525, 25505. **This exemption provides that you may *have* a loaded firearm while you are on property you lawfully possess; it does not say that you may *carry* a loaded firearm there.
Home or Privately Held Property of Another	Are you at someone else's private business, home, or private property that is lawfully owned or possessed by that person?	No	Yes* P.C. § 26383	Yes P.C. § 26405(b)	No	In order to meet any of these exemptions, if you have permission to carry the firearm from the property owner or person who lawfully possesses the property. In order for the permission to be valid, the property owner must be able to lawfully carry on his or her property under P.C. § 25605. *This exemption applies only when you are outside of a vehicle. But you may be able to carry the handgun openly in your vehicle if you meet another exemption.

Exemptions Based on Where you Are

Where Are You?	Description	Can You Carry an Unloaded Handgun Concealed?	Can You Carry an Unloaded Handgun Openly?	Can You Carry an Unloaded "Firearm That Is Not a Handgun"?	Can You Carry a Loaded Firearm?	Notes and Comments
Your Private Business	Are you in your place of business?	Yes* P.C. § 25605(a)	Yes P.C. § 25605	Yes P.C. §§ 25605(a), 26405(a)	Yes** P.C. § 26035	*You may also transport a handgun unloaded and in a locked container directly between your place of residence, place of business, or other privately held property that you own. P.C. § 25525, 25505. **It is unclear whether you can *carry* a loaded firearm within your business if it is located in a "public place." This exemption only provides that you may *have* a loaded firearm in your business if you have it for a lawful purpose connected with your business.
Private Business of Another	Are you in someone else's private business, residence, or privately owned property?	No	Yes* P.C. § 26383	Yes P.C. § 26405(b)	No	In order to meet any of these exemptions, you must have permission from the property owner to carry on their property. But, in order for the permission to be valid, the property owner must themselves be able to lawfully carry on their property. *This exemption only applies when you are outside of a vehicle. But, you may be able to carry the handgun openly in your vehicle if you meet another exemption.

CHAPTER 7: FIREARM CARRY RESTRICTION EXEMPTIONS AND TRANSPORTING FIREARMS | 323

Category	Question				Notes
Campsites or Temporary Residences	Are you at a campsite or temporary residence?	No*	No	Maybe** P.C. § 26055	*You may transport an unloaded handgun in a locked container when going to or from your campsite, if you are taking the handgun for the purpose of self-defense. P.C. § 25550(a). But keep in mind that you are still subject to any other restrictions or rules made by other governmental agencies that regulate the transportation or possession of firearms on parks or campgrounds. P.C. § 25550(b). **This exemption only provides that you may *have* a loaded firearm at your temporary residence or campsite; it does not say that you may *carry* a loaded firearm there. Therefore, it is unclear whether or not you can carry a loaded firearm in a temporary residence or campsite without a Carry License.
Club or Organization Meetings	Are you at a meeting of a club or organization, organized for the purpose of lawfully collecting and displaying handguns or other firearms?	Yes P.C. § 25515	No	No	In order to meet this exemption, you must actually be a member of the club or organization and the firearm must be unloaded and in a locked container while you are at the meeting of the club or organization. You may also transport the handgun when going directly to or from a meeting of the club or organization if it is unloaded and in a locked container. P.C. § 25505.
School Zones	Are you in a school zone (defined in Chapter 8)?	No	Yes P.C. § 26370	Yes P.C. § 26405(n)	No	In order to meet any of these exemptions, your carrying of the firearm must not be prohibited by the Gun-Free School Zone restriction (P.C. § 626.9). (See Chapter 8).

Exemptions Based on Where You Are

Where Are You?	Description	Can You Carry An Unloaded Handgun Concealed?	Can You Carry An Unloaded Handgun Openly?	Can You Carry An Unloaded "Firearm That Is Not A Handgun"?	Can You Carry A Loaded Firearm?	Notes And Comments
Gun Shows	Are you at a gun show, swap meet, or similar event where the public is invited, for the purpose of displaying your firearm?	Yes* P.C. § 25535	Yes** P.C. § 26369	Yes** P.C. § 26405(m)	No	*This exemption applies only to transporting an unloaded handgun to and from the event in a locked container. P.C. § 25505. This exemption also applies to any gun shows or events as defined by Section 478.100 of Title 27 of the Code of Federal Regulations for transferring the firearm via lawful private transfer. **These exemptions apply to gun shows conducted pursuant to Article 1 (commencing with Section 27200) and Article 2 (commencing with Section 27300) of Chapter 3 of Division 6 of the Penal Code. The exemption to the open carry restriction applies only when you are carrying outside of a vehicle.
Nonprofit Auctions, Raffles, or Similar Events	Are you at an auction, raffle, or similar event of a nonprofit public benefit or mutual benefit corporation?	No	Yes P.C. § 26384	Yes P.C. § 26405(z)	No	In order to meet any of these exemptions, the firearm must be: (1) a firearm that is going to be auctioned, raffled, or otherwise sold for the benefit of the nonprofit or a firearm that you bought at the auction; and (2) it must be delivered by a firearms dealer.
State or Local Public Buildings	Are you at a place protected by P.C. § 171b (i.e., any state or local public building or at a meeting place required to be open to the public)?	No	Yes P.C. § 26371	Yes P.C. § 26405(o)	No	In order to meet any of these exemptions, you must be one of the persons listed in P.C. § 171b(b).

CHAPTER 7: FIREARM CARRY RESTRICTION EXEMPTIONS AND TRANSPORTING FIREARMS | **325**

State Capital or Legislative Offices	Are you in a place protected by P.C. § 171c (*i.e.*, the State Capital or its grounds, any legislative office, any office of the Governor or other constitutional officer, or any hearing room in which a committee of the Senate or Assembly is conducting a hearing)?	No	Yes P.C. § 26385	Yes P.C. § 26405(aa)	No	In order to meet any of these exemptions, you must have permission to carry the firearm from the Chief Sergeants at Arms of the State Assembly *and* the State Senate.
Governor's Mansion or Other Constitutional Officers' Residences	Are you in, or on a place protected by P.C. § 171d (*i.e.*, the grounds of the Governor's Mansion, or any other residence of the Governor, constitutional officer, or Member of the Legislature)?	No	Yes P.C. § 26386	Yes P.C. § 26405(ab)	No	In order to meet any of these exemptions, you must be one of the persons listed in P.C. § 171d.
Airports or Passenger Vessel Terminals	Are you in an airport or passenger vessel terminal (see Chapter 8)?	No	Yes P.C. § 26391	Yes P.C. § 26405(ag)	No	In order to meet any of these exemptions, you must be one of the persons listed in P.C. § 171.5(d).
Sterile Areas of Public Transit Facilities	Are you in an area protected by P.C. § 171.7 (*i.e.*, a sterile area of a public transit facility) (see Chapter 8)?	No	Yes P.C. § 26387	Yes P.C. § 26405(ac)	No	In order to meet any of these exemptions, you must be responsible for the security of the public transit system and authorized in writing by the public transit authority's security coordinator to possess the firearm.
Publicly Owned Land	Are you on publicly owned land?	No	Yes P.C. § 26388	Yes P.C. § 26405(ad)	No	In order to meet any of these exemptions, your possession and use of the firearm must be specifically permitted by the managing agency of that land. You must also be in lawful possession of the firearm.
Navigable Waters of California	Are you on navigable waters held in public trust of California?	No	No	Yes P.C. § 26405(ai)	No	In order to meet this exemption, your possession and use of the firearm must be specifically permitted by the managing agency of the navigable waters. You must also be in lawful possession of the firearm.

EXEMPTIONS BASED ON THE ACTIVITY YOU ENGAGE IN					
WHAT ARE YOU DOING?	DESCRIPTION	CAN YOU CARRY AN UNLOADED HANDGUN CONCEALED?	CAN YOU CARRY AN UNLOADED HANDGUN OPENLY?	CAN YOU CARRY AN UNLOADED "FIREARM THAT IS NOT A HANDGUN"?	CAN YOU CARRY A LOADED FIREARM?	NOTES AND COMMENTS
Shooting at a Target Range	Are you at an established target range for the purpose of practice shooting with a firearm?	No*	Yes** P.C. § 26377	Yes*** P.C. § 26405(f), (t)	Yes**** P.C. § 26005(a)	*But you may transport a handgun for the purpose of practice shooting directly to or from a target range that has a regulatory or business license. But, the handgun must be unloaded and kept in a locked container while it is being transported. P.C. § 25540, 25505. **This exemption applies only while you are using the handgun at an *established public or private* target range. ***This exemption applies only when you are using a firearm at an *established public* target range. ****This exemption applies only when you are using a target range for the purpose of practice shooting with the firearm.
Hunting at the Shooting Club	Are you a member of a shooting club and hunting on the club's premises?	Yes* P.C. § 25640	Yes* P.C. § 26366	Yes* P.C. § 26405(j)	Yes P.C. § 26005(b)	*Note that you would be exempted under these restrictions regardless of whether you are a member of a shooting club or are shooting on club premises because you would be exempted under the much broader exemptions listed in the "hunting" section above (unless you are hunting in a city that has a local law that requires membership in the club to hunt). There are no specific exemptions for the concealed, open, or "firearm that is not a handgun" restrictions that apply only to members of shooting clubs.

CHAPTER 7: FIREARM CARRY RESTRICTION EXEMPTIONS AND TRANSPORTING FIREARMS | 327

Hunting	Are you a licensed hunter and out hunting?	Yes* P.C. § 25640	Yes* P.C. § 26366	Yes* P.C. § 26405(j)	Yes** P.C. § 26040	*These exemptions only allow you to carry firearms when you are actually engaged in hunting. You may also transport your firearm to and from your hunting expedition. **The loaded restriction is not in force in areas where you are allowed to hunt because these places are generally in unincorporated areas where it is lawful to discharge a firearm. But, where the restriction does apply, you are exempted if you are actually engaged in hunting, you are in an area within an incorporated city, and ***you are hunting at a place and time that is not prohibited by the city council***. *Note*: You may also carry a loaded or unloaded rocket, rocket propelled projectile launcher, or similar device designed primarily for emergency or distress signaling purposes while in a permitted hunting area or traveling to or from a permitted hunting area and carrying a valid California permit or license to hunt. P.C. §§ 26060, 26362, 26405(f).
Training Your Dog for Hunting	Are you a licensed hunter training your dog for the purpose of using the dog for hunting not prohibited by law?	No	Yes* P.C. § 26366.5	Yes* P.C. § 26405(af)	No	*These exemptions also allow you to transport the firearm when you are going to and from the place you are training your dog.

Exemptions Based on The Activity You Engage In

What Are You Doing?	Description	Can You Carry an Unloaded Handgun Concealed?	Can You Carry an Unloaded Handgun Openly?	Can You Carry an Unloaded "Firearm That Is Not a Handgun"?	Can You Carry a Loaded Firearm?	Notes and Comments
Fishing	Are you a licensed fisherman on a fishing expedition?	Yes* P.C. § 25640	No**	No**	No**	*This exemption allows you to carry the firearm when you are going to or returning from your fishing expedition. **Keep in mind that the restrictions on carrying unloaded handguns openly, "firearms that are not handguns," and loaded firearms do not apply to unincorporated areas where it is lawful to discharge a firearm. This is likely why there aren't any exemptions to these restrictions for fishing as fishing often takes place in such areas.
Camping	Are you camping?	No*	No	No	Maybe** P.C. §26055	*You may also transport an unloaded handgun in a locked container when going to or from your campsite if you are taking the handgun for the purpose of self-defense while at the lawful campsite. P.C. § 25550(a). But, you are still subject to any other restrictions or rules made by governmental agencies that may regulate the transportation or possession of firearms on parks or campgrounds. P.C. § 25550(b). **This exemption only provides that you may have a loaded firearm at your temporary residence or campsite; it does not say that you may carry a loaded firearm there. So, it is unclear whether you may carry a loaded firearm in a temporary residence or campsite without a Carry License.

CHAPTER 7: FIREARM CARRY RESTRICTION EXEMPTIONS AND TRANSPORTING FIREARMS | 329

Parading with Military or Civil Org.	Are you parading with a military or civil organization?	Yes* P.C. § 25625	Yes** P.C. § 26364	Yes** P.C. § 26405(h)	No	In order to meet any of these exemptions, you must be a duly authorized member of the military or civil organization you are parading with. *This exemption applies only when you are going to and from the place where you are meeting your military or civil organization to parade. **These exemptions apply when you are at the meeting place of your military or civil organization, while parading, or while you are rehearsing or practicing for the parade.
Parading with Non-Profit or Tax Exempt Org.	Are you on official parade duty or at a ceremonial occasion of an organization chartered by the Congress of the United States or a nonprofit mutual or public benefit corporation recognized by the IRS as such?	No	Yes P.C. § 26368	Yes P.C. § 26405(l)	No	In order to meet any of these exemptions, you must be a member of the organization, nonprofit, or public benefit corporation.
Taking Your Firearm to Sell, Repair, Loan, or Transfer	Are you transporting your firearm to a business or private residence to sell, loan, or transfer that firearm or to have it lawfully repaired?	Yes* P.C. § 25530	No	No	No	*In order to for this exemption to apply, you must transport the handgun unloaded and in a locked container, and your course of travel should only include necessary deviations. P.C. § 25505.
Engaging in Firearm Related Activities at a Business	Are you at a fixed place of business and (1) engaging in activities that are related to the selling, making, repairing, transferring, pawning of a firearm; (2) using a firearm; or (3) engaging in firearms training?	No	Yes* P.C. § 26374	Yes* P.C. § 26405(q)	No	*In order to meet these exemptions, you must be at a fixed place of business licensed to conduct, and does in fact conduct, as a regular course of business, activities related to selling, making, repairing, transferring, pawning, or using the firearm, or firearms training.

Exemptions Based on The Activity You Engage In

What Are You Doing?	Description	Can You Carry an Unloaded Handgun Concealed?	Can You Carry an Unloaded Handgun Openly?	Can You Carry an Unloaded "Firearm That Is Not a Handgun"?	Can You Carry a Loaded Firearm?	Notes and Comments
Buying, Renting, or Receiving a Firearm	Are you participating in a transaction to buy/sell, loan, or transfer/receive a firearm?	No	Yes* P.C. § 26373	No	No	*This exemption applies only if the handgun is possessed on private property, and you must have permission of the owner or lessee of that private property to carry and possesses that handgun.
Taking a Found Firearm to Law Enforcement	Did you find a firearm and now want to transport it to a law enforcement agency to comply with your duties as a finder under the law (see Cal. Civ. Code § 2080.1(a))?	Yes* P.C. § 25570	Yes*	Yes* P.C. § 26406	No	* In order to for this exemption to apply, you must transport the handgun unloaded and in a locked container, and your course of travel should only include necessary deviations. P.C. § 25505. And, before transporting the handgun to the law enforcement agency, you must give them notice that you will be transporting the firearm there.
Taking a Firearm to Report Information	Are you taking a firearm to report information regarding the acquisition, ownership, destruction, or disposal of that firearm?	Yes* P.C. § 25560	Yes** P.C. § 26379(b)	Yes*** P.C. § 26405(v)(2)	No	In order to meet any of these exemptions, the firearm must be the firearm that you are reporting to the DOJ. * In order to for this exemption to apply, you must transport the handgun unloaded and in a locked container, and your course of travel should only include necessary deviations. P.C. § 25505 **This exemption applies only when you are outside of a vehicle incident to taking the firearm to report the information. But, you may be able to carry the handgun openly in your vehicle if you meet another exemption. ***This exemption only applies incident to taking the firearm to report the information.

CHAPTER 7: FIREARM CARRY RESTRICTION EXEMPTIONS AND TRANSPORTING FIREARMS | 331

Scenario	Question	Answer	Citation	Notes
Crime Victim Taking Firearm to Law Enforcement	Are you taking a firearm to law enforcement because you were a victim of a crime, took the firearm from the person who was committing the crime against you, and now want to transport that firearm to a law enforcement agency?	Yes* P.C. § 25570	Yes* P.C. § 26406	No	* In order to for this exemption to apply, you must transport the handgun unloaded and in a locked container, and your course of travel should only include necessary deviations. P.C. § 25505. And, before transporting the handgun to the law enforcement agency, you must give them notice that you will be transporting the firearm there.
Delivering Your Firearm to a "Gun Buyback"	Are you selling, delivering, or transferring a firearm to a government entity as part of a voluntary program in which the government is buying weapons from private individuals (i.e., a "gun buyback" event)?	Yes* P.C. § 25565	Yes** P.C. § 26379(c)	Yes P.C. § 26405(v)(3)	No	Keep in mind that these exemptions only apply to the specific firearm that you are selling in the "gun buyback" event. *This exemption only allows you to transport a handgun to the "gun buyback" event. The handgun must be unloaded and in a locked container while it is being transported and your course of travel should only include necessary deviations. P.C. § 25505. **This exemption applies only when you are outside of a vehicle. But, you may be able to carry the handgun openly in your vehicle if you meet another exemption.
Taking Your Firearm to Report it After Bringing it into the State	Are you a personal firearm importer transporting your firearm in order to comply with the personal firearm importer requirements (see Chapter 5)?	Yes* P.C. § 25575	Yes** P.C. § 26379(a)	Yes*** P.C. § 26405(v)(1)	No	*This exemption only allows you to transport a handgun to be reported/transferred/turned in under the personal firearm importer requirements. The handgun must be unloaded and in a locked container while it is being transported and your course of travel should only include necessary deviations. P.C. § 25505. **This exemption applies only when you are outside of a vehicle and incident to an activity associated with the requirements of a personal firearm importer. But, you may be able to carry the handgun openly in your vehicle if you meet another exemption. ***This exemption applies incident to complying with the requirements of a personal firearm importer.

EXEMPTIONS BASED ON THE ACTIVITY YOU ENGAGE IN

WHAT ARE YOU DOING?	DESCRIPTION	CAN YOU CARRY AN UNLOADED HANDGUN CONCEALED?	CAN YOU CARRY AN UNLOADED HANDGUN OPENLY?	CAN YOU CARRY AN UNLOADED "FIREARM THAT IS NOT A HANDGUN"?	CAN YOU CARRY A LOADED FIREARM?	NOTES AND COMMENTS
Transporting Your "Curio or Relic" to Comply with the Registration Requirement	Are you a licensed collector (see Chapter 3) who acquired a "curio or relic" from outside of California and are taking it to comply with the requirements of P.C. § 27565 (having to do with licensed collectors bringing "curio and relic" firearms into the state)?	Yes* P.C. § 25580	Yes** P.C. § 26379(a)	Yes*** P.C. § 26405(v)(1)	No	*This exemption only allows you to transport a handgun to be reported as required by P.C. § 27565. The handgun must be unloaded and in a locked container while it is being transported and your course of travel should only include necessary deviations. P.C. § 25505. **This exemption applies only when you are outside of a vehicle incident to reporting the handgun per P.C. § 27565. But, you may be able to carry the handgun openly in your vehicle if you meet another exemption. ***This exemption applies only to situations incident to the reporting requirement.
Taking A Firearm You Obtained by Operation of Law to Report it	Are you a person complying with the requirements of an intra-familial or operation of law transfer?	Yes* P.C. § 25555	Yes** P.C. § 26379(d),(e)	Yes*** P.C. § 26405(v)(4), (5)	No	*This exemption only allows you to transport a handgun to comply with the requirements of the transfer. The handgun must be unloaded and in a locked container while it is being transported and your course of travel should only include necessary deviations. P.C. § 25505. **This exemption applies only when you are outside of a vehicle and incident to the transfer. But, you may be able to carry the handgun openly in your vehicle if you meet another exemption. ***This exemption applies only to situations incident to the transfer of the firearm.

Exemption	Question					Notes
Taking Your Firearm to Obtain an Identification Number	Are you transporting your firearm to get an identification number assigned to that firearm (under P.C. § 23910)?	Yes* P.C. § 25585	Yes** P.C. § 26376	Yes*** P.C. § 26405(s)	No	*This exemption only allows you to transport a handgun for the purpose of obtaining an identification number or mark. The handgun must be unloaded and in a locked container while it is being transported and your course of travel should only include necessary deviations. P.C. § 25505. **This exemption applies only when you are outside of a vehicle and incident to obtaining an identification number or mark. But, you may be able to carry the handgun openly in your vehicle if you meet another exemption. ***This exemption applies only to situations incident getting the identification mark.
Storing an Emergency Signaling Device on a Fishing Vessel or Aircraft	Are you making or attempting to make a lawful arrest?	No	Yes* P.C. § 26362	Yes* P.C. § 26405(f)	Yes* P.C. § 26060	*These exemptions only allow you to store a loaded or unloaded rocket, rocket propelled projectile launcher, or similar device designed primarily for emergency or distress signaling purposes on a fishing vessel or aircraft.
Carrying at the Request of a Sheriff or Chief	Did a sheriff, chief of police, or other head of a municipal police department request that you carry a firearm?	No	Yes P.C. § 26382	Yes P.C. § 26405(y)	No	N/A
Acting in Self Defense When There is a Restraining Order	Are you in "grave danger" from a person against whom you have a restraining order?	Yes P.C. § 25600	Yes P.C. § 26362	Yes P.C. § 26405(d), (f)	Yes P.C. § 26045(b)	In order to meet any of these exemptions, the court must have issued the restraining order after finding that the person posed a threat to your life or safety. Keep in mind that these exemptions may not apply where there is a *mutual* restraining order. Also, the belief that you are in "grave danger" must be reasonable.

Exemptions Based on The Activity You Engage In

What Are You Doing?	Description	Can You Carry an Unloaded Handgun Concealed?	Can You Carry an Unloaded Handgun Openly?	Can You Carry an Unloaded "Firearm That Is Not a Handgun"?	Can You Carry a Loaded Firearm?	Notes and Comments
Acting in Self Defense, Absent a Restraining Order	Are you, another person, or your or another person's property in immediate, "grave danger"?	No	Yes P.C. § 26362	Yes P.C. § 26405(f)	Yes P.C. § 26045(a)	In order to meet any of these exemptions, you or another person must be in "immediate grave danger." "Immediate" in this circumstance means the brief interval before and after law enforcement has been notified of the danger and before they arrive.
Taking a Safety or Hunter Safety Class	Are you going to, or coming from a recognized safety or hunter safety class in which you are a participant?	Yes* P.C. §25520	No	No	No	*This exemption only allows you to transport a handgun directly to or from a recognized safety or hunter safety class. The handgun must be unloaded and in a locked container while it is being transported and your course of travel should only include necessary deviations. P.C. § 25505.
Training to Become a Sworn Officer	Are you training to become a sworn peace officer?	No	Yes* P.C. § 26380	Yes* P.C. § 26405(w)	No	*These exemptions apply only when you are carrying the firearm incident to, and during the course and scope of, your training to become a sworn peace officer as part of a study approved by the Commission on POST.
Training for a Carry License	Are you training to obtain a Carry License?	No	Yes* P.C. § 26381	Yes* P.C. § 26405(x)	No	*These exemptions apply only when you are carrying the firearm incident to, and during the course and scope of, a course of study necessary to obtain your license or authorized by a person who may legally to issue the license under Chapter 4 (commencing with P.C. § 26150).

CHAPTER 7: FIREARM CARRY RESTRICTION EXEMPTIONS AND TRANSPORTING FIREARMS | 335

	Question				
Taking Your Firearm to a Licensing Agency	Are you transporting your firearm to a place where Carry Licenses are issued for the purpose of determining whether you will be issued the license?	Yes* P.C. § 25545	No	No	*This exemption allows you to transport your firearm directly to and from a place designated to issue licenses under P.C. §§ 26150, 26155, 26170, or 26215. And, this exemption applies only when the issuing agency requests that you bring the firearm to them so they can determine whether to issue you a license. Keep in mind, the handgun must be unloaded and in a locked container while it is being transported and your course of travel should only include necessary deviations. P.C. § 25505.
Participating in a Motion Picture	Are you an authorized participant in a motion picture, television, or video production, or entertainment event?	Yes* P.C. § 25510(a)	Yes** P.C. § 26375	Yes** P.C. § 26405(r)	No	In order to meet any of these three exemptions, you must be lawfully using the firearm as part of the entertainment production or event. *This exemption also allows you to transport the handgun unloaded and in a locked container when going to or from the entertainment production or event. **Not only do these exemptions apply while you are making the motion picture, but also while you are rehearsing or practicing for that production or event.
Supplying Firearms to a Motion Picture	Are you an authorized employee or agent of a supplier of firearms that is supplying firearms to a motion picture, television or video production, or entertainment event?	Yes* P.C. § 25510(b)	Yes** P.C. § 26375	Yes** P.C. § 26405(r)	No	*The concealed carry exemption also allows you to transport the handgun unloaded and in a locked container when going directly to and from the entertainment production or event. **Not only do these exemptions apply while you are making the motion picture, but also while you are rehearsing or practicing for that production or event.
Participating in a Sporting Event	Are you going to or from a recognized sporting event involving a firearm in which you are a participant?	Yes* P.C. §25520	No	No	No	*This exemption only allows you to transport a handgun directly to or from a recognized safety or hunter safety class. The handgun must be unloaded and in a locked container while it is being transported and your course of travel should only include necessary deviations. P.C. § 25505.

Exemptions Based on The Activity You Engage In

What Are You Doing?	Description	Can You Carry an Unloaded Handgun Concealed?	Can You Carry an Unloaded Handgun Openly?	Can You Carry an Unloaded "Firearm That Is Not a Handgun"?	Can You Carry a Loaded Firearm?	Notes and Comments
Making a Lawful Arrest	Are you making or attempting to make a lawful arrest?	No	Yes* P.C. § 26372	Yes* P.C. § 26405(p)	Yes* P.C. §26050	*Beware, these exemptions only apply when you are actually making or attempting to make a *lawful* arrest.
Transporting Your Firearm for Any Lawful Purpose	Are you transporting your firearm for a lawful purpose (Chapter 7, Section (III)(E)(2))?	Yes* P.C. § 25610	Yes** P.C. § 26389	Yes*** P.C. § 26405(c)	No	*In order for this exemption to apply, you must be over the age of 18 and not prohibited from possessing firearms. If you are transporting a handgun in a vehicle, it must be locked in the vehicle's trunk or in a locked container. But, if you are transporting a handgun outside of a car, this exemption only applies if you are carrying it directly to or from a motor vehicle in a locked container. Keep in mind, you may also transport a handgun between any place you may lawfully carry the handgun concealed, open, or loaded so long it is unloaded and in a locked container. P.C. § 25590. **This exemption applies only when you are transporting the unloaded handgun in a vehicle. Moreover, the handgun must be unloaded and carried in either the trunk of the vehicle or a locked container. ***You may transport your long gun inside your vehicle in any manner as long as it is unloaded, unless you are in certain areas, such as a gun free school zone (see Chapter 8). If you are transporting the firearm outside of the vehicle, the firearm must be in a locked container or "encased," as discussed in Chapter 7, Section (V). Moreover, your course of travel should only include necessary deviations, unless you must meet another exemption to this restriction.

CHAPTER 8:
PLACES WHERE FIREARM POSSESSION IS PROHIBITED AND FIREARM USE IS RESTRICTED

As explained in previous chapters, the regulation of firearm possession in California is primarily based on whether the firearm is in a "private" or "public" place, "carried" or "possessed," "loaded" or "unloaded," and/or "concealed."

In addition to these categorical restrictions, both California and federal law completely prohibit firearms in specific places, or, if firearms are allowed at all, restrict who may possess them and in what manner they may be possessed. Sometimes the scope of these restrictions is not as clear as it should be. California and federal laws impose different, and sometimes overlapping, restrictions. You need to know where and what these areas are so you don't violate the law.

The following Sections discuss when and where you can, or more appropriately, when and where you *cannot* possess a firearm.

While this book covers mostly federal and state laws, keep in mind that cities and counties can pass certain laws about where and how you may possess firearms. For example, the Los Angeles Municipal Code regulates the possession of firearm parts (*e.g.*, a frame, receiver, or firearm barrel) and ammunition at the Los Angeles International Airport.[1]

Many local municipal codes also prohibit discharging firearms.[2] In Los Angeles County, for example, there are a large number of "districts" where discharging a firearm is prohibited.[3] The most common local restrictions prohibit or regulate firearm possession in city or county public parks.[4]

---

[1] L.A., CAL., MUN. CODE § 55.17. "Ammunition" is defined in Penal Code (P.C.) section 16150.

[2] The California state legislature has provided in California Government Code (Cal. Gov't Code) section 25840 that a county "board of supervisors may prohibit and prevent the unnecessary firing and discharge of firearms on or into the highways and other public places and may pass all necessary ordinances regulating or forbidding such acts." *See, e.g.*, L.A. CNTY. CODE §§ 17.04.620, 19.12.1420(p).

[3] Descriptions of these districts can be very specific and in some cases border on the absurd. *See* L.A. CNTY. CODE §§ 13.66.130, 17.04.620, 19.12.1420(o).

[4] *See Calguns Foundation, Inc. v. Cnty. of San Mateo*, 218 Cal. App. 4th 661 (2013) (upholding such an ordinance in the face of a preemption challenge).

If you plan on possessing a firearm in public, familiarize yourself with both your city's and county's applicable regulations and the state and federal restrictions discussed below. Though local governments are somewhat limited in the types of firearm restrictions they can have, knowing these additional local rules may save hours of your life and thousands of dollars in attorneys' fees if you must prove you were acting lawfully.

I. FIREARM POSSESSION IN GOVERNMENT BUILDINGS

A. Federal Law

Under federal law, it is generally illegal to knowingly possess or bring a firearm or other dangerous weapon[5] into a federal facility. A "federal facility" is any building or part thereof owned or leased by the federal government where federal employees regularly report for work.[6] Exceptions to this rule exist for officers, agents, and state or U.S. employees performing their official law enforcement duties; federal officials and military members, if authorized by law to possess a firearm; or those carrying firearms for hunting or other lawful purposes.[7]

Anyone who "knowingly possesses or causes to be present a firearm or other dangerous weapon in a federal facility (other than a federal court facility), or attempts to do so, shall be fined . . . or imprisoned not more than 1 year, or both."[8] Anyone knowingly possessing a firearm or other dangerous weapon in a federal *court* facility, or even attempting to do so, can be fined and/or imprisoned for up to two years.[9] Anyone using, or attempting to use, a firearm to commit a crime in a federal facility can be fined and/or imprisoned for up to five years.[10] You cannot, however, be convicted of bringing a firearm into a federal facility unless the facility is clearly labeled or you had actual notice of this restriction.[11]

B. California Law

It is illegal to bring a loaded firearm into, or possess "a loaded firearm within, the State Capitol, any legislative office, any office of the Governor or other constitutional officer, or any hearing room in which any committee of the Senate or Assembly is

---

[5] A "'dangerous weapon' means a weapon, device, instrument, material, or substance, animate or inanimate, that is used for, or is readily capable of, causing death or serious bodily injury . . . ." It does not include pocket knives with a blade less than 2 ½ inches long. 18 U.S.C. § 930(g)(2).

[6] 18 U.S.C. § 930(g)(1).

[7] 18 U.S.C. § 930(d). This "other lawful purpose" exception does not apply to federal courts and is unclear as to what activities it does apply. 18 U.S.C. § 930(e)(2).

[8] 18 U.S.C. § 930(a).

[9] 18 U.S.C. § 930(e).

[10] 18 U.S.C. § 930(b).

[11] 18 U.S.C. § 930(h).

conducting a hearing, or upon the grounds of the State Capitol, which is bounded by 10th, L, 15th, and N Streets in the City of Sacramento . . . ."[12]

It is also illegal to possess or bring a loaded firearm onto the grounds of or within the Governor's Mansion or any other residence of the Governor, a constitutional officer, or any member of the Legislature.[13] These offenses are "wobblers," punishable as either felonies or misdemeanors.[14]

California peace officers may examine any firearm in any place where possessing a loaded firearm is prohibited by California Penal Code (P.C.) sections 171c or 171d. Refusing to allow a peace officer to inspect your firearm in such a place or, as explained in Chapter 6, while in most "public places," is grounds for arrest.[15]

Both the prohibition on loaded firearms in the State Capitol and related offices, and in the Governor's mansion and on its grounds have exceptions for certain authorized peace officers, those summoned by law enforcement to assist in making an arrest or preserving the peace, and holders of a valid Carry License[16] (see Chapter 7).[17] The prohibition on loaded firearms in the State Capitol and related offices also has an exception for those with permission from the Chief Sergeants at Arms of both the State Assembly and Senate.[18] And the prohibition on loaded firearms in the Governor's mansion and on its grounds or any other residence of the Governor, other constitutional officer, or member of the legislature also has exceptions for military members performing their duties and other persons authorized by the occupants of the specified residences.[19]

Anyone who possesses firearms, knives with a blade longer than four inches that is either fixed or capable of being fixed in an unguarded position, switchblade knives,[20] generally prohibited weapons,[21] tasers, stun guns, or anything that expels a metallic projectile such as a BB or pellet through air or CO_2 pressure or spring action, or any spot marker or paint gun in any state or local public building or public meeting, violates California law.[22]

---

[12] P.C. § 171c.

[13] P.C. § 171d.

[14] P.C. §§ 171c, 171d. Although the definition of "loaded" is discussed thoroughly in Chapter 6, for purposes of P.C. sections 171c and 171d, "loaded" means whenever both the firearm and unexpended ammunition are immediately possessed by the same person. *See* P.C. § 171e. This means the ammunition does *not* have to be in the firearm to be "loaded" in this context.

[15] P.C. §§ 171e, 25850(b).

[16] A Carry License is also widely known as a "CCW" (carry concealed weapon). *See* P.C. § 16360.

[17] P.C. § 171c(b). Notably absent from those exempt are military personnel while performing their duties.

[18] But, only a peace officer acting within the scope of his or her employment may carry a firearm on the floor of the Assembly or in a committee room when the Assembly is in session or during a meeting of a committee or subcommittee. CAL. H.R. RES. 1 § 117.7A (2015-2016).

[19] P.C. § 171d.

[20] As described in P.C. section 17235.

[21] Listed in P.C. section 16590. *See* Chapter 10 for further information.

[22] P.C. section 171b provides a definition for "state or local public building," which includes any buildings, or part of a building, the state or local government owns or leases where government employees regularly go to perform their official duties. It includes courthouses, but not government employees' residences. *See also* CAL. GOV'T CODE §§ 11120, 54950 (discussing which places are intended for public business).

This prohibition does not apply to:

(1) Those possessing or transporting weapons into court for evidence as long as they are not a party to the action;[23]

(2) Authorized peace officers,[24] retired peace officers with authorization to carry concealed weapons,[25] full-time paid peace officers of another state or the federal government who are carrying out official duties while in California, or those summoned by a peace officer to assist with an arrest or preserving the peace;[26]

(3) Those with a valid Carry License;[27]

(4) Those with written permission from an authorized official in charge of state or local government building security;[28]

(5) Those who lawfully reside in, own, or possess those portions of the building that are not owned or leased by the state or local government;[29]

(6) Those hired by the building's owner or manager who have permission to possess firearms in those areas they lawfully reside in, own, or lawfully possess that the state or local government does not own or lease;[30] *or,*

(7) Those who lawfully bring a weapon to a gun show for sale or trade.[31]

II. FIREARM POSSESSION IN "SCHOOL ZONES"

Though exceptions exist, it is generally unlawful under both California and federal law to possess a firearm – whether loaded or unloaded – in an area you know, or reasonably should know, is a "school zone."[32] There are both California and federal laws covering gun possession in school zones. Because California and federal laws exist independently of each other, it is important to remember that you may be prosecuted for violating either state and/or federal law. So you must comply with both.

---

[23] P.C. § 171b(b)(2)(B).

[24] As defined in P.C. sections 830-832.9.

[25] As described in P.C. sections 25450-25475.

[26] P.C. § 171b(b)(2)(A).

[27] P.C. § 171b(b)(3). Although no law prohibits the carrying of firearms into a state courthouse with a valid Carry License, most state court policies prohibit carrying firearms into a courthouse by anyone other than law enforcement.

[28] P.C. § 171b(b)(4).

[29] P.C. § 171b(b)(5).

[30] P.C. 171b(b)(6). This exemption only applies to those who are "licensed or registered in accordance with, and acting within the course and scope of" their duties as private investigators and/or alarm company operators. *See* Cal. Bus. & Prof. Code §§ 7512-7514, 7590-7590.5.

[31] P.C. § 171b(b)(7)(B).

[32] P.C. § 626.9(b); *see* 18 U.S.C. § 922(q)(2)(A).

A. Federal Law

Federal law defines a "school zone" as an area that is "in, or on the grounds of, a public, parochial or private school; or within a distance of 1,000 feet from the ground of a public, parochial or private school."[33] But, note that unlike California law (see below), federal law does not restrict firearms on college campuses or universities.

Although it is generally illegal to possess a firearm in a "school zone" under federal law,[34] there are some exceptions to this restriction. Specifically, the following people and situations are exempt from the federal firearm restriction in a "school zone":

(1) Individuals who are on private property that is not part of school grounds; *or*

(2) Certain state-licensed individuals;[35]

(3) When the firearm is unloaded and in a locked container or locked firearm rack on a motor vehicle;

(4) Individuals who are in a school-approved program;

(5) Individuals who have contracted with a school to possess a firearm;

(6) Law enforcement officers acting in their official capacity; *or,*

(7) Individuals carrying unloaded while going over school premises to gain access to lawful hunting lands if the school authorizes the entry.[36]

Note that while California's exception, explained below, requires handguns be in a locked container and long guns to be transported according to California law[37] when in a "school zone," federal law additionally requires that long guns also be in locked containers.[38] Because federal law places stricter restrictions on all types of firearms, you should follow the federal restrictions regarding transportation in order to comply with both state and federal law.

---

[33] 18 U.S.C. § 921(a)(25)-(26).

[34] 18 U.S.C. § 922(q)(2)(A). The federal "school zone" restriction, however, only applies to a firearm that "has moved in or otherwise affects interstate or foreign commerce." The restriction likely still applies to nearly all firearms because even "homemade" firearms contain parts that have "moved in" or "affect" interstate commerce.

[35] For this exception to apply, federal law requires "the individual possessing the firearm [be] licensed to do so by the State in which the school zone is located or a political subdivision of the State, and the law of the State or political subdivision requires that, before an individual obtains such a license, the law enforcement authorities of the State or political subdivision verify that the individual is qualified under law to receive the license." 18 U.S.C. § 922(q)(2)(B)(ii).

[36] 18 U.S.C. § 922(q)(2)(B).

[37] As discussed in Chapter 6, long guns (unless they are "assault weapons") do not need to be in a locked container when transported in a vehicle.

[38] *See* 18 U.S.C. § 922(q)(2)(B).

B. California Law

California's Gun-Free School Zone Act defines "school zone" as "an area in, or on the grounds of, a public or private school providing instruction in kindergarten or grades 1 to 12, inclusive, or within a distance of 1,000 feet from the grounds of the public or private school."[39] Though this law is somewhat unclear, to be on the safe side you should measure the 1,000 feet starting from the school's *perimeter*, not its center-point. This advice is especially warranted since violating a "school zone" law may be a felony with mandatory jail time.

 Curiously, California does not require "school zones" to be marked,[40] so the 1,000-foot "school zone" border is often difficult to determine. Whether you know, or reasonably should know, you are in a "school zone" will be a question of fact for a jury to decide if you are prosecuted – which is an expensive process – so be careful around schools!

The California Gun-Free School Zone Act (but not federal law) also generally prohibits possessing firearms, whether loaded or unloaded, at university or college campuses and their buildings for student housing, teaching, research, or administration.[41] Either offense is a felony, but possessing a "loaded"[42] firearm on university or college property where possession is prohibited has a steeper sentence.[43]

The following people are exempted from California's "school zone" (*i.e.*, the grounds of the school and 1,000 feet from the school grounds) and university/college campus firearm prohibitions:

(1) An individual who is on an existing shooting range at a school, university, or college campus (P.C. § 626.9(n));

(2) An individual who is a duly appointed California peace officer,[44] either a federal officer or one from another state carrying out official duties, an individual summoned by any of those officers to make an arrest or keep the peace, or any military members performing their duties (P.C. § 626.9(l));

---

[39] P.C. § 626.9(e)(1).

[40] P.C. § 626.9(k).

[41] Unlike "school zones," which need not be marked as such, universities and colleges must "post a prominent notice at primary entrances on noncontiguous property [*i.e.*, property not connected to the campus] stating that firearms are prohibited on that property." P.C. § 626.9(h)-(i).

[42] The term "loaded" in this context "when there is an unexpended cartridge or shell, consisting of a case that holds a charge of powder and a bullet or shot, in, or attached in any manner to, the firearm, including, but not limited to, in the firing chamber, magazine, or clip thereof attached to the firearm." P.C. § 626.9(j). A muzzle-loading firearm is considered to be "loaded" in this context "when it is capped or primed and has a powder charge and ball or shot in the barrel or cylinder." P.C. § 626.9(j).

[43] P.C. § 626.9(h)-(i). This general prohibition is notwithstanding P.C. section 25605's general exception to the firearm restriction in one's residence. *See People v. Anaim*, 47 Cal. App. 4th 401 (1996) (depublished) (defendant violated the Gun-Free School Zone Act because he possessed a loaded firearm on university property even though the university-owned apartment complex was his residence). Post-*Heller* (see Chapter 1), this may change. But until it does, you cannot lawfully have a firearm in your residence if your residence is part of university property and marked as such.

[44] As defined in P.C. section 830.

(3) An armored vehicle guard[45] performing his or her duties (P.C. § 626.9(l));

(4) A security guard authorized to carry loaded firearms (P.C. § 626.9(m));[46]

(5) An honorably retired peace officer authorized to carry concealed or loaded firearms (P.C. § 626.9(o)); *or*,(6) A peace officer[47] who is authorized to carry a firearm by the appointing agency.[48]

(7) An individual who is participating in a program involving shooting sports or activities (including, but not limited to, trap shooting, skeet shooting, sporting clays, and pistol shooting) that is sanctioned by a school, school district, college, university, or other governing body of the institution, and that occurs on the grounds of a public or private school or university or college campus; *or*

(8) An individual who is participating in a state-certified hunter education program pursuant to Fish and Game Code section 3051, as long as he or she does not possess live ammunition in a school building.[49]

Under current California law, "school zones" (*i.e.*, the grounds of the school and 1,000 feet from the school grounds) have additional exceptions including:

(1) When the firearm is lawfully possessed in a residence, place of business, or on private property *as long as* such places are not part of the school *grounds* (*i.e.*, on campus)[50] (P.C. § 626.9(c)(1));

(2) Any handgun being lawfully transported (meaning handguns that are unloaded and *either* in a "locked container"[51] or in the locked trunk of a car) (P.C. § 626.9(c)(2));

(3) When you reasonably believe you are in "grave danger because of circumstances forming the basis of a current restraining order issued by a court against another person or persons who has or have been found to pose a threat to . . . [your] life or safety" (P.C. § 626.9(c)(3));[52]

---

[45] As defined in Cal. Bus. & Prof. Code section 7582.1(d).

[46] P.C. §§ 26000-26060.

[47] Appointed under P.C. section 830.6.

[48] P.C. §§ 25450, 25650, 25900-25910, 26020 , 26300(c)(2).

[49] P.C. § 626.9(q).

[50] Public streets are considered easements and are therefore not considered to be "private property." *See People v. Tapia*, 129 Cal. App. 4th 1153 (2005). That means if you live within 1,000 feet of the grounds of a public or private school, the public street and sidewalk in front of your house would not be considered "private property" for purposes of this exemption and would likely still be considered part of the "school zone."

[51] *See* Chapter 7 for a definition of "locked container" and how to lawfully transport firearms.

[52] This exception may not include mutual restraining order circumstances and does not include the general exception to the carrying loaded restriction for "carrying of any loaded firearm under circumstances where it would otherwise be lawful, by a person who reasonably believes that any person or the property of any person is in immediate, grave danger and that the carrying of the weapon is necessary for the preservation of that person or property." P.C. § 26045.

(4) When the firearm is possessed by individuals exempt from the general concealed firearm prohibition per specific Penal Code provisions (P.C. § 626.9(c)(4));[53] *or*,

(5) Any long gun being lawfully transported in accordance with California law.[54]

California law also provides an exemption that allows Carry License[55] holders to carry a firearm within the 1,000 feet "school zone" border.[56] But this exemption does not allow Carry License holders to carry a firearm on "school grounds."

C. California and Federal Discharge Restrictions

California and federal "school zone" laws also prohibit knowingly or recklessly *discharging*, or attempting to discharge, a firearm in a "school zone."[57] They both exempt discharging a firearm on private property, though.[58] Federal law further exempts discharging a firearm if the activity is part of a school-approved program, in accordance with a school contract, or by law enforcement officers acting in their official capacity.[59]

Be careful differentiating between California and federal "school zone" exemptions. You can be prosecuted for violating *either* federal or California law. An exception to one will not necessarily exempt you from prosecution under the other.

III. AMMUNITION & WEAPON POSSESSION ON "SCHOOL GROUNDS"

Federal law does not generally regulate the possession of ammunition on "school grounds." But, California law prohibits the carrying of ammunition, reloaded am-

---

[53] The Penal Code sections listing these exemptions are: P.C. sections 25615 (transporting unloaded handguns by a licensed person who manufactures, imports, wholesales, repairs, or deals with firearms in their business); 25625 (authorized military or civil organizations carrying firearms while parading or going to and from their organization); 25630 (guards, financial institution employees, or common carriers while working); and 25645 (operating a licensed common carrier to transport unloaded firearms per federal law). *See also* Chapter 7.

[54] P.C. § 626.9(c)(5).

[55] Issued under Chapter 4 (commencing with P.C. section 26150) of Division 5 of Title 4 of Part 6.

[56] P.C. § 626.9(c).

[57] P.C. § 626.9(d); 18 U.S.C. § 922(q)(3)(A). As with the possession restriction, for the federal discharge prohibition to apply, the firearm must have moved in, or affected, interstate or foreign commerce, *and* the person must have *known* it was a "school zone."

[58] P.C. § 626.9(d); 18 U.S.C. § 922(q)(3)(B)(i). But beware of local discharge restrictions.

[59] 18 U.S.C. § 922(q)(3)(B)(ii)-(iv).

munition, and weapons[60] on "school grounds."[61] Unlike the restriction on possessing firearms on school grounds, which discusses and defines what a school (or "school zone") is, it is not entirely clear what is meant by "school grounds" for the ammunition restriction. Is this limited to elementary schools or does it also apply to high schools and/or universities? The legislature did not provide any guidance concerning this restriction.

Sworn law enforcement officers acting within the scope of their duties and persons exempt under P.C. section 25450 (*i.e.*, law enforcement officers exempt from the carrying concealed restriction discussed in Chapter 7) may carry ammunition onto school grounds.[62]

The ammunition restriction also does *not* apply to:

(1) A duly appointed peace officer as defined in Chapter 4.5 (beginning with P.C. section 830) of Title 3 of Part 2;

(2) A full-time paid peace officer of another state or the federal government who is carrying out official duties while in California;

(3) Any person summoned by any of these officers to help make an arrest or preserving the peace while that person is actually engaged in assisting the officer;

(4) A member of the military forces of this state or of the U.S. who is engaged in the performance of his or her duties;

(5) An armored vehicle guard, who is engaged in the performance of his or her duties, as defined in subdivision (d) of Section 7582.1 of the California Business and Professions Code;

(6) Any peace officer listed in P.C. sections 830.1, 830.2, or 830.33(a), whether active or honorably retired;

(7) Any other duly appointed peace officer;

(8) Any honorably retired peace officer listed in P.C. section 830.5(c);

(9) Any other honorably retired peace officer who during the course and scope of his or her appointment as a peace officer was authorized to, and did, carry a firearm; *or*,

---

[60] Under California law, a person can also be prosecuted for a misdemeanor or a felony for bringing or possessing any dirk; dagger; ice pick; knife having a blade longer than two and a half inches; folding knife with a blade that locks into place; razor with an unregulated blade; taser; stun gun; instrument that expels a metallic projectile, such as a BB or a pellet, through the force of air pressure, CO_2 pressure, or spring action; or spot marker gun on the grounds of, or within, any public or private school providing instruction in kindergarten or any of grades 1 to 12. P.C. § 626.10(a)(1). It is also a misdemeanor to bring or possess a razor blade or box cutter onto "school grounds." P.C. § 626.10(a)(2). In addition, a person can be prosecuted for a misdemeanor or a felony for brining or possessing a dirk; dagger; ice pick; or knife having a fixed blade longer than two and a half inches on the grounds of, or within, any private university, the University of California, the California State University, or the California Community Colleges. P.C. § 626.10(b).

[61] P.C. §§ 626.91, 30310.

[62] P.C. § 30310(a).

(10) A person carrying ammunition or reloaded ammunition onto school grounds that is in a motor vehicle at all times and is within a "locked container"[63] or within the locked trunk of the vehicle.[64]

Notice, however, that there is no longer an exception to the ammunition restriction for Carry License holders.

IV. FIREARM POSSESSION IN AIRPORTS, ON AIRPLANES, AND ON COMMON CARRIERS

A. Possession in Airport "Sterile Areas"

1. Federal Law

Under federal law, you can be imprisoned for up to ten years if you have a concealed "dangerous weapon" that would be accessible to you while on, or trying to get on, most commercial flights.[65] This restriction does not apply to government law enforcement officers authorized to carry firearms in their official capacity, those authorized by the Federal Aviation Administration (FAA) or the Secretary of Transportation, or those transporting "unloaded" firearms in baggage not accessible to them during flight as long as the air carrier is notified about every firearm.[66]

Note that there is no exception to these restrictions for holders of a valid Carry License. These licensees can be charged just like anyone else for possessing firearms in a "sterile area" of an airport or for attempting to bring a firearm onto a plane.

The federal Transportation Safety Authority (TSA) can also separately fine you up to $3,000 (or up to $7,500 if the firearm is loaded).[67] If this happens, the TSA will normally send you a letter informing you of the violation and your options, which include paying a civil fine, submitting evidence that the violation did not occur, submitting information to reduce the fine, or requesting an informal conference or a formal hearing. If you get a letter like this, hiring an attorney experienced in firearms law to respond is strongly advised.

---

[63] A "locked container" is "a secure container that is fully enclosed and locked by a padlock, keylock, combination lock, or similar locking device." P.C. § 16850. But the term "does not include the utility or glove compartment of a motor vehicle." P.C. § 16850.

[64] P.C. § 30310(b).

[65] 49 U.S.C. § 46505(b)(1). This statute only applies to aircraft operating in "air transportation" or "intrastate air transportation." "Air transportation" is defined to include international transportation, transportation between states, and transportation of mail by aircraft; and "intrastate air transportation" is defined as transportation by a common carrier of passengers entirely in the same state, by turbojet-powered aircraft capable of carrying at least 30 passengers. 49 U.S.C. § 40102(a)(5), (a)(27). But, if you are flying on a plane that is not covered by this statute, there are other federal and state laws that may otherwise prohibit you from bringing a firearm on a plane. *See, e.g.*, 14 C.F.R. § 135.119. Be sure to check with the aircraft operator before even arriving at the airport with a firearm.

[66] 49 U.S.C. § 46505(d).

[67] *See* Transportation Security Administration, Enforcement Sanction Guidance Policy, available at https://www.tsa.gov/sites/default/files/enforcement_sanction_guidance_policy.pdf (last visited Sept. 10, 2020).

2. California Law

Under California law, it is generally illegal to knowingly possess firearms, frames, receivers, barrels, firearm magazines, BB devices, imitation firearms, tasers or stun guns,[68] or ammunition, in a "sterile area"[69] of an airport.[70] A "passenger vessel terminal" is "a harbor or port facility . . . regularly serv[ing] scheduled commuter or passenger operations."[71] Exceptions to this restriction include:

(1) Authorized peace officers and those summoned to assist them;

(2) Retired peace officers with Carry Licenses issued pursuant to P.C. section 25450;

(3) Individuals with written authorization from an airport security coordinator; *and,*

(4) Individuals responsible for passenger vessel terminal security who have written authorization pursuant to an approved U.S. Coast Guard facility security plan.[72]

Laws regulating firearms or ammunition in airports are most commonly violated by people who simply forget they have a firearm or ammunition in their carry-on bags. This may seem unbelievable to those who do not regularly use firearms, but in fact, people sometimes use the same bags to carry other personal items as they use to carry firearms. Depending on the weight of the firearm and the type of bag, this is a common mistake.

Although California laws prohibiting possession at airports generally have a "knowing" requirement – meaning you may not be found guilty of the offense if you legitimately forgot the firearm was in your bag – prosecutors are typically skeptical. Adding to the difficulty, people usually see their bag being removed from the x-ray conveyor belt and wonder why. At that point, they usually remember the firearm in their bag and say something along the lines of, "That's my bag. There's a gun in there." This "admission" becomes very difficult to disprove or explain.

Don't let this mistake happen to you. Take any firearm out of the bag when you get home from the range or other lawful activity. As a general rule never use your range bag as a carry-on! No matter how thorough you are in cleaning it out, one round of ammunition is enough to cause problems.

Also, to be clear, barring any local ordinance to the contrary, you may lawfully possess firearms and ammunition in places outside airport "sterile areas" as long as you are complying with other applicable laws like those that apply generally in public

---

[68] As defined in P.C. section 244.5.
[69] "Sterile area" is defined in P.C. section 171.5(a)(3).
[70] P.C. § 171.5(b).
[71] P.C. § 171.5(a)(2).
[72] P.C. § 171.5(d).

places. You can also lawfully transport unloaded firearms on planes in *checked* luggage.[73]

B. Possession on Commercial Airplanes

Federal law generally prohibits having firearms and ammunition accessible on commercial or charter aircraft, and even private aircraft over a certain passenger or payload capacity.[74] Law enforcement officers authorized to carry firearms on duty who have completed the "Law Enforcement Officers Flying Armed" training program, and whose employer has determined a need exists to carry the firearm while on the aircraft, are allowed to carry firearms on airplanes as long as they declare the firearm to the aircraft operator, keep it concealed – but never in the overhead compartment – and on their person if in uniform, and notify the pilot and crew members of its location. If the flight does *not* require screening, those officers are not required to have special approval from their agency as long as they comply with all other requirements.[75]

This law enforcement exception does not apply to any officer who has been drinking alcohol, nor may officers drink alcohol while on the aircraft if carrying a firearm.[76]

C. Possession on Amtrak Trains

As of December 15, 2010, stations that accept checked baggage allow passengers to transport unloaded firearms in checked baggage under specific conditions. Among the requirements are:

(1) Passengers must declare to Amtrak their intent to transport a firearm at the time the reservation is made (online reservations for checking firearms are not accepted), or at least 24 hours before departure;

(2) The firearm must be unloaded and in their checked baggage; *and,*

(3) Transportation of the firearm must comply with other carriage regulations (*i.e.*, unloaded, hard-sided locked container, etc.).[77]

Check www.amtrak.com for further information about taking firearms on Amtrak trains. Even though you may be able to lawfully transport firearms on Amtrak trains, you must still follow any other applicable regulations when transporting the firearm to the train. For example, if you plan to board an Amtrak train at a "public

---

[73] P.C. § 171.5(g). See Chapter 7 for how to lawfully transport unloaded firearms in checked luggage and for problems that may arise in airports like New Jersey or New York City.

[74] *See* 49 C.F.R. §§ 1544.201(d), 1544.1(a)(1); *see also* 14 C.F.R. §§ 119.1(a), 135.119.

[75] *See* 49 C.F.R. §§ 1544.201(d), 1544.219, 1544.221. Air marshals are covered by a different set of laws. *See* 49 C.F.R. § 1544.223.

[76] *See* 49 C.F.R. § 1544.219(c).

[77] *See Firearms in Checked Baggage,* AMTRAK, https://www.amtrak.com/firearms-in-checked-baggage (last visited Sept. 10, 2020).

transportation facility," you might have problems getting the firearm to the train as you cannot knowingly possess firearms in the "sterile area" of the facility (see below).

D. Possession on Greyhound Buses

Greyhound Lines, Inc. prohibits transporting firearms and ammunition on their buses.[78] Though this is their rule, not a law, you could still be prosecuted for trespassing or for a similar violation if you break this rule.

E. Possession on All Other Common Carriers

If you cross state lines with a common carrier, even if the carrier allows firearm possession, federal law requires you to declare and surrender the firearm to the carrier operator for the duration of the trip.[79]

Also, federal law only protects you from state prosecution for violating a state's firearms laws if your firearm is not immediately accessible.[80] This means, if you enter a state on a carrier where it is illegal to possess a firearm without a permit (*e.g.*, New Jersey) and you do not have that permit, federal law does *not* protect you from prosecution under that state's laws if a firearm is in your carry-on bag and not stored away in a place where you cannot readily access it.[81]

F. Possession in Harbors & Ports

Under California law, it is generally illegal to knowingly possess firearms, frames, receivers, barrels, firearm magazines, BB devices, imitation firearms, tasers or stun guns,[82] or ammunition, in a "sterile area"[83] of a passenger vessel terminal.[84] A "passenger vessel terminal" is "a harbor or port facility . . . regularly serv[ing] scheduled commuter or passenger operations."[85] Exceptions to this restriction include:

(1) Authorized peace officers and those summoned to assist them;

(2) Retired peace officers with Carry Licenses issued pursuant to P.C. section 25450;

(3) Individuals with written authorization from an airport security coordinator; *and*,

---

[78] *Baggage Information*, GREYHOUND, https://www.greyhound.com/en/help-and-info/travel-info/baggage (last visited Sept. 10, 2020).
[79] 18 U.S.C. § 922(e).
[80] 18 U.S.C. § 926A (part of FOPA).
[81] See Chapter 7 for properly transporting firearms across state lines and consequences for not doing so properly.
[82] As defined in P.C. section 244.5.
[83] "Sterile area" is defined in P.C. section 171.5(a)(3).
[84] P.C. § 171.5(2).
[85] P.C. § 171.5(a)(2).

(4) Individuals responsible for passenger vessel terminal security who have written authorization pursuant to an approved U.S. Coast Guard facility security plan.[86]

G. Possession in "Sterile Area" of Public Transportation Facility

Under California law, it is generally illegal for a person to knowingly possess any firearm[87] within the "sterile area" of a public transportation facility, if the "sterile area"[88] is posted with a statement providing reasonable notice that prosecution may result from possession of these items.[89]

A "public transportation facility" is any land, building, or equipment that has as its primary purpose the operation of a public transit system or that provides services to the passengers of a public transportation system.[90] This includes any vehicles in the public transportation system that transport people for hire, such as "motor vehicles, street cars, trackless trolleys, buses, light rail systems, rapid transit systems, subways, trains, [and] jitneys."[91]

The following people are exempt from this restriction:

(1) Authorized peace officers and those summoned to assist them;

(2) Retired peace officers with Carry Licenses issued pursuant to P.C. section 25450;

(3) A person responsible for the security of the public transportation system and who has been authorized by the public transit authority's security coordinator, in writing, to possess a weapon specified in P.C. section 171(b);

(4) A person who is exempt from the prohibition against carrying concealed handguns, if they are carrying the handgun in accordance with the terms and conditions of an exemption specified in Article 2 (beginning with P.C. section 25450) of Chapter 2 of Division 5 of Title 4 of Part 6 of the Penal Code, or P.C. sections 25615 to 25655, inclusive;[92] *and,*

---

[86] P.C. § 171.5(d).

[87] This restriction includes any imitation firearm as defined in P.C. section 417.4; instrument that expels a metallic projectile, such as a BB or pellet, through the force of air pressure, CO_2 pressure, or spring action; spot marker or paint gun; metal military practice hand grenade; metal or plastic replica hand grenade; unauthorized tear case weapon, or undetectable knife as described in P.C. section 17290.

[88] For purposes of this restriction, a "sterile area" is "any portion of a public transit facility that is generally controlled in a manner consisted with the public transit authority's security plan." P.C. § 171.7(a)(2).

[89] P.C. § 171.7(b).

[90] P.C. § 171.7(a)(1).

[91] P.C. § 171.7(a)(1).

[92] This exemption is somewhat redundant given that P.C. section 171.7(c) already provides exemptions for most of the people listed in these code sections. For example, P.C. section 171.7 already provides an exemption for authorized peace officers and honorably retired peace officers with Carry Licenses under P.C. section 25450. *See* P.C. § 171.7(c)(1)(B). But,this exemption also exempts peace officers and retired peace officers with Carry Licenses under P.C. section 25450. P.C. § 171.7(c)(2). Additionally, this code section also provides that persons carrying in

(5) Any person who possess a tear gas weapon if the possession is permitted by Division 11 (beginning with P.C. section 22810) of Title 3 of Part 6 of the Penal Code.[93]

V. FIREARM POSSESSION IN PARKS, FORESTS, AND REFUGES

A. Federal Lands

1. National Parks and Wildlife Refuges

Federal law allows firearm possession on National Park land and within National Wildlife Refuge Systems as long as you are not otherwise prohibited from possession,[94] and you comply with the state law where the National Park System or National Wildlife Refuge System is located.[95]

This means, while federal law allows for firearm possession in National Parks and Wildlife Refuges, California's carry restrictions still apply, as do their exceptions, which include lawfully transporting a firearm to an activity where carrying a firearm is permitted, such as hunting, camping, target shooting, etc., or if discharging firearms is allowed in that area.[96]

Though federal law allows *possessing* firearms in National Park land and within National Wildlife Refuge Systems, as long as you comply with the state law where the park or refuge is located, *discharging* firearms is a different story. Discharging firearms on National Wildlife Refuges is federally prohibited unless specifically au-

---

accordance with the following code sections are also exempt from California's restriction on possessing firearms in "sterile area" of a "public transportation facility": P.C. sections 25615 (Concealed carry exemption for possession or transportation of unloaded firearms in lawful course of business), 25620 (Concealed carry exemptions for members of the Army, Navy, Air Force, Coast Guard, Marine Corps, or National Guard); 25625 (Concealed carry exemption for authorized military or civil organization members in relation to parading) 25630 (Concealed carry exemption for guards or messengers of common carriers, banks, or financial institutions when shipping things of value); 25636 (Concealed carry exemption for use or transport of firearms for use at target ranges); 25640 (Concealed carry exemption for licensed hunters or fisherman); 25645 (Concealed carry exemptions the transportation of firearms by common carriers); 25650 (Concealed carry exemption for honorably retired federal officers or agents); 25655 (Concealed carry exemption for people with valid Carry Licenses). But, note that anyone meeting these restrictions is still prohibited from possessing any imitation firearm as defined in P.C. section 417.4; instrument that expels a metallic projectile, such as a BB or pellet, through the force of air pressure, CO_2 pressure, or spring action; spot marker or paint gun; metal military practice hand grenade; metal or plastic replica hand grenade; unauthorized tear case weapon, or undetectable knife as described in P.C. section 17290 while in the "sterile area" of the airport.

[93] P.C. § 171.7(c).

[94] 16 U.S.C. § 1a-7b. *See* Chapter 4 for who is prohibited from possessing firearms.

[95] H.R. 627, § 512(b) (2009) (codified as 16 U.S.C. § 1a-7b). Prior to this law changing, *United States v. Masciandaro*, 638 F.3d 458 (4th Cir. 2011), was decided. In this case, the petitioner fell asleep in his car on National Park property. A federal park ranger woke him and found a loaded handgun in a backpack in his trunk. Unfortunately, this incident occurred before firearms were allowed in National Park land. The Fourth Circuit upheld Masciandaro's conviction. Additionally, it noted that Second Amendment rights outside the home, and the appropriate standards for if and how those rights can be regulated by the government, is still uncertain. So make sure you comply with state laws in National Parks.

[96] See Chapter 7 for the specific restrictions and exceptions.

thorized.[97] National Parks and Refuges, or specified areas within those parks and refuges, in California may be open for hunting as outlined in 36 Code of Federal Regulations (C.F.R.) Part 7 and 50 C.F.R. section 32.24, but are still subject to California laws and requirements.

2. National Forests

National Forests are not to be confused with National Parks. These are two separate types of lands regulated by different portions of the federal code and government (the Department of Agriculture and the Department of the Interior, respectively).

Within the National Forest System it is unlawful to discharge "a firearm or any other implement capable of taking human life, causing injury, or damaging property":

(1) In or within 150 yards of a residence, building, campsite, developed recreation site or occupied area;

(2) Across or on a National Forest System road or a body of water adjacent thereto, or in any manner or place whereby any person or property is exposed to injury or damage as a result of such discharge; *or*,

(3) Into or within any cave.[98]

The use of tracer bullets and incendiary ammunition is also prohibited in the National Forest System.[99] The Department of Agriculture Forest Service also has discretion to close or restrict those areas where discharging firearms is lawful.[100]

3. Bureau of Land Management (BLM) and Other Federally Protected Areas

The Bureau of Land Management's (BLM) California policy is to allow the use of firearms on public lands,[101] as provided for in state law, and to cooperate with state authorities in the enforcement of firearms regulations.[102] It is still unlawful, however, to discharge or use firearms on developed recreation sites and areas[103] unless authorized.[104] The BLM can also limit hunting and discharging firearms to protect

---

[97] 50 C.F.R. § 27.41.
[98] 36 C.F.R. § 261.10(d).
[99] 36 C.F.R. § 261.5(b). Tracers are also illegal "destructive devices" under California law. See Chapter 10.
[100] 36 C.F.R. § 261.58(m).
[101] Maps of BLM land are available at: https://www.blm.gov/maps (last visited Sept. 10, 2020).
[102] *See California Recreational Shooting*, U.S. Dept. of the Interior, Bureau of Land Management, https://www.blm.gov/programs/recreation-programs/recreational-shooting/california (last updated Aug. 12, 2018).
[103] "Developed recreation sites and areas means sites and areas that contain structures or capital improvements primarily used by the public for recreation purposes. Such sites or areas may include such features as: Delineated spaces for parking, camping or boat launching; sanitary facilities; potable water; grills or fire rings; tables; or controlled access." 43 C.F.R. § 8360.0-5.
[104] 43 C.F.R. § 8365.2-5.

certain locations. Before you head to BLM land to use your firearms, contact the local BLM office for information on where they think you can lawfully shoot.

4. United States Army Corps of Engineers (USACE) Managed Land

USACE manages almost 12 million acres of land and water.[105] The law is currently unclear about whether firearms may be lawfully possessed on USACE land. In the past, USACE has taken the position that laws permitting firearms in National Parks and Wildlife refuges do not apply to USACE managed land. Congressional attempts to specifically amend the law to permit firearms on this land have thus far failed.[106] However, a recent legal challenge in the Ninth Circuit against USACE's policies was successful at both the preliminary injunction and permanent injunction stage.[107] Currently, the appeal of that victory is in limbo because the government was given leeway to determine how it would like to proceed before further litigation. In the meantime, given USACE's policies have not been clarified, it is advisable to refrain from possessing firearms on USACE land, or to confirm USACE's policy before entering these areas with a firearm.

B. California State Lands

Firearms are generally prohibited in the state park system[108] and are only permitted in areas (including state marine recreational management areas) that are developed for the use of firearms.[109] There are some exceptions to this general restriction. Specifically, a person can possess a firearm in:

(1) Underwater parks or designated archery ranges where the Department of Parks and Recreation finds that it is in its best interest;

(2) Lands open to lawful hunting; *and,*

(3) Unloaded firearms that are inoperable or stored to prevent their ready use within either a temporary lodging or a mechanical mode of conveyance (*e.g.*, car, bike, RV, boat, etc., but not a horse).[110]

---

[105] *Environmental Stewardship Program Statistics*, U.S. ARMY CORPS OF ENGINEERS, http://www.usace.army.mil/Media/FactSheets/FactSheetArticleView/tabid/219/Article/173/environmental-stewardship-program-statistics.aspx (last visited Sept. 10, 2020).

[106] Kevin Freking, *Senate rejects firearms on Army Corps of Engineers lands, boosting gun control supporters*, FOX NEWS (May 8, 2013), http://www.foxnews.com/us/2013/05/08/senate-rejects-firearms-on-army-corps-engineers-lands-boosting-gun-control/ (last visited Sept. 10, 2020). But, in 2015, Republican lawmakers in both the House and the Senate introduced two companion bills (H.R. 578 and S. 263) to amend this law. *See* Chris Eger, *Bill Filed to Lift Army Corps of Engineers' Ban on Guns*, GUNS.COM (Feb. 2, 2015), *available at* http://www.guns.com/2015/02/02/bills-filed-to-lift-army-corps-of-engineers-ban-on-guns/ (last visited Sept. 10, 2020). As of the date of publication, these bills have not been passed.

[107] *See Morris v. U.S. Army Corps of Engineers*, 990 F. Supp. 2d 1082 (D. Idaho 2014); *Morris v. United States Army Corps of Eng'rs*, 60 F.Supp.3d 1120 (D. Idaho 2014); see also Chapter 7.

[108] The Department of Parks and Recreation controls the state park system (*i.e.*, California state parks, park property, recreation areas, natural reserves, etc.). CAL. CODE REGS. tit. 14, §§ 4300, 4313. This restriction includes "any weapon, firearm, spear, bow and arrow, trap, net, or device capable of injuring, or killing any person or animal, or capturing any animal, or damaging any public or private property." CAL. CODE REGS. tit. 14, § 4313(a).

[109] *See* CAL. CODE REGS. tit. 14, § 4501 (allowing hunting in specific state park lands).

[110] CAL. CODE REGS. tit. 14, § 4313.

The restrictions listed above are separate from those in "state wildlife areas." Firearms are generally prohibited from possessing, discharging, and using any firearms in "state wildlife areas," except:

(1) Where the Department of Fish and Wildlife has designated a hunting area or shooting site;

(2) When the person has been issued a permit by the Department of Fish and Wildlife;

(3) As authorized for dog training in a designated area;

(4) When fishing with bow and arrow tackle as defined in Cal. Code Regs. title 14, section 550(b)(9) and allowed in Cal. Code Regs. title 14, section 550(h); *or,*

(5) When dispatching a trapped animal as provided in Cal. Code Regs. title 14, section 465.5(g)(1) and 550(ee).[111]

Nonetheless, even in state wildlife areas where a person may be exempted from the general restriction, the use and discharge of firearms can be limited (as to the type/quantity of ammunition, type of firearm, and when the firearm may be used) and in some cases outright banned.[112]

California also designates "State Game Refuges." Unless you have a permit or specific authorization, it is illegal to possess or discharge a firearm (or BB device or bow and arrow) in a game refuge, with few exceptions.[113] Firearms *can* be transported through a game refuge, but only if they are taken apart or encased and unloaded.[114] Also, when traveling on something other than a public highway, public thoroughfare, or right of way within a State Game Refuge, you have to give the Department of Fish and Game at least 24 hours' notice that you will be transporting a firearm. You have to give your name and address, the name of the refuge, the approximate route, and the approximate time when you intend to travel through the refuge.[115]

The state has also created "ecological reserves"[116] where possessing and discharging firearms is generally prohibited except by law enforcement and in areas that allow hunting.[117] The California Fish and Game Code (Cal. Fish & Game Code) and its companion regulations are full of intricate and specific prohibitions on all sorts of activity involving firearms. Before you enter state-owned lands, you should contact the state entity in charge of the land and ask what the law, regulations, or policies are with respect to firearms. Respectfully request such information in writ-

---

[111] CAL. CODE REGS. tit.14, §§ 550(cc).
[112] CAL. CODE REGS. tit.14, §§ 550, 551, 552.
[113] CAL. FISH & GAME CODE § 10500.
[114] CAL. FISH & GAME CODE § 10506.
[115] CAL. FISH & GAME CODE § 10506.
[116] These areas are outlined in Cal. Code Regs. title 14, section 630.
[117] *See* CAL. CODE REGS. tit. 14, §§ 550(cc)(4)(B), 630.

ing. If they are unable to do so, you should speak with an attorney experienced in firearms law before entering state land with a firearm.

1. Other Parks

Be aware that city, county, state, and national parks may be run by different government agencies that have different rules and regulations. As discussed at the beginning of this chapter, local ordinances also often restrict possessing firearms in city or county public parks. If you plan on visiting one of these parks, call ahead, check the park's website, and familiarize yourself with the rules regarding firearms *before* you go.

VI. FIREARM POSSESSION IN UNITED STATES AND INTERNATIONAL WATERS

Federal, state, local and/or another country's laws may apply depending on where your boat is in the water. Federal, state, and local firearms laws apply in waters within California's baseline boundary (coastline),[118] called its "internal waters."[119] To lawfully possess firearms on your boat while in "internal waters," you need to know how your boat is classified because "internal waters" are likely "public places" where general firearm restrictions apply.[120]

Three nautical miles[121] from the state's coastline is the state's "seaward boundary." All waters within this three-mile stretch are subject to federal and California firearms laws. Local laws do not apply.[122] You may therefore possess firearms in these waters as long as you comply with state and federal law. But this is no easy task, as knowing *how* you are supposed to lawfully possess a firearm depends on whether you are in a restricted "public place." If you are not, then there are generally no restrictions on possessing firearms. But if you are in such a place, then how you possess firearms depends on whether your boat is considered a residence, vehicle, or place of business.[123] You may also be a licensed fisherman who is exempt from the concealed carry laws.[124]

---

[118] Except where otherwise provided, the baseline boundary is the low-water line along the coast. *See* UNITED NATIONS CONVENTION ON THE LAW OF THE SEA, (hereinafter, "UNCLOS") 27, art. 5, *available at* http://www.un.org/depts/los/convention_agreements/texts/unclos/unclos_e.pdf (last visited Sept. 10, 2020). Note that the U.S. has never ratified UNCLOS in its entirety but has selected a few sections for adoption via presidential proclamation. It is therefore not controlling law, but its descriptions of the various maritime zones are generally accurate.

[119] "Internal waters" includes rivers, bays, and harbors. *See* SCOTT JASPER, SECURING FREEDOM IN THE GLOBAL COMMONS 52 (2010).

[120] See Chapters 6 & 7.

[121] All "miles" in this section refer to nautical miles unless otherwise specified (1 "nautical mile" is approximately 1.15 statute miles).

[122] *See People v. Weeren*, 26 Cal. 3d 654, 661-63, 665 (1980); *see also* 43 U.S.C. §§ 1301(b), 1312.

[123] *See* Chapter 7.

[124] P.C. § 25640. See also Chapter 7.

Since there are no express California restrictions on discharging firearms in this area, the legality of doing so depends on whether it is a restricted "public place," which is sometimes unclear. Whether it is such a "public place" may depend on how close you are to land and other vessels at the time. What is clear, however, is that California does ban discharging a firearm in certain other areas. For example, the discharge ban also includes the "sea otter translocation zone" surrounding San Nicolas Island (except for government employees performing their duties).[125] Possessing and discharging firearms in certain marine areas and ecological reserves is also prohibited.[126]

From the "seaward boundary" to the 12-mile mark is the U.S.'s "territorial waters," where only federal firearms laws apply.[127] There are no real restrictions on possessing a "regular" firearm within this twelve mile zone because federal law does not generally regulate where and how a non-prohibited person can *possess* firearms.[128]

From the baseline out to 200 miles from the coastline is the "exclusive economic zone" (EEZ).[129] From the end of the EEZ to 350 miles from the coastline (or to the end of subsurface land, whichever is shorter) is the "continental shelf."[130] The U.S. has generally asserted authority over natural resources in the continental shelf region beyond the EEZ. Because firearms are not natural resources, the federal government likely does not assert jurisdiction over them in that region.

Past the "continental shelf" you will either be in international waters or waters belonging to another country. It appears U.S. firearms laws generally do not apply in the EEZ or on the "continental shelf." But, the first twelve miles of the EEZ is called the "contiguous zone."[131] In this zone, federal pollution, taxation, customs, and immigration laws, and possibly international laws, may apply.[132] Though it is unclear what, if any, firearm or ammunition possession restrictions apply, if you are boating in the "contiguous zone," be sure to check the laws concerning pollution, as expended bullets, shot, and casings may bring you under the purview of pollution laws.

Again, even if federal firearms laws apply beyond U.S. "territorial waters" (*i.e.*, past the 12-mile mark) – perhaps under a "flag of the state" theory, where the law of

---

[125] CAL. FISH & GAME CODE § 8664.2. See this section for the coordinates of the areas around San Nicolas Island.

[126] See Cal. Code Regs. title 14, sections 630 and 632 for a list of areas and specific restrictions.

[127] *See* UNCLOS 27, arts. 3-4, *available at* http://www.un.org/depts/los/convention_agreements/texts/unclos/unclos_e.pdf (last visited Sept. 10, 2020). The U.S. accepted this portion of UNCLOS via Presidential Proclamation in 1988. *See* Proclamation No. 5928, 54 Fed. Reg. 777 (Dec. 27, 1988).

[128] Unless it is a National Firearms (NFA) firearm as discussed in Chapters 3 and 10.

[129] *See* UNCLOS 43-44, arts. 55-57, *available at* http://www.un.org/depts/los/convention_agreements/texts/unclos/unclos_e.pdf (last visited Sept. 10, 2020).

[130] *See* UNCLOS 53-54, art. 76, *available at* http://www.un.org/depts/los/convention_agreements/texts/unclos/unclos_e.pdf (last visited Sept. 10, 2020).

[131] *See* UNCLOS 35, art. 33, *available at* http://www.un.org/depts/los/convention_agreements/texts/unclos/unclos_e.pdf (last visited Sept. 10, 2020). To be clear, the first 24 miles past the "seaward boundary" is considered the "contiguous zone." The U.S. accepted this portion of UNCLOS via Presidential Proclamation in 1999. *See* Proclamation No. 7219, 64 Fed. Reg. 48, 701 (Aug. 2, 1999).

[132] *See* UNCLOS 35, art. 33, *available at* http://www.un.org/depts/los/convention_agreements/texts/unclos/unclos_e.pdf (last visited Sept. 10, 2020).

the state (country) a boat originally embarks from is controlling – federal law has very few restrictions on firearm possession, aside from possessing NFA firearms and certain individuals prohibited from possessing firearms under the Gun Control Act (GCA).

Finally, if you will be boating in Canadian, Mexican, or another country's waters, you should learn that country's firearms law and act accordingly. Also, check with the ATF and Customs and Border Protection, as you may have to get a permit and/or fulfill other requirements in order to enter another country's waters or re-enter U.S. waters with firearms.

This is a simplified overview of the laws concerning firearms on boats. Specific questions concerning your boating activities with firearms should be directed to a maritime attorney.

VII. FIREARM POSSESSION AT PROTEST EVENTS

California law prohibits carrying concealed, loaded, or deadly weapons while picketing or engaging in other informational activities in public that relate to a concerted refusal to work.[133] Violating this is a misdemeanor that results in a 10-year firearm prohibition under P.C. section 29805, and there is no exception for those with a valid Carry License.[134]

VIII. FIREARM POSSESSION AND POLITICIANS

Under federal law, Congress has directed and authorized the U.S. Secret Service to protect the President of the United States as well as other presidential personnel and their family members, where it is warranted. So, although federal possession laws do not expressly mention the President, the Secret Service can protect the President from private party firearm possession if it threatens the President.

Law enforcement personnel are thus not authorized to arrest or charge peaceful demonstrators who do not pose a threat to the President and who are not violating any laws. But whether the Secret Service considers someone a threat is left to its discretion.

---

[133] P.C. § 17510.
[134] P.C. § 17510.

IX. OTHER RESTRICTED PLACES UNDER CALIFORNIA LAW

A. Gun Shows

You must be at least age 18 to go to gun shows or events, unless you are accompanied by a parent, grandparent, or legal guardian.[135] Except for sworn peace officers, show/event security, and vendors, any firearm you bring to the gun show or event must be checked, cleared of any ammunition, and secured to prevent it from being operated. Before you will be allowed to enter the show, an identification tag or sticker must also be attached to it identifying the owner[136] and explaining that sales must go through an FFL.[137] And as of 2020, members of the public carrying ammunition into the show must also similarly check, secure, and tag all ammunition.[138] Except for sworn peace officers, security, and vendors, you cannot possess a firearm with ammunition designed to be fired in that firearm at the same time as you are attending a gun show.[139] And you must show your government-issued photo identification to law enforcement upon request if you bring a firearm or ammunition to the gun show.[140]

B. Polling Places

Any person possessing a firearm at a polling place without city or county written authorization can be prosecuted with a felony or a misdemeanor.[141] Unless a peace officer, security guard, or security personnel meets an exception discussed below, they are in violation of this section as well. This restriction does not apply to:

(1) An unarmed uniformed guard or security personnel who is at the polling place to cast his or her vote;

(2) A peace officer conducting official business or who is at the polling place to cast a vote;

(3) A private guard or security personnel hired or arranged for by an elections official; *or,*

(4) A private guard or security personnel hired or arranged for by the owner or manager of the polling place, as long as not hired solely for Election Day.[142]

In addition, a person can be prosecuted with a felony or misdemeanor if they hire or arrange for a person in possession of firearm or a uniformed peace officer,

---

[135] P.C. § 27335.
[136] Including the owner's signature, printed name, and government-issued identification.
[137] P.C. § 27340.
[138] P.C. § 27340(c).
[139] P.C. § 27330.
[140] P.C. § 27345.
[141] Cal. Elections Code § 18544(a).
[142] Cal. Elections Code § 18544(b).

private guard, security guard, or any person wearing a uniform of a peace officer, guard, or security personnel to be stationed in the immediate vicinity of, or posted at, a polling place without written authorization.[143] Note that, just like "sterile areas" in airports, there is *no* exception to the above restrictions for valid Carry License holders. They can be charged just like anyone else for possessing firearms at a polling place.

C. Playgrounds and Youth Centers

If you unlawfully draw a firearm in a rude, angry, or threatening manner while you are knowingly on, or within, the grounds of certain child care facilities, or carry a firearm in violation of the concealed and/or loaded firearm restriction in public while on or around a playground or youth center when it is open for business, classes, or school-related programs, or whenever minors are using it, you can be prosecuted with a felony or misdemeanor.[144] Those who brandish or carry concealed and/or loaded lawfully should not be in violation of this law.

A "playground" is "any park or recreational area specifically designed to be used by children that has play equipment installed, including public grounds designed for athletic activities such as baseball, football, soccer, or basketball, or any similar facility located on public or private school grounds, or on city or county parks."[145] A "youth center" is "any public or private facility that is used to host recreational or social activities for minors while minors are present."[146]

X. RESTRICTING FIREARM POSSESSION BY PRIVATE BUSINESSES

After a number of gun owners began carrying firearms inside grocery stores, shopping centers, and restaurants in protest of carry restrictions, private businesses and restaurants began adopting policies prohibiting people from bringing firearms into their establishments. For example, some national businesses, such as Buffalo Wild Wings, Costco, Whole Foods Market, Target, and Starbucks have either prohibited firearms inside their stores[147] or have requested that patrons not carry firearms inside their stores.[148] Some have even gone as far as checking patron's bags and purses

---

[143] CAL. ELECTIONS CODE § 18545. But, this restriction does not apply to the owner or manager of the facility or property in which the polling place is located if the private security guard or security personnel is not hired or arranged solely for the day on which the election is held. CAL. ELECTIONS CODE § 18545.

[144] P.C. §§ 417(a-b), 25400, 25850, 626.95(a).

[145] P.C. § 626.95(c)(1).

[146] P.C. § 626.95(c)(2).

[147] *See Personal Firearms/Guns in Costco Stores*, COSTCO.COM, *available at* https://customerservice.costco.com/app/answers/detail/a_id/709/kw/guns (last visited Sept. 10, 2020); *see also 8 Companies That Have Actually Banned Guns*, THE HUFFINGTON POST (Sep. 18, 2013), *available at* http://www.huffingtonpost.com/2013/09/18/company-gun-bans_n_3948309.html (last visited Sept. 10, 2020).

[148] *See Target Addresses Firearms in Stores*, TARGET (July 2, 2014), *available at* https://corporate.target.com/article/2014/07/target-addresses-firearms-in-stores (last visited Sept. 10, 2020); *see also* Open letter from Howard

for weapons before they enter the establishment. But are these store policies legal in California? And can stores enforce them?

The simple answer to this question is, yes. Although private business cannot arbitrarily exclude customers from their property based on things like race, ethnicity, gender, religion, sexual orientation, medical condition, disability, genetic information, or martial status,[149] California law does not regulate or prohibit private business owners from establishing policies that prohibit firearms inside their stores, restaurants, or businesses.

These policies generally do not carry the weight of the law, meaning that if you lawfully carry a firearm inside a store that has a "no gun" policy in place, you have not committed a criminal act. But, if someone inside the store asks you to leave the premises because you are carrying a firearm in violation of a store policy, then you can be arrested and charged with trespassing[150] if you refuse to leave the store.

Note that although the practice of openly carrying a firearm might be considered a form of protected speech under the First Amendment, private business owners are not government entities and therefore do not violate your right to free speech by prohibiting firearms inside their stores or asking patrons who are carrying firearms to leave the premises.

XI. GENERAL FIREARM DISCHARGE RESTRICTIONS

Outside of specific areas like state parks and refuges owned by the state, California does not generally regulate non-negligent[151] or non-felonious discharge of firearms, leaving it to local entities or those that manage public lands to regulate instead. You should therefore generally look to local laws to determine where it is lawful to discharge firearms.

That being said, California makes it unlawful for you to discharge a firearm at an *unoccupied* motor vehicle or *uninhabited* building or dwelling house *without the owner's permission*.[152]

California also makes it unlawful to discharge "any firearm or other deadly weapon within 150 yards of any occupied dwelling house, residence, or other building or any barn or other outbuilding" related to it, without being the owner or person possessing the premises, or without having the owner or lawful possessor's permission.[153] It is also illegal to shoot a firearm from or onto a public road or high-

---

Schultz, CEO of Starbucks Coffee (Sep. 17, 2013), *available at* https://news.starbucks.com/views/open-letter-from- (last visited Sept. 10, 2020).

[149] *See* 42 U.S.C § 2000a; CAL. CIV. CODE § 51.

[150] *See* P.C. § 602.

[151] *See* P.C. § 246.3(a)-(b) (making a willful discharge of a firearm in such a *grossly negligent* manner is a possible felony, and a misdemeanor if done so with a BB device).

[152] P.C. § 247(b).

[153] CAL. FISH & GAME CODE § 3004(a).

way[154] or to "intentionally discharge a firearm or release an arrow or crossbow bolt over or across a public road or other established way open to the public, in an unsafe and reckless manner."[155] It is also unlawful to "willfully and maliciously" shoot a firearm at an *unoccupied* aircraft.[156] Likewise, you cannot "discharge any firearm within 500 feet of any magazine or any explosive manufacturing plant."[157]

If permitted in the first place, the discharge of firearms in any of the five California state forests is prohibited in the vicinity of camps or within 150 yards of designated camping areas, "residence sites, recreation grounds and areas, and over lakes or other bodies of water adjacent to or within such areas, whereby any person is exposed to injury as a result of such discharge."[158] The California Fish & Game Code also prohibits *discharging* firearms in certain specified refuges.[159]

If you enter private lands, be wary of trespassing. "It is unlawful to enter land for the purpose of discharging a firearm or taking or destroying a mammal or bird, including waterfowl, on that land without having first obtained written permission from the owner, or the owner's agent, or the person in lawful possession of that land, if either of the following is true":

(1) The land belongs to or is occupied by another person and is either under cultivation or enclosed by a fence; *or*,

(2) There are signs of any size and wording forbidding trespass or hunting or both displayed along all exterior boundaries of the land, at intervals not less than three to the mile, and at all roads and trails entering the land, including land temporarily inundated by water flowing outside the established banks of a river, stream, slough, or other waterway, which fairly advise a person about to enter the land that the use of the land is so restricted.[160]

Also, except for lawful self-defense, aiming or pointing a laser scope[161] or laser pointer[162] at anyone in a threatening manner to cause them fear of bodily harm is a misdemeanor.[163]

---

[154] P.C. § 374c.
[155] Cal. Fish & Game Code § 3004(b).
[156] P.C. § 247(a).
[157] Cal. Health & Saf. Code § 12084.
[158] Cal. Code Regs. tit. 14, § 1413.
[159] Cal. Fish & Game Code § 10662. For example, certain areas of California Fish & Game District 4D in Riverside County are outlined in Cal. Fish & Game Code section 10837.
[160] Cal. Fish & Game Code § 2016. See also P.C. § 602(l).
[161] A "laser scope" is "a portable battery-powered device capable of being attached to a firearm and capable of projecting a laser light on objects at a distance." The "laser scope" does not need to be attached to a firearm to be a crime. P.C. § 417.25(a-b).
[162] A "laser pointer" is "any hand held laser beam device or demonstration laser product that emits a single point of light amplified by the stimulated emission of radiation that is visible to the human eye." P.C. § 417.25(c).
[163] P.C. § 417.25(a).

"[W]illfully and maliciously discharg[ing] a laser at an aircraft,"[164] whether it is moving or not, is also a crime.[165] This rule does not apply to laser development activity by, or on behalf of, the U.S. Armed Forces.[166]

XII. SHOOTING RANGE USE RESTRICTIONS

A well-established range can provide an environment where you can discharge your firearm without fear of criminal prosecution.[167] For the first-time shooter going to the range, make sure you contact the range ahead of time and get information on the kinds of firearms they allow (some ranges are handguns or rifles or shotguns only). If you are bringing ammunition to the range, inquire into what kinds of ammunition you can bring (some ranges do not allow you to shoot steel-jacketed, steel-core, or semi-jacketed ammunition, etc.), what kind of eye/ear wear they require, and whether they provide such protection. If you plan on renting firearms, ask whether the range has firearms for rent and, if so, what the requirements are to rent (ID, age restrictions, number of persons, etc.).

XIII. SUGGESTIONS FOR SHOOTING IN PUBLIC

If you have found a place where you may lawfully shoot, here are some tips:

(1) Since areas where you can discharge your firearm may be closed or restricted, contact the respective state and/or national authorities in these areas *before* shooting. They will be your best authority as to where you can lawfully shoot in these areas. When possible, get the name of the person you spoke with and get their permission in writing beforehand.

(2) Know your surroundings. Even if you find a place to shoot lawfully, you may be near an area where the sound of firearms being fired is not appreciated. Contact law enforcement to let them know where you plan to shoot and ask for suggestions to avoid complaints.

(3) Shoot only at retrievable, freestanding targets and do not attach targets to living plants or against rocks, plants, or solid objects. Under federal law, it is illegal to deface/destroy trees, signs, or other objects on federal land that are for the public's enjoyment.[168]

(4) Watch the area behind your intended target. Make certain no one can enter into the area where you are shooting without you seeing them first. Try to

---

[164] "Aircraft" means any contrivance intended for and capable of transporting persons through the airspace. P.C. § 247.5.
[165] P.C. § 247.5.
[166] P.C. § 247.5.
[167] Keep in mind that law enforcement members frequent firearm ranges for firearm qualification and training. Make certain the firearms you possess and your activities are lawful.
[168] 43 C.F.R. § 8365.1-5(a)(1).

choose a place with a natural backstop or berm. Never shoot where you don't know where your rounds will land.

(5) Leave the area as you found it. Pick up your trash, spent casings, targets, etc. If you are using clays or any other launch targets, do not launch them into areas where you cannot go and retrieve pieces later, such as cliffs, steep hillsides, or water.

(6) Discharging firearms directly into the air on the Fourth of July, New Year's Eve, or really *anytime*, is a horrible idea and may subject you to criminal and/or civil liability.

For more information on where to shoot and how to shoot safely, visit the websites of the NRA (http://home.nra.org/), CRPA (http://www.crpa.org/), and the National Shooting Sports Foundation (NSSF) (http://www.nssf.org/).

CHAPTER 9:
REGULATION OF "ASSAULT WEAPONS" AND .50 BMG RIFLES

California law expressly forbids any person in the state from manufacturing, causing to be manufactured, distributing, transporting, importing into the state, keeping for sale, offering for sale, exposing for sale, giving, or lending any firearm classified by California as an "assault weapon."[1] It is also illegal for any person in the state to possess any firearm classified by California as an "assault weapon."[2]

What exactly is an "assault weapon" according to California? Generally, there are two types. First, there are those semiautomatic firearms expressly listed by their make and model as "assault weapons."[3] Second, there are those firearms identified as "assault weapons" based on their features and/or characteristics.[4]

These types can be further separated into different categories. Firearms expressly listed by the Legislature in the 1989 "Assault Weapons Control Act" ("AWCA") and the subsequent 1991 amendment are commonly known as "Category 1" "assault weapons."[5] Firearms that were added to this list by DOJ through its regulatory authority are commonly known as "Category 2" "assault weapons." Finally, those firearms identified as "assault weapons" based on their features and/or characteristics are commonly known as "Category 3" "assault weapons."

---

[1] P.C. § 30600(a). Violations of this restriction are a felony punishable with up to eight years in prison. *Id.*
[2] P.C. § 30605(a). Violations of this restriction are a wobbler punishable by imprisonment in a county jail for up to one year. *Id.*
[3] *See* P.C. § 30510; *see also* CAL. CODE REGS . tit. 11, §§ 5495-5499.
[4] *See* P.C. § 30515.
[5] P.C. §§ 30500-31115.

I. "ASSAULT WEAPON" DEFINED

A. Category 1 "Assault Weapons"

Firearms listed in the 1989 AWCA and those added in 1991, which included: "Made in China AK, AKM, AKS, AK47, AK47S, 56, 56S, 84S, and 86S," are commonly known as Category 1 "assault weapons."[6] They are the same firearms specifically named by make and model in P.C. section 30510.[7] They had to be registered with DOJ on or before March 31, 1992.[8] See the AWIG for representative photos of each Category 1 "assault weapon."

Today, it is no longer possible to register a Category 1 "assault weapon."

Examples of Category 1 "Assault Weapons"

Intratec TEC-9

B. Category 2 "Assault Weapons"

In 2000 the California Supreme Court upheld the validity of the AWCA, including the DOJ "add-on" provision, in the face of a lawsuit challenging its constitutionality.[9]

As a result, DOJ added over sixty Colt AR-15 and AK "series" firearms to the list of restricted "assault weapons," making those firearms illegal to possess in California if not registered by the applicable deadline. These new additions are referred

---

[6] P.C. § 30510. See the "Assault Weapon" list at the end of this chapter.

[7] P.C. § 30510 ; *see also* CAL. CODE REGS. tit. 11, § 5495.

[8] CAL. DEPT. OF JUSTICE, OFFICE OF THE ATTORNEY GENERAL, ASSAULT WEAPONS IDENTIFICATION GUIDE, (3rd ed. Nov. 2001), *available at* http://oag.ca.gov/sites/all/files/agweb/pdfs/firearms/forms/awguide.pdf (last visited Oct. 9, 2020).

[9] *Kasler v. Lockyer*, 23 Cal. 4th 472 (2000). DOJ has been unable to use this provision to add to the prohibited "assault weapons" list since January 1, 2007, because it was statutorily "unsettled" – meaning it expired – by the passage of AB 2728, and the list has remained fixed ever since.

to as Category 2 "assault weapons," and the deadline to register them was January 23, 2001. These added Category 2 "assault weapons" are listed in Cal. Code Regs. title 11, section 5499. The public education program advising people that these guns had been "series" designated as "assault weapons" was meager. Many people did not realize these firearms had become Category 2 "series" "assault weapons" and did not realize the firearms now needed to be registered.

If a firearm is not currently listed as an "assault weapon" in the Penal Code, California Code of Regulations, or the AWIG, it is not a Category 1 or 2 "assault weapon." If a firearm does not have the same manufacturer and model designation as the ones on the list, it also is not a Category 1 or 2 "assault weapon."

A number of manufacturers have made California-compliant firearms similar to the ones on the list with different model designations. These firearms cannot be considered "assault weapons" under Category 1 or 2. They could, however, still meet the definition of a Category 3 "assault weapon" depending on the firearm's features, as discussed below.

DOJ has argued, somewhat inconsistently, that Category 1 and 2 "assault weapons" are "assault weapons" at the bare receiver/frame level – regardless of any other particular characteristic. This is debatable because frames and receivers are considered "firearms" under certain Penal Code sections,[10] but *not* under the AWCA. Under the AWCA, therefore, a frame or receiver should not be considered a "firearm." For a frame or receiver to be considered an "assault weapon," it first must be considered a "firearm" that is either a semiautomatic rifle, pistol, or shotgun.[11]

Since a bare frame or receiver alone cannot function as a firearm at all because it does not have the characteristics of a rifle, pistol, or shotgun, and particularly not in a manner to justify designating it "semiautomatic,"[12] a fully functioning "make and model" firearm should be present to be a "firearm" under the AWCA, not just a frame or a receiver.

Nevertheless, since DOJ may disagree, it is not recommended that you possess even bare firearm frames/receivers listed by make and model as "assault weapons" unless they are registered.

---

[10] P.C. § 16520.
[11] P.C. § 30510.
[12] A shotgun with a revolving cylinder does not need to be semiautomatic. P.C. § 30515(a)(8).

Examples of Category 2 "Assault Weapons"

Norinco MAK 90

Colt AR-15 Semi-Automatic Rifle

CATEGORY 1 "ASSAULT WEAPONS"
RIFLES

- Any AK series including but not limited to the following models:
  - Made in China AK, AKM, AK47, AK47S, 56, 56S, 84S, and 86S
  - Norinco 56, 56S, 84S and 86S
  - Poly Technologies AKS and AK47
  - MAAI AK47 and ARM
- Any of the following MAC types:
  - RPB Industries Inc. sM10 and sM11
  - SWD Incrporated M11
- Armalite AR-180
- Beretta AR-10
- Bushmaster Assault Rifle
- Calico M-900
- CETME Sporter
- Colt AR-15 series
- Daewoo K-1, K-2, Max 1, Max 2, AR 100, and AR 110C
- Fabrique Nationale FAL, LAR, FNC, 308 Match, and Sporter
- HK-91, HK-93, HK-94, and HK-PSG-1
- J&R ENG M-68
- MAS 223
- SKS with detachable magazine
- SIG AMT, PE 57, SG 550, and SG 551
- Springfield Armory BM59 and SAR-48
- Sterling MK-6
- UZI and Galil
- Valmet M62S, M71S, and M78S
- Weaver Arms Nighthawk
- Steyr AUG

CATEGORY 2 "ASSAULT WEAPONS"
RIFLES

- American Arms AK-C47, AK-F 39, AK-F 47, AK-Y 39
- American Spirit ASA Model
- Armalite AR 10 (all), Golden Eagle, M15 (all)
- Arsenal SLG (all), SLR (all)
- B-West AK-47 (all)
- Bushmaster XM15 (all)
- Colt AR-15 (all), Law Enforcement (6920), Match Target (all), Sporter (all)
- Dalphon B.F.D.
- DPMS Panther (all)
- Eagle Arms EA-15 AS H-Bar, EA-15 E1, M15 (all)
- Frankford Arsenal Ar-15 (all)
- Hesse Arms, Model 47 (all), Wieger STG 940 Rifle, HAR 15A2 (all)
- Inter Ordinance - Monroe, NC AK-47 (all), NC M-97, NC RPK
- Kalashnikov USA Hunter Rifle/Saiga
- Knights RAS (all), SR-15 (all), SR-25 (all)
- Les Bauer Ultimate AR (all)
- MAADI CO AK, 47, ARM, MISR (all), MISTR (all)
- Made in China AK, AKM, AKS, AK47-, 56, 56S, 84S, 86S
- Mitchel Arms, Inc. AK-47, AK-47 Cal .308 (all), M-76, M-90, RPK
- Norinco 56, 56 S, 81 S (all), 84 S, 86 (all), 86 S, AK-47 (all), Hunter Rifle, MAK 90, NHM 90, 90-2, 91 Sport, RPK Rifle
- Ohio Ordinance Works (o.o.w.) AK-74, ROMAK 991
- Olympic Arms AR-15, Car-97, PCR (all)
- Ordnance, Inc. AR-15
- Palmetto SGA (all)
- Poly Technologies AKS, AK47
- Professional Ordinance, Inc. Carbon 15 Rifle
- PWA All Models
- Rock River Arms, Inc. Car A2, Car A4 Flattop, LE Tactical Carbine, NM A2-DCM Legal, Standard A-2, Standard A-4 Flattop
- Valmet 76 S, Hunter Rifle
- Wilson Combat AR-15
- WUM WUM (all)

CATEGORY 1 "ASSAULT WEAPONS" PISTOLS	CATEGORY 2 "ASSAULT WEAPONS" PISTOLS

• UZI
• Encom MP-9 and MP-5
• The following MAC Types
   • RPB Industries Inc. sM10 and sM11
   • SWD Incorporated M-11
   • Advanced Armament Inc. M-11
   • Military Armament Corp. Ingram M-11
• Intratec Tec-9
• Sites Spectre
• Sterling MK-7
• Calico M-950
• Bushmaster Pistiol
	• MARS Pistol
	• Professional Ordnance, Inc. Carbon 15 Pistol

C. Category 3 "Assault Weapons"

1. A Brief History

In 1999, the AWCA was again amended to define "assault weapons" a third way: generically by a firearm's characteristics.[13] This new classification, commonly referred to as "Category 3," resulted in many semiautomatic firearms equipped with a "detachable magazine" and additional prohibited features being classified by California as "assault weapons" regardless of their make or model. Notably, none of the expressly identified prohibited features altered the firearm's rate of fire.

In the years following the creation of Category 3 "assault weapons," firearm owners and manufactures converted firearms by removing the expressly prohibited characteristics, thereby preventing the firearm from being labeled an "assault weapon" under this classification. Some would convert their semiautomatic firearms to non-semiautomatic actions, while others would convert their centerfire rifles to rimfire. Although these conversions may still remove a firearm out of the definition of an "assault weapon," most gun owners and manufacturers did not choose to use these methods to make their firearms California compliant. Instead, most chose to remove the firearm's capability of accepting a detachable magazine by installing a magazine lock commonly known as a "Bullet Button."

Standard magazine releases for a "detachable magazine" usually operate with the push of a finger, meaning no "tool" is required to release the magazine. A "Bullet Button," however, replaces the standard one-piece magazine release button with a two-piece assembly that cannot be operated with just the push of a finger. The outer

---
[13] P.C. § 30515.

button directly replaces the standard magazine release button in shape and size but without actuating the spring that allows magazine removal. The much smaller inner button sits recessed within the outer button and becomes the firearm's true magazine removal mechanism. Since the inner button is too small and recessed to be pushed by a finger; a tool is needed to push the inner button to release the magazine so it can be removed. The most common "tool" used to push the recessed button and remove the magazine is the tip of a bullet--hence, the name "Bullet Button." Because a tool is needed to release the magazine, firearms equipped with a "Bullet Button" do not have the capacity to accept a "detachable magazine" for purposes of California's "assault weapon" restrictions.

California's Category 3 classification remained unchanged for well over a decade. But then on July 1, 2016, Governor Jerry Brown signed AB 1135 and SB 880 into law. These identical[14] bills amended the definition of a Category 3 "assault weapon" by replacing the phrase "capacity to accept a detachable magazine" with "does not have a fixed magazine." In doing so, the amendment was meant to prohibit firearm owners from using "Bullet Buttons" as a means of avoiding California's restrictions. And in 2020, Governor Gavin Newsom signed SB 118 into law, which now also classified certain "other" firearms that cannot legally be classified as rifles, pistols, or shotguns as "assault weapons" in the same manner as other "Category 3" classifications.

Current Category 3 "assault weapon" definitions as applied to rifles, pistols, shotguns, and "other" type firearms are discussed below.

2. Category 3 Rifles

Since January 1, 2017, a rifle is considered a Category 3 "assault weapon" if it meets any of the following three definitions::

(1) It is semiautomatic, centerfire, does not have a "fixed magazine," and has any one of the following:

   (a) A pistol grip that protrudes conspicuously beneath the action of the weapon;

   (b) A thumbhole stock;

   (c) A folding or telescoping stock;

   (d) A grenade launcher or flare launcher;

   (e) A flash suppressor; or,

   (f) A forward pistol grip.[15]

---

[14] SB 880 and AB 1135 were practically identical for all intents and purposes. Technically, they were never reconciled when they were passed, so both are current California law. As a result, there are two versions of P.C. section 30680 in existence due to a slight variation in wording between AB 1135 and SB 880. The Legislature needs to fix this for housekeeping purposes, but it does not substantively affect the analysis discussed later in detail.

[15] P.C. § 30515(a)(1).

(2) It is semiautomatic, centerfire, and has a fixed magazine with the capacity to accept more than 10 rounds[16]; or,

(3) It is semiautomatic, centerfire, and has an overall length of less than 30 inches.[17]

As used above, the term "fixed magazine" means "an ammunition feeding device contained in, or permanently attached to, a firearm in such a manner that the device cannot be removed without disassembly of the firearm action."[18]

Example of a Category 3 Rifle

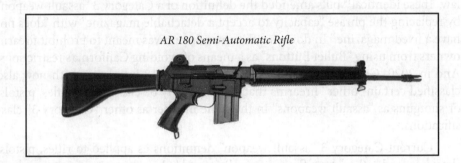

AR 180 Semi-Automatic Rifle

3. Category 3 Pistols

Since January 1, 2017, a pistol is considered a Category 3 "assault weapon" if it meets either of the following two definitions:

(1) It is semiautomatic, does not have a "fixed magazine," and has any one of the following:

    (a) A threaded barrel, capable of accepting a flash suppressor, forward handgrip, or silencer;

    (b) A second handgrip;

    (c) A shroud that is attached to, or partially or completely encircles, the barrel that allows the bearer to fire the weapon without burning the bearer's hand, except a slide that encloses the barrel; *or*,

    (d) The capacity to accept a detachable magazine at some location outside of the pistol grip.[19]

---

[16] P.C. § 30515(a)(2).
[17] P.C. § 30515(a)(3).
[18] P.C. § 30515(b).
[19] P.C. § 30515(a)(4).

(2) It is semiautomatic and has a fixed magazine with the capacity to accept more than 10 rounds.[20]

Note that unlike rifles, a pistol need not be "centerfire" to be classified as an "assault weapon" under California law.

Threaded barrel from a Ruger 22.45

4. Category 3 Shotguns

Prior to January 1, 2017, a shotgun did not have "the ability to accept a detachable magazine" if it was equipped with a magazine locking device like a "Bullet Button." Although SB 880 and AB 1135 did not change the definition of an "assault weapon" as applied to shotguns under Penal Code section 30515, DOJ adopted a new definition for the phrase "[a]bility to accept a detachable magazine" that states "with respect to a semiautomatic shotgun, it does not have a fixed magazine."[21]

In effect, DOJ's regulatory definition classified any semiautomatic shotgun equipped with a magazine lock such as a "Bullet-Button" as an "assault weapon"—at least in the opinion of DOJ. But with the enactment of SB 118 in 2020, California law has now been amended to align with DOJ's regulations.[22] As a result of this change, California law classifies the following types of shotguns as "assault weapons":

(1) A semiautomatic shotgun that has both of the following:

    (a) A folding or telescoping stock, *and*

    (b) A pistol grip that protrudes conspicuously beneath the action of the weapon, thumbhole stock, or vertical handgrip.[23]

---

[20] P.C. § 30515(a)(5).

[21] CAL. CODE REGS. tit. 11, § 5471(a).

[22] CRPA has filed a lawsuit challenging DOJ's "assault weapon" regulations, including the DOJ's regulations requiring certain shotguns to be registered as "assault weapons." That lawsuit, titled Villanueva v. Becerra, Case No. 17-CECG-03093, is currently on appeal. But the superior court's decision in the case has stated that DOJ's regulations, including for "Bullet Button" shotguns, "properly carry out the Legislative intent." DOJ has argued that its interpretation is based on the Legislative intent of SB 880 and AB 1135. But the regulation DOJ adopted regarding the definition of "ability to accept a detachable magazine" only applies for purposes of registration, not general enforcement of California's "assault weapon" laws. Further, although the Penal Code now supports this position, at the time DOJ adopted its regulation, it did not specifically prohibit the pos- session or even transfer of "bullet-button shotguns"—regardless if the shotgun was properly registered. Make sure you subscribe to NRA and CRPA email alerts to stay informed on any updates regarding this case.

[23] P.C. § 30515(a)(6).

(2) Any semiautomatic shotgun that does not have a fixed magazine[24]; or

(3) Any shotgun with a revolving cylinder.[25]

If you failed to timely register a shotgun that was previously required to be equipped with a "bullet button" and you still currently possess that firearm, you should seek the assistance of a skilled firearms attorney immediately. Additionally, separating the upper and lower receiver or otherwise disassembling the shotgun so it can no longer function in a semiautomatic nature may help you avoid criminal charges should you be contacted by law enforcement.[26]

5. "Other" Category 3 Firearms That Are Not Rifles, Pistols, or Shotguns

With the adoption of SB 118 in 2020, California law also now labels as "assault weapons" certain firearms otherwise incapable of being legally classified as a rifle, pistol, or shotgun.[27] This includes any firearm meeting the following definitions:

(1) A semiautomatic centerfire firearm that is not a rifle, pistol or shotgun that does not have a fixed magazine, but that has any one of the following:

   (a) A pistol grip that protrudes conspicuously beneath the action of the weapon;

   (b) A thumbhole stock;

   (c) A folding or telescoping stock;

   (d) A grenade launcher or flare launcher;

   (e) A flash suppressor;

   (f) A forward pistol grip;

   (g) A threaded barrel, capable of accepting a flash suppressor, forward handgrip, or silencer;

   (h) A second handgrip;

   (i) A shroud that is attached to, or partially or completely encircles, the barrel that allows the bearer to fire the weapon without burning the bearer's hand, except a slide that encloses the barrel; or

   (j) The capacity to accept a detachable magazine at some location outside of the pistol grip.[28]

---

[24] P.C. § 30515(a)(7).
[25] P.C. § 30515(a)(8).
[26] *See* Cal. Code Regs. tit. 11, § 5471(hh) (stating a firearm is not considered "semiautomatic" if it is lacking a firing pin, bolt carrier, gas tube, or some other crucial part of the firearm).
[27] P.C. § 30515(a)(9-11).
[28] P.C. § 30515(a)(9)(A-J).

(2) A semiautomatic, centerfire firearm that is not a rifle, pistol, or shotgun, that has a fixed magazine with the capacity to accept more than 10 rounds[29]; or,

(3) A semiautomatic centerfire firearm that is not a rifle, pistol, or shotgun, that has an overall length of less than 30 inches.[30]

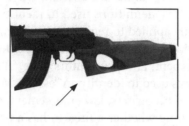

Example of a conspicuously protruding pistol grip   *Example of a thumbhole stock*   *Example of a forward pistol grip*

Individuals who lawfully possessed a firearm meeting any of the above definitions may continue to lawfully possess such firearms provided the following conditions are satisfied:

- Prior to September 1, 2020, the person would have been eligible to register the firearm pursuant to subdivision (c) of Penal Code section 30900;
- The person lawfully possessed the firearm prior to September 1, 2020; and,
- The person registers the firearm by January 1, 2022, as an "assault weapon" in accordance with subdivision (c) of Penal Code section 30900.[31]

In connection with the above, SB 118 also adds subdivision (c) to Penal Code section 90300, which outlines the basic procedures required for registering a newly classified "assault weapon" before January 1, 2022. Registrations can only be submitted after DOJ has adopted regulations implementing subdivision (c)'s registration requirements.[32] At this time, DOJ has yet to propose, let alone adopt, any such regulations. But it is anticipated DOJ's regulations will closely mirror that of the registration regulations it adopted in connection with SB 880 and AB 1135. But unlike past "assault weapon" registrations, SB 118's changes make clear that joint-registrations will not be permitted.[33]

---

[29] P.C. § 30515(a)(10).
[30] P.C. § 30515(a)(11).
[31] P.C. § 30685. Readers should also note that SB 118's provisions classifying "other" firearms as "assault weapons" appear to be in direct response to a new and unique firearm design from Franklin Armory referred to as the "Title 1." In response, Franklin Armory, with the support of CRPA, is challenging SB 118 in court. Be sure to subscribe to CRPA email alerts to be notified of detailed information regarding the registration process and any updates regarding the lawsuit.
[32] P.C. § 30900(c)(1).
[33] P.C. § 30955(b).

a. DOJ's Regulatory Definitions Applicable to The Identification of "Assault Weapons."

In August 2017, DOJ adopted regulations applicable to the registration of firearms classified as "assault weapons" under SB 880 and AB 1135 while simultaneously repealing all prior regulatory definitions used to identify "assault weapons."[34] But these new regulations only applied to registration, not enforcement of California's "assault weapon" restrictions.[35] This resulted in unintended consequences affecting gun owners, law enforcement, and prosecutors alike. There were no legal definitions for any of the features used to identify an "assault weapon" under Penal Code sections 30510 or 30515. Gun owners, law enforcement, and prosecutors lost crucial guidance in determining whether a firearm has a prohibited feature or characteristic that would result in the firearm being classified as an "assault weapon."

Finally recognizing its own error, DOJ proposed a new regulation in May 2018 that simply read:

> *The definitions of terms [adopted pursuant to DOJ's "assault weapon" registration regulations] shall apply to the identification of assault weapons pursuant to Penal Code section 30515.*[36]

The proposed regulation sought to expand DOJ's previously adopted "assault weapon" definitions (only applicable for registration purposes) to apply for all purposes, including general enforcement of California's "assault weapon" laws. In other words, DOJ was attempting to do exactly what OAL previously rejected.

This regulation was ultimately approved by California's Office of Administrative Law ("OAL") in January 2019. Below, we list these definitions with additional analysis and commentary on each:

(1) "'Ability to accept a detachable magazine' means with respect to a semiautomatic shotgun it does not have a fixed magazine."[37]

> *As discussed above, DOJ's definition of "ability to accept a detachable magazine" shoehorned semiautomatic shotguns with "bullet buttons" into the definition of "assault weapons." While we believe DOJ is wrong as discussed above, given the current uncertainty surrounding the issue gun owners are advised to treat such shotguns as "assault weapons" that had to have been registered, modified, or removed from the state before July 1, 2018.*

(2) "'Action' means the working mechanism of a semiautomatic firearm, which is the combination of the receiver or frame and breech bolt together with

---

[34] *See* CAL. CODE REGS. tit. 11, §§ 5459-5478.
[35] *See* CAL. CODE REGS. tit. 11, § 5471 (stating that "for purposes of [registration] the following definitions shall apply.")
[36] CAL. CODE. REGS. tit. 11 § 5460.
[37] CAL. CODE. REGS. tit. 11, § 5471(a).

the other parts of the mechanism by which a firearm is loaded fired and unloaded."[38]

(3) "'Barrel' means the tube usually metal and cylindrical through which a projectile or shot charge is fired. Barrels may have a rifled or smooth bore."[39]

(4) "'Barrel length' means the length of the barrel measured as follows: Without consideration of any extensions or protrusions rearward of the closed bolt or breech-face the approved procedure for measuring barrel length is to measure from the closed bolt (or breech-face) to the furthermost end of the barrel or permanently attached muzzle device. Permanent methods of attachment include full-fusion gas or electric steel-seam welding, high-temperature (1100°F) silver soldering, or blind pinning with the pin head welded over. Barrels are measured by inserting a dowel rod into the barrel until the rod stops against the closed bolt or breech-face. The rod is then marked at the furthermost end of the barrel or permanently attached muzzle device, withdrawn from the barrel, and measured."[40]

This definition is odd because the new law does not redefine the definition for "assault weapon" based on barrel length. This appears to be DOJ, again through regulation, molding the law into what it thinks it should be. It will remain to be seen if law enforcement and/or the courts will attempt to use this definition for other things like "short-barreled" rifles and "short-barreled" shotguns.

(5) "'Bullet' means the projectile expelled from a gun. It is not synonymous with a cartridge. Bullets can be of many materials, shapes, weights, and constructions such as solid lead, lead with a jacket of harder metal, round-nosed, flat-nosed. hollow-pointed, et cetera."[41]

(6) "'Bullet-button' means a product requiring a tool to remove an ammunition feeding device or magazine by depressing a recessed button or lever shielded by a magazine lock. A bullet-button equipped fully functional semiautomatic firearm does not meet the fixed magazine definition under Penal Code section 30515(b)."[42]

(7) "'Bore' means the interior of a firearm's barrel excluding the chamber."[43]

(8) "'Caliber' means the nominal diameter of a projectile of a rifled firearm or the diameter between lands in a rifled barrel. In the United States, caliber is usually expressed in hundreds of an inch; in Great Britain in thousandths of an inch; in Europe and elsewhere in millimeters."[44]

---

[38] CAL. CODE. REGS. tit. 11, § 5471(b).
[39] CAL. CODE. REGS. tit. 11, § 5471(c).
[40] CAL. CODE. REGS. tit. 11, § 5471(d).
[41] CAL. CODE. REGS. tit. 11, § 5471(e).
[42] CAL. CODE. REGS. tit. 11, § 5471(f).
[43] CAL. CODE. REGS. tit. 11, § 5471(g).
[44] CAL. CODE. REGS. tit. 11, § 5471(h).

(9) "'Cartridge' means a complete round of ammunition that consists of a primer, a case, propellant powder and one or more projectiles."[45]

(10) "'Centerfire' means a cartridge with its primer located in the center of the base of the case."[46]

(11) "'Contained in' means that the magazine cannot be released from the firearm while the action is assembled. For AR-15 style firearms this means the magazine cannot be released from the firearm while the upper receiver and lower receiver are joined together."[47]

(12) "'Department' means the California Department of Justice."[48]

(13) "'Detachable magazine' means any ammunition feeding device that can be removed readily from the firearm without disassembly of the firearm action or use of a tool. A bullet or ammunition cartridge is considered a tool. An ammunition feeding device includes any belted or linked ammunition, but does not include clips, en bloc clips, or stripper clips that load cartridges into the magazine. [ ] An AR-15 style firearm that has a bullet-button style magazine release with a magnet left on the bullet-button constitutes a detachable magazine. An AR-15 style firearm lacking a magazine catch assembly (magazine catch, magazine catch spring and magazine release button) constitutes a detachable magazine. An AK-47 style firearm lacking a magazine catch assembly (magazine catch, spring and rivet/pin) constitutes a detachable magazine."[49]

The second half of this definition appears to be DOJ extending what it thinks the law should be. As mentioned before, we know DOJ's opinion was that "bullet buttons" with magnets or other items within them constituted "detachable magazines." This position, while far from ideal, was debatable because a "tool" was still required. Through its new definition, DOJ has effectively slammed the door on the debate.

We are aware of past instances where law enforcement has come across firearms that lack a "magazine catch assembly." Law enforcement attempted to classify firearms in this situation as capable of accepting a detachable magazine. Of course, there is a question of whether the firearms, without a magazine catch, are capable of accepting any magazine, let alone a "detachable" one.

(14) "'Disassembly of the firearm action' means the fire control assembly is detached from the action in such a way that the action has been interrupted and will not function. For example, disassembling the action on a two part receiver, like that on an AR-15 style firearm, would require [1] the rear take

---

[45] CAL. CODE. REGS. tit. 11, § 5471(i).
[46] CAL. CODE. REGS. tit. 11, § 5471(j).
[47] CAL. CODE. REGS. tit. 11, § 5471(k).
[48] CAL. CODE. REGS. tit. 11, § 5471(l).
[49] CAL. CODE. REGS. tit. 11, § 5471(m).

down pin to be removed, [2] the upper receiver lifted upwards and away from the lower receiver using the front pivot pin as the fulcrum, before the magazine may be removed."[50]

This phrase, when first used in the Penal Code to define "fixed magazine," caused a lot of confusion because the "action" of a firearm has a rather fluid meaning.[51] And the public had concerns about the amount of "disassembly" required by the Penal Code. DOJ appears to clear some of these concerns. DOJ also appears to lend its approval to devices that prevent the removal of the magazine unless the upper receiver of an AR-15 style firearm is tilted up. As a result, and explained in more detail later in this Chapter, certain aftermarket parts should take a firearm out of the new definition of "assault weapon" because they make it so that the magazine can only be removed by (1) releasing the takedown pin and (2) swinging the upper receiver away from the lower receiver. Hence, these aftermarket products make it so that the magazine cannot be removed without "disassembling the firearm's action" (as that term is defined by DOJ's regulations), which means that there is a "fixed magazine" and no "assault weapon" under the new definition of "assault weapon."

(15) "'Featureless' means a semiautomatic firearm (rifle, pistol, or shotgun) lacking the characteristics associated with that weapon, as listed in Penal Code section 30515."[52]

DOJ's definition isn't entirely clear. DOJ references the characteristics listed in Penal Code section 30515, but it never states which characteristics it means. For example, for rifles, "semiautomatic," "centerfire," "does not have a fixed magazine," "pistol grip," "flash suppressor," etc. can all be lumped together into "characteristics." While there are some firearms that lack all of the characteristics listed in section 30515, they come nowhere near approaching the definition of an "assault weapon."

"Featureless" as that term is most commonly used by the public usually refers to a rifle that will have the following characteristics: semiautomatic, centerfire, and does not have a fixed magazine (or prior to 2017, may have had "the capacity to accept a detachable magazine") but didn't have any of the additional, required features that would cause the rifle to meet the definition

---

[50] CAL. CODE. REGS. tit. 11, § 5471(n).

[51] For example, some sources define "action" as "[t]he mechanism of a gun, usually breechloading, by which it is loaded, fired, and unloaded." John Quick, DICTIONARY OF WEAPONS & MILITARY TERMS 3 (Harold B. Crawford et al., 1973). Other sources say that "the action of a firearm is the method of firing, expelling the spent casing, and chambering a new one, as mechanically facilitated by the design of the firearm." Kevin Inouye, THE THEATRICAL FIREARMS HANDBOOK 19 (CRS Press 2014). And others think of an "action" as "[t]he part of a firearm that load, fires, and ejects a cartridge. Includes lever action, pump action, bolt action, and semi-automatic. The first three are found in weapons that fire a single shot. Firearms that can shoot multiple rounds ("repeaters") include all these types of actions, but only the semi- automatic does not require manual operation between rounds. A truly 'automatic' action is found on a machine gun." *Firearms Handout, Firearms Definitions,* TENNESSEE STATE COURTS, http://www.tncourts.gov/sites/default/files/docs/firearmshandout_1.pdf (last visited Oct. 9, 2020).

[52] CAL. CODE. REGS. tit. 11 , § 5471(o).

of an *"assault weapon" under P.C. section 30515(a)(1), i.e., a pistol grip that protrudes conspicuously beneath the action of the weapon, a thumbhole stock, a folding or telescoping stock, a grenade launcher or flare launcher, a flash suppressor, and a forward pistol grip).*

With the above definition, it is unclear what DOJ means by "featureless." Maybe DOJ should have requested public comment before simply enacting the regulations.

(16) "'Fixed magazine' means an ammunition feeding device contained in, or permanently attached to, a firearm in such a manner that the device cannot be removed without disassembly of the firearm action."[53]

(17) "'Flare launcher' means a device used to launch signal flares."[54]

(18) "'Flash suppressor' means any device attached to the end of the barrel, that is designed, intended, or functions to perceptibly reduce or redirect muzzle flash from the shooter's field of vision. A hybrid device that has either advertised flash suppressing properties or functionally has flash suppressing properties would be deemed a flash suppressor. A device labeled or identified by its manufacturer as a flash hider would be deemed a flash suppressor."[55]

The original, horrible definition of "flash suppressor" remains from the original regulation. It is still unclear what or how much flash must be "perceptibly reduced" for a device to meet the definition of a "flash suppressor." But DOJ made a bad definition worse by tacking on new second and third sentences to the definition. We know that law enforcement, in order to attempt to determine whether a device is a flash suppressor, would turn to instruction manuals for certain firearms and see what the manufacturer calls the device. Now, DOJ has codified the practice into a regulation. Now, a device, according to DOJ, can meet the definition of "flash suppressor" just by being called that no matter if the device reduces muzzle flash. Based on this definition, if the device increased the muzzle flash but was called a "flash hider" by its manufacturer, it would be a "flash suppressor" under California law. Good thing this theory doesn't apply to other California laws or a person could be prosecuted for possession of a destructive device for possessing a pack of "Bazooka Joe" bubble gum.

(19) "'FMBUS' means a Firearm Manufactured By Unlicensed Subject."[56]

This on its face is just an acronym, but it lends a little guidance into DOJ's thought process. "Unlicensed subject" is not a firearm industry term but a law

---

[53] CAL. CODE. REGS. tit. 11, § 5471(p).
[54] CAL. CODE. REGS. tit. 11, § 5471(q).
[55] CAL. CODE. REGS. tit. 11, § 5471(r).
[56] CAL. CODE. REGS. tit. 11, § 5471(s).

enforcement term. A "subject" is often what law enforcement refer to when it is talking about a person who is the subject of a criminal investigation.

(20) "'Forward pistol grip' means a grip that allows for a pistol style grasp forward of the trigger."[57]

(21) "'Frame' means the receiver of a pistol."[58]

(22) "'Grenade launcher' means a device capable of launching a grenade."[59]

(23) "'Permanently attached to' means the magazine is welded, epoxied, or riveted into the magazine well A firearm with a magazine housed in a sealed magazine well and then welded, epoxied, or riveted into the sealed magazine well meets the definition of 'permanently attached to.'"[60]

(24) "'Overall length of less than 30 inches' with respect to a centerfire rifle means the rifle has been measured in the shortest possible configuration that the weapon will function/fire and the measurement is less than 30 inches. Folding and telescoping stocks shall be collapsed prior to measurement. The approved method for measuring the length of the rifle is to measure the firearm from the end of the barrel, or permanently attached muzzle device, if so equipped, to that part of the stock that is furthest from the end of the barrel, or permanently attached muzzle device. (Prior to taking a measurement the owner must also check any muzzle devices for how they are attached to the barrel.)"[61]

This definition is odd in that the "assault weapon" definition for semiautomatic centerfire rifles less than 30 inches in length was unchanged by the recent legislation. They were illegal to possess before January 1, 2017 and remained illegal thereafter. DOJ's definition is odd unless DOJ wanted to make a firm case for what it considered illegal to possess, as it did with its other regulations. Even odder is the fact that the "assault weapon" registration system appears to allow for the registration of rifles less than 30 inches in length, despite the Penal Code clearly not allowing for the registration of that type of firearm (discussed later).

(25) "'Pistol' means any device designed to be used as a weapon, from which a projectile is expelled by the force of any explosion, or other form of combustion, and that has a barrel less than 16 inches in length. This definition includes AR-15 style pistols with pistol buffer tubes attached. Pistol buffer tubes typically have smooth metal with no guide on the bottom for rifle stocks to be attached, and they sometimes have a foam pad on the end of the tube farthest from the receiver."[62]

---

[57] CAL. CODE. REGS. tit. 11, § 5471(t).
[58] CAL. CODE. REGS. tit. 11, § 5471(u).
[59] CAL. CODE. REGS. tit. 11, § 5471(v).
[60] CAL. CODE. REGS. tit. 11, § 5471(w).
[61] CAL. CODE. REGS. tit. 11, § 5471(x).
[62] CAL. CODE. REGS. tit. 11, § 5471(y).

(26) "'Pistol grip that protrudes conspicuously beneath the action of the weapon' means a grip that allows for a pistol style grasp in which the web of the trigger hand (between the thumb and index finger) can be placed beneath or below the top of the exposed portion of the trigger while firing. This definition includes pistol grips on bullpup firearm designs."[63]

(27) "'Receiver' means the basic unit of a firearm which houses the firing and breech mechanisms and to which the barrel and stock are assembled."[64]

(28) "'Receiver, lower' means the lower part of a two part receiver."[65]

(29) "'Receiver, unfinished' means a precursor part to a firearm that is not yet legally a firearm. Unfinished receivers may be found in various levels of completion. As more finishing work is completed the precursor part gradually becomes a firearm. Some just have the shape of an AR-15 lower receiver for example, but are solid metal. Some have been worked on and the magazine well has been machined open. Firearms Manufactured by Unlicensed Subjects (FMBUS) began as unfinished receivers."[66]

(30) "'Receiver, upper' means the top portion of a two part receiver."[67]

(31) "'Rifle' means a weapon designed or redesigned, made or remade, and intended to be fired from the shoulder and designed or redesigned and made or remade to use the energy of the explosive in a fixed cartridge to fire only a single projectile through a rifled bore for each single pull of the trigger."[68]

(32) "'Rimfire' means a rimmed or flanged cartridge with the priming mixture located in the rim of the case."[69]

(33) "'Second handgrip' means a grip that allows the shooter to grip the pistol with their nontrigger hand. The second hand grip often has a grip texture to assist the shooter in weapon control."[70]

(34) "'Semiautomatic' means a firearm functionally able to fire a single cartridge, eject the empty case, and reload the chamber each time the trigger is pulled and released. Further, certain necessary mechanical parts that will allow a firearm to function in a semiautomatic nature must be present for a weapon to be deemed semiautomatic. A weapon clearly designed to be semiautomatic but lacking a firing pin, bolt carrier, gas tube, or some other crucial part of the firearm is not semiautomatic for purposes of Penal Code sections 30515, 30600, 30605(a), and 30900.

---

[63] CAL. CODE. REGS. tit. 11, § 5471(z).
[64] CAL. CODE. REGS. tit. 11, § 5471(aa).
[65] CAL. CODE. REGS. tit. 11, § 5471(bb).
[66] CAL. CODE. REGS. tit. 11, § 5471(cc).
[67] CAL. CODE. REGS. tit. 11, § 5471(dd).
[68] CAL. CODE. REGS. tit. 11, § 5471(ee).
[69] CAL. CODE. REGS. tit. 11, § 5471(ff).
[70] CAL. CODE. REGS. tit. 11, § 5471(gg).

(a) A mechanically whole semiautomatic firearm merely lacking ammunition and a proper magazine is a semiautomatic firearm.

(b) A mechanically whole semiautomatic firearm disabled by a gun lock or other firearm safety device is a semiautomatic firearm. (All necessary parts are present, once the gun lock or firearm safety device is removed, and weapon can be loaded with a magazine and proper ammunition.)

(c) With regards to an AR-15 style firearm, if a complete upper receiver and a complete lower receiver are completely detached from one another, but still in the possession or under the custody or control of the same person, the firearm is not a semiautomatic firearm.

(d) A stripped AR-15 lower receiver, when sold at a California gun store, is not a semiautomatic firearm. (The action type, among other things, is undetermined.)"[71]

As is apparent from the definition above, if the firearm is broken or missing a key component that would prevent it from functioning, the firearm cannot be considered semiautomatic and, therefore, it cannot be considered to be an "assault weapon." Only shotguns with revolving cylinders don't need to be semiautomatic in order to meet the definition of an "assault weapon." Therefore, before anyone can determine whether a firearm meets the definition of an "assault weapon," they must physically inspect the firearm or personally see the firearm function while it is in an illegal configuration. But, as discussed later, there may still be a problem if a person possesses the parts to make an illegal "assault weapon" and has the intent to put the firearm together in an illegal configuration.

(35) "'Shotgun with a revolving cylinder' means a shotgun that holds its ammunition in a cylinder that acts as a chamber much like a revolver. To meet this definition the shotgun's cylinder must mechanically revolve or rotate each time the weapon is fired. A cylinder that must be manually rotated by the shooter does not qualify as a revolving cylinder."[72]

While the regulations define "rifle," they overlook "shotgun." One would assume that "shotgun," used here and elsewhere, requires the firearm to have a smooth bore barrel.

(36) "'Shroud' means a heat shield that is attached to, or partially or completely encircles the barrel, allowing the shooter to fire the weapon with one hand and grasp the firearm over the barrel with the other hand without burning the shooter's hand. A slide that encloses the barrel is not a shroud."[73]

---

[71] Cal. Code. Regs. tit. 11, § 5471(hh).
[72] Cal. Code. Regs. tit. 11, § 5471(ii).
[73] Cal. Code. Regs. tit. 11, § 5471(jj).

(37) "'Spigot' means a muzzle device on some firearms that are intended to fire grenades. The spigot is what the grenade is attached to prior to the launching of a grenade."[74]

(38) "'Stock' means the part of a rifle, carbine, or shotgun to which the receiver is attached and which provides a means for holding the weapon to the shoulder. A stock may be fixed, folding, or telescoping."[75]

(39) "'Stock, fixed' means a stock that does not move, fold, or telescope."[76]

(40) "'Stock, folding' means a stock which is hinged in some fashion to the receiver to allow the stock to be folded next to the receiver to reduce the overall length of the firearm. This definition includes under folding and over folding stocks."[77]

(41) "'Stock, telescoping' means a stock which is shortened or lengthened by allowing one section to telescope into another portion. On AR-15 style firearms, the buffer tube or receiver extension acts as the fixed part of the stock on which the telescoping butt stock slides or telescopes."[78]

(42) "'Those weapons with an ammunition feeding device that can be readily removed from the firearm with the use of a tool' includes functional semiautomatic rifles, pistols, and shotguns with bullet-button style magazine releases. These weapons do not have a fixed magazine."[79]

(43) "'Thumbhole stock' means a stock with a hole that allows the thumb of the trigger hand to penetrate into or through the stock while firing."[80]

(44) "'Threaded barrel, capable of accepting a flash suppressor, forward handgrip, or silencer' means a threaded barrel able to accept a flash suppressor, forward handgrip, or silencer, and includes a threaded barrel with any one of those features already mounted on it. Some firearms have "lugs" in lieu of threads on the end of the barrel. These lugs are used to attach some versions of silencers. For purposes of this definition a lugged barrel is the same as a threaded barrel."[81]

D. Making Firearms That Would Otherwise Be Classified as "Assault Weapons" Compliant with California Law

There may be ways to configure a firearm so it will not be classified as an "assault weapon."

---

[74] CAL. CODE. REGS. tit. 11, § 5471(kk).
[75] CAL. CODE. REGS. tit. 11, § 5471(ll).
[76] CAL. CODE. REGS. tit. 11, § 5471(mm).
[77] CAL. CODE. REGS. tit. 11, § 5471(nn).
[78] CAL. CODE. REGS. tit. 11, § 5471(oo).
[79] CAL. CODE. REGS. tit. 11, § 5471(pp).
[80] CAL. CODE. REGS. tit. 11, § 5471(qq).
[81] CAL. CODE. REGS., tit. 11, § 5471(rr).

1. Aftermarket Parts

There are some aftermarket parts, such as the AR-15 MR2 Magazine Lock and the Bullet Button Reloaded, which, according to the regulations, appear to make it so that AR-15 firearms have a "fixed magazine." These products work by making it so that the magazine can only be removed by "disassembling the action" of the firearm by removing the rear takedown pin and swinging the upper receiver away from the lower receiver. Because the upper receiver must be swung away from the lower receiver to remove the magazine, these products should take a firearm out of the new definition of an "assault weapon" because the magazine would be fixed in the sense that it could not be removed without disassembling the firearm's action.

The foregoing devices should require "disassembly of the firearm action." Lastly, note that a rifle can still be an "assault weapon" if a magazine is used that holds more than 10 rounds or if the rifle is less than 30 inches (and, of course, if the rifle is on the make/model list, this "fix" does not work).

2. Compliant Features

Alternatively, you could take your firearm out of the definition of an "assault weapon" (both for the new and old Category 3 "assault weapons") by removing all the prohibited features from the firearm (making the firearm "featureless" as mentioned above). For AR and AK style rifles, this would typically mean removing the pistol grip, folding or telescoping stock, and any other prohibited features present on the firearm (often referred to as a "featureless build").

Or, some shooters add stocks or attachments that modify the shooter's grip. These attachments attach to Ruger Mini-14, AR-15 and AK-47 type receivers, replacing the pistol grip and/or stock, which takes them out of Category 3 "assault weapon" status – assuming they have no other prohibited characteristics. By installing these attachments, one must always be careful whether the attachment can be considered a "pistol grip that protrudes beneath the action of the weapon." In order to be a "pistol grip," the grip, according to California regulations, must: (1) allow a "pistol style grasp" (2) where "the web of the trigger hand (between the thumb and index finger) can be placed beneath or below the top of the exposed portion of the trigger while firing."[82] Make certain that any grip or stock marketed as "California compliant" does not meet both of these criteria.

Removing or altering the pistol grip only works for rifles with "off-list lowers" that are otherwise lawful in California. Adding these items to rifles that are considered Category 1 or 2 "assault weapons," however, does *not* make those rifles lawful. In addition, keep in mind that even if you remove restricted features or use after-

---

[82] Cal. Code. Regs. tit. 11, § 5471(z).

market features, the firearm may still meet one of the other definitions of "assault weapon" some other way.

E. Possessing the Parts of an "Assault Weapon"

If you merely possess parts that, if assembled, would make a "machinegun," you can be prosecuted for possessing a "machinegun."[83] The same is usually true if you possess parts that, if assembled, would only make a "short-barreled shotgun"[84] or "short-barreled rifle."[85] But, the same is not true for "assault weapons." Possessing unassembled parts that, if assembled, would make a firearm an "assault weapon" is *not* considered "possession" of an "assault weapon." This is because, as mentioned above in the regulations, a firearm that is disassembled is not considered to be "semiautomatic."[86] Because a firearm must be "semiautomatic" in almost all instances before it can meet the definition of an "assault weapon," a firearm in pieces (i.e., a disassembled firearm) should not be considered an "assault weapon."

The Penal Code defines "assault weapons" as "rifles," "pistols," or "shotguns" listed by make and model, or that have certain features, not mere *parts* of a firearm.[87] Nothing prohibits having mere "assault weapon" *parts*, even if those parts can be assembled into a complete "assault weapon." In other words, a firearm, as assembled, is either an "assault weapon" or it is not. Having parts around that might turn a firearm into one does not change the analysis. But continuing to possess an unregistered receiver for a firearm listed by make and model as a California "assault weapon" is still playing with fire given law enforcement's interpretation of the law.

In 2013, a case opened the door a crack for potential criminal liability for attempted possession or manufacturing of an "assault weapon" even if you merely possess the parts of an "assault weapon."[88] The Orange County District Attorney's Office presented this novel theory in *People v. Nguyen*.[89] Nguyen, who was prohibited from possessing firearms as a result of a prior felony conviction, purchased all of the parts and an 80% receiver[90] and he put work into completing the receiver.[91] When law enforcement came by his auto shop during an investigation, Nguyen discussed possessing the parts with the officers, how he obtained them, and his intent to make an "AK-47."[92] At the time of the investigation, some of these parts were incomplete and he did not possess a magazine lock, which, at the time, would have

---

[83] P.C. § 16880.
[84] P.C. § 17180.
[85] P.C. § 17170.
[86] Cal. Code. Regs. tit. 11, § 5471(hh).
[87] P.C. §§ 30510, 30515.
[88] *See People v. Nguyen*, 212 Cal. App. 4th 1311 (2013).
[89] *People v. Nguyen* 212 Cal. App. 4th 1311 (2013).
[90] Discussed in Chapter 4.
[91] *See People v. Nguyen*, 212 Cal. App. 4th 1311, 1315-16 (2013).
[92] *People v. Nguyen*, 212 Cal. App. 4th 1311, 1316 (2013).

made the firearm California compliant.[93] The District Attorney's office charged him with *attempted* manufacturing and *attempted* possession of an "assault weapon." He was convicted and appealed.[94]

The Court of Appeal affirmed the conviction, reasoning that Nguyen violated the laws for attempted manufacturing and possession because he admitted to having the intent to make an "AK-47," he admitted to gathering all of the parts, he had the ability to complete the firearm, and he apparently would have done so if law enforcement had not shown up.[95]

The moral to be learned from this case is, do not discuss any of your intentions with law enforcement because your statements can and will be used against you.

II. .50 BMG RIFLES

Outside of some limited exceptions, all .50 BMG rifles must have been registered with DOJ prior to April 30, 2006.[96] A .50 BMG[97] rifle is a centerfire rifle that is not already an "assault weapon" or a "machinegun"[98] and can fire a .50 BMG cartridge. It does not include "antique firearms" or "curios or relics."[99]

A .50 BMG cartridge is a cartridge for firing from a centerfire rifle that has the following criteria:

(1) An overall length of 5.54 inches from the base to the tip of the bullet;

(2) The bullet diameter for the cartridge is from .510 to, and including, .511 inch;

(3) The case base diameter for the cartridge is from .800 inch to, and including, .804 inch; *and,*

(4) The cartridge case length is 3.91 inches.[100]

To be clear, just because a firearm is chambered in .50 BMG does not necessarily mean it is a .50 BMG rifle; the firearm must be a "rifle." In order to be a "rifle," the firearm should be "intended to be fired from the shoulder . . . ."[101] For example, a firearm chambered in .50 BMG, without a stock, that is fired from a mount using

---

[93] *People v. Nguyen*, 212 Cal. App. 4th 1311, 1316 (2013).
[94] *People v. Nguyen*, 212 Cal. App. 4th 1311, 1317 (2013).
[95] *People v. Nguyen*, 212 Cal. App. 4th 1311, 1323 (2013).
[96] P.C. § 30905 (also stating that registration is only available to .50 BMG rifles that were lawfully possessed prior to January 1, 2005).
[97] "BMG" is the abbreviation for Browning Machine Gun. Keep in mind that under California law, a .50 BMG rifle is not a "machinegun." It is a rifle that can fire a .50 BMG cartridge.
[98] P.C. § 30530(a). *See also* P.C. § 16880(a) (defining a "machinegun" as "any weapon that shoots, is designed to shoot, or can readily be restored to . . . automatically [shoot] more than one shot, without manual reloading, by . . . [one] function of the trigger").
[99] P.C. § 30530(b). See Chapters 3 and 5 for "antique firearm" and "curio and relics" definitions.
[100] P.C. § 30525.
[101] P.C. § 17090 (defining "rifle" generally for purposes of defining "short-barreled rifle").

spade grips is not a .50 BMG rifle and thus need not be registered to be lawfully possessed in California. Since many law enforcement officers are unaware of this distinction, know that even a legal firearm chambered in .50 BMG may still cause law enforcement issues.

Example of a .50 BMG Rifle: A Barrett Model 95

III. "ASSAULT WEAPON" AND .50 BMG RIFLE USE RESTRICTIONS

With few exceptions, anyone in California who manufactures, distributes, transports, imports, sells, gives, or lends any "assault weapon" or .50 BMG rifle is guilty of a felony. And if you transfer, loan, sell, or give an "assault weapon" or .50 BMG rifle to a minor, an additional one-year penalty could be added to your sentence.[102]

Mere possession of a Category 1, Category 2, and Category 3 "assault weapon" or .50 BMG rifle that is not properly registered to you may also result in a felony or misdemeanor conviction for "assault weapons" and a misdemeanor for .50 BMG rifles.[103] Category 3 "assault weapons" that meet the definition of "assault weapon" from before January 1, 2017 are, and remain, illegal to possess.[104] And firearms that became "assault weapons" on January 1, 2017 as a result of the change in law are also illegal to possess in their present configuration if they were not registered by July 1, 2018 (discussed below).[105] And transporting one improperly can result in a separate felony charge (or a misdemeanor) *even if it is registered to you*.[106] You can be prosecuted for any of these violations even if you lawfully obtained the "assault weapon" or .50 BMG rifle before the law requiring their registration took effect if you did not properly register it.

For the first year after the window for registering "assault weapons" and .50 BMG rifles closes, the violation for possession can only be charged as an infraction

---

[102] P.C. § 30600(a)-(b).

[103] P.C. §§ 30605, 30610. Mere possession of an "assault weapon" is also considered a crime of "moral turpitude," *i.e.* the possession of such an "assault weapon" demonstrates a "general willingness to do evil." *People v. Gabriel*, 206 Cal. App. 4th 450, 458 (2012).

[104] *Cf* P.C. § 30515 (2016) with P.C. § 30515 (2017). A firearm "that has the capacity to accept a detachable magazine" is a firearm "that does not have a fixed magazine[.]" And the other pre-2017 definitions of "assault weapon" in P.C. section 30515 that do not use those terms are worded exactly the same in 2017.

[105] P.C. § 30680.

[106] P.C. §§ 30600(a), 30945.

in certain circumstances. For some reason, however, the same conduct that was an infraction several years ago is now a felony or misdemeanor with possible jail time and a possible lifetime ban on your right to possess a firearm. After the window closed for registering newly-defined "assault weapons" (on July 1, 2018), first time offenders of the new restrictions may also be charged as infractions in certain circumstances (see below). Also, the same conduct that would have resulted in an infraction for the first offense will be treated as a felony or a misdemeanor.

In 1991, former P.C. section 12289 was added to the Penal Code allowing for "assault weapon" registration education and notification programs.[107] Despite the legislature's mandate that DOJ create an education and notification program, California's confusing "assault weapon" laws have not become any clearer in the 25 years since the AWCA was passed. Law-abiding citizens with no criminal history are *still* being prosecuted today for possessing firearms they were unaware met the "assault weapon" definition even though they may have lawfully purchased them years ago.

Interestingly, when the California Legislature passed SB 880 and AB 1135, they failed to include any kind of notice provisions in these bills. As a result, there will likely be thousands of law-abiding citizens who will, once again, be unaware of the fact that their once legal to possess firearms are considered illegal "assault weapons" after January 1, 2017.

A. Civil Compromise for Illegally Possessing an "Assault Weapon" or .50 BMG Rifle

Prior to the enactment of AB 879 in 2019, California law allowed government attorneys to settle criminal cases involving charges of "assault weapons" and/or .50 BMG rifle possession with a civil compromise in lieu of a criminal conviction.[108] The adoption of AB 879 has expanded the authority of government attorneys so that they can also settle criminal cases involving charges of manufacture, importation, keeping for sale, offering or exposing for sale, giving, or lending any "assault weapon" and/or .50BMG rifle with a civil compromise in lieu of a criminal conviction (no longer just possession).[109]

This allows those individuals charged with violations of California's "assault weapon" and/or .50BMG rifle restrictions a way to resolve their case without the consequences of a criminal conviction. In such instances, the individual will almost certainly have to surrender the firearm to law enforcement permanently and pay a fine. The availability of this option, however, is subject to the sole discretion of the prosecuting agency.

---

[107] P.C. § 12289 (currently codified at P.C. § 31115).
[108] P.C. § 30800.
[109] P.C. §30800(b)(1)..

B. Infraction for First Violation of Possessing an "Assault Weapon"

As explained above, any person who possesses an unregistered "assault weapon" can generally be convicted of a misdemeanor or a felony. But, first time offenses are generally treated as infractions if the person was found in possession of no more than two firearms in compliance with P.C. section 30945[110] and all the person meets all the following conditions:

(1) The person proves that he or she lawfully possessed the "assault weapon" prior to the date it was defined as an "assault weapon";

(2) The person has not previously been convicted of a violation of P.C. sections 30600-30675 (an unlawful act relating to an "assault weapons" or .50 BMG rifle);

(3) The person was found to be in possession of the "assault weapon" within one year following the end of the one-year registration period established under P.C. section 30900 (discussed later); *and,*

(4) The person relinquished the firearm to law enforcement under P.C. section 31100 (transportation of "assault weapon" or .50 BMG rifle to police or sheriff's office for relinquishment).[111]

IV. EXCEPTIONS TO "ASSAULT WEAPON" AND .50 BMG RIFLE LAWS

A. Law Enforcement and Other Government Agencies

The general "assault weapon" and .50 BMG rifle possession restrictions do not apply to their sale, purchase, import, or possession "by the [DOJ], police departments, sheriffs' offices, marshals' offices, the Department of Corrections and Rehabilitation, the Department of the California Highway Patrol, district attorneys' offices, the Department of Fish and Wildlife, the Department of Parks and Recreation, or the military or naval forces of this state or of the United States, or any federal law enforcement agency for use in the discharge of their official duties."[112]

Sworn peace officers who are members of the agencies may also possess and use "assault weapons or . . . 50 BMG rifle[s] . . . for law enforcement purposes, *whether on or off duty.*"[113]

---

[110] Meaning a registered "assault weapon."
[111] P.C. § 30605.
[112] P.C. § 30625.
[113] P.C. § 30630(a) (emphasis added).

B. Peace Officers and Federal Law Enforcement Acquiring "Assault Weapons" and .50 BMG Rifles

Sworn peace officers may also acquire, register, and possess "assault weapons" or .50 BMG rifles if authorized in writing by the head of their agency.[114] They must also register their "assault weapon" with DOJ within 90 days of receiving it (or one year for .50 BMG rifles) and include a copy of the required authorization with their registration.[115] This is the only exception that allows *registering* a newly acquired "assault weapon" and/or .50 BMG rifle.

Unlike the "law enforcement purposes" exception for *agency*-owned "assault weapons," this exception does *not* limit an officer's "assault weapon" or .50 BMG rifle use. This means that an officer obtaining an "assault weapon" or .50 BMG rifle under this exception is not limited to only using it for "law enforcement purposes."[116]

Federal law enforcement members may also purchase, receive, and possess "assault weapons" or .50 BMG rifles if they are authorized by their employer to possess the firearm.[117]

And, due to a lawsuit I filed in August 2016, the Los Angeles Superior Court ruled in September 2017 that reserve peace officers are also entitled to the peace officer exemptions for the acquisition, possession, and use of "assault weapons," so long as they are authorized by their department.[118].

C. Carrying "Assault Weapons" Under the Law Enforcement Officer Safety Act (LEOSA)

As explained in Chapter 7, the exemption provided by the Law Enforcement Officer Safety Act (LEOSA) allows qualified law enforcement officers (QLEOs) and qualified retired law enforcement officers (QRLEOs) to possess and carry concealed any firearm that meets the definition of a "firearm" under 18 U.S.C. section 921(a)(2). 18 U.S.C. section 921(a)(3) defines the term "firearm" as:

(1) Any weapon (including a starter gun) which will or is designed to or may readily be converted to expel a projectile by the action;

(2) Any firearm muffler or firearm silencer; *or,*

---

[114] P.C. § 30630(b)(1).

[115] P.C. § 30630(b)(1)-(3).

[116] An AG opinion states that any peace officer who legally purchased and registered an "assault weapon" or .50 BMG rifle under this exception cannot continue to possess it after retiring. Opinion No. 09-901, 93 Ops. Cal. Atty. Gen. 130 (2010), *available at* http://oag.ca.gov/system/files/opinions/pdfs/09-901.pdf (last visited Oct. 9, 2020). This opinion is still disputed and not binding law but may be persuasive to courts interpreting the law.

[117] P.C. § 30630(c).

[118] *Llanos v. Harris*, Case BS163796 (L.A. Sup. Ct. Sept. 2017). The court also issued an injunction preventing DOJ from refusing to register an "assault weapon" acquired by any California sworn reserve peace officer who is eligible and authorized by the head of the officer's agency to possess and use this firearm for law enforcement purposes in compliance with Penal Code Section 30630(b).

(3) Any destructive device.[119]

The term "firearm" also includes ammunition not expressly prohibited by federal law (like armor piercing handgun ammunition) or subject to provisions of the National Firearms Act (NFA) (like destructive devices and machineguns).[120]

The term "firearm" under LEOSA, however, does not include any "machinegun" (as defined in 26 U.S.C. section 5848),[121] "silencer" (as defined under 18 U.S.C. 921),[122] or "destructive device" (as the term is defined under 18 U.S.C. 921).[123]

Interestingly, while a QLEO or QRLEO could not possess or carry a "machinegun," "silencer," or "destructive device" under LEOSA, they may be able to possess "assault weapons" even though state law prohibits them from doing so because "assault weapons" are considered to "firearms" for purposes of this exemption. Although this is a rather odd distinction because some states, such as California, generally ban these types of firearm, this language suggests that Congress intended to allow QLEOs and QRLEOs to carry firearms that may potentially be prohibited by state laws.

But, even though the law seems to allow QLEOs and QRLEOs to possess and carry "assault weapons," I strongly suggest not attempting to push this apparent loophole in the law until Congress or a court clarifies the exception.

D. Estate Executor and Inheritance

An executor or administrator of an estate cannot be prosecuted for possessing or transporting an "assault weapon" or .50 BMG rifle properly registered (or lawfully possessed by a sworn peace officer pursuant to P.C. section 30630(a)) if it is being lawfully disposed of as authorized by a probate court.[124]

If you inherit title to a properly registered "assault weapon," you must make it permanently inoperable, sell it to an FFL with an "assault weapon" permit, obtain a Dangerous Weapons Permit from DOJ, or remove it from California within 90 days (180 days for .50 BMG rifles) of receiving it.[125]

E. Loaning and Returning an "Assault Weapon" or .50 BMG Rifle

If you lawfully possess an "assault weapon" or .50 BMG rifle, you may lend it to someone else as long as the person you lend it to is at least age 18[126] and is not

---

[119] 18 U.S.C. § 921(a)(3). See also Chapter 3.
[120] 18 U.S.C. § 926B(e)(2).
[121] 18 U.S.C. §§ 926B(e)(3)(A), 926C(e)(1)(C)(i).
[122] 18 U.S.C. §§ 926B(e)(3)(B), 926C(e)(1)(C)(ii).
[123] 18 U.S.C. §§ 926B(e)(3)(C), 926C(e)(1)(C)(iii).
[124] P.C. § 30655.
[125] P.C. §§ 30915, 30935.
[126] Anyone under age 18 cannot even *touch* an "assault weapon." No exceptions. *See* P.C. § 30660.

otherwise prohibited from possessing, receiving, owning, or purchasing a firearm, *the registered owner remains in the presence of the "assault weapon" or .50 BMG rifle,* and the "assault weapon" or .50 BMG rifle is possessed at any of the places it is permissible to use an "assault weapon" listed in Section IX.[127]

Parents often run into problems at ranges when they allow their children to shoot their registered "assault weapon." Remember, the age restriction for the loan of an "assault weapon" is 18 years and older. I know of parents who have been thrown off ranges when they allow their son or daughter to shoot their "assault weapons." Thankfully I am aware of no arrests or criminal prosecutions for this innocuous practice.

Also, keep in mind that the list of places where possession is legal and the list of places where it is permissible to loan are not identical, so cross reference both to make sure what you want to do is expressly legal.[128]

F. Nonresident Possession at Match or Competition

Subject to the transportation requirements,[129] California non-residents over age 18 who are not otherwise prohibited from possessing firearms may possess and import "assault weapons" or .50 BMG rifles in California if they are "going directly to or coming directly from an organized competitive match or league competition that involves the use of an assault weapon or a .50 BMG rifle."[130] For this exception to apply, the competition or match must take place at a "target range that holds a regulatory or business license for the purpose of practice shooting at that target range" or a "target range of a public or private club or origination that is organized for the purpose of practice shooting at targets."[131] In addition, "[t]he match or competition ... [must be] sponsored by, conducted under the auspices of, or approved by, a law enforcement agency or a nationally or state recognized entity that fosters proficiency in, or promotes education about, firearms."[132] Because the law says you must be going directly to or from the approved locations, detours are risky.

G. California Department of Justice Permits

Today anyone other than certain peace officers can, *in theory*, acquire an "assault weapon" or .50 BMG rifle in California if they first obtain a Dangerous Weapons Permit.[133] The permit process involves filling out a six-page form with references,

---

[127] P.C. § 30660.
[128] *See* P.C. §§ 30660(3), 3030945.
[129] "Assault weapons" and .50 BMG rifles must be transported according to P.C. section 25610 or 25505.
[130] P.C. § 30665(a).
[131] P.C. § 30665(b).
[132] P.C. § 30665(c).
[133] P.C. §§ 31000, 32650; Cal. Code Regs. tit. 11, § 4128. For the Dangerous Weapons License/Permit Application, see *Dangerous Weapons License/Permit(s) Application*, Cal. Dept. of Justice, http://oag.ca.gov/sites/all/files/agweb/pdfs/firearms/forms/pdf/FD030DWApp.pdf (last visited Oct. 9, 2020).

fingerprints, and a statement of "good cause," and it is the same process used to acquire a "machinegun" license and a "destructive device" permit in California.[134]

For "good cause" you must give "clear and convincing evidence that there is a bona fide market or public necessity for the issuance of a dangerous weapons license or permit and that . . . [you will not] endanger[] public safety."[135] "Good cause" includes the following:

(1) Sales to and/or manufacture for sales to law enforcement, military and/or other Dangerous Weapon Permit holders;

(2) Training, research and development; and/or manufacturing pursuant to government contract;

(3) Use and/or manufacture of dangerous weapons as props in commercial motion picture, television production, or other commercial entertainment events;

(4) Possession for the purpose of maintaining a collection of destructive devices as defined in P.C. section 16460 but such possession shall not be allowed for short-barreled shotguns, short-barreled rifles, machineguns or "*assault weapons*";

(5) Repair and maintenance of dangerous weapons lawfully possessed by others; or

(6) Use of dangerous weapons in activities sanctioned by government military agencies by members of those agencies;

(7) The sale of assault weapons and/or the manufacture of assault weapons for the sale to, purchase by, or possession of assault weapons by: the agencies listed in P.C. section 30625 and the officers described in P.C. section 30630; entities and persons who have been issued assault weapon permits; entities outside the state who have, in effect, a federal firearms dealer's license solely for the purpose of distribution to an entity listed within this paragraph; federal law enforcement and military agencies; law enforcement and military agencies of other states; and foreign governments and agencies approved by the United States State Department; or,

(8) Use of dangerous weapons for the design, manufacture, demonstration, and sales of dangerous weapons accessories to law enforcement, military and/or other Dangerous Weapon Permit Holders.[136]

In the highly unlikely event that DOJ gives you a Dangerous Weapons Permit, you are required to *annually* renew it along with paying a renewal and inspection

---

[134] Out-of-state residents who have lawfully acquired an "assault weapon" or a .50 BMG rifle before moving to California cannot simply register their firearms; they must get a Dangerous Weapons Permit first. P.C. §§ 30925, 30940.

[135] CAL. CODE REGS. tit. 11, § 4128(c).

[136] CAL. CODE REGS. tit. 11, § 4128. *See also* P.C. § 31005 (giving DOJ authority to issue "assault weapons" permits upon a finding of "good cause").

fee of up to $1,500, keep an inventory of all "dangerous weapons," and store them in a safe place.[137] If you have less than five devices that require the permit, only one inspection every five years is required.[138]

H. "Licensed Gun Dealer" Exceptions

For purposes of "assault weapons" and .50 BMG rifles, "licensed gun dealers" are those who not only possess a standard license to sell firearms (as discussed in Chapter 5),[139] but who *also* possess Dangerous Weapons Permit for "assault weapons" and/or .50 BMG rifles.[140]

1. Service or Repair

"Licensed gun dealers" can take possession of "assault weapons" or .50 BMG rifles to service or repair them from a lawfully registered owner or Dangerous Weapons Permit holder. The "licensed gun dealer" may also give possession of them to a gunsmith to help with the service or repair as long as the gunsmith is employed by, or has a contract with, the dealer for gunsmithing[141] services.[142]

Despite being able to take possession of an "assault weapon" for service or repair, DOJ has taken the position that these FFLs cannot convert an "assault weapon" into a California compliant firearm for the purposes of sales.[143] This kind of action may be considered "manufacturing," which is not usually covered by a Dangerous Weapons Permit.

2. Other Special Allowances

These "licensed gun dealers" may also transport an "assault weapon" or .50 BMG rifle between dealers or to out-of-state dealers per the NFA,[144] display firearms at licensed state or local government gun shows, sell them to out-of-state residents, or sell them to someone with a Dangerous Weapons Permit.[145]

---

[137] CAL. CODE REGS. tit. 11, §§ 4129, 4130, 4145.

[138] CAL. CODE REGS. tit. 11, § 4145(b).

[139] Having the "standard license to sell firearms" means that you are a California-licensed firearms dealer (i.e., someone licensed per P.C. sections 26700 to 26915, inclusive).

[140] P.C. § 16790.

[141] For this exception the gunsmith must have an FFL of his or her own and a business license required by a state or local governmental agency. P.C. § 31050(c).

[142] P.C. § 31050.

[143] *Important Notice Re: Dangerous Weapons*, CALIFORNIA DEPARTMENT OF JUSTICE, BUREAU OF FIREARMS (on file with authors of this book).

[144] NFA firearms are discussed in Chapter 3. Almost all "assault weapons" and .50 BMG rifles are not "firearms" under the NFA, showing that the legislature did not know what it was doing when writing these laws. Also, remember that transporting "assault weapons" has specific requirements discussed in Section IX(A) of this chapter and in Chapter 7.

[145] P.C. § 31055.

V. ACQUIRING NEW "ASSAULT WEAPONS" OR .50 BMG RIFLES

A. Registration (with the exception of newly classified "other" firearms)

As mentioned above, registration periods for 50 BMG rifles, Category 1 and Category 2 "assault weapons," and firearms meeting the old definition of Category 3 "assault weapons" have long passed.[146] With the exception of peace officers, DOJ no longer accepts registration applications for these firearms.

In the past, a lot of folks believe that their firearms were registered as "assault weapons" when they originally purchased their firearm from the dealer. But in order to have properly registered a firearm as an "assault weapon" or .50 BMG rifle, you must have submitted an application to DOJ that required you to provide the firearms description and all unique identification marks, your full name and address, date of birth, thumbprint, and other pieces of information, and you were required to pay the requisite fee to process the application ($20 for an "assault weapon," and $25 for a .50 BMG rifle).[147]

If you properly sent in your registration for an "assault weapon" or .50 BMG rifle within the specified time period and all of the information was accurately provided, the registration should have been entered into DOJ's Automated Firearm System (AFS) database, and you should have received a confirmation notice.[148] If you have a firearm that should have been registered as an "assault weapon" but was not, there will be no record in the AFS for the firearm as an "assault weapon." In other words, if your "assault weapon" is not registered to you as an "assault weapon" in the AFS, you may be possessing it illegally.

There have been reports of DOJ inadvertently omitting "assault weapon" registrations for an "assault weapons" from the AFS, and in the past, an ex-DOJ official testified to the unreliability of the AFS system for keeping accurate firearm disposition records (not just "assault weapon" records). It is therefore wise to keep the confirmation notice of your "assault weapon" registration in a safe place, along with copies saved in paper and electronic format. Some "assault weapon" owners keep a copy of their registration in the hollow space of their "assault weapons" pistol grip or buttstock in case law enforcement asks them about it. That's smart.

---

[146] All of the deadlines for registering Category 1, Category 2, and Category 3 "assault weapons" have passed. April 30, 2006, was the most recent deadline applying to the registration of .50 BMG rifles. P.C. § 30905.

[147] P.C. §§ 30900(c-d) ("assault weapons"), 30905(b)-(c) (.50 BMG rifles).

[148] In such situations, it may be possible to update or correct your AFS records. See Chapter 5, Section XIII.A.5.

Table 9.1

QUICK REVIEW OF REGISTRATION DEADLINES FOR ASSAULT WEAPONS AND .50 BMG RIFLES[147]		
FIREARM	**DESCRIPTION OF FIREARM**	**REGISTRATION DATE**[161]
Category 1 "Assault Weapons"	Firearms listed in the 1989 Assault Weapons Control Act and those added later to the Penal Code are considered Category 1 assault weapons. These firearms are specifically named in P.C. § 30510.	Category 1 "assault weapons" must have been registered with DOJ before March 31, 1992.
Category 2 "Assault Weapons"	AR-15 and AK "series" firearms that were added through the "add on procedure" are considered Category 2 "assault weapons." These firearms are listed in Cal. Code Regs. tit. 11, § 5499.	Category 2 "assault weapons" must have been registered with DOJ before January 23, 2001.
Pre-2017 Category 3 "Assault Weapons"	Firearms with certain features that are listed in P.C. § 30515 are considered Category 3 "assault weapons."	Category 3 "assault weapons" must have been registered with DOJ before December 31, 2000.
.50 BMG Rifles	A .50 BMG rifle is a centerfire rifle that is not already an "assault weapon" or a "machinegun" and can fire a .50 BMG cartridge. See Section IV for a complete discussion of what kind of rifle is considered a .50 BMG rifle.	Must have been registered before April 30, 2006.[148]
Category 3 "Assault Weapons"	Semiautomatic, centerfire rifles and semiautomatic handguns that do not have a "fixed magazine," and contain one (or more) of the features listed in P.C. § 30515 are now considered Category 3 "assault weapons."	Firearms newly-classified as Category 3 "assault weapons" after January 1, 2017 must have been registered with DOJ before July 1, 2018. Semiautomatic shotguns with "bullet buttons" attached must also have been registered before July 1, 2018.

---

[149] All of the tables within this book are paraphrases of the law and are not a complete summary of each subject area. Please review the corresponding sections within this chapter for a more in-depth discussion of each topic and for the applicable statutes and/or case law that is paraphrased within the tables.

[150] The registration dates for all three categories of "assault weapons" can be found in the AWIG. *See* CAL. DEPT. OF JUSTICE, OFFICE OF THE ATTORNEY GENERAL, ASSAULT WEAPONS IDENTIFICATION GUIDE, (3rd ed. Nov. 2001), *available at* http://oag.ca.gov/sites/all/files/agweb/pdfs/firearms/forms/awguide.pdf (last visited Oct. 9, 2020).

Category 3 "Assault Weapons" Added After January 1, 2021	A semiautomatic centerfire firearm that is not a rifle, pistol, or shotgun, and contains one (or more) of the features listed in P.C. § 30515(a)(9), (a)(10), or (a)(11) will be considered Category 3 "assault weapons" starting on January 1, 2021.	Firearms newly-classified as Category 3 "assault weapons" after January 1, 2021 must be registered with DOJ prior to January 1, 2022 (but the person must have possessed the gun and been eligible to register it before September 1, 2020).

1. Post-Registration Modification of "Bullet Buttons" of Registered Assault Weapons Is Prohibited

DOJ has declared that you are prohibited from changing the release mechanism for the ammunition feeding device on any "assault weapon" registered under the new regulations.[151] But this restriction does not apply to: (1) the repair or like-kind replacement of the mechanism, or (2) firearm undergoing the deregistration process.[152]

According to DOJ, this is because "[a]ny alteration to the release mechanism converts the assault weapon into a different weapon from the one that was registered."[153] So, you cannot modify or remove the "bullet button" on your firearm.

Yet, DOJ doesn't specify that other modifications are prohibited. Hence, you should be able to change other parts of the firearms (e.g., stocks, muzzle attachments, forward grips, etc.), so long as you don't make anything that would otherwise be illegal in and of itself, i.e., a short-barreled rifle or shotgun, machinegun, destructive device, or "any other weapon."

2. Voluntary Deregistration

You can voluntarily deregister your firearm as an "assault weapon" if:

(1) You no longer possess the "assault weapon;" *or*,

(2) The firearm has been modified or reconfigured to no longer meet the definition of an "assault weapon."[154]

If the firearm is deregistered, DOJ will delete the "assault weapon" registration for the specified firearm(s).[155] Once deregistered, the firearm cannot be possessed in the state in its "assault weapon" configuration, unless another exception to the "assault weapon" restrictions applies.

---

[151] Cal. Code Regs. tit. 11, § 5477(a).
[152] Cal. Code Regs. tit. 11, § 5477(b), (c).
[153] Cal. Code Regs. tit. 11, § 5477(a).
[154] Cal. Code Regs. tit. 11, § 5478.
[155] Cal. Code Regs. tit. 11, § 5478(b).

B. Alternatives to Registration

Those who own newly-designated Category 3 "assault weapons" and who do not want to register them—or failed to register them—may have some other options to avoid the registration requirements of the law. These include:

(1) Removing the firearm from California;

(2) Lawfully selling or transferring the firearm;

(3) Surrendering the firearm to law enforcement;

(4) Rendering the firearm permanently inoperable; *and,*

(5) Properly configuring the firearm so that it is no longer classified as an "assault weapon."

VI. MOVING INTO CALIFORNIA WITH AN "ASSAULT WEAPON" OR .50 BMG RIFLE

If you plan on moving to California and bringing an "assault weapon" or .50 BMG rifle, you must get a Dangerous Weapons Permit from DOJ *before* you can bring your firearm into California. Alternatively, you can have the firearm sent to an FFL who has a Dangerous Weapons Permit in California, and once you get a Dangerous Weapons Permit, *then* the FFL will redeliver the firearm to you.[156] If the FFL is prohibited from delivering the firearm to you, either because you did not obtain the required permit or because you are prohibited from owning firearms in general (see Chapter 4), the FFL will keep possession or lawfully dispose of it according to California law.[157] There is little chance DOJ will issue this permit to you.

You always have the option to render your "assault weapon" California compliant before bringing it into the state. This means modifying your non-make/model prohibited "assault weapon" into a configuration that does not meet the definition of an "assault weapon" (discussed throughout this chapter). You will still have to meet the requirements of a "personal firearm importer" (discussed in Chapter 5) if you are moving to the state with the firearm.

VII. LAWFULLY USING "ASSAULT WEAPONS" AND .50 BMG RIFLES

Unless DOJ issues you a permit for additional uses, you may only possess an "assault weapon" or .50 BMG rifle *registered to you*:

(1) At your residence, place of business, or other property you own or on the property of another with their express permission;

---

[156] P.C. §§ 30925, 30940.
[157] *See* P.C. §§ 30925 ("assault weapons"), 30940 (.50 BMG rifles).

(2) While on the premises of a target range of a public or private club or organization organized for the purpose of practicing shooting at targets;

(3) While on a target range that holds a regulatory or business license for the purpose of practicing shooting at that target range;

(4) While on the premises of a shooting club licensed pursuant to the California Fish and Game Code;

(5) While attending any exhibition, display, or educational project that is about firearms and that is sponsored by, conducted under the auspices of, or approved by a law enforcement agency or a nationally or state recognized entity that fosters proficiency in, or promotes education about, firearms;

(6) While on publicly owned land, if the possession and use of an "assault weapon" is specifically permitted by the managing agency of the land; *or,*

(7) While transporting the assault weapon or .50 BMG rifle between any of the places mentioned here, or to any FFL (who also has a dangerous weapons permit) for service or repair.[158]

If you want to use an "assault weapon" or .50 BMG rifle for something other than the things above, you have to get a Dangerous Weapons Permit from DOJ first.[159]

A. Transporting Registered "Assault Weapons" and .50 BMG Rifles

Firearms meeting the definition of an "assault weapon" must be transported like handguns, even if they are non-handguns, meaning that they must be transported unloaded and in a "locked container."[160] Only the registered owner of the "assault weapon" may lawfully transport it and only between the places and activities where you can lawfully use your "assault weapons," which are listed above.

VIII. WHAT TO DO IF YOU THINK YOU HAVE AN "ASSAULT WEAPON" OR .50 BMG RIFLE THAT YOU AREN'T SURE IS LEGAL

A. Determine if It *Is* an "Assault Weapon" or .50 BMG Rifle

Using the above information, determine if your firearm meets the definition of an "assault weapon" or .50 BMG rifle. As discussed above, some of the laws prohibiting "assault weapons" were passed with little fanfare. No doubt thousands of Califor-

---

[158] P.C. § 30945.
[159] P.C. § 31000(a).
[160] P.C. § 30945(g).

nia residents are unknowingly "in possession" of unregistered "assault weapons." If you have any doubts about your firearm, ask an attorney familiar with California firearms law.

B. Determine If Your "Assault Weapon" or .50 BMG Rifle Was Registered

If you do not know or *think* that you registered your "assault weapon" or .50 BMG rifle, you may request a list of all firearms of which you are the registered owner by submitting an Automated Firearms System Record Request to DOJ. This form can be found at http://ag.ca.gov/firearms/forms/pdf/AFSPrivateCitizen.pdf.

If you know or believe you registered your "assault weapon" or .50 BMG rifle but no registration record appears in DOJ's system, you should contact an attorney experienced in firearms law immediately for possible options.

Often people are confused and believe that filling out the Form 4473 and DROS form (discussed in Chapter 5) registers their firearm as an "assault weapon." They are incorrect. A separate form needs to be filled out and sent to DOJ registering their firearm as an "assault weapon." If you did not do this or don't remember doing this, there is a strong chance your firearm is not registered as an "assault weapon."

C. If Your "Assault Weapon" or .50 BMG Rifle Is Unregistered

If you possess an unregistered "assault weapon" or .50 BMG rifle and do not meet any of the above exceptions, that is illegal under California law. Unfortunately, there is no way for you to register an "assault weapon" or .50 BMG rifle now (with the exception of newly designated "other" firearms). If you possess an unregistered "assault weapon" or .50 BMG rifle that cannot be registered, you should contact an attorney with experience in California firearms law immediately to determine what to do with it.

IX. "ASSAULT WEAPONS" LISTED BY NAME[161]

A. Combined Listing of Category 1 and Category 2 "Assault Weapons"

Table 9.2 on the following page lists Category 1 and Category 2 "Assault Weapons." Italicized models are Category 1 "assault weapons" and were required to be registered on or before March 31, 1992. Non-italicized models are Category 2 "assault weapons" and were required to be registered with the Department of Justice on or before January 23, 2001. Category 3 "assault weapons" are not included in this table.

---

[161] This list is from the AWIG. *See* CALIFORNIA ATTORNEY GENERAL, CALIFORNIA ASSAULT WEAPONS IDENTIFICATION GUIDE 82-84 (3d ed., 2001), *available at* http://oag.ca.gov/sites/all/files/agweb/pdfs/firearms/forms/pdf/awguide.pdf (last visited Oct. 9, 2020).

Table 9.2

RIFLES		
American Arms	**American Spirit**	**Armalite**
AK-C 47	ASA Model	AR 10 (all)
AK-F 39		*AR-180*
AK-F 47		Golden Eagle
AK-Y 39		M15 (all)
Arsenal	**Beretta**	**Bushmaster**
SLG (all)	*AR-70*	*Assault Rifle*
SLR (all)		XM15 (all)
B-West	**Calico**	**Colt**
AK-47 (all)	M-900	*AR-15 (all)*
		Law Enforcement (6920)
		Match Target (all)
		Sporter (all)
Daewoo	**Dalphon**	**DPMS**
AR100, AR110C	B.F.D.	Panther (all)
K-1, K-2		
Max 1, Max 2		
Eagle Arms	**Fabrique Nationale**	**Frankford Arsenal**
EA-15 A2 H-BAR	*308 Match, Sporter*	AR-15 (all)
EA-15 E1	*FAL, LAR, FNC*	
M15 (all)		
Hesse Arms	**HK**	**IMI**
HAR 15A2 (all)	*91, 94, PSG-1*	*Galil*
Model 47 (all)	93	*Uzi*
Wieger STG 940 Rifle		
Inter Ordnance - Monroe, NC	**J&R ENG**	**Kalashnikov USA**
AK-47 (all)	M-68	Hunter Rifle / Saiga
M-97		
RPK		

Rifles

Knights	Les Baer	MAADI CO
RAS (all)	Ultimate AR (all)	*AK 47*
SR-15 (all)		*ARM*
SR-25 (all)		*MISR (all)*
		MISTR (all)

Made in China	Made in Spain	MAS
56	*CETME Sporter*	*223*
56S		
84S		
86S		
AK		
AK47		
AKM		
AKS		

Mitchell Arms, Inc.	Norinco	Ohio Ordnance Works (O.O.W.)
AK-47 (all)	56	AK-74
AK-47 Cal .308 (all)	56 S	ROMAK 991
M-76	81 S (all)	
M-90	84 S	
RPK	86 (all)	
	86 S	
	AK-47 (all)	
	Hunter Rifle	
	MAK 90	
	NHM 90, 90-2, 91 Sport	
	RPK Rifle	
	SKS w/ detachable magazine	

Olympic Arms	Ordnance, Inc.	Palmetto
AR-15	AR-15	SGA (all)
Car-97		
PCR (all)		

Poly Technologies	Professional Ordnance, Inc.	PWA
AK47	Carbon 15 Rifle	All Models
AKS		

RIFLES		
Rock River Arms, Inc. Car A2 Car A4 Flattop LE Tactical Carbine NM A2 - DCM Legal Standard A-2 Standard A-4 Flattop	**RPB Industries, Inc.** *sM10, sM11*	**SIG** *AMT, PE-57* *SG 550, SG 551*
Springfield Armory *BM59, SAR-48*	**Sterling** *MK-6*	**Steyr** *AUG*
SWD Incorporated *M11*	**Valmet** *76 S* Hunter Rifle *M62S, M71S, M78S*	**Weaver Arms** *Nighthawk*
Wilson Combat AR-15	**WUM** WUM (all)	

PISTOLS		
Advance Armament Inc. *M11*	**Bushmaster** *Pistol*	**Calico** *M-950*
Encom *MP-9* *MP-45*	**IMI** *UZI*	**Intratec** *TEC-9*
MARS Pistol	**Military Armament Corp.** *M-11*	**RPB Industries Inc.** *sM10, sM11*
Sites *Spectre*	**Sterling** *MK-7*	**SWD Incorporated** *M11*

Shotguns		
Cobray	**Franchi**	
Streetsweeper	*SPAS 12*	
S/S Inc.	*LAW 12*	
SS/12		
Striker 12		

CHAPTER 10:
OTHER HEAVILY REGULATED FIREARMS AND DEVICES

As discussed throughout this book, California and federal laws often differ and overlap. To comply with laws about heavily regulated firearms and devices, you must comply with both state and federal requirements.

Unlike California law, federal law does not have many restrictions on what types of firearms a person may possess. But there is one notable exception: the National Firearms Act (NFA). Items meeting the NFA's unusual definition of "firearm"[1] have a separate set of federal requirements you must meet before you can lawfully possess them. These requirements are discussed briefly at the end of this chapter.

If you want to possess any of the items described below, believe you already possess them, and/or have questions on whether your possession of them is legal, you should contact an attorney experienced in firearms law immediately.

I. "MACHINEGUNS"

Under both California and federal law, a "machinegun" is "any weapon which shoots, is designed to shoot, or can be [easily] restored to . . . automatically [shoot,] more than one shot, without manual reloading, by a single function of the trigger."[2] A "machinegun" "also include[s] the frame or receiver[,] . . . any part designed solely and exclusively, or combination of parts designed and intended, for use in converting a weapon into a machinegun, . . . [any weapon the Bureau of Alcohol, Tobacco, Firearms, and Explosives (ATF) consid-

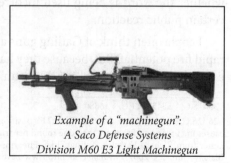

Example of a "machinegun": A Saco Defense Systems Division M60 E3 Light Machinegun

---

[1] See Chapter 3 for "firearm" definitions.
[2] 26 U.S.C. § 5845(b); P.C. § 16880.

ers easily convertible to a 'machinegun,'[3] or] any combination of parts from which a machinegun can be assembled if" they were under the same person's possession or control.[4]

These parts vary in size and description. For some firearms you only need a specially shaped metal piece that will allow a firearm to fire fully automatic (a.k.a. an auto or conversion sear). So this one single part could be considered a "machinegun." For other firearms, small mechanisms that attach to the firearm or replace internal parts are all you need. These metal parts and pieces can be considered "machineguns" by themselves even if you do not possess the actual firearm they are designed to be used with.

An auto sear, a part of a "machinegun," is specifically addressed under the law. The ATF has interpreted the NFA to include auto sears in the definition of a "machinegun."[5] Therefore, you may not possess an auto sear unless it is properly registered under the NFA.[6]

Another way a firearm may be considered a "machinegun" is if its parts wear out over time, causing the firearm to fire two shots per trigger pull. Although this is incorrect because a firearm with worn parts isn't *designed* to shoot fully automatic, under these circumstances, law enforcement might believe you have created or modified your firearm into a "machinegun." If this happens to you, take your firearm apart and to a gunsmith as soon as possible.

The term "automatic" firearm is used and abused a lot. An "automatic" firearm is simply one that "automatically" loads another round into the chamber after a round is discharged. The term can include "semiautomatic," meaning one shot per trigger pull, and "fully automatic," meaning rounds will continue to fire as long as the trigger is pressed down or until the firearm runs out of ammunition. The media often uses the phrases "automatic weapon" or "automatic firearms." Because the term "automatic" can include many firearm types – ranging from semiautomatic pistols to tank-mounted "machineguns" – pay attention to how the word is used. The next time you come across an "automatic" firearm in a news story, consider whether the word is being used incorrectly, or whether it is being used to elicit a certain public reaction.

People often think of Gatling guns as "machineguns" because of their relatively rapid fire potential. But, because they have no trigger and instead are crank-operated, they cannot meet the "machinegun" definition. Their ammunition feeding de-

---

[3] 26 U.S.C. § 5845(b); P.C. § 16880.

[4] 26 U.S.C. § 5845(b); P.C. § 16880. The ATF's position is that a shoestring attached to a semiautomatic rifle that causes the firearm to fire more than one round per trigger pull is, when attached to the firearm, a "machinegun." Letter from Richard Vasquez, Acting Chief, Firearms Technology Branch, U.S. Department of Justice, to Brian Blakely (Jun. 25, 2007), *available at* http://www.everydaynodaysoff.com/2010/01/25/shoestring-machine-gun/ (last visited Oct. 9, 2020). This position is a modification of a previous ATF opinion which stated a shoestring, by itself, could be a "machinegun."

[5] ATF Rul. 81-4 (1981), *available at* http://www.atf.gov/file/55331/download (last visited Oct. 9, 2020); 27 C.F.R. § 479.11.

[6] *United States v. Dodson*, 519 Fed. App'x. 344 (6th Cir. 2013).

vices, however, likely constitute "large-capacity magazines" and are thus regulated as such, as discussed below.

A. Prohibitions

Under federal law, it can be legal to acquire a "machinegun" that was lawfully possessed before May 19, 1986, as long as you comply with the strict requirements for transferring and possessing NFA firearms discussed in Section XII of this chapter. But even if you meet the federal NFA requirements to lawfully possess a "machinegun," you must also meet one of the exceptions to California's general ban on possessing them (explained below).[7]

It is generally illegal for anyone to knowingly possess, transport, manufacture, sell, or convert an existing firearm into a "machinegun" under both California and federal law.[8] Severe penalties exist for violating this prohibition, including potentially years in prison following a California felony conviction,[9] and up to 10 years and/or a fine of no more than $10,000 for violating federal law.[10]

Given the stiff penalties for violating California and federal "machinegun" laws, you should be sure to take certain precautions if you inadvertently come into possession of one of these firearms. For example, you may discover that granddad's WWII souvenir from Italy is actually a "machinegun." Alternatively, a deceased family member could leave you such a firearm in their will. If you come into possession of an unregistered NFA firearm, the ATF suggests that you contact your nearest ATF office.[11] But, given the sensitivity of this issue and the potential criminal liability for possessing such an item, you should first consult an attorney experienced in firearms law to understand your full range of options.

B. California Exceptions to "Machinegun" Restrictions

California law provides for a few narrow exceptions to the restrictions on possessing "machineguns." These exceptions, discussed below, are limited to certain law enforcement agencies and military forces, and those possessing certain permits.

---

[7] 26 U.S.C. § 5812(a). "Applications [for NFA firearms] shall be denied if the transfer, receipt, or possession of the firearm would place the transferee in violation of law." 26 U.S.C. § 5812(a).

[8] P.C. § 32625; 18 U.S.C. § 922(o); 26 U.S.C. § 5861, *declared unconstitutional as applied to law enforcement officers by U.S. v. Vest*, 448 F. Supp. 3d 1002 (S.D. Ill. 2006).

[9] P.C. § 32625.

[10] 26 U.S.C. § 5871.

[11] *Firearms- Frequently Asked Questions- National Firearms Act (NFA)*, U.S. DEPT. OF JUSTICE, BUREAU OF ALCOHOL, TOBACCO, FIREARMS AND EXPLOSIVES, http://www.atf.gov/qa-category/national-firearms-act-nfa#unregistered-possession (last visited Oct. 9, 2020).

1. Law Enforcement and Military

Certain law enforcement agencies and military forces may receive and possess "machineguns," including ones made after 1986.[12] Though such agencies and military forces are exempt from the NFA tax[13] (discussed below), they still must register the "machineguns."[14]

2. Permits to Possess, Manufacture, and Transport

Upon satisfactorily showing that "good cause" exists, the California Department of Justice (DOJ) may issue you a permit to possess, manufacture, or transport "machineguns."[15] These permits must be renewed annually.[16] Unless you are involved with law enforcement, the military, a business that supports, advises, trains, or supervises these organizations, or the entertainment industry, it is unlikely you will be able to establish the "good cause" required to obtain this permit.[17]

If you are able to obtain the permit, it must be kept on you or with the "machinegun" and must be made available for law enforcement inspection.[18] DOJ will also annually inspect the license holder for proper security and safe storage of any "machinegun," and to confirm the "machinegun" inventory.[19]

DOJ may revoke the permit at any time if it determines that your need for the "machinegun" has ceased, the "machinegun" was used for an unauthorized purpose, or you failed to exercise great care in retaining custody of any firearm possessed under the permit.[20]

Federal law does not require a separate permit to lawfully *possess* "machineguns."[21] But it does require that you get California's "machinegun" permit, or otherwise be exempt from the "machinegun" restriction. Without a permit or exemption, the ATF will deny the transfer. And since it is almost impossible for common people to obtain such a permit from DOJ (and most people do not fall

---

[12] The federal exception to the ban on "machineguns" made after 1986 includes "a transfer to or by, or possession by or under the authority of, the United States or any department or agency thereof or a State, or a department, agency, or political subdivision thereof." 18 U.S.C. § 922(o)(2)(A). Under California law, these entities' personnel may possess "machineguns" too, but only while acting within the scope of their duties. P.C. § 32610(a).

[13] 26 U.S.C. §§ 5852, 5853; 27 C.F.R. §§ 479.89-479.90.

[14] Unless the firearms are possessed or under the control of the U.S., the "machineguns" must be registered in the National Firearms Registration and Transfer Record. 26 U.S.C. § 5841. Federal law also allows certain government entities to acquire and register NFA firearms (including "machineguns") for official use when the firearm has been abandoned or forfeited. 27 C.F.R. § 479.104.

[15] P.C. § 32650.

[16] P.C. § 32655(d).

[17] *See* CAL. CODE REGS. tit. 11, § 4128(c)(1)-(7). See Chapter 9 for examples.

[18] P.C. § 32660.

[19] P.C. § 32670. If a permittee has fewer than five "machineguns," however, the inspection is only once every five years, unless DOJ determines additional inspections are necessary. P.C. § 32670(b).

[20] P.C. § 32665.

[21] Remember, federal law still requires registration and importer, dealer, and manufacturing licenses.

under an exemption), the fact that you can theoretically own a "machinegun" in California under federal law is practically irrelevant.

C. Licenses to Sell "Machineguns"

The ATF may grant licenses to engage in the business of selling "machineguns."[22] But, for the license to be valid in California, you must get a separate license from DOJ, renew it annually, and comply with numerous regulations.[23]

D. "Bump Stocks" in the Context of Machinegun Restrictions

Also known as "bump-fire stocks," bump stocks were catapulted into the spotlight recently due to their apparent usage by the gunman in the 2017 Las Vegas mass shooting. Bump stocks allow people to "bump fire" semiautomatic firearms. Simply put, "bump fire" is the act of using a semiautomatic firearm's recoil in part to discharge the firearm. Further analyses and descriptions of bump stocks are located under Section III(F) of this chapter, which discusses multiburst trigger activators.

1. Bump Stocks Under Federal Law

On December 18, 2018, the federal government amended Bureau of Alcohol, Tobacco, Firearms, and Explosive ("ATF") regulations clarifying that bump stocks fall within the definition of a "machinegun" under federal law, making such devices generally illegal to possess.[24] Individuals were required under the rule to divest themselves of any such items by March 26, 2019.[25] A lawsuit has been filed challenging the regulations as a violation of federal rulemaking requirements, and is currently pending before the Tenth Circuit.[26]

2. Bump Stocks Under California Law

Following the enactment of SB 1346 in 2018, bump stocks have been labeled "multiburst trigger activators" within the meaning of California law, and are therefore generally illegal to possess in the state regardless of current federal restrictions.[27] California defines a bump stock as "a device that uses a spring, piston, or similar mechanism to push back against the recoil of a firearm, thereby moving the firearm

---

[22] 18 U.S.C. § 923(a); 26 U.S.C. § 5802; 27 C.F.R. § 478.44.
[23] See P.C. §§ 32700-32720.
[24] See https://www.atf.gov/rules-and-regulations/bump-stocks.
[25] See https://www.atf.gov/rules-and-regulations/bump-stocks.
[26] *Aposhian v. Barr*, Case No. 19-4036 (10th Cir. 2019). On September 4, 2020, the Tenth Circuit issued an order for the case to be reheard by a larger "en banc" panel, vacating the Court's prior May 7, 2020 judgment. Briefing at the en banc stage is now underway.
[27] P.C. § 16930(b)(1); *see also* P.C. § 32900 (prohibiting manufacture, importation, sale, giving, lending, or possessing any "multiburst trigger activator" in California).

in a back-and-forth motion and facilitating the rapid reset and activation of the trigger by a stationary finger."[28]

II. "DESTRUCTIVE DEVICES"

"Destructive device" definitions vary between California and federal law. Under federal law a "destructive device" is any of the following weapons:

(1) Any explosive, incendiary, or poison gas:

   (a) bomb,

   (b) grenade,

   (c) rocket having a propellant charge of more than four ounces,

   (d) missile having an explosive or incendiary charge of more than one-quarter ounce,

   (e) mine,

   (f) similar device; or,

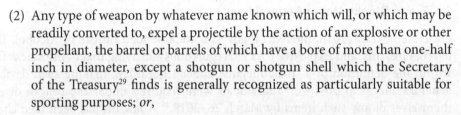

A grenade is considered a "destructive device" under both California and federal law

(2) Any type of weapon by whatever name known which will, or which may be readily converted to, expel a projectile by the action of an explosive or other propellant, the barrel or barrels of which have a bore of more than one-half inch in diameter, except a shotgun or shotgun shell which the Secretary of the Treasury[29] finds is generally recognized as particularly suitable for sporting purposes; or,

(3) Any combination of parts either designed or intended for use in converting any device into a destructive device as defined in subparagraphs (1) and (2) and from which a destructive device may be readily assembled.[30]

Under federal law the term "destructive device" does not include:

(1) Any device which is neither designed nor redesigned for use as a weapon;[31]

(2) Any device, although originally designed for use as a weapon, which is redesigned for use as a signaling, pyrotechnic, line throwing, safety, or similar device;

---

[28] P.C. § 16930(b)(1).

[29] The NFA is part of the Internal Revenue Code, which is typically under the Secretary of the Treasury. After the events of September 11, 2001, the ATF was placed under the supervision of the U.S. Attorney General (AG). So, while the NFA refers to the Secretary of the Treasury, these references now actually mean the U.S. AG.

[30] 26 U.S.C. § 5845(f). The definition of "destructive device" under the Gun Control Act (GCA) is phrased slightly different than the NFA definition. See 18 U.S.C. § 921(a)(4).

[31] It is important to note that in order to be a "destructive device" under state and federal law the device must be a weapon. What constitutes a "weapon" under California law is discussed in Chapter 3.

(3) Surplus ordnance sold, loaned, or given by the Secretary of the Army pursuant to federal codes; or,

(4) Any other device which the Secretary finds is not likely to be used as a weapon, or is an antique or a rifle that the owner intends to use solely for sporting purposes.[32]

Much like they do with "machineguns," the ATF strictly regulates transferring "destructive devices." A "destructive device" is an NFA "firearm" and, if it is regulated under California law, it *can only be* lawfully acquired and possessed if, in addition to meeting the strict federal requirements discussed in Section XII of this chapter, your possession falls within one of California's exceptions.

Under California law, a "destructive device" is any of the following *weapons*:

(1) Any projectile containing any explosive or incendiary material or any other chemical substance, including, but not limited to, that which is commonly known as tracer or incendiary ammunition, except tracer ammunition manufactured for use in shotguns;

(2) Any bomb,[33] grenade, explosive missile, or similar device or any launching device therefor;

(3) Any weapon of a caliber greater than 0.60 caliber which fires fixed ammunition, or any ammunition therefor, other than:

(a) a shotgun (smooth or rifled bore) conforming to the definition of a "destructive device" found in 27 C.F.R. section 479.11(b);

(b) shotgun ammunition (single projectile or shot);

(c) an antique rifle;[34]

(d) an antique cannon;[35] or,

(4) Any rocket, rocket-propelled projectile, or similar device of a diameter greater than 0.60 inch, or any launching device therefor, and any rocket, rocket-propelled projectile, or similar device containing any explosive or incendiary material or any other chemical substance, other than the propellant for that device, except those devices as are designed primarily for emergency or distress signaling purposes;

---

[32] 26 U.S.C. § 5845(f).

[33] A California court defined the term "bomb" as "a device carrying an explosive charge fused to blow up or detonate under certain conditions." *People v. Morse*, 2 Cal. App. 4th 620, 647 n. 8 (1992); CALCRIM No. 2570.

[34] The term "antique rifle" means a firearm conforming to the definition of an "antique firearm" in 27 C.F.R. section 479.11. P.C. § 16180.

[35] For this section, the term "antique cannon" "means any cannon manufactured before January 1, 1899, which has been [made] incapable of firing or for which ammunition is no longer manufactured in the [U.S.] and is not readily available in the ordinary channels of commercial trade." P.C. § 16160. With the internet, what "ordinary channels of commercial trade" means may change in coming years. Please see www.CalGunLawsBook.com for a more detailed discussion on this topic.

(5) Any breakable container that contains a flammable liquid with a flash point of 150 degrees Fahrenheit or less and has a wick or similar device capable of being ignited (*i.e.*, devices like a Molotov cocktail), other than a device which is commercially manufactured primarily for the purpose of illumination (*i.e.*, tiki torches); *or*,

(6) Any sealed device with dry ice (CO_2) (*i.e.*, a dry ice bomb) or other chemically reactive substances assembled for the purpose of causing an explosion by a chemical reaction.[36]

Under California law it is generally illegal for any person or entity to possess,[37] sell, offer for sale, knowingly transport,[38] make or intend to make,[39] import, export, manufacture, or use in business any "destructive device" in the state without a valid permit.[40] Federal law likewise restricts activities like importing, manufacturing, dealing, transporting, and possessing "destructive devices."[41]

Under California law, unlawful possession of a "destructive device" can be punished as a misdemeanor or a felony.[42] Possession of a "destructive device" is punishable as a felony if your possession is reckless or malicious and you possess the "destructive device":

(1) On a public street or highway;

(2) In or near any:

    (a) Theater;

    (b) Hall;

    (c) School;

    (d) College;

    (e) Church;

    (f) Hotel;

    (g) Other public building;

    (h) Private habitation; *or*,

(3) In, on, or near any:

    (a) Aircraft;

    (b) Railway passenger train;

---

[36] P.C. § 16460(a)(1)-(6). "A bullet containing or carrying an explosive agent is not a destructive device...." P.C. § 16460(b). But it may be considered ammunition "containing ... an explosive agent[]" as discussed in P.C. section 30210(b).

[37] P.C. § 18710.

[38] P.C. § 18730.

[39] P.C. § 18720.

[40] P.C. § 18900.

[41] 18 U.S.C. § 923; 26 U.S.C. § 5871. The federal definition of "destructive device" is slightly different from California's. *See* 26 U.S.C. § 5845 (defining "destructive device").

[42] P.C. § 18710.

(c) Car;

(d) Cable road;

(e) Cable car;

(f) Vessel engaged in carrying passengers for hire; *or*,

(g) Other public place ordinarily passed by human beings.[43]

The unlawful sale, offer for sale, or knowing transportation of a "destructive device" is a felony punishable by up to four years in prison.[44] It is also a felony to possess any substance, material, or combination of substances or materials, intending to make a destructive device or explosive without the proper permit.[45] If, however, the "destructive device" that is unlawfully possessed, sold, offered for sale, or transported is fixed ammunition greater than .60 caliber, the first offense is only a misdemeanor.[46] Any offenses committed after that can be a misdemeanor or a felony.[47]

Regardless of whether it is a misdemeanor or a felony offense, under California law, any conviction involving a "destructive device" is ineligible for probation or a suspended sentence, meaning jail or prison time will almost certainly be imposed.[48]

A. Permits

If you are a dealer, manufacturer, importer, or exporter of "destructive devices" or if you use a "destructive device" in a motion picture or television studio, you must first get a special permit from DOJ and renew it annually.[49] Likewise, if you or your firm or corporation does not fall into any of these categories and you wish to possess or transport a "destructive device," you must obtain a permit from DOJ and meet specific criteria.[50] Similar to "machinegun" inspections, DOJ may inspect places where "destructive devices" are kept.[51] Such inspections are held annually. If the permit holder has less than five "destructive devices," DOJ will only inspect every five years, unless they determine additional inspections are necessary.[52]

---

[43] P.C. § 18715.
[44] P.C. § 18730.
[45] P.C. § 18720.
[46] P.C. § 18735.
[47] P.C. § 18735.
[48] P.C. § 18780.
[49] P.C. §§ 18900(a), 18905(b).
[50] P.C. § 18900(b).
[51] P.C. § 18910.
[52] P.C. § 18910(b).

B. Exceptions for Peace Officers, Firefighters, and Military

Certain peace officers,[53] including those in DOJ authorized by the California Attorney General (AG), military personnel, and national guardsmen, may purchase, possess, transport, store, or use a "destructive device" "while on duty and acting within the scope and course of employment."[54]

Exceptions also apply to any equipment considered a "destructive device" that is used by a fire department or fire protection or firefighting agency in the course of fire suppression by "any person who is a regularly employed and paid officer, employee, or member of a fire department or fire protection or firefighting agency of the . . . state, [local or federal government,] while on duty and acting within the scope and course of employment."[55]

C. 37mm Flare Launchers v. Grenade Launchers and 22mm Grenade Launchers v. Flash Suppressors/Muzzle Brakes

Some firearm enthusiasts possess 37mm *flare* launchers. These devices are typically stand-alone launchers or attach under the barrel of a rifle.[56] Because flare launchers closely resemble 40mm *grenade* launchers, law enforcement often mistakes them for "destructive devices." But they are not. You should make sure that any launcher you have is the 37mm variety, not the 40mm version.

As mentioned above, in order to be a "destructive device" under state and federal law, a 37mm *flare* launcher must be considered a weapon. The ATF has issued a ruling saying that 37mm flare guns are not destructive devices so long as they are not possessed with "anti-personnel" ammunition.[57] The same rule should apply for California law; however, there is no case law telling us so and no opinion from DOJ confirming it.

Also, even though 37mm launchers are available nationwide, some California law enforcement agencies still classify them as "destructive devices," claiming that a 37mm grenade exists *somewhere* that can launch from the device. You should therefore carefully consider whether you want to possess one and what your local law enforcement agency's position is.

A similar attempt has been made by certain law enforcement agencies to say that any muzzle attachments are "grenade launchers." Under this theory muzzle devices (flash suppressors and/or muzzle brakes) measuring 22mm in diameter (a common dimension) are alleged to be "grenade launchers." These law enforce-

---

[53] Those listed in P.C. sections 830.1 and 830.2.
[54] P.C. § 18800(a).
[55] P.C. § 18800(b).
[56] Note that when a flare or grenade launcher is attached to a semiautomatic centerfire rifle that does not have a "fixed magazine," the rifle meets the restricted "assault weapon" definition in California (see Chapter 9).
[57] ATF Rul. 95-3 (1995), *available at* http://www.atf.gov/file/55446/download (last visited Oct. 9, 2020). *See* Chapter 3.

ment agencies theorize that there are devices that can attach to a 22mm flash suppressor/muzzle brake, making these devices capable of holding a grenade. When a blank cartridge is inserted into the rifle and discharged, the grenade then shoots off the end of the device. There are also 22mm grenades that fit on the ends of rifle muzzles that either catch a discharged bullet or use the force of a discharged blank to launch. Often it is only the law enforcement agency that is aware of this process, and the firearm owner does not possess the grenade, device that attaches to the flash suppressor or muzzle brake, or blank cartridge. Much like the 37mm flare launchers, typical flash suppressors and muzzle brakes are not considered "weapons" by themselves.

There are other devices that do attach to rifle muzzles designed solely for the purpose of launching a grenade. These devices are also 22mm in diameter but are specifically designed to launch grenades. Usually, the manufacturer will explicitly list these devices as "grenade launchers" in the firearm's packaging material or manual. DOJ has information concerning one type of these devices on their website.[58] If you possess a device described by the manufacturer as a "grenade launcher," you should contact an attorney experienced in firearms law immediately.

D. Cannons

Cannons represent an interesting question with respect to their legality under both state and federal law. Remember first that in order to be a "destructive device" the cannon must be a "weapon." If the cannon is solely decorative or designed solely for signaling purposes, it should not fall under the definition of a "destructive device." Under California law, "antique rifles" and "antique cannons" are exempt from the definition of "destructive devices" as are "antiques" under federal law.

Oddly, the definition of "antique rifle" under California law means "a firearm conforming to the definition of an 'antique firearm' in Section 479.11 of Title 27 of the Code of Federal Regulations [(C.F.R.)]."[59] "An antique firearm" under the Code of Federal Regulations is "[a]ny firearm not designed or redesigned for using rim fire or conventional center fire ignition with fixed ammunition and manufactured in or before 1898 (including any matchlock, flintlock, percussion cap, or similar type of ignition system or replica thereof, whether actually manufactured before or after the year 1898) and also any firearm using fixed ammunition manufactured in or before 1898, for which ammunition is no longer manufactured in the United States and is not readily available in the ordinary channels of commercial trade."[60]

While there are a number of ways a cannon can be exempt from California and federal restrictions on "destructive devices," one should take precautions not

---

[58] *See Public Notice - Zastava SKS Carbines*, CAL. DEPT. OF JUSTICE, OFFICE OF THE ATTORNEY GENERAL, http://oag.ca.gov/firearms/zastava (last visited Oct. 9, 2020).
[59] P.C. § 16180.
[60] 27 C.F.R. § 479.11.

to violate California's restriction on "zip guns" (discussed in Section III(H) of this chapter).

III. "GENERALLY PROHIBITED WEAPONS"

Former P.C. section 12020 was an extremely long statutory provision that generally prohibited the manufacturing, importing, selling, gifting, loaning, or possessing of an odd array of weapons and related equipment. That provision had numerous exceptions, some of which related to all the listed weapons, while others only related to one specific type. This means that people interested in a particular weapon's legality had to read a lot of irrelevant material before finding the portion of former P.C. section 12020 relevant to them.[61]

To ease confusion and eliminate this problem, the Penal Code was revised to separate former P.C. section 12020 and its subdivisions out. As a result of this revision, the prohibited items were separated out in new sections according to the specific firearm, equipment, or device to which they pertain. For example, the restriction on "cane guns" can now be found in a separate section specifically concerning "cane guns." Some of these items are "firearms" and some are not.

For most of these items, manufacturing, importing, keeping for sale, offering or exposing for sale, giving, lending, and possessing are illegal.[62] All are now listed as "generally prohibited weapons" under P.C. section 16590, and each is defined in its own additional code section. As of the date of this book's publication, P.C. section 16590 lists the following as "generally prohibited weapons" in California:

(1) An air gauge knife (P.C. section 20310);

(2) Ammunition that contains or consists of a flechette dart (P.C. section 30210);

(3) A ballistic knife (P.C. section 21110);

(4) A belt buckle knife (P.C. section 20410);

(5) A bullet containing or carrying an explosive agent (P.C. section 30210);

(6) A camouflaging firearm container (P.C. section 24310);

(7) A cane gun (P.C. section 24410);

(8) A cane sword (P.C. section 20510);

(9) A concealed dirk or dagger (P.C. section 21310);

(10) A concealed explosive substance, other than fixed ammunition (P.C. section 19100);

---

[61] *Nonsubstantive Reorganization of Deadly Weapon Statutes Recommendation*, 38 Cal. L. Revision Comm'n Reports 217, 245 (2009).

[62] P.C. section 16590 contains a list of the "generally prohibited weapons" and the code sections restricting them.

(11) A firearm that is not immediately recognizable as a firearm (P.C. section 24510);

(12) A "large-capacity magazine" (P.C. section 32310);

(13) A leaded cane or an instrument or weapon of kind commonly known as a billy, blackjack, sandbag, sandclub, sap, or slungshot (P.C. section 22210);

(14) A lipstick case knife (P.C. section 20610);

(15) Metal knuckles (P.C. section 21810);

(16) A metal military practice handgrenade or metal replica handgrenade (P.C. section 19200);

(17) A multiburst trigger activator (P.C. section 32900);

(18) A nunchaku (P.C. section 22010);

(19) A shobi-zue (P.C. section 20710);

(20) A short-barreled rifle or short-barreled shotgun (P.C. section 33215);

(21) A shuriken (P.C. section 22410);

(22) An unconventional pistol (P.C. section 31500);

(23) An undetectable firearm (P.C. section 24610);

(24) A wallet gun (P.C. section 24710);

(25) A writing pen knife (P.C. section 20910); and,

(26) A zip gun (P.C. section 33600).

As applied here, the restrictions against "large-capacity magazines" are discussed in more detail below. There are also restrictions on "large-capacity magazine conversion kits," but these items were not added to the list of "generally prohibited weapons." However, the exceptions for "generally prohibited weapons" apply to "large-capacity magazine conversion kits." (discussed below).

If you are concerned that you possess any of the above-listed items or if you have questions about them, you should refer directly to the Penal Code and the sections defining these items. And, as always, when in doubt consult an attorney knowledgeable in California weapons laws.

A. "Cane Gun"

"Cane guns"⁶³ are "any firearm mounted or enclosed in a stick, staff, rod, crutch, or similar device, designed to be, or capable of being used as, an aid in walking, if the firearm may be fired while mounted or enclosed therein."⁶⁴ "Cane guns" were popular in the mid-1850s and served not only as a walking accessory but also for self-defense.⁶⁵

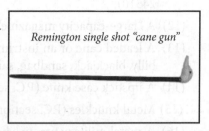
Remington single shot "cane gun"

B. "Wallet Gun"

"'[W]allet gun'⁶⁶ means any firearm mounted or enclosed in a case, resembling a wallet, designed to be or capable of being carried in a pocket or purse, if the firearm may be fired while mounted or enclosed in the case."⁶⁷ Because of its shape and size, a "wallet gun" can look and feel like an actual wallet. These devices are also problematic under the federal law's "any other weapon" definition.⁶⁸

 Interestingly enough, the "wallet" is not illegal under California law by itself, nor is the "gun" necessarily illegal by itself. Once the "gun" is mounted or enclosed in the "wallet," however, it becomes illegal. This means you could lawfully possess either the "wallet" or the "gun" by themselves or both, as long as the "gun" is not "mounted or enclosed" or you did not intend to mount or enclose⁶⁹ it in the "wallet." But we recommend that you don't possess both, even if the "gun" is not "mounted or enclosed" in the "wallet."

Example of a wallet gun

The device also may not need to be a conventional wallet. Certain holsters come dangerously close to a "wallet gun" by allowing you to shoot firearms while they are mounted or enclosed in them, and could fall under the definition.

---

⁶³ Prohibited via P.C. section 24410.

⁶⁴ P.C. § 16330.

⁶⁵ *Remington Cane Guns*, THE REMINGTON SOCIETY OF AMERICA, http://www.remingtonsociety.org/remington-cane-guns/ (last visited Oct. 9, 2020).

⁶⁶ Contraband pursuant to P.C. section 24710.

⁶⁷ P.C. § 17330.

⁶⁸ 26 U.S.C. § 5845(e).

⁶⁹ As discussed in Chapter 9, according to the *Nguyen* case, the possession of the parts of an illegal weapon can be problematic if you have the intent to make an illegal weapon with these parts.

C. "Undetectable Firearm"

An "undetectable firearm"[70] is any weapon that satisfies either of the following:

(1) After removal of grips, stocks, and magazines, the weapon is not as detectable as the Security Exemplar by a walk-through metal detector calibrated and operated to detect the Security Exemplar; *or*

(2) Any major component of the weapon defined by federal law that, when inspected by x-ray machines commonly used at airports, does not generate an image that accurately depicts the shape of the component. Barium sulfate or other compounds may be used to make the component.[71]

In the past, lawmakers were concerned that firearms made out of composite materials or polymers would not show up in metal detectors or x-ray machines. These concerns proved baseless. These firearms, such as most Glock models (high-tech polymer based, corrosion resistant, 86% lighter,[72] and tougher than steel), still have enough metal to be easily detected by metal detectors and x-ray machines, especially when loaded.

Note that if you plan to make your own plastic or polymer 3D printed firearm, you must incorporate some kind of metal into the design in order to make the firearm detectable. For example, Defense Distributed, the group that created the first fully 3D printed handgun, incorporated a six-ounce chuck of steel into the body of the firearm in order to make the firearm detectable by a walk-through metal detector.[73]

D. Firearms Not "Immediately Recognizable" as Firearms

The Penal Code does not specifically define "immediately recognizable" or a "firearm that is not immediately recognizable." Nevertheless, it is illegal under P.C. section 24510. So, exactly what is prohibited by this California statute is unclear. Obvious examples are firearms disguised as cell phones and the "Braverman Stinger."[74] The "Palm Pistol"[75] is also arguably covered.

Example of a palm pistol: a Chicago Firearms Co. Protector Palm Pistol

---

[70] P.C. section 24610 prohibits "undetectable firearms."

[71] P.C. § 17280. See 18 U.S.C. section 922(p) for a comparison to federal law.

[72] *See* Glock *"Safe Action" Pistol*, GLOCK.COM, https://us.glock.com/technology/safe-action (last visited Oct. 9, 2020).

[73] To learn more about 3D printed firearms, see Chapter 5.

[74] *See Stinger Penguns*, PENGUN.COM, http://pengun.com/ (last visited Oct. 9, 2020).

[75] *See* John B. Snow, *Strange Guns: Palm Pistol*, OUTDOOR LIFE (Apr. 13, 2011), http://www.outdoorlife.com/blogs/gun-shots/2011/04/strange-guns-palm-pistol (last visited Oct. 9, 2020).

Painting a firearm to resemble a BB device or an imitation firearm by adding a fluorescent orange tip or other painting is highly risky. It is also likely illegal because it might be considered disguising a real firearm as an imitation firearm and thus not "immediately recognizable" as a firearm.

E. "Camouflaging Firearm Container"

A "camouflaging firearm container"[76] is a container that meets the following criteria:

(1) It is designed and intended to enclose a firearm;

(2) It is designed and intended to allow the firing of the enclosed firearm by external controls while the firearm is in the container; *and,*

(3) It is not readily recognizable as containing a firearm.[77]

A common "camouflaging firearm container" is a "briefcase gun" where a firearm is mounted inside of a normal-looking briefcase. The case has an internal mechanism that allows the operator to discharge the firearm by either pulling a trigger on the briefcase handle or by pushing a secret button somewhere on the case.

F. "Multiburst Trigger Activator"

A "multiburst trigger activator"[78] means one of the following:

(1) A device designed or redesigned to be attached to, built into, or used in conjunction with, a semiautomatic firearm, which allows the firearm to discharge two or more shots in a burst by activating the device; *or,*

(2) A manual or power-driven trigger-activating device constructed and designed so that when attached to, built into, or used in conjunction with, a semiautomatic firearm it increases the rate of fire of that firearm.[79]

Any person in California who possesses, gives, lends, tries to sell, imports into California, or causes to be manufactured any multiburst trigger activator can be punished by either a misdemeanor or felony conviction ("wobbler").[80] And if the "multiburst trigger activator" is attached to a firearm, the firearm will likely be confiscated and destroyed along with the device.[81]

---

[76] Illegal under P.C. section 24310.

[77] P.C. § 16320(a). "'Camouflaging firearm container' does not include any camouflaging covering used while . . . lawful[ly] hunting or while going to or returning from a lawful hunting expedition." P.C. § 16320(b).

[78] Considered contraband under P.C. section 32900.

[79] P.C. § 16930(a). *See also* P.C. §§ 32900 (prohibiting the manufacture, importation, sale, supply, or possession of any "multiburst trigger activator), 32990 (labeling "multiburst trigger activators" as a "nuisance" subject to confiscation and summary destruction).

[80] P.C. § 32900.

[81] P.C. § 32990.

Common examples of "multiburst trigger activators" include the "Hell-Fire" or "Hellstorm 2000." While differing in design, both function under the same principle. They are marketed to assist a user in bump-firing a gun by attaching to the firearm's trigger guard and putting forward spring tension on the trigger. In theory, this added tension assists a user in engaging the trigger mechanism in rapid succession by utilizing the firearm's recoil (aka "bump-firing").

For decades, "bump stocks" did not meet California's original definition of "multiburst trigger activator." Bump stocks are neither "burst fire" or "trigger activating" devices and therefore did not meet the definition of a "multiburst trigger activator." But in 2018 with SB 1346, the California Legislature "clarified" this definition of "multiburst trigger activator" to specifically include "bump stocks," as well as "burst triggers," "trigger cranks," and other similar devices. As a result, the following four devices now meet the above definition of "multiburst trigger activator":

(1) A device that uses a spring, piston, or similar mechanism to push back against the recoil of a firearm, thereby moving the firearm in a back-and-forth motion and facilitating the rapid reset and activation of the trigger by a stationary finger. These devices are commonly known as bump stocks, bump fire stocks, or bump fire stock attachments.

(2) A device placed within the trigger guard of a firearm that uses a spring to push back against the recoil of the firearm causing the finger in the trigger guard to move back and forth and rapidly activate the trigger. These devices are commonly known as burst triggers.

(3) A mechanical device that activates the trigger of the firearm in rapid succession by turning a crank. These devices are commonly known as trigger cranks, gat cranks, gat triggers, or trigger actuators.

(4) Any aftermarket trigger or trigger system that, if installed, allows more than one round to be fired with a single depression of the trigger.[82]

So, "bump stocks" are specifically prohibited under California law as "multiburst trigger activators." Interestingly, California Attorney General Xavier Becerra issued a press release in 2017 claiming "bump stocks" are illegal "multiburst trigger activators" that have been prohibited in California *since 1990*.[83] But the recent amendment to the law clarifying that "bump stocks" are "multiburst trigger activators," coupled with the lack of prosecutions for bump stocks prior to this amendment, raise serious doubt as to the veracity of the Attorney General's claim.

---

[82] P.C. § 16930(b).
[83] *See California Department of Justice Issues Advisory Reminding Gun Retailers That Bump Stocks Are Illegal*, https://oag.ca.gov/news/press-releases/california-department-justice-issues-advisory-reminding-gun-retailers-bump (Oct. 19, 2017).

G. "Short-Barreled Shotguns" and "Short-Barreled Rifles"

Both California and federal law restrict possessing and transferring shotguns and rifles if they are under a certain length.[84]

1. "Short-Barreled Shotguns"

Two separate definitions exist under federal law for restricted shotguns of certain lengths. The Gun Control Act (GCA) has one, and the National Firearms Act (NFA) does too.

Under the GCA, "[t]he term 'short-barreled shotgun' means a shotgun having one or more barrels less than eighteen inches in length and any weapon made from a shotgun (whether by alteration, modification or otherwise) if such a weapon as modified has an overall length of less than twenty-six inches."[85] The GCA defines "shotgun" as "a weapon designed or redesigned, made or remade, and intended to be fired from the shoulder and designed or redesigned and made or remade to use the energy of an explosive to fire through a smooth bore either a number of ball shot or a single projectile for each single pull of the trigger."[86]

The GCA restricts transferring and transporting firearms meeting this definition but does not generally restrict possessing them.[87] The GCA does, however, add additional penalties if these firearms are possessed while committing a crime.[88]

In contrast to the GCA, the NFA does *not* refer to shotguns of prohibited lengths as "short-barreled shotguns," but instead describes them by their physical dimensions. The NFA specifically restricts "shotguns" with one or more barrels less than 18 inches long and weapons made from "shotguns" with overall lengths of less than 26 inches or that have one or more barrels that are less than 18 inches long.[89] The NFA defines the term "shotgun" the same way as the GCA, but additionally includes "any such weapon which may be readily restored to fire a *fixed shotgun shell*."[90]

Like all NFA firearms, "shotguns" restricted based on length can be lawfully acquired, possessed, and transferred under federal law *as long as* you meet all of the NFA requirements discussed in Section XII of this chapter. As noted below, how-

---

[84] P.C. § 33215; 18 U.S.C. § 922; 26 U.S.C. § 5861.

[85] 18 U.S.C. § 921(a)(6).

[86] 18 U.S.C. § 921(a)(5).

[87] 18 U.S.C. § 922(a)(4), (b)(4).

[88] 18 U.S.C. § 924(c)(1)(B).

[89] Note that the NFA has an additional category of restricted short-barreled shotguns that the GCA does not, *i.e.*, weapons made from a "shotgun" that have one or more barrels less than 18 inches long. This means that a firearm no longer meeting the "shotgun" definition (*e.g.*, one not intended to be fired from the shoulder) but made from a "shotgun" is restricted under the NFA but not necessarily under the GCA. The NFA also restricts "weapons with combination shotgun and rifle barrels 12 inches or more, less than 18 inches in length, from which only a single discharge can be made from either barrel without manual reloading, and shall include any such weapon which may be readily restored to fire." Those are discussed in the "any other weapon" section. 27 C.F.R. § 479.11.

[90] 26 U.S.C. § 5845(d) (emphasis added).

ever, the possession of most NFA firearms is strictly prohibited under California law, even if they can be lawfully possessed under federal law.

Under both the GCA and the NFA, a firearm has to actually be a "shotgun" – meaning it must be "intended to be fired from the shoulder" – or made from a "shotgun" to be federally restricted as a "short-barreled shotgun." This may sound obvious based on the name, but as mentioned below, California law considers any "firearm" with certain dimensions that fires fixed shotgun shells, even handguns, to be "short-barreled shotguns." Because this is not the case under federal law, firearms like the Taurus Judge and Smith & Wesson Governor (handguns designed to shoot .410 shotgun shells) are legal under federal law but not under California law.[91]

Example of a short-barreled shotgun

California's "short-barreled shotgun" definition is different from the federal definitions for "shotguns" that are restricted based on their length. Under California law a "short-barreled shotgun" means any of the following:

(1) A *firearm* that is designed or redesigned to fire a fixed shotgun shell and has a barrel or barrels of less than 18 inches in length; *or*

(2) A *firearm* that has an overall length of less than 26 inches and that is designed or redesigned to fire a fixed shotgun shell; *or*

(3) Any weapon made from a shotgun (whether by alteration, modification, or otherwise) if that weapon, as modified, has an overall length of less than 26 inches or a barrel or barrels of less than 18 inches in length; *or*

(4) Any device that may be readily restored to fire a fixed shotgun shell and, when so restored, is a device defined in subdivisions (1) to (3), inclusive; *or*

(5) Any part, or combination of parts, designed and intended to convert a device into a device defined in subdivisions (1) to (3), inclusive, or any combination of parts from which a device defined in subdivisions (1) to (3), inclusive, can be readily assembled if those parts are in the possession or under the control of the same person.[92]

Know that the California "short-barreled shotgun" definition above does not require the firearm to actually *be* a "shotgun."[93] Any *firearm* "designed or redesigned"

---

[91] C. D. Michel, *Judging the Judges – Illegal Firearms in California?*, CALGUNLAWS.COM (June 13, 2011), http://www.CalGunLaws.com/wp-content/uploads/2012/09/Judging-the-Judges-Illegal-Firearms-in-California.pdf (last visited Oct. 9, 2020).

[92] P.C. § 17180.

[93] *See* P.C. § 17190 (defining "shotgun" for purposes of defining "short-barreled shotgun" as "a weapon designed or redesigned, made or remade, and intended to be fired from the shoulder and designed or redesigned and made or remade to use the energy of the explosive in a fixed shotgun shell to fire through a smooth bore either a number of projectiles (ball shot) or a single projectile for each pull of the trigger.") *See also* Chapter 3.

to shoot fixed shotgun ammunition can be a "short-barreled shotgun" if it fails to meet the length requirements. In fact, even a handgun can be considered one.[94]

"Short-barreled shotguns" are generally restricted under California law the same way as all "generally prohibited weapons" listed in P.C. section 16590.

2. "Short-Barreled Rifles"

As with shotguns, two separate federal definitions exist under the GCA and the NFA for restricted "rifles" of certain lengths.

Under the GCA a "short-barreled rifle" "means a rifle having one or more barrels less than sixteen inches in length and any weapon made from a rifle (whether by alteration, modification, or otherwise) if such weapon, as modified, has an overall length of less than twenty-six inches."[95] The GCA defines the term "rifle" as "a weapon designed or redesigned, made or remade, and intended to be fired from the shoulder and designed or redesigned and made or remade to use the energy of an explosive to fire only a single projectile through a rifled bore for each single pull of the trigger."[96] The GCA restricts these rifles the same way it does "short-barreled shotguns" as described above.

Example of a short-barreled rifle

As with shotguns, the NFA also does *not* refer to rifles with prohibited lengths as "short-barreled," but instead describes them by their physical dimensions. It specifically restricts "rifles" with one or more barrels less than 16 inches long and weapons made from a "rifle" with an overall length of less than 26 inches or that have one or more barrels that are less than 16 inches long.[97] The NFA also defines "rifle" the same way the GCA does, but additionally includes "any such weapon which may be readily restored to fire a fixed cartridge."[98]

Under the NFA, "short-barreled rifles" are restricted the same way shotguns are restricted as described above.

"Short-barreled rifles are illegal simply because they are short, which makes them 'suitable for unlawful purposes because of their concealability and ease of handling.'"[99] This is also the case with "short-barreled shotguns." This can be a problem because the prosecution can use circumstantial evidence to show that you

---

[94] P.C. §§ 16530(b), 16640(b).

[95] 18 U.S.C. § 921(a)(8).

[96] 18 U.S.C. § 921(a)(7).

[97] 26 U.S.C. § 5845(a)(3)-(4). Note that, as with shotguns, the NFA has an additional restricted "short-barreled rifle" category not found in the GCA, *i.e.*, weapons made from a "rifle" that have one or more barrels less than 16 inches long. 26 U.S.C. § 5845(a)(3). The same implications apply as for shotguns discussed above.

[98] 26 U.S.C. § 5845(c).

[99] *People v. King*, 38 Cal. 4th 617, 627 (2006) (citing *People v. Rooney*, 17 Cal. App. 4th 1207, 1211 (1993)); *see also People v. Stinson*, 8 Cal. App. 3d 497, 500 (1970).

knew a firearm was unusually short and could be classified as a "short-barreled shotgun/rifle."[100]

Under California law, a "short-barreled rifle" is any of the following:

(1) A rifle[101] having a barrel or barrels of less than 16 inches in length;

(2) A rifle with an overall length of less than 26 inches;

(3) Any weapon made from a rifle (whether by alteration, modification, or otherwise) if that weapon, as modified, has an overall length of less than 26 inches or a barrel or barrels of less than 16 inches in length;

(4) Any device which may be readily restored to fire a fixed cartridge which, when so restored, is a device defined in subdivisions (1) to (3), inclusive;[102] or,

(5) Any part, or combination of parts, designed and intended to convert a device into a device defined in subdivisions (1) to (3), inclusive, or any combination of parts from which a device defined in subdivisions (1) to (3), inclusive, may be readily assembled if those parts are in the possession or under the control of the same person.[103]

"Short-barreled rifles" are generally subject to the same restrictions under California law as all "generally prohibited weapons" listed in P.C. section 16590.

While the Penal Code does not specify how a rifle or shotgun's "overall length" is determined, California law enforcement will measure any "short-barreled shotgun/rifle" with the firearm in its shortest configuration (*e.g.*, with its stock folded).[104] Meanwhile, federal law enforcement measures firearms in their lengthiest configuration (*e.g.*, with a folding stock extended) to determine whether the firearm is a "short-barreled shotgun/rifle."[105]

As explained by the ATF, the proper way to measure barrel length is by inserting a rod down the barrel from the muzzle through the chamber to the back of the breach.[106] This should be standard practice but is often overlooked by California

---

[100] *People v. King*, 38 Cal. 4th 617, 627-28 (2006).

[101] See P.C. section 17090 for the California definition of "rifle." *See also* Chapter 3.

[102] Note that under both California law and the federal NFA, a firearm must fire a "fixed cartridge" to be a "rifle," but to be a restricted "short-barreled rifle" it only needs to be *readily able to be restored* to fire a "fixed cartridge," so be careful. Interestingly, if the firearm does not meet either of these definitions (*i.e.*, it does not and cannot be readily made to fire a "fixed cartridge"), it cannot be a "short-barreled rifle" under California law or the federal NFA. This means that you could lawfully possess a muzzle-loading firearm that would otherwise be considered a restricted "short-barreled rifle" based on its length without violating California law or the federal NFA. Such a firearm *would*, however, still be subject to the federal GCA limitations on transfers explained above.

[103] P.C. § 17170.

[104] *People v. Rooney*, 17 Cal. App. 4th 1207, 1211-13 (1993).

[105] 27 C.F.R. § 479.11 (stating in pertinent part: "The overall length of a weapon made from a shotgun or rifle is the distance between the extreme ends of the weapon measured along a line parallel to the center line of the bore").

[106] *See* U.S. Dept. of Justice, Bureaus of Alcohol, Tobacco, Firearms, and Explosives, ATF National Firearms Act Handbook 6 (2009), *available at* https://www.atf.gov/firearms/docs/guide/atf-national-firearms-act-handbook-atf-p-53208/download (last visited Oct. 9, 2020) ("The ATF procedure for measuring barrel length is to measure from the closed bolt (or breech-face) to the furthermost end of the barrel or permanently attached

law enforcement who incorrectly exclude the chamber in measuring overall barrel length. It does not help that California has not universally adopted the federal method, even though DOJ regulations say that the federal method applies for "ghost gun" registration.[107]

3. Possession of Parts Constituting "Short-Barreled Shotguns/Rifles"

Note that, under both California and federal law, mere parts can be considered a "short-barreled shotgun/rifle" if, when combined, they could readily be made into one.[108] In *United States v. Thompson/Center Arms Co.*, the U.S. Supreme Court explained that pistol parts and carbine kits – parts that can be assembled to create either a handgun or a rifle – are not necessarily a "short-barreled rifle" under federal law if the parts could possibly be assembled in a way that would *not* constitute a "short-barreled rifle." The court clarified, however, that if the parts, when assembled, could *only* create a "short-barreled rifle," or are so assembled, then the parts would themselves be considered a restricted "short-barreled rifle."[109] The Ninth Circuit Court of Appeals (the controlling Court of Appeals for California) further explained that "an aggregation of weapons parts may not constitute [an NFA] firearm if the parts have an apparent legal purpose other than the creation of such a firearm" (*e.g.*, a "short-barreled rifle" under federal law).[110]

Parts kits that are used to make firearms into pistols or rifles like those considered by the U.S. Supreme Court in the *Thompson* case – with a receiver that you can attach both the parts for a pistol (a short barrel and pistol grip) and the parts for a rifle (a long barrel and shoulder stock) – have caused a lot of confusion. Because of *Thompson* and its progeny, case law has explained that such kits are legal unless the parts can *only* be, or *are*, configured in a way to create a "short-barreled rifle" (this is not such a problem with shotguns). But people run into problems when they attach their pistol barrel and shoulder stock to the receiver. This kind of firearm is one designed to be fired from the shoulder with a rifled barrel, but the barrel (and usually the overall length of the firearm) is too short under both California and federal law, thereby creating a "short-barreled rifle." Having the wrong parts attached at the wrong time can subject you to serious criminal charges.

---

muzzle device. Permanent methods of attachment include full-fusion gas or electric steel-seam welding, high-temperature (1100°F) silver soldering, or blind pinning with the pin head welded over. Barrels are measured by inserting a dowel rod into the barrel until the rod stops against the bolt or breech-face. The rod is then marked at the furthermost end of the barrel or permanently attached muzzle device, withdrawn from the barrel, and measured.").

[107] *See* CAL. CODE. REGS. tit. 11, § 5507(c).

[108] P.C. §§ 17170(d)-(e) (rifles), 17180(d)-(e) (shotguns).

[109] *United States v. Thompson/Center Arms Co.*, 504 U.S. 505, 511-12 (1992) (plurality opinion).

[110] *United States v. Kwan*, 300 Fed. App'x. 485 (9th Cir. 2008) (citing *United States v. Thompson/Center Arms Co.*, 504 U.S. 505, 512-13 (1992)); *see also United States v. Kent*, 175 F.3d 870 (11th Cir. 1999). For more in-depth analysis of this and other federal firearms law related topics, see STEPHEN P. HALBROOK, FIREARMS LAW DESKBOOK (West 2011-2012 ed. 2011).

4. Pistol Stabilizing Braces

Attaching a pistol stabilizing brace (*e.g.*, a Sig Sauer SB15 Pistol Stabilizing Brace) to a buffer tube equipped pistol does not convert it into a "short-barreled rifle" under California or federal law. But it may be considered a "short-barreled rifle" depending on how the shooter *uses or modifies* the forearm brace.

A pistol stabilizing brace is a device that is meant to aid shooters – especially with those who have limited strength or mobility due to a handicap – in operating rifle-caliber or large caliber pistols. These devices look like short stocks on the end of the pistol and attach to the shooter's forearm by a Velcro strap, which allows the weight the firearm to be distributed evenly in order to improve accuracy and reduce the recoil felt by the shooter.

Generally, attaching a pistol stabilizing brace to a buffer tube equipped pistol and using it as it is intended to be used (*i.e.*, as a forearm brace) does not convert the firearm into a "short-barreled rifle" because the resulting firearm is still a pistol, meaning it is not intended to be fired from the shoulder – a requirement that must be met before a firearm can be a "short-barreled rifle" under both California and federal law.[111]

The ATF's position on pistol-stabilizing braces has repeatedly changed over the years. On March 5, 2014, the ATF originally decided that using a pistol-stabilizing brace as a shoulder stock does not change the classification of the weapon or transform the pistol into a "short-barreled rifle."[112]

Then, in a series of letters between November 2014 and January 2015, the ATF changed course and said that using an arm brace as a shoulder stock on a pistol "redesigned" the firearm into an NFA "short-barreled rifle." On November 10, 2014, the ATF explained (in response to an inquiry about the Sig Sauer SB15 Arm Brace) that attaching a stabilizing brace to the pistol alone does not change the pistol into a "short-barreled rifle" under federal law. But, if the brace stabilizer was used as a shoulder stock, it would then be classified as a "rifle" and therefore considered a "short-barreled rifle" under federal law.[113] On December 15, 2014, the ATF issued another letter supporting this decision, finding that attaching a Shockwave Blade AR Pistol Stabilizer to a pistol does not convert the weapon into a "short-barreled rifle" for purposes of federal law as long as it is used as originally designed and not used as a shoulder stock.[114] Later, in an open letter released on January 16, 2015, the

---

[111] As with California law, before a firearm can be considered a "short-barreled rifle" under federal law, it must first be a "rifle," meaning that it must be intended to be fired from the shoulder. 26 U.S.C. § 5845(a), (c).

[112] Letter from Earl Griffith, Chief, Firearms Technology Branch to Sergeant Joe Bradley, Greenwood Police Department (Mar. 5, 2014), *available at* http://www.gunsandammo.com/files/2014/04/S72-LEGAL-B1404030900021.jpg (last visited Oct. 9, 2020).

[113] Letter from Max M. Kingery, Acting Chief, Firearms Technology Industry Services Branch to Anonymous (Nov. 10, 2014), *available at* https://princelaw.files.wordpress.com/2014/12/sig-brace-nov-2014.pdf (last visited Oct. 9, 2020).

[114] Letter from Michael R. Curtis, Acting Chief, Firearms Technology Industry Services Brach to Martin Ewer, Owner, Shockwave Technologies (Dec. 15, 2014), *available at* http://shockwavetechnologies.com/site/?p=2114 (last visited Oct. 9, 2020).

ATF stated that any person who intends to use or uses a pistol stabilizing brace as a shoulder stock converts the firearm into a "short-barreled rifle" under the NFA.[115]

The reasoning outlined in these letters raises an obvious question: how does merely shifting the firearm from the arm to the shoulder "convert" or "redesign" the firearm into a rifle? On March 21, 2017, the ATF attempted to clarify this issue by stating that one may use an arm brace as a shoulder stock in an "incidental", "situational" or "sporadic" manner.[116] But, attaching a stabilizing brace that is not in its "original approved condition" to a pistol may convert it into a "short-barreled rifle" under the NFA.[117] As explained earlier in this chapter, the NFA defines a "rifle" as any "weapon, designed or redesigned, made or remade, and intended to be fired from the shoulder."

Although neither the NFA nor GCA define the term "redesign," in the ATF's opinion, any affirmative steps" to configure the device as a shoulder stock constitute a "redesign" of the firearm into a "rifle."[118] Examples of some affirmative steps include, but are not limited to: (1) "configuring the brace so as to permanently affix it to the end of a buffer tube, (thereby creating a length that has no other purpose than to facilitate its use as a stock); (2) removing the arm-strap; or (3) otherwise undermining its ability to be used as a brace."[119] So any person who consistently uses a pistol stabilizing brace as a shoulder stock regardless of the situation, or at any time connects a pistol stabilizing brace that is not in its "original approved condition" to a pistol with a rifled barrel under 16 inches as a shoulder stock has "redesigned" the firearm into a "short-barreled rifle" for purposes of the NFA.[120]

The ATF has repeatedly changed its position on this issue. The most recent example is ATF's August 3, 2020 "Cease and Desist" letter to Q, LLC, regarding the Honey Badger firearm.[121] In this letter, ATF states the Honey Badger's features indicate it is intended to be fired from the shoulder. Coupled with the firearm's barrel of less than 16 inches, ATF states the firearm therefore meets the definition of a

---

[115] Open Letter on the Redesign of "Stabilizing Braces" from Max M. Kingery, Acting Chief, Firearms Technology Criminal Branch, Firearms and Ammunition Technology Division, Bureau of Alcohol, Tobacco, Firearms, and Explosives (Jan. 16, 2015), *available at* https://www.atf.gov/file/11816/download (last visited Oct. 9, 2020).

[116] Letter from Marvin G. Richardson, Assistant Director of Enforcement Programs and Services, Bureau of Alcohol, Tobacco, Firearms and Explosives (Mar. 21, 2017), *available at* https://www.sigsauer.com/wp-content/uploads/2017/04/atf-letter-march-21-2017.pdf (last visited Oct. 9, 2020).

[117] Letter from Marvin G Richardson, Assistant Director of Enforcement Programs and Services, Bureau of Alcohol, Tobacco, Firearms and Explosives (Mar. 21, 2017), *available at* https://www.sigsauer.com/wp-content/uploads/2017/04/atf-letter-march-21-2017.pdf (last visited Oct. 9, 2020).

[118] 26 U.S.C. § 5845(a).

[119] Letter from Marvin G Richardson, Assistant Director of Enforcement Programs and Services, Bureau of Alcohol, Tobacco, Firearms and Explosives (Mar. 21, 2017), *available at* https://www.sigsauer.com/wp-content/uploads/2017/04/atf-letter-march-21-2017.pdf (last visited Oct. 9, 2020.

[120] Note that because almost all buffer tube equipped pistols are based on the AR15 platform and have rifled barrels. Therefore, even if a stabilizing brace is attached to an AR pistol, it would not fall under the definition of "any other weapon" under the NFA because it is designed to be gripped by one hand (see Section XII(A) of this chapter).

[121] More information regarding ATF's determination, including a copy of ATF's letter, can be found on Q, LCC's website at https://www.liveqordie.com/wp-content/uploads/2020/10/Q-Honey-Badger-Pistol-Notification-10-06-2020-With-Links-1.pdf.

"short-barreled rifle" under the NFA. What is not clear from ATF's letter, however, is why it considers the Honey Badger's brace as one that "is designed and intended to be fired from the shoulder." What's more, whether ATF's letter signals a shift in its policy towards stabilizing braces in general remains to be seen.

Although there is no case law on the matter in California, presumably law enforcement would likely apply the same analysis in determining whether a buffer tube equipped pistol is an illegal "short-barreled rifle" under California law if a person attaches a stabilizing brace to the pistol with the intent of using it as, or actually uses it as, a shoulder stock.

Therefore, if you plan on attaching and using a stabilizer brace on a buffer tube attached pistol in California, we still suggest you use it as intended (i.e., as a forearm brace).

H. "Zip Gun"

Under California law, a "zip gun"[122] is any weapon or device that meets all of the following:

(1) It was not imported as a firearm by a licensed importer;[123]

(2) It was not originally designed to be a firearm by a licensed manufacturer;[124]

(3) No tax was paid on the weapon or device, nor was it exempt from a tax;[125] *and,*

(4) It is made or altered to expel a projectile by the force of an explosion or other form of combustion.[126]

"Zip guns" are typically small homemade firearms. They are usually destroyed once fired. This does not mean, however, that a larger, sturdier item could not be considered a "zip gun." In the past, some law enforcement agencies have claimed that *all* firearms made from raw materials are "zip guns."[127] But that is incorrect. It is not necessarily illegal for people to assemble or build firearms for their own personal use (see Chapter 5).

Example of a "zip gun": this one was made in prison with metal parts

Firearms made to expel projectiles by combustive force, but that have been made from raw materials, have clearly not been imported as a firearm, nor would

---

[122] Illegal under P.C. section 33600.
[123] Licensed pursuant to 18 U.S.C. section 923.
[124] Licensed pursuant to 18 U.S.C. section 923.
[125] This exemption is granted under 26 U.S.C. sections 4181, 4216-4227 and the regulations issued pursuant thereto.
[126] P.C. § 17360.
[127] If the "zip gun" is created from a receiver acquired from an FFL, a tax would have been paid.

taxes be paid on them.[128] The issue, then, is about the firearm's *design*. If you make a brand-new firearm from an original design (*i.e.*, not based on an existing firearm design), you have arguably created a "zip gun" unless you are a licensed firearm manufacturer (see Chapter 5). This means that, if you create a firearm based on a licensed firearm manufacturer's design, it should *not* be considered a "zip gun" under the above criteria.

I. "Unconventional Pistol"

Under California law, an "unconventional pistol"[129] is a firearm: (1) without a rifled bore, and (2) that "has a barrel or barrels of less than 18 inches in length or has an overall length of less than 26 inches."[130]

J. "Large-Capacity Magazine" and "Large-Capacity Magazine Conversion Kits"

1. Definition

Under California law, a "large-capacity magazine" is "any ammunition feeding device with the capacity to accept more than 10 rounds," but it does *not* include:

(1) A feeding device that has been permanently altered so that it cannot accommodate more than 10 rounds;

(2) A .22 caliber tube ammunition feeding device; *or,*

(3) A tubular magazine that is contained in a lever-action firearm.[131]

California law does not explain further what a "large-capacity magazine" is, but in the definition of "detachable magazine," an "ammunition feeding device" includes "any belted or linked ammunition" but not "clips, en bloc clips, or stripper clips that load cartridges into the magazine."[132]

Ammunition feeding devices of any size and capacity may be permanently[133] altered to make them unable to accept more than ten rounds. If this happens, they lose their "large-capacity magazine" status and thus are not restricted.

---

[128] There is an argument to be made that if the "zip gun" was manufactured for personal use, no tax was due, and therefore the gun was exempt from the tax requirement. But the ins and outs of federal tax law far exceed the scope of this book.

[129] Contraband under P.C. section 31500.

[130] P.C. § 17270.

[131] P.C. § 16740.

[132] CAL. CODE REGS. tit. 11, § 5471(m).

[133] Whether an alteration is "permanent" can affect the magazine's legal status and is not always clear. In fact, DOJ attempted to define "permanently altered" in the California Code of Regulations but deleted the definition. *See Notice of Modification to Text of Proposed Regulations*, CALIFORNIA DEPT. OF JUSTICE, OFFICE OF THE ATTORNEY GENERAL, http://oag.ca.gov/sites/all/files/agweb/pdfs/firearms/regs/sb23rev.pdf (last visited Oct. 9, 2020).

Some law enforcement agencies have tried to cram an eleventh round into magazines designed, sold, and used as ones with a ten-round maximum capacity. Some magazines' springs will allow this and still function, even though they are not designed to accept that eleventh round. Though this scenario is unlikely and uncommon, it is worth trying to force an eleventh round into a magazine to see if it is considered a "large-capacity magazine" (explained below).

DOJ attempted to define the phrase "permanently altered" in the proposed emergency regulations for "large-capacity magazines" that it submitted to the Office of Administrative Law on December 23, 2016. Specifically, DOJ's proposed regulations stated that individuals must do the following to "permanently alte[r] the magazine's feeding device" in order to keep the magazine after the July 1, 2017 ban on "large-capacity magazines" was supposed to go into effect:

(1) A large-capacity magazine that is a box type can have its capacity permanently reduced by using both of the following methods

(a) Inserting a rigid magazine capacity reduction device, also known as a magazine block, into the magazine body and then affixing the floor plate of the magazine to the body of the magazine with permanent epoxy. Metal magazines with metal floor plates have the option of being either welded closed or permanently epoxied closed once the magazine block(s) have been inserted. Due to magazine manufacturing variations (such as drum magazines or tubular magazines) it may be necessary to insert multiple magazine blocks in order to reduce the capacity to 10 rounds; and

(b) Once the capacity of the magazine has been reduced by inserting a rigid magazine block into the magazine, it shall be riveted in place through either the floor plate or side wall of the magazine body.

(2) A large-capacity magazine that is a drum or tubular style can be permanently reduced by using any of the following methods:

(a) Drum magazines generally come in two styles: those that are fed from the neck of the magazine (neck fed drum magazines and those that open from the side and are loaded once a lid or cover is opened up (clam shell drum magazines)

(i) A neck fed drum magazine needs a specific number of "dummy rounds" inserted into the neck fed magazine drum and then the "dummy rounds" needs to be epoxied in place in an attempt at reducing the capacity of the neck fed drum magazine. The actual numbers of dummy rounds vary per neck fed drum magazine depending on its original capacity. For example, a 50 round neck fed drum magazine needs 40 dummy rounds epoxied in place so that no more than 10 rounds could be loaded. Once these dummy rounds are permanently epoxied into place the lid shall be closed and also permanently epoxied closed. Due to the internal moving parts of these magazines, a rivet securing the lid or cover is not possible in most cases. Armatac AR-15 style magazines are one example of this type of magazine.

(ii.) Clam shell drum magazines are fed by opening the cover or lid and then loading the magazine. This magazine type cannot be loaded via the neck because of its design. Examples of this type are the AK-47 style Suomi, PPSH 41 and Thompson "Tommy Gun" drum magazines. If the capacity is reduced down to 10 rounds or less, (as described above), and the cover or lid is epoxied closed, the magazine could never be reloaded once the 10 rounds are fired. This magazine type is not a good candidate for reduction to 10 rounds or less and shall be disposed of by other means if not permanently altered as described in this section.

(b) A tubular magazine that has more than a 10 round capacity shall have its capacity permanently reduced by insertion of a magazine block and use of permanent epoxy to hold the block in place. Then, a rivet shall secure the block in place by penetrating the tubular magazine and the magazine block.[134]

In these same regulations, DOJ also attempted to define "large-capacity magazine" for dual tube shotguns. According to the withdrawn regulations, "[o]ne or more magazines each having a 10 round or less capacity, that are then attached to each other with tape, a plastic or metal coupler, or welded together would not be deemed a large-capacity magazine unless one of the following circumstances exist:

(1) The internal magazines of a firearm are part of a design function in which the combined ammunition capacity exceeds 10 rounds, and can be fired by the shooter without manipulating the magazine selector switch. An example of this type of firearm is the Standard Manufacturing DP-12 pump shotgun. If the tubular magazines are permanently altered to reduce their capacity to 10 rounds or less as described in this section, then this firearm would not be deemed a large-capacity magazine.

(2) The internal magazines of a firearm are part of a design function in which the combined ammunition capacity exceeds 10 rounds and the firearm has a selector switch that allows the shooter to alternatingly use ammunition from more than one tubular magazine without having to manually switch the ammunition feeding process. An example of this type of firearm is the UTAS MAKINE LTD., MODEL: UTS-15, pump shotgun which has two seven-round tubular magazines. If the tubular magazines are permanently altered to reduce their capacity to 10 rounds or less as described in this section, then this firearm would not be deemed a large-capacity magazine. Alternatively, if the UTS-15 magazine selector switch was modified so that the shooter had to manually switch the ammunition feed from one tube to another, then this firearm would not be deemed a large-capacity

---

[134] Proposed Cal. Code. Regs. tit. 11 § 5491(b)(1), (b)(2) (2016).

magazine. If a firearm with multiple tubular magazines, each having a 10 round or less capacity, must be manually switched from one tube to the other tube to us each group of ammunition, this type of firearm would not be deemed a large-capacity magazine. An example of this type of firearm is the KEL TEC, KSG shotgun which has two seven-round tubular magazines. While the tubes can collectively hold 14 rounds, the shooter must manually switch magazines. Another example of this type of firearm is the SRM-1216 semi- automatic shotgun that has four four-round tubular magazines welded together. After firing the first four rounds the shooter must manually rotate the quad magazine clockwise to enable firing of the next group of four rounds. If a version of this firearm was manufactured that mechanically rotated the quad ammunition tubes it would be deemed a large-capacity magazine.[135]

Because these regulations were withdrawn following opposition to them by the NRA and CRPA and other pro-Second Amendment advocates, they never became law. Nevertheless, they are a good indication of DOJ's position on the requirements.

2. *Duncan v. Becerra* and California's Attempt to Ban "Possession" of "Large-Capacity" Magazines

In 2016, California enacted Proposition 63 and SB 1446, both of which attempted to ban mere possession of magazines capable of holding more than 10 rounds in addition to the restrictions discussed above. But CRPA, with the support of NRA, filed a lawsuit challenging the new law titled *Duncan v. Becerra*.[136] In June 2019, mere days before the law was set to take effect, CRPA was successful in obtaining an injunction.

Then on March 29, 2019, CRPA succeeded in obtaining a permanent injunction which, in addition to prohibiting the state from enforcing its "possession" ban, also prohibited the state from enforcing its existing restrictions regarding the acquisition of magazines capable of holding more than 10 rounds. This resulted in tens of thousands of California gun owners lawfully purchasing 10+ round magazines for the first time in nearly two decades. It has been estimated that millions of magazines were sold in a matter of days widely known as "Freedom Week" among California gun owners.

The permanent injunction was ultimately stayed pending an appeal to the Ninth Circuit. On August 14, 2020, a three-judge panel upheld the injunction, but that decision likely did not have any immediate effect on the enforcement of the statewide ban previously enjoined by the District Court, in part because the stay that was issued remains in effect "pending *final* resolution" of the appeal. On August 28, 2020,

---

[135] Proposed CAL. CODE. REGS. tit. 11 § 5491(b)(4), (b)(5) (2016).
[136] *Duncan v. Becerra*, Case No. 3:17-cv-01017-BEN-JLB (2017).

the Attorney General requested the case be reheard by a larger "en banc" panel of the Ninth Circuit, meaning that the appeal has yet to be "finally" resolved.

For now, gun owners who currently possess magazines capable of hold more than 10 rounds, whether acquired before January 1, 2000 or during "Freedom Week," can continue to lawfully possess them while the case is pending appeal. Be sure to visit the CRPA website for updates regarding the *Duncan* lawsuit as well as other important Second Amendment litigation in California.

3. Restricted Activity for "Large-Capacity Magazines"

Like most of the items discussed in this chapter, under California law it is generally illegal to manufacture or cause to be manufactured, import, keep for sale, offer or expose for sale, give, lend, buy, or receive a "large-capacity magazine."[137]

Prior to the passage of Senate Bill (SB) 1446 and Proposition 63 (Prop. 63), it was not generally illegal to possess a "large-capacity magazine" under California law.[138] Beginning July 1, 2017, unless you meet one of the exceptions outlined below, it would have been illegal to possess "large-capacity magazines" throughout California. But due to the efforts of our office in the U.S. District Court in San Diego for the *Duncan v. Becerra* case, the enforcement of the ban on "large-capacity magazine" has been enjoined for the time being.[139] At the time of this book's writing, we do not know where the law and our case will end up.[140] You should monitor the status of the *Duncan v. Becerra* case to make certain you are compliant.[141]

Meanwhile, note that violations of this general restriction are treated differently under SB 1446 and Prop. 63. Under SB 1446, any person who possesses a "large-capacity magazine" in California is guilty of an infraction, punishable by a fine not to exceed $100 for the first offense, $250 for the second offense, and $500 for any subsequent offenses.[142] On the other hand, a violation of this restriction under Prop. 63 is treated as an infraction, punishable by a fine not to exceed $100 per magazine; or a misdemeanor, punishable by a fine not to exceed $100, imprisonment in a county jail not to exceed one year, or by both fine and imprisonment.[143]

---

[137] P.C. § 32310(a).

[138] Although it was not generally unlawful to possess a "large-capacity magazine" under California law, some cities, such as San Francisco and Los Angeles, had passed ordinances that made it illegal to possess "large-capacity magazines" within their respective city limits (see below).

[139] *Duncan v. Becerra*, 2017 WL 2813727(S.D. Cal., June 29, 2017, No. 3:17-CV-1017-BEN).

[140] On March 29, 2019, the court issued a permanent injunction against all of California's magazine restrictions, including the restrictions against the acquisition of such magazines. But before California's Attorney General could take the case out of the lower court, the Judge issued a partial stay of his permanent injunction that took effect on April 5, 2019. The stay leaves in place the injunction against California's "possession" restriction but allows continued enforcement of the acquisition restrictions.

[141] You can monitor the case by visiting https://michellawyers.com/duncan-v-becerra/.

[142] *See* SB 1446, 2015-2016 Leg., Reg. Sess. (Cal. 2016), *available at* http://leginfo.legislature.ca.gov/faces/billNavClient.xhtml?bill_id=201520160SB1446 (last visited Oct. 9, 2020).

[143] *See* OFFICE OF THE ATTORNEY GENERAL, FULL TEXT OF PROPOSITION 63, *available at* https://www.oag.ca.gov/system/files/initiatives/pdfs/15-0098%20(Firearms)_0.pdf (last visited Oct. 9, 2020); P.C. § 32310(c).

Prop. 63 appears to trump SB 1446, so any person who violates this general restriction on the possession of "large-capacity magazines" may be charged with an infraction or misdemeanor.

If the restriction on the possession of "large-capacity magazines" had not been stayed by the *Duncan* case, you would have had to do one of the following under SB 1446 before July 1, 2017:

(1) Remove the "large-capacity magazine" from the state;

(2) Sell the "large-capacity magazine" to a licensed firearms dealer;

(3) Destroy the "large-capacity magazine"; *or*,

(4) Surrender the "large-capacity magazine" to a law enforcement agency for destruction.[144]

In contrast, Prop. 63 only provides three different methods for disposing of your "large-capacity magazine":

(1) Remove the "large-capacity magazine" from the state;

(2) Sell the "large-capacity magazine" to a licensed firearms dealer; *or*,

(3) Surrender the "large-capacity magazine" to a law enforcement agency for destruction.[145]

Once again, Prop. 63 appears to trump SB 1446 in this case.

Although it is not included within the new law, an individual could theoretically also lawfully dispose of their "large-capacity magazine" by converting it to a magazine that holds ten rounds or less. At this point, the magazine would no longer fit within the definition of a "large-capacity magazine" because the magazine would no longer be able to hold more than ten rounds. Therefore, the magazine would no longer fall under any of the restrictions above. As further discussed above, DOJ's proposed (and withdrawn) regulations attempted to address this. But, again, the regulations never became law and the possession restriction was enjoined. How this matter will be resolved remains to be seen as of the time of the writing of this book.

4. Restricted Activity for "Large-Capacity Magazine Conversion Kits"

Along with the restrictions on "large-capacity magazines," it is also unlawful under California law to manufacture, cause to be manufactured, import into the state, keep for sale, offer or expose for sale, give, lend, buy, or receive any "large-capacity magazine conversion kit."[146] Notice that unlike with "large-capacity magazines," the

---

[144] *See* SB 1446, 2015-2016 Leg., Reg. Sess. (Cal. 2016), *available at* http://leginfo.legislature.ca.gov/faces/billNavClient.xhtml?bill_id=201520160SB1446 (last visited Oct. 9, 2020); OFFICE OF THE ATTORNEY GENERAL, FULL TEXT OF PROPOSITION 63, *available at* http://www.oag.ca.gov/system/files/initiatives/pdfs/15-0098%20%28Firearms%29_0.pdf (last visited Oct. 9, 2020).

[145] *See* SB 1446, 2015-2016 Leg., Reg. Sess. (Cal. 2016), *available at* http://leginfo.legislature.ca.gov/faces/billNavClient.xhtml?bill_id=201520160SB1446 (last visited Oct. 9, 2020); P.C. § 32310(d).

[146] P.C. § 32311.

Legislature and Lt. Governor Newsom did not attempt to ban the possession of "large-capacity magazine conversion kits." Therefore, possession of a "large-capacity magazine conversion kit" in California is still allowed regardless of our lawsuit.

A "conversion kit" is defined as "a device or combination of parts of a fully functioning large capacity magazine, including, but not limited to, the body, spring, follower, and floor plate or end plate, capable of converting an ammunition feeding device into a large capacity magazine."[147]

Due to the problematic definition of "conversion kit," there is still a great deal of confusion over what magazine parts and/or accessories are restricted by this section. Magazine extenders that are capable of converting an ammunition feeding device into a "large-capacity magazine" are likely to be treated as prohibited "conversion kit" devices under this section. In fact, DOJ's defunct regulations attempted to say as much.[148]

It is also unknown at this time what items will be considered a "combination of parts" of a fully functioning large-capacity magazine capable of converting an ammunition feeding device into a large-capacity magazine. Because "large-capacity magazine" rebuild kits do not really "convert" an existing magazine into a "large-capacity magazine," a plain reading of the law suggests that rebuild kits, *i.e.* parts kits, are not prohibited.

According to the author's statements about the intent of the law, the law was intended to ban the sale of these rebuild kits. The confusion seems to have arisen based on the author's misunderstanding of how a rebuild kit can be used to assemble a "large-capacity magazine," rather than to "convert" an existing magazine into a "large-capacity magazine." If a court finds the definition of a conversion kit is not clear on its face, it may turn to the bill's legislative history for clarification. And while the author's comments alone may not be enough to convince a court that the law applies to rebuild kits, for the time being there is risk of criminal prosecution for transferring them.[149]

Neither the language of AB 48 nor its legislative history suggests that magazines that are not "large-capacity magazines," or their parts, were intended to be restricted as "conversion kits." Due to the ambiguous nature of the law, however, it is difficult to predict how law enforcement agencies and prosecutors will interpret and enforce this section. Nothing in this book is intended to suggest that the law prohibits the sale of any individual part(s), whether interchangeable with a "low-capacity" magazine or not.

---

[147] P.C. § 32311.
[148] Proposed CAL. CODE. REGS. tit. 11, § 5492(a) (2016).

[149] In 2013, the San Francisco City Attorney's Office filed a lawsuit alleging unfair business practices against three online vendors and a gun show company for selling "large-capacity magazine" rebuild kits. The City Attorney alleged that the disassembled parts kits are still unlawful "large-capacity magazines," and that the sellers knowingly assisted in the unlawful manufacture of "large-capacity magazines." Ultimately, this case was settled outside of court, with the vendors agreeing to pay $15,000 and discontinuing the sales of "large-capacity magazines" to California customers.

It is *not* illegal to merely possess a "conversion kit." This means that those who possessed a "large-capacity magazine conversion kit" prior to P.C. section 32311, which took effect on January 1, 2014, may continue to possess them so long as they are not assembled into, or used to assemble, a "large-capacity magazine." Again, be careful. This does not mean law enforcement agencies cannot prosecute you for a "large-capacity magazine conversion kit" found in your possession if they can prove you imported, manufactured, bought, received, or sold it after January 1, 2014.

If you lawfully possess a "large-capacity magazine" that requires repair, the Penal Code expressly authorizes transfers of "large-capacity magazines" to a licensed firearms dealer for repairs.[150] And owners of lawfully obtained "large-capacity magazines" who have parts kits acquired prior to January 1, 2014, are not prohibited from making the repairs themselves.

DOJ's withdrawn regulations also discuss "large-capacity magazine conversion kits," stating that disassembled "large-capacity magazines" that may be "readily assembled" and that "is in the possession of or under the control of the same person is a large -capacity magazine conversion kit."[151] The withdrawn regulations also state that a grip extension whose sole purpose is to increase grip space on the magazine is not a "large-capacity magazine conversion kit."[152] And DOJ wanted to continue to allow those in lawful possession of "large-capacity magazines" to disassemble the magazines for cleaning, maintenance, or other lawful purpose without running afoul of the restrictions on "large-capacity magazine conversion kits."[153] It bears repeating, though, that these proposed regulations are *not* California law. Rather, they may be used as insight to what DOJ thinks the law should be.

5. Local Restrictions on "Large-Capacity Magazines"

Currently, two cities in California – the City of San Francisco and Sunnyvale– have enacted laws that make it illegal to possess "large-capacity magazines,"[154] regardless of whether the magazines are assembled or disassembled.[155] The city of Los Angeles used to have such laws,[156] but it repealed its ordinances in response to the NRA

---

[150] P.C. § 32425.
[151] Proposed CAL. CODE. REGS. tit. 11, § 5492(b) (2016).
[152] Proposed CAL. CODE. REGS. tit. 11, § 5492(c) (2016).
[153] Proposed CAL. CODE. REGS. tit. 11, § 5492(d) (2016).
[154] San Francisco and Sunnyvale both define the term "large capacity magazine" as "any detachable feeding device with the capacity to accept more than" ten rounds, but does not have an exception for a feeding device that has been permanently altered so that it cannot accommodate more than ten rounds, a .22 caliber tubular ammunition feeding device, or a tubular magazine that is contained in a level-action firearm as allowed by the California Penal Code. S.F., CAL., POLICE CODE § 619; SUNNYVALE, CAL., MUN. CODE § 9.44.050(a)(1)-(3).
[155] S.F., CAL., POLICE CODE § 619; Sunnyvale, CAL., MUN. CODE § 9.44.050.
[156] A ban similar to Los Angeles's ban on "large-capacity" magazines was found to be constitutional under the Second Amendment by the United States Court of Appeals for the Second Circuit in *New York State Rifle & Pistol Association v. Cuomo*, 804 F.3d 242 (2d Cir. 2015), *cert. denied sub nom. Shew v. Malloy*, 136 S.Ct. 2486 (2016).

and CRPA's pre-litigation demands in the *Bosenko v. City of Los Angeles* case.[157] Because of this repeal, and because *Duncan v. Becerra* enjoined the state-wide ban on "large-capacity magazine" possession, there is currently no law prohibiting the possession of "large-capacity magazines" in the City of Los Angeles at the time of the book's publication. This may change, though, depending on the outcome of the *Duncan v. Becerra* case.

Meanwhile, the restrictions from San Francisco and Sunnyvale still apply, regardless of the state-wide enjoinment. There are some exceptions to these general restrictions, however. Specifically, the following people and entities are exempt from San Francisco's ban on the possession of "large-capacity magazines":

(1) Any government officer, agent, or employee, member of the armed forces of the United States, or peace officer, to the extent that such person is otherwise authorized to possess a "large-capacity magazine" in connection with his or her official duties;

(2) A licensed firearms dealer;

(3) A gunsmith for the purposes of maintenance, repair, or modification of the "large-capacity magazine";

(4) Any entity that operates an armored vehicle business under the laws of the state, and an authorized employee of such entity, while in the course and scope of his or her employment for purposes that pertain to the entity's armored vehicle business;

(5) Any person, corporation, or other entity that manufactures "large-capacity magazines" for a government officer, agent, or employee, member of the armed forces of the United States, or peace officer;

(6) Any person using the "large-capacity magazine" solely as a prop for motion picture, television, or video production, or entertainment event;

(7) Any holder of a special weapon's permit issued under P.C. section 33300 (permit for "short-barreled rifle" or "short-barreled shotgun"), 32650 (permit for possession, manufacture, or transportation of machineguns), 32700 (license to sell machineguns), 31000 ("assault weapons" and .50 BMG permit), or 18900 (permit to conduct business using, or to possess or transport "destructive devices");

(8) Any person issued a permit under P.C. section 32315 by DOJ upon a showing of "good cause" for the possession, transportation, or sale of "large-capacity magazines" between a person licensed under P.C. sections 26700 to 26915 and an out-of-state client, when those activities are in accordance with the terms and conditions of that permit;

(9) Any federal, state, or local historical society, museum or institutional collection that is open to the public, provided that the large-capacity

---

[157] *Bosenko v. City of Los Angeles*, BS158682, (LA Sup. Ct. 2015).

magazine" is properly housed, secured form unauthorized handling and unloaded;

(10) Any person who finds a "large-capacity magazine," if the person is not prohibited form possessing firearm or ammunition under federal or California law, and the person possesses the "large-capacity magazine" no longer than is necessary to deliver or transport the same to a law enforcement agency for that agency's disposition according to law;

(11) A forensic laboratory or any authorized agent or employee thereof in the course and scope of his or her authorized activities;

(12) Any person in the business of selling or transferring "large-capacity magazines" in accordance with P.C. section 32310 who is in possession of a "large-capacity magazine" solely for the purpose of doing so; *and,*

(13) Any person lawfully in possession of a firearm that the person has obtained prior to January 1, 2000, if no magazine that holds ten or less rounds of ammunition is compatible with that firearm and the person possess the "large-capacity magazine" solely for use with that firearm.[158]

Unlike San Francisco, Sunnyvale only exempts the following people and entities from its ban on "large capacity magazines":

(1) Any federal, state, county, or city agencies that are charged with the enforcement of any law, or use by agency employees in the discharge of their official duties;

(2) Any government officer, agent or employee, member of the armed forces of the United States, or peace officer, to the extent that such person is otherwise authorized to possess a "large-capacity magazine" and does so while acting within the course and scope of his or her duties;

(3) A forensic laboratory or any authorized agent or employee thereof in the course and scope of his or her duties;

(4) Any entity that operates an armored vehicle business pursuant to the laws of the state, and an authorized employee of such entity, while the course and scope of his or her employment for purposes that pertain to the entity's armored vehicle business;

(5) Any person who has been issued a license or permit by the California Department of Justice pursuant to Penal Code Sections 18900, 26500-26915, 31000, 32315, 32650, 32700-32720, or 33300, when the possession of a "large-capacity magazine" is in accordance with that license or permit;

---

[158] S.F., Cal., Police Code § 619.

(6) A licensed gunsmith for purposes of maintenance, repair or modification of the "large-capacity magazine";

(7) Any person who finds a "large-capacity magazine," if the person is not prohibited from possessing firearms or ammunition pursuant to federal or state law, and the person possesses the "large-capacity magazine" no longer than is reasonably necessary to deliver or transport the same to a law enforcement agency;

(8) Any person lawfully in possession of a firearm that the person obtained prior to January 1, 2000, if no magazine that holds fewer than 10 rounds of ammunition is compatible with the firearm and the person possesses the large-capacity magazine solely for use with that firearm; *and,*

(9) Any retired peace officer holding a valid Carry License.[159]

Under Sunnyvale and San Francisco's restrictions, persons who possessed "large-capacity magazines" when these laws went into effect were given a grace period during which they were required to surrender their "large-capacity magazines" to law enforcement, remove them from the city, or sell or transfer them to a dealer with a dangerous weapons permit.[160] But these grace periods have ended.

Moreover, note that San Francisco and Sunnyvale *do not* exempt visitors or people passing through the state from the restrictions on "large-capacity magazines," even if the magazines are in a locked container or the trunk of a car. Therefore, you should be cautious when you are traveling through California with "large-capacity magazines" because although they may be legal in the city you currently live in, you can be held criminally liable for possessing them if you pass into the city limits of San Francisco or Sunnyvale.

Again, these local laws are not currently affected by the injunction on the statewide possession ban. Depending on how *Duncan v. Becerra* plays out, though, these local laws may be affected in the future.

IV. EXCEPTIONS TO CALIFORNIA LAW FOR "GENERALLY PROHIBITED WEAPONS," "LARGE-CAPACITY MAGAZINE CONVERSION KITS," AND THE BAN ON "LARGE-CAPACITY MAGAZINE" POSSESSION

Former P.C. section 12020(b) combined all 32 exceptions to the "generally prohibited weapons" restrictions into one large list. Those exceptions are now laid out as one exception per section number. Unless otherwise indicated, the following

---

[159] SUNNYVALE, CAL., MUN. CODE § 9.44.050(c). Note that currently, only Sunnyvale exempts retired peace officers from the restriction on "large-capacity magazines."

[160] S.F., CAL., POLICE CODE § 619; SUNNYVALE, CAL., MUN. CODE § 9.44.050.

exceptions apply to each of the above firearms, weapons, devices, and ammunition that are considered "generally prohibited weapons" and listed in P.C. section 16590.

As discussed above, when the law was changed on January 1, 2014, to include restrictions on "large-capacity magazine conversion kits," these items were not added to the list of "generally prohibited weapons." Regardless of this obvious oversight, all of the exceptions to the restrictions for "generally prohibited weapons" extend to "large-capacity magazine conversion kits."[161]

It is also important to note that the following exemptions also apply to the general prohibition on the possession of "large-capacity magazines," which would have gone into effect on July 1, 2017 (see above).

A. "Antique Firearms"

An item is not considered a "generally prohibited weapon" if it is an "antique firearm."[162] See Chapter 3 for the definition of "antique firearm" applicable to "generally prohibited weapons."[163]

B. "Curios or Relics"

Certain firearms and ammunition are not prohibited if they are lawfully possessed "curios or relics" under federal law.[164] "Curios or relics" are of special interest to collectors for "some quality other than [those] associated with firearms intended for sporting use or as offensive or defensive weapons."[165] See Chapter 3 for the definition of "curios or relics."

C. "Any Other Weapons"

A "generally prohibited weapon" meeting the NFA definition of "any other weapon" (defined below) is legal to possess if you are not otherwise generally prohibited from possessing these firearms under the GCA.[166]

D. Historical Society, Museum, or Institutional Collection

The "generally prohibited weapons" restrictions "do not apply to any instrument or device that is possessed by a federal, state, or local historical society, museum,

---

[161] P.C. § 32311.
[162] P.C. § 17700.
[163] P.C. § 16170(c).
[164] P.C. § 17705. For example, someone not prohibited from possessing firearms under 18 U.S.C section 922.
[165] 27 C.F.R. § 478.11.
[166] P.C. § 17710. Oddly, it is the NFA, not the GCA, that strictly regulates "any other weapons." It is unclear why the California legislature said GCA instead of NFA, or if it was a mistake. While the GCA regulates who may lawfully possess firearms under federal law (i.e., prohibited persons), "any other weapons," like other NFA firearms, are highly regulated.

or institutional collection that is open to the public," as long as they are "properly housed," "secured from unauthorized handling," and, "if the instrument or device is a firearm, it is unloaded."[167]

In addition, the version of P.C. section 32406 implemented by SB 1446 states that the ban on "large-capacity magazine" possession does not apply to these entities (i.e., "[a] federal, state, or local historical society, museum or institutional society, or museum or institutional collection, that is open to the public"), "provided that the "large-capacity magazine is unloaded, properly housed within secured premises, and secured from unauthorized handling."[168]

E. Media or Entertainment Events

The "generally prohibited weapons" restrictions (other than those for "short-barreled shotguns/rifles") do not apply when they are "possessed or used during the course of a motion picture, television, or video production or entertainment event by an authorized participant therein in the course of making that production or event or by an authorized employee or agent of the entity producing that production or event."[169]

F. People Who Sell Items to Historical Societies, Museums, Institutional Collections, or Entertainment Events

The "generally prohibited weapons" restrictions (other than those for "short-barreled shotguns/rifles") do not apply when they are "sold by, manufactured by, exposed or kept for sale by, possessed by, imported by, or lent by" those whose business it is to sell instruments or devices to historical societies, museums or institutional collections, or entertainment events while "engaging in transactions with those entities."[170]

G. Law Enforcement Firearm Purchases and Those Who Sell to Law Enforcement

The "generally prohibited weapons" restrictions (other than those for "short-barreled shotguns/rifles") do not apply to selling, possessing, or purchasing "any weapon, device, or ammunition" (other than "short-barreled shotguns/rifles") that is used by any law enforcement agency in discharging their official duties. Nor does it restrict their possession by any federal, state, or local peace officers when on duty and authorized by the agency and when the possession is "within the course and

---

[167] P.C. § 17715.
[168] P.C. § 32406(b).
[169] P.C. § 17720.
[170] P.C. § 17725.

scope of the[ir] ... duties."¹⁷¹ The "generally prohibited weapons" restrictions also do not apply (other than those for "short-barreled shotguns/rifles") when "sold by, manufactured by, exposed or kept for sale by, possessed by, imported by, or lent by" anyone whose business it is to sell these items to law enforcement agencies "when engaging in transactions with those entities."[172]

H. Transporting Most "Generally Prohibited Weapons" to Law Enforcement

The "generally prohibited weapons" restrictions do not apply to the *non-firearm devices* listed therein when possessed by someone who is allowed to possess firearms or ammunition (see Chapter 4) if the non-firearm device is possessed no longer than necessary to transport it to a law enforcement agency to turn it in.[173]

The "generally prohibited weapons" restrictions (other than those for "short-barreled shotguns/rifles") do not apply to the *firearms* listed therein when possessed by someone allowed to possess firearms or ammunition, as long as they are possessed no longer than necessary to transport them, in a locked container,[174] to a law enforcement agency.[175] Such persons must also give prior notice that they are transporting the firearms for disposition.[176]

I. Forensic Laboratory

The "generally prohibited weapons" restrictions (other than those for "short-barreled shotguns/rifles") do not apply to a forensic laboratory's possession of "any weapon, device, or ammunition," including possession by its authorized agents or employees, as long as in the course of authorized activities.[177]

In addition, the version of P.C. section 32406 implemented by SB 1446 states that the ban on "large-capacity magazine" possession also does not apply to "[a] forensic laboratory, or an authorized agent or employee thereof in the course and scope of his or her authorized activities."[178]

---

[171] P.C. § 17730(a)-(b).
[172] P.C. § 17730(c).
[173] P.C. § 17735.
[174] As defined in P.C. section 16850.
[175] P.C. § 17740.
[176] P.C. § 17740(d).
[177] P.C. § 17745.
[178] P.C., § 32406(d).

V. ADDITIONAL CALIFORNIA LAW EXCEPTIONS FOR "LARGE-CAPACITY MAGAZINE" AND "LARGE-CAPACITY MAGAZINE CONVERSION KIT" RESTRICTIONS

Recall that since January 1, 2000, it has been generally illegal for anyone to manufacture, import, sell, or give any "large-capacity magazine." And recall that the restrictions on the possession of "large-capacity magazines" in California should have gone into place on July 1, 2017.

In addition to the exceptions for "generally prohibited weapons" discussed above, which include "large-capacity magazines," there are a number of exceptions that only apply to "large-capacity magazines." These exceptions are discussed in further detail below.

When California law was changed in 2014 to add the restrictions on "large-capacity magazine conversion kits," the California legislature did not amend certain code sections to specifically include the phrase "large-capacity magazine conversion kits" and many of the exceptions do not even reference "large-capacity magazine conversion kits." Nevertheless, many of the following exceptions apply to "large-capacity conversion kits." The Penal Code section restricting "large-capacity magazine conversion kits" specifically references the following exceptions for "large-capacity magazines" to include "large-capacity magazine conversion kits."[179] Consequently, the following exceptions to the restrictions on "large-capacity magazines" extend to "large-capacity magazine conversion kits" as well.

A. Law Enforcement Agencies

The general "large-capacity magazine" and "large-capacity magazine conversion kit" restrictions do not apply to selling, giving, lending, importing, purchasing, or the possession of any "large-capacity magazine" to or by any government agency charged with enforcing any law for use in "discharg[ing] . . . their official duties, whether on or off duty, and where the use is authorized by the agency and is within the course and scope of their duties."[180]

B. Use During a Basic Training Course Prescribed by the Commission on Peace Officer Standards and Training

In 2017, the California Legislature added section 32455 to the law to, among other things, provide peace officer cadets with an exception to "large-capacity magazine"

---

[179] P.C. § 32311(a).
[180] P.C. § 32400.

restrictions.[181] Consequently, the general "large-capacity magazine" and "large-capacity magazine conversion kit" restrictions do not apply to:

(1) The sale, gift, or loan of a "large-capacity magazine" to a person enrolled in the course of basic training prescribed by the Commission on Peace Officer Standards and Training, or any other course certified by the Commission; or,

(2) The possession of, or purchase by, that enrolled person.[182]

But, the sale, gift, loan, possession, or purchase of the "large-capacity magazine" must only be for purposes of participating in the course during the period of enrollment.[183]

Also, upon completion of the course, the "large-capacity magazine" must be removed from the state, sold to a licensed firearms dealer, or surrendered to a law enforcement agency, unless an exemption applies.[184] There is a question of how this new law will play out in the context the injunction on the possession of "large-capacity magazines." We know that there is no ban on possession of "large-capacity magazines" as of the writing of this book, and that the injunction is likely to last into 2020. It would appear that in order to still meet the exceptions to the restrictions on acquiring "large-capacity magazines," the magazines would likely need to be transferred. It is also likely that the other exceptions to P.C. section 32310 (i.e., the prohibition on manufacture, import, sale, gift, loan, purchase, receipt, or possession of "large-capacity magazines") mentioned in P.C. section 32455 (*i.e.*, the new law discussed in this section) is in reference to the exception carved out for law enforcement (discussed immediately below). Therefore, if a person does not meet an exception to the restrictions on acquiring "large-capacity magazines" after his or her training is over, he or she may want to strongly consider getting rid of the "large-capacity magazine" at that time.

C. Peace Officers

The general "large-capacity magazine" and "large-capacity magazine conversion kit" restrictions do not apply to selling to, lending to, transferring to, purchasing, receiving, possessing, or importing into this state a "large-capacity magazine" "by a sworn peace officer[185] . . . authorized to carry a firearm in the course and scope of that officer's duties."[186]

---

[181] *See* AB 693, 2017-2018 Leg., Reg. Sess. (Cal. 2017), *available at* https://leginfo.legislature.ca.gov/faces/billCompareClient.xhtml?bill_id=201720180AB693 (last visited Oct. 9, 2020).
[182] P.C. § 32455.
[183] P.C. § 32455.
[184] P.C. § 32455.
[185] As defined in P.C. sections 830-832.9.
[186] P.C. § 32405.

1. Federal Law Enforcement

Prior to the passage of SB 1446 and Prop. 63, federal law enforcement officers were not allowed to purchase or receive "large-capacity magazines" because they were not defined as "peace officers" under California law. [187] For years, DOJ allowed federal law enforcement to purchase "large-capacity magazines," even though they were not exempted from the general restriction. But, after DOJ noticed that federal law enforcement was not included in the general peace officer exemption (see above) a couple of years ago, they stopped allowing these purchases.

Then, SB 1446 and Prop. 63 amended the "peace officer" exception in P.C. section 32405 to include sworn federal law enforcement officers. Now, sworn federal law enforcement officers who are authorized to carry a firearm in the course and scope of their duties may also purchase, receive, and possess "large-capacity magazines."[188]

2. Honorably Retired Sworn Peace Officers & Federal Law Enforcement Officers

The general restriction on the possession of "large-capacity magazines" "does not apply to any honorably retired sworn peace officer[189] . . . or any honorably retired sworn federal law enforcement officer, who was authorized to carry a firearm in the course and scope of the officer's duties."[190]

The term "'honorably retired' includes any peace officer who has qualified for, and has accepted, a service or disability retirement. . . . [it] does not include an officer who has agreed to a service retirement in lieu of termination."[191]

This exception expressed in P.C. section 32406 was added by both Prop. 63 and SB 1446 to California's body of law. But, Prop. 63 and SB 1446 added different versions of P.C. section 32406. Since July 2018, the term "honorably retired" also includes a retired level I reserve officer who meets the requirements specified in P.C. section 26300(c)(2).[192]

Under the section 32406 added by Prop. 63, only authorized honorably retired peace officers and honorably retired federal law enforcement officers are exempt

---

[187] See P.C. §§ 830-832.9.
[188] P.C. § 32405.
[189] As defined in P.C. sections 830-832.9
[190] P.C. § 32406.
[191] P.C. §§ 16990, 32406.
[192] P.C. § 16990(a)(2). P.C. section 26300(c)(2) pertains to a retired reserve officer who (1) was authorized to, and did, carry a firearm during the course and scope of his or her appointment as a peace officer, (2) has an endorsement on the officer's identification certificate stating that the issuing agency approves the officer's carrying of a concealed and loaded firearm, and (3) was a level I reserve officer as described in P.C. section 832.6(a)(1) and has served in the aggregate the minimum amount of time as specified by the retiree's agency's policy as a level I reserve officer, provided that the policy shall not set an aggregate term requirement that is less than 10 years or more than 20 years. Service as a reserve officer, other than a level I reserve officer prior to January 1, 1997, shall not count toward the accrual of time required by this section. P.C. § 26300(c).

from the restriction on possession of "large-capacity magazines." The section added by SB 1446 also prohibited , honorably retired peace officers and honorably retired federal law enforcement officers.[193] Currently, *both* versions of P.C. section 32406 are in existence, and both of them are California law. Despite having the same section number in the Penal Code and saying different things, both delineate the exceptions to the general restriction on the possession of "large-capacity magazines" and need to be understood.

D. Dealer Acquisition

The general "large-capacity magazine" and "large-capacity magazine conversion kit" restrictions do "not apply to the possession, sale, or purchase of any large-capacity magazine to or by a" licensed firearms dealer.[194]

E. Loans Between Individuals

The general "large-capacity magazine" and "large-capacity magazine conversion kit" restrictions do not apply to loaning a lawfully possessed "large-capacity magazine" to any individual who is not otherwise prohibited from possessing firearms (see Chapter 4), as long as the exchange occurs at a location where "large-capacity magazines" are lawful. The lender must also stay in the recipient's "accessible vicinity."[195]

F. Dealer or Gunsmith Loan for Maintenance/Repair

The general "large-capacity magazine" and "large-capacity magazine conversion kit" restrictions do not apply to lending or giving a "large-capacity magazine" to, or possession of that magazine by, a Federal Firearms Licensee (FFL)[196] or gunsmith for maintenance, repair, or modification. It also does not apply to an FFL or gunsmith returning it to the lawful possessor.[197]

G. Importing or Selling Between Out-of-State Clients With a Permit

The general "large-capacity magazine" and "large-capacity magazine conversion kit" restrictions do not apply to those FFLs issued a permit to import, possess,

---

[193] *See* SB 1446, 2015-2016 Leg., Reg Sess. (Cal. 2016), *available at* http://leginfo.legislature.ca.gov/faces/billNavClient.xhtml?bill_id=201520160SB1446 (last visited Oct. 9, 2020).

[194] P.C. § 32410. *See also* P.C. §§ 26700-26915.

[195] P.C. § 32415.

[196] P.C. §§ 26700-26915.

[197] P.C. § 32425.

transport, or sell "large-capacity magazines"[198] between themselves and out-of-state clients.[199] The terms and conditions for these permits can be found on the permit application at the DOJ website.[200] Once the magazine is in-state, in order to be transferred lawfully, another exception to the general restriction must be used (*i.e.*, sell to law enforcement or the entertainment industry).

H. Entities Operating An Armored Vehicle Business

The general "large-capacity magazine" and "large-capacity magazine conversion kit" restrictions do not apply to the selling, giving, lending, possession, importing, or purchasing of "large-capacity magazines" to or by entities lawfully operating armored vehicle businesses.[201]

The general "large-capacity magazine" restrictions do not apply to those entities lending "large-capacity magazines" to their "authorized employees, while in the course and scope of employment for purposes that pertain to the entity's armored vehicle business," or those employees returning them to the business," or to the possession of those "large-capacity magazines" by those authorized employees.[202]

I. Manufacturing "Large-Capacity Magazines" by Law Enforcement

The general "large-capacity magazine" and "large-capacity magazine conversion kit" restrictions do not apply to manufacturing "large-capacity magazines":

(1) By any law enforcement agency for use by their employees in the discharge of their official duties, whether on or off duty, and where the use is authorized by the agency and is within the course and scope of their duties;

(2) For use by sworn officers[203] authorized to carry a firearm in the course and scope of their duties; *or,*

(3) For export or for sale to government agencies or the military per federal regulations.[204]

---

[198] P.C. § 32315.
[199] P.C. § 32430.
[200] *Large Capacity Magazine Permit Application (BOF 050).]*, CALIFORNIA DEPT. OF JUSTICE, BUREAU OF FIREARMS, http://ag.ca.gov/firearms/forms/pdf/CLlcmpapp.pdf (last visited Oct. 9, 2020).
[201] P.C. § 32435(a).
[202] P.C. § 32435(b-c).
[203] Defined in P.C. sections 830-832.9.
[204] P.C. § 32440.

J. Entertainment Industry Props

The general "large-capacity magazine" and "large-capacity magazine conversion kit" restrictions do not apply when a "large-capacity magazine" is loaned "solely as a prop for a motion picture, television, or video production."[205]

K. Purchase by Special Weapons Permit Holder

The general "large-capacity magazine" and "large-capacity magazine conversion kit" restrictions do not apply when a special weapons permit[206] holder purchases or possesses a "large-capacity magazine" to:

(1) Use solely as a prop for a motion picture, television, or video production;

(2) Export pursuant to federal regulations; *or*,

(3) Resell it "to law enforcement agencies, government agencies, or the military, pursuant to applicable federal regulations."[207]

L. Receipt or Disposition by Trustees, Executors, or Administrators

According to the version of P.C. section 32406 implemented by SB 1446, the ban on the possession of "large-capacity magazines" does not apply to the receipt or disposition of a "large-capacity magazine" by:

(1) A trustee of a trust that includes a "large-capacity magazine," *or*,

(2) An executor or administrator of an estate, including an estate that is subject to probate, that includes a large-capacity magazine.[208]

M. Finding and Delivering "Large-Capacity Magazines" to Law Enforcement

According to the version of P.C. section 32406 implemented by SB 1446, the ban on the possession of "large-capacity magazines" does not apply to a person who finds a "large-capacity magazine," if:

(1) The person is not prohibited from possessing firearms or ammunition; *and*,

---

[205] P.C. § 32445.

[206] Special weapons permits are issued per P.C. sections 31000 ("assault weapons" permit), 32650 (permit to possess, manufacture, or transport machineguns), 33300 (permit for "short-barreled rifle" or "short-barreled shotgun"), 18900-18910 (permit to conduct business using, or to possess or transport "destructive devices"), 32700-32720 (license to sell machineguns).

[207] P.C. § 32450.

[208] P.C. § 32406(e).

(2) The person possessed the "large-capacity magazine" no longer than necessary to deliver or transport it to the nearest law enforcement agency.[209]

N. Possessing the "Large-Capacity Magazine" Solely for Use with a Firearm that Is Lawfully-Obtained Prior to 2000 that Is Incompatible with Magazines Holding 10 or Fewer Rounds

According to the version of P.C. section 32406 implemented by SB 1446, the ban on the possession of "large-capacity magazines" does not apply to a person:

(1) (Who is lawfully in possession of a firearm that he or she obtained prior to January 1, 2000, if no magazine that holds 10 or fewer rounds of ammunition is compatible with that firearm; *and*,

(2) Who possesses the "large-capacity magazine" solely for use with that firearm.[210]

We strongly advise you to use this exception with caution. If the ban on the possession of "large-capacity magazines" ever becomes enforceable, law enforcement will likely be suspicious of any "large-capacity magazine" they encounter. Therefore, you may likely be cited and/or arrested for possessing a "large-capacity magazine," and you or your attorney will have to explain this exception to a prosecutor, judge, or jury.

VI. ADDITIONAL EXCEPTIONS TO CALIFORNIA LAW FOR RESTRICTIONS ON "SHORT-BARRELED SHOTGUNS/RIFLES"

There are two additional exceptions to the general ban on possessing "short-barreled shotguns/rifles." Both exceptions, however, are conditioned on you also meeting the requirements to lawfully possess or make an NFA firearm.

A. Law Enforcement Agencies

The "short-barreled rifle" and "short-barreled shotgun" restrictions do not apply to sales to, purchases by, or possession by a "police department, sheriff's office, marshal's office, the California Highway Patrol, the Department of Justice, the Department of Corrections and Rehabilitation, or the military or naval forces . . . for use in the discharge of their official duties."[211] Peace officers who are "members of a police department, sheriff's office, marshal's office, the California Highway Patrol, the Department of Justice, or the Department of Corrections and Rehabilitation"

---

[209] P.C. § 32406(c).
[210] P.C. § 32406(f).
[211] P.C. § 33220.

may also possess "short-barreled rifles" and/or "short-barreled shotguns" "when on duty and the use is authorized by the agency and is within the course and scope of their duties, and the officers have completed a training course in the use of these weapons certified by the Commission on Peace Officer Standards and Training."[212] Though law enforcement agencies are exempt from the NFA tax, they must comply with the other requirements, including registration.

B. Permit Authorization

"Short-barreled rifle" and "short-barreled shotgun" restrictions do not apply when DOJ authorizes the manufacture, possession, transportation, or sale of "short-barreled shotguns" or "short-barreled rifles" by issuing a permit.[213]

A Dangerous Weapons Permit can be obtained from DOJ by submitting an application to DOJ's Bureau of Firearms.[214]

One must have "good cause" for this permit, including showing DOJ that issuing the permit does not endanger public safety. "Good cause" for obtaining a permit relating to "short-barreled shotguns" or "short-barreled rifles" *only* exists when:

(1) The permit is sought for the manufacture, possession, or use with blank cartridges of a "short-barreled rifle" or "short-barreled shotgun," solely as a prop for a motion picture, television, or video production or entertainment event; *or*

(2) The permit is sought for the manufacture of, exposing for sale, keeping for sale, sale of, importation or lending of "short-barreled rifles" or "short-barreled shotguns" to certain law enforcement entities by persons who are licensed as dealers or manufacturers under the NFA.[215]

VII. "SILENCERS"/"SOUND SUPPRESSORS"

The NFA regulates "silencers" (which are considered "firearms" under the NFA), but does not provide a definition. Instead, the NFA refers to the GCA's definition.[216] Under the GCA, a "firearm silencer" and "firearm muffler" "mean any device for silencing, muffling, or diminishing the report of a portable firearm, including any combination of parts, designed or redesigned, and intended for use in assembling or fabricating a firearm silencer or firearm muffler, and any part intended only for use in such assembly or fabrication."[217]

---

[212] P.C. § 33220.
[213] P.C. § 33225 (issued per P.C. sections 33300-33320 and in compliance with federal law).
[214] *Dangerous Weapons License/Permit(s) Application*, CALIFORNIA DEPT. OF JUSTICE, BUREAU OF FIREARMS, https://oag.ca.gov/sites/all/files/agweb/pdfs/firearms/forms/FD030DWapp.pdf (last visited Oct. 9, 2020).
[215] P.C. § 33300. *See also* P.C. § 33220 (providing the approved law enforcement entities for whom "short-barreled shotguns" and "short-barreled rifles" may be manufactured).
[216] 26 U.S.C. § 5845(a) (defining a "silencer" as that in 18 U.S.C. section 921).
[217] 18 U.S.C. § 921(a)(24) (emphasis added).

Certain silencers, and the rifles they attach to, received a lot of attention in the media in late 2017 as being exempt from federal restrictions. These silencers attach to muzzle-loading rifles and, as a result, are not regulated under federal law. This is because most muzzle-loading rifles meet the definition of "antique firearms" under the GCA and NFA and, thus, are not considered "firearms" under the GCA and NFA. In turn, this means that the silencers that attach to "antique" muzzle-loading rifles are not "any device for silencing, muffling, or diminishing the report of a portable *firearm*." Hence, silencers that attach to "antique" muzzle-loading rifles are not prohibited by federal law.[218] This is not the case under California law, though, because California's definition of an "antique firearm" is not as generous as the federal definition.

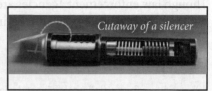

Cutaway of a silencer

"Silencers" are generally prohibited in California. The Penal Code defines "silencer" as follows:

> [A]ny device or attachment of any kind designed, used, or intended for use in silencing, diminishing, or muffling the report of a firearm. The term "silencer" also includes any combination of parts, designed or redesigned, and intended for use in assembling or fabricating a silencer [including] any part intended only for use in assembly or fabrication of a silencer.[219]

Unlawfully possessing a "silencer" is a felony.[220]

In California, "the sale to, purchase by, or possession of silencers by" certain law enforcement agencies[221] or state or U.S. military forces for "use in the discharge of their official duties" is lawful.[222] Members of these law enforcement agencies (provided they are regular, salaried, full-time peace officers) and members of the military may possess "silencers" "when [they are] on duty and when the use of silencers is authorized by the agency and is within the course and scope of their duties."[223]

Also, FFLs and manufacturers (who are also licensed under the NFA) may manufacture, possess, transport, sell, or transfer "silencers" to any of the entities listed above.[224]

Unlike highly regulated firearms and devices (*i.e.*, machineguns, "assault weapons," destructive devices), there is no special permit required under California law to deal in or possess "silencers." You simply have to meet one of the above criteria. As mentioned above, silencers for muzzle-loading firearms are likely to be consid-

---

[218] *See* Letter from Michael R. Curtis, Chief of the Firearms Technology Industry Services Branch of the Bureau of Alcohol, Tobacco, Firearms and Explosives, to Stephen P. Halbrook (Jan. 23, 2017).
[219] P.C. § 17210.
[220] P.C. § 33410.
[221] These law enforcement agencies are specified in P.C. section 830.1.
[222] P.C. § 33415(a).
[223] P.C. § 33415(b).
[224] P.C. § 33415(c).

ered "silencers" under California law. As mentioned in Chapter 3, California law exempts "antique firearms" from a certain list of California Penal Code sections.[225] If a Penal Code section is mentioned on this list, then the section's corresponding restrictions on "firearms" do not apply to "antiques" (because "antique firearms" are not considered to be "firearms" for purposes of these sections). On the other hand, if a Penal Code section corresponding to a restriction on "firearms" is *not* mentioned in that list, then the restriction will apply to all firearms ("antique" or otherwise). And the definition of "silencer" and the restrictions on these devices are not on that list. Therefore, silencers are still considered "silencers" under California law, even when they are made only for "antique firearms."

The practice of attaching homemade devices to the end of a firearm to make it look "cooler" is risky because the device could be considered by law enforcement to be a "silencer." The ATF has reportedly considered simple homemade items, such as copper pot scrubbers used with fiberglass insulation, oil filters, and solvent traps, to be "silencers" when people use them as silencers, which means that they would be subject to the NFA "firearm" requirements. Also, beware that some law enforcement agencies confuse "silencers" with barrel extensions and devices that look like "silencers" (but are not). It is not uncommon for law enforcement to discover a long pipe-like item that might fit on the end of a firearm and incorrectly believe it to be a "silencer." Certain firearms come with or have the ability to install items that have the same outward appearance as a "silencer."

Example of a homemade silencer

I strongly suggest you reconsider keeping items like these. If law enforcement stumbles across them, your attorney will have some explaining to do, usually in the context of a felony criminal case where you are the defendant.

VIII. OBLITERATED OR COVERED SERIAL NUMBERS

Under federal law, "[i]t shall be unlawful for any person knowingly to [1] transport, ship, or receive, in interstate or foreign commerce, any firearm which has had the importer's or manufacturer's serial number removed, obliterated, or altered or [2] to possess or receive any firearm which has had the importer's or manufacturer's serial number removed, obliterated, or altered and has, at any time, been shipped or transported in interstate or foreign commerce."[226]

Contrary to the federal restriction on obliterating *serial numbers*, California's rule is much more restrictive. Under California law, it is a felony to change, alter,

---

[225] *See* P.C. § 16170.
[226] 18 U.S.C. § 922(k).

remove, or obliterate either the name of a firearm maker, its model, the manufacturer's number, or other identification mark on any firearm without first receiving written permission from DOJ.[227] There are no exceptions. This means that if you enjoy modifying and refurbishing firearms, you have to be very careful not to remove the manufacturer's or model's name, and certainly not the serial number.

Even if you are not the one who actually altered the firearm's *identifying marks*, it is a misdemeanor under California law to possess, receive, transfer, or offer for sale any firearm, knowing that the name of the maker, model, manufacturer's number, or other identification mark has been changed, altered, removed, or obliterated.[228] This restriction does not apply to such a firearm being acquired or possessed by any:

(1) State or U.S. military members while on duty and acting within the scope of their employment;

(2) Peace officers while on duty acting within the scope of their employment;[229] *or,*

(3) Forensic laboratory employees while on duty and acting within the scope of their employment.[230]

Nor do they apply to firearm possession and disposition by someone who:

(1) Is not prohibited by state or federal law from possessing, receiving, purchasing, or owning a firearm (see Chapter 4);

(2) Possessed the firearm no longer than necessary to deliver it to law enforcement for lawful disposition; *and,*

(3) Gave prior notice to law enforcement, then transported the firearm in a locked container (as defined in P.C. section 16850) and in accordance with the law to law enforcement for its lawful disposition.[231]

Currently, it is generally lawful to possess a firearm *without* identifying marks because, as explained in Chapter 5, not all firearms must have identifying marks in the first place, *e.g.*, lawfully home-built firearms.[232] Problems arises when already existing identifying marks are altered. But, be mindful of the new regulations on "assault weapons" made by unlicensed persons (discussed in Chapter 9) and the new laws on "ghost guns," which require individuals to obtain a serial number or

---

[227] P.C. § 23900.

[228] P.C. § 23920. At least one court has upheld a conviction for possessing a firearm with an obliterated serial number over a Second Amendment challenge. *United States v. Marzzarella*, 614 F.3d 85 (3d Cir. 2010). Though not a California case, the result here would almost certainly be the same – California's prohibition and your conviction will probably be upheld.

[229] These officers are described in the Penal Code commencing with section 830.

[230] P.C. § 23925(a)-(c).

[231] P.C. § 23925(d).

[232] If requested, DOJ "may assign a distinguishing number or identification mark to any firearm" if it lacks one or if the previous one was destroyed or obliterated. P.C. § 23910.

identification mark for any homemade firearms that they currently own or plan to create after July 1, 2018 (see Chapter 5).

Possessing a firearm with its serial number or identification number covered from view seems clearly illegal under P.C. section 537e. But, since P.C. section 23920 says it is only unlawful if the marks are "changed, altered, removed, or obliterated," it is unclear whether it is legal to *temporarily* cover a firearm's otherwise valid and intact identification marks (*e.g.*, with tape). According to P.C. section 537e:

> Any person who knowingly . . . has in his or her possession any personal property from which the manufacturer's serial number, identification number, electronic serial number, or any other distinguishing number or identification mark has been removed, defaced, *covered*, altered, or destroyed, is guilty of a public offense. . . .[233]

P.C. sections 23920 and 537e seem to conflict because P.C. section 537e covers almost all of the prohibited activity in P.C. section 23920, making P.C. section 23920 somewhat redundant.

When statutes are inconsistent with each other, or when a specific statute covers almost the same things as a more general law does, the more specific law usually applies.[234] This means that since P.C. section 23920 is more specific, it should be followed with respect to firearm identifying marks.

IX. "UNSAFE" HANDGUNS

DOJ maintains the Roster of Handguns Certified for Sale in California.[235] With certain exceptions, California residents cannot buy handguns not appearing on the Roster *from FFLs*. Those not listed on the Roster are legally referred to as "unsafe" handguns, though this description is not factually accurate.[236]

It is illegal for "any person in this state who manufactures or causes to be manufactured, imports into the state for sale, keeps for sale, offers or exposes for sale, gives, or lends"[237] an "unsafe handgun," subject to the limited exceptions discussed below. Simple possession of a handgun not on the Roster is legal. Handguns that you've possessed before the "unsafe" handgun law took effect, handguns you ac-

---

[233] P.C. § 537e (emphasis added).

[234] *People v. Vessell*, 36 Cal. App. 4th 285, 289 (1995); *People v. Jenkins*, 28 Cal. 3d 494, 505-06 (1980); *People v. Gilbert*, 1 Cal. 3d 475, 481 (1969).

[235] DOJ's Roster can be searched by a handgun's make, model, type, barrel length, or caliber, or when the handgun is scheduled to be removed from the Roster. *See Roster of Handguns Certified for Sale*, CALIFORNIA DEPT. OF JUSTICE, BUREAU OF FIREARMS, *available at* http://certguns.doj.ca.gov/ (last visited Oct. 9, 2020).

[236] In 2015, a district court held that the limitations imposed under the Unsafe Handgun Act do not violate the Second Amendment. *Peña v. Lindley*, 2:09-CV-01185-KJM-CKD (E.D. Cal. Feb. 25, 2015), *available at* http://michellawyers.com/wp-content/uploads/2012/06/February-25-2015-Order.pdf (last visited Oct. 9, 2020). In August 2018, the Ninth Circuit Court of Appeals affirmed the district court's order. The plaintiffs have filed a petition with the United States Supreme Court to rehear the case, but the Supreme Court denied certiorari in *Pena v. Horan*, 2020 U.S. LEXIS 3180 (U.S., June 15, 2020).

[237] P.C. § 32000.

quired through PPTs that were not on the Roster, and handguns that might have fallen off the Roster are all still lawful for you to possess, provided they are not illegal for some other reason (like meeting the definition of an "assault weapon").

Depending on the handgun type (whether a revolver or a pistol), handguns must meet certain "safety" criteria before they can be placed on the Roster.[238] Firearm manufacturers must have their handguns tested and pay a fee before their handguns can be put on the Roster, and must also pay an annual renewal fee.[239] The annual fee is due before January 1 of each year. Every year, we have people contact us in a panic because of all the handguns they see dropping off the Roster as of the first of the year. Don't panic. January 1 is just the renewal date. Nothing requires a manufacturer to renew the handgun on the Roster. It is entirely up to the manufacturer to renew the handgun or not.

Typically, if a handgun is not on the Roster, the manufacturer has not submitted it for DOJ testing or has allowed it to drop off the list by not paying the annual fee, or the firearm cannot meet California's so called "safety" requirements because of its design.

In order to be available for sale, the handgun must not be "unsafe." As backwards as that sounds, that is how California law is written. And with the enactment of AB 2847 in 2020, California's definition of "unsafe handgun" has been amended in the context of its microstamping requirement.

In general, the following handguns are considered "unsafe" under P.C. section 31910:

For revolvers:

(1) It does not have a safety device that, either automatically in the case of a double-action firing mechanism, or by manual operation in the case of a single-action firing mechanism, causes the hammer to retract to a point where the firing pin does not rest upon the primer of the cartridge;

(2) It does not meet the firing requirement for handguns; *or,*

(3) It does not meet the drop safety requirement for handguns.[240]

For all pistols (semiautomatic, centerfire, rimfire, or otherwise):

(1) It does not have a positive manually operated safety device, as determined by standards relating to imported guns issued by the ATF;

(2) It does not meet the firing requirement for handguns; *or,*

(3) It does not meet the drop safety requirement for handguns.[241]

---

[238] P.C. § 31910. See also P.C. sections 31905, 31900, 32010 for the requirements.
[239] P.C. § 32015.
[240] P.C. § 31910.
[241] P.C. § 31910.

For centerfire semiautomatic pistols:

(1) It does not have a chamber load indicator;

(2) If equipped with a detachable magazine, it does not have a magazine disconnect mechanism; or,

(3) It is not designed and equipped with microstamping technology.

For rimfire semiautomatic pistols::

(1) If equipped with a detachable magazine, it does not have a magazine disconnect mechanism;

(2) It is not designed and equipped with microstamping technology.

As applied to the above, a "magazine disconnect mechanism" is defined as a mechanism that prevents a semiautomatic pistol from operating while the magazine is not inserted into the firearm.[242] And a "chamber load indicator" is defined as a device that plainly indicates a cartridge is in the firing chamber.[243]

A. "Microstamping" Requirement

The concept of "microstamping" ammunition gained recognition a number of years ago. In theory "microstamping" is the process of laser-engraving a pistol's make, model, and serial number on parts of a firearm, typically its firing pin, so that the information is stamped on the cartridge casing or primer upon discharging the pistol. This means that when the casing is ejected from the pistol after being shot, you can examine it under a microscope and theoretically know what pistol it was shot from. Let's be clear: the addition of microstamping does not make the handgun "safer." This is not a "safety" feature. It is a law enforcement one. Microstamping does not help to prevent the negligent discharge of a firearm.

Since May 17, 2013, California has required microstamping on two or more places on the interior surface or internal working parts of a pistol for it to be approved for sale in California. Consequently, no semiautomatic pistols, barring limited exceptions, have been added to California's Roster since. But with the passage of AB 2847, microstamping will only be required on one or more places of a pistol as of July 1, 2022. Although this change should make it easier for manufacturers to comply with California's microstamping requirements in theory, the reality is that microstamping has thus far proven unreliable and unrealistic to manufacture—if not impossible.

---

[242] P.C. § 16900.
[243] P.C. § 16380.

Such problems are well documented. First, the technology itself was determined to be unreliable by a University of California, Davis, study.[244] Because microstamping is laser engraved on firearm parts, it takes little effort to remove or render impressions illegible. The parts of the pistol microstamping is placed on can be easily replaced with parts that do not possess microstamping. Microstamping was alleged to be a fantastic crime-fighting tool, and proponents of the technology claim that the additional costs of microstamping will only add a few dollars to the cost of firearms. They seem to forget that parts, individually stamped and intended for certain firearms, must be tracked and installed in the specific serialized firearm they are intended for. This type of tracking and matching is time consuming and expensive, especially when you consider that most manufactures obtain different parts of firearms from different manufacturers. Proponents also fail to take into account the problem that, if the microstamped part proves faulty, a replacement must be found (with the same microscopic number) before the firearm can be sent to California.

Casings might also be stamped with multiple numbers before they are considered unusable. Hopefully, law enforcement agents realize that the casing they have at a murder scene only matches your firearm because you used (and left) that casing at a range a year before. Lastly, this technology does not pre- vent a criminal from "seeding" a crime scene with casings from rounds they picked up at a firearm range the day before.

Microstamping also creates problems for pistols already listed on the Roster. Because California law is so poorly written, whenever a manufacturer makes a non-cosmetic change to their firearm, it is viewed by DOJ as a "new" firearm. Under the current interpretation of the "unsafe" handgun law, this "new" handgun must be retested for it to be sold in California. Because of microstamping, these "new" hand- guns cannot be resubmitted for testing and consequently, cannot be sold in California. Ironically, newer, safer, state-of-the-art pistols cannot be sold in California because of California's "unsafe" handgun laws.

Firearms already listed on California's Roster do not need to be equipped with microstamping. However, as a result of AB 2847, anytime a new handgun is added to the Roster after July 1, 2022, DOJ will be required to remove three semiautomatic pistols that were added to the Roster before July 1, 2022, and lack a chamber load indicator, magazine disconnect mechanism, or microstamping technology. The three pistols to be removed will be selected based on their dates of addition to the Roster, beginning with the pistol added on the earliest date and continuing from there. Whether a new handgun equipped with microstamping can be manufactured and added to the Roster, however, remains to be seen.

---

[244] David Howitt, Frederic A. Tulleners & Michael T. Beddow, *What Micro Serialized Firing Pins Can Add to Firearm Identification in Forensic Science: How Viable are Micro-Marked Firing Pin Impressions as Evidence?*, FORENSIC SCIENCE GRADUATE GROUP, UNIV. OF CAL., DAVIS, *available at* http://www.firearmsid.com/pdfs/microserialnumber.pdf (last visited Oct. 9, 2020).

As of the publication of this book, no firearms with microstamping technology have been added to the Roster, let alone manufactured and sold to the general public.[245]

1. "Smart Gun" Technology

Another topic that has received attention recently is "smart gun" technology, which is technology that is intended to limit firearm operability to the owner of the gun through different types of mechanisms.[246] This is unproven technology that carries large risks since most of the "smart gun" solutions include electrical and/or battery-powered mechanisms of questionable reliability, which could prevent the operability of a firearm.

During the 2013 legislative session, Senator Mark DeSaulnier introduced Senate Bill (SB) 293, which would have required that any new firearm added to the DOJ Roster contain "smart gun" technology two years after the date when there were two firearms on the Roster with "smart gun" technology. This recent effort failed; however, there may be renewed attempts to require this type of technology in future firearms.

If the ill-conceived "smart gun" bill had passed, it could have resulted in a requirement that all handguns on California's Roster possess "smart gun" technology."

B. Exceptions to the "Unsafe" Handgun Roster Requirement

Under certain circumstances, you may be able to acquire firearms that are not on the Roster. See below for a list of these exceptions and circumstances where such a transfer may be permitted.

1. Law Enforcement and Military

The restriction on "unsafe handguns" does not apply if the handgun is sold to, or purchased by, DOJ, a police department, a sheriff's official, a marshal's office, the Department of Corrections and Rehabilitation, the California Highway Patrol, any district attorney's office, any federal law enforcement agency, or the military or naval forces of this state or of the United States for use in the discharge of their official

---

[245] As of the date of publication, two separate court cases have been brought challenging the microstamping law. One case lost at the state appellate court level, but the California Supreme Court granted review of it *See National Shooting Sports Foundation v. State of California*, 6 Cal.App.5th 298 (2016), *reh'g denied* (Dec. 15, 2016); *National Shooting Sports Foundation v. State of California*, 215 Cal.Rptr.3d 1 (Cal. 2017). The other case lost at the federal district court level and at the Ninth Circuit, but the plaintiffs are planning to file a petition with the United States Supreme Court. *Pena v. Lindley*, No. 2:09-CV-011185-KJM-CKD (E.D. Cal. Feb. 25, 2015), *available at* http://michellawyers.com/wp-content/uploads/2012/06/February-25-2015-Order.pdf (last visited Oct. 9, 2020). While these cases are being appealed, microstamping is here for the foreseeable future.

[246] *Debate Over Futuristic 'Smart Gun' Technology Resumes as Gun Control Issue Takes Center Stage in National Politics*, N.Y. DAILY NEWS (Jan. 28, 2013, 10:53 AM), http://www.nydailynews.com/news/national/futuristic-smart-gun-technology-gun-control-solution-threat-2nd-amendment-article-1.1249466 (last visited Oct. 9, 2020).

duties.²⁴⁷ The restriction on "unsafe handguns" also does not apply to the sale to, or purchase by, sworn members of these agencies.²⁴⁸

Before January 1, 2014, federal law enforcement was not included in this exemption. Nevertheless, for years DOJ allowed federal law enforcement to purchase non-Roster handguns. That changed in 2013 when DOJ presumably "discovered" federal law enforcement was not included in the exception. Following the uproar from federal law enforcement officers, the Legislature quickly changed the law and included them in this list of exempt individuals.²⁴⁹

2. Purchase of a State-Issued Handgun to Spouse or Domestic Partner of a Peace Officer Who Died in the Line of Duty

The restrictions on "unsafe handguns" do not apply to the sale, purchase, or delivery of a state-issued handgun to a spouse or domestic partner of a peace officer²⁵⁰ who was employed by the State of California and died in the line of duty.²⁵¹ But, these transfers must still be processed through an FFL (when an FFL is required).²⁵²

3. Private Party, Spousal, Operation of Law, Etc. Transfers

The restriction on "unsafe handgun" transfers does not apply to Private Party Transfers (PPT) (as further discussed below), pawn or consignment sales, intra-family transfers, operation of law transfers, or other specifically described transfers.²⁵³ These transfers, however, must still go through an FFL (when an FFL is required), as was discussed in detail in Chapter 5. The return of handguns in these situations is also exempted from the "unsafe" handgun restriction.

4. Specified State Agencies/Departments and their "Sworn Members"

Until January 1, 2021, California law exempts specified state agencies and their "sworn members" who have satisfactorily completed a firearms training course prescribed by the Commission on Peace Officer Standards and Training (POST) pursuant to Penal Code section 832. These agencies include:

(1) The Department of Parks and Recreation;

---

²⁴⁷ P.C. § 32000(b)(4). While this exemption provides for the sale and purchase of "unsafe handguns" to law enforcement and the military, it does not actually say how those firearms are supposed to be imported into the state so that they can actually be sold and purchased. Nonetheless, DOJ has stated that it is implied from this exemption that "unsafe handguns" can be imported into the state in order to be sold to, or purchased by, law enforcement or military.

²⁴⁸ P.C. § 32000(b)(4).

²⁴⁹ See AB 169, 2013-2014 Leg., Reg. Sess. (Cal. 2013) (creating the new exception for federal officers at P.C. section 32000(b)(4)).

²⁵⁰ As defined in Chapter 4.5 (commencing with P.C. section 830) of Title 3 of Part 2 of the Penal Code.

²⁵¹ P.C. § 32000; CAL. PUB. CONTRACT CODE § 10334(d).

²⁵² P.C. § 10334(d).

²⁵³ P.C. § 32110.

(2) The Department of Alcoholic Beverage Control;

(3) The Division of Investigation of the Department of Consumer Affairs; (4) The Department of Motor Vehicles;

(5) The Fraud Division of the Department of Insurance;

(6) The State Department of State Hospitals;

(7) The Department of Fish and Wildlife;

(8) The State Department of Developmental Services;

(9) The Department of Forestry and Fire Protection;

(10) A county probation department;

(11) The Los Angeles World Airports, as defined in P.C. section 830.15;

(12) A K-12 public school district for use by a school police officer, as defined in P.C. section 830.32;

(13) A municipal water district for use by a park ranger, as described in P.C. section 830.34;

(14) A county for use by a welfare fraud investigator or inspector, as described in P.C. section 830.35;

(15) A county for use by the coroner or the deputy coroner, as described in P.C. section 830.35;

(16) The Supreme Court and the courts of appeal for use by marshals of the Supreme Court and bailiffs of the courts of appeal, and coordinators of security for the judicial branch, as described in P.C. section 830.36;

(17) A fire department or fire protection agency of a county, city, city and county, district, or the state for use by either of the following:

　(a) A member of an arson-investigating unit, regularly paid and employed in that capacity under P.C. section 830.37; *or,*

　(b) A member other than a member of an arson-investigating unit, regularly paid and employed in that capacity under P.C. section 830.37; *and,*(18)　The University of California Police Department, or the California State University Police Departments, as described in P.C. section 830.2

(19) A California Community College police department, as described in P.C. section 830.32; *and*

(20) A harbor or port district or other entity employing peace officers described in P.C. section 830.33(b), the San Diego Unified Port District Harbor Police, and the Harbor Department of the City of Los Angeles.[254]

---

[254] P.C. § 32000(b)(6).

(21) (Beginning Jan. 1, 2021) Local agencies employing park rangers described in subdivision (b) of Penal Code section 830.31.[255]

But with the passage of AB 2699 in 2020, several new limits for this exception as applied to "sworn members" of the above listed specified agencies will take effect January 1, 2021. From that point forward, the exception will only apply if the handgun is "for use as a service weapon," meaning the handgun cannot be solely for personal use by "sworn members" of the above listed agencies.[256] What's more, "sworn members" will also be required to complete a POST basic course and a live-fire qualification at least once every six months as a condition of carrying that handgun.[257]

AB 2699 also lists additional state agencies as exempt from California's roster effective January 1, 2021. But unlike the above, sworn members of these newly listed agencies are not exempt in an individual capacity.[258] Instead, only the agencies themselves are exempt, meaning officers of these agencies cannot purchase the handgun in an individual capacity. These newly listed agencies include:

(1) The California Horse Racing Board;

(2) The State Department of Health Care Services;

(3) The State Department of Public Health;

(4) The State Department of Social Services;

(5) The Department of Toxic Substances Control;

(6) The Office of Statewide Health Planning and Development;

(7) The Public Employees' Retirement System;

(8) The Department of Housing and Community Development;

(9) Investigators of the Department of Business Oversight;

(10) The Law Enforcement Branch of the Office of Emergency Services;

(11) The California State Lottery; and,

(12) The Franchise Tax Board.[259]

Under P.C. section 32000 firearms dealers are expressly prohibited from "processing the sale or transfer of an unsafe handgun between a person who has obtained an unsafe handgun pursuant to the exception for specified agencies and their sworn members and a person who is not exempt from the *requirements* of [P.C. section 32000]."[260] The language used in this restriction is somewhat odd. It

---

[255] P.C. § 32000(b)(6)(U) (effective Jan. 1, 2021).
[256] P.C. § 32000(b)(6) (effective Jan. 1, 2021).
[257] P.C. § 32000(b)(6) (effective Jan. 1, 2021).
[258] P.C. § 32000(b)(7)(B) (effective Jan. 1, 2021).
[259] P.C. § 32000(b)(7)(A) (effective Jan. 1, 2021).
[260] P.C. § 32000(c)(1).

seems like the Legislature was attempting to restrict to whom a person could transfer an "unsafe handgun," namely to individuals who fall under an exemption listed in P.C. section 32000.

But, there are multiple issues with the way this restriction is phrased. First, the restriction does not state that a person who has acquired an "unsafe handgun" under the exemptions above cannot transfer an "unsafe handgun" to a person who is not exempt from the requirements of P.C. section 32000 at all. Instead, it states that a *dealer* cannot process these transactions. So, it appears that if the transaction does not need to be processed through a dealer, such as an intra-familial transfer or operation of law transfer as discussed in Chapter 5, then the transaction would not be prohibited under California law. In other words, individuals who obtain an "unsafe handgun" under the exemption above can freely transfer the "unsafe handgun" through operation of law of law or intra-familial transfer.

In addition, it appears that the Legislature may have overlooked that fact that there are numerous other exemptions to the *requirements* of P.C. section 32000.[261] For example, as explained above, PPTs, pawn or consignment sales, and other specifically described transfers are all exempt from the requirements of P.C. section 32000.[262] Therefore, it would appear that a firearms dealer would not be restricted from processing a PPT of an "unsafe handgun", regardless of whether the individual receiving the firearm falls under an exemption listed in P.C. section 32000 because the transaction itself is exempt from the requirements of P.C. section 32000.

In an apparent attempt at enhanced enforcement of the above transfer restrictions, AB 2699 requires DOJ to maintain a database of handguns acquired pursuant to the exceptions, which will include data available to DOJ from purchases and transfers made prior to January 1, 2021. Using this information, DOJ will notify those persons or entities of the prohibitions regarding subsequent sales or transfers.

AB 2699 also requires persons to report any sale or transfer of the handgun acquired pursuant to these exceptions within 72 hours to DOJ.[263] In addition to potential criminal penalties, AB 2699 imposes a civil penalty of up to $10,000 for an unlawful sale or transfer or failure to notify DOJ of a sale or transfer.[264]

Any person who obtains an "unsafe handgun" under this exception must, when leaving their handgun unattended[265] in a vehicle,[266] adhere to the storage requirements stated in P.C. section 32000 (which we explain in Chapter 5).

---

[261] *See* P.C. §§ 32100-32110.

[262] P.C. § 32110.

[263] Processing the sale or transfer through a California licensed firearms dealer will satisfy this notification requirement. P.C. § 32000(e)(2) (effective Jan. 1, 2021). Otherwise, the seller will be required to notify DOJ in a format prescribed by DOJ, which will presumably involve the use of a form which DOJ has yet to develop. *Id.*

[264] P.C. § 32000(a)(2-3) (effective Jan. 1, 2021).

[265] A vehicle is considered to be "'unattended' when a person who is lawfully carrying or transporting a handgun in the vehicle is not within close proximity to the vehicle to reasonably prevent unauthorized access to the vehicle or its contents." P.C. § 32000(c)(2)(C)(ii).

[266] A "'vehicle' is a device by which any person or property may be propelled, moved, or drawn upon a highway, excepting a device moved exclusively by human power or used exclusively upon stationary rails or tracks." CAL.

5. Testing and Prototypes

Firearms sent into the state for testing and employees or agents of entities sending their firearms into the state for testing are also exempt.[267]

6. "Curios or Relics"

Firearms listed as "curios or relics," as defined in 27 C.F.R. section 478.11, are exempt.[268]

7. Repairs

The Penal Code allows for a handgun to be delivered to a California-licensed firearms dealer for purposes of repair. The return of the handgun is also exempt.[269]

8. Pistols Used as Props and Loans to Consultant-Evaluators

Oddly, only semiautomatic pistols are exempt from the "unsafe handgun" restrictions when they are sold, loaned, or transferred to use "solely as a prop during the course of a motion picture, television, or video production by an authorized participant therein in the course of making that production or event or by an authorized employee or agent of the entity producing that production or event."[270] It appears that, according to the California legislature, movies and television productions using revolvers are out of luck.

The loaning and the return of handguns to a "consultant-evaluator"[271] are also exempt from the Roster requirements.[272]

9. Certain Handguns Exempt From the Roster

Certain handguns are exempt from the Roster requirement. All "curios or relics," as defined in 27 C.F.R. section 478.11, are exempt.[273] Single-action revolvers with at least a five-cartridge capacity and barrel lengths of at least three inches are also exempt if the firearm meets any of the following specifications:

Veh. Code § 670; P.C. § 32000(c)(2)(C)(i).

[267] P.C. § 32000(b)(1-2).

[268] P.C. §§ 32000(b)(3); 32110(c), 32110(g). "Curios or relics" are also discussed in Chapter 3.

[269] P.C. § 32110(d-e).

[270] P.C. § 32110(h).

[271] "'[C]onsultant-evaluator' means a consultant or evaluator who, in the course of that person's profession is loaned firearms from a person licensed pursuant to Chapter 44 (commencing with Section 921) of Title 18 of the United States Code and the regulations issued pursuant thereto, for research or evaluation, and has a current certificate of eligibility issued pursuant to Section 26710." P.C. § 16410.

[272] P.C. § 32110(e), 32110(i), 32110(j), 32110(k).

[273] P.C. § 32000(b)(3); *see* Chapter 3.

(1) It was originally manufactured prior to 1900 and is a "curio or relic," as defined in 27 C.F.R. section 478.11; *or*

(2) It has an overall length measured parallel to the barrel of at least 7½ inches when the handle, frame or receiver, and barrel are assembled; *or*

(3) It has an overall length measured parallel to the barrel of at least 7½ inches when the handle, frame or receiver, and barrel are assembled and is currently lawful to import into the U.S. per 18 U.S.C. section 925(d)(3).[274]

Certain pistols designed expressly for Olympic target shooting events are also exempt.[275]

In the summer of 2014, the California Legislature passed AB 1964, which limited the number of pistols exempt from the "unsafe handgun" restriction.[276] Sincef January 1, 2015, the Roster requirement does not apply to single-shot pistols with a break top or bolt action, a barrel length of six inches or more, and "an overall length of at least 10½ inches when the handle, frame or receiver, and barrel are assembled."[277] But, even if a single-shot pistol meets these requirements, it will still be subject to Roster requirements if it is a semiautomatic pistol that has been temporarily or permanently altered so that it will not fire in a semiautomatic mode.[278]

Prior to January 1, 2015, any semiautomatic pistols with a barrel length of not less than six inches and that had an overall length of at least 10 ½ inches when the handle frame or receiver, and barrel were assembled that had been temporarily or permanently altered so that they could not fire in semiautomatic mode fell under this exception. As a result, people could purchase semiautomatic handguns that had been converted into single-shot pistols. Typically, this was done buying the pistol from an out-of-state FFL. That FFL (if he or she has a manufacturer's license) or another FFL (with a manufacturer's license) would then install a longer barrel so that the pistol meets the length requirements for the exception to apply and insert a mechanism to make the handgun a single-shot pistol. This modified single-shot pistol would then be sent to an FFL in California. The California FFL would then note in the Dealer's Record of Sale (DROS) form that the handgun is exempt from these Roster requirements because of its dimensions and because it is single-shot, and the transfer would be conducted like any other handgun transaction.

AB 1964 closed this so-called "loophole" that some Californians used to buy certain pistols not on the approved Roster. As a result, now only single shot pis-

---

[274] P.C. § 32100(a).

[275] *See* P.C. § 32105; Cal. Code Regs. tit. 11, § 5455 (listing exempt Olympic pistols).

[276] *See* AB 1964, 2013-2014, Leg. Counsel's Digest (Cal. 2014), *available at* http://leginfo.legislature.ca.gov/faces/billNavClient.xhtml?bill_id=201320140AB1964 (last visited Oct. 9, 2020).

[277] P.C. § 32100(b).

[278] P.C. § 32100(b).

tols (*i.e.*, handguns that have not been altered to be single-shot) can fall under the "single-shot" exemption.[279]

As a practical matter, DOJ's Roster has greatly limited the number of handguns available for purchase in California, such as through its microstamping requirement that took effect in May 2013. As a result of the microstamping requirement, the DOJ's Newly Added Firearms list has not seen much activity since May 2013, as the microstamping requirement cannot be met by manufacturers of certain pistols. Meanwhile, hundreds of firearms fell of the list since May 2013 and can no longer be sold by retailers in California.

A way for manufacturers to get firearms on the Roster is for the firearm to be "similar" to one already on the Roster.[280] Firearms determined to be "similar" to handguns already on the roster can be added to the Roster without testing. Generally, the changes must be purely cosmetic.

X. AMMUNITION RESTRICTIONS

There are several different types of prohibited ammunition under California and federal law.

A. Ammunition With "Flechette Darts" and "Explosive Agents"

Under California law, it is illegal to manufacture, cause to be manufactured, import into the state, offer or expose for sale, give, lend, or possess ammunition with a "flechette dart" or "[a]ny bullet containing or carrying an explosive agent."[281]

A "flechette dart" is a dart that can be "fired from a firearm, that measures approximately one inch in length, with tail fins that take up approximately five-sixteenths of an inch of the body."[282]

The Penal Code does not say what constitutes a "bullet containing or carrying an explosive agent," only that tracer ammunition manufactured for shotguns does not qualify.[283] One case, however, found a defendant guilty of possessing ammunition with an explosive agent when he possessed a hollow point bullet[284] with a

---

[279] For example, in 2015, DOJ determined that the Franklin Armory model SE-SSP was a semi-automatic pistol that had been temporarily altered so that it will not fire in a semiautomatic mode. Therefore, the single-shot pistol exemption did not apply to the firearm, despite the fact that the firearm was not semiautomatic to begin with.

[280] P.C. § 32030.

[281] P.C. § 30210.

[282] P.C. § 16570.

[283] P.C. § 30215.

[284] A "hollow point bullet" is a "bullet with a cavity in the nose, exposing the lead core, to facilitate expansion upon impact. Hollow point cartridges are used for hunting, self-defense, police use and other situations to avoid over-penetration." NATIONAL SHOOTING SPORTS FOUNDATION INC., THE WRITER'S GUIDE TO FIREARMS & AMMUNITION 9 (2012).

primer[285] wedged into the hollow portion of the bullet and held in place by paraffin wax.[286]

Hence, although undefined in the Penal Code, any ammunition with an additional explosive agent designed to explode after being fired, or once the bullet strikes its target, may violate California law.

Both ammunition with "flechette darts" and ammunition with an explosive agent are listed among the "generally prohibited weapons." The exceptions for those weapons and devices would therefore apply to these two kinds of ammunition, where applicable, as well.

B. Armor-Piercing Handgun Ammunition

Both California and federal law have restrictions on "armor-piercing ammunition." Under the GCA, "armor-piercing ammunition" is:

(1) A projectile or projectile core which may be used in a handgun and which is constructed entirely (excluding the presence of traces of other substances) from one or a combination of tungsten alloys, steel, iron, brass, bronze, beryllium copper, or depleted uranium; or,

(2) A full jacketed projectile larger than .22 caliber designed and intended for use in a handgun and whose jacket has a weight of more than 25 percent of the total weight of the projectile.[287]

The phrase "'armor-piercing ammunition' does not include shotgun shot required by Federal or State environmental or game regulations for hunting purposes, a frangible projectile designed for target shooting, a projectile which the [U.S. AG] finds is primarily intended to be used for sporting purposes, or any other projectile or projectile core which the [U.S. AG] finds is intended to be used for industrial purposes, including a charge used in an oil and gas well perforating device."[288]

Federal law restricts manufacturing and importing "armor-piercing ammunition," unless it is manufactured for:

(1) The use of the U.S., any department or agency of the U.S., any State, or any department, agency, or political subdivision of a State;

(2) The purpose of exportation; or,

(3) AG-authorized testing or experimentation. This exception also applies to importation.[289]

---

[285] "Primer" is defined as an "ignition component consisting of a brass or gilding metal cup, priming mixture, anvil and foiling disc. It creates a spark when hit by a firing pin, igniting the propellant powder." NATIONAL SHOOTING SPORTS FOUNDATION INC., THE WRITER'S GUIDE TO FIREARMS & AMMUNITION 15 (2012).

[286] *People v. Lanham*, 230 Cal. App. 3d 1396 (1991).

[287] 18 U.S.C. § 921(a)(17)(B).

[288] 18 U.S.C. § 921(a)(17)(C).

[289] 18 U.S.C. § 922(a)(7).

Further, those who manufacture or import "armor-piercing ammunition" may not sell or deliver it unless the sale or delivery is also for:

(1) The use by the U.S., any department or agency of the U.S., any State, or any department, agency, or political subdivision of a State;

(2) Exportation; *or*,

(3) U.S. AG-authorized testing or experimentation.[290]

It is also illegal for any federally licensed firearm importer, manufacturer, dealer, or collector to sell or deliver "armor-piercing ammunition" to another person without recording that person's information[291] into the FFL's records.[292]

Under California law, it is illegal for a person or entity to knowingly possess, manufacture, import, sell, or transport "handgun ammunition" primarily designed to penetrate metal or armor.[293] This includes "any ammunition, except a shotgun shell or ammunition primarily designed for use in a rifle, that is designed primarily to penetrate a body vest or body shield, and has either of the following characteristics":

(1) A projectile or projectile core constructed entirely, excluding the presence of traces of other substances, from one or a combination of tungsten alloys, steel, iron, brass, beryllium copper, or depleted uranium, or any equivalent material of similar density or hardness; *or*,

(2) The ammunition is primarily manufactured or designed, by virtue of its shape, cross-sectional density, or any coating applied thereto, including but not limited to, ammunition commonly known as "KTW ammunition," to breach or penetrate a body vest or body shield when fired from a handgun.[294]

Military personnel, police agencies, persons with permits, and other persons listed in P.C. sections 30325 and 30330 are exempt from this prohibition.

1. The Attempt to Ban "Green Tip" Ammunition

In 2015, the ATF attempted to ban M855 and SS109 "green tip" rifle ammunition in 5.56 and .233 calibers when it quietly released a proposal to adopt a new regulatory framework for determining whether certain types of ammunition were "primarily intended for sporting purposes" and therefore exempt from the federal restrictions on "armor piercing ammunition."[295]

---

[290] 18 U.S.C. § 922(a)(8).

[291] 18 U.S.C. § 922(b)(5) ("name, age, and place of residence of such person if the person is an individual, or the identity and principal and local places of business of such person if the person is a corporation or other business entity").

[292] The records are those required to be kept pursuant to 18 U.S.C. section 923. 18 U.S.C. § 922(b)(5).

[293] P.C. §§ 30315, 30320.

[294] P.C. § 16660.

[295] *ATF Framework For Determining Whether Certain Projectiles Are "Primarily Intended For Sporting Purposes" Within the Meaning of 18 U.S.C. 921(a)(17)(C)*, Bureau of Alcohol, Tobacco, Firearms, and Explosives, *available at* https://www.atf.gov/file/11266/download (last visited Oct. 9, 2020).

"Green tip" ammunition has been considered exempt from the federal restriction since 1986, when the ATF held that 5.56mm ammunition fell under the "sporting purposes" exemption because of its well-documented use during target shooting with rifles. Yet, under the proposed framework, "green tip" ammunition would no longer be exempt from the federal restriction because when a 5.56mm bullet is "loaded into M855 or SS109 cartridges," it can be used in AR-platform handguns, which were very popular among firearm enthusiasts.[296] Under the ATF's proposed regulations, "green tip" ammunition would no longer fall under the "sporting purposes" exemption because it could be used in a handgun that was not "single-shot."[297]

Barely a week after issuing its proposal, the ATF began to pull back from its controversial decision to change the regulatory framework and its decision to ban "green tip" ammunition after it has received over 80,000 comments from the public—most of which were very critical of the ATF's decision.[298] Moreover, 299 members of Congress (241 in the House[299] and 58 in the Senate) signed on to letters to the former ATF Director B. Todd Jones urging him to rescind the proposal.[300] Given this opposition, the ATF did not issue a final framework and moved away from their decision to ban "green tip" ammunition.[301]

Although the ATF backed off their decision to ban "green tip" ammunition, gun owners should keep in mind that they are not safe yet and the government may still try to ban this type of ammunition in the future. In retrospect, it seems clear that the ban itself was a backdoor attempt to limit the public's access to AR style firearms and restrict gun ownership.

---

[296] *ATF Framework For Determining Whether Certain Projectiles Are "Primarily Intended For Sporting Purposes" Within the Meaning of 18 U.S.C. 921(a)(17)(C)*, BUREAU OF ALCOHOL, TOBACCO, FIREARMS, AND EXPLOSIVES, *available at* https://www.atf.gov/file/11266/download (last visited Oct. 9, 2020).

[297] For purposes of the ATF's proposed regulations, a "single shot handgun" was defined as "a break-open or bolt action handgun that can accept only a single cartridge manually and does not accept or use a magazine or other ammunition feeding device. The term does not include a pocket pistol or derringer-type firearm." *ATF Framework For Determining Whether Certain Projectiles Are "Primarily Intended For Sporting Purposes" Within the Meaning of 18 U.S.C. 921(a)(17)(C)*, BUREAU OF ALCOHOL, TOBACCO, FIREARMS, AND EXPLOSIVES, *available at* https://www.atf.gov/file/11266/download (last visited Oct. 9, 2020).

[298] *See Special Advisory: Notice to Those Commenting on the Armor Piercing Ammunition Exemption Framework*, BUREAU OF ALCOHOL, TOBACCO, FIREARMS, AND EXPLOSIVES (Mar. 10, 2015), *available at* https://www.atf.gov/news/pr/notice-those-commenting-armor-piercing-ammunition-exemption-framework (last visited Oct. 9, 2020).

[299] *See Congress Halts ATF Attempt to Ban 'Green Tip' Bullets*, NBC29.COM (Mar. 24, 2015), *available at* http://www.nbc29.com/story/28356908/congress-halts-atf-attempt-to-ban-green-tip-bullets (last visited Oct. 9, 2020).

[300] Letter to B. Todd Jones, Director, Bureau of Alcohol, Tobacco, Firearms, and Explosives from United States Senate (Mar. 9, 2015), *available at* http://judiciary.house.gov/wp-content/uploads/2016/02/030415_ATF-Letter.pdf (last visited Oct. 9, 2020).

[301] *See Special Advisory: Notice to Those Commenting on the Armor Piercing Ammunition Exemption Framework*, BUREAU OF ALCOHOL, TOBACCO, FIREARMS, AND EXPLOSIVES (Mar. 10, 2015), *available at* https://www.atf.gov/news/pr/notice-those-commenting-armor-piercing-ammunition-exemption-framework (last visited Oct. 9, 2020).

C. Tracer Ammunition

As mentioned above, any projectile with an explosive or incendiary material or other chemical substance like tracer ammunition (except tracer ammunition made for shotgun use) is illegal to possess in California without proper permits and/or licensing, as it meets one of the state's definitions of a "destructive device."[302] Specific military members, peace officers, firefighters, permit holders, and other groups listed in P.C. sections 18800 and 18900 may possess and use "destructive devices," including tracer ammunition.

For some reason, tracer ammunition is lumped in with "destructive devices" and consequently carries that stigma in California. In fact, tracer ammunition is generally available in most states and can be purchased over the Internet. Firearm enthusiasts, often with no criminal record, unknowingly violate California's law when they are discovered with tracer ammunition they lawfully purchased in another state. Because this ammunition is readily available in other states, it is common for people to not know that they cannot possess it in California.

D. Lead-Based Ammunition Used in Hunting Applications

Federal law limits the types of ammunition that can be used to hunt certain animals. For example, federal law prohibits using lead shot when hunting waterfowl.[303] In addition, California currently prohibits using projectiles with more than 1% lead when hunting big game (deer, black bear, wild pig, elk, pronghorn antelope, and bighorn sheep),[304] non-game birds, or non-game mammals[305] in designated California condor range areas.[306] In California condor range areas, it is also illegal for hunters to possess the combination of:

(1) Lead-based ammunition; *and*

(2) A firearm capable of firing that lead-based ammunition, even if the lead-based ammunition is not being used for hunting.[307]

Different states have different regulations related to the use of lead-based ammunition, but the limitations on lead-based ammunition across the country are generally related to migratory bird hunting or other forms of hunting occurring near some type of water source (*e.g.*, river, pond, lake).[308]

---

[302] P.C. §§ 16460(a) (defining "destructive device"), 18720, 18900 (permit requirement).

[303] 50 C.F.R. §§ 20.21(j), 20.108.

[304] CAL. FISH & GAME CODE § 3004.5; CAL. CODE REGS. tit. 14, §§ 350, 353(h).

[305] CAL. CODE REGS. tit. 14, § 475(f).

[306] CAL. FISH & GAME CODE § 3004.5(a). For the California Condor range, *see Ridley-Tree Condor Preservation Act*, CAL. DEPT. OF FISH & GAME, https://nrm.dfg.ca.gov/FileHandler.ashx?DocumentID=82802 (last visited Oct. 9, 2020).

[307] CAL. CODE REGS. tit. 14, §§ 353(h), 475(f).

[308] *State Regulations*, HUNTFORTRUTH.ORG, http://www.huntfortruth.org/legal/state-regulations/ (last visited Oct. 9, 2020).

CHAPTER 10: OTHER HEAVILY REGULATED FIREARMS AND DEVICES | **473**

By the end of this decade, it will be illegal to hunt in California using traditional lead-based ammunition. In 2013, California Governor Jerry Brown signed a bill into law (AB 711) which required that the California Fish & Game Commission (referred to in this section as the Commission) to enact regulations to make it illegal for anyone in California to take any game or non-game animal with lead-based ammunition.[309] The Commission adopted regulations (as it was required to do by law) shortly after AB 711 passed. As of the date of this book's publication, all firearms used for hunting in California must generally use lead-free ammunition.[310]

1. General Exceptions to the Lead Ammunition Restrictions

a. Possession of Handguns for Self-Defense

The lead ammunition restrictions are "[not] intended to prohibit the possession of [handguns] containing lead ammunition, provided that the firearm is possessed for personal protection and is not used to take or assist in the take of wildlife."[311] In other words, you may carry a handgun that contains lead ammunition while hunting, provided that you are only carrying the handgun for personal protection and it is not used to take, or assist in taking, any wildlife.

b. Temporary Exception for "Calibers" that Are Commercially Unavailable in Non-lead Due to Federal "Armor Piercing Ammunition" Restrictions

The lead ammunition restrictions "shall be temporarily suspended for a specific hunting season and caliber upon a finding by the [California Department of Fish and Wildlife] director that non-lead ammunition of a specific caliber is not commercially available from any manufacturer because of federal prohibitions relating to armor-piercing ammunition . . . ."[312]

This exception attempts to account for the potential unavailability of some "non-lead ammunition" because of the federal restrictions on "armor piercing ammunition" (explained above). As the federal government can declare that a given projectile meets the definition of "armor piercing ammunition" at any time, if a particular "caliber"[313] of certified ammunition is not commercially available because of federal law, this exception requires that the director of the California Department

---

[309] CAL. FISH & GAME CODE § 3004.5(i); Letter from Edmund G. Brown, Governor of California, to the Members of the California State Assembly (Oct. 11, 2013), *available at* http://gov.ca.gov/docs/AB_711_2013_Signing_Message.pdf (last visited Oct. 9, 2020).

[310] It is generally "unlawful to use, or possess with any firearm capable of firing, any projectile(s) not certified as non-lead when taking any wildlife for any purpose in the state." CAL. CODE REGS. tit. 14, § 250.1(d)(3).

[311] CAL. CODE REGS. tit. 14, § 250.1(c)(3).

[312] CAL. FISH & GAME CODE § 3004.5(b),(j)(1).

[313] Unfortunately, the term "caliber" is not defined for purposes of this exception and there isn't really much guidance on what projectiles would even be included. Many bullets of the same caliber can be loaded in different size cartridges. For example, the same .30 caliber bullet can be loaded into a .300 Savage, .308 Winchester, .30-06 Springfield, .300 Remington Short Action Ultra Magnum, .300 Winchester Short Magnum, .300 H&H Magnum, .308 Norma Magnum, 300 Winchester Magnum, 300 Weatherby Magnum, 300 Remington Ultra Magnum, and 30-378 Weatherby Magnum, all of which are distinct cartridges that serve a specific purpose with their unique performance characteristics. *See ATF Framework For Determining Whether Certain Projectiles Are "Primarily Intended*

of Fish and Wildlife temporarily suspend California's ban and allow the use of non-certified ammunition in that "caliber."

Note that this exception does not apply "when taking big game mammals, nongame birds, or nongame mammals in" any California condor range area. This means that this exception will only apply in California Condor range areas when hunting small game.

c. Law Enforcement Engaged in Official Duties Exception

Law enforcement and other government official are exempt from the restriction on lead ammunition, but only if they are "carrying out a statutory duty required by law."[314] This means that law enforcement officers engaging in recreational hunting are not exempt from the lead ammunition restrictions.

2. Penalties for Violating Restriction on Lead Ammunition

Except when waterfowl are involved,[315] anyone who violates the restrictions on the use of lead ammunition can be punished with a fine of $500, and if it is their second offense, a fine between $1,000 to $5,000.[316]

XI. OTHER REGULATED DEVICES

A. BB Guns

California law does not use the term "BB gun" but rather "BB device." A "BB device" is anything "that expels a projectile, such as a BB or a pellet, through . . . air pressure, gas pressure, or spring action, or any spot marker gun."[317] This means that any spot marker gun or device expelling any projectile through air pressure, gas pressure, or spring action will be considered a "BB device."[318] Devices that meet the definition of "BB device" are not "firearms."[319]

For Sporting Purposes" Within the Meaning of 18 U.S.C. 921(a)(17)(C), BUREAU OF ALCOHOL, TOBACCO, FIREARMS, AND EXPLOSIVES, *available at* https://www.atf.gov/file/11266/download (last visited Oct. 9, 2020).

[314] CAL. FISH & GAME CODE § 3004.5(h).

[315] Violations of the federal regulations governing waterfowl can result in a misdemeanor, which can carry a fine up to $15,000 and imprisonment for up to six months, 16 U.S.C. § 707(a), as well as civil penalties and seizure of property, see 50 C.F.R. §§ 11.1, 12.1. In addition to the federal regulations, violations of state regulations can result in an infraction punishable as a fine between $100 and $1,000, or a misdemeanor. CAL. FISH & GAME CODE § 12000.

[316] CAL. FISH & GAME CODE § 3004.5(g).

[317] P.C. § 16250.

[318] P.C. § 16250(a). This is due to SB 199, which was signed into law in September 2014. *See* SB 199, 2013-2014, Leg. Counsel's Digest (Cal. 2014), *available at* https://leginfo.legislature.ca.gov/faces/billNavClient.xhtml?bill_id=201320140SB199 (last visited Oct. 9, 2020).

319 Remember that in order to be a "firearm," there must be combustion. P.C. § 16250. "Firearms" are discussed and defined in Chapter 3.

It's illegal to sell "BB devices" to minors, and no one may loan or give a "BB device" to a minor without permission from that minor's parent or legal guardian.[320]

Example of a "BB gun"

Despite generally being considered a nonlethal weapon, a BB gun used while committing a robbery is a "dangerous weapon," according to a decision by the California Court of Appeal.[321] Under California law, a person who uses a deadly or "dangerous weapon" in the commission of a felony can receive an additional jail sentence on top of the jail sentence they receive for a felony conviction. These are referred to as sentence enhancements.[322] So don't think you won't face serious charges just because you use a BB gun to commit a crime and not a real firearm.

B. Toy Guns a.k.a. "Imitation Firearms"

When discussing "imitation firearms," it is best to start with federal law and work back to California law. Under federal law, it is illegal for anyone "to manufacture, enter into commerce, ship, transport, or receive any toy, look-alike, or imitation firearm unless such firearm contains, or has affixed to it, a marking approved by the Secretary of Commerce . . . ."[323]

Unless there is an exception or the Secretary of Commerce has provided for an alternate marking or device,[324] "each toy, look-alike, or imitation firearm shall have as an integral part, permanently affixed, a blaze orange plug inserted in the barrel of such toy, look-alike, or imitation firearm. Such plug shall be recessed no more than 6 millimeters from the muzzle end of the bar-rel of such firearm."[325]

A "'look-alike firearm' means any imitation of any original firearm which was manufactured, designed, and produced since 1898, including and limited to toy guns, water guns, replica nonguns, and airsoft guns firing nonmetallic projectiles."[326] A "look-alike firearm" does not include "any look-alike, nonfiring, collector replica of an antique firearm developed prior to 1898, or traditional BB, paint-ball, or pellet-firing air guns that expel a projectile through the force of air pressure."[327] That is

---

[320] P.C. §§ 19910, 19915.
[321] *In re Bartholomew D.*, 131 Cal. App. 4th 317, 322-26 (2005).
[322] P.C. § 12022(b).
[323] 15 U.S.C. § 5001(a).
[324] The Secretary of Commerce has promulgated a number of regulations concerning alternate markings and identifies how to request a waiver from the marking requirement if you seek to use an imitation firearm in the entertainment industry. *See* 15 U.S.C. § 50001(b)(2);15 C.F.R. §§ 272.1-272.5.
[325] 15 U.S.C. § 5001(b)(1).
[326] 15 U.S.C. § 5001(c).
[327] 15 U.S.C. § 5001(c).

why certain airsoft guns need the orange tips while BB guns that fire metallic pellets do not, despite looking in all other respects identical.

Going back to California law, an "imitation firearm" is "any BB device, toy gun, replica of a firearm, or other device [including "a protective case for a cellular telephone"] that is so substantially similar" in color and overall appearance to an existing firearm that a reasonable person would think it is a firearm.[328]

Anyone who modifies an "imitation firearm" to look more like a firearm is guilty of a misdemeanor.[329] This does not apply to manufacturers, importers, or imitation firearm distributors or those who lawfully use imitation firearms for theatrical, film, or television productions.[330] Manufacturers, importers, or distributors of imitation firearms who fail to comply with federal law or regulations relating to the markings of "a toy, look-alike, or imitation firearm (discussed above) can be prosecuted criminally under California law.[331]

California puts additional burdens on those who purchase, sell, manufacture, ship, transport, distribute, or receive (by mail order or in any other manner) "imitation firearms" for commercial purposes, unless the firearm is:

(1) Only for "export" (interstate or internationally) in commerce;

(2) Only "for lawful use in theatrical productions, including motion picture, television, and stage productions";

(3) For "a certified or regulated sporting event or competition";

(4) For "military or civil defense activities, or ceremonial activities"; *or,*

(5) For public displays authorized by public or private schools.[332]

But, these restrictions (relating to the purchase, sale, manufacture, shipping, transporting, distribution, or receipt of "imitation firearms" in P.C. section 20165) do not include: non-firing collector's replicas that are "historically significant and offered for sale in conjunction with a wall plaque or presentation case"; a *"BB device"*; or a "device where the entire exterior surface of the device is white, bright red, bright orange, bright yellow, bright green, bright blue, bright pink, or bright purple, either" by itself or predominantly "with other colors in any pattern, as provided by federal regulations governing imitation firearms, or where the entire device is constructed of transparent or translucent materials that permit unmistakable observation of the device's complete contents, as provided by federal regulations governing imitation firearms."[333]

---

[328] P.C. § 16700(a)(1-2).
[329] P.C. § 20150(a).
[330] P.C. § 20150(b-c).
[331] P.C. § 20155.
[332] P.C. § 20165.
[333] P.C. § 16700(b).

Yet, only the following types of BB devices will be exempt from the restrictions on the purchase, sale, manufacture, shipment, transportation, distribution, or receipt (by mail order or in any other manner) of "imitation firearms" for commercial purposes under P.C. section 20165:

(1) A BB device that expels a projectile that is neither 6mm nor 8mm caliber;

(2) A BB device that is an airsoft gun expelling a 6mm or 8 mm caliber projectile, only if it has the blaze orange ring on the barrel required by federal law, a trigger guard entirely covered in fluorescent colors; *or*

(3) If it is configured as a handgun, a two-centimeter-wide adhesive band[334] around the circumference of a fluorescently-colored protruding pistol grip; *or,*

(4) If it is configured as a rifle or long gun, a two centimeter wide adhesive band[335] around the circumference of any two of the following: the protruding pistol grip, the buttstock, or a protruding ammunition magazine or clip.[336]

Also as of January 1, 2016, spot marker guns that expel a projectile greater than 10 mm caliber will be exempt from these restrictions, as they too will not be considered to be "imitation firearms for purposes of P.C. section 20165."[337] As will "a nonfiring collector's replica that is historically significant, and is offered for sale in conjunction with a wall plaque or presentation case."[338]

While we may think we know what an "airsoft gun" is, the Legislature did not do the California public and retailers any favors in defining the term. It is still not yet known what items the Legislature meant to regulate as "airsoft guns" and what items are covered under this restriction. This is yet another example of the legislators in Sacramento, and particularly Senator de León (again), drafting legislation that does not provide a clear indication of what is legal or illegal in California.

Finally, a person cannot openly display or expose an "imitation firearm" in a "public place"[339] unless it is:

(1) Packaged or concealed so it is not subject to public viewing;

(2) Displayed or exposed for commerce, including commercial film or video productions, or for service, repair, or restoration;

---

[334] This adhesive band needs to be in place before the BB device is sold to a customer and must be applied in a manner where it is not intended for removal. P.C. § 16700(c).

[335] This adhesive band needs to be in place before the BB device is sold to a customer and must be applied in a manner where it is not intended for removal. P.C. § 16700(c).

[336] P.C. § 16700(b)(3), 16700(b)(4), 16700(d). This is due to the passing of SB 199. *See* SB 199, 2013-2014, Leg. Counsel's Digest (Cal. 2014) *available at* https://leginfo.legislature.ca.gov/faces/billNavClient.xhtml?bill_id=201320140SB199 (last visited Oct. 9, 2020).

[337] P.C. § 16700(b)(2), 16700(b)(2).

[338] P.C. § 16700(b)(1), 16700(b)(1).

[339] A "public place" is any "area open to the public" including streets; sidewalks; bridges; alleys; plazas; parks; driveways; front yards; parking lots; automobiles, whether moving or not; buildings open to the general public, including those that serve food or drink or provide entertainment; and the doorways and entrances to buildings or dwellings, including public schools and colleges or universities. P.C. § 20170(b).

(3) Used for a theatrical, movie, video, television, or stage production;

(4) Used in conjunction with a certified or regulated sporting event or competition;

(5) Used in conjunction with lawful hunting or pest-control activities;

(6) Used or possessed at a certified or regulated shooting range;

(7) Used at a fair, exhibition, exposition, or other similar activity for which the proper permits have been obtained;

(8) Used in military, civil defense, or civic activities, including flag ceremonies, color guards, parades, award presentations, historical reenactments, and memorials;

(9) Used for public displays authorized by any school or museum;

(10) Used in a parade, ceremony, or other similar activity for which proper permits have been obtained;

(11) Displayed on a wall plaque or in a presentation case;

(12) Used where discharging a firearm is lawful; or,

(13) "The entire exterior surface of the imitation firearm is white, bright red, bright orange, bright yellow, bright green, bright blue, bright pink, or bright purple," either by itself or mainly with other colors, or "the entire device is constructed of transparent or translucent material that permits unmistakable observation of the device's complete contents." Merely having an orange tip is not enough. "The entire surface must be colored or transparent or translucent."[340]

Also, even if you meet one of the above "displaying" exceptions, you may still be prosecuted for possessing the device[341] at a state or local public building or meeting,[342] in an airport,[343] or on school grounds.[344]

C. "Tear Gas," "Less Lethal Weapons," and "Stun Guns"

1. "Tear Gas," Pepper Spray, and Mace

"Tear gas" is a catch-all term in California that "includes any liquid, gaseous or solid substance intended to produce temporary physical discomfort or permanent

---

[340] P.C. § 20175.

[341] *See* P.C. § 20180(c) ("[n]othing in Section 20170, 20175, or this section shall be construed to preclude prosecution for a violation of Section 171b, 171.5, or 626.10").

[342] P.C. § 171b.

[343] P.C. § 171.5.

[344] P.C. § 626.10.

injury through being vaporized or otherwise dispersed in the air."[345] Obviously, "tear gas" includes items like mace and pepper spray.

A "tear gas weapon" is:

Example of pepper spray

(1) Any shell, cartridge, or bomb capable of being discharged or exploded, when the discharge or explosion will cause or permit the release or emission of tear gas; *or*,

(2) Any revolver, pistol, fountain pen gun, billy, or other form of device, portable or fixed, intended for the projection or release of tear gas, except those regularly manufactured and sold for use with firearm ammunition.[346]

Most people may purchase and use "tear gas" and "tear gas weapons" (the devices must only expel the "tear gas" by aerosol spray and have no more than two and a half ounces net weight of aerosol spray)[347] if they use them for self-defense purposes. Using "tear gas" or a "tear gas weapon" for a purpose other than self-defense is a crime.[348] The following people, however, are prohibited from purchasing, possessing, or using "tear gas" or "tear gas weapons":

(1) Persons convicted of a felony or any crime involving an assault;

(2) Those convicted of misusing tear gas; *or*,

(3) Persons addicted to any narcotic drug.[349]

It is further unlawful for minors to possess a "tear gas weapon" and for people to sell or give "tear gas" or a "tear gas weapon" to a minor unless the minor is at least age 16 and is accompanied by, or has written consent from, a parent or guardian.[350] Parents, legal guardians, or other persons who allow minors over age 16 to possess "tear gas" may, however, be civilly liable if the minor misuses it.[351]

Many "tear gas" devices on the market store their contents in a form other than aerosol spray. It is questionable whether these devices are legal for ordinary citizens to possess in California.

---

[345] P.C. § 17240(a). "Tear gas" does not include substances such as an "economic poison," as listed in the Food and Agricultural Code sections 12751-13192, "provided that the substance is not intended to be used to produce discomfort or injury to human beings." P.C. § 17240(b).

[346] P.C. § 17250.

[347] P.C. § 22810(e)(1).

[348] P.C. § 22810(g).

[349] P.C. § 22810(a-b).

[350] P.C. §§ 22810(c-d), 22815(a-b).

[351] P.C. § 22815(c) This encompasses persons who authorized the provision of tear gas to a minor by signing a statement of consent or accompanying the minor when he or she obtained the tear gas or tear gas..

Specified peace officers, custodial officers, military personnel, and private investigators/patrol guards are exempt from "tear gas" and "tear gas weapon" restrictions.[352]

For additional laws about permissible "tear gas" amounts that may be possessed, warning label and instruction requirements, and permits for using "tear gas" for anything other than self-defense, see P.C. sections 22810-23025.

2. "Less Lethal Weapons"

A "less lethal weapon" is any device "designed to or that has been converted to expel or propel less lethal ammunition[353] by any action, mechanism, or process for the purpose of incapacitating, immobilizing, or stunning a human being through the infliction of any less than lethal impairment of physical condition, function, or senses, including physical pain or discomfort.[354] It is unnecessary for the weapon to "leave any lasting or permanent incapacitation, discomfort, pain, or other injury or disability to be a less lethal weapon."[355]

A "less lethal weapon" includes the weapon's frame or receiver "but does not include any of the following unless the part or weapon has been converted" as described in the previous paragraph:

(1) A pistol, revolver, or firearm;

(2) A machinegun;

(3) A rifle or shotgun using fixed ammunition consisting of standard primer and powder and not capable of being concealed upon the person;

(4) A pistol, rifle, or shotgun that is a firearm having a barrel less than 0.18 inches in diameter and that is designed to expel a projectile by any mechanical means or by compressed air or gas;

(5) When used as designed or intended by the manufacturer, any weapon that is commonly regarded as a toy gun, and that as a toy gun is incapable of inflicting any impairment of physical condition, function, or senses;

(6) A "destructive device";

(7) A "tear gas weapon";

(8) A bow or crossbow designed to shoot arrows;

---

[352] P.C. §§ 22820, 22825, 22830, 22835.

[353] "Less lethal ammunition" is any ammunition "designed to be used in any less than lethal weapon or any other kind of weapon (including . . . any firearm, pistol, revolver, shotgun, rifle, or spring, compressed air, or compressed gas weapon)" and, "[w]hen used in . . . [any] weapon, it is designed to immobilize, incapacitate, or stun a human being through the infliction of any less than lethal impairment of physical condition, function, or senses, including physical pain or discomfort." P.C. § 16770.

[354] P.C. § 16780(a).

[355] P.C. § 16780(a).

(9) A device commonly known as a slingshot;

(10) A device designed for the firing of stud cartridges, explosive rivets, or similar industrial ammunition;

(11) A device designed for signaling, illumination, or safety; or,

(12) An "assault weapon."[356]

Selling a "less lethal weapon" to anyone under the age of 18 years is a misdemeanor.[357]

3. "Stun Guns"

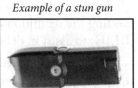

Example of a stun gun

A "stun gun" is "any item except a less lethal weapon used or intended to be used as either an offensive or defensive weapon that is capable of temporarily immobilizing a person by the infliction of an electrical charge."[358] A "stun gun" is not a "less lethal weapon."

As with "tear gas weapons," most people may purchase, possess, and use a "stun gun." But, the following people cannot:

(1) Those convicted of a felony, misusing a stun gun, or any crime involving an assault;

(2) Those addicted to narcotic drugs; or,

(3) Minors (it is illegal for you to sell or furnish a "stun gun" to a minor and it is illegal for a minor to possess a "stun gun" unless the minor is age 16 or older and has written parental or legal guardian consent).[359]

D. "Blowguns"

A "blowgun" is a hollow tube through which a dart is propelled by force of breath.[360] "Blowgun ammunition" is the "dart designed and intended for use in [the] blowgun."[361]

Unless an individual falls under an exception,[362] manufacturing, selling, offering for sale, possessing, or using a "blowgun" or "blowgun ammunition" is unlawful in California.[363]

---

[356] P.C. § 16780(b).
[357] P.C. § 19405.
[358] P.C. § 17230.
[359] P.C. § 22610 (referencing P.C. section 244.5 governing stun gun misuse).
[360] P.C. § 16270.
[361] P.C. § 16280.
[362] This includes zookeepers, animal control officers, Fish and Game personnel, certain humane officers, and veterinarians "in the course and scope of their business in order to administer medicine to animals." P.C. § 20015.
[363] P.C. § 20010.

E. 3D-Printed Guns

3D-printed firearms, as discussed in Chapter 5, may also have restrictions under California and federal law based on their design and how they are made. You should exercise caution in making, obtaining, or possessing these types of firearms since their specifications could make them subject to some of the prohibitions and restrictions discussed in this chapter.

First, they may be subject to the "undetectable firearms" laws depending on the material they are made of. Both California and federal law contain provisions requiring firearms to be detectable in walk-through metal detectors and x-ray machines commonly used at airports.[364]

Second, under California law, a 3D-printed firearm also has the potential of meeting the definition of a "zip gun." See the discussion of "zip guns" in Section (III)(H) to assist in determining whether your firearm is compliant.

Third, a 3D-printed firearm could be considered an "unconventional pistol," which is a prohibited weapon under California law as discussed above. It is unclear from the information available about these firearms whether they have a rifled bore or instead have a smooth bore. Therefore, depending on the length of the 3D-printed firearm, it could fall under the definition of an "unconventional pistol."

In 2013, a bill was introduced in Congress that attempted to regulate these types of firearms, but the bill failed to pass out of the federal legislature.[365] But, California law requires these firearms to be registered and will require permission to be obtained before they are made.[366]

F. Sniperscopes (Night Vision Scopes) and Laser Scopes or Laser Pointers

It is illegal to knowingly buy, sell, receive, dispose of, conceal, or have in your possession a "sniperscope" under California law.[367]

---

[364] *See* P.C. §§ 24610, 17280(a); 18 U.S.C. § 922(p)(1)(A) (discussed above).

[365] *See* H.R. 1474, 113th Cong. (2013). *See also* H.R. 3626, 113th Cong. (2013). On December 2, 2013, the House of Representatives passed H.R. 3626, which extends the Undetectable Firearms Act of 1988 for ten more years without tightening any of the restrictions already outlined in the Act. Kasie Hunt & Carrie Dann, *Senate to Vote on Extension of Undetectable Gun Ban*, NBCNEWS.COM (Dec. 9, 2013, 11:16 PM), http://www.nbcnews.com/news/other/senate-extends-ban-undetectable-guns-nixes-tighter-restrictions-f2D11717122 (last visited Oct. 9, 2020). The Act restricts the manufacture, sale, and possession of guns that cannot be detected by x-ray machines or metal detectors, as discussed above in Section III(C) of this chapter. Democrats, however, have tried to tack on language to the bill that would create tighter restrictions on plastic weapons produced by 3D-printing technology because, as they argue, under the current law gun makers can easily meet the Act's requirements by simply adding an easily detachable metal piece to the firearm. Kasie Hunt & Carrie Dann, *Senate to Vote on Extension of Undetectable Gun Ban*, NBCNEWS.COM (Dec. 9, 2013, 1:16 PM), http://www.nbcnews.com/news/other/senate-extends-ban-undetectable-guns-nixes-tighter-restrictions-f2D11717122(last visited Oct. 9, 2020). On December 9, 2013, the Senate passed H.R. 3626 with unanimous consent, and President Barack Obama signed the bill into law the same day.

[366] *See* P.C. sections 29180 through 29184.

[367] P.C. § 468.

Although the term "sniperscope" might sound broad, California law defines it very narrowly and not in a way that you would think. A "sniperscope" is "any attachment, device or similar contrivance designed for or adaptable to use on a firearm which, through the use of a projected infrared light source and electronic telescope, enables the operator thereof to visually determine and locate the presence of objects during the nighttime."[368]

The restrictions on "sniperscopes" do not apply to "member[s] of the armed forces of the United States or [to] police officers, peace officers, or law enforcement officers authorized by the properly constituted authorities for the enforcement of law or ordinances" when they are authorized to use or possess "sniperscopes."[369] The restriction also does not extend to the use or possession of "sniperscopes" "when used solely for scientific research or educational purposes."[370]

The language of this restriction is odd because there are a number of similar scopes that do not meet the definition of a "sniperscope." This is likely because P.C. section 468 was enacted in 1958. At that time technology like electronic scopes that project infrared light enabling a person to see objects at night was, no doubt, cutting edge technology. But there have been great strides in firearm optics since that time. There are a variety of low soluble light or nighttime rifle scopes that do not require the use of a projected infrared light to illuminate a target. Nevertheless, one should be mindful as some modern scopes do have an infrared light source and others have the ability to turn on an infrared light in low-light conditions. Additionally, some scopes come with a laser range finder. These are not an "infrared light source" and are not intended to allow the operator to "visually determine and locate the presence of objects during the nighttime." Lastly, infrared lasers are also used as sights for handguns and rifles that project a small dot on the intended target. These sights, of course, do not possess an electronic telescope or assist in nighttime vision.

Every person who aims or points a "laser scope" or "laser pointer" "at another person in a threatening manner with the specific intent to cause a reasonable person fear of bodily harm," except in self-defense, is in violation of California law.[371] In other words, the possession of these items is lawful. A person runs afoul of California law only when these items are used to threaten another person with the intent to give that person a "fear of bodily harm." The laser scope does not need to be attached to a firearm to be used illegally.

Under this law, a "laser scope" is "a portable battery-powered device capable of being attached to a firearm and capable of projecting a laser light on objects at a distance."[372] And a "laser pointer" is "any hand held laser beam device or demon-

---

[368] P.C. § 468.
[369] P.C. § 468.
[370] P.C. § 468.
[371] P.C. § 417.25(a).
[372] P.C. § 417.25(b).

stration laser product that emits a single point of light amplified by the stimulated emission of radiation that is visible to the human eye."[373]

XII. NATIONAL FIREARMS ACT – FIREARM POSSESSION

Unlike California law, federal law allows those who can lawfully possess firearms to possess certain "machineguns," "destructive devices," "short-barreled shotguns/rifles," "silencers," and "any other weapons" – also known as "NFA firearms."

A. "Any Other Weapon" Defined

Although "machineguns," "destructive devices," "short-barreled shotguns/rifles," and "silencers" are all regulated under California law (discussed above), the "any other weapons" category is unique to the NFA. The NFA defines "any other weapon" as:

(1) Any weapon or device capable of being concealed on the person from which a shot can be discharged through the energy of an explosive;

(2) A pistol or a revolver having a barrel with a smooth bore designed or redesigned to fire a fixed shotgun shell;

(3) Weapons less than 18 inches in total length with combined shotgun and rifle barrels of 12 inches or more "from which only a single discharge can be made from either barrel without manual reloading"; or,

(4) Any weapon described above that may be readily restored to fire.[374]

"Any other weapon" does not include pistols or revolvers[375] with rifled bores or weapons for firing from the shoulder "and not capable of firing fixed ammunition" (e.g., a blunderbuss or musket).[376] This means these firearms cannot be considered and regulated as "any other weapons."

Be careful, handguns with forward grips may meet the definition of "any other weapon" (in addition to possibly meeting the "assault weapon" definition discussed in Chapter 9).[377] Despite the fact that these handguns meet the general definition of "pistol" and "revolver" under California law (see Chapter 3), they likely are not "pistols" or "revolvers" under the federal definition because they are no longer de-

---

[373] P.C. § 417.25(c).

[374] 26 U.S.C. § 5845(e).

[375] According to 27 C.F.R. section 479.11, a "pistol" is "[a] weapon originally designed, made, and intended to fire a projectile (bullet) from one or more barrels when held in one hand, and having (a) a chamber(s) as an integral part(s) of, or permanently aligned with, the bore(s); and (b) a short stock designed to be gripped by one hand and at an angle to and extending below the line of the bore(s)." A "revolver" is "[a] projectile weapon, of the pistol type, having a breechloading chambered cylinder so arranged that the cocking of the hammer or movement of the trigger rotates it and brings the next cartridge in line with the barrel for firing." 27 C.F.R. § 479.11.

[376] 26 U.S.C. § 5845(e).

[377] See U.S. Dept. of Justice, Bureaus of Alcohol, Tobacco, Firearms, and Explosives, ATF National Firearms Act Handbook 9 (2009).

signed, made, or intended to fire a projectile when "held in one hand," which is a precondition to being a "pistol" or "revolver."[378] But they still fall under the definition of "any other weapon" since they *are* firearms with rifled bores that are "capable of being concealed on the person."

Nail guns may also fall under the definition of "any other weapon" if they are used as weapons.[379]

Unlike other NFA firearms ("machineguns," "silencers," "short-barreled shotguns/rifles"), most items meeting the "any other weapon" definition *can* be possessed, imported, or transferred (to persons age 21 or older) in California as long as they satisfy the respective NFA requirements.

B. Transferring NFA Firearms

To transfer an NFA firearm, you must be the registered owner of the firearm, file the proper ATF forms, and make sure the applicable transfer tax is paid.[380] The ATF must also approve the transfer,[381] and the transferee generally must notify the local chief of police, sheriff of the county, head of the state police, state or local district attorney or prosecutor, or such other authority where the transferee resides.[382] It is otherwise illegal to possess unregistered NFA firearms.[383] If you want to *build* one of these types of firearms, you must have the proper permission from the federal government and, if you are in the business of making NFA firearms, a federal license and tax stamp.[384]

Though federal law makes it much easier to lawfully obtain and own those items constituting NFA firearms, this will not help you much if you are a California resident. As mentioned above, California requires an additional permit (or exception) to possess most of these items, which is nearly impossible to obtain for "normal" people. And the ATF will not approve the transfer of an NFA firearm where state or local law would be violated by doing so.[385]

---

[378] *See* U.S. DEPT. OF JUSTICE, BUREAUS OF ALCOHOL, TOBACCO, FIREARMS, AND EXPLOSIVES, ATF NATIONAL FIREARMS ACT HANDBOOK 9 (2009); *see also* 27 C.F.R. § 479.11. In order to be a "pistol" under the Code of Federal Regulations, the firearm must be designed to be "held in one hand." 27 C.F.R. § 479.11. Therefore, a pistol with a forward grip would not fit within this definition. But this distinction isn't as clear with "revolvers" that are modified to have a forward grip. In order to be a revolver under the Code of Federal Regulations, the firearm must be "of the pistol type." 27 C.F.R. § 479.11. While it is not clear what the phrase "of the pistol type" means, it is likely that a revolver with a forward grip would not fall under this definition, as "of the pistol type" most likely denotes that it must be designed to be "held in one hand."

[379] *See Open Letter on the Redesign of "Stabilizing Brace,"* BUREAU OF ALCOHOL, TOBACCO, FIREARMS, AND EXPLOSIVES, https://www.atf.gov/file/11816/download (last visited Oct. 9, 2020).

[380] The tax is $200 generally or $5 for "any other weapons." 26 U.S.C. § 5811(a).

[381] 26 U.S.C. § 5812(b); 27 C.F.R. § 479.86.

[382] 27 C.F.R. § 479.85.

[383] *United States v. Freed*, 401 U.S. 601, 607 (1971).

[384] 18 U.S.C. § 922(a)(1)(A); 26 U.S.C. §§ 5822, 5801, 5802.

[385] 26 U.S.C. § 5812(a); 27 C.F.R. § 479.85.

Nevertheless, people have found a way to avoid some federal restrictions and procedures associated with getting an NFA firearm by creating a legal document known as an NFA Trust or "Gun Trust." These are discussed in Chapter 5.

XIII. EXPLOSIVES

A. "Fireworks" and "Explosives"

"Fireworks" and "explosives" are wide and varying topics with special state and federal laws regulating their transportation, importation, sale, and possession.[386] "Explosives" are especially a concern for firearm enthusiasts who enjoy reloading their own ammunition.

B. Ambiguity Concerning the Amount of Black Powder a Person Can Possess

The amount of smokeless and black powder a person may legally possess can be located in Chapter 3. But there appears to be a conflict in the law concerning the actual amount of *black powder* that a person may legally possess in California.

The conflict exists between California Health and Safety Code (Cal. Health & Saf. Code) sections 12001 and Cal. Health & Saf. Code section 12101.

Cal. Health & Saf. Code sections 12000-12405 regulate the use, transportation, and possession of "explosives."[387] The term "explosives," as used and defined within this part of the California Health & Safety Code, specifically includes smokeless and black powder.[388] Yet, the sections, as provided in section 12001, do not apply to the possession of "[b]*lack powder* in quantities of 25 pounds or less in the hands of a retailer having a permit . . . and in quantities of five pounds or less in the hands of all others[,]" or to "*smokeless powder* in quantities of 20 pounds or less [when] used, possessed, stored, sold, or transported" if it is "exempted under, or authorized by, the Federal Organized Crime Control Act of 1970[389] . . . and applicable federal regulations thereunder."[390] In other words, Cal. Health & Saf. Code section 12001 essentially says that quantities of black powder of five pounds or less are not "ex-

---

[386] *See, e.g.*, CAL. HEALTH & SAF. CODE §§ 12500-12759. *See also* CAL. CODE REGS. tit. 19, §§ 979-1039; 27 C.F.R. §§ 555.221-555.224; 18 U.S.C. § 842. There may also be other relevant statutes, regulations, or local municipal codes that address fireworks and pyrotechnics. Those are beyond the scope of this book, however, so if you have specific questions, you should consult an attorney who specializes in that area of law.

[387] *See* CAL. HEALTH & SAF. CODE §§ 12000-12405.

[388] CAL. HEALTH & SAF. CODE § 12000.

[389] *See* 18 U.S.C. §§ 831-837. The Federal Organized Crime Control Act of 1970 includes exemptions for both black powder (*i.e.*, "black powder in quantities not to exceed fifty pounds . . . intended to be used solely for sporting, recreational, or cultural purposes in antique firearms as defined in section 921(a)(16) of title 18 of the United States Code") and smokeless powder (smokeless is construed by the ATF as falling under the "small arms ammunition components thereof"). 18 U.S.C. § 845(a)(4)-(5). Federal regulation 27 C.F.R. section 555.141 also contains exemptions for smokeless and black powder.

[390] CAL. HEALTH & SAF. CODE § 12001 (emphasis added).

plosives," and are therefore exempt from this entire part of the California Health & Safety Code.

In contrast, Cal. Health & Saf. Code section 12101 restricts anyone from receiving, storing, or possessing "explosives" without a *permit*. The "chapter" concerning permits (meaning Chapter 4 of the Cal. Health & Saf. Code), however, provides an exemption to the permit requirement in Cal. Health & Saf. Code section 12102. This statute exempts the possession of 20 pounds or less of smokeless powder, or *one pound or less of black sporting powder* from the permit requirement, provided that: (1) the smokeless powder is intended only for hand-loading small arms ammunition of .75 caliber or less; or (2) the black sporting powder is intended for loading of small arms or small arms ammunition of .75 caliber or less.[391] This seems to indicate that a person would need a permit to possess more than one pound of black powder.

This is clearly a conflict in the law. Cal. Health & Saf. Code section 12001 provides that quantities of black powder in five pounds or less are not considered "explosives," and are therefore exempt from the entire "explosives" part of the California Health & Safety Code. Following this understanding, a person would not need a permit to receive, store, or possess black powder in quantities of five pounds or less because it is not considered an "explosive" under the statute. Therefore, the added language of Cal. Health & Saf. Code section 12102, which seems to indicate that a permit would be needed if you are looking to possess black powder in quantities of *one* pound or more, doesn't make sense because you wouldn't need a permit to possess black powder in quantities of *five* pounds or less, as explained above.

If this was litigated, however, a court must follow the maxim that the legislature is deemed to be aware of existing laws and judicial decisions in effect at the time the legislation is enacted.[392] And when there is a conflict in the law that cannot be harmonized, the later statue enacted prevails.[393] In this case, both Cal. Health & Saf. Code sections 12001 and 12102 were added at the same time in 1967. But the subsection of Cal. Health & Saf. Code section 12001 that exempts black powder in quantities of five pounds or less from the definition of "explosive" was enacted four years after the most recent amendment to Cal. Health & Saf. Code section 12102 and therefore should trump the one pound or less language contained in Cal. Health & Saf. Code 12102. Consequently, the five pound restriction on the possession of black powder should be controlling. Still, out of an abundance of caution, you might want to carry black powder in quantities of one pound or less.

---

[391] CAL. HEALTH & SAF. CODE § 12102.

[392] *Fiscal v. City and Cnty. of San Francisco*, 158 Cal. App. 4th 895, 908 (1999).

[393] *Cal. Corr. Peace Officer Assn. v. Dep't of Corr.*, 72 Cal. App. 4th 1331, 1337 (1999).

C. Binary Exploding Targets

A number of people have been arrested and prosecuted for possessing and/or using binary exploding targets (*i.e.*, products like Tannerite, White Lightning, etc.). These individuals have been charged with possession of destructive devices or explosives for possessing these targets. While the law concerning these substances is complex and delves into an area outside the scope of this book, I strongly advise against possessing and/or using these substances in the state of California.

XIV. IGNORANCE OF THE LAW IS NO EXCUSE

Despite California's massive amount of confusing laws about which firearms and devices are, and are not, legal, ignorance of the law is no excuse. You essentially violate California and federal law if you knowingly possess an item that is something California prohibits you from possessing.[394] It does not matter if you did not know it was illegal.[395]

In some rare instances, however, you may be able to use the "entrapment by estoppel" defense. "Entrapment by estoppel" means that a government representative has informed you that a certain act is lawful, then prosecutes you for that same act.[396] For example, if California law enforcement informs you that a certain firearm is legal in California and then you are arrested because the firearm is actually *illegal* under California law, you might be able to claim "entrapment by estoppel" to defend yourself since law enforcement previously informed you that the firearm was legal.

In general, however, the law expects you as a firearm owner to be familiar with all of the laws discussed above, and those that might not be mentioned as well.

---

[394] *See, e.g., In re Jorge M.*, 23 Cal. 4th 866, 869-70 (2000) (the state must prove defendant knew that he possessed it and knew or reasonably should have known the firearm was prohibited by make and model or its features, but need not prove defendant knew of the law banning unregistered "assault weapon" possession or that the make, model, or features caused the firearm to be classified as an "assault weapon").

[395] *People v. King*, 38 Cal. 4th 617, 627 (2006) ("[T]he prosecution must prove that the item had the necessary characteristic to fall within the statutory description. It must also prove that the defendant knew of the characteristic. That is, it must prove that a defendant charged with possession of a short-barreled rifle knew the rifle was unusually short, but the defendant need not know the rifle's actual dimensions. Similarly, a defendant charged with illegally possessing a cane sword must know that the cane contained a sword, and a defendant charged with possessing a writing pen knife must know that the pen contained a stabbing instrument. Knowledge can, of course, be proved circumstantially. Further, the prosecution need not prove that the defendant knew there was a law against possessing the item, nor that the defendant intended to break or violate the law."); *see People v. Taylor*, 4 Cal. App. 2d 220, 223 (1935) ("It is clear from a reading of the transcript herein that the sole proof on the part of the prosecution which tended to establish the crime charged was the fact of possession by defendant of the proscribed cartridges. There was no proof that he had knowledge of their character as tear gas shells, nor was there any evidence from which such knowledge could be inferred . . . . Without proof of the fact of possession by defendant of an instrumentality capable of discharging these cartridges found in his pocket, there was no sufficient evidence in this case to sustain a conviction.").

[396] *United States v. Batterjee*, 361 F.3d 1210, 1216-17 (9th Cir. 2004).

Index

#

3D printing *207–208, 482–483*
22mm grenade launchers, grenade launchers, and "destructive devices" *416*
30 day requirement for handgun purchases/infrequent sales *156*
37mm flare launchers as "destructive devices" *54, 416*
.50 BMG rifles *365, 387–406*
   acquiring new *396–401*
   civil compromise for illegal possession *389*
   Dangerous Weapons Permits for *393–394*
   determining legality of *400–401*
   estate executor and inheritance *392–393*
   exceptions to laws for *390–395*
   gun trusts and *190–191*
   law enforcement and government agencies, exemptions for *390–392*
   lawful use of *399–400*
   LEOSA and *391*
   loaning and returning *392–393*
   moving into California with *399*
   nonresident possession at match or competition *393–394*
   other exemptions for *395*
   registered, how to determine if *401*
   registration *396–398*
   restrictions and penalties *388–390*
   service or repair by licensed gun dealer, exemption for *395*
   transportation of *400*
   transporting in motor vehicles *270*
   unregistered, possession of *401*
80% receivers *35, 39, 206–207*
5150 commitment *99–100*
5250 commitment *97, 97, 200*

A

Acquiring firearms. *See* Loaning firearms; *See* Private Party Transfers (PPTs); *See* Transfers of Firearms; *See* Purchasing firearms
Add-on provision *366*
AFS database *396. See also* Automated Firearm System (AFS) database.
Aftermarket parts
   "assault weapons," in the context of *378, 385*
   bump stocks *423*
   flash suppressors and other muzzle devices *416*
   "multiburst trigger activators" *422–423*
   parts kits and restrictions against "short-barreled shotguns/rifles" *428–429*
   pistol stabilizing braces *429–431*
   "silencers"/"sound suppressors" *32, 453–455*
Age restrictions. *See* Minors (under age 18); *See* Persons under 21
Airport and airline restrictions
   commercial airlines, possession on *348*
   possession in "sterile areas," California Law *347–348*
   possession in "sterile areas," federal law *346*
   transporting firearms on planes *306–309*
Airsoft guns *477*

Aliens
    defined *112*
    exemptions to firearm restriction prohibitions *112-113*
    firearms, possession of *112-113*
    purchasing firearms by *129-130*
    right to possess, ATF on *113-114*
Ammunition. *See also* Ammunition; *See also* Ammunition, acquisition of
    airplanes, transporting on *306*
    armor-piercing handgun ammunition, restrictions against *469-471*
    California law definitions *56-58*
    California, types unlawful in *227*
    deactivated *57-58*
    defined *55-60*
    "explosive" *227*
    "flechette darts" and "explosive agents" *468-469*
    green tip, attempt to ban *470-471*
    lead-based *472-478*. *See also* Lead-based ammunition
    minors, possession restrictions for *67*
    in National Forest System *352*
    on school grounds *344-346*
    parts *58-59*
    possession by minors (under 18) *69*
    powder, regulation of *58*
    restrictions against types of *468-480*
    shipping of *228-230, 237*
    storage requirements *218*
    tracer ammunition *472*
    transporting into Cal., exemptions to prohibition to *237-238*
    TSA regulations for transport of *307*
Ammunition, acquisition of *227-238*
    authorization to purchase
    background checks
    exceptions to requirements for *230-231*
    face-to-face transaction requirement *229-233*
    licensed ammunition vendors *228-229*
    recording purchaser information *231-232*
    regulation efforts
    sales and transfers *228-237*
    transporting ammunition into California *237-238*
    updating AFS records for DOJ electronic approval...*235*
    vendors, definition of *228-229*
Amtrak trains
    possession on *348*
    transporting firearms on *309*
"Antique firearms"
    California definition *49*
    cannons as *417-418*
    carrying restrictions, exemptions on *253, 280*
    federal law definitions *46-48*
    "generally prohibited weapons," exceptions to *443*
    infrequent sales requirement, exceptions to *160*
    minors, transfers or loans to *67*
    PPTs *190*
    purchases of *192*
    "silencers" as *454*
"Any other weapon," defined *484-486*

AR-15 semiautomatic rifle *34*
Armed criminal action *249*
Armed Prohibited Persons System (APPS) *64–66*
  aggressive enforcement of *15, 65*
  firearm denials reported to law enforcement *64–65*
  removal of name from *65*
Armored vehicle businesses *450*
Armor-piercing ammunition *469–471*
Army Corps of Engineers (USACE) Managed Land *353*
"Assault weapons" *365–406*
  acquiring new *396–401*
  Category 1 *366, 396, 397, 401–406*
  Category 1, defined *370*
  Category 2 *366–369, 396, 397, 401–406*
  Category 3 *370–393*. *See also* Category 3 "assault weapons"
  civil compromise for illegal possession *389*
  Dangerous Weapons Permits *393–394*. *See also* Dangerous Weapons Permit (DWP)
  defined *37, 366–394*
  determining if weapon is "assault weapon" *400*
  determining legality of *400–401*
  DOJ regulations *38*
  estate executors, exemption for *392–393*
  exceptions to laws for *390–395*
  infraction for first violation of illegal possession *390*
  inheritance of *392*
  law enforcement and government agencies, exemptions for *390–392*
  Law Enforcement Officer Safety Act (LEOSA) and *391–392*
  lawful use of *399–400*
  licensed gun dealers, exceptions to restrictions for *395*
  listed by name *401–406*
  loaning and returning of *392–393*
  locked container requirement *270*
  making "assault weapons" California compliant *384–385*
  moving into California with *399*
  non-NFA gun trusts and *190–191*
  nonresident possession at match or competition *393*
  possessing parts of *386–387*
  post-registration modification of registered firearms *398*
  registered, how to determine if *401*
  registration, alternatives to *399*
  registration deadlines for *397*
  registration of *132*
  restrictions and penalties *388–390*
  sales to minors *177*
  service or repair by licensed gun dealers *395–396*
  transporting *270, 400*
  unregistered weapon, possession of *401*
  voluntary deregistration of *398*
Assault Weapon Identification Guide (AWIG) *27–28*
Assault Weapons Control Act (AWCA, Cal.) *27*
Assembling firearms. *See* Building firearms
Attorneys, how to choose *7–8*
Auctions of non-handguns *195*
Automated Firearm System (AFS) database *396*
AWCA. *See* Assault Weapons Control Act (AWCA, Cal.)
AWIG (Assault Weapon Identification Guide) *27–28*

B

Background checks for purchasing firearms *131–132*
Ballot initiative process *13*
Bang sticks *51–52*
Barrel length *377*
Basic training courses, "large-capacity" magazines/conversion kits use in *446–447*
Battery, firearm restriction due to conviction of *78–79, 82–83*
BB guns/devices *474–475, 477*
Belemjian v. Harris (Cal. Sup. Ct. 2015) *148*
Bicycles, carrying restrictions for *270–271, 310*
Binary exploding targets *488*
Black powder *307, 486–487*
"Blowguns" *481*
Boats
  as place of business *267*
  as residence *266–267*
  in public places *271*
  transporting firearms on *311*
Bosenko v. City of Los Angeles (LA Sup. Ct. 2015) *440*
Braverman Stinger *421*
Briefcase gun *422*
Bringing firearms into California *213–216, 399*
  "assault weapons" or 0.50 BMG rifles, moving in with *399*
  as visitors *213*
  DOJ Bureau of Firearms on *213*
  moving into Cal. *213–215*
Bringing/transporting ammunition into California *237–238*
"Build parties" *206–207*
Building firearms *197–205*
  3D printing *207*
  applying for serial numbers *208–209*
  "build parties" *206–207*
  engraving serial numbers *210–211*
  engraving serial numbers, deadlines for *211*
  from 80% receivers *206–207*
  from prefabricated frames or receivers *198*
  manufacturing "large-capacity" magazines by law enforcement *450*
  registration requirements for *208–212*
"Bullet button" firearms *37, 377, 398*
Bump stocks
  as "multiburst trigger activators" *423*
  California law *411*
  federal law *411*
  "machinegun" restrictions *411–412*
Bureau of Land Management (BLM), possession of firearms in *352–353*
Buses
  Greyhound, possession on *349*
  transporting firearms on *308–309*
Businesses, restricting possession by *265–266*
Buying firearms. *See* Purchasing firearms

C

California compliant parts in context of "assault weapons" *385*
California Constitution, right to self-defense and *20*
California Dealer's Record of Sale (DROS) form *121–122*

California Department of Justice (DOJ)
  "asssault weapon" permits *393–394*
  DROS delays *115–117*
  LEOSA and *304*
  Roster of Handguns Certified for Sale (Roster) *457–462, 466–468*
California Firearms Application Reporting System (CFARS) *208*
California Legislature
  Democratic majority, effect of *9–10*
  DROS delays *116*
  firearms restrictions, expansion of *79–80*
  GVROs, creation of *105*
California regulatory environment *9–30*
  ballot initiative process *13*
  California legal scheme *25–30*
  gun ban lobby *14*
  gun law politics *9–22*
  gun violence research *17–19*
  law enforcement *15*
  local laws *11–13*
  preemption doctrine *22–25*
  pro-gun lobby *15–16*
California Rifle and Pistol Association (CRPA)
  as lobbyists *15–16*
  Local Ordinance Project (LOP) *13*
  safe shooting, information on *363*
California state buildings, firearm possession in *338–340*
California state lands, firearm possession on *353–355*
  ecological reserves *354*
  other parks *355*
  state game refuges *354–355*
  state park system *353–354*
  state wildlife areas *354*
California state statutes
  federal laws and *26–28*
  government bias in *29–30*
"Camouflaging" firearm containers *422*
Campsites, carry restrictions against *264–265*
"Cane guns" *420*
Cannons *417–418*
Carry exemptions table *312–336*
Carrying firearms *239–260. See also* Carry restrictions; *See also* Places with prohibitions or restrictions
  carry concealed weapon licenses (CCWs) *286–293. See also* Carry Licenses
  carry, defined *239–240*
  "carrying" versus "having" *266*
  concealed carry law *241–244. See also* Concealed carry
  concealed handgun, exemptions for *263*
  firearms other than handguns, restrictions against *252–254*
  in a vehicle, defined *240*
  loaded carry law *244–250*
  on/upon the person, defined *240–241*
  open carry of handguns, restrictions for *250*
  places where restrictions apply *254–258*
  public place, defined *255–256*
  public street, defined *257–258*
  regulations under Fish and Game Code (Cal.) *245*
Carry Licenses

application forms, AG *291*
application process and fees *291–292*
criteria for issuance *287–290*
"good cause" requirement *288*
"good moral character" requirement *288–289*
issued in other states *294*
license amendments *293–294*
license restrictions *293–294*
loaded handguns *286–293*
moving out of jurisdiction *292*
physical license, form of *293*
residency requirement *289*
revocation of *292*
for temporary residence or campsite *264*
training course requirement *289–290*
written policy for, issuing authorities' mandatory *290*
Carry restrictions. *See* Firearm carry restrictions
Category 1 "assault weapons" *366, 396, 397, 401–406*
Category 2 "assault weapons" *366–369, 396, 397, 401–406*
Category 3 "assault weapons" *370–393*
   aftermarket parts, compliance of *385*
   brief history..*370*
   defined *370–373*
   making compliant *384–385*
   "other" Category 3 firearms that are not rifles, pistols, or shotguns *374*
   pistols *372*
   rifles *371*
   shotguns *373*
CCW (carry concealed weapon). *See* Carry Licenses
Certified Instructors for Firearm Safety test *137*
Child care facilities, possession at *359*
Clark, People v. (Cal. App. 1996) *248*
Collector's license (Type 03 FFL) *192*
Common carriers, possession on *349*
Community Care Facilities, firearm storage in *223*
Concealed carry *241–243*. *See also* Carry Licenses
   carrying concealed, restrictions against *241–242*
   concealed, meaning of *243*
   conditional exemptions for handguns *274–276*
   exemptions to restrictions against *263, 274–277*
   handguns, summary of *244*
Constitution, U.S.
   Full Faith and Credit Clause *87*
   right to keep and bear arms. *See* Right to keep and bear arms
   Second Amendment. *See* Second Amendment
   Supremacy Clause *23*
Court opinions, how to read *7*
Coyote booby traps *52*
Criminal convictions resulting in loss of firearm possession rights. *See also* Felonies; *See also* Misdemeanors
   California restrictions *70–89*
   criminal history, obtaining *117*
   determining firearm prohibitions *63–65, 117–118*
   duplicate laws for *5–6*
   federal restrictions *70–71*
   felony convictions *71*
   not guilty by reason of insanity and *98*

violent crimes, California law on *72–81*
Criminal records, how to obtain *117–118*
Criminal storage of firearms *216–218, 225*
"Curios or relics"
  defined *49–50*
  "generally prohibited weapons," exceptions to *443*
  purchases of *192–195*
  "unsafe" handgun restrictions, exemptions for *466, 466–467*

D

Dangerous Weapons Control Act (DWCA) *25, 27*
Dangerous Weapons Permit (DWP) *181, 186, 392–394, 393–395, 453, 399–400*
Dangerous Weapons Recodification Act (Cal. 2010) *27–28*
Day care centers, firearm storage in *223*
Dealers of firearms
  ammunition vendor license requirement, exception *228*
  California license requirements *120, 159–160*
  CFR definition of *158–159*
  federal requirements for *158–159*
  "large-capacity" magazines/conversion kits and *449*
  loans to, for maintenance/repair *449*
  out-of-state dealers *160–161*
  sales to young people *177*
  transfers and loans to young people *176–177*
Dealer's Record of Sale (DROS)
  delays *115–116*
  fees for *65, 131*
  forms for *121–122*
  for PPTs *155–157*
Defense of others, right to. *See* Right to self-defense or defense of others
"Destructive devices" *412–417*
  37mm flare launchers v. grenade launchers *416*
  California definition *413–414*
  cannons *417*
  exceptions for peace officers, firefighters, and military *416*
  federal definition *412–413*
  "generally prohibited weapons" *418–441*. *See also* "Generally prohibited weapons"
  permits for *415–416*
  possession of, laws on *414–415*
Detachable magazines *376, 378*
Dillard, People v. (Cal. App. 1984) *244*
Discharge restrictions *360–361*
Dishonorable discharge from armed forces, prohibitions on gun ownership following *114*
Disordered sex offenders *98*
District of Columbia v. Heller (U.S. 2008) *19–20, 20, 29*
Divorce, firearms transfers and *182–183*
Domestic violence, firearm restrictions due to. *See also* Misdemeanor crime of domestic violence (MCDV)
  California restrictions against ownership following convictions for *72*
  federal ownership restrictions for *80–85, 102*
DROS form. *See* Dealer's Record of Sale (DROS)
Drug addiction, firearm restrictions due to
  ATF definition of *92–93*
  ATF open letter to FFLs on *93*
  federal law, restrictions against possession under *92–94*
  firearm possession, California restrictions for *94*

unlawful drug use, federal law on 93
Dual residency, gun purchases and 130–131
Duncan v. Becerra (S.D. Cal. 2017) 436, 440
  Freedom Week 435
Duplicate laws for same crime 5–6
DWCA (Dangerous Weapons Control Act) 25, 27–28

E

"Encased" firearms 281
Entertainment Firearm Permit (EFP) 191
Entertainment industry props
  exception to "large-capacity" magazines/conversion kits restrictions 451
  exemption to "unsafe handgun" restrictions, pistols used as props as 466
Estates, firearms included in 183–184
  "assault weapons" and .50BMG rifles 392–393
  "large-capacity" magazines/conversion kits 451
Evictions due to arrests for certain firearm nuisances 89
Exceptions, to prohibited persons possessing firearms 108–111
Exceptions to transferring firearms through FFLs . *See also* Transfers of firearms; *See also* Federal Firearms Licensees (FFLs)
  "antique firearms" 192
  "curios or relics" 192–195
  Entertainment Firearm Permit (EFP) 191
  federal exceptions 180–181
  "gun buybacks" 196
  gun trusts 185–191. *See also* Gun trusts
  intra-familial transactions 180–181
  nonprofit auctions of non-handguns 195
  "Operation of Law" transfers 183–184
  other limited exceptions 197
  spouses or domestic partners, transfers between 182–183
Explosive-powered nail guns 55
"Explosives" 486–488
  ammunition with "explosive agents" 468–469
  binary exploding targets 488
  black powder 307, 486–487
  federal definition 58–59
  "fireworks" 486
Ex post facto prohibitions and firearm possession 89–90

F

Face-to-face transaction requirement for ammunition 229–230
Families. *See also* Domestic violence, firearm restrictions due to; *See* Intra-familial transfers
  gun trusts, intra-familial transfers and 188
  immediate family 105–106, 180–181, 189, 280, 284
  MCDV and. *See* Misdemeanor crime of domestic violence (MCDV)
  transfers of firearms in 180–181
Family day care homes, firearm storage in 223
Federal convictions, possession rights and 70–71
Federal facilities, defined 338
Federal Firearms Licensees (FFLs) 119–120. *See also* Dealers of Firearms
  age requirements for buyers 122, 176
  "antique firearms", sales of 192
  armor-piercing ammunition, sales of 470
  "assault weapons" 392, 395, 399–400
  background checks by 131–132

   Cal. DROS Form *121–122*
   exceptions to transfer requirements . *See also* Exceptions to transferring firearms through FFLs
   Firearm Safety Cerificate requirements *137–148*
   firearm safety device requirements *135–136*
   frame or receiver, purchasing *198*
   gun shows *358*
   interstate private party transfers *162–163, 187*
   "large capacity" magazines, maintenance or repair of *449*
   military personnel, sales to *104*
   PPTs and *155–157, 155–159*
   registration requirements and *104–105*
   residency requirements for buyers from *130*
   restraining orders against individuals, storage of firearms with *104*
   semiautomatic handguns converted to single shot pistols, sales of *467*
   "silencers" *454*
   transfers between spouses or domestic partners *182–183*
   transfers of rifles/shotguns, federal law on *107, 160–161*
   Type 03 FFL *192–195*
   Type 07 FFL (manufacturer) *210*
   "unsafe" handguns, transfers of *457*
   waiting period for purchases through *133–134, 154, 156–157*
Federal lands, firearm possession on *351*
   federal property, carrying firearms on *293*
   National Forests *352*
   National Parks and Wildlife Refuges *351–352*
Federal law and California law, confusion between *26–28*
Federal law enforcement officer. *See* Law enforcement and peace officers
"Feel Good" laws *14*
Felonies. *See also* Wobblers
   "assault weapons," not properly registered *388*
   California ownership restrictions for *70–71, 87–88*
   carrying concealed handguns as potential felony *276*
   carrying loaded firearms as potential felony *244–246*
   convictions of offenses listed in P.C. sections 23515(a), (b), and (d), and 417(a)(2) *74*
   "destructive devices", reckless or malicious possession of *414*
   "destructive devices", unlawful sale of *415*
   false statement on carry license application *291*
   federal ownership restrictions for *70–71, 87–88*
   firearm prohibitions based on outstanding warrant for *91–92*
   Governor's mansion, carrying firearms in *339*
   handgun sales not using FFLs *155*
   loaded while committing a felony/in sensitive places *249*
   "machineguns" and *409*
   misdemeanor violations of P.C. section 273.5 as *72–73*
   "multiburst trigger activators" and *422*
   obliterated or covered serial numbers as *455–457*
   playgrounds and youth centers, carrying firearms in *359*
   registration as safeguard against *132*
   restricted public places, possessing loaded firearms in as potential felony *245–246*
   "school zones", possession of firearms in *342*
   serial numbers, changing, altering or removing of *455*
   "silencers", unlawful possession of *454*
   violations of "assault weapon" restrictions *388–390*
   "violent crimes" resulting in lifetime firearm possession restrictions *73–75*
FFL. *See* Federal Firearms Licensees (FFLs)
Firearm acquisition. *See* Transfers of firearms; *See* Purchasing firearms; *See* Loaning firearms

Firearm carry restrictions. *See also* Carrying firearms; *See also* Carry Licenses; *See also* Firearm concealed and loaded carry restriction exemptions, peace officers
  airplanes, transporting fir earms on 306–309
  bus or other public transportation, transporting on 308
  carrying exemptions table 312–336
  compliance with California fir earms laws, suggestions for 311–312
  exemption for possessory interest 263–264
  exemptions 261–336
  exemptions based on activity engaged in 326–336
  exemptions based on location 321–325. *See also* Public places, restrictions to carrying in
  exemptions based on who you are 314–320
  exemptions for active and retired peace officers 294–305. *See also* Firearm concealed and loaded carry restriction exemptions, peace officers
  exemptions for concealed handguns 263, 273–276
  exemptions for firearms that are not handguns 263–264, 281–286
  exemptions for loaded firearms 262, 276–278
  exemptions for open carry of handguns 278–280
  hunting or fishing 272–273
  license to carry loaded handgun 286–293
  "locked container" or "encased" 281
  public places, restrictions in 264–272
  state lines, transporting across 308
Firearm concealed and loaded carry restriction exemptions, peace officers 294–305
  current California peace officers 294–295
  current federal and out-of-state officers 296
  current reserve peace officers 295
  LEOSA and 300–306
  other current officers 295
  retired California peace officers 297–298
  retired federal peace officers 299
  retired reserve California peace officers 299–300
Firearm Ownership Record 132
Firearm possession
  aliens, restrictions for 112–113
  Armed Prohibited Persons System (APPS) 64–66
  "assault weapons," possessing parts of 386–388
  by minors 68. *See also* Minors (under age 18)
  by minors, restrictions for 66–67
  California convictions, effect in other states 90
  criminal convictions and 70–89. *See* Criminal convictions resulting in loss of firearm possession rights
  defined 62–63
  determining eligibility to possess 117–118
  dishonorable discharge from armed forces, restrictions for 114
  eligibility, determination of 117–118
  exceptions for possession by prohibited persons 108–112
  ex post facto prohibitions on 89–90
  federal restrictions against 115
  five-year restrictions 80
  "fugitives from justice," federal prohibition for 90–91
  justifiable possession exception for prohibited persons 111
  juvenile offenses, restrictions for 84–87
  lifetime restrictions under California law 72–76, 74
  MCDV restrictions 80–84. *See* Misdemeanor crime of domestic violence (MCDV)
  mental health related restrictions 95–102. *See also* Mental health related firearm restrictions
  misdemeanor convictions, restrictions for 75–84
  momentary possession exception for prohibited persons 110–111

under NFA *484–485*
outstanding warrants for felony or certain misdemeanors, prohibitions based on *91–92*
places prohibited *337–363*
probation or parole, restrictions for persons on *87–88*
prohibitions during purchases *63–65*
public property, prohibition on *12*
renouncing U.S. citizenship, restrictions for persons *114*
restraining orders, restrictions based on *102–108*. *See also* Restraining orders, firearm prohibitions for subjects of
self-defense exception to prohibited persons possessing *108–111*
ten-year restrictions *75–80*
transporting "generally prohibited weapons" to law enforcement *445*
violent crimes resulting in lifetime restrictions *73–75*
"Firearm Safety" test *137*
Firearm Safety Certificates (FSC)
    exemptions *137–146*
    for purchasing firearms *137–138*
Firearm safety devices *135*
Firearm sales. *See* Purchasing firearms
Firearms dealers. *See* Dealers of firearms
Firearms, defined *31–60, 407–412*. *See also* Firearm subgroup definitions
    under California law *35–39*
    California's definition, history of *36*
    Due Process *50–51*
    under federal law *31–35*
    frames or receivers, California definition of *37–38*
    frames or receivers, federal definition of *34*
    LEOSA definitions *305*
    non-functioning *35, 38–39*
    precursor (80%) receivers *35, 39*
    projectiles *51*
Firearms not immediately recognizable as firearms *421*
Firearms, ownership of *61–118*. *See also* Firearm possession
    determining place of residence *151–155*
    Form 4473 requirements *120–121*
    "large-capacity" magazines, use with firearms obtained prior to 2000 *452*
    ownership, defined *63*
    place restrictions against *337–362*
    purchasing from licensed dealers *120–152*
Firearms, purchasing of *119–238*. *See* Purchasing firearms
Firearm storage *216–225*
    in community care facilities *223*
    criminal storage *225*
    criminal storage, exceptions to *217*
    handguns
    handguns in unattended vehicles *219–222*
    loaded firearms *216–217*
    local laws *222–223*
    misdemeanor violations *224*
    residing with person prohibited from possessing *218–219, 225*
    unattended vehicles, by law enforcement officers *221–222*
Firearm subgroup definitions *39–50*
    "antique firearms" *46–49*
    "curios or relics" *49–50*
    expressly exempted items *55*
    handguns *39–42*
    long guns *43–44*

    other firearms *45*
    pistols *40–41*
    revolvers *41–42*
    rifles *42–43*
    shotguns *43*
    weapons *45–46*
"Fireworks" *486*
Fishing, carrying exemption while *272–273*
Fixed magazines, defined *372*
Flare guns *53–54*
Flare launchers, 37 mm *54*
Flash suppressors/muzzle brakes *416, 380*
"Flechette darts" *468–469*
Forensic laboratories *445*
Form 4473 requirements *120–121*
Frames or receivers *34*
    as "assault weapons" per DOJ argument *367*
    California definition of *37–38*
    defined *381*
    defined per DOJ "assault weapon" regulations *382*
    federal law definition of *34*
    incomplete receivers *35*
    precursor receivers *35*
    prefabricated for building firearms *198*
FSC. *See* Firearm Safety Certificates (FSC)
"Fugitives from justice," firearm possession and *90–91*

G

Gatling guns *408–409*
"Generally prohibited weapons" *418–441*. *See also* "Generally prohibited weapons," exceptions to restrictions; *See also* "Generally prohibited weapons," exceptions to restrictions against "large capacity magazines"; *See also* "Generally prohibited weapons," exceptions to restrictions against "short-barreled shotguns/rifles"
    "camouflaging firearm containers" *422*
    "cane guns" *420*
    firearms not immediately recognizable as firearms *421*
    "large-capacity" magazines and conversion kits *432–442*. *See also* "Large-capacity" magazines
    "multiburst trigger activators" *422–423*
    pistol stabilizing braces *429–431*
    "short-barreled shotguns/rifles" *424–431*
    "unconventional pistols" *432*
    undetectable firearms *420–421*
    "wallet guns" *420*
    "zip guns" *431–432*
"Generally prohibited weapons," exceptions to restrictions.
    "antique firearms" *443*
    "any other weapons" *443*
    "curios or relics" *443*
    forensic laboratories *445–446*
    historical societies, museums, institutional collections, or entertainment events, sales to *443, 444–445*
    law enforcement, sales to *444–446*
    media or entertainment events *444*
"Generally prohibited weapons," exceptions to restrictions against "large capacity magazines" *446–452*
    armored vehicle businesses *450*
    basic training courses for peace officers *446*
    dealer acquisition *449*

dealer or gunsmith loan for maintenance/repair *449*
  entertainment industry props *451*
  federal law enforcement *448*
  finding and delivering to law enforcement *451*
  firearm lawfully-obtained prior to 2000 that is incompatible with magazines holding 10 or fewer rounds, solely for use with *452*
  honorably retired sworn peace officers *448–449*
  importing or selling between out-of-state clients with a permit *449*
  law enforcement agencies *446–447*
  loans between individuals *449–450*
  manufacturing "large-capacity" magazines by law enforcement *450*
  peace officers *447–450*
  special weapons permit holders, purchases by *451*
  trustees, executors, or administrators, receipt or disposition by *451–452*
"Generally prohibited weapons," exceptions to restrictions against "short-barreled shotguns/rifles" *452–453*
  law enforcement agencies *452*
  permit authorizations *453–454*
"Ghost guns"
  DOJ regulations *37, 49*
  registration requirements for *208, 428*
  serial numbers or identification marks *456*
Glock handguns *10*
Government bias in California state statutes *29–30*
Government buildings, firearm possession in *338–340*
"Grave danger" exemption *271–272*
"Gray Areas" and Test Cases *28–29*
Green tip ammunition *470–471*
Grenade launchers and 22m grenade launchers as "destructive devices" *416, 381*
Greyhound buses, firearm possession on *310, 349*
Gun ban lobby *14*
"Gun buybacks" *196*
Gun Control Act (GCA)
  "antique firearms" defined *46–48*
  dealer, defined *158*
  firearms, defined *31–32*
  handguns, defined *39*
  LEOSA and *300*
Gun-Free School Zone restrictions. *See also* "School zones"
  ammunition and weapon possession on school grounds *344–346*
  exemptions to *278, 323, 336*
  school zone, defined *342*
  storage of firearms and *252, 255*
  ten-year firearms restrictions for *312*
Gun law politics *9–18*
  ballot initiative process *13*
  "feel good" laws *14*
  gun violence research *17–19*
  legislative process *9–11*
  local laws *11–13*
  overaggressive law enforcement *15*
  pro-gun lobby *15–16*
Gun Owners of California *11, 15*
Gun safety *1–2, 147–148*
Gun shows/traders *158, 160, 358*
Gun trusts *185–191*
  NFA trusts *185–186*
  non-NFA trusts in California *186–191*. *See also* Non-NFA gun trusts

Gun violence research *17–19*
"Gun Violence Restraining Orders" (GVROs) *80, 105–108*

H

Hale, People v. (Cal. App. 1974) *243*
Handguns.
   3D printing *207*
   ammunition for *57*
   antique, transfers to minors *67, 192*
   armor-piercing handgun ammunition *469–471*
   California law definition of *40*
   concealed carry law *241–244*. *See also* Concealed carry
   concealed, exemptions for carrying *263, 273–276, 314–335*
   "curios or relics," transfers of *194*
   defined *39–42*
   exceptions to criminal storage of *217*
   exemptions for openly carrying unloaded handguns *262–263*
   exemptions for "unsafe" handgun roster requirement *466–468*
   exemptions to possessions restrictions for minors *68–69*
   federal definition of *39*
   Firearm Safety Certificate *137–148*
   Handgun Safety Certificate *137*
   infrequent sales of *160*
   license to carry loaded handguns *286–293*
   loaning to minors *176*
   minors, ammunition possession restrictions for *67*
   minors, possession restrictions for *66–67*
   minors, sales to *177–178*
   one handgun per 30 day requirement *156*
   open carry restriction exemptions *278–280, 314–335*
   open carry restrictions *250*
   pistols *40–41*
   private party transfers of *155–157*
   proof of residency for purchase of *151–155*
   purchase requirements *120–152*
   required locking devices and warnings for *135–136*
   revolvers *41–42*
   "Saturday Night Specials" *10*
   shipping of *163*
   storage of *224*
   "unsafe" handgun *457–465*
   "unsafe" handguns in unattended vehicles *221–222, 221–224*
Harbors & ports, firearm possession in *349–350*
Hard cases *268*
Heller, District of Columbia v. (U.S. 2008) *19, 29*
Hunting
   California Fish & Game Code regulations for *273*
   carrying exemption while *272–273*
   lead-based ammunitions, restrictions against *472–478*. *See also* Lead-based ammunition licenses for
Hurtado, People v. (Cal. App. 1996) *111*

I

Identification requirements for firearm purchases from dealers
   California *124–125*

DROS fees *131*
dual residency and *130–131*
federal *123–125*
Identity, proof of *125*
   for military personnel *129*
   for non-citizens (aliens) *129–130*
   providing proof of ID *122–130*
   REAL IDs, Non-REAL IDs, and AB 60 *125–126*
Ignorance of the law is no excuse *488*
Imitation firearms *475–478*
Incendiary ammunition *352*
Incomplete receivers *35, 206*
Incorporated cities *252, 261*
Indicted persons *114*
Infrequent sales/30-day requirement for handgun purchases *156*
Initiative process *13*
Insanity. *See* Mental health related firearm restrictions
Internal waters, firearm possession in *355*
International waters, firearm possession in *355*
Interstate firearm purchases and transfers *158–170, 160–169*
   checklist for *163*
   exemptions to restrictions against out-of-state transfers *164–170*
   "large capacity" magazines/conversion kits *449*
   PPTs *162–164*
   shipping *163–164*
   transfers from out-of-state dealers *160–161*
Intra-familial transfers
   change in law for long guns *181*
   divorce and *182*
   non-NFA gun trusts and *188*
   of long guns to minors *189*
   "Operation of Law" transfers *183–184, 189*

J

James v. State (Cal. App. 2014) *83–84*
Justifiable possession of firearms *111*
Juvenile offenses and firearm prohibitions *84–86*
Juvenile Parole Board *295*

K

King, People v. (Cal. 1978) *109–110*

L

"Large-capacity" magazines. *See also* "Generally prohibited weapons," exceptions to restrictions against "large capacity magazines"
   "antique firearms", exemptions to restrictions for *443*
   as "generally prohibited weapons" *432–442*
   California restrictions, exceptions to *442–452*
   conversion kits, restricted activity for *437–439*
   "curios or relics," exemptions to restrictions for *443*
   definition *432–435*
   Duncan v. Becerra, injunction from *436*
   entertainment industry props, exemptions to restrictions for *451*
   federal law enforcement, exemption from restrictions for *448*
   FFLs or gunsmiths, loans for maintenance/repair *449*
   forensic laboratories, exceptions to restrictions for *445–446*

Gatling guns *408–409*
"generally prohibited weapons," in context of *432*
gun trusts and *191*
historical society, museum, or institutional collection, exceptions to restrictions for *443*
honorably retired peace officers, exception to restrictions for *448–449*
law enforcement agencies, exemptions to restrictions for *444–447*
law enforcement, manufacturing by *450*
lawfully-obtained firearms prior to 2000, possession of *452*
LEOSA, in context of *305*
limitations of non-NFA trusts as applied to *190*
loans of *446, 449*
local restrictions against *439–442*
media or entertainment events, exceptions to restrictions for *444*
NFA definitions of "any other weapons", exceptions from restrictions for *443*
people who sell items to historical societies, museums, institutional collections, or entertainment events, exceptions to *restrictions for 444–445*
restricted activity for "large-capacity" magazines *436–437*
special weapons permit holders, purchases by *451*
transporting to law enforcement, exceptions to restrictions for *445, 451*
trustees, executors, or administrators, receipt or disposition by *451*
Laser scopes/pointers *361, 482–483*
Law enforcement and peace officers
  Armed Prohibited Persons System (APPS) *64–65*
  armor-piercing ammunition, exemption from restriction on *470*
  "assault weapons"/.50BMG rifles, exceptions to restrictions for *391–393*
  basic training course for Commission on Peace Officer Standards and Training *150, 221, 277, 279, 284, 290, 446–447, 151*
  deadly weapon, meaning to *95*
  "destructive devices", exceptions to restrictions for *416*
  exemptions on carry restrictions for *294–305*. *See also* Firearm concealed and loaded carry restriction exemptions, peace officers
  Form 4473 exemption for *121*
  "generally prohibited weapons,"use by *444*
  handguns in locked vehicles, storage of *219*
  "large-capacity" magazine and conversion kit restrictions, exceptions for *444–446, 450–452*
  lead-based ammunition restriction, exception for *474, xxv*
  LEOSA *300–306*. *See also* Law Enforcement Officers Safety Act (LEOSA)
  "machineguns," exceptions to restrictions for *410*
  overagressive enforcement *15*
  purchase of firearms by, ID requirements
  "short-barreled shotguns/rifles," exceptions to restrictions for *452*
  storage of handguns in unattended vehicles by *221–222*
  transporting most "generally prohibited weapons" to law enforcement *445*
  "unsafe" handguns exceptions for *461–462*
  "unsafe" handguns exceptions for specified agencies *462*
Law Enforcement Officers Safety Act (LEOSA) *300–306*
  "assault weapons," carrying under *391–392*
  California DOJ and *304*
  firearm, defined in *305*
  firearms, types one may carry *304–305*
  limits on *304–305*
  QLEO definition and ID requirements *300–301*
  QRLEO definition and ID requirements *301–303*
  reserve officers and *305*
"Lawful purpose" requirement in motor vehicles as an exemption to carry restrictions *269*
Laws, how to read and determine application *4–7*
Lawyers, how to choose *7–8*
Lead-based ammunition *472–478*

    certain hunting applications, use in *472–480*
    exception for calibers commercially unavailable in non-lead *473, xxv*
    exceptions to general restrictions *473–474, xxv*
    law enforcement engaged in official duties exception *474, xxv*
    penalties for violating restrictions against *474*
    self-defense exception to restrictions *473, xxv*
Legislative intent *5*
Lenity, rule of *5*
LEOSA. *See* Law Enforcement Officers Safety Act (LEOSA)
"Less lethal weapons" *480–481*
Licensed ammunition vendors *57, 228, 230–231, 237–238*
Licensed Ammunition Vendors *228*
Licensed firearm dealers. *See also* Federal Firearms Licensees (FFLs); *See also* Dealers of firearms
    ammunition vendors and *228*
    "assault weapons" and .50 BMG rifles, exceptions *396–401*
    "large-capacity" magazines and exceptions for *449*
    non-NFA gun trusts *188–190*
    obtaining firearms from *120–153. See also* Purchasing firearms
    "unsafe" handguns and exceptions for *465*
License to carry concealed or loaded weapon. *See* Carry Licenses
Lifetime ownership restrictions for firearms *70–74*
Loaded carry law *244–250. See also* Carrying firearms; *See also* Carry Licenses
    armed criminal action, loaded definition for *249*
    definition of "loaded" *247–250*
    exemptions *262*
    Fish and Game Code, loaded definition in *249*
    general definition, loaded *247–249*
    loaded firearm restrictions *244–246*
Loaning firearms
    "assault weapons" or .50 BMG rifles *392–393*
    exemptions *170–174*
    "Firearm Safety" Certificate exemptions *137–146*
    gun trusts, in the context of *190*
    to adults *169–174*
    to consultant-evaluators, exception to Roster requirements *466*
    to young people *176–178*
Lobbyists
    gun ban lobby *14*
    pro-gun lobby *15–16*
Local laws *4, 11–13*
    on firearm storage *222–223*
    on "large-capacity" magazines, restrictions against *439–442*
    on mandatory lock storage *11*
    on mandatory lost/stolen reporting *11, 14*
    prohibiting possession of firearms on public property *12*
    on public gatherings with firearm limitations *12*
Local Ordinance Project (LOP) *13*
"Locked container" storage, as exemptions to carry restrictions *268–269, 281*
Locking devices, requirements for purchase *135–136*
Lock storage, cities requiring mandatory *11*
Long guns. *See also* Non-handguns
    auction, raffle, or similar event by a nonprofit corporation *195*
    carrying restrictions resulting from AB 1527 *252–254*
    "curios or relics" *193*
    defined *43–44*
    examples *44*

gun-safe affidavits and *136*
"school zone" possession *341*
shipping *163*
transfers to minors via gun trusts *181, 189*
Look-alike firearms *475–478*
Los Angeles
 "large capacity" magazines, local law on *439*
 local laws for *11–12*
 local storage laws *222*
 sympathy for anti-gun legislation *25*
Lost/stolen reporting *226–227*
 cities requiring *11*
 false reports of *226*
Lu v. County of Los Angeles (Cal. App. unpublished) *286*

M

Mace *478–480*
"Machineguns"
 bump stocks and *411–412*
 California exceptions to restrictions *409–410*
 defined *33–35, 43, 45, 305, 387*
 law enforcement and military exceptions to restrictions *410*
 LEOSA and *392*
 licenses to sell *411*
 non-functioning *39*
 permits to possess, manufacture, and transport *410–411*
 prohibitions *409*
Manufacturing firearms. *See* Building firearms
Marijuana, drug addiction restrictions and *92–94*
McDonald v. Chicago (U.S., 2010) *19, 30*
MCDV. *See* Misdemeanor crime of domestic violence (MCDV)
Media or entertainment events, exceptions to "generally prohibited weapons" restrictions *444*
Mental health related firearm restrictions *95–102*
 California commitments resulting in federal restrictions *97*
 California ownership restrictions, table of *101*
 commitments under California Welfare and Institutions Code *97*
 conservatorship, individuals under *99–100*
 dangerous/gravely disabled persons *99–100*
 dangerous inpatients *97*
 federal restrictions *96–97*
 incompetency to stand trial *98*
 intensive treatment, individuals committed to *100*
 mental disorders, illnesses or disordered sex offenders *98*
 mental health, federal definitions of *96–97*
 not guilty by reason of insanity *98*
 psychotherapist, communicating threats to *97*
Mental health restrictions
 California law summary *101*
"Microstamping" *459–461*
Military personnel
 armor-piercing ammunition, exemption from restriction on *470*
 carrying restrictions, exceptions to *276–278, 319, 329, 339, 342, 345*
 "destructive devices", exceptions for *416*
 "machinegun" restrictions, exceptions to *410*
 obliterated serial number restrictions, exceptions to *456*

purchase of firearms by *125, 129, 152, 154*
"short-barreled shotguns/rifles" restrictions, exceptions to *452*
"silencer" restrictions, exceptions to *454*
"tear gas" restrictions, exceptions to *478-479*
"unsafe" handguns restrictions, exceptions to *461-462*
Minors (under age 18). *See also* Persons under 21
   ammunition restrictions under California law *67-68*
   "antique firearms", ownership restrictions for *67*
   BB guns restrictions *475*
   carry license restrictions *287*
   dealers sales to *176-177*
   firearm and ammunitions possession restrictions for *66-69*
   gun trusts and transfers of long guns to *189*
   handguns, exemptions to federal restrictions for *68-69*
   handguns, possession restrictions for *67*
   juvenile offenses, restrictions against ownership for *84-87*
   playgrounds and youth centers, firearm possession on *359*
   possession restrictions, summary of *69*
   purchasing firearms by *177*
   shotgun and rifle possession restrictions *66*
   "stun gun" restrictions *481*
   "tear gas" restrictions *479*
   transfer of long guns to *181*
   transferring and loaning firearms to *176-178*
   transferring firearms to, exceptions
Misdemeanor crime of domestic violence (MCDV) *80-84*
   battery against spouse, cohabitant, fiancé *82-83*
   California offenses that may be MCDVs *81-84*
   injuring a spouse, cohabitant, fiancé *81-82*
   other California crimes that may be considered MCDV *84*
Misdemeanors
   bringing or transporting ammunition into California improperly *237*
   concealed carry as *242, 244*
   face-to-face transaction requirement for ammunition sales, violation of *229-230*
   false reports of lost or stolen firearms *226*
   false statement on Carry License application *291*
   firearm possession at protest events *357*
   five-year restrictions for *80*
   illegal carrying of loaded firearms *245-246*
   illegal carrying of registered firearms *132*
   improper modification of "imitation firearm" *476*
   improper storage of firearms *224*
   "less lethal firearms," sales to minors *481*
   lifetime restrictions for *72*
   obliterated or covered serial numbers *456*
   openly carrying unloaded handgun improperly *250-251*
   possessing loaded firearm in restricted public place *245*
   possession of unregistered .50 BMG rifles *388*
   possession of unregistered "assault weapons" *390*
   restrictions against ownership for *75-89*
   ten-year restrictions for *72, 75-80*
   unlawful carry of non-handguns, penalties for *253-254*
   unlawful possession of "destructive devices" *414*
Motorcycles, carrying restrictions for *270-271, 310*
Motor homes, carry restrictions for *266, 310*
Motor vehicles *267-270*. *See also* Vehicles, carry restrictions for

allowing others to carry firearms in your vehicle 251
"assault weapons" and .50 BMG rifles, transporting in 270
discharging firearms in 360
"lawful purpose" requirement 269
locked container requirement 268-269
transporting firearms across state lines 308
transporting firearms in 310
Moving into California with firearms. *See* Bringing firearms into California
"Multiburst trigger activators" 422-423
Muzzle brakes/flash suppressors as "destructive devices" 416

N

Nail guns 55
National Firearms Act (NFA)
   "antique firearms", defined 48-49
   "any other weapon", defined 484-486
   "destructive devices", defined 413
   firearm, defined 31-33
   firearm possession 407-408, 484-485
   frame or receiver, defined 34
   losing firearm status, ATF on 33
   NFA tax 33, 65, 94, 453
   NFA trusts 185-186
   rifle, defined 42
   "short-barreled rifles," defined 426
   "short-barreled shotguns," defined 424-426
   shotgun, defined 43
   "silencers," defined 453
   transferring NFA firearms 485
National Forests, firearm possession in 352
National Instant Criminal Background Check System (NICS) 63
National Parks
   firearm possession in 351-352
   rangers, concealed carry in 296
National Rifle Association (NRA)
   as lobbyists 15-16
   Guide to the Interstate Transportation of Firearms 309
   legislative debates, role in 10
   rules for gun safety 1
   safe shooting, information on 363
National Shooting Sports Foundation (NSSF) 15, 363
National Wildlife Refuge Systems 351
NFA. *See* National Firearms Act (NFA)
NFA trusts 185-186
Nguyen, People v. (Cal. App. 4th 2013) 386
Night vision scopes (sniperscopes) 482-483
Non-functioning firearms 35, 38-39
Non-handguns
   carrying exemptions for 263-264, 281-286
   carrying restrictions against 239, 252-254
   defined 253
   infrequent transfer requirements 159
   loans to minors
   nonprofit auctions of 195
   penalties for unlawful carry 253-254

required processing of PPTs by FFL 155
transfer to immediate family members 252
transfer to minor by parent, guardian or grandparent 181
transportation in vehicles 252
Non-NFA gun trusts 186–191
   "antique firearms" transfers through 190
   application of California laws on loaning firearms 190
   "assault weapons," limitations on as applied to 190–191
   Cal. firearm transfer laws in context of 186–187
   exceptions to transfers through Licensed Firearms Dealer 188–190
   intra-familial transfers 188
   "large-capacity" magazines and 191
   taking title by "Operation of Law" 189
   transfers between spouses 188
   transfers of long guns to minors by immediate family members 189
Nuisance violations 89

O

Oakland
   local storage laws 222
   mandatory lock storage 11
   prohibition of possession of firearm/ammunition on public property 12
Obliterated or covered serial numbers 455–457
Omnibus Consolidated Appropriations Bill (U.S., 1996) 18
One handgun purchase every 30 days rule
Open carry
   firearms other than handguns 252–254
   handguns 250–251
   people and activities exempt from restrictions 278–280
   unloaded handguns, exemptions for 262–263
"Operation of Law" transfers 183–184, 189
   exception to "unsafe" handgun restrictions 462
   non-NFA trusts and
   spouses, transfers between 188
Other states, effect of California prohibitions on 90
Out-of-state law enforcement officers. *See* Law enforcement and peace officers
Out-of-state transfers
   "curios or relics" 193
   exemptions to Cal. restrictions against firearm transfers 164–170
   firearm transfers from out-of-state dealers 160–162
   interstate private party transfers 162–164
   registration with DOJ required of Type 03 FFLs 194
   restriction on bringing ammunition into Cal. 237–238
   shipping firearms 163–164
   transporting firearms across state lines 308–310
Outstanding warrants, firearm prohibitions based on 91–92
Ownership, defined 63
Ownership of firearms. *See* Firearm possession
Ownership of firearms, California definition of 63

P

Palm Pistol 421
Palm Springs local storage laws 222
"Paperweights". *See* Non-functioning firearms
Passenger vessel terminal, defined 347, 349

Peace officers. *See* Law enforcement and peace officers
Pellecer, People v. (Cal. App. 2013) *240–241*
People v.
   Clark (Cal. App. 1996) *248*
   Dillard (Cal. App. 1984) *244*
   Hale (Cal. App. 1974) *243*
   Hurtado (Cal. App. 1996) *111*
   King (Cal. 1978) *109–110*
   Nguyen (Cal. App. 4th 2013) *386*
   Pellecer (Cal. App. 2013) *240–241*
   Squier (Cal. App. 1993) *5*
   Wade (Cal. 2016) *241*
Pepper spray *478–480*
Permits
   Entertainment Firearm Permits *191*
   for "destructive devices" *415–416*
   for "machineguns", to possess, manufacture, and transport *410–411*
   for "short-barreled shotguns/rifles" *453*
   special weapons permits for "large capacity" magazines/conversion kits *451*
   to import or sell "large-capacity" magazines between FFL and out-of-state clients *449*
Personal Firearms Eligibility Check (PFEC) *95, 122, 210*
Personal firearms importers *165*
Persons prohibited from possessing firearms
   aliens *112-113*
   Cal. conviction, effect in other states *90*
   California conviction, effect in other states *90*
   convictions listed under P.C. section 23515 and 417(a)(2) *73–74*
   convictions of P.C. section 273.5 and certain "violent crimes" *72–74*
   dishonorable discharge from armed forces *114*
   due to drug addiction and use *92–94*
   exceptions to *108–112*
   ex post facto prohibitions, application of *89*
   for felony convictions *70–71*
   five-year prohibitions *80*
   for misdemeanor convictions *75–84*
   "fugitives from justice" *90*
   indicted persons *114*
   justifiable possession exception *111*
   juvenile offenders *84–87*
   lifetime restrictions *70–74, 80–84*
   mental health related *95–102*
   misdemeanor crime of domestic violence (MCDV) *80–84*
   momentary possession exception *110–111*
   notice required for *88–89*
   outstanding warrants, persons subject to *91–92*
   persons on probation or parole *87–88*
   persons renouncing U.S. citizenship *114*
   prohibited persons, defined *61*
   restraining orders *102–108*
   self-defense exception *108–111*
   ten-year prohibitions *75–80*
   violent crimes, lifetime restriction and *73–75*
Persons under 21. *See also* Minors (under age 18)
   obtaining firearms, restrictions against *176–177, 198*
   serial number applications and *209*
Pistols

"assault weapons," Categories 1 and 2 *370*
"assault weapons," Categories 1 and 2, listed by name *404*
"assault weapons," Category 3 *372*
   defined *40–41, 198, 381*
   props, use as *466*
   semiautomatic *41*
   "unconventional" *432*
   "unsafe" handguns, exemptions to restrictions for *467*
Pistol stabilizing braces *429–431*
Places with prohibitions or restrictions *337–363. See also* Public places, restrictions to carrying in
   airplanes *306–309, 348*
   airport "sterile areas," possession in *346–348*
   Amtrak trains *309, 348–349*
   Army Corps of Engineers managed land *353*
   Bureau of Land Management (BLM) and other federally protected areas *352–353*
   buses and other common carriers *308–309, 349*
   California state lands and other parks *353–355*
   common carriers, possession on *349*
   discharge restrictions *360–361*
   government buildings, California law *338–340*
   government buildings, federal law *338*
   Greyhound buses, possession on *349*
   gun shows *358*
   harbors & ports *349–350*
   National Forests *352*
   National Parks and Wildlife Refuges *351–352*
   parks, forests, and refuges, possession in *351–355*
   playgrounds and youth centers *359*
   politicians, firearm possession and *357*
   polling places *358–359*
   private businesses, restrictions by *359–360*
   protest events, firearm possession at *357*
   public transportation facilities, "sterile areas" *350*
   refuges, under California Fish and Game Code *361*
   school grounds *344–346*
   "school zones" *340–344*
   shooting range use restrictions *362*
   suggestions for shooting in public *362–363*
   United States and international waters *355–357*
Playgrounds, California restricted places *359*
Point of contact state, California as *63*
Polling places *358–359*
Ports, possession in *349–350*
Possession of firearms. *See* Firearm possession
POST Commission *150, 277, 279, 284, 290, 151, 295, 318, 334*
Potato guns *52–53*
Precursors *38, 39*
   as firearms *35*
   authorization to purchase firearm precursor parts *203–204*
   building own firearms *198-199*
   exceptions to new restrictions on precursor part sales *201-206*
   face-to-face transaction requirement *200-201*
   licensed precursor part vendor *199-200*
   persons prohibited from possessing firearm precursor parts *203*
   recording of firearm precursor part purchaser or transferr information *202-203*
   restrction against bringing firearm precursor parts into California *205*

Preemption Doctrine
  California *23–25*
  federal *22–23*
Prefabricated frame or receiver, building firearms from *198*
Private businesses, firearm possession restrictions by *359–360*
Private Party Transfers (PPTs) *155–157*
  checklist for *157*
  exception to one handgun every 30-day restriction *149–150*
  interstate *162–169*
  non-NFA trusts and *187*
  non-profit auctions of non-handguns *195*
  "unsafe" handgun transfers as *458, 462, 465*
Private property, firearm possession restrictions and exemptions *276–278*
Probation or parole, restrictions against ownership/possession for *87–88*
Pro-gun lobby *15–16*
Prohibitions to firearm possession
  persons prohibited from possessing firearms *63–65.* See also Criminal convictions resulting in loss of firearm possession rights;
    See also Persons prohibited from possessing firearms
  places prohibited *337–363.* See also Places with prohibitions or restrictions
Projectiles *51*
Proposition 63 (2016) *5, 14, 23, 46, 56, 226–227, 236–238, 436–437, 448–449*
Proposition 64 (2016) *94*
Proprietary, possessory, or substantial ownership interest requirement *263*
Protest events, firearm possession at *357*
Public gatherings, cities with firearm limitations for *12*
Public places, restrictions to carrying in *250–260* See also Transportation of firearms; See also Places with prohibitions or restrictions
  boats in public places *271*
  business or other private property open to public *265–266*
  carrying firearms that are not handguns *263–264*
  carrying loaded firearms in *244–250, 262*
  concealed carry law *241–244*
  exemptions *264–272*
  motorcycles and bicycles in public places *270–271*
  motor vehicles *267–270*
  open carry of handguns *250–251*
  public place, defined *255–256*
  public property, cities prohibiting on *12*
  temporary residences and campsites *264–265*
  vehicles or boats as places of business in public places *267*
  vehicles or boats as residences in public places *266–267*
Public street, defined *257–258*
Public transportation facilities, possession in *349–350*
Public transportation, transporting firearms on *308–309*
  airports, airplanes, and common carriers *346–350*
  Amtrak trains *309, 348–349*
  buses and other public transportation *310–311*
  Greyhound buses *310*
  possession in harbors & ports *349–350*
  possession in sterile area of public transportation facility *350*
  possession on all other common carriers *349*
Purchasing ammunition. See Ammunition, acquisition of
Purchasing firearms *119–238.* See also Selling firearms
  aliens *129–130*
  "assault weapons" or .50 BMG rifles, new *396–401*
  background checks *131–132*
  confusion regarding AFS record requirement after January 1, 2014 *134*

Dealer Record of Sales fees *131*
determining eligibility for *117*
determining when prohibitions apply *63–64*
DROS delays *115–117*
exceptions to transferring firearms through FFL in Cal. *180–196*
exemptions to restrictions against out-of-state transfers *164–170*
federal form 4473 requirements *120–121*
Firearm Safe-Handling Demonstration *147–148*
Firearm Safety Certificate exemptions *137–146*
Firearm Safety Certificate requirements *137–138*
Firearm Safety test *137*
from FFLs *120–153*. See also Federal Firearms Licensees (FFLs)
handgun purchase requirements *149–154*
minors under age 18 *177–178*
nonprofit auctions *195*
one handgun every 30 days requirement *149–150*
out-of-state dealers, transfers from *160*
proof of identity, age, and address *122–130*
proof of residency for handguns *151–155*
REAL IDs, non-REAL IDs, and AB 60 *125–128*
registration at time of purchase *132–133*
registration of "assault weapons" or .50 BMG rifles *396–398*
required locking devices and warnings *135–136*
requirements, quick guide *154–155*
voluntary registration *132*
waiting period *133–134*
waiting period, exemptions to *133–134*
young people under 21 *176–177*

Q

Qualified law enforcement officers (QLEO), carry exemptions for *300–301, 304–305*. See also Law Enforcement Officers Safety Act (LEOSA)

R

Rash v. Lungren (Cal. App. 1997) *79–80*
REAL IDs *125–126*
Receivers. See also 80% receivers
  building firearms from *198–199*
  California definition of *37–38*
  federal definition of *34*
  possible designation as "assault weapons" *367*
Registration of firearms
  .50 BMG rifles *387–388*
  "assault weapons" *191, 366, 374, 396–398*
  "assault weapons," alternatives to registration *399*
  at time of purchase *132–133*
  confusion regarding requirement to register after January 1, 2014 *133*
  "curio or relic" by Type 03 FFL, registration of *194–195*
  deadlines after moving into California *213–215*
  determining if your "assault weapon" or .50 BMG rifle was registered *401*
  DOJ Bureau of Firearms, forms available from *132*
  joint registration, lack of law regarding *188*
  NFA firearms *408–409*
  peace officer exception for "assault weapon" registration deadlines *391*
  post-registration modification of "bullet button assault weapons" *398*

registration deadlines *397*
requirements for building your own firearms *198, 208-212*
voluntary deregistration of "assault weapons" *398*
voluntary registration *132*
relics. *See* "Curios or relics"
Renouncing U.S. citizenship, firearm possession prohibition after *114*
Reorganization of the Dangerous Weapons Control Act *27-28*
Reporting lost or stolen firearms. *See* Lost/stolen reporting
Report of Operation of Law or Intra-Familial Firearm Transaction form *181, 185, 189*
Reserve officers. *See* Law enforcement and peace officers
Residence
   aliens *129-130*
   carrying loaded handgun, residency requirement for license to *289*
   determining place of *151-152*
   dual residency *130-131, 161-162*
   establishing residency and moving into California with firearms *213-216*
   exemption for carrying concealed in *263-264*
   exemption for carrying loaded firearms in *263*
   exemption for carrying unloaded handguns in *263*
   members of military stationed in Cal. *129*
   proof of address for *123-125*
   proof of residency for handgun purchases *151-155, 155*
   residing with prohibited person *218-219, 225*
   state of residency *161-162*
   temporary residences and campsites *264-265*
   vehicle or boat as *266-267*
Residential care facilities, firearm storage in *223*
Restraining orders, firearm prohibitions for subjects of *102-107*
   federal law on *102, 107*
   "grave danger" exemption *271*
   "gun violence restraining orders" *80, 105-108*
Retired law enfocement officers. *See* Law enforcement and peace officers
Revolvers
   defined *41-42*
   exemptions for "unsafe" handgun restrictions *466-467*
   "unsafe" handguns *458*
Rifles *10*. *See also* Non-handguns
   .50 BMG rifles. *See* .50 BMG rifles
   AR-15 semiautomatic *34*
   "assault weapons," Category 1 and 2, listed by name *402-404*
   "assault weapons," Category 3 definition *371*
   defined *42-43, 382*
   exceptions to restrictions against "short-barreled rifles" *452-453*
   possession restrictions for minors *66*
   "short-barreled" *426-428*. *See also* "Short-barreled shotguns/rifles"
Right to keep and bear arms *19-22*
   2d amendment standards of review *21-22*
   California law on *20*
   current litigation, primary issues being addressed in *20-22*
   U.S. Constitution *19-20*
Right to self-defense or defense of others *19-22*
   exceptions for prohibited person *108-111*
   exceptions to criminal storage and *217*
   in Cal. Constitution *20*
   lead-based ammunition, use for *473, xxv*
   social utility of firearms and *2*

"tear gas" and *479*
Roberti-Roos Assault Weapons Control ACT (AWCA). *See also* Assault Weapons Control Act (AWCA, Cal.)
Roster of Firearm Safety Devices Certified for Sale *136*
Roster of Handguns Certified for Sale *221, 457*
Rule of lenity *5*

S

Safe-handling demonstrations *147–148*
Safety devices *135–136, 154, 192, 216, 383*
Sales of firearms. *See* Selling firearms
San Francisco
    "large-capacity" magazines, restrictions against *439–442*
    limitations on public gatherings with firearms *12*
    local storage laws *222*
    mandatory lock storage *11*
    mandatory lost/stolen reporting *11*
    prohibitions for possessing firearms on public property *12*
    sympathy for anti-gun legislation *25*
Santa Cruz, local storage laws *222*
"Saturday Night Specials" *10*
School grounds, ammunition & weapon possession on *224, 344–346, 359*
"School zones" *340–344*. *See also* Gun-Free School Zone restrictions
    California's Gun-Free School Zone Act *342–344*
    discharge restrictions in *344*
    firearm possession in, California law *342–344*
    firearm possession in, federal law *341–342*
Second Amendment. *See* Right to keep and bear arms
    campsites, right to firearms on *456*
    government bias and firearm laws *29*
    pro-gun lobby and *13, 15–16*
    right to bear arms and *19–22*
    U.S. Supreme Court decisions regarding *9*
Self-defense, right to. *See* Right to self-defense or defense of others
Selling firearms. *See also* Transfers of firearms; *See also* Minors (under age 18); *See also* Purchasing firearms; *See also* Persons under 21
    California law for dealers *120, 180–195*
    dealer license requirements *158–159*
    DOJ's Roster of handguns that FFLs can sell in Cal. *457–459*
    DROS form for *121–122*
    federal law for dealers *158–159*
    "machineguns," licenses to sell *411*
    proof of identity, age, and address. *See also* Identification requirements for firearm purchases from dealers
    registration at time of purchase *132–133*
    required locking devices and warnings *135–136*
    to historical societies, museums, institutional collections, or entertainment events *444–445*
    to law enforcement *444*
Selling your firearms. *See also* Purchasing firearms
Semiautomatic firearms
    semiautomatic, defined *382*
    semiautomatic pistols *41, 458–459*
Serial numbers. *See also* Building firearms
    deadlines to engrave and upload required digital images when building your own firearms *211*
    engraving, when building your own firearms *210–211*
    firearms exempt from AB 857s serialization requirements *212–213*
    obliterated or covered *455–457*
    Unique Serial Number Applications *208*

Shark killers 51–52
Shipping firearms 163–164
Shirey v. Los Angeles County Civil Service Commis (Cal. App. 2013) 83
Shooting clubs, exemptions pertaining to 173, 273, 276–277, 477, 400
Shooting range use restrictions 362
"Short-barreled shotguns/rifles" 424–431, 440. *See also* "Generally prohibited weapons," exceptions to restrictions against "short-barreled shotguns/rifles"
    DOJs definition of barrel length for "assault weapon" registration 466
    law enforcement agencies, exceptions to restrictions for 452
    permit authorizations for 453–454
    pistol stabilizing braces 429–431
    possession of parts constituting 428–429
    "short-barreled rifles" 426–428
    "short-barreled shotguns" 424–426
Shotguns
    "assault weapons," Category 1 and 2, listed by name 405
    "assault weapons," Category 3 definition 373
    defined 43
    minors, ownership restrictions for 66
    with revolving cylinders, defined 383
    "short-barreled" 424–426, 452–453
Signal launchers 53–54
"Silencers"/"sound suppressors" 453–455
    Gun Control Act and 32
    LEOSA and 391
    National Firearms Act and 185–186, 484–486
"Smart gun" technology 461
Sniperscopes (Night Vision Scopes) 482–483
Special weapons permits 138, 451
Spot marker guns 477
Spouses or domestic partners. *See also* Domestic violence, firearm restrictions due to; *See also* Families
    divorce and firearms transfers 182–183
    firearm transfers between 182
    gun trusts and 188
"Spud guns" 52–53
Squier, People v. (Cal. App. 1993) 5
State courts, carrying firearms in 293
"Sterile areas," firearm possession in 346–348, 350–351
Stolen firearms 6, 226–227. *See* Lost/stolen reporting
Storing firearms. *See* Firearm storage
"Stun guns" 481
Sunnyvale
    "large capacity" magazines, restrictions against 13, 439–442
    storage laws in 11, 222
    sympathy for anti-gun legislation 25

T

Tasers 51–52, 349
"Tear gas," pepper spray, and mace 51, 351, 478–480
Temporary Carry Licenses 286–287
Temporary residences, carry restrictions in 264–265
Testing and prototypes as exceptions to "unsafe" handgun restrictions 466
Theft or loss of firearms 5, 11, 226–227. *See also* Stolen firearms; *See also* Lost/stolen reporting
Thompson/Center Arms Co, U.S. v. (U.S. 1992) 428
Tiburon, local laws 11, 222

TITAN Gun Vault 268–269
Toy guns a.k.a. "imitation firearms" 475–478
Tracer ammunition 352, 413, 472
Transfers of firearms. *See also* Minors (under age 18); *See also* Purchasing firearms; *See also* Exceptions to transferring firearms through FFLs; *See also* Gun trusts; *See also* Persons under 21; *See also* Private Party Transfers (PPTs); *See also* Selling firearms
  "antique firearms" 192
  "assault weapons" and 388, 399
  between spouses or domestic partners 182
  "curio or relic" firearms 192–195
  "destructive devices" 413
  divorce and 182
  with Entertainment Firearm Permit (EFP) 191
  exceptions to transferring firearms through FFL in Cal.
  "generally prohibited weapons," exceptions to limitations on 442–445
  "gun buybacks" 196
  gun trusts, tranfers through 185–191
  infrequent transfer requirement 159–160
  interstate private party transfers 162–163
  intra-familial transfers, California law on 180–181
  "large-capacity magazines" and 437–439, 442–451
  limitations of gun trusts with "assault weapons" and "large-capacity magazines" 190–191
  loaning firearms to adults 169–174
  "machineguns" and 409–411
  nonprofit auction of non-handguns 195
  "Operation of Law" transfers 183–184
  out-of-state dealers, from 160–162
  out-of-state transfers, exemptions to limitations on 164–170
  private party transfers 155–157
  prohibited persons to FFL 104
  purchasing from licensed firearms dealers 119–153
  requirement to conduct through licensed firearm dealers 119–120
  shipping, interstate 163–164
  "short-barreled" shotguns/rifles and 424
  transporting "generally prohibited weapons" to law enforcement 445
  "unsafe handgun" 461–466
  to young people 66–67, 176–178
Transmutation 182–184, 188–189
Transportation of firearms 306–310. *See also* Public places, restrictions to carrying in; *See also* Vehicles, carry restrictions for; *See also* Carrying firearms; *See also* Public transportation, transporting firearms on
  across state lines 308–309
  airplanes, transporting on 306–309
  "assault weapons" and .50 BMG Rifles 400
  buses or other public transportation, transporting on 308–309
  coming into California with firearms 213–216
  possession of firearms in airports, on airplanes, and on common carriers 346–350
  quick tips for public and private transportation 309–310
  transporting "generally prohibited weapons" to law enforcement 445
Traumatic conditions, P.C. section 273.5 and firearm prohibition 82
Trusts. *See* Gun trusts
Type 03 FFL (collector's license) 192–195

U

"Unconventional pistols" 207, 432, 482–483
"Undetectable firearms" 207, 420–421
Unincorporated areas 252–255, 258, 261, 263–264, 272, 327–328

Unique Serial Number Applications 208
United States Army Corps of Engineers (USACE) Managed Land, possession of firearms on 353
United States v. Castleman (U.S. 2014) 83–84
United States v. Thompson/Center Arms Co. (U.S. 1992) 428
Unlawful detainer actions for firearm related nuisance arrests 89
"Unsafe handguns"
   certain handguns exempt from Roster requirement. 466–468
   exceptions to Roster requirement 461–466
"Unsafe" handguns 457–465
   "curios or relics" exemption 466
   in unattended vehicles of law enforcement officers 221–222
   law enforcement and military exception 461–463
   loans to consultant-evaluators 466
   "microstamping" and 459–461
   peace officers from specified agencies, exceptions for 462
   pistols used as props 466
   private party and other designated transfers, exception for 462
   purchase by spouse of peace officer who died in line of duty 462
   repairs, exception for 466
   Roster requirement 457–459, 466–468
   "smart gun" technology 461
   testing and prototypes, exception for 466
"Unsafe" handguns
   definitions applicable for 41–42
Unsafe Handgun Act 11, 457
U.S. and international waters, firearm possession in 355–357
Utility compartments, legality of gun storage in 268, 270, 310

V

Vehicles, carry restrictions for. *See also* Motor vehicles; *See also* Public transportation, transporting firearms on
   armored vehicle business, exception to "large-capacity magazine" restrictions for 450
   as places of business, exemption to general public carry restrictions 267
   as residence, exemption to general public carry restrictions 266–267
   carry requirements 267–271
   "lawful purpose" requirement 269
   locked container requirement 268–269
   motorcycles and bicycles, carrying via 270–271
   storage of handguns in unattended 219–222
   storage of "unsafe" handguns in unattended vehicles by law enforcement 221–222
   transporting "assault weapons" and .50 BMG rifles 270
   unloaded firearms in public places 267–270
Violent crimes, lifetime restrictions for certain convictions 72, 74–75

W

Wade, People v. (Cal. 2016) 241
Waiting period for purchasing firearms 133–135, 154–157, 194
"Wallet guns" 420
Warning labels 135
Warrant, effect on firearm eligibility if outstanding 91–92
Weapons
   "any other weapon," defined under NFA 484–486
   defined 45–46
   "generally prohibited weapons" 418–441. *See also* "Generally prohibited weapons"
   "less lethal weapons" 480–481
   possession on "school grounds" 344–346

Wildlife Refuges, firearm possession in *351-352*
Wobblers
  concealed carry as *72, 242*
  defined *242*
  polling places, possessing firearms in *358*
  violation for bringing loaded firearm on residence of Governor or Legislature *339*
  violation for possessing loaded firearm *245-246*
  violation involving "multiburst trigger activator" *422*
  violation of lifetime restrictions following P.C. section 273.5 convictions *72-73*

Y

Young people. *See* Minors (under age 18); *See* Persons under 21
Youth centers, possession on grounds of *359*

Z

"Zip guns" *207, 431-432*

ABOUT THE AUTHORS

C.D. "Chuck" Michel is Senior Counsel and owner of Michel & Associates, P.C., a boutique law firm located in Long Beach, California. The firm's practice focuses on adversarial litigation and regulatory compliance advice. Areas of practice include firearms law, constitutional law, civil rights advocacy, criminal law, business litigation, land use law, employment law and environmental law. The firm's website is www.MichelLawyers.com.

Mr. Michel has been litigating civil and criminal firearms cases since 1991. He is recognized as one of the leading national authorities on firearms laws. For over two decades, he has played a significant role in advocating and defending individual civil and constitutional rights, particularly Second Amendment rights, and in helping to shape related legislation. He has been instrumental in crafting some of the most important legal challenges to legislation that infringes on rights guaranteed by the Constitution. His clients include the National Rifle Association (NRA), the California Rifle & Pistol Association (CRPA) Foundation, *FFLGuard*, gun manufacturers, wholesalers, retailers, and individual gun owners. He has represented thousands of individuals and companies charged with violating California's confusing firearms laws. He has litigated hundreds of cases and been trial counsel in scores of jury trials, many of which were high profile and attracted state and national media attention. As an attorney for the NRA, Mr. Michel has been a stakeholder in drafting legislation to protect California gun owners and an advocate in opposing ill-conceived legislation. Mr. Michel and his law firm have donated over 2 million dollars worth of *pro bono* legal work to the NRA and the CRPA Foundation.

Among many other victories, Mr. Michel won the NRA-sponsored lawsuit that struck down Proposition H – the San Francisco law that would have banned the civilian possession of handguns in the city. He also led the successful CRPA Foundation lawsuit that struck down Assembly Bill 962, an anti-gun politician's attempt to severely restrict and require registration of all ammunition purchases. Mr. Michel filed prestigious, influential, and unprecedented *amicus* briefs on behalf of dozens of California district attorneys in both the 2008 *District of Columbia v. Heller* and the 2010 *McDonald v. Chicago* Supreme Court gun-rights cases. He has been honored with numerous awards for his legal successes, including awards for his civil rights advocacy, trial advocacy skills, writing skills, and *pro bono* work.

Mr. Michel has served as a spokesperson for the NRA, CRPA, other civil rights group clients, and individual clients. He has appeared on dozens of television and radio interviews and been quoted in thousands of newspaper articles. He has had articles and editorials published in the *Los Angeles Times*, the *Los Angeles Daily Journal*, and other state and national newspapers and magazines.

"Professor" Michel has also taught classes in Firearms Law and Law Practice Management as an adjunct professor at Chapman University Dale E. Fowler School of Law in Orange, California.

Mr. Michel graduated near the top of his classes from both Rutgers University in New Jersey in 1980 and from Loyola Law School in Los Angeles in 1989. He began his legal career with a coveted judicial clerkship for U.S. District Court Judge William J. Rea in Los Angeles. He worked as a criminal prosecutor for the Los Angeles County District Attorney's Office and several Southern California cities and as an advocate with the Los Angeles Federal Public Defender's office. Mr. Michel also practiced environmental and general civil litigation as an attorney at the renowned international law firm of O'Melveny & Myers, LLP. While at O'Melveny, Mr. Michel represented clients ranging from individuals to multinational corporations. Among many other cases and clients, he represented Exxon in connection with the Exxon Valdez oil spill and served as staff counsel to the "Christopher Commission" which investigated the Los Angeles Police Department after the Rodney King incident.

Mr. Michel grew up in what used to be rural New Jersey at a time when neighbors wished him luck as he walked out his back door and into the woods behind his house to go rabbit hunting before high school – these days the neighbors would call the SWAT team on a high school student with a gun. His father was a businessman who loved teaching others, including his three sons, the shooting sports as an NRA instructor. Some of Mr. Michel's fondest childhood memories are of backyard plinking contests with his entire family. He is striving to pass this firearm heritage along to his own sons and hopes that they will be able to pass it on to future generations of free Americans.

Matthew D. Cubeiro is a Partner at Michel & Associates, P.C. His primary practice areas include firearms-related regulatory compliance, legislative analysis, firearms-related local ordinance issues, and general civil litigation. In addition to practicing law, Mr. Cubeiro is dedicated to teaching the knowledge, skills, and attitude necessary for the safe and enjoyable use of firearms. He is certified by the National Rifle Association as an instructor in Home Firearm Safety, Metallic Cartridge Reloading, Pistol, Rifle, Refuse to Be A Victim, Personal Protection in the Home, and Personal Protection Outside the Home disciplines. He is also a certified Range Safety Officer, and routinely volunteers his time to teach both members of the public and law enforcement on California gun laws and the legal requirements for using a firearm in self-defense.

Mr. Cubeiro is a graduate of Western State University where he received his Juris Doctorate with Honors and Certificate in Criminal Law Studies. Before law school, he earned his Bachelor of Arts in business administration with honors from Chapman University

Recruiter ID: XP025815
Date: _____

NRA MEMBERSHIP APPLICATION

☐ NEW MEMBER   ☐ RENEWAL # _____ (Current or past NRA Member)

NAME: _____
                    FIRST   LAST

ADDRESS: _____
                    STREET   CITY   STATE   ZIP

PHONE: (____) _____   **BIRTHDATE:** ____ / ____ / ____

E-MAIL (Required for Digital Magazine): _____

MEMBERSHIP TYPE
☐ **1 YEAR:** $35 (Reg. $45)
☐ **3 YEARS:** $85 (Reg. $100)
☐ **5 YEARS:** $125 (Reg. $150)
☐ **1 YEAR JUNIOR (18 AND UNDER):** $15
☐ **ASSOCIATE (NO MAGAZINE):** $10

LIFE MEMBERSHIP
☐ **LIFE:** $1,000 (Reg. $1,500)
☐ **JUNIOR LIFE:** $500 (Reg. $750)
  *18 and Under
☐ **DISTINGUISHED LIFE:** $500 (Reg. $750)
  *Aged 65+ or Disabled Veteran
☐ **EASY PAY LIFE:** $25 DOWN PAYMENT
  +$25 per quarter until fully paid

SELECT ONE FREE MAGAZINE (Additional subscriptions add $9.95 per year):
☐ AMERICAN RIFLEMAN   ☐ AMERICAN HUNTER   ☐ AMERICA'S 1ST FREEDOM   ☐ SHOOTING ILLUSTRATED

DELIVERY METHOD: ☐ PRINT   ☐ DIGITAL (e-mail required)

PAYMENT TYPE: ☐ CHECK OR MONEY ORDER *(PAYABLE TO NRA)*   ☐ CREDIT CARD
CARD TYPE: ☐ VISA   ☐ MASTERCARD   ☐ AMEX   ☐ DISCOVER   **EXP. DATE**

MO   YR

SIGNATURE (CC# only): _____

PLEASE RETURN APPLICATION BY MAIL TO:
National Rifle Association
c/o Recruiting Programs
11250 Waples Mill RD
Fairfax, VA 22030

Contributions, gifts or membership dues made or paid to the National Rifle Association of America are not refundable or transferable and are not deductible as charitable contributions for Federal income tax purposes. $3.75 of the membership dues are designated for magazine subscription. **Foreign postage add $5 for Canada, $10 for all other countries.**

Membership starts the day of processing of dues payments by NRA. Three dollars and seventy-five cents of the annual membership fee is designated for magazine subscription. Insurance benefits are subject to the conditions contained in the Master Policy on file at NRA headquarters at the time a claim arises. There are special exclusions and limitations to such policy. Furthermore, NRA and the Insurers specifically reserve the right to alter or change any conditions in the Master Policy, including, but not limited to, reductions in the amount of coverage, and the cancellation or non-renewal of such policy. Annual Junior members are not eligible for insurance benefits. Affinity card available for applicants who meet all the credit criteria. The moving discount is off the Interstate Commerce Commission approved tariff rate. For specific state-by-state disclosures, please visit http://www.nra.org/NRA-UniformDisclosureStatement.pdf

WHY JOIN THE NRA?
800-392-VOTE • www.NRAILA.org

NRA Membership Benefits

These basic membership benefits are automatically included with your NRA Annual Membership or Life Membership, along with special members-only discounts and services.

- An official NRA Membership ID card - showing your Membership ID number and expiration date or Life Member status. You should carry this card with you at all times.
- With all regular memberships, you will get a choice of subscription to American Rifleman, American Hunter, or America's 1st Freedom.
- Junior members receive a subscription to Insights.
- Annual members receive $5,000 of Accidental Death and Dismemberment coverage at NO COST to you. The plan covers accidents at, or to and from, an NRA event; and accidents that occur during the use of firearms or hunting equipment while hunting. Insurance must be activated at time of renewal. (Does not include Junior membership.)
- Life members receive $10,000 of Accidental Death and Dismemberment coverage at NO COST to you. The plan covers accidents at, or to and from, an NRA event; and accidents that occur during the use of firearms or hunting equipment while hunting. Insurance must be activated at time of upgrade to Life member status
- Law Enforcement Officers, that are NRA members, killed in the line of duty will have $25,000 in coverage.
- $2,500 of ArmsCare coverage with your NRA membership. This plan covers insured firearms, air guns, bows and arrows against theft, accidental loss, and damage. Insurance must be activated.

  For purposes of insurance, NRA members must be current active members of the NRA whose name appears on the NRA membership list. Activation is required.

- New and Enhanced insurance coverages through the NRA Endorsed Insurance Programs. Enroll on-line for Life, Health and Accident and Individual Property and Liability insurance or call Toll free 1-877-NRA-3006 (1-877-672-3006.) New Commercial Property Liability Insurance Program for NRA Affiliated Clubs and Business Alliance Members, visit on-line or call Toll Free 1-877-487-5407.
- The most important benefit of NRA membership, however, is the defense of your Constitutional right to keep and bear arms, both nationally and in California. NRA-ILA tracks the issues and alerts members about legislation involving firearms and hunting at the federal, state and local levels of government. Successful legislative action begins with you -- the individual member. For information regarding legislative action or to become an ILA grassroots volunteer, call 1-800-392-8683.
- NRA Institute for Legislative Action representatives are your voice on Capitol Hill and in Sacramento.
- Your NRA Membership dues payment receipt allows you to immediately enter NRA registered tournaments.

For real American values, shop NRAstore.com,
where 100% of the profits go directly to support vital NRA programs
Request a catalog • 888-607-6007 • Shop online: www.NRAstore.com

Membership starts the day of processing of dues payments by NRA. Insurance benefits are subject to the conditions contained in the Master Policy on file at NRA Headquarters at the time a claim arises. There are special exclusions and limitations to such policy. Furthermore, NRA and its Insurers specifically reserve the right to alter or change any conditions in the Master Policy; including but not limited to, reductions in the amount of coverage, and the cancellation or non-renewal of such policy. Annual Junior members are not eligible for insurance benefits. Affinity card available for applicants who meet all credit criteria. The moving discount is off the Interstate Commerce Commission approved tariff rate. $3.75 of membership dues are designated for magazine subscriptions. For specific state by state disclosures, please visit www.NRA.org/NRAUniformDisclosureStatement.pdf

CALIFORNIA RIFLE & PISTOL ASSOCIATION
CRPA MEMBERSHIP APPLICATION FORM

STRENGTH IN MEMBERS

Ways to Join:

Return this form by mail to
California Rifle & Pistol Association
271 E. Imperial Highway, Suite #620
Fullerton, CA 92835

Or

Become a member online at:
www.CRPA.ORG

Or

Call the office:
(800) 305-2772

CRPA Membership Levels

✓	Membership Option	Price
	1 Year Membership	$35
	5 Year Membership	$150
	2A Sustaining Membership	$17.91 / Month
	Life Membership	$500 Or four $135 / quarterly payments
		Veteran Discount: 10% off any of the above memberships
	Senior Life Membership	$275 Or four $75 / quarterly payments
	Defender Life Member	$1000 + Life Membership
	Activist Life Member	$1500 + Defender Membership
	Patriot Life Member	$1500 + Activist Membership

Check next to membership of choice   ☐ Auto Renewal

Name: _____   DOB: / /

Address: _____

City: _____ State: _____ ZIP: _____

Home Phone: (   ) _____   Mobile Phone: (   ) _____

Email: _____

PAYMENT INFORMATION:

Card #: _____   Exp. Date: /

Membership: $ _____   Additional: $ _____   Total: $ _____   Check: # _____

*A portion of CRPA membership dues are used for lobbying and political activities. The portion used for these purposes is 25% of the total cost of membership paid.

BE SAFE. SHOOT STRAIGHT. *FIGHT BACK!*

MICHEL & ASSOCIATES, P.C.
Attorneys at Law

Helping Firearms Owners, Businesses, Ranges and Clubs Nationwide

---

FIREARMS | ENVIRONMENTAL | LAND USE | CIVIL RIGHTS ADVOCACY
LABOR & EMPLOYMENT | CIVIL LITIGATION | CRIMINAL DEFENSE

Michel & Associates, P.C. is a full-service law firm representing businesses throughout the country. Owner C.D. "Chuck" Michel leads a team of over a dozen highly qualified and experienced attorneys with extensive experience in a variety of legal specialties. The firm has been litigating civil and criminal firearm cases since 1991.

Some law firms undermine your right to keep and bear arms by providing *pro bono* legal services to politicians who would deprive you of your Second Amendment rights. This *pro bono* work is subsidized through the legal fees paid by business clients. Since it was formed, **Michel & Associates has provided over $3 million worth of** *pro bono* **legal service to indigent gun owners, and to the non-profit associations that protect your rights.** Shop for your legal service provider carefully so you don't inadvertently subsidize the gun ban lobby!

As attorneys for the NRA, CRPA, firearm manufacturers, wholesalers, and retailers, the lawyers at Michel & Associates have litigated thousands of cases involving civil rights issues, including Second Amendment challenges, in both state and federal trial and appellate courts. They have represented many clients in high-profile cases that have garnered national media attention, and have appeared as spokespersons for the NRA and CRPA.

Mr. Michel is frequently quoted concerning Second Amendment rights by the major daily newspapers, and by television and radio stations. He is the author of *California Firearms Laws, A Guide to State and Federal Firearm Regulations* (available at CalGunLawsbook.com). Mr. Michel has been honored and profiled in recognition of his corporate and civil-rights work in multiple periodicals and by the NRA, which awarded him its prestigious *Defender of Justice* Award in 2013. Professor Michel also teaches *Firearms Law* and *Law Practice Management* at Chapman University School of Law.

LEGAL *FIREPOWER*

- Civil Litigation
- Restoration of Gun Rights
- Gun Seizures & Returns
- Inventory Cataloging
- Restraining Order Removal
- Criminal Defense
- Hunter & Hunting Protection
- Regulatory Compliance Checks
- Governmental Licensing & Permits
- Range Protection & Development
- Range Environmental Issues
- Explosives & Destructive Devices
- Entertainment Industry Props
- & Much More

Michel & Associates, P.C.
180 East Ocean Boulevard, Suite 200
Long Beach, California 90802
(562) 216-4444
www.michellawyers.com

Free Gun Law Info
www.calgunlaws.com

MORE LAWYERS | MORE EXPERIENCE | MORE RELATIONSHIPS | MORE RESOURCES | MORE RESULTS

Coming Soon from Coldaw Publishing

Gun Owner's Guide to Restoring Your Gun Rights

Gun Truths: A Compilation of Research & Empirical Studies Proving that Gun Control Laws Fail

Freedom Week

Gun Owner's Guide to Police Encounters: Know All Your Constitutional Rights & Avoid Becoming an Accidental Criminal

Gun Owner's Guide to Firearm Seizure, Surrender, and Return

Gun Owner's Guide to the Law of Self-Defense & Use of Force in California

Notes

Notes

Notes

Notes

Notes

Notes

Notes